A Grammar of Upper Tanana

A Grammar of Upper Tanana

Volume 1: Phonology, lexical classes, morphology

Olga Lovick

University of Nebraska Press

Lincoln

This book is published as part of the Recovering Languages and Literacies of the Americas initiative. Recovering Languages and Literacies is generously supported by the Andrew W. Mellon Foundation.

Library of Congress Cataloging-in-Publication Data
Names: Lovick, Olga Charlotte, author.
Title: A grammar of Upper Tanana.
Description: Lincoln: University of Nebraska Press, [2019]—Contents: volume 1. Phonology, lexical classes, morphology / Olga Lovick. | Includes bibliographical references.
Identifiers: LCCN 2019014268
ISBN 9781496213150 (volume 1: cloth: alk. paper)
ISBN 9781496222275 (volume 1: paperback)
ISBN 9781496219190 (volume 1: epub)
ISBN 9781496219206 (volume 1: mobi)
ISBN 9781496219213 (volume 1: pdf)
Subjects: LCSH: Upper Tanana language—Grammar.
Classification: LCC pm641.z9 u67 2019 | DDC 497/.2—dc23
LC record available at https://lccn.loc.gov/2019014268

Contents

List of Tables xxxv

List of Figures xxxviii

List of Maps xxxix

List of Abbreviations xl

Acknowledgments xliii

Preface xlvi

I Background

1 About this grammar **2**
- 1.1 Scope and aim 2
- 1.2 Data 4
  - 1.2.1 Sources 4
  - 1.2.2 Relationship between naturalistic and elicited data . 5
  - 1.2.3 Data presentation and glossing conventions 6
- 1.3 Fieldwork and linguistic competence 10
- 1.4 Why two volumes? 11

2 About Upper Tanana **13**
- 2.1 Name 13
- 2.2 Defining Upper Tanana 14
- 2.3 The Dene language family 14
- 2.4 Geographical location 17
- 2.5 Prior research 19
- 2.6 Speaker numbers and language vitality 20

3 **Dialects** **23**
3.1 Traditional bands and current dialects 23
3.2 Phonological dialect differences 24
3.2.1 Realization of *ə in stems 24
3.2.2 Realization of *ə in prefixes 25
3.2.3 Realization of vocalic suffixes 26
3.2.4 Realization of nasal consonants in onsets 26
3.2.5 Low tone 28
3.2.6 High tone 29
3.2.7 Realization of /ɔ/ 29
3.2.8 Realization of /i͡o/, /ĩ͜õ/ 30
3.2.9 Miscellaneous phonological differences 30
3.3 Lexical differences 31
3.4 Morphological differences 31
3.4.1 Realization of the *i*- perfective 31
3.4.2 Adverbial-derivational prefix strings 31
3.4.3 Reciprocal object *łi*- 32
3.4.4 Conjugation marker following P+*tüh* ‘over P’ 32
3.4.5 Prefixes of directionals 32
3.5 Summary 32

4 **Some cultural background** **34**
4.1 *Įįjih* 34
4.1.1 Linguistic aspects of *įįjih* 36
4.2 Stories and storytelling 37
4.3 Story characters 38
4.3.1 Yamaagn Teeshyaay and Tsa’ Ushyąą 38
4.3.2 *Gǫǫ* 39
4.3.3 *Che’ t’iin* ‘Tailed People’ 39
4.3.4 Raven 40
4.3.5 Other sentient beings 40
4.4 Summary 40

II **Phonology**

5 **Consonants** **42**
5.1 Oral stops and affricates 42
5.1.1 Aspirated oral stops and affricates 42

5.1.1.1 Aspirated oral stops 42
5.1.1.2 Aspirated affricates 44
5.1.2 Unaspirated oral stops and affricates 45
5.1.2.1 Unaspirated oral stops 45
5.1.2.2 Unaspirated affricates 47
5.1.3 Ejective stops and affricates 48
5.1.3.1 Ejective oral stops 49
5.1.3.2 Ejective affricates 49
5.2 Fricatives 50
5.2.1 Voiceless fricatives 51
5.2.2 Voiced fricatives 53
5.3 Sonorants 54
5.3.1 Voiceless sonorants 54
5.3.2 Voiced sonorants 54
5.3.2.1 Denasalization of /m/, /n/ in onset position 56
5.4 Summary 57

6 Vowels **59**
6.1 Oral vowels 59
6.1.1 /i/ and /iː/ 59
6.1.2 /e/ and /eː/ 60
6.1.3 /a/ and /aː/ 61
6.1.4 /o/ and /oː/ 61
6.1.5 /u/ and /uː/ 62
6.1.6 /ɔ/ and /ɔː/ 63
6.1.7 /ʌ/ 63
6.1.8 /i͡a/ 64
6.1.9 /i͡o/ 64
6.2 Nasal vowels 65
6.2.1 /ĩ/ and /ĩː/ 66
6.2.2 /ã/ and /ãː/ 66
6.2.3 /õ/ and /õː/ 67
6.2.4 /ɔ̃/ and /ɔ̃ː/ 68
6.2.5 /ʌ̃/ 68
6.2.6 /ĩ͜ã/ 69
6.2.7 /ĩ͜õ/ 69
6.3 Vowel length 70
6.4 Summary 70

7 Tone 72
7.1 No tonal specification 72
7.2 Low tone 72
7.2.1 Contour tone 74
7.3 High tone 75
7.4 Illustration of tonal contrasts 77
7.5 The phonetic realization of tones: an instrumental study . . 78
7.5.1 Data and methods 79
7.5.2 Results: Northway 80
7.5.3 Results: Tetlin 83
7.6 Summary 83

8 A historical perspective on the sound system 85
8.1 Consonant developments 86
8.1.1 Changes in onset position 86
8.1.1.1 Obstruents 86
8.1.1.1.1 No change 87
8.1.1.1.2 The Great Northern Series Shift 87
8.1.1.2 Sonorants 89
8.1.2 Changes in coda position 90
8.1.2.1 Obstruents 90
8.1.2.1.1 Stops 91
8.1.2.1.2 Affricates 91
8.1.2.1.3 Fricatives 92
8.1.2.2 Sonorants 93
8.1.2.3 Final consonant clusters 94
8.1.3 Consonant developments: general tendencies 95
8.1.3.1 Devoicing 95
8.1.3.2 Absorption into the stem vowel 95
8.1.3.3 Neutralization and deletion 95
8.2 Vowel developments 96
8.2.1 Full vowels 96
8.2.1.1 *i· 96
8.2.1.2 *e· 97
8.2.1.3 *a· 97
8.2.1.4 *u· 98
8.2.2 Reduced vowels 100
8.2.2.1 *ə 100
8.2.2.2 *α 100

8.2.2.3 *ʊ 100
8.2.3 Absorption of features into the vowel 100
8.2.3.1 Nasality 100
8.2.3.2 Constriction 103
8.2.3.3 Labialization 104
8.3 Summary 104

9 Stem-initial fricative lenition **105**
9.1 Fricative lenition in noun stems 105
9.1.1 Morphological conditions 105
9.1.2 Fricative lenition in noun stems as an optional process 107
9.2 Fricative lenition in verb stems 108
9.2.1 Morphological conditions 108
9.2.1.1 Fricative lenition following D- 109
9.2.1.2 Frequent lenition following L- 111
9.2.1.3 Optional fricative lenition following Ø- . 111
9.2.1.4 No fricative lenition following H- 111
9.3 Illustration of fricative lenition 112
9.3.1 Partial voicing 113
9.3.2 Reduced intensity and duration 113
9.3.3 Lenis fricatives versus affricates 115
9.4 Phonemic status of lenis fricatives 115
9.5 Summary 116

10 Syllable structure **119**
10.1 Stem syllables 119
10.1.1 Onset of stem syllables 119
10.1.1.1 Simple onsets 119
10.1.1.2 Complex onsets 120
10.1.1.3 Stems without an onset consonant 121
10.1.2 Rhyme 121
10.1.2.1 Nucleus 122
10.1.2.2 Coda 122
10.1.2.3 More on /t, k/- final stems 123
10.2 Prefix syllables 125
10.2.1 Onset of prefix syllables 125
10.2.1.1 Simple onsets 125
10.2.1.2 Syllables without onset consonant 126
10.2.1.3 Complex onsets 126

10.2.2 Rhyme of prefix syllables 127
10.2.2.1 Nucleus 127
10.2.2.1.1 Vocalic nucleus 127
10.2.2.1.2 Consonantal nucleus 127
10.2.2.2 Coda of prefix syllables 128
10.3 Incorporated roots 128
10.4 Summary 129

11 Light and heavy stems **131**
11.1 Heavy stems as the result of synchronous suffixation 131
11.1.1 No or glottal coda consonant 132
11.1.2 Stems ending in /n̥, j̊, ɬ/ 133
11.1.3 Stems ending in /tʰ, kʰ/ 134
11.2 Inherently heavy stems 134
11.3 Summary 135

12 The practical orthography **136**
12.1 Comparison of orthographies 136
12.1.1 Spelling of consonants 136
12.1.2 Spelling of vowels 138
12.2 The orthography used in this grammar 139
12.2.1 <ä> and <a> 139
12.2.2 Tone 139
12.2.3 Lenis fricatives 140
12.2.4 Word-initial glottal stop, <w> and <y> 141
12.2.5 Capitalization 141
12.2.6 Phonological variation and standardization 142
12.3 Summary 143

III Lexical categories

13 Nouns **146**
13.1 Stem nouns 147
13.2 Affixed stems 147
13.2.1 Suffixed stems 147
13.2.1.1 Suffix -v 147
13.2.1.2 Suffix *-ł* 148
13.2.1.3 Suffix -’ 148
13.2.2 Prefixed stems 149

13.2.2.1 Prefix *ch'-* 149
13.2.2.2 Prefix *į́į-, ii-* 150
13.2.2.3 Prefix *hu-* 150
13.2.2.4 Prefix *ǫǫ-, oo-* 150
13.2.2.5 Adverbial prefixes 151
13.2.2.6 Prefix *n-* 151
13.2.2.7 Prefix *di-* 152
13.2.2.8 Prefix *nah-, naa-* 152
13.2.2.9 Prefix *ni-, nii-, nih-* 153
13.3 Other disyllabic stems 153
13.4 Compound nouns 154
13.4.1 Noun + noun compounds 154
13.4.1.1 Noun + noun:POSS 155
13.4.1.2 Noun + noun 157
13.4.2 Noun + verb 158
13.4.3 Noun + modifier compounds 159
13.4.4 Noun + postposition compounds 160
13.4.5 Compounding as a recursive process 161
13.5 Deverbal nouns 161
13.5.1 Subject nominalization 162
13.5.2 Direct object nominalization 163
13.5.3 Postpositional object nominalization 164
13.5.4 Deverbal nouns in compounds 165
13.6 Loanwords 165
13.7 Summary 167

14 Verbs **168**
14.1 Structure 168
14.2 Semantics 169
14.2.1 Active verbs 169
14.2.2 Neuter verbs 170
14.3 Functions 171
14.3.1 Verb phrases as predicates 171
14.3.2 Verb phrases as attributes 171
14.4 Summary 172

15 Free postpositions **173**
15.1 Properties 173
15.1.1 Compatibility with verb themes 173

15.1.2 Separability of free postpositions 175
15.1.3 Free postpositions and conjugation markers 175
15.2 Inventory 176
15.2.1 Postpositions of place 176
15.2.1.1 P+*dą'* 'at P' 176
15.2.1.2 P+*dänh, danh* 'at P' 177
15.2.1.3 P+*tah* 'among P, in the area of P' 178
15.2.1.4 P+*ts'änh* 'from P' 179
15.2.1.5 P+*ch'a'* 'from P' 180
15.2.1.6 P+*nts'ą̈'* 'toward P' 181
15.2.1.7 P+*ttheh* 'in front of P' 182
15.2.1.8 P+*k'eh* 'behind P, following P' 182
15.2.1.9 P+*k'e'* 'not reaching P' 183
15.2.1.10 P+*k'üü* 'next to P' 183
15.2.1.11 P+*t'aat, t'aa* 'underneath P' 184
15.2.1.12 P+*k'it* 'on top of P' 184
15.2.1.13 P+*shyiit* 'inside P, into P' 185
15.2.1.14 P+*tüh* 'over, across' 186
15.2.1.15 P+*taagn, tag* 'meandering through P' . . . 186
15.2.1.16 P+*aanah* 'around (in a circular motion)' . 187
15.2.1.17 P+*maagn* 'around P, at the edge of P' . . . 187
15.2.1.18 P+*aaxah* 'in the vicinity of P' 187
15.2.1.19 P+*ch'ąą* 'opposite P, a little ways from P' . 188
15.2.1.20 P+*ahch'aa* 'far from P' 189
15.2.1.21 P+*daachiit* 'blocking P's way' 189
15.2.1.22 P+*naał* 'in front of P's eyes' 189
15.2.1.23 P+*nänht'aagn, naht'aag, nuht'aag* 'behind P's back' 190
15.2.1.24 P+*tthiit'aag* 'on top of P' 190
15.2.1.25 P+*tthiłt'aagn* 'behind P's head' 191
15.2.1.26 P+*daategn, daatagn* 'between P' 191
15.2.1.27 P+*nia* 'in the middle of P' 192
15.2.1.28 P+*tth'itohnia, tthitohnia* 'in the middle of P (water)' 193
15.2.1.29 P+*eekeh* 'halfway up P, on the side of P' . . 194
15.2.1.30 P+*uudih* 'all the way P' 194
15.2.2 Temporal postpositions 194
15.2.2.1 P+*dą'* 'when P (PST)' 194
15.2.2.2 P+*de'* 'when P (FUT)' 195

15.2.2.3 P+*tah* 'when P' . . . 196
15.2.2.4 P+*ttheh* 'before P' . . . 197
15.2.2.5 P+*naattheh* 'long before P' . . . 197
15.2.2.6 P+*k'ehtl'üdn* 'after P's death' . . . 198
15.2.2.7 P+*uudih* 'all P long' . . . 198
15.2.3 Participant postpositions . . . 199
15.2.3.1 P+*xah, aa* 'for P, about P' . . . 199
15.2.3.2 P+*eh, eł* 'with P' . . . 201
15.2.3.3 P+*k'eh* 'like P' . . . 203
15.2.3.4 P+*kah* 'in quest of P, to get P' . . . 204
15.2.3.5 P+*de' kah* 'to see if P' . . . 204
15.2.3.6 P+*doo* 'waiting for P' . . . 205
15.2.3.7 P+*ehdänh, ehdanh* 'without P, lacking P' . . 205
15.2.3.8 P+*kįį'* 'subsisting on P' . . . 205
15.2.3.9 P+*k'įįl* 'on account of P, through P's fault' 206
15.2.3.10 P+*k'eexaagn* 'on account of P, through P's fault' . . . 206
15.2.3.11 P+*k'ia'* 'on account of P' . . . 206
15.2.3.12 P+*k'etl'aa(t)* 'in P's place, following P' . . . 207
15.2.3.13 P+*ch'a'* 'for fear of P, tired of P' . . . 207
15.2.4 Comparative postpositions . . . 207
15.2.4.1 P+*k'eh* 'like P, as __ as P' . . . 208
15.2.4.2 P+*k'e'* 'less than P' . . . 208
15.2.4.3 P+*ch'ashyiit* 'more than P' . . . 208
15.2.4.4 P+*ch'ahnoo* 'lots more than P' . . . 209
15.3 Summary . . . 209

16 Adverbs **211**
16.1 Functions . . . 211
16.2 Adverb formation . . . 212
16.2.1 Stem adverbs . . . 212
16.2.2 Complex adverbs . . . 213
16.2.2.1 Adverb stem plus other material . . . 213
16.2.2.2 Adverbs from postpositional phrases . . . 214
16.2.2.3 Adverbs from verb phrases . . . 215
16.2.3 Adverbializers . . . 215
16.3 Semantic categorization . . . 217
16.3.1 Spatial adverbs . . . 217
16.3.2 Temporal adverbs . . . 218

16.3.3 Aspectual adverbs 219
16.3.4 Manner adverbs 220
16.3.5 Degree adverbs 222
16.4 Summary 223

17 Directionals **224**
17.1 Directional stems 225
17.1.1 Forms 226
17.1.1.1 *ne'* 'upriver' 227
17.1.1.2 *da'* 'downriver' 228
17.1.1.3 *negn'* 'upland, up the shore' 230
17.1.1.4 *tthän'* 'downland, toward water' 233
17.1.1.5 *degn'* 'up above, uphill' 234
17.1.1.6 *shyign'* 'down below, downhill' 236
17.1.1.7 *naan'* 'across' 237
17.1.1.8 *noo'* 'ahead' 239
17.1.1.9 *'än* 'out' 240
17.1.2 Semantics 241
17.1.2.1 *ne'* 'upriver, backward' 241
17.1.2.2 *da'* 'downriver' 244
17.1.2.3 *negn'* 'upland, up the shore, back (in a boat, house)' 244
17.1.2.4 *tthän'* 'downland, toward water' 245
17.1.2.5 *degn'* 'up above, uphill' 246
17.1.2.6 *shyign'* 'down below, downhill, on the ground' 246
17.1.2.7 *naan'* 'across' 246
17.1.2.8 *noo'* 'ahead, into the open, by the hearth, a long way away, a long time in the future' 247
17.1.2.9 *'än'* 'out, away, off to the side' 249
17.2 Prefixes 250
17.2.1 Prefix order 250
17.2.2 Semantics of directional prefixes 252
17.2.2.1 *hu-* 'AR'- 252
17.2.2.2 *tth'i-* 'straight out' 253
17.2.2.3 Distance distinction: *da-, na-, ya-, a-* . . 254
17.2.2.4 *ha-* 'ADJC'- 258
17.3 High tone on directional stems 259
17.4 Summary 261

18 Adjectives and modifiers **263**
18.1 Adjectives 264
18.1.1 Functions 264
18.1.2 Inventory 265
18.1.2.1 *abah* 'ouch' 265
18.1.2.2 *elih* 'cold' 266
18.1.2.3 *elok* 'hot' 266
18.1.2.4 *idzii'* 'scary' 266
18.1.2.5 *įįjih* 'taboo, forbidden' 267
18.1.2.6 *choh* 'big' 267
18.1.2.7 *teejuh* 'poor, pitiful, cute, respectful' . . . 267
18.1.2.8 *t'ayaadn, ayaa* 'filthy, disgusting' 268
18.1.2.9 *tsin'įį, tsinaa'įį* 'thank you (very much), (very) grateful' 268
18.2 Modifiers 269
18.2.1 Functions 269
18.2.2 Inventory 269
18.2.2.1 *choh* 'big' 269
18.2.2.2 *gaay* 'young, small' 270
18.2.2.3 *guuy* 'small, tiny' 271
18.2.2.4 *su', suu'* 'pretty, good' 272
18.2.2.5 *shyuh* 'full, complete' 272
18.2.2.6 *teejuh* 'poor, pitiful' 273
18.2.2.7 *tleegn* 'dirty, rotten' 273
18.3 Summary 274

19 Pronouns **275**
19.1 Personal pronouns 275
19.1.1 Inventory 275
19.1.2 Functions 275
19.1.2.1 Identification of individuals 276
19.1.2.2 Emphasis and contrast 277
19.1.2.3 Pronoun + *shyįį'* 'by oneself' 278
19.2 Demonstrative pronouns 279
19.3 Interrogative proforms 279
19.3.1 Inventory 280
19.3.2 Functions 280
19.3.2.1 Interrogative proforms in questions 280
19.3.2.2 Indefinite and negative proforms 282

19.3.2.2.1 *doo* 'someone, whoever, nobody' 282
19.3.2.2.2 *dii* 'something, whatever, everything, nothing' 284
19.3.2.2.3 *nts'ąą'* 'however, no way' 285
19.3.2.2.4 *nduugn* 'somewhere, wherever' . 286
19.3.2.2.5 *ndee* 'somewhere, any place' . . 286
19.3.2.2.6 *nday* 'somewhere' 287
19.3.2.2.7 No indefinite adverb 'whenever, never' 287
19.4 Summary 287

20 Numerals 289
20.1 Cardinal numerals 289
20.1.1 Dialectal variation 289
20.1.2 Morphological structure of numerals 290
20.1.3 Numerals greater than 10 292
20.1.4 No animacy-based distinction 292
20.1.5 Fractions 292
20.2 Other number words 293
20.2.1 Ordinal numbers 293
20.2.2 X times 293
20.2.3 No incorporation of numerals 294
20.3 Use of numerals 294
20.3.1 Numbers of special significance 296
20.3.1.1 Four times 297
20.3.1.2 Two people 299
20.3.1.3 Three units of time 299
20.4 Summary 300

21 Other minor word categories 302
21.1 Non-verbal predicates 302
21.1.1 O *nde'* 'give me o' 302
21.1.2 O *na'* 'take o, here is o' 303
21.1.3 *aan* 'come in, come here' 304
21.1.4 *duk* 'get ready, go' 304
21.1.5 *(t)thee' (de')* 'wait' 305
21.1.6 O+*kol* 'O NEGEX, there is no o' 305
21.2 Interjections 306
21.2.1 *iih* 'oh no! yuck' 306

21.2.2 *edzee'* 'oh my! goodness!' 307
21.2.3 *adzu'* 'oops! oh!' 307
21.2.4 *ohįį* 'if only' 307
21.2.5 *ayt'oo* 'okay, all right' 308
21.2.6 *hǫǫ'shyįį', ayshyįį'* 'that's all' 308
21.3 One-word responses 309
21.3.1 *ąą* 'yes' 309
21.3.2 *duka'* 'all right, okay' 309
21.3.3 *ina', ena'* 'no' 310
21.3.4 *sǫ'* 'don't' 311
21.3.5 *le'e, le'* 'I don't know' 311
21.4 Miscellaneous function words 311
21.4.1 Quantifiers 311
21.4.2 Coordinating conjunctions 312
21.4.3 Discourse markers 312
21.4.4 Modal particles 312
21.4.5 Polarity particles 312
21.4.6 Plural enclitic *tin* 313
21.5 Summary 313

IV Morphology

22 Possessor inflection **316**
22.1 Different types of possession 316
22.1.1 Obligatorily possessed nouns 316
22.1.2 Optionally possessed nouns 317
22.2 Possessive morphology 318
22.2.1 Possessive suffixes 318
22.2.1.1 Alienable possessive suffix 319
22.2.1.2 Inalienable possessive suffix 319
22.2.2 Possessor prefixes 321
22.2.2.1 First- and second-person possessor prefixes 321
22.2.2.1.1 First-person singular *sh-* 321
22.2.2.1.2 Second-person singular *n-* . . . 321
22.2.2.1.3 First-person plural *nee-* 322
22.2.2.1.4 Second-person plural *nuh-* . . 323
22.2.2.2 Third-person possessor prefixes 323
22.2.2.2.1 Third-person singular *u-/mb-* . 323

22.2.2.2.2 Third-person plural *hu-* 324
22.2.2.2.3 Disjunct third-person (singular) *i-/y-* 325
22.2.2.2.4 Disjunct third-person plural *hii-* 325
22.2.2.3 Coreferential possessor and subject 326
22.2.2.3.1 Reflexive *d-* 326
22.2.2.3.2 Reciprocal *nił-* 327
22.2.2.4 Other possessor prefixes 328
22.2.2.4.1 Areal *hu-* 328
22.2.2.4.2 Indefinite *ch'-* 328
22.2.3 Effects on the stem 329
22.2.3.1 Stem-initial fricative lenition 329
22.2.3.2 Irregular possessed stems 329
22.2.4 Restrictions on possessive morphology 330
22.2.4.1 Semantic restrictions 330
22.2.4.2 Morphological restrictions 331
22.2.5 Double possession (not attested) 334
22.3 Other possessive constructions 335
22.3.1 __ P+*ts'änh* '__ belonging to P, P's __' 335
22.3.2 Possession of deverbal nouns 336
22.4 Syntactic comments 338
22.4.1 Noun phrases and possessor prefixes 338
22.4.2 Recursion 339
22.5 Summary 340

23 Inflection of postpositions **342**
23.1 First- and second-person postpositional objects 342
23.1.1 First-person singular *sh-* 343
23.1.2 Second-person singular *n-* 343
23.1.3 First-person plural *nee-* 343
23.1.4 Second-person plural *nuh-* 344
23.2 Third-person postpositional objects 344
23.2.1 Third-person singular *u-/mb-* 344
23.2.2 Third-person plural *hu-* 345
23.2.3 Disjunct third-person (singular) *i-/y-* 346
23.2.4 Disjunct hird-person plural *hii-* 347
23.3 Coreferential postpositional object and subject 348
23.3.1 Reflexive *d-* 348

23.3.2 Reciprocal *nitł/łi-* 349
23.4 Other postpositional object prefixes 350
23.4.1 Areal *hu-* 350
23.4.2 Indefinite *ch'-* 350
23.5 Summary 351

24 Verbal morphology: An overview **352**
24.1 Conjunct and disjunct prefixes 353
24.2 The verb theme 353
24.3 Morpheme order and discontinuous morphology 354
24.4 Derivation 356
24.4.1 Aspectual derivation 356
24.4.2 Non-aspectual derivation 356
24.4.3 Superaspectual derivations 357
24.5 Inflection 359
24.6 Verbs without (overt) prefixes 359
24.6.1 The peg prefix 360
24.6.2 Bare stem verbs 361
24.7 Summary 361

25 Verb theme categories **362**
25.1 Active versus neuter verb theme categories 363
25.2 Active verb theme categories 365
25.2.1 Motion themes 365
25.2.1.1 Aspectual derivations of motion themes . 366
25.2.1.2 Non-aspectual derivations of motion themes 367
25.2.1.3 Superaspectual derivations 368
25.2.2 Successive themes 371
25.2.2.1 Derivations 371
25.2.3 Operative themes 372
25.2.3.1 Operative-durative themes 373
25.2.3.1.1 Derivations 373
25.2.3.2 Operative-onomatopoetic themes 374
25.2.3.2.1 Derivations 374
25.2.3.3 Operative-repetitive$_1$ themes 374
25.2.3.3.1 Derivations 375
25.2.3.4 Operative-repetitive$_2$ themes 375
25.2.3.4.1 Derivations 375
25.2.3.5 Operative-reversative themes 375

25.2.3.5.1 Derivations 376
25.2.3.6 Operative-persistive themes 376
25.2.3.6.1 Derivations 376
25.2.4 Conversive themes 376
25.2.4.1 Conversive-conclusive themes 376
25.2.4.1.1 Derivations 377
25.2.4.2 Conversive-reversative themes 378
25.2.4.2.1 Derivations 378
25.2.4.3 Conversive-continuative themes 379
25.2.4.3.1 Derivations 379
25.2.4.4 Conversive-repetitive$_2$ themes 379
25.2.4.4.1 Derivations 379
25.3 Neuter verb theme categories 379
25.3.1 Extension themes 380
25.3.1.1 Derivations 380
25.3.2 Neuter verb themes with (dh, aa) conjugation prefixes 381
25.3.2.1 Classificatory themes 381
25.3.2.1.1 Derivations 382
25.3.2.2 Positional themes 383
25.3.2.2.1 Derivations 383
25.3.2.3 Stative 384
25.3.2.3.1 Derivations 384
25.3.3 Neuter verbs with (Ø, aa) conjugation markers . . . 385
25.3.3.1 Dimensional 385
25.3.3.1.1 Derivations 387
25.3.3.1.1.1 Comparative derivation . 387
25.3.3.1.1.2 Transitional derivation . 388
25.3.3.2 Descriptive 389
25.3.3.2.1 Derivations 389
25.4 Summary 390

26 Verb stem 392
26.1 Phonology 392
26.1.1 Verb stems with variable onset consonant 392
26.2 Morphology: Verb stem variation 395
26.2.1 Aspectual variation 396
26.2.1.1 Stem variation in the neuter 396
26.2.1.2 Stem variation in the transitional 398
26.2.1.3 Stem variation in the momentaneous . . . 398

26.2.1.4 Stem variation in the durative 399
26.2.1.5 Stem variation in the semelfactive 400
26.2.1.6 Stem variation in the conclusive 401
26.2.1.7 Stem variation in the perambulative . . . 401
26.2.1.8 Stem variation in the continuative 401
26.2.1.9 Stem variation in the reversative 403
26.2.1.10 Stem variation in the onomatopoetic . . . 403
26.2.1.11 Stem variation in the repetitive$_1$ 404
26.2.1.12 Stem variation in the repetitive$_2$ 404
26.2.1.13 Stem variation in the persistive 405
26.2.1.14 Irregular stems 405
26.2.2 Superaspectual stem variation 405
26.2.2.1 Stem variation in the customary 406
26.2.2.2 Stem variation in the progressive 406
26.2.2.3 Stem variation in the distributive 407
26.3 Suppletive stems 408
26.4 Summary 408

27 Voice/valence markers **409**
27.1 Phonology 409
27.1.1 Voice/valence marker Ø- 410
27.1.1.1 Lenition after Ø- 410
27.1.1.2 Ø- in verbs with no onset consonant . . . 410
27.1.2 Voice/valence marker D- 410
27.1.2.1 "D-effect": D- before stem-initial consonants 410
27.1.2.1.1 Lenition after D- 411
27.1.2.1.2 D- plus /ʔ/ 411
27.1.2.2 D- in stems without an onset consonant . 412
27.1.3 Voice/valence marker H- 412
27.1.3.1 No lenition after H- 412
27.1.3.2 H- in stems without an onset consonant . 412
27.1.4 Voice/valence marker L- 412
27.1.4.1 Lenition after L- 412
27.1.4.2 L- in verb stems without onset consonant 413
27.2 Thematic voice/valence markers 413
27.3 Productive (derivational) uses of the voice/valence prefixes . . 414
27.3.1 Voice/valence prefix changes to H- 414
27.3.1.1 Causativization 414

27.3.1.2 Possessive transitivization 416
27.3.1.3 Comparative derivation 417
27.3.1.4 Other transitivization 417
27.3.1.5 Intensification 418
27.3.2 Voice/valence prefix changes to D- or L- 419
27.3.2.1 Transitivity decrease 421
27.3.2.1.1 Passivization 421
27.3.2.1.2 Reflexive 423
27.3.2.1.3 Self-benefactives 424
27.3.2.1.4 Reciprocals 425
27.3.2.1.5 Other transitivity reduction . . 427
27.3.2.2 Iterative 428
27.3.2.2.1 Iterative in intransitive themes . 428
27.3.2.2.2 Iterative in transitive themes . . 429
27.3.2.3 Perambulative 430
27.4 Summary 431

28 Subject marking **432**
28.1 First person 433
28.1.1 Phonology 433
28.1.1.1 Glottal stop insertion 434
28.1.1.2 Nasalization of *ag-* 435
28.1.2 Functions 435
28.1.2.1 Indexing the speaker 435
28.1.2.2 Indexing the subject of the matrix clause . 436
28.2 Second person 436
28.2.1 Phonology of the second-person singular subject prefix 436
28.2.1.1 Glottal stop insertion 437
28.2.1.2 Denasalization before L- 438
28.2.2 Phonology of the second-person plural subject . . . 438
28.2.2.1 Glottal stop insertion 439
28.2.3 Functions of the second-person subject prefixes . . . 440
28.2.3.1 Second-person subject in declarative sentences 440
28.2.3.2 Second-person subjects in questions . . . 440
28.2.3.3 Second person subject prefixes in requests 440
28.3 Syntax of inner subject prefixes 441
28.3.1 Pronominal prefixes 441
28.3.2 Inner subject prefixes with free noun phrases 441

28.3.3 Inner subject prefixes with coreferential free pronouns 442
28.4 Summary 443

29 Conjugation and mode prefixes 444
29.1 Imperfective Ø- 445
29.1.1 The Ø- imperfective 446
29.1.2 The *aa*- imperfective 446
29.1.3 The *n*- imperfective 447
29.1.4 The *i*- imperfective 448
29.2 Perfective *į*- 449
29.2.1 The Ø- perfective 449
29.2.2 The *aa*- perfective 452
29.2.3 The *n*- perfective 453
29.2.4 The *dh*- perfective 455
29.2.5 The *i*- perfective 456
29.3 Optative *u*- 457
29.4 Negative perfective *i*- 459
29.5 Summary 461

30 Qualifiers 462
30.1 Inventory and order 463
30.2 The *i*- qualifier 463
30.3 The *n*- qualifier 464
30.3.1 Functions 465
30.3.1.1 Errative 465
30.3.1.2 *n*- as gender prefix 465
30.3.1.3 Other derivational uses of *n*- 466
30.3.1.4 *n*- in themes of seeing and hiding 466
30.3.1.5 Lexicalized *n*- qualifier 467
30.3.2 Phonology 467
30.4 The *d*- qualifier 468
30.4.1 Functions 468
30.4.1.1 *d*- as gender prefix 469
30.4.1.2 *d*- in self-benefactives 469
30.4.1.3 Lexicalized *d*- qualifier 469
30.4.2 Phonology 470
30.5 The *dh*- qualifier 472
30.5.1 Position and function 472
30.5.2 Phonology 472

30.6 The *t*- qualifier . . . 473
30.6.1 Functions of the *t*- qualifier . . . 473
30.6.1.1 Inceptive derivations in motion themes . . 474
30.6.1.2 Inceptive perfective . . . 474
30.6.1.3 Future . . . 475
30.6.1.4 Lexicalized *t*-qualifier . . . 476
30.6.2 Phonology . . . 476
30.7 The *u*- qualifier . . . 478
30.7.1 Functions . . . 479
30.7.1.1 The *u*- qualifier in successive verb themes 479
30.7.1.2 The *u*- qualifier in motion verbs . . . 481
30.7.1.3 Lexicalized *u*- qualifier . . . 481
30.7.2 Phonology . . . 482
30.8 The *hu*-qualifier . . . 482
30.8.1 Pronominal or qualifier? . . . 483
30.8.1.1 Areal gender . . . 483
30.8.1.2 Lexicalized areal . . . 484
30.8.2 Phonology . . . 484
30.9 Summary . . . 487

31 Pronominal prefixes **488**
31.1 Outer subject prefixes . . . 488
31.1.1 Third-person (singular) subject Ø- . . . 488
31.1.1.1 Functions . . . 489
31.1.1.2 Syntax . . . 490
31.1.1.3 Phonology . . . 490
31.1.2 Third-person plural subject *h*- . . . 491
31.1.2.1 Functions . . . 491
31.1.2.1.1 (Human) plural subject prefix . 491
31.1.2.1.2 Nonspecific human subject prefix 492
31.1.2.2 Syntax . . . 493
31.1.2.3 Phonology . . . 493
31.1.2.3.1 Schwa insertion . . . 493
31.1.2.3.2 Expansion to *hih*- . . . 494
31.1.2.3.3 Resyllabification of *h*- . . . 494
31.1.3 First-person plural subject *ts'*- . . . 495
31.1.3.1 Functions . . . 495
31.1.3.1.1 Indexing group including the speaker . . . 495

31.1.3.1.2 Indexing the subject of the matrix clause 496
31.1.3.1.3 *ts'*- in prohibitive constructions 497
31.1.3.1.4 Impersonal uses of *ts'*- 497
31.1.3.2 Syntax 498
31.1.3.3 Phonology 499
31.1.3.3.1 Schwa insertion 499
31.1.3.3.2 Qualifier absorption 499
31.1.3.3.3 Indefinite object absorption . . 500
31.1.4 Indefinite subject *ch'*- 501
31.1.4.1 Functions 501
31.1.4.2 Syntax 502
31.1.4.3 Phonology 503
31.1.5 Areal subject *hu*- 503
31.1.5.1 Functions 503
31.1.5.2 Syntax 503
31.1.5.2.1 Coreferential noun phrases . . . 503
31.1.5.2.2 Dummy subject 504
31.1.5.3 Phonology 504
31.1.5.3.1 Coalescence with iterative prefix 504
31.1.5.3.2 Coalescence with conjugation and mode markers 505
31.2 Direct object prefixes 505
31.2.1 First- and second-person direct object prefixes . . . 505
31.2.1.1 First-person singular direct object *sh*- . . 505
31.2.1.1.1 Functions 505
31.2.1.1.1.1 Indexing the speaker . . 505
31.2.1.1.1.2 Indexing the subject of the matrix clause 506
31.2.1.1.2 Syntax 506
31.2.1.1.3 Phonology 506
31.2.1.2 Second-person singular direct object *n*- . 507
31.2.1.2.1 Functions 507
31.2.1.2.2 Syntax 507
31.2.1.2.3 Phonology 507
31.2.1.3 First-person plural direct object *nee*- . . . 508
31.2.1.3.1 Functions 508
31.2.1.3.2 Syntax 508
31.2.1.3.3 Phonology 509

31.2.1.4 Second-person plural direct object *nuh-* . 509
31.2.1.4.1 Functions 509
31.2.1.4.2 Syntax 509
31.2.1.4.3 Phonology 509
31.2.2 Third-person direct object prefixes 510
31.2.2.1 Unmarked third-person (singular) object . 510
31.2.2.2 Third-person plural direct object *hu-* . . . 510
31.2.2.2.1 Functions 510
31.2.2.2.2 Syntax 511
31.2.2.2.3 Phonology 511
31.2.2.3 Disjunct hird-person (singular) *i/y-* . . . 511
31.2.2.3.1 Functions 511
31.2.2.3.2 Syntax 512
31.2.2.3.3 Phonology 512
31.2.2.4 Disjunct third-person plural *hii/hiiy-* . . . 512
31.2.2.4.1 Function 512
31.2.2.4.2 Syntax 513
31.2.2.4.3 Phonology 513
31.2.3 Coreferential subject and direct object 513
31.2.3.1 Reflexive singular direct object *id-* 513
31.2.3.1.1 Functions 513
31.2.3.1.2 Syntax 514
31.2.3.1.3 Phonology 514
31.2.3.2 Plural reflexive direct object *ihd-* 514
31.2.3.2.1 Function 514
31.2.3.2.2 Syntax 515
31.2.3.2.3 Phonology 515
31.2.3.3 Reciprocal object 515
31.2.3.3.1 Function 515
31.2.3.3.1.1 Productive use 515
31.2.3.3.1.2 Lexicalized use 516
31.2.3.3.2 Syntax 516
31.2.3.3.3 Phonology 517
31.2.3.3.3.1 Allomorph *łi-* 517
31.2.4 Other direct object prefixes 517
31.2.4.1 Areal object *hu-* 517
31.2.4.1.1 Functions 518
31.2.4.1.2 Syntax 518

31.2.4.1.2.1 Co-occurrence with noun phrases 518
31.2.4.1.2.2 Introducing complement clauses 518
31.2.4.1.3 Phonology 519
31.2.4.1.3.1 *ho-* versus *hu-* 519
31.2.4.1.3.2 Coalescence with iterative 519
31.2.4.1.3.3 Coalescence with conjugation markers 519
31.2.4.2 Indefinite direct object *ch'-* 519
31.2.4.2.1 Functions 519
31.2.4.2.1.1 Unknown or unelaborated referent 520
31.2.4.2.1.2 Lexicalized use 521
31.2.4.2.2 Syntax 521
31.2.4.2.3 Phonology 521
31.2.4.2.3.1 Epenthesis 521
31.2.4.2.3.2 Qualifier absorption . . 521
31.2.4.2.3.3 Absorption into *ts'-* . . 522
31.3 Summary 522

32 Distributive prefix **524**
32.1 Position 524
32.2 Phonology 525
32.3 Function 525
32.3.1 Indefinite object *ch'-* + first-person plural subject *ts'-* 525
32.3.2 Pejorative *ts'-* and first-person plural subject *ts'-* . . 526
32.3.3 Exception 527
32.4 Redistribution of distributive functions 527
32.4.1 Iterative and distributive 528
32.5 Summary 530

33 Incorporated roots **531**
33.1 Position 531
33.2 Inventory of incorporates 531
33.2.1 Body parts 532
33.2.1.1 *tthi-* 'head' 532
33.2.1.2 *xa-* 'hair' 532
33.2.1.3 *nii-* 'mind' 532

33.2.1.4 *naak-* 'eye' 533
33.2.1.5 *dzii-* 'hearing, inner ear' 533
33.2.1.6 *da-* 'mouth' 533
33.2.1.7 *thaa-* 'mouth' 534
33.2.1.8 *thah-* 'voice' 534
33.2.1.9 *thii(n)-* 'neck' 535
33.2.1.10 *dzii-, dzeeyh-* 'heart' 535
33.2.1.11 *thu(u)-* 'skin' 535
33.2.1.12 *gaan', gą̨ą̨'-* 'arm' 536
33.2.1.13 *ła-* 'hand' 536
33.2.1.14 *tl'a-* 'buttocks, stern' 537
33.2.1.15 *nän, nan-* 'back' 537
33.2.1.16 *chi-* 'tail' 537
33.2.1.17 *got-* 'knee' 538
33.2.1.18 *ki̱-, ke-* 'foot' 538

33.2.2 Other stems 538
33.2.2.1 *'eeł-* 'trap' 538
33.2.2.2 *chin-* 'moving as a group' 539
33.2.2.3 *dli-* 'cold' 539
33.2.2.4 *dlįǫ-* 'snare' 539
33.2.2.5 *dloh-* 'laugh' 539
33.2.2.6 *kon'-* 'fire' 540
33.2.2.7 *łįǫ'-, łǫǫ-* 'drag' 540
33.2.2.8 *kał-* 'patch' 540
33.2.2.9 *neeł-* 'group of people' 541
33.2.2.10 *sa-, saa-* 'sun' 541
33.2.2.11 *säł-* 'hollering' 541
33.2.2.12 *shya-* 'noise' 542
33.2.2.13 *shyah-* 'house' 542
33.2.2.14 *shyia-* 'knot' 542
33.2.2.15 *(ch'u)shyoo-* 'whistle' 542
33.2.2.16 *ta-* 'water' 543
33.2.2.17 *tät-* 'cane' 543
33.2.2.18 *tl'uuł-* 'rope' 543
33.2.2.19 *tsaa-* 'cache' 543
33.2.2.20 *tsüh-, tsaa-* 'cry' 544
33.2.2.21 *tsüü-* 'whip' 544
33.2.2.22 *tsiił-* 'snow' 544
33.2.2.23 *tthee-* 'bark' 544

33.2.2.24 *tthii-* 'rock' 545
33.2.2.25 *xał-* 'sled' 545
33.2.2.26 *xał-* 'club' 545
33.2.2.27 *xeeł-* 'darkness' 546
33.2.2.28 *xeeł-* 'pack' 546
33.2.3 Incorporates with no corresponding free stem 546
33.2.3.1 *chi-* 'pretend' 546
33.2.3.2 *ch'edzi-* 'quadruped' 547
33.2.3.3 *ła-* 'sagging, deteriotating' 547
33.2.3.4 *mbäł-, mbał-* 'sleep' 547
33.2.3.5 *ta-* 'skin' 548
33.2.3.6 *thaa-* 'fighting' 548
33.2.3.7 *thi-, shi-* 'in fright' 549
33.2.3.8 *xa-* 'weapon' 549
33.2.3.9 *xeeł* 'cramped, crippled' 550
33.3 Incorporated roots, not stems 550
33.4 Phonological properties 553
33.4.1 Truncation of incorporates 553
33.4.2 Glottal stop insertion 553
33.5 The syntax of incorporates 553
33.5.1 Incorporates as arguments 554
33.5.2 Incorporates as adverbials 556
33.6 Productivity and lexicalization 557
33.7 Incorporation and language endangerment 561
33.8 Summary 561

34 Iterative prefix **562**
34.1 Position 562
34.2 Functions 562
34.2.1 Iterative prefix string 563
34.2.1.1 Iterative indicating simple repetition . . . 563
34.2.1.2 Iterative in transitive themes: 'another o' . 563
34.2.1.3 Iterative plus customary superaspect . . . 564
34.2.1.4 Iterative in motion themes: return to origin 564
34.2.1.5 Iterative in neuter themes: return to a previous state 565
34.2.1.6 Iterative in cyclical events 566
34.2.1.7 Overlaps in meaning 567
34.2.2 Lexicalized iterative prefix 567

34.2.3 "Distributive" functions 568
34.2.3.1 Distributive derivations 568
34.2.3.2 Lexicalized "distributive" 569
34.3 Phonology 569
34.3.1 Iterative absorption 570
34.3.2 Coalescence with areal prefix 570
34.4 Summary 570

35 Adverbial-derivational prefixes **572**
35.1 Adverbial-derivational prefixes and aspectual prefix strings . 573
35.2 Inventory 575
35.2.1 Directional adverbial-derivational prefixes 575
35.2.1.1 *ch'a-* 'away, out' 575
35.2.1.1.1 ch'a#(n, n) 'away, out' 575
35.2.1.2 *da-* 'orifice' 576
35.2.1.2.1 da# (n, n) 'into dwelling' 576
35.2.1.2.2 da#n (Ø, dh) 'filling, full' 576
35.2.1.2.3 da#t+n (dh, aa) 'full' 576
35.2.1.2.4 da# (Ø, dh) 'closing off' 577
35.2.1.3 *da-* 'up, on' 577
35.2.1.3.1 da# (?, dh) 'up, ascending' . . . 577
35.2.1.3.2 da# (dh, aa) 'up, at an elevation' 578
35.2.1.3.3 da+tl'a# (Ø, dh) 'up onto shore' 578
35.2.1.3.4 k'i+da#, k'e+da# (?, dh) 'upon' . 579
35.2.1.4 *dzi-* 'dividing' 579
35.2.1.4.1 dzi# (?, ?) 'over edge' 579
35.2.1.4.2 dzi+na# (Ø, aa) 'down over edge' 580
35.2.1.4.3 sdzi# (Ø, dh) 'split, apart' . . . 580
35.2.1.4.4 sdzi# (Ø, aa) 'split' 580
35.2.1.5 *ha-* 'up and out' 581
35.2.1.5.1 ha# (Ø, aa) 'up and out, out from below' 581
35.2.1.5.2 ha# (Ø, dh) 'off, into a pattern' . 581
35.2.1.6 *ha-* '?' 582
35.2.1.6.1 ha# (?, ?) 'turn around' 582
35.2.1.7 *k̲i-* 'against, up' 582
35.2.1.7.1 ki# (Ø, aa) 'up, climbing' 582
35.2.1.7.2 ski# (n, n) 'across' 583
35.2.1.7.3 ski# (n, aa) 'across' 583

35.2.1.7.4 sts'a+ke# (?, dh) 'around in a circle' 584
35.2.1.7.5 ki+tl'a# (?, dh) 'to shore' 584
35.2.1.7.6 ki+tl'a# (Ø, aa) 'ashore' 585
35.2.1.7.7 ti+ki# (?, aa) 'off trail' 585
35.2.1.7.8 *he-* (Ø, n) 'against' 585
35.2.1.8 *k'i-* 'on' 586
35.2.1.8.1 k'i# (?, n) 'to the trail' 586
35.2.1.8.2 k'e# (Ø, aa) 'along the trail' . . 586
35.2.1.8.3 ti+k'i# (?, aa) 'onto the trail' . . 586
35.2.1.8.4 nił+k'i# (Ø, dh) 'back and forth' 587
35.2.1.9 *k'i-* 'by the wayside' 587
35.2.1.9.1 k'e# (?, dh?) 'by the wayside' . . 587
35.2.1.10 *na-* 'iterative' 588
35.2.1.10.1 na#t+D (aa, n), łoo#(t) (aa, n) 'perambulative' 588
35.2.1.10.2 na+ke#(d) (Ø, dh) 'around and back, around and over' 590
35.2.1.10.3 sna+ke# (?, ?) 'around in a circle' 591
35.2.1.11 *na-* 'down' 591
35.2.1.11.1 na# (Ø, aa) 'down' 591
35.2.1.11.2 na# (dh, aa) 'down' 591
35.2.1.12 *ni-* 'terminative' 592
35.2.1.12.1 ni# (n, n) 'to a point, stopping' . 592
35.2.1.12.2 ni# (n, aa) 'to a point, stopping' 592
35.2.1.12.3 ni# (i, i), ni# (Ø, dh) 'up vertically' 592
35.2.1.13 *taa-* 'down' 593
35.2.1.13.1 taa# (?, n) 'down' 593
35.2.1.14 *ta-* 'off to the side' 593
35.2.1.14.1 ta#t+n (?, dh) 'off to the side' . 593
35.2.1.14.2 sta# 'away' (n, n) 594
35.2.1.15 *ta-* 'among' 595
35.2.1.15.1 ta# (Ø, aa) 'distribute' 595
35.2.1.16 *ta-* 'into the water' 595
35.2.1.16.1 ta# (Ø, aa) 'into the water' . . . 595
35.2.1.16.2 ta# (?, ?) 'upland' 596
35.2.1.16.3 ta# (Ø, aa) 'upland' 596
35.2.1.17 *ti-* 'submerged in water, underwater' . . . 597
35.2.1.17.1 ti# (Ø, n) 'underwater' 597

35.2.1.17.2 ti# (dh, aa) 'underwater' 598
35.2.1.18 *ti-* 'out of enclosure, out into the open' . . 598
35.2.1.18.1 ti# (n, n) 'out into the open' . . 598
35.2.1.18.2 ti+ki# (Ø, aa) 'off the trail' . . . 598
35.2.1.19 *t'a-* 'under, out and down' 599
35.2.1.19.1 t'a# (Ø, aa) 'under, out and down' 599
35.2.1.19.2 t'a# (Ø, aa) '?' 599
35.2.1.19.3 s+t'a# (Ø, aa) 'up?' 600
35.2.1.20 *tth'a-* 'out and away' 600
35.2.1.20.1 tth'a# (Ø, aa) 'out and away' . . 600
35.2.1.21 *tthi-* 'into the fire, into the open' 601
35.2.1.21.1 tthi#d (Ø, aa) 'into the fire, into the open' 601
35.2.1.21.2 tthi# (n, n) 'out' 602
35.2.1.22 *tth'i-* 'straight out' 602
35.2.1.22.1 tth'i# (Ø, dh) 'straight out' . . . 602
35.2.1.22.2 tth'i# (dh, aa) 'straight out' . . . 602
35.2.1.23 *ts'i-* 'wake' 603
35.2.1.23.1 ts'i# (n, n) 'wake' 603
35.2.1.24 *ya-* 'continuously' 603
35.2.1.24.1 ya# (Ø, ?) 'continously' 603
35.2.1.25 *ya-* 'into air' (Ø, aa) 603
35.2.1.25.1 ya+ha# (?, aa) 'out into the air' . 604
35.2.2 Nondirectional adverbial-derivational prefixes 604
35.2.2.1 *da-* 'ADMIR, excessively'- 604
35.2.2.1.1 da#t+H (dh, ?) 'ADMIR, excessively' 604
35.2.2.2 *dzi-* 'mourn' 605
35.2.2.2.1 dzi# (Ø, aa) 'mourn' 605
35.2.2.3 *ha-* 'spot, look around' 605
35.2.2.3.1 ha#d+L (?, n) 'spot' 605
35.2.2.3.2 P+kah ## ha#ch'+(uu)+d+L (Ø, aa) 'look around for P' 605
35.2.2.4 *ha-* 'completely' (Ø?, aa) 606
35.2.2.4.1 ha# (?, aa) 'completely' 606
35.2.2.5 *k'i-* 'severing' 606
35.2.2.5.1 k'i#G (Ø, n) 'severing' 606
35.2.2.5.2 k'i# (?, dh) 'figure out' 607
35.2.2.5.3 ni+k'i#hu+d 'figure out' 607

35.2.2.6 *ła*-'completely' 608
35.2.2.6.1 ła#t+(n) (? dh), ła# (?, n) 'completely' 608
35.2.2.6.2 ła# (?, n) 'drown' 609
35.2.2.7 *na*- 'continuative' 609
35.2.2.7.1 na#(t)+D (aa, dh) 'continuative' 609
35.2.2.7.2 k'i+na# (?, aa) 'taking revenge' . 610
35.2.2.7.3 nat'u# (Ø, aa) 'skinning' 611
35.2.2.8 *shi*- '?' 611
35.2.2.8.1 shi#n (?, dh) 'intensely' 611
35.2.2.8.2 shi#n+L (?, dh) 'ceaselessly, uncontrollably' 612
35.2.2.9 *ti*- 'tired' 613
35.2.2.9.1 ti# (aa, aa) 'tired' 613
35.2.2.10 *tthi*- 'into pieces' 613
35.2.2.10.1 tthi#(?, n) 'into pieces' 613
35.2.3 Adjectival adverbial-derivational prefixes 613
35.2.3.1 ts'#__+v́ 'pejorative' 613
35.2.3.2 *ts'a*- 'bad' 614
35.3 Summary 615

36 Bound postpositions **616**
36.1 Bound versus free postpositions 616
36.1.1 Inseparability 617
36.1.2 Voice/valence prefix changes 618
36.1.3 Change in conjugation prefix 619
36.1.4 Semantic bleaching 620
36.2 Inventory 621
36.2.1 P+*a*- 'teaching P' 621
36.2.2 P+*i*-, Ø- 'acting on P' 621
36.2.3 P+*dzi*- 'splitting P' 623
36.2.4 P+*k'a*- 'taking care of P' 623
36.2.5 P+*k'etaa*- 'according to P, as P told S' 624
36.2.6 P+*k'i*- 'trading with P' 624
36.2.7 P+*k'ii*- 'into P (hole, depression)' 625
36.2.8 P+*k'ii*- 'rubbing P' 626
36.2.9 P+*na*- 'around P' 626
36.2.10 P+*t'a*- 'catching up with P, against P' 626
36.2.11 P+*t'a*- 'obstructing P, snagging on P' 627

36.2.12 P+*tl'a-* 'handing to P' . . . 628
36.2.13 P+*tl'a-, da-* 'exterminating P' . . . 628
36.3 Comparison to Ahtna . . . 629
36.4 Summary . . . 630

37 Verbal suffixes **631**
37.1 Inventory . . . 631
37.1.1 The nominalizing suffix -v . . . 631
37.1.1.1 Phonology . . . 631
37.1.1.2 Functions . . . 631
37.1.2 The imperative suffix -v . . . 633
37.1.2.1 Phonology . . . 633
37.1.2.2 Functions . . . 633
37.1.3 The negative suffix -v́ . . . 634
37.1.3.1 Phonology . . . 634
37.1.3.2 Functions . . . 634
37.2 Co-occurrence and ordering of suffixes . . . 635
37.3 Summary . . . 636

References **637**

List of Tables

2.1 Development of stem-final alveolar and postalveolar affricates and fricatives 16
2.2 Development of vowels preceding these affricates and fricatives 16
3.1 Dialects and speaker numbers 24
5.1 The consonants of Upper Tanana 43
6.1 The short oral monophthongs of Upper Tanana 59
6.2 The vowels of Upper Tanana 65
7.1 Syllable count, Mrs. Demit-Barnes 79
7.2 Syllable count, Mrs. Northway 80
7.3 Syllable count, Mrs. David 80
7.4 Tonal distinctions, all syllables, Mrs. Demit-Barnes 81
7.5 Tonal distinctions, verb stems only, Mrs. Demit-Barnes . . 81
7.6 Tonal distinctions, all syllables, Mrs. Northway 82
7.7 Tonal distinctions, verb stems only, Mrs. Northway 82
7.8 Tonal distinctions, all syllables, Mrs. David 83
8.1 Consonant development summary 86
8.2 Development of *t, *d, *t’, *tl, *dl, *tl’, *ʔ in onsets 87
8.3 Great Northern Series Shift 89
8.4 Development of *n, *ŋ^{y}, *ŋ$^{y}_{2}$, *w in onsets 90
8.5 Development of *d, *t’, *g^{y}, *k’^{y}, *ɢ, *q’, *ʔ in codas 91
8.6 Development of *dl, *tł’, *dz, *dž, *dž^{r}, *ts’, *tš’, *tš’^{r} in codas 92
8.7 Development of *ł, *l, *z, *s, *š, *ž, *ž^{r}, *x^{y}, *x̣, *ɣ̇ in codas . 93
8.8 Development of *w, *n, *ŋ^{y}, *y in codas 94
8.9 Neutralization and deletion of coda obstruents 96
8.10 Vowel development (summary) 97
8.11 Development of *i· 97
8.12 Development of *e· 98
8.13 Development of *a· 99
8.14 Development of *u· 99
8.15 Development of *ə 101

8.16 Development of *ɑ 102
8.17 Development of *ʊ 102
8.18 The origin of nasality from *n, *ŋʸ in codas 103
8.19 The origin of low tone from constriction 103
8.20 Vowel rounding originating in labial consonants 104
9.1 Voiceless and voiced fricatives 105
9.2 Lenis fricatives in the speech of Mrs. David (T) 108
9.3 Lenis fricatives in the speech of Mrs. Brewer (N) 108
9.4 Lenis fricatives in verbs with D-voice/valence marker 110
9.5 No lenition of /x/ following D-voice/valence marker 110
9.6 Fortis and lenis fricatives in verbs with a L-voice/valence marker 111
9.7 Fortis or lenis fricatives in verbs with a Ø-voice/valence marker 112
9.8 Fortis fricatives in verbs with H-voice/valence marker 112
12.1 Comparison of orthographies (consonants) 137
12.2 Comparison of orthographies (vowels) 138
14.1 The Upper Tanana verb, represented as a template 168
17.1 Directional stems in Pre-Proto-Dene and Upper Tanana . . 226
17.2 Directional prefixes in Upper Tanana, from Brucks (2015, 57) 250
19.1 Personal pronouns 275
19.2 Interrogative proforms 280
19.3 Indefinite and negative proforms 283
20.1 Numerals 1–10 289
20.2 Numerals 10–100, UTOLAF14Nov2401 292
23.1 Possessor, postpositional object, and direct object prefixes . 342
24.1 The Upper Tanana verb, represented as a template 352
24.2 Some verb themes mapped onto the template 355
26.1 Vowel-initial verbs 392
26.2 Inflection of verbs with D-voice/valence marker in themes with a stem without an onset consonant 394
26.3 Onset variation in 'classify PL.O, RO' 394
26.4 Stem variation in the neuter 397
26.5 Stem variation in the transitional 398
26.6 Stem variation in the momentaneous 399
26.7 Stem variation in the durative 400
26.8 Stem variation in the semelfactive 401
26.9 Stem variation in the conclusive 402
26.10 Stem variation in the perambulative 402
26.11 Stem variation in the continuative 403

26.12 Stem variation in the reversative 403
26.13 Stem variation in the onomatopoetic 404
26.14 Stem variation in the repetitive$_1$ 404
26.15 Stem suffixation patterns in the repetitive$_2$ 404
26.16 Stem variation in the persistive 405
26.17 Irregular verb stem variation 405
26.18 Stem variation in the customary superaspect 406
26.19 Stem variation in the progressive 407
26.20 Stem variation in the distributive 407
26.21 Suppletive stem sets 408
27.1 Insertion of onset consonant 410
27.2 D- in vowel-initial verbs 412
28.1 Inner-subject voice/valence prefix portmanteaus in the Ø-imperfective 433
29.1 Possible conjugation/mode prefix combinations 445
29.2 Surface forms in the Ø- imperfective 446
29.3 Surface forms in the *aa*- imperfective 447
29.4 Surface forms in the *n*- imperfective 448
29.5 Surface forms in the *i*- imperfective 449
29.6 Surface forms in the Ø- perfective 450
29.7 Surface forms in the *aa*- perfective 452
29.8 Surface forms in the *n*- perfective 454
29.9 Surface forms in the *dh*- perfective 455
29.10 Surface forms in the *i*- perfective 456
29.11 Surface forms in the optative 458
29.12 Surface forms in the negative perfective 460
30.1 The qualifier zone in the template following Kari (1993, 52) 463
32.1 Iterative and distributive morphemes in Alaskan Dene . . . 528
36.1 Postpositions in Ahtna and Upper Tanana 629

List of Figures

7.1 Contrast between unmarked and low-marked syllables, Mrs. Demit-Barnes (N) . . . 77
7.2 Contrast between unmarked and high-marked verb stem, Mrs. Demit-Barnes (N) . . . 78
7.3 Tonal distinctions, Mrs. Demit-Barnes . . . 81
7.4 Tonal distinctions, Mrs. Northway . . . 82
7.5 Tonal distinctions, Mrs. David . . . 83
9.1 Partially voiced stem initial fricative [θ̬] in *taniinishthiit* 'I am depressed' . . . 113
9.2 Fortis stem-initial fricative [s] in *sǫǫ* 'robin' and lenis fricative [s̬] in *et-suuk* 's/he is noisy' . . . 114
9.3 Fortis [x] and lenis [x̬] in *xeeł na'ishxeeł* 'I am carrying the pack back' . . . 115
9.4 Aspirated affricate [t͡sʰ], unaspirated affricate [t͡s], oral stop + lenis fricative [ts̬] . . . 117
17.1 The meaning difference between the areal suffix (in the form *hanogn* 'an area upland'; left panel) and the areal prefix (in the form *hunegn'* 'the upland area'; right panel) . . . 254
17.2 High tone on *degn'* 'up:ALL', speaker: Mrs. David (T) . . . 260
17.3 High tone on *hadǫǫ* 'NTRL:downriver:ABL', speaker: Mrs. Demit-Barnes) . . . 260
17.4 High tone on *ya'än* 'DSTL:OUT:ALL' and *atthuugn* 'NTRL:waterward:AR', speaker: Mrs. Tyone (S) . . . 261

List of Maps

1 Indigenous Peoples and Languages of Alaska (Krauss et al. 2010) 15
2 The Upper Tanana language area 18
3 The area surrounding Tetlin and Northway 19
4 Schematic map of the Alaskan part of the Upper Tanana area 225

List of Abbreviations

AA	aa-conjugation marker
ABL	ablative
adj.	adjective
ADM	admirative
adv.	adverb
ADVZR	adverbializer
AJC	adjacent
ALL	allative
AO	animate object
AR	areal
ASRT	assertive
AVERT	avertive
B	Beaver Creek dialect
CMP	complementizer
CMPL	completive
CNJ	conjugation
CO	compact object
CON	conative
CONC	conclusive
CONT	continuative
CT	contrastive topic
CUST	customary
D	D-voice/valence marker
DEM	demonstrative
DES	desire
desc.	descriptive verb theme category
DH	dh-conjugation marker
dim.	dimensional verb theme category
DSTR	distributive

DSTL	distal
DUR	durative
EMPH	emphasis
ERR	errative
EVID	evidential
ext.	extension verb theme category
FO	fabric-like object
FOC	focus
FUT	future
G, GEN	gender
H	H-voice/valence marker
IGN	ignorance
IMP	imperative
IMPSL	impersonal
inc.	incorporate
INC	inceptive
INDF	indefinite
INTS	intensifier
IPV	imperfective
IT	iterative
L	L-voice/valence marker
LO	linear object
LRO	long rigid object
MED	medial
MIR	mirative
MOM	momentaneous
mot.	motion verb theme category
n.	noun
N	n-conjugation marker
N	Northway dialect
NEG	negation, negative
NEGEX	negative existential
neut.	neuter verb theme category
NEUT	neuter
NOM	nominalizer
NTRL	neutral distance
O, o	direct object
ONOM	onomapoetic
OOC	object in open container

op.	operative verb theme category
OPT	optative
P, P	postpositional object
PASS	passive
PEJ	pejorative
PL	plural
PNCT	punctual
pos.	positional verb theme category
POSS	possessed
POT	potential
PP	postposition
PRMB	perambulative
PROG	progressive
PROH	prohibitive
PROX	proximate
PSR	possessor
PST	past
PURP	purposive
PFV	perfective
Q	question
QUAL	qualifier
RECP	reciprocal
REFL	reflexive
REP_1	$repetitive_1$
REP_2	$repetitive_2$
REV	reversative
RO	rope-like object
S	subject
S	Scottie Creek dialect
SEM	semelfactive
SG	singular
stat.	stative verb theme category
suc.	successive verb theme category
T	Tetlin dialect
TERM	terminative
TRNS	transitional
U	Upper Nabesna dialect
v.	verb
VV	voice/valence marker

Acknowledgments

This grammar would not have been possible without the work and dedication of my Upper Tanana teachers and friends. I want to express my deep appreciation and gratitude to Mr. and Mrs. Roy and Avis Sam, Mrs. Sherry Demit-Barnes, and Mrs. Rosa Brewer, all from Northway, and to Mr. Roy H. David Sr. and Mrs. Ida Joe, from Tetlin. I dearly miss my late friends and teachers Mrs. Cora H. David (Tetlin) and Mrs. Darlene Northway (Northway), both of whom were important contributors who left us too early. I am grateful for the time I spent with all of you, learning about your language and culture and enjoying your company. It is a pleasure and a privilege to work with you. Tsinah'įį!

More occasional contributors include (from Beaver Creek) Mrs. Jenny Sanford, now residing in Mentasta; (from Tetlin) Mrs. Yvonne John and the late Mrs. Stella Sam; and (from Northway) Mrs. Ada Gallen, Mrs. Martha Sam, Mr. Julius Sam, Mr. Oscar Jimmie (all deceased now), and Mr. Harry Frank. I cannot thank you all enough for your patience, your time, and your teaching. Tsinah'įį to you as well!

I also want to thank the contributors' families (in particular Dale Brewer, Lydia David, Rowena Paul, Howard Sam, and Rowena Sam) for making me feel welcome and comfortable while I was working with the Elders.

Special thanks go to Dr. Polly Hyslop from Northway, now an assistant professor at the University of Alaska Fairbanks, for introducing me in the community and for being a friend for all of these years.

Among the many linguists who helped along the way, I want to particularly acknowledge Dr. James Kari for getting me started in the Upper Tanana area (and in Alaska!) and for his many detailed comments on a draft of this grammar. A reviewer who can catch mistakes in the data is a rare privilege. Thank you, Jim!

Dr. Siri Tuttle served as my postdoctoral mentor during my first two years working with Upper Tanana (2006–2008). We later cooperated on a grant on Alaskan Dene grammar. I hope we'll continue our conversations about grammatical structures: there is so much left to learn!

There are many other linguists who discussed Dene grammar with me, sent me papers that I had difficulty accessing otherwise, or offered advice and encouragement. If I try to make a list, I am bound to forget some of you. Thank you all, and please feel yourself included!

On a personal note, I want to thank Joe and Julius—for limiting domestic catastrophes when I am away on fieldwork, for putting up with me on days when the writing isn't coming, or maybe just for putting up with me in general. Your love means the world to me.

Special thanks go to Nero, Mephistopheles, and the late Kubla Khan, for taking on countless shifts of snoozing in my office and knowing unerringly which piece of paper to sit on.

Over the years my work on Upper Tanana was funded by several sources, and while not all funding was dedicated to grammar research, the data collected for other projects ultimately fed into this grammar. Thus I gratefully acknowledge support from the following sources:

2007 Foundation for Endangered Languages, "Upper Tanana Grammar Resource for Teachers"

2009 Jacobs Fund, "Tetlin Histories as Told by Upper Tanana Athabascan Elder Cora David"

2010 Phillips Fund,"Conversation in Upper Tanana Athabascan"

2011–2012 Endangered Languages Fund, "Transcription, Translation, and Annotation of Upper Tanana Athabascan (ISO 639-3: TAU) Materials"

2011–2012 University of Regina SSHRC Cohort funding, "Documenting Old-Time Stories from Northway, Alaska"

2012–2015 Social Sciences and Humanities Research Council of Canada (SSHRC) Insight Development Grant, "Talking Animals, Talking to Animals: Documentation Of Old-Time Stories in Upper Tanana Athabascan"

2012–2015 National Science Foundation grant, "Alaskan Athabascan Grammar Database Development: Koyukon (KOY), Lower Tanana (TAA), And Upper Tanana (TAU)" (PI: Siri Tuttle, University of Alaska Fairbanks)

I began working on this grammar during a sabbatical from the First Nations University of Canada (2014–2015).

I want to thank all of the above individuals, institutions, and agencies for their support. All errors of fact or representation are mine.

Preface

When I first visited Northway in August 2006 (and Tetlin a few months later), Polly Hyslop introduced me to the elders who would become my friends, saying, “This is Olga. She’s going to write our book.” I would smile and nod, even though we were probably thinking about different books.

What Polly and the elders meant with “their book” was stories: traditional stories explaining why the world is the way it is, oral histories situating the Upper Tanana in their environment, teachings that provide guidance to the young, and memoirs of a way of life that has all but disappeared now. There are several bilingual story collections of this kind: Mary Tyone (1996), edited by James Kari; Cora H. David, edited by me (2011, 2017); and Avis Sam, Sherry Demit-Barnes, and Darlene Northway, edited jointly by me and Caleb Brucks (forthcoming).

What I was thinking of when Polly introduced me, was, however, this book: a detailed grammatical account. Upper Tanana is the first language I ever worked on where practically no grammatical information is available. Moreover, the same is true for the other languages of eastern Alaska (Ahtna being the notable exception). This lack of grammatical resources is a severe obstacle for language teaching, especially given the small number of fluent speakers.

While this grammar is not a set of lessons, I hope that it can still be useful to language teachers. Its intended audience are individuals with some degree of linguistic training; this includes fully trained linguists but also community members who have taken only a few linguistics classes. I made every effort to keep this grammar as accessible as possible, which involves minimizing jargon, sticking to established Athabascanist (Deneologist!) terminology, and providing numerous examples from natural speech.

Although this may not be the book that the Upper Tanana elders envisaged when we began working thirteen years ago, it is the book that I have been wanting to write for a long time. It contains my best understanding of this truly beautiful language. Other groups have demonstrated that it is possible to revitalize a language based on solid documentation. It is my fierce hope that this grammar, together with the corpus of narratives and other data that have been amassed in the past, will be part of bringing the Upper Tanana language back from the brink.

In this spirit, I offer this book to the Upper Tanana speakers past, present, and, most important: future.

Part I

Background

1 About this grammar

After refining the scope and aim of this grammar, I describe the data as well as the different data presentation formats. I discuss my level of fluency in Upper Tanana as well as my level of involvement in the communities where it is spoken. Finally, I offer a rationale for my decision to split this grammar into two volumes.

1.1. Scope and aim

The goal of this grammar is to provide a complete description of the Upper Tanana language as spoken in the neighboring communities of Tetlin and Northway, Alaska. While there are several detailed accounts of Alaskan Dene phonology and morphology (e.g., Tenenbaum [1978] for Dena'ina verb morphology and semantics, Kari [1979] for Ahtna verb structure and verb theme categories, Leer [1979] for comparative Dene stem phonology, and Holton [2000] for Tanacross phonology and morphology) and several detailed stem dictionaries (Kari [1990] for Ahtna and Jetté and Jones [2000] for Koyukon), there is to date no comprehensive grammatical account of any Alaskan Dene language. This grammar is my contribution to filling this gap.

The documentation history of Upper Tanana spans only about sixty years (see chap. 2.5). Even during this short time period the language has undergone changes, due at least in part to the pressures of colonization. Many materials collected by prior researchers are not accessible; others are hard for contemporary speakers to interpret. Thus I limit this description to Upper Tanana as spoken during the time of my fieldwork there, 2006 until the present. I offer comparisons to older materials where available.

I limit the scope of the grammar to the Northway and Tetlin dialects (see chap. 3), for several reasons. First, these two dialects are the most vital. Not only did this allow me to work with several speakers per dialect, but it also makes them the most promising candidates for revitalization efforts. The Beaver Creek dialect is spoken in the Yukon Territory, and thus inside the sphere of influence of the Yukon Native Language Centre. No opportunity for in-depth research presented itself. I was fortunate to work a few times with Mrs. Jenny Sanford, a speaker of the Beaver Creek dialect living in Mentasta (on the Alaskan side of the border). Some data provided by Mrs. Sanford is included in this grammar, but my knowledge of her dialect remains incomplete, and I am not often able to comment on structural differences. The remaining two dialects (Upper Nabesna and Scottie Creek) are no longer vital. Both are documented in the work of Dr. James Kari. Extensive lexical data from these dialects is contained in Kari (1997b) and place-names data in Kari (1997a). He edited a bilingual collection of narratives in the Scottie Creek dialect (Tyone 1996) and collected many materials in the Upper Nabesna dialect that are not published. However, it was not possible for me to work with speakers of either dialect to explore these materials in greater depth. The last speaker of the Scottie Creek dialect (Mrs. Mary Tyone) passed away several years before I began working in the region, and the few remaining speakers of the Upper Nabesna dialect were not interested in doing language work with me. I could only respect this decision. For the above reasons, focusing on the Northway and Tetlin dialects, where multiple speakers professed clear interest in working with me, was a natural decision.

This grammar is written in the framework of Basic Linguistic Theory (Dixon 2009), which aims to describe a language informally on its own terms using concepts informed both by traditional grammar and by typology. I prioritize description over (theoretical) explanation. Although explanations are included in many places throughout the grammar, I agree with Matthew S. Dryer (2006) that description comes first and explanation is a second step (see, however, Rice [2006] for an examination of how [formal] linguistic theory can contribute to grammar writing).

The audience of this grammar is anyone with an interest in learning about the Upper Tanana language. This includes professional linguists but also Upper Tanana language teachers and learners. Readers with no or only a small amount of linguistic training may find this grammar difficult to use; I hope to prepare a more accessible "learners' grammar" for those readers once this more technical grammar is completed. To accommodate learners and teachers as well as linguists of different backgrounds, I have attempted to minimize the use of specialized Deneologist terminology.

The elders who contributed to this grammar requested that I emphasize the concept of *įįjih* 'forbidden, taboo' as it pertains to proper ways of speaking (see chap. 4.1). They are particularly concerned that learners of Upper Tanana are not aware of *įįjih* in linguistic practice. During our work elders often pointed out constructions illustrating or violating *įįjih*. Their commentary is included where appropriate to make this information available to learners and teachers.

1.2. Data

I discuss three related topics here: data sources, the relationship between elicited and naturalistic data, and data presentation.

1.2.1. Sources

Most of the data I draw on in this grammar comes from narrative text. Elicited data is used primarily to illustrate pronunciations and paradigm formation or in cases where no naturalistic data was available (e.g., negative evidence or accidental gaps). I also use data collected by other researchers, notably Dr. James Kari and the Reverend Paul Milanowski.

The main reason for the emphasis on naturalistic data stems from the elders' clearly stated desire that I record, transcribe, translate, and eventually publish their stories. They patiently (or not so patiently) answer questions about the structure of a word or sentence, or discuss the meaning of a word, but this is always with the understanding that doing so will advance our main endeavor: the documentation of Upper Tanana stories. In their view, the study of grammar is the means, not the end. As a result, much of my research continues to focus on the collection of stories, and I have assembled a corpus of more than eight thousand utterances from narrative text. The corpus is continuously being reviewed and edited by myself in conjunction with speakers. Including this rich data in the grammar was an obvious decision.

Several elders who contributed find grammar work dreadfully tedious and have no compunctions letting me know about this. As a result, much of the grammar work I did prior to 2012 was "snuck in" on the sly as part of story transcription and translation. This changed in 2013 as my colleague Dr. Siri Tuttle (Alaska Native Language Center, University of Alaska Fairbanks) and I began to identify gaps in the structural documentation of Alaskan Dene languages. Even though the corpus of stories was expanding rapidly at the time, it became clear that many gaps could not be filled simply by analyzing that corpus. By alternating work on stories with brief elicitation sessions on grammatical topics, I was able to fill many gaps. Working extensively with elicited data benefited my understanding of the textual data considerably, and in this way the two tasks of story annotation and grammar writing became truly complementary. I am deeply grateful to the elders for participating in this despite the linguist-induced tedium.

1.2.2. Relationship between naturalistic and elicited data

The dual process of supplementing naturalistic with elicited data raised some concerns about the validity of the latter. A simple example comes from third-person plural subject marking of verbs. Upper Tanana verbs contain pronominal prefixes indexing the subject and (when applicable) the direct and postpositional object. There are three persons and two numbers (disregarding for now the areal and indefinite subject prefixes), resulting in six possible forms. In elicitation, speakers will produce a paradigm like the one given in (1).

(1) Ø- imperfective of d+L+xoh, 'play' (UT Notebook #3, 78)
 a. 1sg dagnxoh
 b. 2sg di̧lxoh
 c. 3sg delxoh
 d. 1pl dzelxoh
 e. 2pl dalxoh
 f. 3pl hihdelxoh

Without going into the details of paradigm construction here, the third-person plural form differs from the third-person singular form in that it has the prefix *hih-* while third-person singular is unmarked; see chap. 31. But although (1) is typical of elicitation, in natural speech we also frequently find verb forms like *delxoh* '3sg plays' with a third-person *plural* subject referent as shown in (2):

(2) a. *Adogn* *dlagn* *xah* *delxoo* *iin* *all*
 NTRL:upland:AR squirrel for 3?:play:IPV:NOM PL all
 hi̧i̧xą̧ą̧. (T)
 3PL:kill.PL.O:PFV
 'They killed all of the ones who had played with the squirrel.'
 UTOLAF13May2403:029

 b. *T'axoh* *hu'eh* *nihni̧i̧deel* *eh* *ch'its'ą̧ą̧'* *Che' t'iin*
 finally 3PL:with 3PL:PL.arrive:PFV:NOM and different Tailed.People
 hiyuusih *dindeey* *tthi'* *eh* *t'eey* *delxoh.* (T)
 3PL>3PL:call.name:IPV people head with ADVZR 3?:play:IPV
 'Finally when they arrived with them, the different ones they call Tailed People were playing with people's heads.' UTCBAF14Jul1805:017

Both times the subject of *delxoh* is clearly plural as indicated by the translation. There is also grammatical evidence for plurality, namely the plural enclitic *iin* in (2a) or the third-person plural postpositional object prefix *hu-* in (2b) that is coreferential to the subject of *delxoh*. The third-person plural subject prefix can be left out precisely because of these other indicators of plurality; thus in elicitation speakers will use it, but in narrative text plurality can be recovered from context. The fact that third-person plural marking is optional cannot be worked out from elicited data, only from contextualized speech.

I recognize, of course, that the line between naturalistic and elicited data can be hard to draw, particularly when data was elicited using methodologies as outlined in the papers in M. Ryan Bochnak and Lisa Matthewson (2015) or Aimée Lahaussois and Marine Vuillermet (2019), which are geared specifically to reduce interferences from the elicitation language. Data elicited by direct translation from English is indicated as such either in the surrounding text or by virtue of having a notebook reference (see 1.2.3).

1.2.3. Data presentation and glossing conventions

Several different types of data are presented in this grammar. Phonological data is presented usually in table format, giving not only the gloss and the orthographic representation, but also a phonological representation and phonetic variants, both in IPA (International Phonetic Alphabet). Word lists are also usually in table format. The lexical entry of a verb is a set of often discontinuous morphemes called a verb theme (see chap. 24.2). Verb themes are listed with '+' signs between morphemes, as is done in related languages. No corpus references are provided for this type of data to avoid a cluttered look.

Regarding the other types of data, I had originally planned to provide full morpheme glosses for all of it. Feedback from colleagues suggested, however, that this is more information than most of them are looking for, and full morpheme glosses add considerably to the bulk of the publication. I adopted the following strategy: when morphological or morphophonemic information is essential (i.e., throughout chapters 22–37 and in several other places), data is presented in the practical orthography and is fully glossed, containing both an interlinear morpheme gloss and a free translation. Most morphemes are separated individually, with the exception of those making up the pre-stem syllable in verbs, which is subject to numerous but very regular morphophonemic processes. This way of glossing is illustrated using two verb forms in (3).

(3) a. *delxoh* (T)
del-xoh
3PL.S:QUAL:Ø.IPV:L-play:IPV
'they played' UTOLAF13May2403:028

b. *hįįxąą* (T)
hįį-xąą
3PL.S:AA.PFV:Ø-kill.PL.O:PFV
'they killed them' UTOLAF13May2403:028

In creating these morpheme glosses, I made the choice to treat the pre-stem syllable as one inflectional "chunk" similar as has been proposed by Antti Arppe et al. (2017) for Tsuut'ina (see also Lovick et al. [2018] for application of this approach to Upper Tanana), rather than glossing each morpheme individually.

However, this way of presenting morphological information adds up, and there are over one thousand numbered examples in this grammar, many of them containing multiple parts. Thus whenever the morphology is *not* relevant to the point under discussion, I present the data in a three-line format: the first line contains the text in practical orthography, the second line is a word gloss containing some grammatical information, and the third line is a free translation. The grammatical information is as follows: verb glosses contain information on participants as well as aspectual information; noun glosses contain information about possessive morphology; preposition glosses contain participant information; directional glosses contain information about the meaning of all prefixes and suffixes. All lexical information about a verb form is summarized in one lexical gloss. This is illustrated in (4) and (5). (4) contains a brief passage from a story by Mrs. Avis Sam (N) with full morpheme glosses, (5) contains the same passage with shorter word glosses.

(4) UTOLVDN07Nov2901:047-049 (N)

a. *Ay tl'aan shta' mǫǫnüü Bill Northway mǫǫsi' di'aat Liza eh chih ay iin chih all neek'eh nahtetdek.*

ay tl'aan *sh-ta'* *m-ǫǫnüü* *Bill* *Northway*
and.then 1SG.PSR-father 3SG.PSR-older.brother Bill Northway

m-ǫǫsi' *d-'aat* *Liza* *eh* *chih* *ay* *iin* *chih* *all*
3SG.PSR-name REFL.PSR-wife Liza and also 3 PL also all

nee-k'eh *na-htet-dek*
1SG.P-following PRMB-3PL.S:INC:IPV:D-PL.go:IPV:CUST

'And then my father's older brother Bill Northway, his wife Liza too, they all followed us.'

b. *Hiixah nįįdeeł k'eh ch'a doodeltsįį.*

hii-xah *nįį-deeł* *k'eh* *ch'a*
3PL.S>3SG.P-for N.PFV:Ø-PL.arrive:PFV like FOC
da-hu-del-tsįį
mouth-AR.S-QUAL:DH.PFV:L-seem:IPV
'It sounded like they arrived for them.'

c. *Niithaat tah hǫǫ' shihinay ch'eładn idhagnnüh.*

niithaat *tah* *hǫǫ'* *sh-hi-nayh* *ch'ehładn*
long.time among thus 1SG.O-3PL.S:Ø.IPV:Ø-say:IPV:NOM some
i-dhagn-nüh
PP-DH.PFV:1SG.S:L-forget:PFV
'It's a long time since they told me that, I forgot some.'

(5) UTOLVDN07Nov2901:047-049 (N)

a. *Ay tl'aan* *shta'* *mǫǫnüü* *Bill* *Northway* *mǫǫsi'*
and.then 1SG:father 3SG:older.brother Bill Northway 3SG:name
di'aat *Liza* *eh* *chih* *ay* *iin* *chih* *all* *neek'eh*
REFL:wife Liza and also 3 PL also all 1PL:following
nahtetdek.
3PL:PL.walk.around:IPV
'And then my father's older brother Bill Northway, his wife Liza too, they all followed us.'

b. *Hiixah* *nįįdeeł* *k'eh* *ch'a* *doodeltsįį.*
3PL>3SG:for PL.arrive:PFV like FOC AR:sound:IPV
'It sounded like they arrived for them.'

c. *Niithaat* *tah* *hǫǫ'* *shihinay* *ch'eładn* *idhagnnüh.*
long.time among thus 3PL>1SG:say:IPV:NOM some 1SG:forget:PFV
'It's a long time since they told me that, I forgot some.'

The three-line format in (5) is not as detailed as the four-line format in (4), but it is easier to read and conserves considerable amount of space.

Most verb themes have only two participants. In those instances, the participants are glossed in the format 3P>1S (5c), with the subject preceding the direct or postpositional object. In forms with three participants, I use the order subject > postpositional object > direct object, e.g., (6):

(6) *utl'a'ih'ąą* (N)
1SG>3SG>3SG:give.CO:PFV
'I gave [the can] to her' UTOLVDN10Jul2724:058

Some utterances are quite long, and not everything is relevant to the point illustrated. In those cases, I indicate which piece is omitted using ... (7):

(7) *T'axoh hu'eh nihnįįdeel eh...* (T)
finally 3PL:with 3PL:PL.arrive:PFV:NOM and
'Finally when they arrived with them, ...' UTCBAF14Jul1805:017

When only a single word is taken out of a longer utterance to illustrate a morphological point, it is given in lower case, without punctuation:

(8) *nihnįįdeel* (T)
ni-hnįį-deel
TERM-3PL.S:N.PFV:Ø-PL.go:PFV:NOM
'they, arriving' UTCBAF14Jul1805:017

Direct speech is indicated both in the text line and in the free translation as shown in (9):

(9) *"Doo iin?" nih.* (T)
who PL say:IPV
'"Who?" he said.' UTCBAF14Jul1805:037

Upper Tanana extensively uses emphatic lengthening and high pitch. The verb form in (10) would ordinarily mean something like 'she started running'; the special prosody indicates that she runs particularly fast. Emphatic lengthening and high pitch is indicated in the transcription by colons after the vowel; the number of colons roughly correlates with the length of the vowel.

(10) *Teltthä:::t!* (N)
3SG:SG.run:INC:PFV
'She took off running at high speed!' UTOLAF12Jul1201:043

Almost all data contains an explicit reference. References such as "UTCBAF14Jul1805:037" in (9) point to the corresponding utterance in the corpus; everything preceding the colon is the recording, and the three digits following the colon indicate the utterance within the recording. Data from my fieldnotes reference the notebook[1] and page number. Recordings, annotations, and scans of my notebooks are all available from the Alaska Native Language Archive. Data from published sources is cited with author, year, and page. Data from the lexical file Kari (1997b) contains no indication of where in the file a form was found, since it is a flat and ever-changing electronic file. The data source usually follows the example; if a text passage is cited, as in (5), the source is indicated in the preamble to the example.

1.3. Fieldwork and linguistic competence

In anthropology it is considered good practice for researchers to position themselves vis-à-vis their research topic. In linguistics this continues to be much less common; Terry Crowley (2007, 156), for example, observes that many grammar authors are "surprisingly reticent" about their level of fluency in the language they describe. I think this is a mistake. Who we are significantly impacts our analysis and our presentation of the data. Our level of fluency of course has bearing on not just these two points but also on the types of data to which we are exposed.

My role in Tetlin and Northway remains that of an outsider. During field trips I elected to stay in the regional center of Tok rather than in one of the villages. This was done in order to avoid giving the impression that I was affiliated more with one village than the other, and it also helped minimize driving. (It was always my intention to work with speakers from both villages.) Staying in Tok had the added benefit of allowing me to not get drawn too deeply into local politics (the political situation in Northway in particular was quite divisive in my first few years there).

My level of fluency in Upper Tanana is up for debate. Originally, my goal had been explicitly *not* to learn the language. While this may sound surprising (given in particular the arguments in Crowley [2007, 154–61] in favor of learning the language), the following anecdote will help explain this.

Sometime before beginning work on Upper Tanana, I did fieldwork on a related language. I was working with an elder, repeating her words and trying to construct words myself. I was beginning to be quite proud of my achievement. But then the elder turned to her daughter, who had been sitting in on our session, and said something along the lines of, "See how well she's speaking? She's just picking it up. Why can't you do this? You're not even making an effort to learn." Needless to say, the daughter from that point on resented my spending time with her mother.

What I learned from this incident was to be mindful of those individuals who, due to assimilatory language policies, never learned their native language and grew up during a time when the social fabric in native Alaska began to disintegrate under the influence of colonization. I did not want to position myself as a "good" language learner at the expense of those who try to learn their language but who are hampered by lack of time and funding, not to mention emotional baggage. I emphatically do not wish to suggest that learning the language is a bad thing. Reverend Milanowski, for example, is a very proficient speaker of the Tetlin dialect, and the community is cognizant of and full of admiration for his skill. I simply felt that in my particular situation, arriving there when I did, making a serious effort to learn the language would not have been appropriate. In another time or place, this could have been different. (An additional challenge was that the language simply is not used for daily communication.)

So, how fluent am I? My oral comprehension is very good. I can follow a narrative or a conversation without problems; I am also able to pick up on many jokes made in the language. I have become fairly adept at translating from one dialect to the other. My intuitions about grammaticality of structures is good. My production, though, remains limited. I can produce short sentences, but I would not be able to maintain my end of a conversation or tell a story. (Actually, there has never been an opportunity—at language gatherings, everyone would much rather listen to the elders than to me!)

1.4. Why two volumes?

This grammar was originally conceived as a single volume. Given the rapidly dwindling number of speakers, it has always been clear that this grammar should be available to the community as soon as possible. I am, however, enjoying the task of compiling it so much that I could easily spend another ten years doing so, adding detail and finding better examples. By then, many more speakers of Upper Tanana would have passed on, making language revitalization even harder. I decided that I needed to find a compromise. At that point the chapters on phonology, lexical categories, morphology, and syntax were almost completed. But while much of the material for the chapters on semantic systems and discourse structure had been compiled, I had not yet begun their analysis.

In the attempt to balance the need for expediency with that for careful analysis, I decided to split the book in two. Volume 1 contains the chapters on phonology, lexical categories, and morphology. Volume 2 will contain the chapters on syntax, semantics, and discourse. This is not ideal, but it makes some material available while allowing me treat the topics in volume 2 with the attention they deserve.

Thus, here is volume 1 of the Grammar of Upper Tanana, and I hope that volume 2 will be on its way soon.

Notes

1. There are some references to notebook #2.5 throughout the grammar. This is not an error: notebook #2.5 had been in hiding for several years and I only found it again after starting notebook #5.

2 About Upper Tanana

This chapter contains background information on Upper Tanana. 2.1 discusses the name used here for both the people and their language. The Upper Tanana language is defined in 2.2 and contextualized within the Dene language family in 2.3. Its geographical location is described in 2.4 and its documentation history summarized in 2.5. The vitality of Upper Tanana today is described in 2.6.

2.1. Name

The name "Upper Tanana" refers to the upper reaches of the Tanana River and its headwaters. The name "Tanana" comes from the Koyukon word *tene no, tenene* 'trail river' (Bright 2004, 478); the Upper Tanana themselves call this river *Tth'itu'*, which Kari (1997b) glosses as 'main river'.

In his original study of Alaskan Dene groups, Cornelius Osgood (1936) used the name "Nabesna" to refer to the Upper Tanana people, an adaptation of the term *Nabesnatánas* used by Lieutenant Allen. The word *Nabesnatánas* appears to be Ahtna in origin, e.g., *Nabaes Na' hwt'aene* 'people of the Nabesna River'. This term became common usage until the publication of *The Upper Tanana Indians* by Robert A. McKennan (1959), who argued in favor of the name "Upper Tanana," since the cultural area encompasses more than just the Nabesna valley. Curiously, cultural anthropologist Marie-Françoise Guédon uses the term "Nabesna" in her French writing (Guédon 2005), but "Upper Tanana" in her English publications (Guédon 1974, 1981).

The English name "Upper Tanana" is nowadays used by outsiders to refer both to the people and to their traditional language. In Upper Tanana, *neek'eh* 'like us' or *nee'aaneegn'* 'our words' refers to the language, and *dineh shyuh* 'complete person' is used as the autonym. None of these terms, however, distinguish the Upper Tanana language and people from other Alaskan Dene languages and groups.

McKennan (1969, 338) notes that the indigenous groups along the Tanana

River form both a linguistic and a cultural continuum with relatively few differences between adjacent groups. Traditionally individuals identified primarily with their "band";[1] nowadays, they identify with their village.

2.2. Defining Upper Tanana

Michael E. Krauss (2000, li) notes that the terms "language" and "dialect" do not adequately capture the linguistic situation in Alaskan Dene. He observes that the traditional lack of central social organization above the band level combined with the seminomadic lifestyle led to the formation of a dialect chain, where each band spoke a distinctive variety that differed slightly from the varieties of neighboring bands. Alaskan Dene traveled extensively, both for subsistence and for social purposes, resulting in frequent contact with speakers of other varieties. This in turn led to extensive passive and active multilingualism. For this reason the concept of "mutual intelligibility," often used to distinguish "languages" from "dialects," is not meaningful in the traditional Alaskan Dene context, and Krauss (2000, li) calls it "irrelevant, artificial, academic."[2]

Yet as Krauss points out, there are also reasons in favor of grouping varieties into constructs we call languages, the development of orthographies and language materials being first and foremost among them. Thus in 1972 Krauss grouped the many varieties of Alaskan Dene into "languages" that can be shown on a map (Krauss 1982). The most recent version of Krauss's map is given in map 1.[3]

The map shows that Upper Tanana is surrounded by other Dene languages: Ahtna to the south and southwest, Tanacross to the west, Han to the north, and Northern and Southern Tutchone to the east. Each of these languages encompasses several varieties. Upper Tanana is defined in contrast to all of these varieties over a particular set of sound changes affecting the stem syllable, described in detail in chap. 8. Put simply, historical stem-final alveolar or postalveolar fricatives or affricates were deleted or simplified, and the preceding vowel was modified. The changes are summarized in tables 2.1 and 2.2. If a variety of Northern Dene has undergone this set of changes, it is considered to be a variety of Upper Tanana; if it has not, then it is classified as belonging to a different language.

2.3. The Dene language family

Upper Tanana is a member of the Dene, or Athabascan, language family. Nowadays the language family is usually referred to as Dene in Canada but continues to be called Athabascan (or Athabaskan)[4] in the United States,

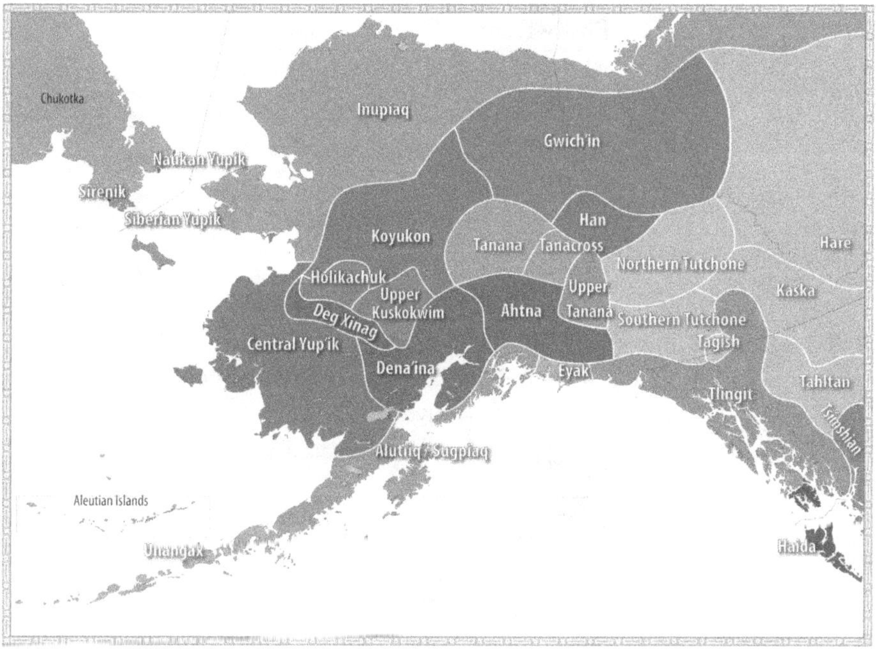

Map 1. Indigenous Peoples and Languages of Alaska (Krauss et al. 2010)

although the use of the term "Dene" is expanding there too.[5] The word "Dene" derives from the word for 'person' in many Dene languages, e.g., *dëne* in Dëne Sųłiné, *diné* in Navajo, or *dineh* in Upper Tanana. The term "Athabascan," on the other hand, is an anglicized version of the Woods Cree word *athapaskāw* 'reedy, area of reeds' referring to Lake Athabasca (Solomon Ratt, Arok Wolvengrey, personal communication). Most of the speakers I work with use the term "Athabascan," but the term "Dene" is gaining traction among younger community members, especially those with an interest in indigenous self-determination. I anticipate that in a few years, Dene will be used across Alaska as well. For this reason I made the decision to refer to the language family as Dene throughout this grammar. I also use the word "Deneologist" to refer to a person studying this language family, as a replacement for the term "Athabascanist."

The Dene language family is part of the Na-Dene phylum, which also includes Eyak and (more distantly related) Tlingit. At a symposium held in Fairbanks in 2008, Edward J. Vajda (2010a, 2010b) suggested a relationship between Na-Dene and Yeniseian; additional papers addressing this question can be found in the volume edited by James Kari and Ben A. Potter (2010).

Proto-Dene	Upper Tanana
*dz, ts’	
*dž, tš’	tʰ + Mod.
*džʳ, tšʳ	
*s, z	
*š, ž	h, Ø + Mod.
*žʳ (, šʳ)	
*x̣, ẏ	h, Ø (+ Mod.)

Table 2.1. Development of stem-final alveolar and postalveolar affricates and fricatives

Proto-Dene	Upper Tanana
*i·, e·	ɪ͡a
*a·	ɘ:
*u·	ɪ͡o, õ:
*ə	ʌ, ɘ
*ɑ	o
*ʊ	o

Table 2.2. Development of vowels preceding these affricates and fricatives

Relationships within the Dene language family are complex. Geographically, three subgroups can be identified: the Pacific Coast languages, the Southern or Apachean languages, and the Northern group. This geographic grouping does not necessarily correspond to genealogical relationships (Krauss and Golla 1981; Krauss 2005). The complexities of genealogical relationships between Dene languages, however, are not germane to this grammar; hence I will use the geographic classification.

The Northern group, to which Upper Tanana belongs, is a dialect continuum reaching from western Alaska almost to the Hudson Bay in the east, and to the Calgary area in Alberta in the south. The Northern group is by far the largest, encompassing about forty languages. These languages differ immensely with respect to vitality: speakers of Dëne Sųłiné in Canada number in the thousands while there only a handful of Lower Tanana speakers.

2.4. Geographical location

The Upper Tanana language area is located in eastern interior Alaska and across the U.S./Canada border in the Yukon Territory. McKennan delimits the Upper Tanana area as follows:

> I might describe their territory as embracing the entire drainage of the Nabesna and Chisana rivers which, coming together, form the Tanana proper; the main Tanana and tributaries down as far as the Tok River, the White River as far east as the old mining camp of Canyon City at the mouth of the Klutlan River, and the Beaver and Snag Rivers, tributaries of the White River. (McKennan 1959, 17)

A map showing the Upper Tanana language area is given in map 2.

Alaskan Dene were traditionally seminomadic, and McKennan (1959) points out that one should not think of the entire area as being continuously settled. Rather, family groups congregated for part of each year at sites that were especially rich in particular resources. The current villages of Tetlin and Northway are located close to such sites, namely Last Tetlin (no longer a permanent settlement) and Fish Camp (still settled). See map 3 for a more detailed view of the Tetlin and Northway area.

Today the majority of Upper Tanana speakers can be found in three permanent settlements: Tetlin and Northway (including Fish Camp) in Alaska, and Beaver Creek in the Yukon. Until recently, Upper Tanana was also spoken in the village of Nabesna and in the Scottie Creek area, but by 2006 all speakers from Nabesna had relocated to Northway, and all speakers of the Scottie Creek dialect had passed away. Some speakers also live in close by communities such as Tok (non-indigenous), Tanacross (Tanacross), or Mentasta (Ahtna), while others have left the Upper Tanana area entirely.

The topography of the Upper Tanana area is quite varied. Today's settlements are located in the Tanana River lowlands, a broad glacial valley dotted with numerous lakes, many of which are connected. Many speakers, however, remember traveling into the Wrangell Mountains in the south or into Ladue country in the north. Family groups traveled frequently to the Tetlin Hills, the Last Tetlin Hills, and the Nutzotin Range (known locally as the "Black Hills").

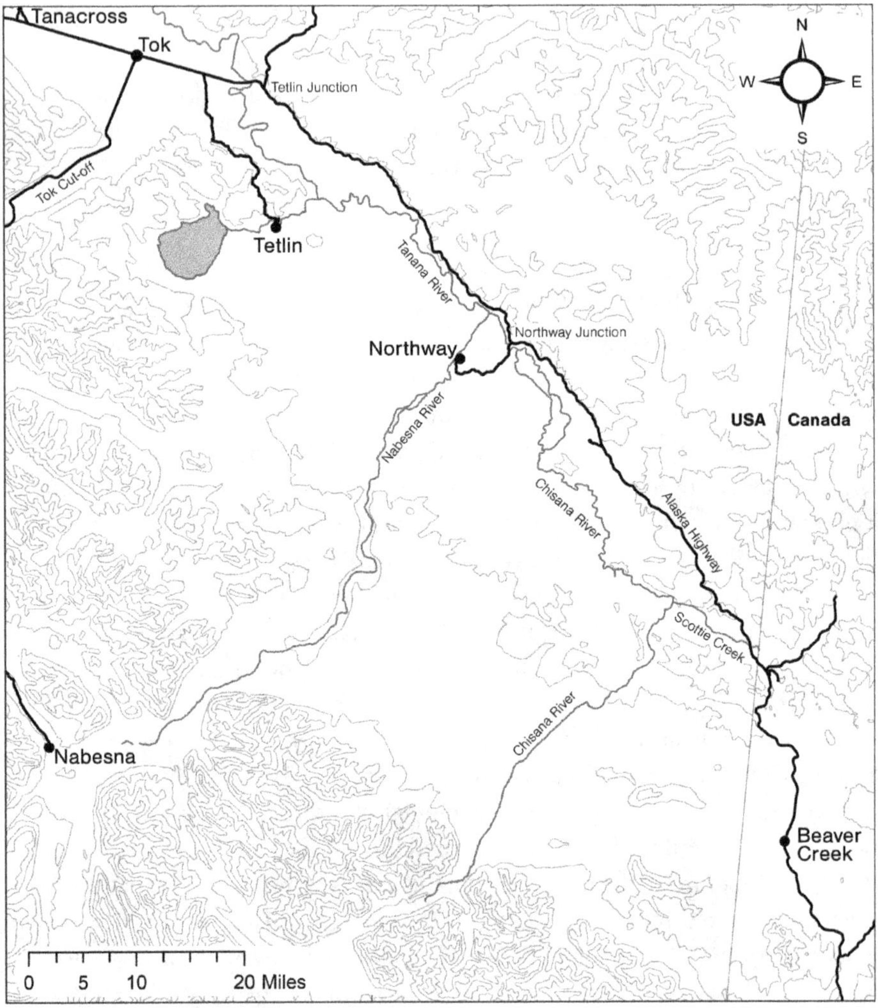

Map 2. The Upper Tanana language area

The climate in this area is notoriously harsh. Summers are short and hot (by Alaskan standards) with temperatures reaching the 70s °F (around 25 °C). Due to the numerous lakes, creeks, swamps, and muskegs in the area, mosquitoes are never in short supply from May through September. Winters are long, with freeze-up occurring in October and breakup taking place in May. Temperatures commonly reach -50 °F (-45.5 °C) in winter, with January and February being the coldest months.

The extremely harsh climate combined with the varied topography contributes significantly to the seminomadic way of life that is traditional in this area.

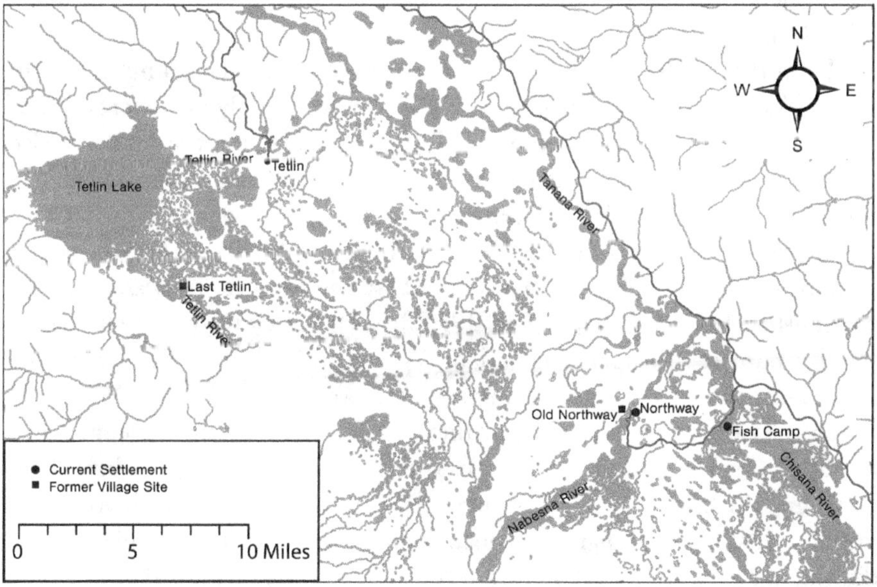

Map 3. The area surrounding Tetlin and Northway

2.5. Prior research

Anthropological research in the Upper Tanana area began with the ethnographic fieldwork by Robert A. McKennan in 1928–1929, published in McKennan (1959, 1969, 1981). McKennan still worked with individuals who remembered the time before intensive contact with white people (the intensive contact period for Upper Tanana begins in the 1910s). McKennan never developed proficiency in the Upper Tanana language; the few Upper Tanana words contained in his writing are so haphazardly spelled that deciphering them is almost impossible.

McKennan's research was followed by a long gap until the work by Albert Heinrich (1957) on the kinship system of the Upper Tanana. While that paper contains only a handful of terms in the Upper Tanana language, they are all spelled consistently and recognizably.

In May 1959 Reverend Paul G. Milanowski Sr. (affiliated with the Wycliffe Bible Institute) came to Tetlin and began working on a Bible translation. His work led to a large number of publications including a paper on the sound system (Milanowski 1961) and a partial Bible translation (Milanowski and John 1966, 1972; Joe, John, and Milanowski 2013). He also contributed significantly to Upper Tanana lexicography through published and unpublished dictionaries (Milanowski and Jimerson 1975; Milanowski and John 1979; Milanowski 2011).

From the 1960s on, the Upper Tanana area was visited by linguists from the Alaska Native Language Center. This resulted mainly in the creation of field notes by Michael E. Krauss and Jeff Leer, all available at the Alaska Native Language Archive, and to the inclusion of Upper Tanana data in comparative work (Krauss and Leer 1981; Leer 1979, 1996a). The research by James Kari was more extensive and includes a story collection by Tyone (1996), edited by Kari; the Upper Tanana Place Names List and Map (Kari 1997a); and an unpublished lexical stem file (Kari 1997b), with additions by myself. There are also numerous Upper Tanana language recordings made by Kari in the holdings of the Alaska Native Language Archive.

In the early 1990s Nobukatsu Minoura conducted linguistic fieldwork in the Upper Tanana area, focusing on dialectology (Minoura 1994) and typology (Minoura 1997, 2004). No recordings of his work sessions are archived. Also in the 1990s, Upper Tanana was documented by Daniel Tlen, affiliated with the Yukon Native Language Centre at the time. His work resulted in a sizeable body of recordings available from the Alaska Native Language Archive and probably underlies much of the literacy materials available from the Yukon Native Language Centre.

2.6. Speaker numbers and language vitality

Viktor K. Golla (2007, 89) reports "at most 100" speakers of Upper Tanana in the United States and about ten in Canada. This estimate was likely too high even at the time of publication. When I began fieldwork on this language in 2006, there were already far fewer than one hundred speakers in total, and many speakers have since passed away. My best estimate is that there are between thirty and fifty fluent speakers of Upper Tanana. Almost all of them are elders, most of them in their seventies or older. Intergenerational transmission stopped in the 1970s, and the language is no longer used as a means of daily communication.[6] Using the criteria developed in the UNESCO Ad Hoc Expert Group on Endangered Languages (2003), Upper Tanana can be classified as "severely endangered."

Still, there is room for cautious optimism. In 2006 I conducted a sociolinguistic survey. One of the more surprising outcomes was the claim made by several participants that "everybody speaks our language"—surprising because this so completely contradicted my observations. Yet it is true that everyone, including quite young children, speaks *some* Upper Tanana and can understand and use basic expressions. In both Northway and Tetlin, there are language and culture classes for youth, where simple vocabulary, basic linguistic structures such as possession, and cultural activities such as singing and dancing are taught. Although I never observed anything like the "language games" described by Barbra A. Meek (2007, 2010) for Kaska, there is nowadays considerable pride among young people in their linguistic and cultural heritage.

Also, several community members are working to reclaim their language. Some of them remember being fluent as children in the 1960s and 1970s; others were never fluent. Polly Hyslop, at the time a PhD student at the University of Alaska Fairbanks, spearheaded the "Upper Tanana Songbook Project," funded through the Alaska Forum for the Humanities, which involved community members recording, transcribing, and translating traditional songs and compiling them into a booklet for use by the community. Jamie Marunde, a young learner from Northway, is building an Upper Tanana language app. A recent large push for the reclamation of Alaskan Dene languages comes from the Doyon Foundation, whose Language Revitalization Program Director Allan Hayton has secured funding to develop online language materials. This work is still in the initial stages, but it promises to be the largest concerted effort for language revitalization in the area to date. These activities clearly illustrate the passion that many individuals have for their ancestral language. It is my fervent hope that they will become the next generation of speakers and, most importantly, teachers.

Notes

1. McKennan (1959, 17) for example distinguishes the Upper Chisana-Upper Nabesna band, the Last Tetling band, the Tetling band, the Mouth of the Nabesna band, and the Scottie Creek band. Chap. 3 shows that these bands largely correspond to dialectal boundaries.

2. Another term could be "colonialist"—to this day, the divisions drawn by linguists and anthropologists do not make sense to the indigenous population there.
3. Some scholars, including Kari (personal communication), also recognize Middle Tanana, formerly spoken in the Salcha/Goodpaster area, in the eastern part of the area labeled "Tanana" on map 1.
4. The spelling *Athabascan* was adopted by the Tanana Chiefs Conference in the 1990s. In other parts of the United States, the spelling *Athabaskan* is used.
5. For example, the annual conference dedicated to the study of this language family changed its name to "Dene Languages Conference" in 2012, following a suggestion made by James Kari.
6. Even fluent speakers whose spouse is also a fluent speaker do not usually use Upper Tanana at home.

3 Dialects

In this chapter the dialects comprising Upper Tanana are described. Several phonological dialect diagnostics were identified by Minoura (1994) (3.2), but there are also lexical (3.3) and morphological (3.4) differences. The chapter focuses on the differences between the Northway and Tetlin dialects, from which the bulk of the data used in this grammar is drawn.

Whenever forms from the Northway and Tetlin dialects are contrasted, the Northway form precedes the Tetlin form.

3.1. Traditional bands and current dialects

In 1928 McKennan (1959, 17) identified five bands: (1) the Upper Chisana-Upper Nabesna band, (2) the Last Tetlin band, (3) the Tetlin band, (4) the Mouth of the Nabesna band, and (5) the Scottie Creek band. The Last Tetlin band has since merged with the Tetlin band. Minoura (1994) also observed significant linguistic variation within the Scottie Creek band, which led him to identify five dialects: (1) the Upper dialect spoken by members of the Upper Chisana-Upper Nabesna band; (2) the Tetlin dialect spoken by members of the Last Tetlin and Tetlin bands;[1] (3) the Northway dialect spoken by what McKennan called the "Mouth of the Nabesna band"; (4) the Scottie Creek dialect proper; (5) and the Canadian or Beaver Creek dialect.

Not all speakers of a particular dialect reside in the community where their dialect was historically spoken. The Scottie Creek band never had a semipermanent settlement (McKennan 1959, 18). All speakers of the Upper (Nabesna) dialect that I have met resided in Northway at the time; most of them have passed away since. A summary of the dialects and the number of known speakers of each dialect is given in table 3.1. The speaker number given for the Beaver Creek dialect is almost certainly too low; I personally know two speakers, but there are several others.

Dialect	No. of speakers	Places of residence
Upper	1+?	Northway
Tetlin	< 10	Tetlin, Tok
Northway	20–50	Northway, Beaver Creek
Scottie Creek	0	(Northway)
Beaver Creek	2+?	Beaver Creek, Mentasta

Table 3.1. Dialects and speaker numbers

3.2. Phonological dialect differences

Upper Tanana dialectology owes much to the work of Nobukatsu Minoura, who conducted an extensive study in the early 1990s. His work, however, needs to be examined with two caveats. One is simply that it is two decades old, and the language has undergone changes since. Secondly Minoura does not distinguish systematically between phonological and phonetic representation, which makes his data difficult to interpret.

Minoura (1994, 174) identifies the following phonological characteristics distinguishing the dialects of Upper Tanana: the realization of *ə, the existence of phonemic low tone, the existence of super-high tone, the realization of /m/ in the onset of syllables not containing nasal sounds, the realization of vocalic suffixes and the resulting opposition between light and heavy stems, the realization of /ɣ̆/, and the realization of /ɬ/ following a long nasal vowel. The last three features distinguish the Beaver Creek dialect from the four Alaskan ones; as I can neither confirm nor deny their relevance, they are not discussed here. Instead I add the realization of /ɔ/ and development of the diphthong /i͡ɔ/.

3.2.1. Realization of *ə in stems

The realization of *ə in stems reliably distinguishes the Tetlin dialect from all other dialects.

In most dialects of Upper Tanana, Proto-Dene *ə in stems has developed in most environments into an unrounded open-mid back vowel /ʌ/ (represented as [ɤ] in Minoura [1994]; but see Tuttle, Lovick, and Núñez-Ortiz [2011] for a motivation of its representation as /ʌ/). In the Tetlin dialect, this vowel has merged with /a/ (11).

(11) Realization of *ə

		Northway		*Tetlin*	
a.	‘PL go FUT’	däł	/tʌ̀ɬ/	dał	/taɬ/
b.	‘firewood’	tsät	/t͡sʰʌtʰ/	tsat	/t͡sʰatʰ/
c.	‘from P’	P+ts’änh	/t͡s’ʌn̥/	P+ts’anh	/t͡s’an̥/
d.	‘towards P’	P+nts’ą̈’	/nt͡s’ʌ̃̀ʔ/	P+nts’ą’	/nt͡s’ãʔ/

Before *gʸ, kʸ, k’ʸ, *ə developed into /e/ in the Northway, Scottie Creek, and Beaver Creek dialects but into /a/ in the Tetlin dialect (12).

(12) Realization of *ə before *gʸ, kʸ, k’ʸ

		Northway		*Tetlin*	
a.	‘osprey’	tth’ek	/t̪͡θ’ekʰ/	tth’ak	/t̪͡θ’akʰ/
b.	‘PL go IPV CUST’	dek	/tekʰ/	dak	/takʰ/
c.	‘all’	łahtthegn	/ɬaht̪͡θʰek/	łahtthag	/ɬaht̪͡θʰak/

Finally, *ə before *ɣ̇ developed into /a/ or /aː/ in the Tetlin dialect, but into /ɔ/ or /ɔː/ in the others. Note that *ɣ̇ itself has disappeared (13a) or weakened to /h/ (13b, c).

(13) Realization of *ə before *ɣ̇

		Northway		*Tetlin*	
a.	‘older brother’	-ǫǫnüü	/õːnɔː/	-oondaa	/õːnaː/
b.	‘forget IPV’	nüh	/nɔh/	nah	/nah/
c.	‘cry IPV’	tsüh	/t͡sʰɔh/	tsah	/t͡sʰah/

3.2.2. Realization of *ə in prefixes

*ə in prefix syllables is variably realized as /e/ or /i/. As pointed out by Minoura (1994, 177), the rules governing the occurrence of one or another of these vowels are complex. While this variation is partially due to surrounding consonants—in both Northway and Tetlin, syllable-initial /ʃ/ and /h/ often trigger the realization of *ə as /i/—Minoura (1994, 177–78) correctly observes that in open syllables, Northway /i/ often corresponds to Tetlin /e/ (14). There is, however, significant variation within each dialect and even speaker.

(14) Realization of *ə in prefixes

		Northway		*Tetlin*	
a.	‘he swam across’	skinįįmįį	/skʰinĩːmĩː/	skenįįmįį	/skʰenĩːmĩː/
b.	‘I climbed up’	ki’ihshyah	/kʰìʔihʃʲah/	ke’ihshyah	/kʰeʔihʃʲah/

c.	'I started to go'	tidhihshyah	/t^{h}ìðihʃ̫ah/	tedhihshyah	/t^{h}eðihʃ̫ah/
d.	'she walks around'	natidaak	/nat^{h}ita:k^{h}/	natedaak	/nat^{h}eta:k^{h}/
e.	'no'	ina'	/ʔinàʔ/	ena'	/ʔenaʔ/

3.2.3. Realization of vocalic suffixes

As discussed in chap. 11 Upper Tanana distinguishes heavy syllables, which contain a vocalic suffix, from light ones, which do not. The realization of this suffix in stems with final /t, k/ is a strong indicator of dialect. In Tetlin the suffix in such stems is realized as a fully voiced oral stop [d, g], which may additionally be followed by a short vowel [ɪ, ə] or a homorganic nasal consonant. In Northway and Scottie Creek the suffix is realized as a fully voiced oral stop followed by a homorganic voiced nasal or, in the case of stems ending in /k/, only as a voiced nasal consonant [ŋ]. Examples are given in (15).

(15) Realization of vocalic suffixes following /t, k/

		Northway		*Tetlin*	
a.	'bald eagle'	tuudn	[t^{h}u:dn]	tuudi	[t^{h}u:d], [t^{h}u:dɪ], [t^{h}u:dn]
b.	'my cane'	shtädn'	[ʃt^{h}ʌ̀dnʔ]	shtad'	[ʃt^{h}adʔ], [ʃt^{h}adəʔ], [ʃt^{h}adnʔ]
c.	'fish'	łuugn	[łu:gŋ], [łu:ŋ]	łuug(e)	[łu:g], [łu:gə], [łu:gŋ]
d.	'my coat'	sh'eegn'	[ʃʔè:gŋʔ], [ʃʔè:ŋʔ]	sh'eeg'	[ʃʔe:gʔ], [ʃʔe:gəʔ], [ʃʔe:gŋʔ]

The realization of vocalic suffixes after /t, k/ is one of the most consistent dialect features and probably contributes to Tetlin speakers' perception that the Northway dialect sounds very nasal.

3.2.4. Realization of nasal consonants in onsets

Another distinction between the Tetlin and Northway dialects, according to Minoura (1994, 180), lies in the realization of /m/ in the onset of syllables without another nasal segment. He claims that it is realized as [^{m}b] in Tetlin but as [m^{b}] in Northway.

While Minoura is right about noting this as a difference between dialects, he omits some crucial information. First, the realization of /m/ in the Tetlin dialect is even more denasalized than Minoura's notation suggests. The examples in (16) come from elicitation sessions with two typical Northway speakers (N1: Mrs. Rosa Brewer and N2: Mrs. Avis Sam), and two typical Tetlin speakers (T1: Mrs. Cora H. David, T2: Mr. Roy H. David Sr.). In three of the elicitation sessions (N1, N2, and T2) I targeted specifically the realization of /m/. When I started looking at denasalization in 2015, speaker T1 had already passed away. Instead, I used recordings from 2006, which targeted vowel realization. Mrs. Brewer (N1) noticed the focus on /m/ early on and commented during the elicitation of *dimbee* 'sheep': "Tetlin is [tibeː], and us, we have *m*, [timeː]. It doesn't matter, you know, they're both the same, alike" (from recording UTOLAF15May1101.wav.) In natural speech all speakers vary more strongly between different realizations than the forms in (16) suggest; I chose the most common form for each word. Note that some words are consistently realized without a trace of nasalization, especially in the Tetlin dialect.

(16) Realization of /m/

			N1	*N2*	*T1*	*T2*
a.	'ouch'	abah	[abah]	[apah]	[apah]	[abah]
b.	'dry fish'	ba'	[bàʔ]	[bàʔ]	[^{m}baʔ]	[baʔ]
c.	'toboggan'	boh	[m^{b}oh]	[^{m}boh]	[^{m}boh]	[boh]
d.	'ptarmigan'	k'atmbah	[k'àt^{h}mah]	[k'àt^{h}m^{b}ah]	[k'at^{h}bah]	[k'at^{hm}bah]
e.	'weasel'	nihmbaay	[nihmaːj]	[nih^{m}baːj]	[nih^{m}baːj]	[nihbaːj]
f.	'sheep'	dimbee	[timeː]	[tipeː]	[ti^{m}beː]	[tibeː]
g.	'fish knife'	mbeetsäl	[meːt͡s^{h}ʌl]	[m^{b}eːt͡s^{h}ʌl]	–	[peːt͡s^{h}al]
h.	'loon'	ts'almbeed	[t͡s'almèːt]	[t͡s'al^{m}bèːt]	[t͡s'alpeːt]	[t͡s'al^{m}beːt]
i.	'gillnet'	tehbįįł	[t^{h}ehmɨ̃̀ːɬ]	[t^{h}ehmɨ̃̀ːɬ]	[t^{h}eh^{m}bɨ̃ːɬ]	[t^{h}eh^{m}bɨ̃ːɬ]
j.	'edge'	maagn	[maːŋ]	[maːgŋ]	[maːgŋ]	[m^{b}aːg]
k.	'lake'	mänh	[mʌn̥]	[mʌn̥]	[man̥]	[man̥]

Second, /n/ is also partially denasalized in the Tetlin dialect (17). /n/ is never denasalized completely, presumably to avoid a merger with /t/; there are several minimal pairs involving these two sounds: e.g., *dät* /tʌɬ/ 'blood' versus *nät* /nʌɬ/ 'wedge' or *de'* /téʔ/ 'vertically up ALL' versus *ne'* /néʔ/ 'upriver ALL'. The data in (17) comes from a variety of sources and reflects the speakers' broad tendencies: Tetlin speakers tend to partially denasalize /n/ especially in stem onsets (unlike /m/, /n/ also occurs in prefix syllables, although it appears to be denasalized less frequently in that position), while Northway speakers do not usually do so. Again there is considerable variation within each individual's speech.

(17) Realization of /n/

			N1	*N2*	*T1*	*T2*
a.	'man'	dineh	[tineh]	[tin^{d}eh]	[tin^{d}eh]	[tin^{d}eh]

b.	'he tells'	naholnek	[naholnek^{h}]	[naholnek^{h}]	[n^{d}ahol^{n}dak^{h}]	[n^{d}ahol^{n}dak^{h}]
c.	'upriver ALL'	ne'	[néʔ]	[néʔ]	[^{n}déʔ]	[n^{d}éʔ]
d.	'moose'	diniign	[tinìːŋ]	[tinìːgŋ]	[tin^{d}iːgŋ]	[tin^{d}iːgŋ]
e.	'my eye'	shnaagn'	[ʃnàːŋʔ]	[ʃnàːŋʔ]	[ʃnaːgŋʔ]	[ʃnaːgʔ]
f.	'fox'	naagädn	[nàːgʌdn]	–	[naːgadə]	[naːgadə]

Overall the data in (16) and (17) demonstrates that denasalization of nasal consonants is primarily a feature of the Tetlin dialect. Commentary like that by Mrs. Brewer quoted above points to the salience of this difference. Due to the considerable variation exhibited by all speakers, denasalization is however not a reliable dialect diagnostic.

3.2.5. Low tone

Minoura (1994, 178) notes that retention of low tone resulting from Proto-Dene constriction (see chap. 7) differs across dialects, with clear and consistent distinctions in the Beaver and Scottie Creek dialects, but less clear retention in the Upper and Northway dialects. He claims that in the Northway dialect "the younger speakers are starting to lose tones and have very unclear tones, while older speakers have steady tones" (178). He further notes that the Tetlin dialect has lost low tone almost entirely, leaving only occasional vestigial tones.

Two and a half decades later I can confirm that the Tetlin dialect does not distinguish low tone. The vestigial low tones Minoura mentions have either been lost as well or were confused with intonational patterns. I however struggle to understand the motivation for his claim that younger Northway speakers are losing low tone, especially given the fact that I have worked with (presumably) those individuals that counted as "younger" in the 1990s. I show in chap. 7.5 that low tone in Northway is realized clearly and consistently.

(18) Low tone

		Northway		*Tetlin*	
a.	'I kept hollering'	na'ihsäł	/nàʔihsʌɬ/	na'ihsał	/naʔihsaɬ/
b.	'we took off'	tseedeeł	/t͡s^{h}èːteːɬ/	tseedeeł	/t͡s^{h}eːteːɬ/
c.	'father'	-ta'	/t^{h}àʔ/	-ta'	/t^{h}aʔ/
d.	'land'	nän'	/nʌ̀nʔ/	nan'	/nanʔ/

In spite of the clarity of tonal distinctions, it is uncertain how salient this dialect difference is for speakers. It does not present a barrier to mutual intelligibility; Northway and Tetlin speakers communicate with each other without the slightest problems. Yet several Northway speakers have told me that I sound like a Tetlin speaker, which is quite possibly due to unclear tonal distinctions in my speech.

3.2.6. High tone

Minoura (1994, 179) observes that "super-high" tone is a characteristic of negative verb stems in the speech of Mrs. Bessie John from Beaver Creek. He notes that she is the only speaker with this distinction. He also quotes Mr. Jack John Justin (Upper dialect) as saying that super-high tone is characteristic of the speech of women in general, but that this does not match his own impressions (Minoura 1994, 180).

As discussed in more detail in chap. 7, I find that high tone is a feature of all speakers with whom I have worked, female and male alike.[2] I am inclined to agree with Mr. Justin insofar as high tone is much more noticeable in women's speech, who regularly slip into falsetto speech in syllables with high tone. The two male speakers with whom I have extensively worked, Mr. Roy H. David Sr. (Tetlin) and Mr. Roy Sam (Northway), however, both also clearly pronounce high tone (see also Brucks and Tuttle [2014]). Contrary to Minoura's claim, high tone is not a dialect diagnostic.

3.2.7. Realization of /ɘ/

A minor dialect difference not reported by Minoura (1994) is the realization of /ɘ/. Tuttle, Lovick, and Núñez-Ortiz (2011, 294) observe that this vowel is backed to [ɤ] in the speech of one of the Northway speakers. I later found that this backed pronunciation is common in Northway as shown in (19). The speaker labels in (19) are the same as those in (17) with the exception of N3, which refers to Mrs. Sherry Demit-Barnes from Northway. Where two forms are given, the first one is more common in the speech of that individual.

(19) Realization of /ɘ/ in Tetlin and Northway

			N1	*N2*	*N3*	*T1*	*T2*
a.	'skin'	thüh	[θɤ̀h]	[θɘ̀h]	[θɤ̀h]	[θɘh]	[θɘh]
b.	'urine'	łüh	[ɬɤh]	[ɬɘh]	[ɬɤh], [ɬɘh]	[ɬɘh]	[ɬɘh]
c.	'hunter'	nahelsüü	[nahelsɤː]	[nahelsɘː]	[nahelsɤː]	[nahelsɘː]	[nahelsɘː]
d.	'snow'	shyüh	[ʃʲɤ̀h]	[ʃʲɘ̀h]	[ʃʲɘ̀h], [ʃʲɤ̀h]	[ʃʲɘh]	[ʃʲɘh]

Unlike most of the previous dialect indicators, this one is not clear-cut. All Tetlin speakers with whom I have worked consistently use [ɘ]. Some Northway speakers such as N1 always use [ɤ]. N2 always uses [ɘ], while N3 alternates freely between the two sounds. Thus one can say that the realization of [ɤ] is a characteristic of the Northway dialect, while the realization as [ɔ] is not indicative of either dialect.

3.2.8. Realization of /i͡o/, /ĩ͜õ/

I observed in earlier work that the diphthongs /ɪ͡o/, /ɪ̃͜õ/ are disappearing in the Tetlin and Northway dialects (Lovick 2011). The oral diphthong /ɪ͡o/ no longer occurs in either dialect; in those dialects the monophthong /u:/ is used instead. The nasal diphthong /ɪ̃͜õ/ occurs regularly in the Scottie Creek dialect, occasionally in the Northway dialect, and never in the Tetlin dialect. Examples are given in chap. 6.1.9 (/ɪ͡o/) and 6.2.7 (/ɪ̃͜õ/).

3.2.9. Miscellaneous phonological differences

There are numerous additional phonological differences between the two dialects. A selection is shown in (20).

(20) Miscellaneous phonological differences

		Northway	*Tetlin*
a.	'dog'	łįį	łii
b.	'cup'	tuutįįł	tuutiił
c.	'louse nits'	shya' ts'įįl'	shya' ts'iil'
d.	'muskrat candy'	nihtsįįl	nihtsiil
e.	'spruce'	ts'ǫǫ	ts'oo
f.	'two'	łaakay	łaakeey
g.	'God'	T'oodįht'ay	T'oodįht'eey
h.	'butterfly'	naalil	laalil
i.	'tea'	ndiil	ldiil
j.	'rosehip'	nihchǫǫ	nchǫǫ
k.	'seagull'	mbohk'ąąy	mbehk'ąąy
l.	'fox'	nuungaay	nǫǫgaay
m.	'grayling'	sheejil	cheejil
n.	'moccasin'	kentsįą	kantsįą
o.	'with, and'	eh	eł

(20a–e) illustrate denasalization in the Tetlin dialect. This process is common but by no means ubiquitous or regular; the stems *tsįį* 'be hungry IPV' , *dįįł* 'do FUT', *k'įįł* 'birch sap, cottonwood sap', *tsǫǫ* 'grandmother' are consistently nasal in both the Tetlin and the Northway dialects, while the stem *nąą* 'mother' occurs occasionally denasalized in many instances in both.

There are also instances where Tetlin has /e:/ before /j/ and Northway has

/a/ (20f, g). In (20h, i) Tetlin /l/ corresponds to Northway /n/. Neither difference is regular; both occur in only a few words. The remaining differences in (20) are also irregular.

3.3. Lexical differences

The study of lexical dialect differences is hampered by the fact that there is considerable contact between the dialects. Speakers of either dialect will recognize and even occasionally use forms that are typical of the other dialect; they only comment on such differences when I ask directly (e.g., when I inquire about the semantic difference between the two verb themes for skinning or hunting in [21a, b]). The list in (21) is not inclusive.

(21) Miscellaneous lexical differences

		Northway	*Tetlin*
a.	'skin small animal'	na+thu#Ø+teeyh	nat'u#Ø+teeyh
b.	'go hunting'	na+xa#ch'+L+shyeeyh	na#t+L+süü
c.	'also'	–	tat'eey
d.	'here, this'	jin	jah
e.	'seven'	łk'idänchii	ahts'ąy uk'et łaakeey
f.	'silverberry'	dämbaa'	xay jign
g.	'according to P'	P+k'eh	P+k'etaa
h.	'1SG'	shiy	shin
i.	'foxtail'	łįįche'	łįįcheexa'

3.4. Morphological differences

There are several minor morphological dialect differences. The following list is likely incomplete.

3.4.1. Realization of the *i*- perfective

The *i*- perfective, which is characterized by an *i*- conjugation marker in forms without an inner subject prefix, is realized clearly in the Northway dialect as /ì/. In the nontonal Tetlin dialect, it is realized as /e/ and seems to have been reanalyzed as a *dh*-perfective. See chap. 29.2.5.

3.4.2. Adverbial-derivational prefix strings

Several prefix strings seem to have dialect restrictions. Sts'a+ke# (?, dh) 'around in a circle' occurs only in the Tetlin dialect; in the Northway dialect na+ke#(d) (Ø, dh) 'around and back, around and over' is used instead.

Da+ki+tl'a (?, aa) 'up onto the shore' and da+tl'a# (Ø, dh) 'onto land' are attested only in the Tetlin dialect; the Northway dialect uses ki+tl'a# (?, dh) 'toward shore' and ki+tl'a# (Ø, aa) 'onto shore' instead. See chap. 35.2.1.7 for examples and discussion.

3.4.3. Reciprocal object *ɬi*-

In the Tetlin and Beaver Creek dialects the reciprocal direct and postpositional object prefix *niɬ*- has the allomorph *ɬi*-; the two allomorphs appear to be in free variation. In the Northway dialect *ɬi*- only occurs in strongly lexicalized contexts, not as a productive object marker. See chap. 31.2.3.3 and 23.3.2 for discussion and examples.

3.4.4. Conjugation marker following P+*tüh* 'over P'

The postposition P+*tüh* 'over P' triggers an *aa*- perfective in the verb in the Tetlin dialect but not in the Northway dialect. The Tetlin form is more consistent with what is reported for related languages (see Kari [1990, 334] for Ahtna or Jetté and Jones [2000, 509] for Koyukon, where the cognate postposition requires (Ø, gh)[3] conjugation prefixes). See chap. 15.2.1.14 for examples.

3.4.5. Prefixes of directionals

The prefix *tth'i*- 'straight out' on directional adverbs is attested only in the Tetlin dialect, while the prefix *ha*- 'ADJC'- is quite common in the Northway dialect but rare in Tetlin. See chap. 17.

I suspect that there are additional morphological dialect differences, but a systematic study still remains to be done. This also holds for syntactic differences.

3.5. Summary

In this chapter the dialects of Upper Tanana are reviewed. Based on phonological criteria, Minoura (1994) identifies five dialects: Tetlin, Upper, Northway, Scottie Creek, and Beaver Creek. These dialects correspond largely to the seminomadic bands reported on by McKennan (1959). Of the five dialects the Scottie Creek dialect is extinct and the Upper dialect almost so; speaker counts for the other three dialects are included where available.

I discuss the phonological dialect differences identified by Minoura (1994), paying particular attention to the Northway and Tetlin dialects. A few minor differences between those two dialects not included in Minoura (1994) are added.

Not surprisingly, there are quite a few lexical differences. A few morphological differences are also reviewed.

It is likely that there are further morphological as well as syntactic differences between the dialects; a more thorough investigation is warranted.

Notes

1. I additionally suspect that there remain dialect distinctions between the Last Tetlin and the Tetlin dialect. The late Mrs. Cora David, one major contributor to this grammar, came from Last Tetlin; her husband Mr. Roy H. David Sr., also a major contributor, and his cousin Mrs. Ida Joe are both from Tetlin. All three identify as Tetlin speakers, yet Mrs. David's language differs considerably from that of the other two. A detailed study of this is in preparation.
2. I further note that high tone also occurs on directional stems and a few other lexical items; see chap. 7.3.
3. This *gh* is cognate to the *aa-* conjugation marker in Upper Tanana.

4 Some cultural background

In this chapter I provide some cultural background that I believe to be helpful for reading this grammar. Hill (2006) comments extensively on the need to include this type of background, and many chapters throughout this grammar rely, implicitly or explicitly, on cultural knowledge possessed by Upper Tanana speakers but not shared beyond their linguistic area.

As the focus of this book lies on grammatical structure, the following discussion of cultural concepts is very brief. More detail can be found in the following ethnographic studies.

McKennan's (1959, 1969, 1981) publications, though published in the second half of the twentieth century, are based on his fieldwork in 1928–1929. They thus contain the earliest ethnographic accounts of Upper Tanana culture. Case (1986), Halpin (1987), and Friend, Holton, and Easton (2007) study subsistence in the Upper Tanana area. The geographic knowledge of Upper Tanana people is documented in Kari (1997a). The social fabric of Upper Tanana culture is explored in Heinrich (1957) and McKennan (1969), and, with the greatest amount of detail, Guédon (1974). Guédon (1981) and Simeone (1995) describe the potlatch, possibly the single most important social event in that area. Guédon (2005) explores the dreamworld, drawing connections between the two important traditions of shamanism and storytelling.

In the following sections, I focus on several aspects of Upper Tanana culture: the concept of *į̨įjih* (section 4.1), stories and storytelling (section 4.2), and the cast of characters within stories (section 4.3).

4.1. *Į̨įjih*

Throughout this grammar I make frequent reference to the concept of *į̨įjih*, which is hard to adequately render in English. Speakers often translate it as 'taboo', 'forbidden', or 'that's a no-no'. Its semantic range is illustrated in (22), taken from a narrative by Mrs. Cora H. David.

(22) Excerpt: UTOLVDN11Jul2901:001–008 (T)

a.

Neenaattheh	*dą’*	*ts’exeey*	*iin*	*tihehaak*	*tah*
1PL:before	at	women	PL	3PL:SG.go.outside:IPV:CUST	when

įįjih	*huhinih.*
taboo	3PL>3PL:say:IPV

‘Long before our time, they called women who have their first period taboo.’

b.

Įįjih.
taboo

‘Taboo.’

c.

Nahugn	*hiiye’aal*	*hut’eey*	*įįjih.*
whatever	3PL>3SG:eat:IPV:NOM	ADVZR	taboo

‘Whatever they eat was restricted.’

d.

Nahugn	*diniign*	*tthįį’*	*neetsay*	*tthįį’*	*hugn*	*t’eey*	*įįjih.*
whatever	moose	meat	1PL:grandfather	meat	all	even	taboo

‘Whatever, moose meat, bear meat, all was forbidden.’

e.

Hiiyehgąy	*tl’aan*	*ay*	*shyiit*	*tah*	*shyi’*
3PL>3SG:dry:PFV:NOM	and	and	there	when	meat

hiiye’įįł.
3PL>3SG:eat:IPV:CUST

‘Having dried it, then they would eat meat.’

f.

Nahugn	*hiishyii*	*tuu*	*etnaa*	*nts’ą’*	*hiishyii*
whatever	3PL>3SG:in	water	drink:IPV:NOM	and	3PL>3SG:in

ch’e’aal	*hut’eey,*	*k’at’eey*	*doo*	*t’eey*	*hiishyii*
INDF.O:eat:IPV:NOM	even	NEG	anyone	even	3PL>3SG:in

chaa’aal	*nts’ą’*	*dihįįshyįį’*	*hiishyiit*	*chih*	*chaa’aał.*
INDF.O:eat:FUT:NEG	and	3PL:alone	3PL>3SG:in	also	INDF.O:eat:FUT

‘They have their own cup and plate; nobody may eat from it, only they may eat from it.’

g.

Įįjih.
taboo

‘It was forbidden.’

h. *Įįjih, ay eł shyįį' ch'a ts'eneeshyaan ts'įįtsuul*
taboo that with only FOC 1PL:grow.up:PFV:NOM 1PL:be.small:IPV
dą'.
when
'*Įįjih*, that's the only way we grew up when we were little.'

Catalogues of prohibitions like the one in (22) are probably the reason why *įįjih* is often translated with 'taboo' or 'forbidden'. But on the day where Mrs. David told me about *įįjih*, she also discussed the proper way to wash one's face, the best food for young children, armbands made from beaver claws as well as wood shavings in their pockets for boys, the correct way to place fish on a drying rack, and so forth. While *įįjih* is strongly associated with hunting luck (Nelson 1983), reducing it to a strategy to avoid spoiling one's luck is an oversimplification. Rather, *įįjih* can be thought of as the sum of all the rituals, large and small, that Guédon (2005, 164–75) lists: puberty and rites of passage; menstruation, delivery, and other female powers and needs; death and rituals associated with it; hunting and ritual relationships with game animals and plants; situations allowing the identification of humanness as opposed to other beings; war, murder, and fighting; encounters between humans and animals as well as humans with special gifts; magical chants; and magic. In the words of Mrs. David:

(23) *Įįjih ay hǫǫ' shyįį' ts'iinįįthįį.* (T)
įįjih 3SG thus only 1PL:think:IPV:CUST
'*Įįjih*, that's the only way we think.' UTOLVDN11Jul2902:014

For a person who grew up in the old way—this includes most of the elders alive today and some of their offspring—attention to *įįjih* is constant and one of the defining characteristics of an Upper Tanana (or Dene) person. A good person keeps their *įįjih* regardless of the circumstances, and many traditional stories contain explicit warnings about the consequences of not doing so.

4.1.1. Linguistic aspects of *įįjih*

Įįjih requires a person to pay attention to their linguistic behavior. This includes vocabulary restrictions such as the avoidance of the words *shoh* '(black) bear' and *ch'iliitthoo'* 'grizzly' by many women. Instead women use terms such as the English word *bear* or, in Tetlin especially, *neetsay* 'our grandfather'. Similarly, there are euphemisms for going to the bathroom (ni+na#D+haak 'SG customarily repeatedly goes to a place'), having one's period (ti#Ø+haak 'SG customarily goes outside'), and going hunting (na+xa#ch'+L+shyeek 'customarily carry PL weapons around'). The killing of a moose is usually referred to with the verb theme inflected for indefinite object (ch'+dh+H+xeh 'kill something'); the word *diniign* 'moose' is not usually mentioned in this context.

Įįjih also leads to the avoidance of certain linguistic structures. For example, it is possible to claim ownership over many items using possessive morphology (see chap. 22). Yet this construction cannot be used to indicate possession of wild animals—while one can say *shliign'* 'my dog', one cannot say *shgah* 'my rabbit' or *shdlegn'* 'my squirrel', either with the interpretation 'my pet rabbit or squirrel' or 'the rabbit or squirrel that I caught'. *Įįjih* disallows both interpretations: there is a strong injunction against owning animals other than dogs, and claiming ownership over a game animal suggests an unwillingness to share.

Communicative behavior is also subject to *įįjih*. Scollon and Scollon (1981) observe that many linguistic behaviors that Anglo-Americans find "normal" are viewed as problematic by Alaskan Dene: an Anglo-American's desire to present herself in the best light might be interpreted as bragging; making explicit plans for the future might be considered reckless behavior with respect to her luck; and her attempts to draw individuals out in conversation can be taken as intrusive. Rushforth and Chisholm (1991) also draw a link between various types of linguistic behavior and the general moral framework of the Bearlake Dene.

Linguistic aspects of *įįjih* are touched upon throughout this grammar.

4.2. Stories and storytelling

Upper Tanana culture is traditionally oral, and many aspects of cultural knowledge were handed down through stories. The importance of storytelling thus cannot be overemphasized. They contain and teach all of the cultural knowledge that an individual needs, from survival and orientation skills to knowledge about how the world came to be the way it is.

Old-time stories are set in "floating time" (Helm and Gillespie 1981) when animals and humans could still communicate (see, e.g., McKennan [1959, 162], Ruppert [1996, ix] for Upper Tanana, Ellanna and Balluta [1982, 39–47] and Fall [1990, 4] for Dena'ina, or Nelson [1983, 24] for Koyukon). The stories serve several purposes: "to entertain, educate and inspire—to cause the reader or listener to think" (Attla [1990, ix]; see also Ellanna and Balluta [1982, 39–47] or Fall [1990, 5–7], among others). Elders compare old-time stories to Bible stories in that the narratives provide the listener with a moral code (de Laguna 1995, 76) and in that magical or miraculous events are common.

Stories are not owned by individuals. Knowledge of the stories is required to be a good Upper Tanana person. But even though everybody *knows* the stories, not every individual is (or feels) qualified to tell them. Old-time stories in particular require that they be told by an elder with a good understanding of the stories' importance and verbal skill to match. Several individuals who told me in 2006 that they were not storytellers have since stepped up to the task of telling stories, as their elders passed on.

Traditionally stories were told in the evenings in winter (Jetté 1908) in a group setting. More recently stories are told at other times of the day and (with a few exceptions) during other seasons. Nowadays they are often told in English since the target audience—young people—no longer understands the traditional language well enough. Fall (1990) and Kari and Fall (2003) report for Dena'ina that for an elder to tell a story, a young person first has to work for them. Upper Tanana elders remember this from their youth, but this is no longer practiced. Elders will gladly tell stories as long as their audience demonstrates understanding and appreciation by listening (rather than just recording) and by responding appropriately and in the right places.[1]

4.3. Story characters

Some of the characters featured in the traditional stories may not be familiar to readers not working with Alaskan Dene groups, so they merit a brief introduction.

4.3.1. Yamaagn Teeshyaay and Tsa' Ushyąą

These two names refer to the same individual; *Yamaagn Teeshyaay* 'the one who went around [the world]' is used in Tetlin and Northway; *Tsa' Ushyąą* 'Smart Beaver' is used in Scottie Creek.

Yamaagn Teeshyaay is a central character of Upper Tanana cosmology. In his travels around the world he encounters many different Peoples, all with their own customs and cultures. Some are harmless (such as the Woodpecker's eating worms or the Ant People having a potlatch), so Yamaagn Teeshyaay either leaves them alone or plays a minor prank on them. Other creatures, however, used to be dangerous to humans, such as the Eagles who consumed human flesh. Whenever Yamaagn Teeshyaay encounters such Peoples, he "straightens them out."

The Yamaagn Teeshyaay story cycle is of great spiritual significance. Several elders have compared him to Jesus; some even suggest that Yamaagn Teeshyaay and Jesus are the same person. To respect this I avoid using long textual examples from Yamaagn Teeshyaay stories, but I have explicit permission from the storytellers to use isolated sentences from these stories.

No complete telling of this story cycle in Upper Tanana is published. McKennan (1959) contains several episodes translated into English. A few episodes of this cycle are included in C. David (2011, 2017), and there are several unpublished partial versions in the holdings of the Alaska Native Language Archive. There is a complete version in Tanacross and English Demit and Joe (2010); the most carefully edited version in any Alaskan Dene language is that by Attla (1990) in Koyukon. That collection even includes a companion volume explaining some of the story motifs (Thompson 1990).

4.3.2. *Gǫǫ*

The word *gǫǫ* literally means 'worm', but it is also used to refer to what is known as the 'Bush Indian' across interior Alaska. This evil creature sneaks around villages attempting to abduct individuals, particularly women and children. Its presence is usually signaled by a whistling noise. *Gǫǫ* are seen year-round. Talking about *Gǫǫ* is *įįjih*, and the stories about *Gǫǫ* should only be told during the storytelling months. When people talk about recent *Gǫǫ* encounters, they do so in veiled allusions such as "You heard they saw one down in Dot Lake," without specifying what "one" refers to. *Gǫǫ* encounters, even when they end well, are terrifying experiences. *Gǫǫ* cast a befuddling spell over their victims. In one instance the victim was eventually rescued but never became quite the person she had been before the abduction.

In Tetlin *Gǫǫ* is also used to refer to a person belonging to non-Dene tribes, especially enemies in old-time wars. Interestingly not all *Gǫǫ* are evil, despite their foreign and intimidating appearance. It is also possible to make jokes about them. Mr. Roy H. David Sr., for example, called his beloved wife Cora *Gǫǫ*. (I was extremely flattered when he started calling me *Gǫǫ gaay* 'little *Gǫǫ*', "because you're her friend.")

Throughout this grammar, I do not translate the word *Gǫǫ*, since no English word fully captures its connotations.

4.3.3. *Che' t'iin* 'Tailed People'

The *Che' t'iin* 'Tailed People' are monkey-like creatures with a long tail. Groups similar to the *Che' t'iin* are known to several Alaskan Dene communities. Different stories are associated with them. In Northway the *Che' t'iin* are part of the Yamaagn Teeshyaay story cycle; after they kill Yamaagn Teeshyaay's wife, he kills the chief of the *Che' t'iin* only to discover that he also needs to kill his shadow, or spirit. In Tetlin the *Che' t'iin* used to occupy a hill close to today's village site. From there they would kill and eat people. The Tetlin people finally smoked them out, killing them all – or so they hope. Mrs. Cora H. David's account of this ends with the chilling: *Jah ts'anh hutshyaak nts'ą' k'a hiits'itnąy hihunąy le' nts'ą' nįįłaag le'* 'To this day, we don't know if they are dead or alive' (C. David 2017, 114).

4.3.4. Raven

In Upper Tanana, as in many other Dene groups (de Laguna 1995), Raven is both a creator and a trickster. Although McKennan (1959) contains numerous Raven stories, I have been able to record only a handful. Apparently Raven (unlike Yamaagn Teeshyaay) seems to have lost a lot of his significance in the Upper Tanana area over the last century.

4.3.5. Other sentient beings

As in many other North American groups, sentience and speech are not ascribed solely to humans but also to animals, plants, and other naturally occurring objects. When this happens, the Upper Tanana name of this object is capitalized in the examples; e.g., (24):

(24)	*"Ąą',*	*stanįltthiit,"*	*yehnih,*	*Ch'aachin'*	*t'eey.*	(T)
	yes	2SG:run.away:IPV	3SG>3SG:say:IPV	tree.stump	even	

'"Yes, run away," the tree stump said to her.'

UTOLVDN14Nov2301:308

4.4. Summary

In this chapter some cultural background is provided. The discussion of *įįjih* as well as an introduction to several characters from traditional stories hopefully facilitate interpretation of many examples in this grammar.

Notes

1. This clashes with my training as a documentary linguist, which requires me to be quiet so as not to spoil the recording.

Part II

Phonology

5 Consonants

Upper Tanana has a large inventory of consonants, with thirty-three phonemic consonants, more than half of them stops or affricates.

The consonants of Upper Tanana are shown in table 5.1. (Historical processes contributing to the development of the system are described in chap. 8.) This inventory is taken from Tuttle, Lovick, and Núñez-Ortiz (2011, 286) but has been reorganized to reflect phonological considerations (see chap. 9 and 11). It also includes one nonphonemic sound [ŋ], which is the realization of /k/ in codas (see 5.3.2 for more discussion). Most of the data in this grammar is presented in the practical orthography; hence the first character in each cell is the orthographic representation followed by a phonemic representation between slashes.

In the following sections each group of sounds is briefly discussed and illustrated. Examples contain a gloss, orthographic and phonemic representation, as well as the most common phonetic variants. Some forms include dialect labels; in the absence of dialect information the form is attested in both Northway and Tetlin.

5.1. Oral stops and affricates

In table 5.1, oral stops and affricates are grouped together, as both groups distinguish aspirated, unaspirated, and ejective articulation.

5.1.1. Aspirated oral stops and affricates

Aspirated oral stops and affricates are always voiceless and are orthographically represented with voiceless symbols (an exception is <tl> for /$\widehat{t\text{ɬ}}^{h}$/). Aspirated oral stops may occur in syllable onsets and codas; aspirated affricates are limited to syllable onsets.

5.1.1.1. Aspirated oral stops In syllable onsets before back vowel, (25a, b; 26a, b) the two aspirated oral stops /t^{h}, k^{h}/ are often pronounced with velar rather than glottal aspiration: [t^{x}, k^{x}].[1] They are fully voiceless in syllable-

	Labial	Dental	Alveolar	Lateral	Postalveolar	Palatal	Velar	Glottal
stops, affricates								
aspirated		tth /t̪͜θʰ/	t /tʰ/ ts /t͡sʰ/	tl /t͡ɬʰ/	ch /t͡ʃʰ/		k /kʰ/	
unaspirated		ddh /t̪͜θ/	d /t/ dz /t͡s/	dl /t͡ɬ/	j /t͡ʃ/		g /k/	’ /ʔ/
ejective		tth’ /t̪͜θ’/	t’ /t’/ ts’ /t͡s’/	tl’ /t͡ɬ’/	ch’ /t͡ʃ’/		k’ /k’/	
fricatives								
voiceless		th /θ/	s /s/	ł /ɬ/	sh /ʃ/	shy /ʃʲ/	x /x/	h /h/
voiced		dh /ð/		l /l/				
sonorants								
voiceless			nh /n̥/			yh /j̊/		
voiced	m /m/		n /n/			y /j/	(gn [ŋ])	

Table 5.1. The consonants of Upper Tanana

final position (25c, d; 26c, d). Before a homorganic stop or affricate /tʰ/ is sometimes unreleased (25d).

/tʰ, kʰ/ occur primarily in stems but are also attested in prefixes (25e, 26e). The morphemes *tät-* 'cane' in (25d) and *naak-* 'eye' in (26d) are incorporated stems.

(25) /tʰ/

a.	'three'	taagn	/tʰa:k/	[tʰa:g], [tˣa:g]
b.	'cane' (N)	tät	/tʰʌ̀tʰ/	[tʰʌ̀tʰ], [tˣʌ̀tʰ]
c.	'hurry up'	hanteey'	/hàntʰe:jʔ/	[hàntʰe:jʔ]
d.	'she walked with cane'	natätjettiin	/natʰʌ̀tʰt͡ʃettʰi:n/	[natʰʌ̀t̚t͡ʃettʰi:n]
e.	'[boat] sank' (T)	tinį̨įłaat	/tʰinĩ:ɬa:tʰ/	[tʰinĩ:ɬa:tʰ]

(26) /kʰ/

a.	'wolf'	tthiikaan	/t͜θʰi:kʰa:n/	[t͜θʰi:kʰa:n], [t͜θʰi:kˣa:n]
b.	'absent'	kol	/kʰól/	[kʰól], [kˣól]
c.	'coat'	eek	/ʔe:kʰ/	[ʔe:kʰ]
d.	'she stared at him'	yenaaknitshyah	/jenà:kʰnitʃʲah/	[jenà:kʰnitʃʲah]
e.	'I see you SG'	nnak-'į̨h	/nnakʰʔĩh/	[nnakʰʔĩh]

5.1.1.2. Aspirated affricates The aspirated affricates /t͜θʰ, t͡sʰ, t͡ɬʰ, t͡ʃʰ/ all contain a strong fricative portion followed by glottal aspiration. All affricates are restricted to syllable onsets.

/t͜θʰ/ occurs in stem syllables (27a–c) and prefixes (27d). Orthographically /t͜θʰ/ is represented as <tth>.

(27) /t͜θʰ/

a.	'it is yellow'	deltthoh	/telt͜θʰoh/	[telt͜θʰoh]
b.	'rock'	tthee	/t͜θʰe:/	[t͜θʰe:]
c.	'waterwards' (N)	tthän'	/t͜θʰʌ̀nʔ/	[t͜θʰʌ̀nʔ]
d.	'he fell into the fire' (N)	tthidaltth'ät	/t͜θʰitalt͜θ'ʌtʰ/	[t͜θʰitalt͜θ'ʌtʰ]

/t͡sʰ/ also occurs in stem syllables (28a, b) and prefixes (28c). It is represented as <ts> in the practical orthography.

(28) /t͡sʰ/

a.	'firewood'	tsät	/t͡sʰʌtʰ/	[t͡sʰʌtʰ]
b.	'he made it'	yehtsį̨į	/jeht͡sʰĩ:/	[jeht͡sʰĩ:]
c.	'let's go'	tsuudeeł	/t͡sʰu:te:ɬ/	[t͡sʰu:te:ɬ]

/t͡ɬʰ/ appears to be restricted to stems (29); it is not attested in prefixes. It is the only aspirated affricate that is spelled with a partly voiced symbol <tl> even though it is always fully voiceless (see also chap. 12).

(29) /t͡ɬʰ/

a.	'algae'	tahtlogn	/tʰaht͡ɬʰok/	[tʰaht͡ɬʰogŋ]
b.	'it is slippery' (N)	hultlät	/hult͡ɬʰʌtʰ/	[hult͡ɬʰʌtʰ]
c.	'mushy, bad'	tleegn	/t͡ɬʰeːk/	[t͡ɬʰeːgŋ]

/t͡ʃʰ/ occurs both in stem syllables (30a, b) and prefixes (30c). It is orthographically represented as <ch>.

(30) /t͡ʃʰ/

a.	'its tail'	uche'	/ut͡ʃʰèʔ/	[ut͡ʃʰèʔ]
b.	'she grabbed it'	yihchuut	/jihʃʰùːtʰ/	[jiht͡ʃʰùːtʰ]
c.	'I will eat it'	nachih'aał	/nat͡ʃʰih'ʔàːɬ/	[nat͡ʃʰih'ʔàːɬ]

5.1.2. Unaspirated oral stops and affricates

Unaspirated oral stops and affricates are underlyingly voiceless but are orthographically represented by characters usually associated with voicing. Unaspirated oral stops may be phonetically voiced in codas; unaspirated affricates are always voiceless.

5.1.2.1. Unaspirated oral stops /t/ occurs in prefixes (31) as well as in stems (32). In prefixes /t/ is always voiceless, regardless of whether it occurs in onsets (31a, b) or codas (31c, d). (Only one prefix can cause an underlying /t/ in a prefix coda: the D- voice/valence marker. While it is phonologically /t/, it is for some reason written with the orthographic symbol for /tʰ/. I made the decision not to change this practice.)

(31) /t/ in prefixes

a.	'I am hungry'	dihtsįį	/tiht͡sʰĩː/	[tiht͡sʰĩː]
b.	'I said to them'	udihnih	/utihnih/	[utihnih]
c.	's/he was killed'	atxąą	/atxãː/	[atxãː]
d.	'she's drinking it'	yetnąą	/jetnãː/	[jetnãː]

In stems the realization of /t/ depends both on its position in the syllable and on the dialect. In stem onsets /t/ is always voiceless [t] (32a–c). In stem codas, /t/ is always the result of suffixation with a vocalic suffix (see chap. 11) and is always fully voiced [d], often followed by a homorganic nasal consonant (N) or a short schwa-vowel (T) ([32d–g]; see also chap. 3).

(32) /t/ in stems

a.	‘I’m sitting’	dhihdah	/ðihtah/	[ðihtah]
b.	‘lynx’	niiduuy	/nì:tu:j/	[nì:tu:j]
c.	‘who’	doo	/to:/	[to:]
d.	‘ant’ (N)	naadodn	/na:tòt/	[na:tòdn]
e.	‘ant’ (T)	naadodi	/na:tot/	[na:todɪ], [na:todə], [na:todn]
f.	‘my belongings’ (N)	s͡ts’ädn’	/s͡ts’ʌtʔ/	[s͡ts’ʌdnʔ]
g.	‘my belongings’ (T)	s͡ts’ade’	/s͡ts’atʔ/	[s͡ts’adʔ], [s͡ts’adəʔ], [s͡ts’adnʔ]

/t/ is written <d> in onsets and, depending on its realization, <d>, <de>, <di>, or <dn> in codas.

/k/ occurs in prefixes as well as in stems. In prefixes it is restricted to the portmanteau morpheme *agn-* /ak/- formed by the first-person singular subject with the L- voice/valence prefix. In this portmanteau /k/ is always fully voiced and often followed by [ŋ], especially in the Northway dialect. The plosive may also disappear altogether in that dialect, leaving only [ŋ] behind (33). /k/ does not occur in the onset of prefix syllables.

(33) /k/ in prefixes

a.	‘I eat it’	agndeeł	/akte:ɬ/	[agte:ɬ], [agŋte:ɬ], [aŋte:ɬ]
b.	‘I’ll see you again’	nanagn’įįł	/nanakʔɨ̀:ɬ/	[nanagʔɨ̀:ɬ], [nanagŋʔɨ̀:ɬ], [nanaŋʔɨ̀:ɬ]

In stems /k/ may occur in onsets (34a–c) as well as in codas (34d–g). In onsets it is always voiceless. /k/ is realized as [k] before front vowel (34a), but [k^{Y}] before back vowel (34b, c). While the words in (34b, c) are recognized when pronounced [kah] and [kõ:], respectively, and are not corrected when produced by language learners, these pronunciations do not usually occur in the speech of native speakers.

/k/ in stem codas is always fully voiced [g]. The voicing is again caused by the presence of vocalic suffixes; see chap. 11. The realization of /k/ in stem codas is a dialect diagnostic as shown in (34d–g) and discussed in chap. 3.

(34) /k/ in stems

a.	‘frozen overflow’	giat	/kɪ͡at^{h}/	[kɪ͡at^{h}]
b.	‘rabbit’	gah	/kah/	[k^{Y}ah]
c.	‘worm’	gǫǫ	/kõ:/	[k^{Y}õ:]
d.	‘three’ (N)	taagn	/t^{h}a:gn/	[t^{h}a:gŋ], [t^{h}a:ŋ]
e.	‘three’ (T)	taag	/t^{h}a:k/	[t^{h}a:g], [t^{h}a:gə], [t^{h}a:gŋ]
f.	‘upwards ALL’ (N)	degn’	/téknʔ/	[tégŋʔ], [téŋʔ]

g. 'upwards ALL' (T) deg̲' /tékʔ/ [tégʔ], [tégəʔ], [tégŋʔ]

/k/ is written <g> in onsets and, depending on its realization, <g>, <ge>, <gi>, or <gn> in codas.

/ʔ/ occurs in stems as well as in prefixes. In stems it may occur in onsets (35a–d) and codas (35d–f); in prefixes it is limited to onsets (35g–i). (35b, f) illustrate that /ʔ/ may occur as the last member of a stem-final consonant cluster. In prefixes, /ʔ/ is epenthetic (35g–i). In word-medial position, /ʔ/ often surfaces as creak on the two surrounding vowels (35i).

(35) /ʔ/

a.	'coat'	eek	/ʔeːkʰ/	[ʔeːkʰ]
b.	'my coat' (N)	sh'̲eegn'	/ʃʔèːkʔ/	[ʃʔèːgŋʔ]
c.	'she's eating'	ch'e'̲aał	/t͡ʃʼeʔàːɬ/	[t͡ʃʼeʔàːɬ]
d.	'no'	ina'̲	/ʔinàʔ/	[ʔinàʔ]
e.	'their tails'	huche'̲	/hut͡ʃʰèʔ/	[hut͡ʃʰèʔ]
f.	'he's holding it'	yuuton'̲	/juːtʰònʔ/	[juːtʰònʔ]
g.	'I'm crying' (T)	ihtsah	/ʔiht͡sʰah/	[ʔiht͡sʰah]
h.	'the sun set'	nasaa'j̲į'ą̲ą	/nasaːʔĩːʔãː/	[nasaːʔĩːʔãː]
i.	'I'm walking back'	na'̲ihdaał	/naʔihtaːɬ/	[naʔihtaːɬ], [na̰ʔḭhtaːɬ], [na̰ḭhtaːɬ]

Glottal stop is written as <'> in word-medial and word-final position; in word-initial position, /ʔ/ is not written at all (35a, d, g).

/ʔ/ in codas often triggers creak in addition to or instead of the glottal stop (36). Creakiness also may affect any additional coda consonants (36c).

(36) Creak before /ʔ/ in codas

a.	'raven'	taatsąą'̲	/tʰaːt͡sʰȁːʔ/	[tʰaːt͡sʰȁːʔ], [tʰaːt͡sʰȁ̰ːʔ], [tʰaːt͡sʰȁ̰ː]
b.	'good'	su'̲	/sùʔ/	[sùʔ/, [sṵ̀ʔ], [sṵ̀]
c.	'coat POSS' (N)	-'eeg̲n̲'	-/ʔèːkʔ/	[ʔèːgŋʔ], [ʔèːŋʔ], [ʔḛ̀ːg̰ŋ̰], [ʔḛ̀ːŋ̰]

5.1.2.2. Unaspirated affricates All unaspirated affricates are restricted to syllable onsets. Contrary to an observation made by Tuttle, Lovick, and Núñez-Ortiz (2011, 285), most unaspirated affricates are voiceless throughout; the exception is /t͡ɬ/, where the fricative portion is voiced.

/t̪θ/ is a very rare consonant attested only in a few stems, never in prefixes. Orthographically, /t̪θ/ is represented as <ddh>.

(37) /t͡θ/

a.	'mountain' (N)	ddhäł	/t͡θʌɬ/	[t͡θʌɬ]
b.	'favourite child' (N)	ddhuugn	/t͡θuːk/	[t͡θuːgŋ]

/t͡s/ is attested in stems (38a–c) as well as in prefixes (38d, e). It is orthographically represented as <dz>.

(38) /t͡s/

a.	'he's dancing'	ch'eldzüh	/t͡ʃ'elt͡səh/	[t͡ʃ'elt͡səh]
b.	'moon'	ch'aldzeegn	/t͡ʃ'alt͡seːkn/	[t͡ʃ'alt͡seːgŋ]
c.	'day'	dziin	/t͡siːn/	[t͡siːn]
d.	'waterfall'	dzina'įįłąy	/t͡sinaʔĩːɬãy/	[t͡sinaʔĩːɬãj]
e.	'we're playing'	dzelxoh	/t͡selxoh/	[t͡selxoh]

/t͡ɬ/ is limited to stem onsets (39). It is always pronounced [t͡l], never [t͡ɬ]. The consistent voicing of the fricative portion of /t͡ɬ/ allows us to perceptually distinguish this affricate from a /t-ɬ/ sequence, as demonstrated in (39c) versus (39d). In the orthography /t͡ɬ/ is represented as <dl>, while /t/+/ɬ/ sequences are written with a hyphen (39d).[2]

(39) /t͡ɬ/

a.	'moss'	dlaat	/t͡ɬaːtʰ/	[t͡laːtʰ]
b.	'it is blue'	deldliat	/telt͡ɬi̯atʰ/	[tet͡li̯atʰ]
c.	'he's laughing' (N)	edloh	/et͡ɬòh/	[et͡lòh]
d.	'she's dragging o back'	O natat-łoo	/natʰatɬoː/	[natʰatɬoː]

/t͡ʃ/ occurs in stems (40a–d) and prefixes (40e). Orthographically it is represented as <j>.

(40) /t͡ʃ/

a.	'I am afraid'	nagnjit	/nakt͡ʃitʰ/	[nagŋt͡ʃitʰ]
b.	'camprobber'	jǫǫ	/t͡ʃõ̀ː/	[t͡ʃõ̀ː]
c.	'berry'	jign	/t͡ʃikn/	[t͡ʃigŋ]
d.	'here' (T)	jah	/t͡ʃah/	[t͡ʃah]
e.	'she's singing'	jeh'ąą	/t͡ʃehʔãː/	[t͡ʃehʔãː]

5.1.3. Ejective stops and affricates

Ejective oral stops and affricates are restricted to syllable onsets. They are always voiceless and strongly glottalized. Weakened pronunciations, such as reported by Rice (1989, 31) for Slave, are very rare. They are always corrected by speakers during the transcription process, suggesting that they are not considered acceptable variants.

5.1.3.1. Ejective oral stops /t'/ occurs in stems (41a–c) and prefixes (41d). It is written <t'>.

(41) /t'/

a.	'aspen'	t'üüh	/t'ɔ̀:h/	[t'ɔ̀:h]
b.	'it is'	nt'eh	/nt'eh/	[nt'eh]
c.	'under P'	P+t'aat	/t'a:tʰ/	[t'a:tʰ]
d.	'I threw them down'	t'a'akdeeł	/t'aʔakʰtè:ɬ/	[t'aʔakʰtè:ɬ]

The ejective stop /t'/ contrasts clearly with the sequence /t/+/ʔ/, which is pronounced as two separate sounds.[3] In the orthography the consonant sequence is marked with a hyphen (42b) to distinguish it from the ejective (42a).

(42) /t'/ vs. /tʔ/

a.	'leaf'	ch'it'ąą'	/t͡ʃ'it'ȁ:ʔ/	[t͡ʃ'it'ȁ:ʔ]
b.	'he brought back O'	O na'at-'ąą	/naʔatʔã:/	[naʔatʔã:]

/k'/ is attested in stem (43a–c) and prefix onsets (43d). It is written <k'>.

(43) /k'/

a.	'willow'	k'ąy'	/k'ȁjʔ/	[k'ȁjʔ]
b.	'she's exercising'	etk'įą	/etk'ĩ͜ã/	[etk'ĩ͜ã]
c.	'NEG'	k'a	/k'à/	[k'à]
d.	'they will land'	k'edahtaadäł	/k'ètahtʰa:tʌ̀ɬ/	[k'ètahtʰa:tʌ̀ɬ]

The realization of /k'/ contrasts with that of /kʰ/+/ʔ/ or /k/+/ʔ/. Again a hyphen is used to distinguish the stop sequences /kʰ/+/ʔ/ (44b) and /k/+/ʔ/ (44c) from the ejective stop (44a).

(44) /k'/ vs. /kʰʔ/, /kʔ/

a.	'she's exercising'	etk'įą	/etk'ĩ͜ã/	[etk'ĩ͜ã]
b.	'I see you SG'	nnak-'įh	/nnakʰʔĩh/	[nnakʰʔĩh]
c.	'I see you SG again'	nannagn'įh	/nannakʔĩ̀:ɬ/	[nannagʔĩ̀:ɬ]

5.1.3.2. Ejective affricates There are four ejective affricates: /t̪θ', t͡s', t͡ɬ', t͡ʃ'/.

/t̪θ'/ occurs in stems (45a–c) and prefixes (45d). It is represented orthographically as <tth'>.

(45) /t͜θ’/

a.	‘ring’ (N)	laatth’üh	/laːt͜θ’əh/	[laːt͜θ’əh]
b.	‘plate’	tth’aak	/t͜θ’àːkʰ/	[t͜θ’àːkʰ]
c.	‘they are sitting’	hihdeltth’ih	/hihtèlt͜θ’ih/	[hihtèlt͜θ’ih]
d.	‘it flew straight’	tth’ineet’ak	/t͜θ’inèːt’akʰ/	[t͜θ’inèːt’akʰ]

/t͡s’/ is attested in stems (46a–c) and prefixes (46d, e). It is written as <ts’>.

(46) /t͡s’/

a.	‘she kissed me’	shnelts’ų’	/ʃnelt͡s’ũ̀ʔ/	[ʃnelt͡s’ũ̀ʔ]
b.	‘spruce’ (T)	ts’oo	/t͡s’oː/	[t͡s’oː]
c.	‘from P’ (T)	P+ts’anh	/t͡s’an̥/	[t͡s’an̥]
d.	‘old lady’	ts’ist’e’	/t͡s’ist’èʔ/	[t͡s’ist’èʔ]
e.	‘we are laughing’	ts’edloh	/t͡s’et͡ɬòh/	[t͡s’et͡lòh]

/t͡ɬ’/ occurs only in stems. Orthographically it is represented as <tl’> (47).

(47) /t͡ɬ’/

a.	‘grass’	tl’oh	/t͡ɬ’oh/	[t͡ɬ’oh]
b.	‘I got dressed’	nadhishtl’ųų	/naðiʃt͡ɬ’ũː/	[naðiʃt͡ɬ’ũː]
c.	‘and then’	tl’aan	/t͡ɬ’àːn/	[t͡ɬ’àːn]

/t͡ʃ’/ is attested in stems (48a–c) as well as in prefixes (48d, e). It is represented orthographically as <ch’>.

(48) /t͡ʃ’/

a.	‘quill’	ch’oh	/t͡ʃ’oh/	[t͡ʃ’oh]
b.	‘it is ripped’	eech’ił	/èːt͡ʃ’iɬ/	[èːt͡ʃ’iɬ]
c.	‘FOC’	ch’a	/t͡ʃ’à/	[t͡ʃ’à]
d.	‘its horns’	ch’ide’	/t͡ʃ’itèʔ/	[t͡ʃ’itèʔ]
e.	‘he’s dancing’	ch’eldzüh	/t͡ʃ’elt͡səh/	[t͡ʃ’elt͡səh]

5.2. Fricatives

The group of sounds labeled “fricatives” in table 5.1 is very heterogeneous including not only sounds that are phonetically classified as fricatives (/θ, ð, s, ɬ, ʃ, x, h/) but also the lateral approximant /l/ and one complex segment /ʃl/. /l/ is classified as a voiced fricative because of its patterning with /ɬ/ (see chap. 11 for more information).

5.2.1. Voiceless fricatives

There are seven voiceless fricatives: /θ, s, ɬ, ʃ, ʆ, x, h/. All of them are allowed in onsets, but only /ɬ/ and /h/ may occur in codas. Under certain conditions /θ, s, ɬ, ʃ, x/ are subject to fricative lenition; this process is described in detail in chap. 9.

/θ/ is limited to stem onsets (49). It is written <th>. When /θ/ occurs in word-medial position, its lenis allophone [θ̬] may occur (49a, c).

(49) /θ/

a.	'I am standing' (N)	na'ihthät	/nàʔihθʌtʰ/	[nàʔihθ̬ʌtʰ]
b.	'belt'	thüh	/θə̀h/	[θə̀h]
c.	'my belt'	shthüü'	/ʃθə̀:ʔ/	[ʃθ̬ə̀:ʔ]
d.	'wait!' (B)	the'	/θeʔ/	[θèʔ]

/s/ may occur in stem (50a, b) and prefix (50c, d) onsets. It is written <s>. When /s/ occurs in word-medial position, its lenis allophone [s̬] may occur (50a, c).

(50) /s/

a.	'it is good'	nsǫǫ	/nsõ:/	[ns̬õ:]
b.	'gaff hook' (N)	säɬ	/sʌ̀ɬ/	[sʌ̀ɬ]
c.	'my gaff hook' (N)	ssäl'	/ssʌ̀lʔ/	[ss̬ʌ̀lʔ]
d.	's/he swam across'	skenįįmįį	/skʰinĩ:mĩ:/	[skʰenĩ:mĩ:]

/ɬ/ occurs both in the onset of stems (51a–c) and prefixes (51e). It may also occur in the coda of light stem syllables (51d) and prefixes (51f). /ɬ/ is represented in the orthography as <ł>. When stem-initial /ɬ/ occurs in word-medial position, its lenis allophone [ɬ̬] may be used (51a, c).

(51) /ɬ/

a.	'it is flowing'	nįįłąyh	/nĩ:ɬãj̊/	[nĩ:ɬ̬ãj̊]
b.	'fish hook'	łoh	/ɬòh/	[ɬòh]
c.	'my fish hook'	shłoo'	/ʃɬò:ʔ/	[ʃɬ̬ò:ʔ]
d.	'crane'	deeł	/te:ɬ/	[te:ɬ]
e.	'she punched her up'	łaytnehgot	/ɬajtʰnèhkòtʰ/	[ɬajtʰnèhkòtʰ]
f.	'they kick each other'	nił'ikihelkayh	/niɬʔikʰìhelkʰaj̊/	[niɬʔikʰìhelkʰaj̊]

/ʃ/ occurs in stem (52a–c) and prefix (52d, e) onsets. It may also occur in prefix codas (52f). It is quite rare in stems, as it has partially merged with the palatalized voiceless fricative /ʆ/. In the orthography /ʃ/ is represented as <sh>.

(52) /ʃ/

a.	'black bear'	shoh	/ʃoh/	[ʃoh]
b.	'summer'	shiin	/ʃiːn/	[ʃiːn]
c.	'1SG' (T)	shin	/ʃin/	[ʃin]
d.	'she said to me'	shehnih	/ʃehnih/	[ʃehnih]
e.	'my father'	shta'	/ʃtʰàʔ/	[ʃtʰàʔ]
f.	'I work'	ishnah	/iʃnah/	[iʃnah]

/ʆ/ is, as the chosen symbol suggests, a voiceless palatalized postalveolar fricative. It differs from /ʃ/ not just with respect to palatalization but is also slightly longer. It is only attested in stem-initial position and is orthographically represented by <shy> (53).

(53) /ʆ/

a.	'it happened'	hutshyaak	/hùtʆaːkʰ/	[hùtʆaːkʰ]
b.	'she breathes'	etshyiyh	/etʆij̊/	[etʆij̊]
c.	'house'	shyah	/ʆah/	[ʆah]
d.	'I jumped into water'	ta'akshyaał	/tʰaʔakʰʆàːɬ/	[tʰaʔakʰʆàːɬ]
e.	'it splashed'	tetshyoh	/tʰetʆoh/	[tʰetʆoh]
f.	'knot'	shyia	/ʆi̯à/	[ʆi̯à]
g.	'vertically down AR'	shyuug	/ʆuːk/	[ʆuːg], [ʆuːgŋ̊]

/ʆ/ is the Upper Tanana reflex of Proto-Dene *y (IPA: [j]) in stem-initial position (53a, b), but it also has partly merged with /ʃ/, the reflex of Proto-Dene *xʸ (53c–g).[4] Because of this partial merger and its complex origins, the status of /ʆ/ in the phonological system of Upper Tanana is challenging to determine. Minoura (1994, 165–66) includes it as a lenis voiceless fricative, alongside [θ̬, s̬, ɬ̬, x̬], which according to him contrast with /θ, s, ɬ, x/ in stem-initial position (in this view, /ʆ/ contrasts with /ʃ/). Since I view the lenis fricatives as morphologically conditioned allophones of /θ, s, ɬ, x/ (see chap. 9.4 for a rationale), I include /ʆ/ among the voiceless fricatives.

/x/ occurs only in stem-initial position. Its realization varies between velar, uvular, and glottal articulation, depending on speaker and speech rate (it is usually [x] or [χ] in careful articulation, but often [h] in less careful speech). It is written as <x>. When noun or verb stem-initial /x/ occurs in word-medial position, its lenis allophone [x̬] (or uvular [χ̬]) may occur (54a, b).[5]

(54) /x/

a.	'she played'	delx̲oh	/telxoh/	[telx̬oh], [telχ̬oh]
b.	'sled'	x̲ał	/xaɬ/	[xaɬ], [χaɬ], [haɬ]
c.	'my sled'	shx̲al	/ʃxàlʔ/	[ʃx̬àlʔ], [ʃχ̬àlʔ]
d.	'for her'	ux̲ah	/uxah/	[uxah], [uχah], [uhah]
e.	'suddenly'	jahx̲än	/t͡ʃahxan/	[t͡ʃahxan], [t͡ʃahχan], [t͡ʃahhan]

/h/ occurs in stems (55a–e) and prefixes (55b, d, e). /h/ occurs both in onsets (55a, b, d) and codas (55c–e). Following /i/ or /iː/, /h/ is often realized as [j̊] (55d–e).

(55) /h/

a.	'she's walking'	aah̲aał	/aːhaːɬ/	[aːhaːɬ]
b.	'he's speaking'	h̲ǫǫh̲eey	/hõːheːj̊/	[hõːheːj̊]
c.	'big'	choh̲	/t͡ʃʰoh/	[t͡ʃʰoh]
d.	'they are playing'	h̲ih̲delxoh̲	/hihtelxoh/	[hihtelxoh], [hij̊telxoh]
e.	'I am sitting'	dhih̲dah̲	/ðihdah/	[ðihdah], [ðij̊dah]

5.2.2. Voiced fricatives

Upper Tanana has only two phonemically voiced fricatives, and both are quite restricted in their occurrence.

The voiced fricative /ð/, represented in the orthography as <dh>, is limited to two morphemes: the *dh-* conjugation prefix (56a) and the *dh-* qualifier (56b, c), which occurs as part of one verb theme and in a few fossilized prohibitives; see chap. 30.5. /ð/ is always fully voiced.

(56) /ð/

a.	'I am sitting'	d̲h̲ihdah	/ðihdah/	[ðihdah]
b.	'he killed sth.'	ch'id̲h̲ehxįį	/t͡ʃʼiðehxĩː/	[t͡ʃʼiðehxĩː]
c.	'be PL quiet!'	dad̲h̲ahnąy	/taðàhnã́j/	[taðàhnã́j]

/l/ may occur both in onsets and codas. In stem onsets (57a, b) it occurs only in a handful of words. In stem codas it is limited to heavy syllables (57c; see chap. 11). The L-voice/valence marker in (57d) is the only prefix that contains /l/. It also occurs in French loanwords as a reflex of the definite article *le* (57e).

(57) /l/

a.	'I don't know'	l̲e'e	/leʔe/	[leʔe]
b.	'butterfly' (T)	l̲aal̲il̲	/laːlil/	[laːlil], [laːlɪl]

c.	'she is small'	ntsuul̲	/n͡tsʰúːl/	[n͡tsʰúːl]
d.	'she is scared'	nel̲jit	/nelt͡ʃitʰ/	[nelt͡ʃitʰ]
e.	'tea' (T)	l̲diil	/ltiːl/	[ltiːl]

5.3. Sonorants

Upper Tanana has both voiced and voiceless sonorants.

5.3.1. Voiceless sonorants

There are two voiceless sonorants: /n̥/ and /j̊/.

/n̥/ is the product of a historical devoicing process of /n/ in stem-final position in light stems (Leer 1996c, 204). Synchronously it contrasts with /n/ in marking the difference between light and heavy stems (see chap. 11); I thus treat it as a phoneme. It is restricted to the stem-final position. Orthographically /n̥/ is represented as <nh> (58).

(58) /n̥/

a.	'muskrat'	dzän̲h̲	/t͡sʌn̥/
b.	'stick'	dichin̲h̲	/tit͡ʃʰin̥/
c.	'he wants o'	O iniithän̲h̲	/ìnìːθʌn̥/

/j̊/ is the product of a historical devoicing process of /j/ in stem-final position. Synchronically the two sounds contrast, marking the difference between light and heavy stems (see chap. 11). /j̊/ is limited to stem codas. /j̊/ begins voiced and ends voiceless; as a result, vowels other than /i/ tend to be slightly diphthongized before /j̊/ (59). The diphthongization of vowels before /j̊/ in turn means that the difference in vowel length between words like (59a, b) and those like (59c) becomes obscured. /j̊/ is often weakened to [h], especially after close vowels (59d).

(59) /j̊/

a.	'knife'	seey̲h̲	/seːj̊/	[se͡ij̊]
b.	'snowshoe'	aay̲h̲	/ʔaːj̊/	[ʔa͡ij̊]
c.	'she vomited'	na'etkuy̲h̲	/naʔatkʰuj̊/	[naʔatkʰu͡ij̊]
d.	'he is breathing'	etshyiy̲h̲	/et͡ʃij̊/	[et͡ʃij̊], [et͡ʃih]

5.3.2. Voiced sonorants

There are three phonemic voiced sonorants and one subphonemic sonorant.

/m/ is the only labial phoneme in Upper Tanana. Orthographically it is represented as <m>, <mb>, or (rarely) <b>, depending on its realization.

/m/ occurs in stem-initial position (60a–c). It also occurs in the consonantal allomorph of the third-person singular possessor and postpositional object prefix *u-/mb-* (60d, e).

(60) /m/

a.	'weasel'	nihmbaay	/nihma:j/
b.	'dry fish'	mba'	/màʔ/
c.	'it is shiny'	delmbiat	/telmi͡atʰ/
d.	'her older sister'	mbaadeh/	/ma:teh]
e.	'with her'	mbeł	/mèɬ/

The realization of /m/ as more or less denasalized is discussed in 5.3.2.1.

/n/ may occur in syllable onsets as well as in codas. Orthographically it is represented as <n> or <nd>. /n/ is a common consonant both in stems (61a–c) and prefixes (61d, e).

(61) /n/

a.	'I am working'	ishnah	/iʃnah/
b.	'2 SG'	nän	/nʌn/
c.	'earth'	nän'	/nʌ̀nʔ/
d.	'your (SG) older sister'	naadeh/	/naˑteh]
e.	'she arrived'	nįįshyah	/nĩ:ʃʲah/

The realization of /n/ as more or less denasalized is discussed in 5.3.2.1.

/j/ occurs in syllable onsets and codas. It is very rare as a stem-initial consonant; there are only a handful of examples besides the forms given in (62a, b).[6] /j/ is also an allomorph of the prefix *i-*/y- '3SG>3SG'- (62c, d); as part of this prefix, it may occur in syllable-initial and syllable-final position. (62e, f) illustrate /j/ in stem-final position, where it is limited to heavy stems (see chap. 11). /j/ is usually written as <y> or <yy> (in certain heavy syllables). /j/ has no allophones other than [j].

(62) /j/

a.	'woman's daughter'	-yaats'e'	/ja:t͡s'èʔ/
b.	'sky'	yaa	/ja:/
c.	'she said to him'	yehnih	/jehnih/
d.	'she punched her up'	łaytnehgot	/ɬajtʰnèhkòtʰ/
e.	'my snowshoe'	sh'aayy'	/ʃʔà:jʔ/
f.	'tiny'	guuy	/kú:j/

[ŋ] is not a phoneme in Upper Tanana; it is instead the reflex of a vocalic suffix following an unaspirated velar oral stop in syllable-final position, especially in the Northway dialect. Orthographically it is represented by <gn>. (63a) demonstrates [ŋ] in the portmanteau morpheme consisting of the first-person singular subject and an L- voice/valence-marker (see chap. 28 for more information on this prefix). The other three forms illustrate the effect of vocalic suffixes: (63b) contains a historical suffix -v that is part of several noun stems, (63c) the alienable possessive suffix -v̀ʔ, and (63d) the negative suffix -v́. (63) demonstrates that the velar plosive is sometimes deleted, and only the velar nasal stop remains.

(63) /ŋ/

a.	'I eat PL.O'	agndeeł	/akte:ɬ/	[agte:ɬ], [agŋte:ɬ], [aŋte:ɬ]
b.	'fish'	łuugn	/ɬu:k/	[ɬu:g], [ɬu:gŋ], [ɬu:ŋ]
c.	'my coat'	sh'eegn'	/ʃʔè:kʔ/	[ʃʔè:gʔ], [ʃʔè:gŋʔ], [ʃʔè:ŋʔ]
d.	'I don't know'	mits'ishniign	/mit͡s'ìʃní:k/	[mit͡s'ìʃní:g], [mit͡s'ìʃní:gŋ], [mit͡s'ìʃní:ŋ]

5.3.2.1. Denasalization of /m/, /n/ in onset position Both /m/ and /n/ may be (partly) denasalized in onset position under certain conditions. /m/ is realized as [m] in words containing either a nasal vowel (64a) or a nasal consonant (64b, c). (64d–g) illustrate the variability of /m/ in stem syllables that do not contain another nasal. Note also that the compound noun in (64g) contains a nasal consonant in the second syllable, which does not appear to block denasalization of the word-initial consonant. (64h) illustrates denasalization of /m/ in a prefix.

(64) Denasalization of /m/

a.	'it is spherical'	ch'ilmǫǫt	/t͡ʃ'ilmõ̀:t/	[t͡ʃ'ilmõ̀:t]
b.	'lake'	mänh	/mʌn̥/	[mʌn̥]
c.	'edge'	maagn	/mà:k/	[mà:gŋ], [mà:ŋ]
d.	'toboggan'	mboh	/moh/	[m^{b}oh], [^{m}oh], [boh], [poh]
e.	'I boiled it'	akmbiah	/ak^{h}mi͡ah/	[ak^{h}mi͡ah], [ak^{h}m^{b}i͡ah], [ak^{hm}bi͡ah], [ak^{h}bi͡ah]
f.	'sheep'	dimbee	/time:/	[time:], [tim^{b}e:], [ti^{m}be:], [tipe:]
g.	'sea gull'	mbohk'ąąy	/mohk'ã̀:j/	[mohk'ã̀:j], [m^{b}ohk'ã̀:j], [^{m}bohk'ã̀:j], [bohk'ã̀:j]
h.	'for her'	mbaa	/ma:/	[ma:], [m^{b}a:], [^{m}ba:]

The situation is similar for /n/. (65) demonstrates that /n/ is pronounced [n] before a nasal vowel (65a) or nasal stop (65b, c). (65d–f) illustrate denasalization of /n/ in stems, (65f) additionally in a prefix onset. (65d–f) also demonstrate that this process does not progress quite to [d] or [t], presumably to avoid a merger with /t/.

(65) Denasalization of /n/

a.	'his mind'	mǫǫn̲įį'	/mõːnìːʔ/	[mõːnì̃ːʔ]
b.	'earth'	n̲än'	/nʌ̀nʔ/	[nʌ̀nʔ]
c.	'fox' (N)	n̲uungaay	/nuːnkaːj/	[nuːnkaːj]
d.	'upriver ALL'	n̲e'	/néʔ/	[néʔ], [n^{d}éʔ], [^{n}déʔ]
e.	'man' (T)	din̲eh	/tineh/	[tineh], [tin^{d}eh], [ti^{n}deh]
f.	'I tell story' (T)	n̲ahogn̲ak	/nahokdak^{h}/	[nahognak^{h}], [n^{d}ahogn^{d}ak^{h}], [^{n}dahog^{n}dak^{h}]

Orthographically /m/ and /n/ are represented consistently as <m>, <n> in syllables containing another nasal. They are represented less consistently as <m>, <mb>, <b> and <n>, <nd> in syllables that do not contain another nasal element; the choice of characters then usually reflects the variant that is present in that particular utterance.

Minoura (1994) claims that the degree of denasalization is indicative of a speaker's dialect; the dialectology of denasalization is discussed in more detail in chap. 3.2.4.

5.4. Summary

In this chapter the consonant inventory of Upper Tanana is presented. This consonant inventory is typical for an Alaskan Dene language. There are thirty-three phonemic consonants, and over half of them of are oral stops or affricates. There is a three-way distinction between plain, aspirated, and ejective stops and affricates. Upper Tanana is typical of eastern Alaskan Dene languages in having voiceless sonorants. Somewhat unusual is the fact that the language has only two voiced fricatives.

More information on the consonant system of Upper Tanana is found in chap. 8, 9, and 11.

Notes

1. Similar findings in Navajo, Dëne Sųłiné, Tłįchǫ, North Slavey, and Tsilhqút'in lead McDonough and Wood (2008) to analyze these sounds as affricates rather than plain stops.

2. /t/+/l/ sequences do not occur.
3. The sequence /tʰ/+/ʔ/ never occurs.
4. *xʸ is a voiceless fronted velar fricative.
5. Fricative lenition does not seem to affect /x/ in prepositional or adverbial stems, as shown in (54d, e).
6. Most stems predicted to begin with /j/ have /ʝ/ as initial consonant.

6 Vowels

Upper Tanana has a large vowel inventory containing up to seven monophthongs and two diphthongs, in addition to phonemic nasality, length, and tone (tone is described in chap. 7). Not all dialects make all distinctions. The monophthongs of Upper Tanana are shown in table 6.1. All vowels may occur long or short (with the exception of /ʌ/, which is always short), and most of them may be oral or nasal. There are also two diphthongs /i͡a/ and /i͡o/ and their nasal counterparts /i͡ą/ and /i͡ǫ/.

	Front	Center		Back
Close	i /i/			u /u/
Mid	e /e/	ü /ɘ/	ä /ʌ/	o /o/
Open		a /a/		

Table 6.1. The short oral monophthongs of Upper Tanana

The historical developments leading to this unusually large vowel inventory are described in chap. 8; the dialectology is described in chap. 3.

6.1. Oral vowels

In the following sections, the seven oral monophthongs and the two oral diphthongs are described.

6.1.1. /i/ and /iː/

The high front vowels /i/ and /iː/ are similar to their IPA values in pronunciation.

/i/ is a short unrounded close front vowel, orthographically represented as <i>. It may occur in prefixes (66a, b) as well as in stems (66c–f). In closed syllables, /i/ is often pronounced [ɪ].

(66) /i/

a.	‘I arrived’	ni̱ni̱hshyah	/nìnihʃʲah/	[nìnihʃʲah], [nìnɪhʃʲah]
b.	‘I’m drinking it’	i̱shnąą	/iʃnãː/	[iʃnãː], [ɪʃnãː]
c.	‘berry’	ji̱gn	/t͡ʃik/	[t͡ʃigŋ], [t͡ʃɪgŋ]
d.	‘she said to him’	yehni̱h	/jehnih/	[jehnih], [jehnɪh]
e.	‘he is breathing’	etshyiyh	/etʃʲij̊/	[etʃʲij̊], [etʃʲɪj̊]
f.	‘butterfly’ (T)	laali̱l	/laːlil/	[laːlil], [laːlɪl]

/iː/ is a long unrounded close front vowel. In addition to being longer than /i/, it is also more tense. Orthographically it is represented as <ii>. It also may occur in prefixes (67a, b) and stems (67c, d).

(67) /iː/

a.	‘I arrived back’	ni̱i̱nishshyah	/nìːniʃʃʲah/	[nìːniʃʃʲah], [nìːnɪʃʃʲah]
b.	‘he wants o’	O ini̱i̱thänh	/ìnìːθʌn̥/	[ìnìːθʌn̥]
c.	‘there’	ishyi̱i̱t	/iʃʲiːtʰ/	[iʃʲiːtʰ]
d.	‘day’	dzi̱i̱n	/t͡siːn/	[t͡siːn]
e.	‘bridge, weir’	tsi̱i̱ł	/t͡sʰiːɬ/	[t͡sʰiːɬ]
f.	‘I was scared’	nagnji̱i̱t	/nakt͡ʃiːtʰ/	[naŋt͡ʃiːtʰ]

6.1.2. /e/ and /eː/

/e/ is a short unrounded mid front vowel, usually closer to IPA [ɛ] than to [e]. /e/ occurs frequently in prefixes (68a, b) but also in a few glottal-closed stems (68c, d). In the Northway dialect /e/ also occurs in a few stems closed by velar consonants (68f); these stems have /a/ in the Tetlin dialect. Orthographically /e/ is represented by <e>.

(68) /e/

a.	‘she’s paddling around’	nate̱tkeek	/natʰetkʰeːkʰ/	[natʰɛtkʰeːkʰ]
b.	‘he’s crying’ (T)	e̱tsaa	/et͡sʰaː/	[ɛt͡sʰaː]
c.	‘ahead of me’	shtthe̱h	/ʃt͡θʰeh/	[ʃt͡θʰɛh]
d.	‘man’	dine̱h	/tineh/	[tinɛh]
e.	‘let her sleep’	uute̱’	/uːtʰèʔ/	[uːtʰɛ̀ʔ]
f.	‘squirrel’ (N)	dle̱gn	/t͡ɬek/	[t͡ɬɛgŋ]

/eː/ is longer, tenser, and closer than /e/. In prefixes it is restricted to the vocalic allomorph of the *dh-* conjugation marker (69a). In stems the pronunciation of /eː/ varies between [ɛː] and [eː] (69b–e). Orthographically /eː/ is represented by <ee>.

(69) /e:/

a.	'she started to go'	teeshyah	/tʰè:ʃʲah/	[tʰè:ʃʲah], [tʰɛ̀:ʃʲah]
b.	'coat'	eek	/ʔe:kʰ/	[ʔe:kʰ], [ʔɛ:kʰ]
c.	'he buys it'	yuukeet	/ju:kʰè:tʰ/	[ju:kʰè:tʰ], [ju:kʰɛ̀:tʰ]
d.	'she's paddling around'	natetkeek	/natʰetkʰe:kʰ/	[natʰɛtkʰe:kʰ]
e.	'ADVZR'	t'eey	/t'e:j/	[t'ɛ:j], [t'e:j]

6.1.3. /a/ and /a:/

/a/ is a short unrounded open central vowel. It occurs in several prefixes (70a, b) as well as in stems (70c, d). It also occurs in the Tetlin dialect where the Northway dialect has /ʌ/ or /e/ resulting from Proto-Dene *ə (see 6.1.7). (70e) is the Tetlin variant of (78b), (70f) that of (68f). /a/ is orthographically represented as <a>.

(70) /a/

a.	'she's paddling around'	natetkeek	/natʰetkʰe:kʰ/	[natʰɛtkʰe:kʰ]
b.	'I am scared'	nagnjit	/nakt͡ʃitʰ/	[nagŋt͡ʃitʰ]
c.	'rabbit'	gah	/kah/	[kah]
d.	'she's asking me'	shuudehkat	/ʃu:tehkʰatʰ/	[ʃu:tehkʰatʰ]
e.	'she's running' (T)	altthal	/alt̪͡θʰaɬ/	[alt̪͡θʰaɬ]
f.	'squirrel' (T)	dlagn	/t͡ɬak/	[t͡ɬag]

/a:/ is a long unrounded open central vowel. It occurs in several prefixes (71a, b) as well as in stems (71c–f).

(71) /a:/

a.	'she will go'	taahaał	/tʰa:ha:ɬ/	[tʰa:ha:ɬ]
b.	'bucket'	naa'ay	/na:ʔaj/	[na:ʔaj]
c.	'wolf'	tthiikaan	/t̪͡θʰi:kʰa:n/	[t̪͡θʰi:kʰa:n]
d.	'snowshoe'	aayh	/ʔa:j̊/	[ʔa:j̊]
e.	'he is nodding yes'	tthi'et-'aak	/t̪͡θʰìʔètʔa:kʰ/	[t̪͡θʰìʔètʔa:kʰ]
f.	'three'	taagn	/tʰa:k/	[tʰa:gŋ]

6.1.4. /o/ and /o:/

/o/ is an open-mid rounded back vowel [ɔ]. It occurs both in prefixes (72a, b) and stems (72c–e), but is restricted to consonant-closed syllables.

(72) /o/

a.	'I should run out'	ti'ogtthiit	/tʰiʔokt̪θʰiːtʰ/	[tʰiʔɔgŋt̪θʰiːtʰ]
b.	'it is smelly' (N)	miholtsänh	/miholt͡sʰʌn̥/	[mihɔlt͡sʰʌn̥]
c.	'there is nothing'	ch'ikol	/t͡ʃʼikʰól/	[t͡ʃʼikʰɔ́l]
d.	'outside'	nah'ogn	/nah'ʔók/	[nah'ʔɔ́g], [nah'ʔɔ́gŋ]
e.	'myknee'	shgot	/ʃkòt/	[ʃkɔ̀t]

/oː/ is a long close-mid rounded back vowel. It occurs in prefixes (73a, b) as well as in stems (73c–e).

(73) /oː/

a.	'I walked around'	łoonihshyah	/ɬoːnihʃʲah/	[ɬoːnihʃʲah]
b.	'he looks back'	noonel'įh	/noːnelʔĩh/	[noːnelʔĩh]
c.	'she's fishing (with hook)'	nach'ehłoo	/nàt͡ʃ'ehɬoː/	[nàt͡ʃ'ehɬoː]
d.	'who'	doo	/toː/	[toː]
e.	'spruce' (T)	ts'oo	/t͡s'òː/	[t͡s'òː]

Both /o/ and /oː/ are relatively rare.

6.1.5. /u/ and /uː/

/u/ is a short rounded close back vowel [u]. It occurs in prefixes (74a–c) as well as in stems (74d–f). In closed prefix syllables (74a, b) it is often pronounced [ʊ]; this leads Milanowski (2011) and Joe, John, and Milanowski (2013) to write this vowel as <ü> in closed prefix syllables rather than the <u> used by other authors. In stem syllables its pronunciation is closer to [u].

(74) /u/

a.	'I see you PL'	nuhnak-'įh	/nuhnakʰʔĩh/	[nʊhnakʰʔĩh], [nuhnakʰʔĩh]
b.	'I will see them'	hutnak-'įįł	/hutnakʰʔĩ̀ːɬ/	[hʊtnakʰʔĩ̀ːɬ], [hutnakʰʔĩ̀ːɬ]
c.	'her mother'	unąą	/unãː/	[unãː]
d.	'(major) river'	tth'itu'	/t̪θ'itʰùʔ/	[t̪θ'itʰùʔ]
e.	'fork' (N)	ch'igugn	/t͡ʃ'ikuk/	[t͡ʃ'ikugŋ]
f.	'it is short'	nįįk'ul	/nĩːk'úl/	[nĩːk'úl]

/uː/ is a long rounded close back vowel. It also occurs in both prefixes (75a, b) and stems (75c–e).

(75) /u:/

a.	'he asks her'	uudehkat	/u:tehkʰat/	[u:tehkʰat]
b.	'we got lost'	nee'ihuushyaak	/ne:ʔihù:ʃʲa:kʰ/	[ne:ʔihù:ʃʲa:kʰ]
c.	'fish'	łuugn	/ɬu:k/	[ɬu:gŋ]
d.	'rope'	tl'uuł	/t͡ɬ'u:ɬ/	[t͡ɬ'u:ɬ]
e.	'he's dragging it'	aałuu	/a:ɬu:/	[a:ɬu:]

/u/ and /u:/ also are not very frequent vowels.

6.1.6. /ə/ and /ə:/

/ə/ and /ə:/ are both restricted to stem syllables. These two vowels are the result of historical stem vowel modifications; see also chap. 8. There is considerable disagreement in the literature about the articulation of these vowels; see Tuttle, Lovick, and Núñez-Ortiz (2011) for an overview as well as for an instrumental study. I follow their analysis here.

/ə/ is a short mid central unrounded vowel, although some Northway speakers back it to [ɤ] (see chap. 3 for more discussion). Orthographically it is represented as <ü> (76).

(76) /ə/

a.	'dipnet'	üh	/ʔə̀h/	[ʔə̀h], [ʔɤ̀h]
b.	'over it'	utüh	/utʰəh/	[utʰəh], [utʰɤh]
c.	'snow'	shyüh	/ʃʲə̀h/	[ʃʲə̀h], [ʃʲɤ̀h]
d.	'it is cold' (N)	neek'üt	/nè:k'ətʰ/	[nè:k'ətʰ], [nè:k'ɤtʰ]
e.	'fish weir' (N)	k'üdn	/k'ət/	[k'ədn], [k'ɤdn]

/ə:/ is a long mid central unrounded vowel. Again, some Northway speakers back it to [ɤ:] (77).

(77) /ə:/

a.	'my older brother' (N)	shoonüü	/ʃo:nə:/	[ʃo:nə:], [ʃo:nɤ:]
b.	'it will snow'	tahshyüü	/tʰahʃʲə̀:/	[tʰahʃʲə̀:], [tʰahʃʲɤ̀:]
c.	'she was cutting it'	yı̨ı̨t'üüt	/jı̃t'ə:tʰ/	[jı̃t'ə:tʰ], [jı̃t'ɤ:tʰ]
d.	'great horned owl'	ch'udzüüdn	t͡ʃ'ut͡sə:t/	[t͡ʃ'ut͡sə:dn], [t͡ʃ'ut͡sɤ:dn]
e.	'cottonwood'	t'üüh	/t'ə̀:h/	[t'ə̀:h], [t'ɤ̀:h]

6.1.7. /ʌ/

The back unrounded vowel /ʌ/ is restricted to stem syllables. It is always short. It is a reflex of Proto-Dene *ə; see also chap. 8.

/ʌ/ is a dialect diagnostic; in the Tetlin dialect /ʌ/ has merged with /a/ (see Minoura [1994], Tuttle, Lovick, and Núñez-Ortiz [2011]; see also chap. 3).

Tuttle, Lovick, and Núñez-Ortiz (2011) observe that the realization of /ʌ/ is somewhat variable in the Northway dialect. Some speakers pronounce it as an open-mid unrounded back vowel [ʌ], others use a close-mid vowel [ɤ] instead, and most speakers vary quite a bit. Orthographically it is represented as <ä>. (78) contrasts Tetlin and Northway pronunciations of the same words and also shows the different pronunciations attested in the Northway dialect.

(78) /ʌ/

a.	'she's running' (T)	alttha̲ł	/alt̪͜θʰaɬ/	[alt̪͜θʰaɬ]
b.	'she's running' (N)	altthä̲ł	/alt̪͜θʰaɬ/	[alt̪͜θʰʌɬ], [alt̪͜θʰɤɬ]
c.	'firewood' (T)	tsa̲t	/t͡sʰatʰ/	[t͡sʰatʰ]
d.	'firewood' (N)	tsä̲t	/t͡sʰʌtʰ/	[t͡sʰʌtʰ], [t͡sʰɤtʰ]
e.	'muskrat' (T)	dza̲nh	/t͡san̥/	[t͡san̥]
f.	'muskrat' (N)	dzä̲nh	/t͡sʌn̥/	[t͡sʌn̥], [t͡sɤn̥]
g.	'white-winged scoter' (T)	nda̲l	/nal/	[ndal]
h.	'white winged scoter' (N)	nä̲l	/nʌ̀l/	[nʌ̀l], [nɤ̀l]

6.1.8. /ɪ͡a/

The diphthong /ɪ͡a/ exists in all dialects. Its phonetic realization ranges from [ɪ͡a] to [e͡a] or [ɛ͡a]. This diphthong is the result of vowel modification following the loss or simplification of stem-final fricatives and affricates; see chap. 8. It occurs only in stem syllables. Orthographically, /ɪ͡a/ is represented as <ia> regardless of pronunciation.

(79) /ɪ͡a/

a.	'my younger sister'	shdi̲a̲'	/ʃtì͜àʔ/	[ʃtì͜àʔ], [ʃtè͜àʔ], [ʃtɛ̀͜àʔ]
b.	'frozen overflow'	gi̲a̲t	/kɪ͡atʰ/	[kɪ͡atʰ], [ke͡atʰ], [kɛ͡atʰ]
c.	'it is blue/green'	deltli̲a̲t	/telt͡ɬì͜àtʰ/	[telt͡ɬì͜àtʰ], [telt͡ɬè͜àtʰ], [telt͡ɬɛ̀͜àtʰ]
d.	'it is long'	nni̲a̲	/nnì͜à/	[nnì͜à], [nnè͜à], [nnɛ̀͜à]
e.	'they sleep'	hehti̲a̲t	/hehtʰɪ͡atʰ/	[hehtʰe͡atʰ], [hehtʰɛ͡atʰ]

6.1.9. /ɪ͡o/

The diphthong /ɪ͡o/ (sometimes represented as /iu/, e.g., Krauss [1962] and Minoura [1994]) is the result of vowel modification following the loss or simplification of stem-final fricatives and affricates (80); see chap. 8. Orthographically it is represented variably as <io> or <iu>. The oral diphthong occurs consistently only in verb stems in the Scottie Creek and Beaver Creek dialects. In the Northway dialect the diphthong is variably realized as [i͡u] or monophthongized to [u:]. In the Tetlin dialect the monophthong /u:/ occurs instead.

(80) /i͡o/ in verb stems

a.	'he is dragging it' (S)	yaałiuh	/ja:ɬi͡o/	[ja:ɬi͡o]
b.	'he is dragging it' (B)	yaałiuh	/ja:ɬi͡o/	[ja:ɬi͡o]
c.	'he is dragging it' (N)	yaałiuh, yaałuuh	/ja:ɬi͡o/, /ja:ɬu:/	[ja:ɬi͡u], [ja:ɬu:]
d.	'he is dragging it' (T)	yaałuuh	/ja:ɬu:/	[ja:ɬu:]
e.	'it is crawling' (S)	aadiuh	/a:ti͡o/	[a:ti͡o]
f.	'it is crawling' (N)	aadiuh, aaduuh	/a:ti͡o/, /a:tu:/	[a:ti͡u], [a:tu:]
g.	'it is crawling' (T)	aaduuh	/a:tu:/	[a:tu:]

/i͡o/ does not occur in noun stems; instead its nasal counterpart /ĩ͜õ/ or the long monophthong /õ:/ is used. See 6.2.7 for discussion.

6.2. Nasal vowels

Upper Tanana phonemically distinguishes nasal from oral vowels. The inventory of nasal monophthongs (table 6.2) is slightly smaller than that of oral monophthongs (given in table 6.1). The two diphthongs also have nasal counterparts /ĩã/ and /ĩõ/.

	Front	Center	Back
Close	ĩ		
Mid		ə̃	ʌ̃ õ
Open		ã	

Table 6.2. The vowels of Upper Tanana

Nasality historically derives from nasal coda consonants, where the feature [+nasal] has spread to the vowel and the nasal consonant has subsequently been deleted. The nasal vowels resulting from the sequences *e+n and *i+n have merged into /ĩ/, and those resulting from *o+n and *u+n have merged into /õ/. Most nasal vowels exhibit a length distinction.

Orthographically, nasality is indicated by an ogonek: <į>, <ąą>, <ų̈> etc.

6.2.1. /ĩ/ and /ĩː/

/ĩ/ is a short close front unrounded nasal vowel. Its realization varies between [ĩ] and [ɪ̃]. It occurs both in prefixes (81a, b) and stems (81c, d). In prefix syllables with the coda consonant /l/, /ĩ/ is frequently denasalized to [i], especially in the Tetlin dialect (81b). This is usually reflected in the orthography.

(81) /ĩ/

a. ‘you SG sang’ jį̲h’a’ /t͡ʃĩhʔàʔ/ [t͡ʃĩhʔàʔ], [t͡ʃɪ̃hʔàʔ]
b. ‘she ran’ į̲ltthät, i̲ltthät /ĩlt̪θʰʌtʰ/ [ĩlt̪θʰʌtʰ], [ɪ̃lt̪θʰʌtʰ], [ilt̪θʰʌtʰ]
c. ‘it is curly’ delts’į̲k /telt͡s’ĩk/ [telt͡s’ĩk], [telt͡s’ɪ̃k]
d. ‘I see him’ nak-’į̲h /nakʰʔĩh/ [nakʰʔĩh], [nakʰʔɪ̃h]

/ĩː/ is the long counterpart of /ĩ/. It also occurs both in prefixes (82a, b) and stems (82b–d). Phonetically it is often very close to [ẽː], especially in prefixes.

(82) /ĩ/

a. ‘sit SG!’ dhį̲į̲dah /ðĩːtah/ [ðĩːtah], [ðẽːtah]
b. ‘she is hungry’ dį̲į̲tsį̲į̲ /tĩːt͡sʰĩː/ [tĩːt͡sʰĩː], [tẽːt͡sʰĩː]
c. ‘only’ shyį̲į̲’ /ʃʲĩ̀ːʔ/ [ʃʲĩ̀ːʔ]
d. ‘birch sap’ k’į̲į̲ł /k’ĩːɬ/ [k’ĩːɬ]

6.2.2. /ã/ and /ãː/

/ã/ is an open central unrounded nasal vowel. It occurs only in stems before /ʔ/ (83a, b) and /j/ (83c–e).

(83) /ã/

a. ‘at P’ P+dą̲’ /tã̀ʔ/ [tã̀ʔ]
b. ‘truly’ łą̲’ /ɬã̀ʔ/ [ɬã̀ʔ]
c. ‘I don’t see him’ k’a nak-’ą̲y /k’à nàkʰʔã́j/ [k’à nàkʰʔã́j]
d. ‘trail’ tą̲y /tʰãj/ [tʰãj]
e. ‘willow’ k’ą̲y’ /k’ã̀jʔ/ [k’ã̀jʔ]

/ãː/ is the long counterpart of /ã/. It occurs only in stems (84).

(84) /ãː/

a. ‘thus’ dą̲ą̲’ /tã̀ːʔ/ [tã̀ːʔ]
b. ‘raven’ taatsą̲ą̲’ /tʰaːt͡sʰã̀ːʔ/ [tʰaːt͡sʰã̀ːʔ]
c. ‘chickadee’ ts’igą̲ą̲k /t͡s’iːkãːkʰ/ [t͡s’iːkãːkʰ]

d. 'I grew up' nidhihshyąą /nìðìhʃʲãː/ [nìðìhʃʲãː]
e. 'he made it' yįįxąą /jĩːxãː/ [jĩːxãː]

6.2.3. /õ/ and /õː/

/õ/ is a close-mid back rounded nasal vowel. Phonetically it can be realized as [õ] and [ʊ̃]; orthographically it is represented as <ǫ> or <ų> depending on its actual pronunciation. It is a relatively rare vowel attested both in prefixes (85a, b) and stems (85c–e).

The distribution of [õ] and [ʊ̃] is rather complicated. In prefixes the most common context for /õ/ is the second-person singular optative portmanteau morpheme, which is realized as [ʊ̃] preceding the H- voice/valence marker (85a), but as [õ] before the L- voice/valence marker (85b). In the latter context the vowel is often denasalized to [o], especially in the Tetlin dialect. In stems the vowel is almost always pronounced [ʊ̃] (85c, d), whereas the vowel of the proclitic *sǫ'* 'don't, PROH' in (85e) is always pronounced [õ].

(85) /õ/

a. 'you SG should die' ųhte' /õhtʰèʔ/ [ʊ̃htʰèʔ]
b. 'take care SG' k'anǫlta' /k'ànõltʰàʔ/ [k'ànõltʰàʔ], [k'ànoltʰàʔ]
c. 'she kissed me' shnelts'ų' /ʃnelt͡s'õ̀ʔ/ [ʃnelt͡s'ʊ̃̀ʔ]
d. 'woodworms' (T) tsat gų' /t͡sʰatʰ kõʔ/ [t͡sʰatʰ kʊ̃ʔ]
e. 'don't, PROH' sǫ' /sõ̀ʔ/ [sõ̀ʔ]

/õː/ is the long counterpart of /õ/. Its realization varies from [õː] to [ũː]. /õː/ occurs in prefixes (86a, b) as well as in stems (86c–f) and particles (86f).

Again, the distribution of [õː] and [ũː] is complicated. When /õː/ is the realization of the second-person singular subject in the optative mode preceding a Ø- voice/valence marker, it is variably realized as [õː] or [ũː] (86a). When it is the realization of the areal subject prefix in the Ø- perfective, it is always [õː], never [ũː] (86b). In many stems it is always realized as [õː] (86b–d). In some stems, it varies freely (86e), and in a handful of stems, it is always realized as [ũː] (86f). The variant [õː] generally seems to be more common than [ũː].

(86) /õː/

a. 'you (s) should sit' ǫǫda', ųųda' /õːtaʔ/ [õːtaʔ], [ũːtaʔ]
b. 'it is good' hǫǫsǫǫ /hõːsõː/ [hõːsõː]
c. 'my grandmother' stsǫǫ /st͡sʰõː/ [st͡sʰõː]
d. 'from downriver' dǫǫ /tõː/ [tõː]

e.	‘worm, monster’	gǫǫ, gųų	/kõ:/	[kõ:], kũ:]
f.	‘it is undercooked’	eltųų	/eltʰũ:/	[eltʰũ:]

It appears that [ũ] and [õ] as well as [ũ:] and [õ:] are neither entirely separate phonemes, nor have they merged entirely.[1]

6.2.4. /ɜ̃/ and /ɜ̃:/

/ɜ̃/ is a mid central unrounded nasal vowel. It is extremely rare and only occurs in a few stems. (87) contains all known examples.

(87) /ɜ̃/

a.	‘leech, snail’	tl’ų̈h	/t͡ɬ’ɜ̃h/	[t͡ɬ’ɜ̃h]
b.	‘he will tear it in half’	łdzitaagų̈h	/ɬt͡sitʰa:kɜ̃h/	[ɬt͡sitʰa:kɜ̃h]
c.	‘it is blue’	nihtl’ų̈h	/niht͡ɬ’ɜ̃̀h/	[niht͡ɬ’ɜ̃̀h]
d.	‘he clubbed it’	yichehtl’ų̈h	/jit͡ʃʰeht͡ɬ’ɜ̃h/	[jit͡ʃʰeht͡ɬ’ɜ̃h]

/ɜ̃:/, the long counterpart of /ɜ̃/, is just as rare. (88) contains all known examples. All forms in (88) are the heavy counterparts of those in (87): (88a) additionally contains the possessive suffix -v’, (88b) the negative suffix -v́, and (88c) the nominalizing suffix -v.

(88) /ɜ̃:/

a.	‘land snail’	nän’ tl’ų̈ų̈’	/nʌnʔ t͡ɬ’ɜ̃̀:ʔ/	[nʌnʔ t͡ɬ’ɜ̃̀:ʔ]
b.	‘he won’t tear it in half’	k’a łdzitaagų̈ų̈	/k’à ɬt͡sitʰà:kɜ̃́:/	[k’à ɬt͡sitʰà:kɜ̃́:]
c.	‘it, being blue’	nihtl’ų̈ų̈	/niht͡ɬ’ɜ̃̀:/	[niht͡ɬ’ɜ̃̀:]

6.2.5. /ʌ̃/

/ʌ̃/ is an open-mid back unrounded nasal vowel. Its realization varies between [ʌ̃] and [ɤ̃]. It only occurs in a few words, most of which are listed in (89). In (89e, f), *ts’ą̈’/ts’ą’* is an adverbializer; there are several other words (not listed in [89]) containing this adverbializer.

In the Tetlin dialect /ʌ̃/ has merged with /ã/. (89) contrasts forms from the Northway and Tetlin dialects.

(89) /ʌ̃/

a.	‘and’ (N)	nts’ą̈’	/nt͡s’ʌ̃̀ʔ/	[nt͡s’ʌ̃̀ʔ], [nt͡s’ɤ̃̀ʔ]
b.	‘and’ (T)	nts’ą’	/nt͡s’ãʔ/	[nt͡s’ãʔ]
c.	‘towards P’ (N)	P+ts’ą̈’	/t͡s’ʌ̃̀ʔ/	[t͡s’ʌ̃̀ʔ], [t͡s’ɤ̃̀ʔ]
d.	‘towards P’ (T)	P+ts’ą’	/t͡s’ãʔ/	[t͡s’ãʔ]

e. ‘one-way clan’ (N) ałts’ą̈’ dineey /ʔaɬt͡s’ʌ̃̀ʔ tine:j/ [ʔaɬt͡s’ʌ̃̀ʔ tine:j], [ʔaɬt͡s’ɤ̃̀ʔ tine:j]

f. ‘one-way clan’ (T) ałts’ą’ dindeey /ʔaɬt͡s’ãʔ tine:j/ [ʔaɬt͡s’ãʔ tinde:j]

6.2.6. /ĩ͜ã/

/ĩ͜ã/ is the nasal counterpart of /i͡a/. Like /i͡a/, /ĩ͜ã/ is the product of vowel modifications following the loss or simplification of stem-final fricatives and affricates (see chap. 8). It occurs only in stems (90).

(90) /ĩ͜ã/

a. ‘wolverine’ nahtsįą /nàht͡sʰĩ̀͜ã̀/ [nàht͡sʰĩ̀͜ã̀]

b. ‘raft’ nįąh /xĩ̀͜ã̀h/ [xĩ̀͜ã̀h]

c. ‘I’m exercising’ ishk’įą /iʃk’ĩ͜ã [iʃk’ĩ͜ã]

d. ‘moccasin’ kentsįą’ /kʰent͡s’ĩ̀͜ã̀ʔ/ [kʰent͡s’ĩ̀͜ã̀ʔ]

6.2.7. /ĩ͜õ/

/ĩ͜õ/ is attested only in noun stems. It is the result of vowel changes after the loss or simplification of stem-final affricates and fricatives (see Lovick [2011] and Tuttle, Lovick, and Núñez-Ortiz [2011] for more discussion; also chap. 8). Unique among the nasal vowels, the nasality of /ĩ͜õ/ does not always originate in a syllable-final nasal consonant but may instead be due to spontaneous nasalization. /ĩ͜õ/ is phonetically [ĩ͜õ]. Orthographically it is represented by <įǫ>. In the Tetlin dialect and in the speech of some Northway speakers, /ĩ͜õ/ has undergone a (partial) merger with [õ:].

(91) /ĩ͡õ/

a. ‘fireweed’ (S) gįǫ /kĩ̀͜õ̀/ [kĩ̀͜õ̀]

b. ‘fireweed’ (N) gįǫ, gǫǫ /kĩ̀͜õ̀/ [kĩ̀͜õ̀], [kõ̀:]

c. ‘fireweed’ (T) gǫǫ /kõ:/ [kõ:]

d. ‘mountain willow’ (S) łįǫ /ɬĩ͜õ/ [ɬĩ͜õ]

e. ‘mountain willow’ (N) łįǫ, łǫǫ /ɬĩ͜õ/ [ɬĩ͜õ], [ɬõ:]

f. ‘mountain willow’ (T) łįǫ /ɬõ:/ [ɬõ:]

g. ‘rosehip’ (S) nchįǫ /nt͡ʃʰĩ͜õ/ [nt͡ʃʰĩ͜õ]

h. ‘rosehip’ (N) nihchǫǫ /niht͡ʃʰõ:/ [niht͡ʃʰõ:]

i. ‘rosehip’ (T) nchǫǫ /nt͡ʃʰõ:/ [nt͡ʃʰõ:]

6.3. Vowel length

As shown in the preceding sections, most monophthongs exhibit a quantity contrast. There are, however, very few (if any) minimal pairs illustrating this distinction. The near-minimal pairs in (92) are due to morphological processes such as the absorption of the iterative prefix *na-* into the preceding vowel in (92a, c) or the presence of a vocalic suffix that deletes the final consonant and then lengthens the remaining vowel in (92d, f). Note that none of the word pairs in (92) are true minimal pairs; the iterative prefix causes additional morphological changes (see chap. 34 and 27 for more information), and stem syllables containing a short vowel require a coda consonant, while stem syllables with a long vowel do not.

(92) Vowel length contrasts

a.	ninihshyah	'I went there'	niinishshyah	'I went there again'
b.	tthee	'rock'	P+ttheh	'ahead of P'
c.	danįįhaayh	'come in!'	daanįįdaayh!	'come back in!'
d.	deltthoh	'it is brown'	deltthoo	'the brown one'
e.	-tu'	'water' (possessed)	tuu	'water'
f.	etsüh	'she's crying' (N)	k'at'eey etsüü	'she's not crying' (N)

Krauss (1964, 121) reconstructs the Proto-Dene vowel system as distinguishing between full and "reduced (shortened and centralized)" vowels. Minoura (1994, 163) claims that Upper Tanana has "partially" reorganized this system into a "long/short vowel system," where contemporary long vowels correspond to Proto-Dene full vowels. Tuttle, Lovick, and Núñez-Ortiz (2011) provide instrumental evidence supporting his claim. They find that in both the Tetlin and Northway dialects long vowels are roughly twice as long as short vowels. In the Tetlin dialect only the two high vowel pairs /i/-/iː/ and /u/-/uː/ exhibit a quality distinction in addition to the length distinction. In the Northway dialect the mid vowel pairs /e/-/eː/, /ɔ/-/ɔː/, and /o/-/oː/ also exhibit a statistically significant quality distinction. In neither dialect is there a quality distinction for the pair /a/-/aː/.

Vowel length is phonemic only for the six monophthong pairs in (92) as well as for their nasal counterparts (see 6.2 for more information). /ʌ/ and /ʌ̃/ are always short; /i͡a/, /ĩ͡ã/, /i͡o/ and /ĩ͡õ/ are always long.

6.4. Summary

In this chapter, the vowel system of Upper Tanana is described. This language has an unusually large vowel system with seven (in Tetlin: six) monophthongs and one or two diphthongs. Six of the monophthongs show a phonemic quantity distinction. Nasality is also phonemic for most vowels. The Northway dialect as spoken by, for example, Mrs. Avis Sam (chosen because she uses the diphthongs /i͡o/ and /ĩ͜õ/, which many Northway speakers do not use) thus distinguishes a total of twenty-six different vowel phonemes—each of which may be tonally unmarked or low-marked.

Notes

1. This is not unusual in this language family. Rice (1989, 81-82) describes a partial merger of [ã], [õ], and [ũ] in Slave while Cook (2004, 2) notes that in Dëne Sųłiné, [o] does not always contrast clearly [u] nor [õ] with [ũ].

7 Tone

Upper Tanana is a tone language distinguishing unmarked, low-marked, and high-marked syllables. In this chapter I review the tonal distinctions (7.1–7.3), illustrate them using pitch tracks (7.4), and present the results of a preliminary instrumental study (7.5).

7.1. No tonal specification

Many syllables in Upper Tanana have no tonal specification. Syllables without tonal specification occur in all dialects.

(93) Unmarked syllables

a.	‘rabbit’	gah	/kah/	[kah]
b.	‘our grandmother’	neetsǫǫ	/neː t͡sʰõː/	[neː t͡sʰõː]
c.	‘I’m walking’	ihhaał	/ihhaːɬ/	[ihhaːɬ]
d.	‘she is scared’	neljit	/nelt͡ʃitʰ/	[nelt͡ʃitʰ]

7.2. Low tone

The Northway, Scottie Creek, and Beaver Creek dialects of Upper Tanana have lexical low tone caused by suprasegmentalization of a historical glottal segment in the syllable rhyme (this is known as “constriction” in the literature; see Krauss [2005, 66] for an overview over the language family and chap. 8 for Upper Tanana-specific comments). The Tetlin and Nabesna dialects have lost this tonal distinction (data for the Tetlin dialect comes from my own research, while information on Nabesna is reported following Minoura [1994]).

In low-marking dialects, low tone may occur in prefix syllables (94a, b) as well as in stems (94c, d). The functional load of lexical tone is very low in this language. Even though individual morphemes contrast with respect to tone as illustrated in (94), there are usually other distinguishing features between tonally marked and unmarked syllables. All data in (94) comes from the Northway dialect.

(94) Lexical low tone

	low-marked			*unmarked*		
a.	'CONT'-	na-	/nà/-	'IT'-	na-	/na/-
b.	'NEG.PFV:1SG.S:ø'	ih-	/ìh/-	'AA.PFV:1SG.S:ø-	ih-	/ih/-
c.	'PL go IPV'	deeł	/tèːɬ/	'PL go PFV	deeł	/teːɬ/
d.	'land'	nän'	/nʌ̀nʔ/	'you SG'	nän	/nʌn/

Only the morphemes in (94d) are free. They are distinguished not only by tone but also by the presence of a stem-final glottal stop in the low-toned form, and the absence of the glottal stop in the unmarked form. The morphemes in (94a–94c) are all bound morphemes that occur in distinct contexts.

(95) contrasts the low-toned continuative prefix with the unmarked iterative prefix. These prefixes occur in different positions in the verb word: the continuative prefix is an adverbial-derivational prefix of position 10; the iterative prefix occurs in position 9 (see chap. 34 and 35). Additionally, the prefixes differ in the effect they have on the voice/valence marker immediately preceding the verb stem as shown in the derived verb forms in (95). The continuative has no influence on the voice/valence marker, which retains its form Ø- (95a). The iterative, however, changes the voice/valence marker to D- (95b) (see chap. 27).

(95) a. *na'ihsäł* /nàʔihsʌɬ/ (N)
na-ih-säł
CONT-ø.IPV:1SG.S:ø-holler:IPV
'I kept hollering' UTOLAF09Aug1202:032

b. *nanishshyah* /naniʃʃʲah/ (N)
na-nish-shyah
IT-N.PFV:1SG.S:D-SG.go:PFV
'I came back' UTOLAF13May2804:002

(96a) illustrates the tonal effects of the negative perfective prefix /ì/-, which forms a portmanteau /ìh/- with the first-person singular subject prefix preceding a Ø- voice/valence marker (see chap. 28 and 29). This portmanteau differs from the *aa*- perfective first person singular subject before Ø- voice/valence marker *ih*- in (96b) only in its tonal specification, yet negative polarity is also indicated in the verb stem and in the negative particle *k'à*.

(96) a. *k'à ìhtsíá* (N)
k'à ìh-tsíá
NEG NEG.PFV:1SG.S:Ø-cry:PFV:NEG
'I hadn't cried' UT Notebook #3, 86

b. *ihtsia'* (N)
ih-tsia'
AA.PFV:1SG.S:Ø-cry:PFV
'I cried' UT Notebook #3, 70

Finding true tonal minimal pairs is surprisingly difficult. (97) might be such a minimal pair, but while the low tone in (97a) is clearly detectable, (97b) was produced with high-rising intonation on the final syllable (an intonation pattern common in polar questions), which obscures the (unmarked) stem tone.

(97) a. *danahdeeł* /tanahtè:ɬ/ (N)
da-nah-deeł
inside-N.IPV:2PL.S:Ø-PL.go:IPV
'come (PL) in! UT Notebook #6, 15

b. *danahdeeł* /tanahte:ɬ/ (N)
da-nah-deeł
inside-N.PFV:2PL.S:Ø-PL.go:PFV
'you (PL) came inside' UT Notebook #6, 15

In his description of Tanacross, Gary Holton (2000, 73) argues that the lack of tonal minimal pairs in that language does not entail that tone has a low functional load, since "the tonal melody resulting from the sequences of tones in a word or phrase is crucial to effective communication" and is thus "fundamental to understanding Tanacross, just as it is with other tonal Athabaskan languages." In Upper Tanana this does not seem to be the case. Mutual intelligibility between the low-marking Northway dialect and the nonmarking Tetlin dialect is not affected. At the same time tone is very salient to Northway speakers, who often correct me for incorrect or unclear realization of low tone.

7.2.1. Contour tone

Unlike closely related Tanacross Upper Tanana is reported to not have contour tones resulting from suffixation processes. Holton (2000, 79) shows that in

Tanacross contour tones result when the tonal specification of stem and suffix differ. Tanacross has high tones where Upper Tanana has low tones, thus the addition of the possessive suffix -v́ʔ in that language results in a rising tone on the possessed noun stems (98a) (form cited after Arnold, Thoman, and Holton [2009, 190]). Minoura (1994, 178) reports instead for Upper Tanana that the low-toned possessive suffix -v̀ʔ causes an unmarked stem syllable to become low-toned (98b).[1]

(98) Lack of contour tones resulting from suffixation

			Unsuffixed		*Suffixed*	
a.	Tanacross	'packsack'	xeeɬ	/xe:ɬ/	-xěel'	/xě:lʔ/
b.	Upper Tanana	'packsack'	xeeɬ	/xe:ɬ/	-xeel'	/xè:lʔ/

I wish to add a caveat to this section: I am not entirely certain that Minoura's claim about the lack of contour tone in Upper Tanana is correct. Phonetic contour tones certainly do occur when an unmarked stem takes a low-marked suffix (99a, b) or a low-marked stem contains an unmarked suffix (99c, d).[2] But while these contours exist, their phonemic status is uncertain.

(99) Contour tones in Upper Tanana?

		Tanacross		*Upper Tanana*		
a.	'packsack POSS'	-xěel'	/xě:lʔ/	-xeel'	/xè:lʔ/	[xê:lʔ]
b.	'eye'	-dǎagh'	/tǎ:ɣʔ/	-naagn'	/nà:kʔ/	[nâ:gŋʔ]
c.	'lynx'	níidûuy	/ní:tû:j/	niiduuy	/ nì:tù:j/	[nì:tǔ:j]
d.	'berry'	jêg	/t͡ʃêk/	jign	/t͡ʃik/	[t͡ʃǐgŋ]

In the materials produced by the Yukon Native Language Centre, the existence of rising tone (marked orthographically by <ǎ>) and some additional unspecified tone marked by <ā> is implied, but while John Ritter (personal communication) indicated in 2007 that he was conducting a thorough study of tonal contrasts in Upper Tanana, neither the data nor the study results have been published or made otherwise available. Such a study is required before the existence of contour tones can be confirmed or disconfirmed for Upper Tanana.

7.3. High tone

Upper Tanana also has a high tone, which may or may not be phonemic but is certainly very salient. Minoura (1994, 179) claims that this "super-high" tone only exists in the speech of the late Mrs. Bessie John from Beaver Creek, but I have observed it in the speech of all speakers of the Northway and Tetlin dialects. It is restricted to only a few contexts.

High tone is part of the negative suffix -v́. (100a–c) contrasts unmarked affirmative verb stems with high-marked negative ones; (100d, e) contrasts low-marked affirmative verb stems with high-marked negative ones.

(100) High tone in negative verb stems

		Affirmative		*Negative*	
a.	‘SG go PFV’ (N, T)	shyah	/ʃʲah/	shyay	/ʃʲáj/
b.	‘see IPV’ (N, T)	’į̄h	/ʔĩh/	’ą̄y	/ʔã́j/
c.	‘PL go IPV’ (T)	deeł	/te:ɬ/	deel	/té:l/
d.	‘PL go IPV’ (N)	deeł	/tè:ɬ/	deel	/té:l/
e.	‘punch PFV’ (N)	got	/kòtʰ/	godn	/kót/

High tone is also a characteristic of most directional forms (101); see chap. 17.3.

(101) High tone in directionals

a.	‘upriver ALL’	ne’	/néʔ/
b.	‘upriver AR’	nuugn	/nú:k/
c.	‘waterwards ALL’	tthän’	/t͜θʰʌ́nʔ/
d.	‘waterwards PNCT’	tthiit	/t͜θʰí:tʰ/
e.	‘vertically down ALL’	shyign’	/ʃʲíkʔ/
f.	‘vertically down ABL’	shyǫǫ	/ʃʲṍ:/

A handful of other stems also bears high tone. (102a–c) are all lexicalized negative stems without affirmative counterparts. *Guuy* ‘tiny’ in (102d) may be related to the modifier *gaay* ‘small’ (which does not always have the high tone), but it is unclear which derivational process is responsible for this. *Shyįį’* ‘only’ in (102e) is realized with a low tone in the Northway dialect, but with a high tone in Tetlin.

(102) High tone in other stems

a.	‘be small IPV’	tsuul	/t͡sʰú:l/
b.	‘be short IPV’	k’ul	/k’úl/
c.	‘NEGEX’	kol	/kʰól/
d.	‘tiny’	guuy	/kú:j/
e.	‘only’ (T)	shyįį’	/ʃʲĩ́:ʔ/

The phonemic status of high tone in Upper Tanana has yet to be determined; its salience is demonstrated in the following sections.

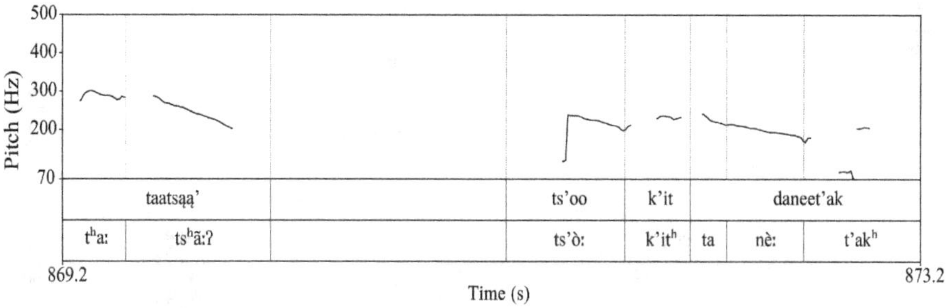

Figure 7.1. Contrast between unmarked and low-marked syllables, Mrs. Demit-Barnes (N)

7.4. Illustration of tonal contrasts

The difference between unmarked and low-marked syllables is illustrated in figure 7.1, a pitch track of (103). While the pitch gently declines over the utterance, the low-marked syllables are noticeably lower in pitch than the unmarked ones.

(103) *Taatsąą' ts'oo k'it daneet'ak.*
/tʰa:t͡sà̃ʔ t͡s'ò: k'it tanè:t'akʰ/
raven spruce on 3SG:SG.fly.up:PFV
'The raven flew onto the spruce.' UTCBAF13Nov0905:080

The contrast between unmarked and high-marked syllables is illustrated using a sentence pair. The first panel of figure 7.2 contains the pitch track of the affirmative sentence in (104a), which contains only unmarked syllables. The second panel of figure 7.2 contains the pitch track of the negative sentence in (104b), which contains not only two low-toned syllables but crucially a high-toned verb stem.[3]

(104) a. *Tthikaan ineljit.*
/t̪θʰikʰa:n inelt͡ʃitʰ/
wolf 3SG:be.scared.of:IPV
'It [e.g., rabbit] is scared of the wolf.' UTCBAF13Nov0805:032

b. *K'at'eey tthikaan ineljidn.*
/k'àt'e:j t̪θʰikʰa:n inìlt͡ʃít/
NEG wolf 3SG:be.scared.of:IPV:NEG
'It [e.g., rabbit] is not scared of the wolf.'
UTCBAF13Nov0805:035

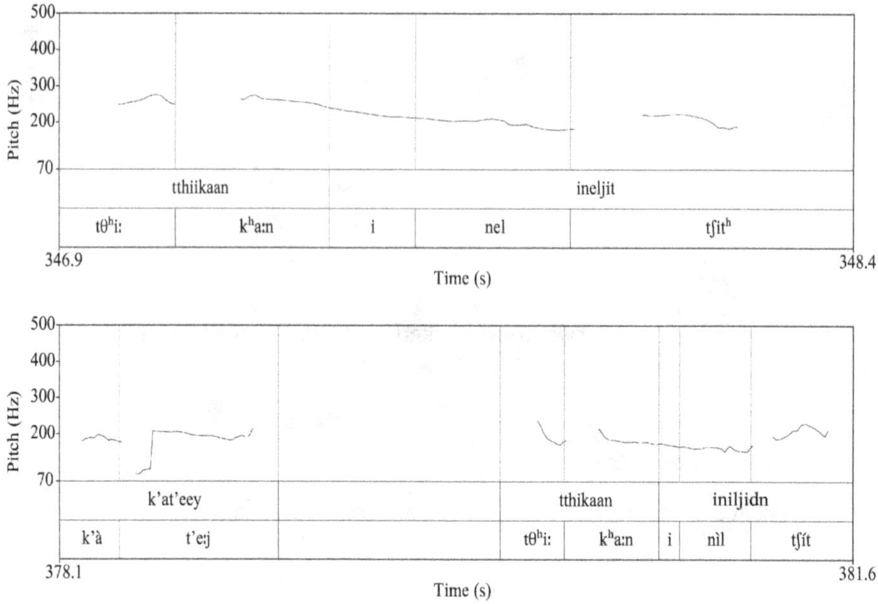

Figure 7.2. Contrast between unmarked and high-marked verb stem, Mrs. Demit-Barnes (N)

7.5. The phonetic realization of tones: an instrumental study

There is to date no detailed instrumental study of the acoustic realization of tonal distinctions in Upper Tanana. Investigating Upper Tanana dialectology, Minoura (1994, 178) claims that the realization of low tone resulting from Proto-Dene constriction is "unclear" and that "younger speakers are starting to lose tones." He further claims that the Tetlin dialect has lost low tone and only retains vestigial tones. Lovick and Tuttle (2011), investigating conversational prosody, agree with Minoura regarding the loss of low tone in Tetlin but do not comment on the realization of low tone in Northway.

Minoura (1994, 179) also comments on the realization of what he calls "super-high" tone. He claims that this is a feature of the Beaver Creek dialect, and that it can be detected in the speech of no speaker other than the late Mrs. Bessie John. He also cites the late Mr. Jack John Justin (Upper dialect), who thought that super-high tone was typical for women's speech, but Minoura notes that this does not conform to his own impressions. Lovick and Tuttle (2011, 133n2) comment however that they observe high tones in the speech of several speakers of the Northway and Tetlin dialects. I have observed high tones in the speech of male as well as female speakers.

In this section an exploratory study of tonal distinctions in the speech of two female speakers from Northway and one female speaker from Tetlin is presented, demonstrating the following three points: (1) low tone is marked consistently in the Northway dialect; (2) the Tetlin dialect does not distinguish low tone; (3) high tone is realized clearly and consistently in both dialects.

7.5.1. Data and methods

The data comes from two female speakers of the Northway dialect, Mrs. Sherry Demit-Barnes and the late Mrs. Darlene Northway, as well as from one female speaker of the Tetlin dialect, the late Mrs. Cora H. David.

Data for Mrs. Demit-Barnes comes from an elicitation session of affirmative and negative verb forms. The list, which attempts to balance affirmative unmarked and low-marked verb stems, was compiled by Dr. Siri Tuttle. It was elicited, recorded, and roughly transcribed into ELAN by Caleb Brucks (Brucks and Tuttle 2014). The transcripts were edited and exported into Praat textgrids by myself. In Praat, the textgrids were edited further: each modal vowel was segmented and coded for word and vowel ID, word category, syllable type, and tonal specification. Word category had the following options: affirmative verb form, negative verb form, noun, postposition, adverb, particle. Syllable type had the following options: verb stem, stem (for all other lexical categories), pre-stem, prefix. Tonal specification had the following options: unmarked, low, and high. F0 was measured using the script **getDurationPitchFormants.praat**, available from https://depts.washington.edu/phonlab/resources/. Statistics on the resulting dataset were calculated using R. A breakdown of the number of syllables in each tonal category is given in table 7.1.

Tone	Affirmative Unm.	Affirmative Low	Negative High	Total
Tokens	389	196	69	655

Table 7.1. Syllable count, Mrs. Demit-Barnes

No comparable elicited dataset is available for Mrs. Northway. Instead I used a narrative text (UTOLAF12Jul1203). The text was chosen because it contains an unusually high number of negative verb forms and contains nonsentive material. The text was transcribed by Caleb Brucks and myself. The edited transcript was exported as a Praat textgrid; from here on the process was identical to that outlined above. A breakdown of the number of syllables in each tonal category is given in table 7.2. Beyond choosing a text with a relatively high number of high-toned syllables due to the number of negative verb forms, I made no attempt to control for tonal distinctions; the distribution of unmarked and low-marked syllables in table 7.2 is thus likely to be representative of Upper Tanana discourse in general.

	Affirmative		Negative	
Tone	Unm.	Low	High	Total
Tokens	281	102	26	409

Table 7.2. Syllable count, Mrs. Northway

The dataset for Mrs. David consists of text UTOLAF12Jul0602 (elicited with help of a storyboard) plus part of a traditional narrative (UTOLAF09Jun2202). Again, these pieces were chosen because they contain a relatively high number of negative verb forms. Both texts were transcribed by myself. The remainder of the process was identical to that outlined above; in coding for low tone (which is not detectable in Mrs. David's speech), I relied on comparison to the Northway dialect. The breakdown of the number of syllables in each category is given in table 7.3.

	Affirmative		Negative	
Tone	Unm.	Low	High	Total
Tokens	363	133	39	535

Table 7.3. Syllable count, Mrs. David

7.5.2. Results: Northway

A graphic representation of the results for Mrs. Demit-Barnes is given in figure 7.3. The box-and-whiskers plot shows that the realization of the three tones differs as expected.

The one-way ANOVA in table 7.4 confirms that the difference in mean between the three categories is significant. Low-marked syllables are on average about 20 Hz lower than unmarked ones; high-marked syllables are on average 14 Hz higher than unmarked ones.

The small difference between unmarked and high-marked syllables is due to some degree to intonational effects. Lovick and Tuttle (2011) observe that

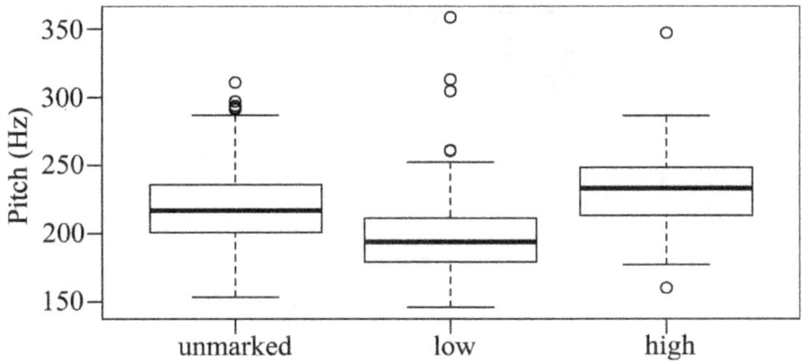

Figure 7.3. Tonal distinctions, Mrs. Demit-Barnes

	Number	Mean (Hz)	PR>|t|
Unm.	389	219	
Low	196	198	2e-16 ***
High	69	233	7.59e-05 ***

Table 7.4. Tonal distinctions, all syllables, Mrs. Demit-Barnes

pitch falls over the course of an utterance. As Upper Tanana is prefixing and verb-final, verb stems tend to occur in utterance-final position. Almost all high-marked syllables are verb stems and thus utterance-final, while most unmarked syllables occur in nonfinal position. To control for this intonational effect, table 7.5 compares only verb stems in utterance-final position. It shows a slightly greater difference in mean between unmarked and high-marked syllables (on average 18 Hz instead of 14 Hz), but also demonstrates that the distinction between unmarked and low-marked syllables is maintained and possibly even exaggerated in final position (40 Hz instead of 20 Hz).

	Number	Mean (Hz)	PR>|t|
Unm.	48	212	
Low	18	172	1.75e-06 ***
High	62	230	0.00137 **

Table 7.5. Tonal distinctions, verb stems only, Mrs. Demit-Barnes

The results for Mrs. Northway are similar, as visualized in figure 7.4. Mrs. Northway speaks generally at a slightly lower pitch and has a much more

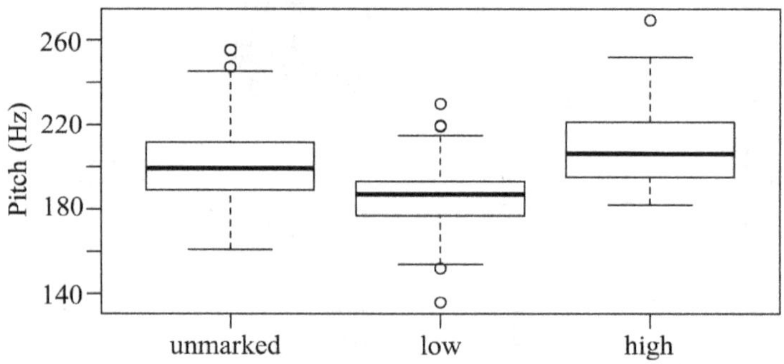

Figure 7.4. Tonal distinctions, Mrs. Northway

narrow pitch range than Mrs. Demit-Barnes. The difference in mean between unmarked and low-marked syllables is about 15 Hz, that between unmarked and high-marked syllables only about 10 Hz. Note however that the one-way ANOVA in table 7.6 finds these differences to be significant.

	Number	Mean (Hz.)	PR>|t|
Unm.	281	201	
Low	102	186	< 2e-16 ***
High	26	211	9.61e-14 ***

Table 7.6. Tonal distinctions, all syllables, Mrs. Northway

When considering only utterance-final verb stem syllables, the distinction between unmarked and high-marked syllables becomes slightly more pronounced (18 Hz instead of 10 Hz), while that between unmarked and low-marked ones all but disappears (table 7.7). This is possibly due to a sampling problem, specifically the small number of low-toned verb stems.

	Number	Mean (Hz.)	PR>|t|
Unm.	38	192	
Low	7	191	0.986443
High	22	210	0.000109 ***

Table 7.7. Tonal distinctions, verb stems only, Mrs. Northway

Thus we find that in the Northway dialect, both low-marked and high-marked syllables are distinguished clearly and consistently from unmarked syllables.

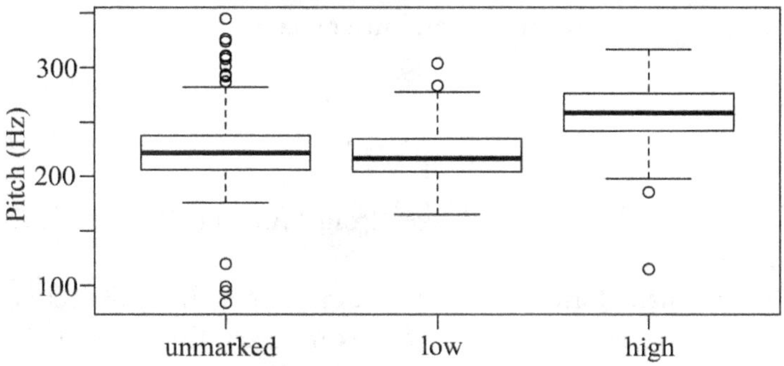

Figure 7.5. Tonal distinctions, Mrs. David

7.5.3. Results: Tetlin

In the speech of Mrs. David from Tetlin, there is no difference between unmarked and low-marked syllables (figure 7.5). While the mean F0 of low-marked syllables is very slightly lower than that of unmarked syllables (about 3 Hz), the pitch ranges overlap almost entirely. High-marked syllables are about 30 Hz higher than unmarked ones. The one-way ANOVA in table 7.8 shows that the mean difference between unmarked and low-marked syllables is not significant, while that between unmarked and high-marked syllables is significant.

	Number	Mean (Hz.)	PR>|t|
Unm.	363	224	
Low	133	221	0.277
High	39	255	1.52e-10 ***

Table 7.8. Tonal distinctions, all syllables, Mrs. David

This shows clearly that in the speech of Mrs. David, low tone is not distinguished, while high tone is realized clearly and consistently.

7.6. Summary

The three tone distinctions—unmarked, low, and high—of Upper Tanana are reviewed briefly and illustrated using pitch tracks. It is noted that the phonemic status of the high tone is unclear, as is that of compound tones. Results from a preliminary instrumental study of tonal distinctions in the Northway and Tetlin dialects are presented briefly.

The interaction between tone and utterance prosody is discussed in volume 2.

Notes

1. While the examples have been taken from Minoura (1994, 178), they have been re-transcribed.
2. All Upper Tanana forms in (99) are from the Northway dialect and come from my own research; Tanacross forms are taken from Arnold, Thoman, and Holton (2009).
3. The pre-stem syllables in the two verb forms in figure 7.2 differ in their tonal specifications, but this difference is not clearly visible in this image.

8 A historical perspective on the sound system

In this chapter the historical developments leading from the sound system of Proto-Dene to that of Upper Tanana are described.

Throughout this chapter reconstructed forms from Proto-Dene (most of them from Leer [1996a] unless otherwise indicated) are compared to synchronic Upper Tanana forms from my own research as well as from Kari (1997b). The vowel symbols in the Proto-Dene column of the tables in this chapter have roughly IPA values, with V' indicating a full (rather than long) vowel. The consonant symbols used to represent Proto-Dene, however, do not have IPA values. Affricates and oral stops represented with voiceless symbols are voiceless aspirated; those represented with voiced symbols are voiceless unaspirated. The haček indicates postalveolar affricates and fricatives; these exist in plain and in retroflex following Leer (1996a, 1996c). Proto-Dene is reconstructed as having a distinction between palatal and uvular (or front and back velar) oral stops and affricates; the palatal series is marked by velar symbols followed by superscript ʸ, the uvular stops by *q, *ɢ, *q', and the uvular fricatives by a dot underneath or above the symbol: *x̣, *ẏ. *y indicates a palatal approximant, *ŋʸ a palatal nasal, and $*ŋ^{y}_{2}$ a different palatal nasal with different reflexes in some of the daughter languages (although not in Upper Tanana).

The term "series" refers to a set of sounds with the same place of articulation, including usually three oral stops or affricates (aspirated, unaspirated, and ejective) and two fricatives (voiceless and voiced).

Consonant developments are described in section 8.1. As onset and coda consonants have developed differently, they are discussed in separate subsections. Vowel developments are described in section 8.2.

8.1. Consonant developments

Table 8.1 summarizes the consonant changes from Proto-Dene to Upper Tanana.

In the Upper Tanana column labeled "Coda," "+ Mod." indicates that the consonant development was accompanied by vowel modifications; when "+ Mod." is in parentheses, the vowel modification took place only under certain conditions.

Place	Proto-Dene	Upper Tanana	
		Onset	Coda
alveolar	*t, *d, *t'	/tʰ, t, t'/	/tʰ/
	*ts, *dz, *ts'	/t͜θʰ, t͜θ, t͜θ'/	/tʰ/ + Mod.
	*s, *z	/θ/	/h/ + Mod.
lateral	*tɬ, *dl, *tl',	/t͡ɬʰ, t͡ɬ, t͡ɬ'/,	/ɬ/
	*ɬ, *l	/ɬ/	/ɬ/
postalveolar	*tš, *dž, *tš'	/t͡sʰ, t͡s, t͡s'/	/tʰ/ + Mod.
	*tšʳ, *džʳ, *tšʳ'	/t͡sʰ, t͡s, t͡s'/	/tʰ/ + Mod.
	*š, *ž	/s/	/h/ + Mod.
	*šʳ, *žʳ	/s/	/h/ + Mod.
palatal	*kʸ, *gʸ, *k'ʸ	/t͡ʃʰ, t͡ʃ, t͡ʃ'/	/kʰ/
	*xʸ, *ɣʸ	/ʃ *or* ʃʲ/	/j̊, h/
uvular	*q, *ɢ, *q'	/kʰ, k, k'/	/kʰ/
	*x̣, *ɣ̇	/x/	/h/ (+ Mod.)
glottal	*ʔ	/ʔ/	/ʔ/
sonorants	*w, *y, *n, *ŋʸ, *ŋʸ₂	/m, j *or* ʃʲ, n, n, n/	/–, j̊, n, n, n/

Table 8.1. Consonant development summary

8.1.1. Changes in onset position

As table 8.1 demonstrates, consonant developments in the onset of syllables are relatively regular.

8.1.1.1. Obstruents We can identify two groups of obstruents based on their historical development. Some have come unchanged from Proto-Dene, while others have participated in a "pull-chain" consonant shift dubbed the "Great Northern Series Shift" by Leer (1996c, 197).

8.1.1.1.1. No change The alveolar oral stop series *t, *d, *t’, the lateral series *tl, *dl, *tl’, and the glottal stop have not been affected by any changes. Examples are given in table 8.2; the Proto-Dene reconstructions are taken from Leer (1996a).

Change	English	Proto-Dene	Upper Tanana	
*t > t^{h}	‘water’	*tu	/t^{h}uː/	tuu
	‘father’	*taʔ	/t^{h}àʔ/	ta’
*d > t	‘horns’	*deʔ	/tèʔ/	de’
	‘crane’	*de·ɬ	/teːɬ/	deeł
*t’ > t’	‘leaf’	*t’a·nʔ	/t’ã̀ːʔ/	t’ąą’
	‘cottonwood’	*t’əɣ̇əs	/t’ɔ̀ːh/	t’üüh
*tɬ > t͡ɬ^{h}	‘rub with grease’	*tɬɑɣ̇	/t͡ɬ^{h}oh/	tloh
	‘classify mushy o’	*tɬe·q’^{w}	/t͡ɬ^{h}èk^{h}/	tleek
*dl > t͡ɬ	‘laugh’	*dlʊ’q’	/t͡ɬòh/	dloh
*D+l	‘be freezing cold’	*D-li·^{w}	/t͡ɬih/	dlih
*tl’ > t͡ɬ’	‘rope’	*tl’u·ɬ	/t͡ɬ’uːɬ/	tl’uuł
	‘rear’	*tl’aʔ	/t͡ɬ’àʔ/	tl’a’
*ɬ > ɬ	‘dog’	*ɬəŋ^{y}	/ɬĩː/	łįį
	‘smoke’	*ɬəd	/ɬʌt^{h}/	łät
*l > ɬ	‘urinate’	*lədž^{r}	/ɬɔh/	łüh
	‘flow’	*ləŋ^{y}	/ɬãj̊/	łąyh
*ʔ > ʔ	‘eat’	*ʔa’·tɬ’	/ʔàːɬ/	’aał
	‘eddy, whirlpool’	*ʔʊ’q’	/ʔòk/	’ok

Table 8.2. Development of *t, *d, *t’, *tl, *dl, *tl’, *ʔ in onsets

8.1.1.1.2. The Great Northern Series Shift The Great Northern Series Shift—systematic fronting of all consonants belonging to the Proto-Dene *ts, *tš, *tš^{w}, *k^{y}, *q series—affects a large number of Northern Dene languages (Leer [1996c, 198] comments that Dena’ina is the only Northern Dene language that has not undergone this shift). Leer (1996c, 197) identifies several stages to this shift: (1) a merger of the two postalveolar *tš and *tš^{w} series into a retroflex *ts^{r} series, (2) fronting of the alveolar *ts series to an interdental series and of the retroflex series to an alveolar series, and finally (3) fronting of the palatal and uvular series to postalveolar and velar series, respectively.[1] These changes are illustrated in table 8.3; reconstructions are again taken from Leer (1996a). Leer (1996a) does not separate *š/ž from *šʳ/žʳ, so I also do not do this. The subsections on *q, *q' are missing from Leer (1996a), so I used the scan of the file slips from Leer (1996b).

Change	English	Proto-Dene	Upper Tanana	
*ts > /t͜θʰ/	'chop'	*tse·tłʔ	/t͜θʰè:ɬ/	ttheeł
	'stone'	*tse·	/t͜θʰe:/	tthee
*dz > /t͜θ/	'mountain'	*dzəł-x	/t͜θʌɬ/	ddhäł
*ts' > /t͜θ'/	'sinew'	*ts'e'·x̣	/t͜θ'è:/	tth'ee
	'hear'	*ts'əɢ	/t͜θ'akʰ/	tth'ak (T)
*s > /θ/	'sand'	*sa·xʸ	/θa:j̊/	thaayh
	'porch, box'	*se·ł	/θe:ɬ/	theeł
*z > /θ/	'think'	*zən	/θʌn̥/	thänh
	'around neck'	*ze·nə	/θi:n/	thiin
*dž > /t͡s/	'caribou'	*wə-džəxʸ	/ut͡sih/	udzih
	'ear'	*džəɣ̇eʔ	/t͡sàkʔ/	dzagn'
*džʳ > /t͡s /	'lower leg'	*džʳ·ad	/t͡sa:tʰ/	dzaat
	'hawk owl'	*tsį·-džʳa·džʳ-v	/t͜θʰìʔt͡sɔ:t/	tthi'dzüüdn
*tš > /t͡sʰ/	'beaver'	*tšaʔ	/t͡sʰàʔ/	tsa'
	'make SG.O'	*tši·	/t͡sʰĩ:/	tsįį
*tšʳ > /t͡sʰ/	'excrement'	*tšʳa·nʔ	/t͡sʰà:nʔ/	tsaan'
	'cry'	*tšʳəɣ̇	/t͡sʰah/	tsah (T)
*tš' > /t͡s'/	'from'	*tš'ən	/t͡s'ʌn̥/	ts'änh
	'spruce'	*tš'e'wə	/t͡s'ò:/	ts'oo
*tš'ʳ > /t͡s'/	'bad'-	*tš'ʳa·	/t͡s'a/-	ts'a-
	'woman'	*tš'ʳe'-qe·	/t͡s'èxeh/	ts'exeh
*š > /s/	'spittle, saliva'	*se·qʔ	/sè:k/	seegn
	'knife'	*še·y-i·	/se:j/	seey
*ž > /s/	'be dark, black'	*žəŋʸ	/sãj̊/	sąyh
	'be good'	*žu·	/sõ:/	sǫǫ
*kʸ > /t͡ʃʰ/	'rain'	*kʸa·n	/t͡ʃʰã:/	chąą
	'stump, base'	*kʸəneʔ	/t͡ʃʰìnʔ/	chin'
*gʸ > /t͡ʃ/	'fear, be afraid'	*gʸəd	/t͡ʃitʰ/	jit
	'berries'	*gʸə'ʸe·	/t͡ʃik/	jign
*k'ʸ > /t͡ʃ'/	'tear, rip'	*k'ʸəl	/t͡ʃ'iɬ/	ch'ił

Change	English	Proto-Dene	Upper Tanana	
	‘veins’	*k’ʸu·ts’(eʔ)	/t͡ʃ’ǫ̀ː/	ch’ǫǫ
*xʸ > /ʃ, ʃʲ/	‘scar’	*xʸə’t’	/ʃitʰ/	shit
	‘black bear’	*xʸɑš	/ʃoh/	shoh
	‘make magic’	*xʸən	/ʃʲin̥/	shyinh
	‘breath’	*xʸi·tš’ʳ	/ʃʲi̯à/	shyia
*q > /kʰ, h/	‘classify OOC’	*qa·	/kʰãː/	kąą
	‘cough’	*qʊs	/kʰoh/	koh
	‘AR’	*qʊ-	/hu/-	hu-
*ɢ > /k/	‘arm’	*ɢa·neʔ	/kàːnʔ/	gaan’
	‘stab, punch’	*ɢʷe’·d	/kòtʰ/	got
*q’ > /k’/	‘arrow’	*q’aʔ	/k’àʔ/	k’a’
	‘on top of’	*q’ə(d)	/k’itʰ/	k’it
*x̣ > /x/	‘pus’	*x̣əz	/xɘh/	xüh
	‘sled’	*x̣ɑdł	/xaɬ/	xał
*ɣ̇ > /x/	‘tooth POSS’	*ɣ̇ɪɪʔ	/xùʔ/	xu’
	‘make PL.O’	*ɣ̇a·n	/xãː/	xąą

Table 8.3. Great Northern Series Shift

Table 8.3 not only demonstrates that the *ts, *tš, *tšʳ, *kʸ, and *q series have all shifted one position to the front, but also illustrates several mergers. In Upper Tanana the *tš series and the *tšʳ series have merged into a /t͡sʰ/ series. The absence of phonemic voiced fricatives in Upper Tanana has resulted in the merger of several voiced/voiceless fricative pairs, e.g., *s, *z to /θ/, *š, *šʳ, *ž, *žʳ to /s/, and *x̣, *ɣ̇ to /x/. The only exception to this fricative merger are the two front velar fricatives. The voiceless fricative *xʸ has developed variably into /ʃ/ and /ʃʲ/. Its voiced counterpart *ɣʸ had already merged with the sonorant *y in Proto-Dene.[2] The change of *q to /h/ seems to affect only prefixes; in stems, *q always developed into /kʰ/.

8.1.1.2. Sonorants Table 8.4 demonstrates the developments of sonorants in onset position. *n, *ŋʸ, and *ŋʸ$_2$ all developed into /n/;[3] *w developed into /m/. *y (which, as stated above, had already merged with the voiced fricative *ɣʸ) developed into /j/ in a handful of morphemes and into /ʃʲ/ in all others. The data in table 8.4 (all from Kari [1997b]) suggests that /j/ as an onset consonant in stems was retained only before /aː/ and turned to /ʃʲ/ in all other environments. The only other morpheme with /j/ as onset consonant is the consonantal allomorph of the object and possessor prefix *i-/y-* '3SG>3SG'-.

Change	English	Proto-Dene	Upper Tanana	
*y > /j, ʃʲ/	'3SG>3SG'	*yə-	/j/-	y-/i-
	'sky'	*ya·	/ja:/	yaa
	'woman's daughter'	*ya·- tš̌'eʔ	/ja:ts'èʔ/	yaats'e'
	'lice'	*yaʔ	/ʃʲàʔ/	shya'
	'grow up PFV'	*ya·ŋ^{y}	/ʃʲã:/	shyąą
	'chase'	*yů·d	/ʃʲù:t^{h}/	shyuut
	'snow (on ground)'	*yəx̣s	/ʃʲəh/	shyüh
*n > /n/	'work'	*na·	/na:/	naa
	'eye'	*na·ɣ̇-əʔ/	/nà:kʔ/	naagn'
	'face'	*ne·nʔ	/nì:nʔ/	niin'
*ŋ^{y} > /n/	'earth, land'	*ŋ^{y}ənʔ	/nʌ̀nʔ/	nän'
	'be long'	*ŋ^{y}e'·z	/ni̯à/	nia
*ŋ$^{y}_{2}$ > /n/	'across'	*ŋ$^{y}_{2}$a·nʔ	/nằ:nʔ/	naan'
	'wedge'	*ŋ$^{y}_{2}$əɬ	/nʌɬ/	näł
*w > /m/	'be round'	*wą·ts'	/mõ̀:(t^{h})/	mǫǫ(t)
	'SG swim IPV'	*we·	/me:j̊/	mbeeyh
	'boil'	*we·dž̌^{r}	/mi͡at^{h}/	mbiat

Table 8.4. Development of *n, *ŋ^{y}, *ŋ$^{y}_{2}$, *w in onsets

8.1.2. Changes in coda position

While the development of onset consonants is relatively predictable, that of coda consonants is quite a bit more complex due to erosion processes, some of which appear to be still ongoing.

8.1.2.1. Obstruents Most stem-final obstruents have undergone dramatic changes. The glottalization of all historically ejective stops and affricates has been suprasegmentalized and now is detectable in the tonal dialects as low tone on the preceding vowel. (In the nontonal Tetlin dialect, all trace of historical glottalization has been lost.) All fricatives other than /ɬ/ and /l/ have been neutralized to /h/, and all apical affricates apart from the lateral ones have been neutralized to /t^{h}/. This neutralization was accompanied by vowel modifications described in section 8.2.

8.1.2.1.1. Stops Table 8.5 illustrates the changes undergone by stops in codas. The aspirated stops *t, *kʸ, and *q are not reconstructed in coda position, hence only unaspirated and ejective stops are included here. Ejective stops affect stem tone; unaspirated stops do not.

	English	Proto-Dene	Upper Tanana	
*d > /tʰ/	'smoke' (*n.*)	*ɬəd	/ɬʌtʰ/	łät
	'stab, punch'	*ɢʷe'·d	/kòtʰ/	got
*t' > /tʰ/	'scar'	*xʸə't'	/ʃitʰ/	shit
	'water algae'	*dla·t'	/t͡ɬàːtʰ/	dlaat
*gʸ > /kʰ/	'remember'	*ni'·gʸ	/nìːkʰ/	niik
	'coat, shirt'	*ʔe·gʸ	/ʔeːkʰ/	eek
*k'ʸ > /kʰ/	'dish, bowl'	*ts'a'·k'ʸ	/t̪͜θ'àːkʰ/	tth'aak
	'be bitter'	*tš'i·k'ʸ	/t͡ʂ'ìːkʰ/	tʂ'iik
*ɢ > /kʰ/	'be lightweight'	*dže·ɢ	/t͡ʂaːkʰ/	dzaak
	'several die off'	*la·ɢ	/ɬaːkʰ/	łaak
*q' > /kʰ, h/	'eddy, whirlpool'	*ʔʊ'q'	/ʔòkʰ/	'ok
	'classify mushy o'	*tɬe·q'ʷ	/ t͡ɬʰèːkʰ/	tleek
	'laugh'	*dlʊ'q'	/t͡ɬòh/	dloh
*ʔ > /ʔ/	'father'	*taʔ/	/tʰàʔ/	ta'
	'horns'	*deʔ	/tèʔ/	de'
	'tooth POSS'	*ɣ̊uʔ	/xùʔ/	xu'

Table 8.5. Development of *d, *t', *gʸ, *k'ʸ, *ɢ, *q', *ʔ in codas

Only three oral stops occur in codas in contemporary Upper Tanana: /tʰ, kʰ, ʔ/.[4] In this position the palatal and uvular series merged into a velar series (Leer 1996c, 198); /kʰ/ may thus have originated as a palatal or uvular stop.

8.1.2.1.2. Affricates Upper Tanana has lost all stem-final affricates. The lateral affricates *dl and *tɬ' have changed to /ɬ/. All other affricate series—*dz, *dž, *džʳ—have been simplified to /tʰ/ or /h/ or have been lost entirely: the data in table 8.6 demonstrates that this process is not entirely regular and predictable, although it seems that coda consonants are retained more consistently in the Tetlin dialect. The loss of the nonlateral affricates additionally triggers vowel modifications; see 8.2.

Again, only unaspirated and ejective affricates are reconstructed in stem-final position. The glottalization of ejective affricates has been suprasegmentalized as phonemic low tone in the tonal dialects.

Change		English	Proto-Dene	Upper Tanana	
*dl	> /ɬ/	'be hollow'	*zu·(d)l	/θu:ɬ/	thuuł
		'sled'	*x̣ɑdł	/xaɬ/	xał
*tł'	> /ɬ/	'eat, chew'	*ʔa·tł'	/ʔà:ɬ/	'aał
		'PL swim'	*ʔʷe·tł'	/ʔè:ɬ/	'eeł
*dz	> /tʰ, h, Ø/	'twist'	*dədz	/tʌtʰ/	dät
	+ Mod.	'step' (*sem.*)	*ʔədz	/ʔɔh/	'üh
		'step' (*dur.*)	*ʔe'·dz	/ʔi͜à/	'ia
*dž	> /tʰ, h, Ø/	'dry wood'	*tšʳədž	/t͡sʰʌtʰ/	tsät
	+ Mod.	'pluck'	*ŋʸ$_2$ədž	/notʰ/	not
		'cartilage'	*gʸį·dž	/t͡ʃɪ͡a/	jia
*džʳ	> /tʰ, h, Ø/	'boil'	*we·džʳ	/mɪ͡ah/	mbiah (N)
	+ Mod.			/mɪ͡atʰ/	mbiat (T)
		'urine'	*lədžʳ	/ɬɔh/	łüh
*ts'	> /tʰ, h, Ø/	'roll'	*wa'ts'	/mõ̀:/	mǫǫ (N)
	+ Mod.			/mõ:tʰ/	mǫǫt (T)
		'suck'	*ts'ųts'	/t͡s'õ̀:/	ts'ǫǫ
*tš'	> /tʰ/	'dance PFV'	*dži·tš'	/t͡si͜àʔ/	dzia' (N)
	+ Mod.			/t͡sɪ͡atʰ/	dziat (T)
		'herd moves'	*ʔa·tš'	/ʔɔ̀:tʰ/	'üüt
*tš'ʳ	> /tʰ, Ø/	'kidney'	*tš'ʳə'tš'ʳ-eʔ	/ts'ʌ̀t/	ts'ädn
		'breath'	*xʸi·tš'ʳ	/ʃi͜à/	shyia

Table 8.6. Development of *dl, *tł', *dz, *dž, *džʳ, *ts', *tš', *tš'ʳ in codas

8.1.2.1.3. Fricatives The development of coda fricatives mirrors that of coda affricates. The lateral fricatives are retained, although *l is devoiced in absolute final position. The apical fricatives *s, *z, *š, *ž, *žʳ (I have not been able to find any examples of *šʳ in coda position, although this may be an oversight of mine) all merge into /h/ or are deleted. Again, this process is not entirely regular; see 8.1.3.3. It is accompanied by vowel modifications (see 8.2).

While palatal and uvular oral stops merge in coda position (see 8.1.2.1.1), the corresponding fricatives have undergone different developments as shown in table 8.7. *xʸ has been fronted to /j̊/ and frequently is weakened to /h/, especially after /i/. *ɣʸ seems to already have merged with *y, which is discussed in section 8.1.2.2. *x̣ and *ɣ̇ have developed into /h/ or been deleted. When followed by a vocalic suffix, *ɣ̇ instead has developed into /k/.

Change	English	Proto-Dene	Upper Tanana	
*ł > /ɬ/	'crane'	*de·ł	/teːɬ/	deeł
	'snare'	*wi'·ł	/mɪ̃̀ːɬ/	mįįł
*l > /ɬ, l/	'be tepid'	*zəl	/θʌɬ/	thäł
	'tongue'	*tsu·l-eʔ	/t͡θʰùːlʔ/	tthuul'
*s > /h, Ø/ + Mod.	'belt'	*səs	/θɔ̀h/	thüh
	'whip PFV'	*tšʳαs	/t͡sʰɔh/	tsüh
	'crawl'	*du·s	/tɪ͡o/, /tuː/	dio, duu
*z > /h, Ø/ + Mod.	'string O'	*ʔe'·z	/ʔɪ͡àh/	'iah
	'be heavy'	*da'·z	/tɔ̀ː/	düü
	'be difficult'	*tšʳa'·z	/t͡ɕʰɔ̀ː/	tsüü
*š > /j̊, h, Ø/ + Mod.	'charcoal'	*t'e'·š	/t'ɪ̯à(h)/	t'ia(h)
	'mittens'	*gʸə'š	/t͡ʃij̊/	jiyh
*ž > Ø + Mod.	'be forked'	*ɢəž	/kɔː/	güü
	'thrush'	*tł'i'·ž	/t͡ɬɪ͡a/	tl'ia
*žʳ > Ø + Mod.	'bicep'	də-yi·(d)žʳeʔ	/tiʃ͡ʲɪ̯àʔ/	dishyia'
*xʸ > /j̊, h/	'bearberry'	*də-nəxʸ-x	/tinaj̊/	dinayh
	'sand'	*sa·xʸ	/θaːj̊/	thaayh
	'caribou'	*wə-džəxʸ	/ut͡sih/	udzih
*x̣ > /h, Ø/	'rabbit'	*ɢαx̣	/kah/	gah
	'nest'	*t'ʊx̣	/t'oh/	t'oh
	'sinew'	*ts'e'·x̣	/t͡θ'èː/	tth'ee
*ɣ̇ > /h, k/	'be brown'	*tsʊɣ̇	/t͡θʰoh/	tthoh
	'grass'	*tł'ʊɣ̇	/t͡ɬ'oh/	tl'oh
	'ear'	*dzəɣ̇eʔ	/t͡sàkʔ/	dzagn'
	'edge'	*wą'·ɣ̇-e	/màːk/	maagn

Table 8.7. Development of *ł, *l, *z, *s, *š, *ž, *žʳ, *xʸ, *x̣, *ɣ̇ in codas

8.1.2.2. Sonorants The development of sonorants in coda position is also rather complex as demonstrated in table 8.8. *ŋʸ$_2$ does not seem to occur in codas. In Leer (1996a) *w is usually written as a superscript or as *m in coda position. It frequently is retained as rounding of the stem vowel but in some cases is deleted without a trace.

*n has two distinct reflexes. If the stem vowel is long (historically: full), or if there is a coda consonant, *n surfaces as nasality on the vowel. If the stem vowel is short and there is no coda consonant, *n needs to remain in the coda to fulfill the phonotactic requirement of bimoraic rhymes (see chap. 10). In that context it is always devoiced to /n̥/.

The reflex of *ŋʸ is a nasal stem vowel. If a stem-final consonant is required, /j/ is inserted.

*y has two distinct reflexes. In word-final position, and rarely before vocalic suffix, the reflex is /j̊/. Before most vocalic suffixes its reflex is more commonly /j/.

	English	Proto-Dene	Upper Tanana	
*w > Ø	'be rotten'	*tɬe·q'ʷ	/t͡ɬ'òk/	tl'ok
	'SG sit'	*da·ʷ	/tah/	dah
	'fly'	*dəŋʸ(w)ʔ	/dã̀jʔ/	dąy'
	'star'	*səmʔ	/sʌ̀nʔ/, /sònʔ/	sän', son'
*n > ṽ, n̥	'kill PL.O'	*ɣ̥̇a·n	/xãː/	xąą
	'see'	*'e·n	/ʔĩh/	'įh
	'leaf'	*t'a·nʔ	/t'ã̀ːʔ/	t'ąą'
	'to'	*tš̌'ənʔ	/t͡s'ʌ̃̀ʔ/	nts'ą̈'
	'from'	*tš̌'ən	/t͡s'ʌ̀n̥/	ts'änh
	'different'	*dən	/dʌn̥/	dänh
*ŋʸ > ṽ, ṽj	'steal'	*ʔi·ŋʸ	/ʔĩː/	'įį
	'dog'	*ɬəŋʸ	/ɬĩː/	łįį
	'dry, dried'	*ɢɑŋʸ	/kãj/	gąy
*y > j̊, y	'wind blows'	*tš̌'ʳəy	/t͡s'aj̊/	ts'ayh
	'spruce roots'	*xɑy	/xaj̊/	xayh
	'knife'	*še·y-i·	/se·j̊/	seeyh
	'man's grandchild'	*tsu·y-e·	/t͜θʰuːj/	tthuuy

Table 8.8. Development of *w, *n, *ŋʸ, *y in codas

8.1.2.3. Final consonant clusters Leer (1996a) also reconstructs coda clusters, usually the result of suffixation processes. With the few exceptions described in chap. 10, Upper Tanana does not allow consonant clusters in codas. Proto-Dene coda clusters have been simplified to adhere to the phonotactic requirements of the daughter language, but the rules governing this process are not fully understood at this time.

8.1.3. Consonant developments: general tendencies

As shown in the preceding subsections Upper Tanana has lost or simplified most stem-final consonants. These changes are somewhat unpredictable, yet three general trends can be identified: (1) devoicing, (2) absorption into the stem vowel, and (3) neutralization and deletion.

8.1.3.1. Devoicing Devoicing affects only fricatives and sonorants, since all Proto-Dene oral stops and affricates are reconstructed as voiceless. Fricatives also are reconstructed as underlyingly voiceless but phonetically voiced in most positions (Krauss 1964, 124). Sonorants are reconstructed as voiced (Krauss and Leer 1981).

As shown above, Upper Tanana does not allow fricatives other than /l/, /ł/, and /h/ in syllable-final position (see also chap. 10). Of these three, voiced /l/ is permitted in coda position only in heavy syllables, i.e., when followed by an underlying vocalic suffix (see chap. 11). Crucially /l/ is *not* the reflex of *l, as *l and *ł have been neutralized to /ł/ in contemporary Upper Tanana. *š and *x^{y} developed into the voiceless sonorant /j̊/. (In some instances, /j̊/ has been weakened to /h/.) The other apical and the velar fricatives have been either deleted or neutralized to /h/; see 8.1.3.3.

8.1.3.2. Absorption into the stem vowel Many instances of syllable-final *n and all instances of syllable-final *ŋ^{y} have been absorbed as nasality into the stem vowel (see 8.2.3.1), while *w in coda position has either disappeared or has been absorbed as labialization into the stem vowel (see 8.2.3.3). The remaining instances of *n as well as all instances of *y, however, surface as voiceless sonorants /n̥/, /j̊/ in contemporary Upper Tanana and become voiced only in heavy syllables.

8.1.3.3. Neutralization and deletion Neutralization and deletion affect primarily obstruents. The extent of this process is summarized in table 8.9, which is a rearrangement of the facts as outlined in Leer (1977) and described in more detail in the previous sections. The data presented above suggests that /t^{h}/ and /j̊/ in particular are undergoing further neutralization and deletion, and in more recent recordings I have noticed that /k^{h}/ in coda position is often deleted in the speech of several speakers.

Extensive neutralization of stem-final obstruents is not unusual in the Dene language family. Leer (1996c, 193) points to a large number of languages where this has taken place, including what he calls the Headwaters languages (Gwich'in, Han, Northern Tutchone, Southern Tutchone, and marginally Upper Tanana) and the dialect continuum sometimes referred to

Proto-Dene	Upper Tanana
*dl, tł' *l, ł	/ł/
*d, t' *dz, ts' *dž, tš' *džʳ, tšʳ	/tʰ, h, Ø/
*s, z *š, ž *žʳ (, šʳ) *x̣, ɣ̇	/h, Ø/
*gʸ, k'ʸ *ɢ, q	/kʰ, Ø/
*xʸ, (y)	/j̊, h, Ø/
*ʔ	ʔ

Table 8.9. Neutralization and deletion of coda obstruents

as Slave (Rice 1989), plus Tłįchǫ). In his analysis of this process in Gwich'in, Leer (1996c, 194) suggests that in that language, the changes affecting coda consonants may have taken as little as five hundred years. Given that the modified vowels remain quite variable in Upper Tanana as discussed in chap. 6, I suspect that the changes in this language may be even more recent.

8.2. Vowel developments

The regular developments of Proto-Dene vowels are summarized in table 8.10 from Leer (1977); exceptions are discussed in the following sections. The term "modified" in table 8.10 refers to vowel changes following the simplification or loss of stem-final affricates and fricatives described in 8.1.2.1.2 and 8.1.2.1.3.

8.2.1. Full vowels

Proto-Dene is reconstructed with four full vowels: *i·, *e·, *a·, *u·.

8.2.1.1. *i· *i· has undergone different developments depending on whether it occurs in the modifying environment. In the nonmodifying environment, *i· has developed into /iː/. In the modifying environment *i· has merged with *e· into /i͡a/. Table 8.11 demonstrates that this process is very regular.

	Proto-Dene	Upper Tanana	
		Unmodified	Modified
Full	*i·	/iː/	/ɪ͡a/
	*e·	/eː/	/ɪ͡a/
	*a·	/aː/	/ɔː/
	*u·	/uː, oː/	/ɪ͡o, ɪ͡u, õː, uː/
Reduced	*ə	/ʌ, a, ɪ/	/ɔ, ʌ/
	*α	/a/	–
	*ʊ	/o, u/	/o/

Table 8.10. Vowel development (summary)

	Change	English	Proto-Dene	Upper Tanana	
non-modified	*i· > /iː/	'remember'	*ni'·gʸ	/nìːkʰ/	niik
		'snare'	*wi'·ɬ	/mı̃̀ːɬ/	mį̱į̱ł
		'steal'	*ʔi·ŋʸ	/ʔĩː/	'į̱į̱
		'make SG.O'	*tši·	/t͡sʰĩː/	tsį̱į̱
modified	*i· > /ɪ͡a/	'breath'	*xʸi·tšʳ	/ʃɪ͡a/	shyia
		'cartilage'	*gʸį·dž	/tʃɪ͡a/	jia
		'dance PFV'	*dži·tš'	/t͡si̯àʔ/	dzia' (N)
				/t͡sɪ͡atʰ/	dziat (T)
		'thrush'	*tƛ'i'·ž	/t͡ɬ'i̯à/	tl'ia
		'bicep'	*də-yi·(d)žʳeʔ	/tiʃi̯àʔ/	dishyia'

Table 8.11. Development of *i·

8.2.1.2. *e· The development of *e· is slightly more complex than that of *i·.*e· and *i· have merged in the modifying environment into /ɪ͡a/. In the nonmodifying environment *e· usually develops into /eː/, with two exceptions. Before /ʔ/, the resulting vowel is short /e/ rather than long /eː/ (this possibly was already the case in Proto-Dene, as the forms in table 8.12 suggest). Before /n/, *e· has developed into /iː/. This last change may be quite recent, since many of these words are spelled with <ee> in Upper Tanana materials developed by Reverend Milanowski or by the Yukon Native Language Centre.

8.2.1.3. *a· Table 8.13 demonstrates that in the nonmodifying environment *a· > /aː/ except before *ʔ, where *a· is shortened /a/. Again it appears that

		English	Proto-Dene	Upper Tanana	
non-modified	*e· > /e:/	'stone'	*tse·	/t̪θʰe:/	tthee
		'coat, shirt'	*ʔe·gʸ	/ʔe:kʰ/	eek
		'crane'	*de·ɬ	/te:ɬ/	deeł
		'sinew'	*ts'e'·x̣	/t̪θ'è:/	tth'ee
	*e· > /e/	'woman's daughter'	*ya·- tš'eʔ	/ja:ts'èʔ/	yaats'e'
		'horns'	*deʔ	/tèʔ/	de'
	*e· > /i:/	'around neck'	*ze·nə	/θi:n/	thiin
		'face'	*ne·nʔ	/nì:nʔ/	niin'
		'see'	*'e·n	/ʔĩh/	'įh
modified	*e· > /i͡a/	'be long'	*ŋʸe'·z	/ni̯à/	nia
		'boil'	*we·džʳ	/mi͡atʰ/	mbiat
		'move by stepping'	*ʔe'·dz	/ʔi̯à/	'ia
		'string o'	*ʔe'·z	/ʔi̯àh/	'iah

Table 8.12. Development of *e·

vowel shortening before glottal stop already occurred in Proto-Dene. In the modifying environment *a· always developed into /ɔ:/.

8.2.1.4. *u· The developments of *u· shown in table 8.14 are even more complex. In the nonmodifying environment it usually developed into /u:/ with two exceptions. Before *ʔ it is shortened to /u/, and before *x̣ it developed into /õ:/. This is an instance of spontaneous nasalization.

In the modifying environment *u· developed differently depending on the lexical category of the stem. In noun stems *u· developed into /ĩ̯õ/, /õ:/ (with /ĩ̯õ/ more common in the Scottie Creek and Beaver Creek dialects and /õ:/ more common in the Tetlin and Northway dialects; see see chap. 3 and 6 for more information; see also Lovick [2011]). Again it appears that nasality developed spontaneously. In verb stems *u· developed into /i͡o/, /u:/. The diphthong is retained consistently only in the Scottie Creek and Beaver Creek dialects and by some speakers of the Northway dialect. Other Northway speakers use the monophthong /u:/, as do all speakers of the Tetlin dialect.

		English	Proto-Dene	Upper Tanana	
non-modified	*a· > /aː/	‘water algae’	*dla·t’	/t͡ɬàːtʰ/	dlaat
		‘eat, chew’	*ʔa·tɬ’	/ʔàːɬ/	’aał
		‘sand’	*sa·xʸ	/θaːj̊/	thaayh
		‘leaf’	*t’a·nʔ	/t’ã̀ːʔ/	t’ąą’
	*a· > /a/	‘father’	*taʔ/	/tʰàʔ/	ta’
		‘rear’	*tl’aʔ	/t͡ɬ’àʔ/	tl’a’
modified		‘herd moves’	*ʔa·tš’	/ʔɘ̀ːtʰ/	’üüt
	*a· > /ɘː/	‘hawk owl’	*tsį·-džʳa·džʳ-v	/t͡θʰìʔt͡sɘːt/	tthi’dzüüdn
		‘be heavy’	*da’·z	/tɘ̀ː(h)/	düü(h)
		‘be difficult’	*tšʳa’·z	/t͡sʰɘ̀ː/	tsüü

Table 8.13. Development of *a

		English	Proto-Dene	Upper Tanana	
non-modified	*u· > /uː/	‘water’	*tu·	/tʰuː/	tuu
		‘be hollow’	*zu·(d)l	/θuːɬ/	thuuł
		‘rope’	*tl’u·ɬ	/t͡ɬ’uːɬ/	tl’uuł
	*u > /u/	‘tooth POSS’	*ɣ̇uʔ	/xùʔ/	xu’
		‘be good’	*žu·	/sõː/	sǫǫ
	*u· > /õː/	‘worm’	*ɢu·x̣	/gõː/	gǫǫ
		‘robin’	*šu·x̣	/sõː/	sǫǫ
modified	*u· > /ĩ͡õ/, /õː/	‘outer bark’	*t’u·ts’	/t’ĩ̀͜õ̀ʔ/,	t’į̨ǫ’ (B, S, N)
				/t’õ̀ː/	t’ǫǫ’ (N, T)
		‘camprobber’	*gʸu·že·	/t͡ʃĩ̀͜õ̀/,	jįǫ (B, S)
				/t͡ʃõ̀ː/	jǫǫ (N, T)
	*u· > /ĩ͡õ/, /uː/	‘crawl’	*du·s	/tĩ͡õ/	dio (B, S, N)
				/tuː/	duu (N, T)
		‘pull o’	*(h)u·z	/hĩ͡õ/	hio (B, S, N)
				/huː/	huu (N, T)

Table 8.14. Development of *u·

8.2.2. Reduced vowels

Proto-Dene is reconstructed with three reduced vowels: *ə, *ɑ, *ʊ.

8.2.2.1. *ə The development of *ə is quite complex, as it is influenced considerably by surrounding consonants. The developments are summarized in table 8.15. The development of *ə serves as a reliable dialect diagnostic between the Northway and the Tetlin dialects as discussed in chap. 3.

In the nonmodifying environment *ə has developed into /i/ whenever it follows any member of the palatal series. This change has taken place in all dialects. Preceding *y, *ŋ^y, and *x^y, *ə has developed into /a/ in all dialects. Preceding *g^y, *ə has developed into /e/[5] in the Northway dialect and into /a/ in the Tetlin dialect. Preceding *ɣ̇, *ə has developed into /ɔ/ in Northway and into /a/ in Tetlin. In all other contexts in the nonmodifying environment *ə has developed into /ʌ/, which has merged with /a/ in the Tetlin dialect. Table 8.15 gives forms from both dialects. Where only one form is given, there is no dialect difference.

In the modifying environment *ə has developed into /ʌ/ (/a/ in Tetlin) or /ɔ/. /ʌ/ usually occurs when the stem is reconstructed with a final affricate, while /ɔ/ occurs in formerly fricative-final stems. There are some exceptions; for example, the stem for 'urine' is affricate-final, yet the Upper Tanana reflex looks as if it came from a fricative-final stem.

8.2.2.2. *ɑ *ɑ has usually developed into /a/, but some stems show /o/ and (in the Northway dialect) /ʌ/ and /e/. The development of *ɑ does not appear to be influenced by the modifying environment (Leer 1977). See table 8.16.

8.2.2.3. *ʊ *ʊ always developed into /o/, regardless of whether it occurs in the nonmodifying or in the modifying environment (see table 8.17). The developments of the form for 'fish trap' are idiosyncratic.

8.2.3. Absorption of features into the vowel

While the developments described in sections 8.2.1 and 8.2.2 explain many phonemic distinctions found in contemporary Upper Tanana, additional distinctions arise from the absorption of features of surrounding consonants in Proto-Dene into the vowel. These include nasality, constriction, and labialization.

8.2.3.1. Nasality While nasality was phonemic in Proto-Dene (Leer 1996c), Upper Tanana has lost all traces thereof. Synchronous nasal vowels derive from the absorption of the historical nasal coda consonants *n, *ŋ^y into the stem vowel as demonstrated in table 8.18.

		English	Proto-Dene	Upper Tanana	
non-modified	*ə > /i/	‘berries’	*gʸə’gʸe·	/t͡ʃìk/	jign
		‘tear, rip’	*k’ʸəl	/t͡ʃ’iɬ/	ch’ił
		‘scar’	*xʸə’t’	/ʃ̂itʰ/	shit
		‘thrust o’	*yəl	/ʃiɬ/	shyił
		‘caribou’	*wə-džəxʸ	/ut͡sih/	udzih
	*ə > /a/	‘wind blows’	*tš’ʳəy	/t͡s’aj̊/	ts’ayh
		‘be dark’	*žəŋʸ	/sãj̊/	sąyh
		‘bearberry’	*də-nəxʸ-x	/tinaj̊/	dinayh
	*ə > /e/, /ʌ/	‘squirrel’	*də-lə’gʸ-əy	/t͡ɬèk/	dlegn (N)
				/t͡ɬak/	dlage (T)
		‘tell story’	*nəgʸ	/nekʰ/	nek (N)
				/nakʰ/	nak (T)
	*ə > /ɘ/, /a/	‘cry’	*tšʳəẏ̥	/t͡sʰɘh/	tsüh (N)
				/t͡sʰah/	tsah (T)
		‘older brother’	*u·nəẏ-e·	/õːnɘː/	ǫǫnüü (N)
				/õːnaː/	ǫǫnaa (T)
	*ə > /ʌ/, /a/	‘smoke’	*łəd	/ɬʌtʰ/	łät (N)
				/ɬatʰ/	łat (T)
		‘torso’	*žə’kʸ	/sʌ̀kʰ/	säk (N)
				/sakʰ/	sak (T)
		‘mountain’	*dzəł-x	/t̪͜θʌɬ/	ddhäł (N)
				/t̪͜θaɬ/	ddhał (T)
		‘to’	*tš’ənʔ	/nt͡s’ʌ̃̀ʔ/	nts’ą̈’ (N)
				/nt͡s’ãʔ/	nts’ą’ (T)
modified	*ə > /ʌ/, /a/	‘kidney’	*tš’ʳə’tš’ʳ-eʔ	/ts’ʌ̀t/	ts’ädn (N)
				/ts’at/	ts’adn (T)
		‘twist’	*dədz	/tʌtʰ/	dät (N)
				/tatʰ/	dat (T)
		‘dry wood’	*tšʳədž	/t͡sʰʌtʰ/	tsät (N)
				/t͡sʰatʰ/	tsat (T)
	*ə > /ɘ/	‘snow’	*yəx̣s	/ʃʲɘh/	shyüh
		‘dipnet’	*ʔə’s	/ʔɘ̀h/	’üh
		‘urine’	*lədžʳ	/ɬɘh/	łüh

Table 8.15. Development of *ə

	English	Proto-Dene	Upper Tanana	
*ɑ > /a/	'sled'	*x̣ɑdɬ	/xaɬ/	xaɬ
	'rabbit'	*ɢɑx̣	/kah/	gah
	'spruce roots'	*xɑy	/xaj̊/	xayh
	'dry, dried'	*ɢɑŋ^{y}	/kãj̊/	ga̧yh
*ɑ > /o/	'rub with grease'	*tɬɑɣ̇	/t͡ɬ^{h}oh/	tloh
	'black bear'	*x^{y}ɑš	/ʃoh/	shoh
ɑ > /ʌ/, /a/	'away ALL'	*ʔɑnʔ	/ʔʌnʔ/	'än' (N)
			/ʔanʔ/	'an (T)
ɑ > /e/, /a/	'one'	*ɬɑ'q'	/ɬek/	łegn (N)
			/ɬak/	łagn (T)

Table 8.16. Development of *ɑ

	English	Proto-Dene	Upper Tanana	
*ʊ > /o/	'eddy, whirlpool'	*ʔʊ'q'	/ʔòk^{h}/	'ok
	'laugh'	*dlʊ'q'	/t͡ɬòh/	dloh
	'nest'	*t'ʊx̣	/t'oh/	t'oh
	'be yellow, tan'	*tsʊɣ̇	/t̪θ^{h}oh/	tthoh
	'grass'	*tɬ'ʊɣ̇	/t͡ɬ'oh/	tl'oh
	'cough'	*qʊs	/k^{h}oh/	koh
	'cloud'	*q'ʊs	/k'oh/	k'oh
	'thorn'	*x̣ʊš	/xoh/	xoh
	'molt'	*k^{y}ʊdž	/t͡ʃ^{h}ot/	chot
	'AREAL'	*qʊ-	/hu/-	hu-
	'fishtrap'	*q'ʊdž	/k'ɘt/	k'üdn (N)
			/k'ʌt/	k'ade (T)

Table 8.17. Development of *ʊ

	English	Proto-Dene	Upper Tanana	
*n > ṽ	'kill PL.O'	*ɣ̇a·n	/xãː/	xąą
	'see'	*ʔe·n	/ʔĩh/	'įh
	'leaf'	*t'a·nʔ	/t'ã̀ːʔ/	t'ąą'
	'to'	*tš'ənʔ	/t͡s'ʌ̃̀ʔ/	nts'ą̈'
*ŋʸ > ṽ, ṽj	'steal'	*ʔi·ŋʸ	/ʔĩː/	'įį
	'dog'	*łəŋʸ	/ɬĩː/	łįį
	'dry, dried'	*ɢɑŋʸ	/kãj̊/	gąyh

Table 8.18. The origin of nasality from *n, *ŋʸ in codas

Nasality also arises spontaneously in stems where *u occurs in the modifying environment; see 8.2.1.4.

8.2.3.2. Constriction The term "constriction" refers to the presence of a feature [+glottal] in the "postvocalic segments of the Pre-PA stem" (Krauss 2005, 66). In Proto-Dene, constriction can be present as final glottal stop or glottalized consonant or as glottalization of the vowel itself. In Upper Tanana, constriction has been suprasegmentalized to low tone, although the Tetlin and Nabesna dialects have subsequently lost this distinction. This is demonstrated in table 8.19.

	English	Proto-Dene	Upper Tanana	
*Vʔ > V̀ʔ	'tooth POSS'	*ɣ̇uʔ	/xùʔ/	xu'
	'horns'	*deʔ	/tèʔ/	de'
	'leaf'	*t'a·nʔ	/t'ã̀ːʔ/	t'ąą'
	'to'	*tš'ənʔ	/t͡s'ʌ̃̀ʔ/	nts'ą̈'
*VC' > V̀C	'dish, bowl'	*ts'a'·k'ʸ	/t̪θ'àːkʰ/	tth'aak
	'eddy, whirlpool'	*ʔʊ'q'	/ʔòkʰ/	'ok
	'PL swim'	*ʔʷe·tł'	/ʔèːɬ/	'eeł
	'herd moves'	*ʔa·tš'	/ʔɔ̀ːtʰ/	'üüt
*V' > V̀	'scar'	*xʸə't'	/ʃitʰ/	shit
	'remember'	*ni'·gʸ	/nìːkʰ/	niik
	'string O'	*ʔe'·z	/ʔi̯àh/	'iah
	'sinew'	*ts'e'·x̣	/t̪θ'èː/	tth'ee

Table 8.19. The origin of low tone from constriction

8.2.3.3. Labialization Labialization is an irregular process. When *a, *e, or *ə occur before or after a labial(ized) consonant, they often are rounded to /o/ or /oː/, as shown in table 8.20. The rules governing this process are not understood at this time.

	English	Proto-Dene	Upper Tanana	
in onset	‘stab, punch’	*ɢʷe’·d	/kòtʰ/	got
	‘roll’	*wa’ts’	/mõ̀ː(tʰ)/	mǫǫ(t)
in coda	‘be rotten’	*tłe·q’ʷ	/t͡ɬʼòk/	tl’ok
	‘star’	*səmʔ	/sʌ̀nʔ/, /sònʔ/	sän’, son’

Table 8.20. Vowel rounding originating in labial consonants

8.3. Summary

In this chapter I show how the sound system of Proto-Dene developed into the sound system of Upper Tanana.

Consonants developed differently depending on their position in the syllable. Upper Tanana, like most Alaskan Dene languages, has participated in the Great Northern Series Shift for onset consonants. Coda consonants in Upper Tanana have a strong tendency to be simplified or deleted.

The development of Proto-Dene vowels was strongly influenced by the surrounding consonants. The neutralization of stem-final affricates and fricatives have resulted in modified vowels. Constriction and nasal consonants have been absorbed into the stem syllable, resulting in phonemic low tone and nasal vowels. Labialized consonants sometimes cause rounding of the stem vowel.

Notes

1. In a recent paper, Kari (2019) suggests that step (2) of this process never took place and that the contemporary interdental series in Northern Dene was already present in Proto-Dene.
2. Leer (1996a) for example cites the verb root ‘breathe’ as *yi·tšʳ, rather than *ɣʸi·tšʳ, which comparison with the noun stem *xʸi·tš’ʳ ‘breath’ could suggest.
3. In some languages these three consonants developed differently from each other; see Krauss and Leer (1981).
4. /t, k/ are limited to heavy syllables, see chap. 11.
5. Kari writes this as <i>, e.g., Kari (1997a, 1997b) and Tyone (1996).

9 Stem-initial fricative lenition

In this chapter stem-initial fricative lenition is described.

The consonant inventory shown in table 5.1 in chap. 5 showed an imbalance between voiceless and voiced fricatives. Table 9.1 repeats the relevant portion, showing that there are only two voiced fricatives. /ð/ is restricted to a few prefixes, while /l/ may occur in codas of heavy stems, in prefixes, and in a few stem onsets. In addition to the two voiced fricatives /ð/ and /l/, Upper Tanana also has morphologically conditioned lenis allophones of voiceless fricatives. Fricative lenition is limited to the stem-initial position.

	Dental	Alveolar	Lateral	Postalv.	Palatal	Velar	Glottal
fricatives							
- voice	th /θ/	s /s/	ł /ɬ/	sh /ʃ/	shy /ʃʲ/	x /x/	h /h/
+ voice	dh /ð/		l /l/				

Table 9.1. Voiceless and voiced fricatives

The morphological conditions for lenis fricatives in nouns and verbs are described in 9.1 and 9.2, respectively. Their phonetic realization is briefly described in 9.3, and their status within the phoneme system of Upper Tanana is discussed in 9.4. Throughout this chapter, lenis fricatives are transcribed as [θ̬, s̬, ɬ̬, x̬,] and, somewhat inconsistently, [ʃʲ].[1]

9.1. Fricative lenition in noun stems

9.1.1. Morphological conditions

In noun stems fricative lenition may apply whenever the stem-initial fricative is not in word-initial position, e.g., in the possessive construction described in chap. 22 or when the stem is part of a complex noun (chap. 13). (105) demonstrates the distinction in optionally possessed noun stems, where fortis fricatives occur in nonpossessed contexts and lenis fricatives occur in the possessive construction.

(105) Fricative lenition in optionally possessed nouns

	English	*Stem*		*Possessed*	
a.	'box'	theeł	[θeːɬ]	-theel'	-[θ̬èːlʔ]
b.	'belt'	thüh	[θə̀h]	-thüü'	-[θ̬ə̀ːʔ]
c.	'gaff hook'	säł	[sʌ̀ɬ]	-säl'	-[s̬ʌ̀lʔ]
d.	'knife'	seeyh	[seːj̊]	-seey'	-[s̬èːjʔ]
e.	'saliva'	seek	[seːkʰ]	-seegn'	-[s̬èːkŋʔ]
f.	'urine'	łüh	[ɬəh]	-łüü'	-[ɬ̬ə̀ːʔ]
g.	'fish hook'	łoh	[ɬòh]	-łoo'	-[ɬ̬òːʔ]
h.	'smoke'	łät	[ɬʌtʰ]	-łädn'	-[ɬʌ̀tnʔ]
i.	'pack'	xeeł	[xeːɬ]	-xeel'	-[x̬èːlʔ]
j.	'sled'	xał	[xaɬ]	-xal'	-[x̬àlʔ]
k.	'raft'	xįąh	[xĩ͜ãh]	-xįą'	-[x̬ĩ̀͜ã̀ʔ]
l.	'louse'	shya'	[ʃʲàʔ]	-shyaa'	-[ʃʲːàʔ]
m.	'house'	shyah	[ʃʲah]	-shyah	-[ʃʲàh]
n.	'snow'	shyüh	[ʃʲə̀h]	-shyüü'	-[ʃʲə̀ːʔ]

In the possessive construction, /θ, s, ɬ, x/ all become lenis [θ̬, s̬, ɬ̬, x̬]. /ʃ/ is very rare in stems (see also 5.2.1) and is not at all attested in possessable noun stems. It has merged almost entirely with /ʃʲ/, which is now used both in nonpossessed and possessed stems (105l–n).

Lenis fricatives are also attested in obligatorily possessed noun stems (106).

(106) Fricative lenition in obligatorily possessed nouns

a.	'windpipe'	-thuul'	-[θ̬ùːlʔ]
b.	'skin'	-thüh	-[θ̬ə̀h]
c.	'mouth'	-thaat	-[θ̬aːtʰ]
d.	'torso'	-sak	-[s̬akʰ]
e.	'man's wife's brother'	-łänh	-[ɬ̬ʌn̥]
f.	'hand'	-įįła'	-[ĩːɬ̬àʔ]
g.	'hair'	-xa'	-[x̬àʔ]
h.	'tooth'	-xu'	-[x̬ùʔ]
i.	'egg'	-xia'	-[x̬ì͡àʔ]
j.	'man's son'	-shye'	-[ʃʲèʔ]
k.	'breath'	-shyiah	-[ʃʲi͡a]
l.	'woman's son'	-shyüüh	-[ʃʲəːh]

Fricative lenition in compounds and prefixed nouns is illustrated in (107).

Note that /ɬ/ either remains fortis [ɬ] (107f–g) or becomes fully voiced [l] (107h, i).

(107) Fricative lenition in complex noun stems

a.	'broth, soup'	tuut̲h̲äł	[tu:θ̬ał]
b.	'snipe'	yaat̲h̲ǫǫ	[jà:θ̬ò̃:]
c.	'Nisüü (clan)'	nis̲üü	[nis̬ə:]
d.	'comb'	tthiis̲eel	[t͡θʰi:s̬e:l]
e.	'falltime'	nooł̲uut	[no:ɬu:tʰ]
f.	'hail'	ch'inł̲uut	[t͡ʃ'inɬu:tʰ]
g.	'branch'	ch'idił̲a'	[t͡ʃ'itiɬàʔ]
h.	'bladder'	ch'il̲uut̲h̲üh	[t͡ʃ'ilu:θ̬ə̀h]
i.	'burl'	ch'il̲ahx̲ia	[t͡ʃ'ilahx̬i͡a]
j.	'brain'	-tthiix̲ą̨ą'	-[t͡θʰi:x̬ã̀:ʔ]
k.	'snow goose'	t'aax̲adn	[t'a:x̬àtn]
l.	'different person'	ch'is̲h̲y̲uuy	-[t͡ʃ'iʃʲu:j]
m.	'widow'	xaas̲h̲y̲aa	[xa:ʃʲã:]

9.1.2. Fricative lenition in noun stems as an optional process

While fricative lenition is possible whenever a noun stem is not in word-initial position, it is almost entirely optional, and I suspect that it may be in the process of disappearing in Upper Tanana. Minoura (1994) treats it as if it were present in all instances (although his transcriptions are not always reliable). This, however, is not actually the case. Even conservative speakers such as the late Mrs. Cora H. David from Tetlin have the lenis fricative in most, but by no means in all, possessed forms, as shown in table 9.2. In her speech, fricatives become lenis whenever preceded by the first-person singular possessor prefix *sh-*. Following other possessive prefixes, the process applies unsystematically in her speech. Data comes from the recording UTOLAF07Feb1302. – indicates that the form was not recorded.

Similar data is shown in table 9.3 for Mrs. Rosa Brewer of Northway. Mrs. Brewer is another conservative speaker, but the data suggests that lenition is again obligatory only in forms with first-person singular possessor and optional in others. Data comes from the recording UTOLAF07Nov2907. – indicates that a particular form was not recorded on this date.

More recent, but much less inclusive,[2] recordings with other speakers show the same tendency: the lenis fricative occurs regularly after the first-person singular possessor prefix and only occasionally elsewhere.

	łįį 'dog'		*seeyh* 'knife'		*xeeł* 'pack'	
1SG	shłiign'	[ʃɬ̬iːkʔ]	sseeyy'	[ss̬eːjʔ]	shxeel'	[ʃx̬eːlʔ]
2SG	nłiign'	[nɬiːkʔ]	nseeyy'	[ns̬eːjʔ]	nxeel'	[nx̬eːlʔ]
3SG	ułiign'	[uɬiːkʔ]	useeyy'	[useːjʔ]	uxeel'	[ux̬eːlʔ]
1PL	neełiign'	[neːɬiːkʔ]	neeseeyy'	[neːs̬eːjʔ]	neexeel'	[neːxeːlʔ]
2PL	nuhłiign'	[nuhɬiːkʔ]	nuhseeyy'	–	nuhxeel'	[nuhx̬eːlʔ]
3PL	hułiign'	[huɬiːkʔ]	huseeyy'	–	huxeel'	[hux̬eːlʔ]

Table 9.2. Lenis fricatives in the speech of Mrs. David (T)

	łįį 'dog'		*seeyh* 'knife'		*thüh* 'belt'	
1SG	shłįįgn'	[ʃɬ̬ĩ̀ːŋʔ]	sseey'	[ss̬èːjʔ]	shthüh	[ʃθ̬əh]
2SG	nłįįgn'	[nɬĩ̀ːŋʔ]	nseey'	[nsèːjʔ]	nthüh	–
3SG	ułįįgn'	[uɬĩ̀ːŋʔ]	useey'	[usèːjʔ]	uthüh	[uθə̀h]
1PL	neełįįgn'	[neːɬĩ̀ːŋʔ]	neeseey'	[neːsèːjʔ]	neethüh'	[neːθə̀h]
2PL	nuhłįįgn'	[nuhɬĩ̀ːŋʔ]	nuhseey'	[nuhs̬èːjʔ]	nuhthüh	–
3PL	hułįįgn'	[huɬĩ̀ːŋʔ]	huseey'	[husèːjʔ]	huthüh	–

Table 9.3. Lenis fricatives in the speech of Mrs. Brewer (N)

9.2. Fricative lenition in verb stems

Fricative lenition also occurs in verb stems (108). Verb stems in Upper Tanana are bound morphemes and occur only in fully inflected verb forms.

(108) Fricative lenition in verb stems

a.	'SG stand IPV'	thät	[θ̬ʌt^{h}]
b.	'worry IPV'	thiit	[θ̬iːt^{h}]
c.	'be black IPV'	sąyh	[s̬ãj̊]
d.	'holler IPV'	säł	[s̬ʌɬ]
e.	'get better PFV'	sǫǫ	[s̬õː]
f.	'drag back PFV'	łuu	[ɬ̬uː]
g.	'urinate again PFV'	łia'	[ɬ̬ì͡àʔ]
h.	'pack back IPV'	xeeł	[x̬èːlʔ]

9.2.1. Morphological conditions

In his description of lenis fricatives in Tanacross, Holton (2001, 399) notes that in that language the segment immediately preceding the stem-initial consonant determines whether lenition takes place. If that segment is underlyingly voiced, then the stem-initial consonant becomes lenis. If it is underlyingly voiceless, the stem-initial consonant remains fortis. (109) illustrates this contrast; note that Holton uses a phonemic, rather than orthographic, transcription.

(109) Lenition after voiced segment in Tanacross (Holton 2001, 399)

a. náʔíhθɛt
'I am standing'

b. náʔinδɛt
'you SG are standing'

In Upper Tanana the distribution of fortis and lenis fricatives is somewhat different. Generally it appears that the process of fricative lenition is becoming less regular, similar to what I observed for nouns. Lenition is not conditioned by the pre-stem segment, but by the underlying morpheme preceding the stem, i.e., by the voice/valence marker. There are four voice/valence markers: Ø-, D-, H-, L-. Of these, D- and L- are considered to be underlyingly voiced (even though the D- voice/valence marker always has the form /t/ and is never phonetically voiced), while Ø- and H- are underlyingly voiceless. Generally D- and L- trigger lenition of the following fricative, while Ø- and H- do not. There are, however, some exceptions, as discussed below.

9.2.1.1. Fricative lenition following D- Fricative lenition is almost obligatory following the D-voice/valence marker. Table 9.4, which combines data from three speakers, illustrates this process in several paradigms.[3] Fricative lenition following a D- voice/valence marker occurs regularly when the stem-initial consonant is /θ, ɬ, s, ʃʲ/. The resulting sequences /tθ̬, tɬ̬, ts̬, tʃʲ/ differ phonetically from the affricates /t͡θ, t͡ɬ, t͡s, t͡ʃ/ as well as from their aspirated counterparts /t͡θʰ, t͡ɬʰ, t͡sʰ, t͡ʃʰ/ (see also section 9.3 for more discussion and examples). The data included in table 9.4 comes from several recordings: sta+nii#D+thiit 'be depressed IPV' comes from recording UTOLAF15May1002, na#O+D+łuu 'drag O around IPV' from UTOLAF15May0803, D+suuk 'be noisy IPV' from UTOLAF15May0703, and na#D+shye' 'recover PFV' from UTOLAF15May0803.

Given that the function of lenition seems to be enhancement of the contrast between affricates and stop-fricative sequences, it not surprising that the paradigm of na#O+D+xeeł 'pack O back' in table 9.5 does not exhibit lenition in most forms, since the verb stem begins with /x/. There is no affricate /t͡x/

	sta+nii#D+thiit 'be depressed IPV'	na#O+D+łuu 'drag O around IPV'	D+suuk 'be noisy IPV'	na#D+shye' 'recover PFV'
1SG	[stʰaniːniʃθ̬iːtʰ]	[naʔiʃɬ̬uː]	[iss̬uːkʰ]	[naʔiʃʃʲèʔ]
2SG	[stʰaniːninθ̬iːtʰ]	[naʔinɬ̬uː]	[ins̬uːkʰ]	[naʔinʃʲèʔ]
3SG	[stʰaniːnet-θ̬iːtʰ]	[naʔat-ɬ̬uː]	[et-s̬uːkʰ]	[naʔetʃʲèʔ]
1PL	[stʰaniːt͡s'inet-θ̬iːtʰ]	[nat͡s'at-ɬ̬uː]	[t͡s'et-s̬uːkʰ]	[nat͡s'etʃʲèʔ]
2PL	[stʰaniːnat-θ̬iːtʰ]	[natʰat-ɬ̬uːkʰ]	[at-s̬uːkʰ]	[naʔatʃʲèʔ]
3PL	[stʰaniːhnet-θ̬iːtʰ]	[nahtʰet-ɬ̬uːkʰ]	[het-s̬uːkʰ]	[nahetʃʲèʔ]
Dial.	T	N	N	N

Table 9.4. Lenis fricatives in verbs with D-voice/valence marker

or /t͡xʰ/ in Upper Tanana with which the sequence /tx/ could be confused. Hence, lenition is not required and frequently does not occur in this context. Data for table 9.5 comes from the recording UTOLAF14Nov2418.

Theme	na#O+D+xeeł 'pack O back IPV'
1SG	[naʔiʃx̬eːɬ]
2SG	[naʔinxeːɬ]
3SG	[najatxeːɬ]
1PL	[nat͡s'atxeːɬ]
2PL	[naʔatxeːɬ]
3PL	[nahatxeːɬ]
Dialect	T

Table 9.5. No lenition of /x/ following D-voice/valence marker

It should be noted that the realization of D+fricative sequences in Upper Tanana is somewhat unusual within the language family. Many other Dene languages exhibit the so-called D-effect, where the D- voice/valence prefix merges with stem-initial consonants (e.g., Rice [1989, 443–45] for Slave, Faltz [1998, 29–31] for Navajo, Gessner [2003, 37–45] for Dakelh, Cook [2004, 70] for Dëne Sųłiné, or Hargus [2007, 341] for Witsuwit'en). In Upper Tanana the D-voice/valence prefix never coalesces with the stem-initial consonant (see also chap. 27); instead, fricative lenition is employed to maximize the contrast between stop-fricative sequences and affricates (see 9.3.3 below).

9.2.1.2. Frequent lenition following L- In verb themes with an L- voice/valence marker fricative lenition occurs frequently, but fortes are also allowed in this environment (table 9.6). Data comes from several recordings: P+ta#uu+d+L+si' 'read P IPV' comes from recording UTOLAF15May0802, na#L+süü 'go hunting IPV' (Tetlin dialect) from UTOLAF15May1001, na#L+süü 'go hunting IPV' (Northway dialect) from UTOLAF15May1102, and d+L+xoh 'play IPV' from UTOLAF14May0803.

	P+ta#uu+d+L+si' 'read P IPV'	na#L+süü 'go hunting IPV'	na#L+süü 'go hunting IPV'	d+L+xoh 'play IPV'
1SG	[tʃ'itʰaʔuːtagŋsìʔ]	[naʔagŋsəː]	[naʔagŋsəː]	[taŋx̬oh]
2SG	[tʃ'itʰaʔuːtĩls̬ìʔ]	[naʔils̬əː]	[naʔĩls̬əː]	[tĩlx̬oh]
3SG	[tʃ'itʰaʔuːtels̬ìʔ]	[naʔelsəː]	[naʔels̬əː]	[telxoh]
1PL	[tʃ'itʰaʔuːt͡sels̬ìʔ]	[nat͡s'els̬əː]	[nat͡s'elsəː]	[t͡selx̬oh]
2PL	[tʃ'itʰaʔuːtals̬ìʔ]	[naʔalsəː]	[naʔals̬əː]	[talx̬oh]
3PL	[tʃ'itʰaʔuhtels̬ìʔ]	[nahelsəː]	[nahels̬əː]	[hihtelx̬oh]
Dial.	N	T	N	N

Table 9.6. Fortis and lenis fricatives in verbs with a L-voice/valence marker

9.2.1.3. Optional fricative lenition following Ø- Table 9.7 demonstrates that while most fricatives are fortis following the Ø- voice/valence marker, lenis fricatives are possible (albeit rather rare) in this environment. Data in table 9.7 again comes from several speakers and recordings: O+Ø+łuu 'drag O IPV' from recording UTOLAF15May0803, Ø+sǫǫ 'be good IPV' from UTOLAF15May0802, O+Ø+thoh 'tan O IPV' from UTOLAF15May1002, and Ø+seek 'spit IPV' from UTOLAF15May0803. Note that in the paradigm of Ø+seek 'spit IPV', lenition is present in all forms, not just in those where the pre-stem segment is voiced. In the paradigm of O+Ø+thoh 'tan O', the stem-initial consonant is fortis when preceded by a voiceless segment; when it follows a voiced segment, it is sometimes lenis and sometimes fortis.

9.2.1.4. No fricative lenition following H- In verb forms that contain an H- voice/valence marker, stem-initial fricatives are always fortis, as shown in table 9.8. The data again comes from several speakers and recordings: O+H+xįį 'kill SG.O PFV' comes from recording UTOLAF15May0802, ch'+H+xał 'drum IPV' from UTOLAF15May1002, O+H+seeł 'carve O IPV' from UTOLAF15May0803, and P+i+na+nii#ch'+H+thät 'SG think about P IPV' from UTOLAF14Nov2005.[4]

	O+Ø+łuu 'drag O IPV'	Ø+sǫǫ 'be good IPV'	O+Ø+thoh 'tan O IPV'	Ø+seek 'spit IPV'
1SG	[ihɬu:]	[ihsõ:]	[ihθoh]	[ihs̬e:kʰ]
2SG	[ĩ:ɬu:]	[ĩ:sõ:]	[ĩ:θ̬oh]	[ĩ:s̬e:kʰ]
3SG	[a:ɬu:]	[nsõ:]	[eθoh]	[es̬e:kʰ]
1PL	[t͡s'a:ɬu:]	[t͡s'ĩ:sõ:]	[t͡s'eθ̬oh]	[t͡s'es̬e:kʰ]
2PL	[ahɬu:]	[ahsõ:]	[ahθoh]	[ahs̬e:kʰ]
3PL	[ha:ɬu:]	[hĩ:sõ:]	[heθoh]	[hes̬e:kʰ]
Dial.	N	N	T	N

Table 9.7. Fortis or lenis fricatives in verbs with a Ø-voice/valence marker

	O+H+xįį 'kill SG.O PFV'	ch'+H+xał 'drum IPV'	O+H+seeł 'carve O IPV'	P+i+na+nii#ch'+H+thät 'SG think about P IPV'
1SG	[ðakʰxĩ:]	[tʃ'akʰxaɬ]	[akʰse:ɬ]	[minani:tʃ'akʰθʌtʰ]
2SG	[ðĩhxĩ:]	[tʃ'ĩhxaɬ]	[ĩhse:ɬ]	[minani:tʃ'ĩhθʌtʰ]
3SG	[ðehxĩ:]	[tʃ'ehxaɬ]	[ehse:ɬ]	[jinani:tʃ'ehθʌtʰ]
1PL	[t͡s'iðehxĩ:]	[nt͡s'ehxaɬ]	[t͡s'ehse:ɬ]	–
2PL	[ðahxĩ:]	[tʃ'ahxaɬ]	[ahse:ɬ]	–
3PL	[hiðehxĩ:]	[tʃ'ihehxaɬ]	[hehse:ɬ]	–
Dial.	N	T	N	T

Table 9.8. Fortis fricatives in verbs with H-voice/valence marker

9.3. Illustration of fricative lenition

The phonetic realization of lenis fricatives is somewhat variable.[5] Leer (1982), describing what he calls semi-voiced fricatives in Tanacross, says that they "begin . . . voiceless and become . . . lenis and voiced immediately preceding the vowel." In an instrumental study of the same language Holton (2001) demonstrates that while some fricatives are partially voiced, lenition usually manifests itself as reduced duration and intensity. Similar observations can be made for Upper Tanana. While a full instrumental study such as that by Holton (2001) is beyond the scope of this grammar, I illustrate the different realizations of lenis fricatives using individual tokens.

9.3.1. Partial voicing

Some lenis fricatives are partially voiced, although they always retain a voiceless portion as well. The stem initial fricative [θ̬] in *taniinishthiit* 'I am depressed' in figure 9.1 contains a relatively long voiced portion highlighted by an arrow. During the voiced portion, the formants of the following vowel are visible, yet the fricative noise in the high frequencies persists. The sound file was produced by Mrs. Demit-Barnes (Northway) as part of the recording UTOLAF15May0802.

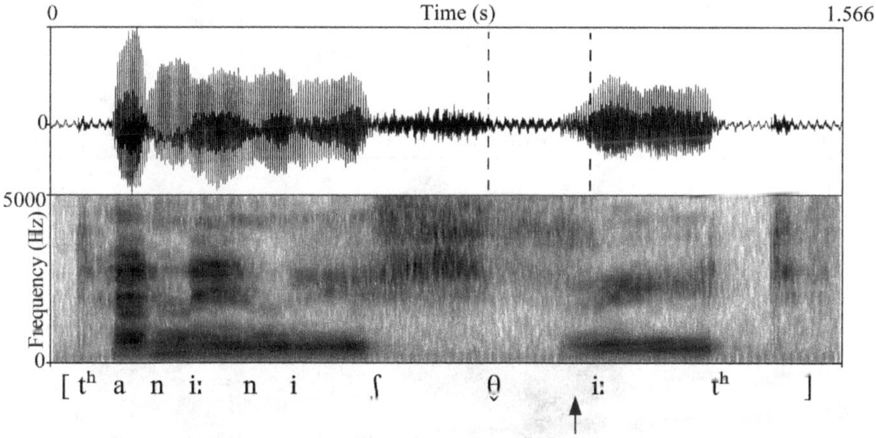

Figure 9.1. Partially voiced stem initial fricative [θ̬] in *taniinishthiit* 'I am depressed'

Figure 9.1 is one of the clearest examples of voicing in lenis fricatives that I have been able to find. Most lenis fricatives show no trace of voicing; instead lenition is realized as reduced amplitude and duration.

9.3.2. Reduced intensity and duration

In the absence of voicing, lenis fricatives are typically quieter as well as shorter than their fortis counterparts. The difference is demonstrated in figure 9.2, which contrasts a fortis fricative in the top panel with a lenis fricative in the bottom panel. The fortis fricative [s] in *sǫǫ* 'robin' is a little over 0.2s in duration, while the corresponding lenis fricative [s̬] in *at-suuk* 'it is noisy' is only about 0.13s. Since I do not use head-mounted microphones in this (or any other) recording, I am loath to comment on the relative intensity of the two fricatives, but the fortis fricative does appear to be louder than the lenis one. The sound file was produced by Mrs. Avis Sam (Northway) as part of recording UTOLAF15May0703.wav.

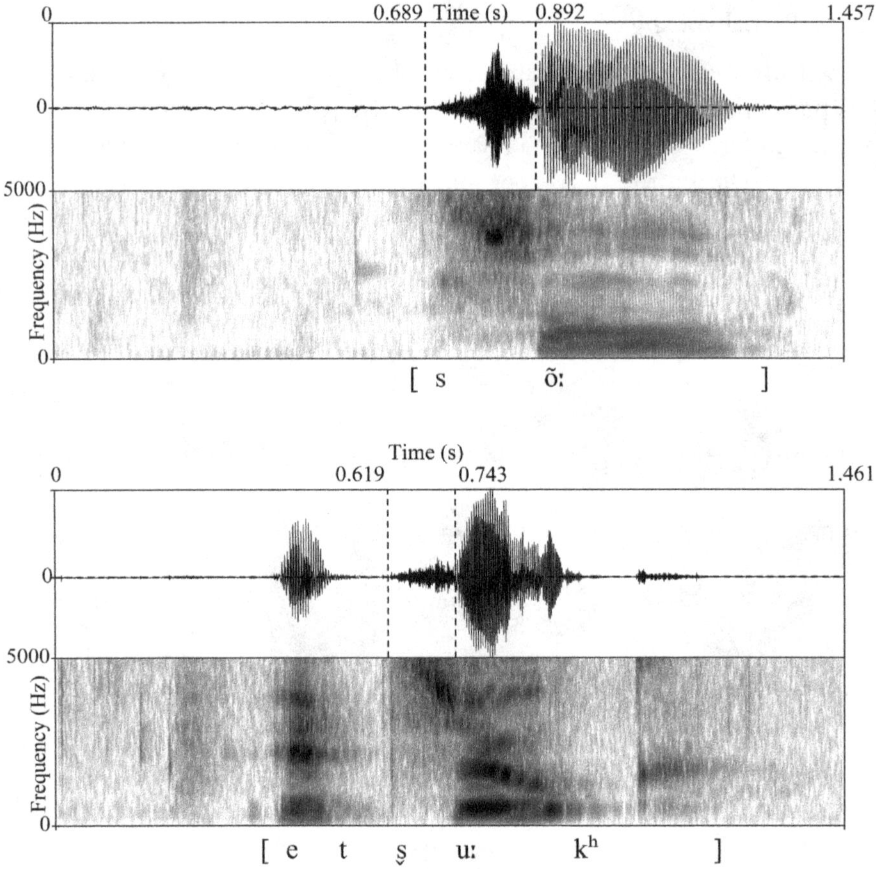

Figure 9.2. Fortis stem-initial fricative [s] in *sǫǫ* 'robin' and lenis fricative [s̬] in *et-suuk* 's/he is noisy'

The same thing is illustrated in figure 9.3, which shows the waveform and spectrogram of *xeeł na'ishxeeł* 'I am carrying the pack back'. Here the fricative in the noun stem is fortis [x], while that of the verb stem is lenis [x̬]. The lenis fricative is both quieter and shorter than the fortis fricative. The sound file was produced by Mrs. Ida Joe (Tetlin) as part of recording UTO-LAF14Nov2418.wav.

This realization of lenis fricatives is significantly more common than the partial voicing demonstrated in 9.3.1. It is likely that the subtlety of this difference is at least partly responsible for the fact that lenis fricatives seem to be disappearing.

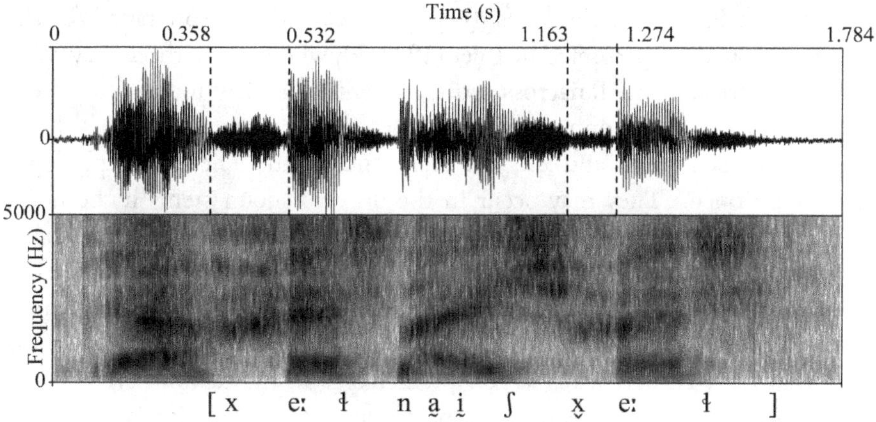

Figure 9.3. Fortis [x] and lenis [x̬] in *xeeł na'ishxeeł* 'I am carrying the pack back'

9.3.3. Lenis fricatives versus affricates

As stated in 9.2.1.1 I suspect that fricative lenition is so common in verb forms with a D-voice/valence marker because of the potential confusion of D+fricative with an affricate in the same place of articulation. The difference is illustrated by figure 9.4, which contrasts aspirated /t͡sʰ/ and unspirated /t͡s/ with the stop-fricative sequence /ts/. The top panel of figure 9.4 shows waveform and spectrogram of the word *shahtsädn ide'* 'lichen'. The aspirated affricate /t͡sʰ/ is about 0.2s in duration and looks like a typical affricate where the stop portion is released into the fricative portion. The middle panel of figure 9.4 contains two tokens of the unaspirated affricate /t͡s/ in the expression *udzih dzaadn thüh* 'caribou shin skin'.[6] The unaspirated affricates again are approximately 0.2s in duration and are released into the fricative portion (the release of /t͡s/ in *udzih* 'caribou' is much more clearly visible than that in *dzaadn* 'shin'). The bottom panel of figure 9.4, in contrast, illustrates the stop-lenis fricative sequence in *dat-sąy* 'it is black'; the release of the oral stop is indicated by an arrow. In the stop-fricative sequence the stop is released completely before the fricative begins. Also, the fricative by itself is about 0.3s, thus slightly longer than the affricates in the panels above. All sound files were produced by Mrs. Avis Sam (Northway) as part of recording UTO-LAF06Nov0105.wav.

9.4. Phonemic status of lenis fricatives

The status of lenis fricatives in the phoneme system of Upper Tanana merits a brief discussion. Minoura (1994, 165) posits a three-way contrast between the fortes /ɬ, θ, s, ʃ, x/, the lenes /θ̬, ɬ̬, s̬, ʃʲ, x̬/, and the 'sonorants' /ð, l/,[7] echoing the analysis presented by Leer (1982, 9), who posits a three-way voice contrast for fricatives in Tanacross. I disagree with this view and prefer to treat the lenis fricatives as allophones of the fortes.

As discussed in 9.1 and 9.2, the occurrence of the lenes is morphologically conditioned. They may occur in the onset of noun stems if the noun is either morphologically possessed or a non-initial part of a complex noun. They occur in verb stems when preceded by a voiced voice/valence marker and occasionally when preceded by a Ø- voice/valence prefix. Treating them as separate phonemes results in an unnecessarily complex phoneme inventory, given that their occurrence is largely predictable. In the cases where it is *not* predictable—i.e., where we would expect a lenis but find a fortis instead—treating them as separate phonemes is even less appropriate, since we would then have to posit a merger of two distinct sets of consonants. For these reasons I suggest that Upper Tanana distinguishes voiced and voiceless fricatives, and that the latter have fortis and lenis allophones, with the lenis allophones occurring in the morphological conditions outlined above.

9.5. Summary

In this chapter lenition of stem-initial fricatives is described. Noun-stem initial fricatives may become lenis when the noun stem is bound; verb-stem initial fricatives may become lenis following voiced voice/valence markers and, less commonly, following the Ø-voice/valence prefix. It is demonstrated that lenition is a somewhat irregular process that is not present in all forms where it could be expected.

The realization of lenis fricatives is somewhat variable. Some of them are partially voiced; in most cases however, they are simply shorter and less intensive than their fortis counterparts. While the discussion of the phonetics of lenis fricatives is very brief, using only a few representative examples, it should be noted that the findings are consistent with those made by Holton (2001) for Tanacross.

In contrast to Leer (1982) and Holton (2001) for Tanacross or Minoura (1994) for Upper Tanana, I treat lenis fricatives as predictable allophones of fortes voiceless fricatives, which contrast phonemically with fully voiced fricatives.

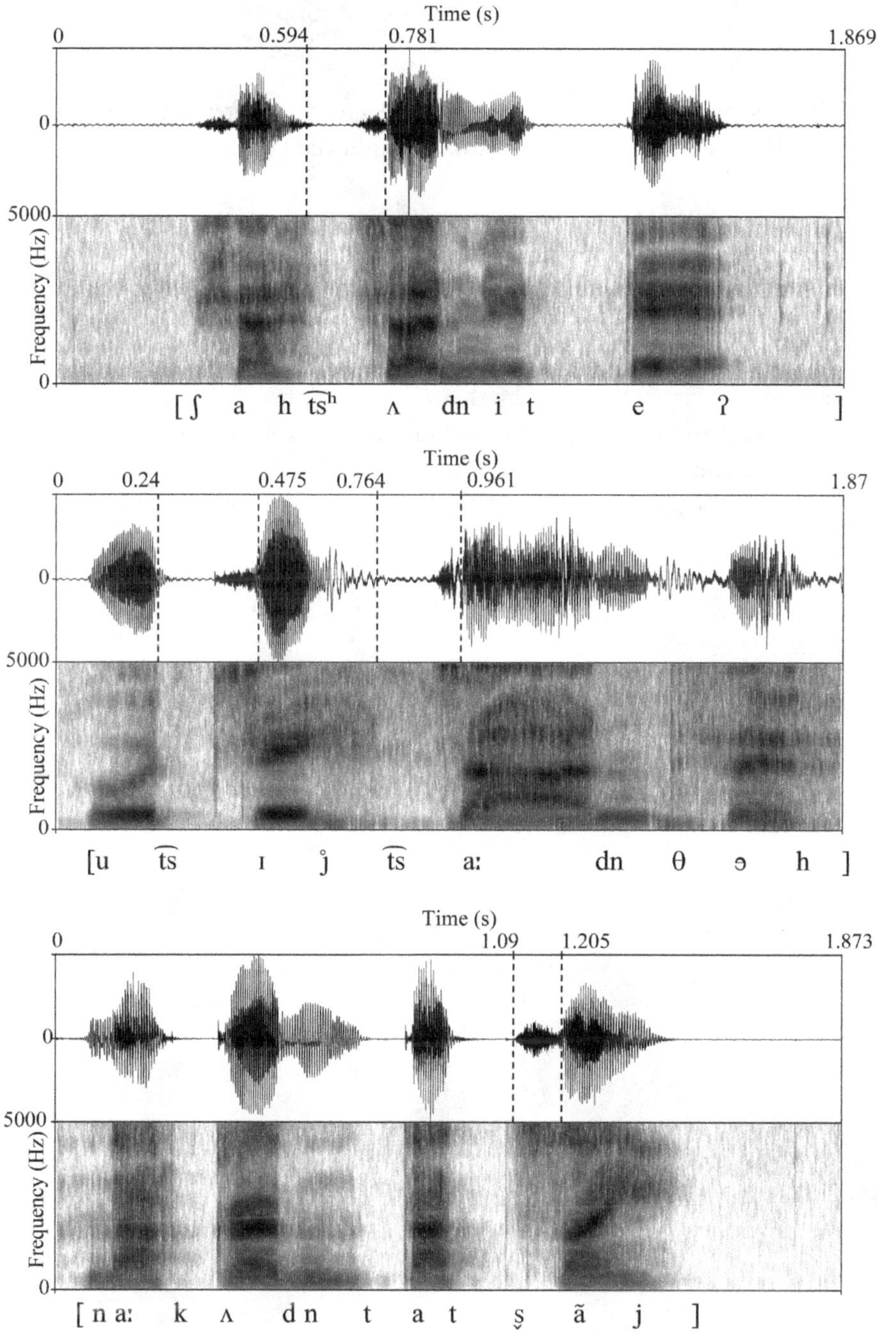

Figure 9.4. Aspirated affricate [t͡sʰ], unaspirated affricate [t͡s], oral stop + lenis fricative [ts̬]

Notes

1. [ʃʲ] is the only fricative that does not have a fortis counterpart. See chap. 5 for a discussion of the special status of [ʃʲ] in the Upper Tanana consonant system.
2. Because speakers get bored with possessive paradigms very quickly, I limited the recordings to only a few forms for each paradigm.
3. In the last two forms of the verb theme na#O+D+łuu 'drag o back', the speaker uses the perambulative rather than the iterative derivation, which introduces a *t-* prefix and changes the verb stem. The stem-initial consonant is however not affected by this.
4. This last verb theme only has singular forms; the corresponding plural theme contains the stem *deek* instead.
5. This variability may also account for some of the irregularities in 9.1 and 9.2.
6. Caribou shin skin is traditionally used to make mukluks.
7. As discussed in chap. 5, I treat these as voiced fricatives rather than sonorants.

10 Syllable structure

In this chapter the structure of stem and prefix syllables is described. Incorporated roots (i.e., roots that serve as verbal prefixes; see chap. 33) share some phonotactic characteristics with stems, others with prefixes.

10.1. Stem syllables

Stem syllables occur in nouns, verbs, adverbs, modifiers, and postpositions. Some other lexical items such as conjunctions or discourse markers also have shapes typical of stem syllables, but not all of them do.

Stem syllables may have the shapes CVː, CVC, CV(ː)C, CV(ː)Cʔ. All stem syllables are required to have an onset consonant, and the rhyme has to be at least bimoraic. A few stem syllables are reconstructed without an initial consonant; if no onset can be supplied from other morphological material, an epenthetic consonant is inserted.

10.1.1. Onset of stem syllables

10.1.1.1. Simple onsets All stem syllables in Upper Tanana are required to have an onset consonant. Almost all consonants may occur in stem onsets (110); the only exceptions are /ð̌, j̊, n̥/ (/ð̌/ is limited to prefix syllables, /j̊, n̥/ to stem codas).

(110) Stem onsets

a.	/t͜θʰ/	‘rock’	tthee	/t͜θʰeː/
b.	/t͜θ/	‘mountain’	ddhäł	/t͜θʌɬ/
c.	/t͜θ’/	‘sinew’	tth’ee	/t͜θ’èː/
d.	/tʰ/	‘among P’	P+tah	/tʰah/
e.	/t/	‘SG sit IPV’	dah	/tah/
f.	/t’/	‘under P’	P+t’aat	/t’aːtʰ/
g.	/t͡sʰ/	‘be hungry IPV’	tsįį	/t͡sʰĩː/
h.	/t͡s/	‘muskrat’	dzänh	/t͡sʌn̥/
i.	/ts’/	‘kiss PFV’	ts’ų’	/t͡s’ò̃ʔ/

j.	/t͡ɬʰ/	‘be mushy’	tlok	/t͡ɬʰòk/
k.	/t͡ɬ/	‘handle PL.O PFV’	dlah	/t͡ɬah/
l.	/t͡ɬ’/	‘rope’	tl’uuł	/t͡ɬ’uːɬ/
m.	/t͡ʃʰ/	‘flat’ (*n.*)	chinh	/t͡ʃʰin̥/
n.	/t͡ʃ/	‘mitten’	jiyh	/t͡ʃij̊/
o.	/t͡ʃ’/	‘rip PFV’	ch’ił	/t͡ʃ’iɬ/
p.	/kʰ/	‘cough IPV’	koh	/kʰoh/
q.	/k/	‘rabbit’	gah	/gah/
r.	/k’/	‘birch’	k’į̨y	/k’ĩːj/
s.	/ʔ/	‘handle CO PFV’	’ą̨ą̨	/ʔãː/
t.	/θ/	‘belt’	thüh	/θə̀h/
u.	/s/	‘star’	sän’	/sʌ̀nʔ/
v.	/ɬ/	‘glacier’	łuut	/ɬuːtʰ/
w.	/l/	‘I don’t know’	le’e	/leʔe/
x.	/ʃ/	‘bear’	shoh	/ʃoh/
y.	/ʃʲ/	‘snow’ (*n.*)	shyüh	/ʃʲə̀h/
z.	/x/	‘play IPV’	xoh	/xoh/
aa.	/h/	‘SG go IPV’	haayh	/haːj̊/
bb.	/m/	‘toboggan’	mboh	/moh/
cc.	/n/	‘animal’	nuun	/nùːn/
dd.	/j/	‘sky’	yaa	/jaː/

10.1.1.2. Complex onsets While stems themselves may have no more than one onset consonant, complex onsets of stem syllables are possible as a result of affixation. Verb stems may only occur as part of fully inflected verb forms, which are required to be at least disyllabic. Noun stems and postpositional stems, on the other hand, can only have a single prefix: a possessor prefix for nouns, and an object prefix for postpositions. Most of these prefixes contain a vowel or a syllabic /n/ (see 10.2.2.1.2), but the first-person singular object or possessor prefix /ʃ/- (with the allomorph /s/- preceding the alveolar affricates or fricative) is not syllabic and forms an onset cluster with the stem-initial consonant. The list of onset clusters in (111) is not inclusive.

(111) Stem onset clusters

a.	/ʃk/	‘my arm’	shgaan’	/ʃkàːnʔ/
b.	/ʃʔ/	‘my snowshoes’	sh’aay’	/ʃʔàːjʔ/
c.	/ʃn/	‘my mother’	shną̨ą̨	/ʃnãː/
d.	/ʃθ/	‘my skin’	shthüü’	/ʃθə̀ːʔ/

e.	/ʃβ/	‘my house’	shyah	/ʃβàh/
f.	/st͡sʰ/	‘my grandfather’	stsay	/st͡sʰaj/
g.	/ss/	‘my knife’	sseey’	/ssè:jʔ/
h.	/ʃt̪θʰ/	‘ahead of me’	shttheh	/ʃt̪θʰeh/
i.	/ʃkʰ/	‘looking for me’	shkah	/ʃkʰah/
j.	/ʃk’/	‘like me’	shk’eh	/ʃk’eh/
k.	/sts’/	‘(away) from me’	sts’änh	/st͡s’ʌn̥/

Thus onset clusters in noun and postposition stem syllables are permissible if the first consonant is /ʃ/ or /s/. Onset clusters are not permitted in verbal stem syllables.

10.1.1.3. Stems without an onset consonant Krauss (1969) reconstructs some Proto-Dene stems as lacking an onset consonant. For these stems to be part of well-formed words, onset consonants need to be inserted.

There are a few stems where the onset consonant requirement may be fulfilled by the possessor or postpositional object prefix, respectively (112).

(112) Noun and postposition stems without onsets

	English	*Stem*		*Inflected*	
a.	‘older sister’	-aadeh	-/a:teh/	shaadeh	/ʃa:teh/
b.	‘mother’s sister’	-aak’ay	-/a:k’aj/	shaak’ay	/ʃa:k’ay/
c.	‘for P’	P+aa	-/a:/	shaa	/ʃa:/

In verb stems reconstructed without an onset consonant (113), the onset consonant requirement may be fulfilled by an epenthetic /h/ or by prefixes adjacent to the stem (see Krauss [1969] for details; also see chap. 26.1.1).

(113) Stems with other morphological material in the onset

a.	‘SG go IPV	haayh	/ha:j̊/
b.	‘SG go IPV + D’	daayh	/ta:j̊/
c.	‘crawl IPV’ (T)	duu	/tu:/
d.	‘drag IPV’ (T)	łuu	/ɬu:/
e.	‘handle PL.O IPV’	łeeyh	/ɬe:j̊/
f.	‘SG go PFV’	shyah	/ʃβah/

10.1.2. Rhyme

The rhyme of a stem syllable is always at least bimoraic. If the nucleus is a short monophthong, then a coda consonant is required; if the nucleus is a long monophthong or diphthong, coda consonants are optional.

10.1.2.1. Nucleus The nucleus of a stem syllable is always one vowel. This vowel may be any monophthong or diphthong, and monophthongs in stem nuclei may be short (114) or long (115).

(114) Stem syllables with short vowel nucleus

a.	/i/	'berry'	jign	/t͡ʃik/
b.	/ĩ/	'see IPV'	'į̨h	/ʔĩh/
c.	/e/	'antlers'	de'	/tèʔ/
d.	/a/	'SG go PFV'	shyah	/ʃʲah/
e.	/ã/	'trail'	tąy	/tʰãj/
f.	/ʌ/	'you SG'	nän	/nʌn/
g.	/ʌ̃/	'towards P' (N)	P+ts'ą̈'	/t͡s'ʌ̃̀ʔ/
h.	/o/	'laugh IPV'	dloh	/t͡ɬòh/
i.	/õ/	'kiss PFV'	ts'ų'	/t͡s'õ̀ʔ/
j.	/ɘː/	'pus'	xüh	/xɘh/
k.	/ɘ̃/	'leech, snail'	tl'ų̈h	/t͡ɬ'ɘ̃h/
l.	/u/	'tooth'	xu'	/xùʔ/

(115) Stem syllables with long vowel or diphthong nucleus

a.	/iː/	'porcupine'	ts'iit	/t͡s'iːtʰ/
b.	/ĩː/	'be hungry IPV'	tsįį	/t͡sʰĩː/
c.	/eː/	'heart'	dzeey	/t͡seːj/
d.	/aː/	'SG go IPV PROG'	haał	/haːɬ/
e.	/ãː/	'leaf'	t'ąą'	/t'ã̀ːʔ/
f.	/oː/	'spruce'	ts'oo	/t͡s'òː/
g.	/õː/	'grandmother'	tsǫǫ'	/t͡sʰõː/
h.	/ɘ/	'pus POSS'	-xüü'	/xɘ̀ːʔ/
i.	/ɘ̃ː/	'leech, snail POSS'	tl'ų̈ų̈'	/t͡ɬ'ɘ̃̀ːʔ/
j.	/uː/	'ice, glacier'	łuut	/ɬuːtʰ/
k.	/ı͡a/	'egg'	xia'	/xı̀͜àʔ/
l.	/ı͡ã/	'early spring'	saanįą	/saːnı̃͜ã/
m.	/ı͡o/	'drag IPV' (N)	łiu	/ɬı͡o/
n.	/ı͡õ/	'fireweed' (N)	gįǫ	/kı̃̀͜õ̀/

10.1.2.2. Coda If the stem nucleus is a short vowel, then at least one coda consonant is required (114). In stems where the nucleus is a long vowel or a diphthong, coda consonants are optional (115).

Only a few consonants are allowed in stem codas: the oral stops /tʰ, t, kʰ, k, ʔ/, the fricatives /ɬ, l, h/, and the sonorants /n̥, n, j̊, j/ (116). Ejective stops, affricates, and most fricatives are not allowed in codas.

(116) Stem syllables with one coda consonant

a.	/tʰ/	'smoke'	łät	/ɬʌtʰ/
b.	/t/	'bald eagle'	tudn (N), tudi (T)	/tʰut/
c.	/kʰ/	'coat'	eek	/ʔeːkʰ/
d.	/k/	'squirrel' (T)	dlag(e)	/t͡ɬak/
e.	/ʔ/	'antlers'	de'	/tèʔ/
f.	/ɬ/	'trap'	eeł	/ʔeːɬ/
g.	/l/	'be short'	k'ul	/k'úl/
h.	/n̥/	'lake'	mänh	/mʌn̥/
i.	/n/	'people'	t'iin	/t'iːn/
j.	/j̊/	'snowshoe'	aayh	/ʔaːj̊/
k.	/j/	'lynx'	niiduuy	/nìːtùːj/

A few stems have complex codas /jʔ, nʔ/ (117).

(117) Stem syllables with complex codas

a.	/jʔ/	'fly'	dąy'	/dã̀jʔ/
b.		'willow'	k'ąy'	/k'ã̀jʔ/
c.	/nʔ/	'earth'	nän'	/nʌ̀nʔ/
d.		'fire'	kon'	/kònʔ/

Complex codas may also be the result of suffixation. Some suffixes only cause voicing of the stem-final consonant (see chap. 11), but others also contain a glottal stop, which may follow /t, k, l, n, j/. The suffix -v̀' used to create the possessed forms in (118) additionally affects the stem tone.

(118) Complex codas

a.	/t + ʔ/	'smoke POSS'	-łädn'	/ɬʌ̀tʔ/
b.	/k + ʔ/	'coat POSS'	-eegn'	/ʔèːkʔ/
c.	/l + ʔ/	'trap POSS'	-eel'	/ʔèːlʔ/
d.	/n + ʔ/	'lake POSS'	-männ'	/mʌ̀nʔ/
e.	/j + ʔ/	'snowshoe POSS'	-aayy'	/ʔàːjʔ/

10.1.2.3. More on /t, k/- final stems Stems ending in /t, k/ are always heavy, which means that they contain a suffix that causes the final consonant to become (phonetically) voiced (see chap. 11). The realization of these stems differs between dialects; see chap. 3.2.3. In the Northway dialect /t, k/ are fully voiced and always followed by a homorganic nasal; the oral stop /k/ then often disappears entirely in this context (119).

(119) /t, k/ in codas (Northway dialect)

a.	/t/	'bald eagle'	/tʰut/	[tʰudn]
b.	/t/	'fish trap'	/k'ɔ̀t/	[k'ɔ̀dn]
c.	/t + ʔ/	'belongings'	/t͡s'ʌtʔ/	[t͡s'ʌdnʔ]
d.	/k/	'fish'	/ɬu:k/	[ɬu:gŋ], [ɬu:ŋ]
e.	/k/	'squirrel'	/t͡ɬek/	[t͡ɬegŋ], [t͡ɬeŋ]
f.	/k + ʔ/	'eye'	/nà:kʔ/	[nà:gŋʔ], [nà:ŋʔ]

In the Tetlin dialect final /t, k/ are fully voiced and may optionally be followed either by a reduced vowel [ə] or (rarely) [ɪ] or by a homorganic nasal. The possible realizations are listed in (120).

(120) /t, k/ in codas (Tetlin dialect)

a.	/t/	'bald eagle'	/tʰut/	[tʰud], [tʰudɪ], [tʰudn]
b.	/t/	'fish trap'	/k'at/	[k'ad], [k'adə], [k'adn]
c.	/t + ʔ/	'belongings'	/t͡s'atʔ/	[t͡s'adʔ], [t͡s'adəʔ], [t͡s'adnʔ]
d.	/k/	'fish'	/ɬu:k/	[ɬu:g], [ɬu:gə], [ɬu:gŋ]
e.	/k/	'squirrel'	/t͡ɬak/	[t͡ɬag], [t͡ɬagə], [t͡ɬagŋ]
f.	/k + ʔ/	'eye'	/na:kʔ/	[na:gʔ], [na:gəʔ], [na:gŋʔ]

This realization of vocalic suffixes shown in (119, 120) led Minoura (1994, 161) to the following statement:

> "The segmental organization of Upper Tanana syllables can be schematized as
>
> (1) $(C_0)C_1V(V)(C_2)$(ə)(ʔ).
>
> This formula (1) consisting of one or two syllables is a recursively occurring unit in Upper Tanana words. In other words Upper Tanana words are, segmentally speaking, made with a recursion of such units. This unit can be considered a kind of 'foot', but this point will not be dealt with in this thesis."

This passage has always struck me as deeply confusing because of the idea that a syllable would contain two vowels separated by a consonant—ordinarily, we would expect a CVCə sequence such as [t͡ɬagə] 'squirrel' from (120e) as consisting of two syllables, not one. And indeed, this is an appropriate approach to surface phonology: the form [t͡ɬagə] is considered by Tetlin speakers as having two beats and hence two syllables. I take issue, however, with calling this "one syllable" or "a kind of foot."

The problem, I suggest, lies in the fact that Minoura mixes several levels of analysis. /t, k/ are the result of historical affixation processes with a vocalic suffix (chap. 11), but as Leer (1996c, 200) points out, these suffixes have been absorbed into the stem syllable and now cause voicing of stem-final consonants. Phonetically forms such as [tʰudɪ] and [tʰudn] contain vocalic and nasal segments after the final stop consonant. Phonemically, however, they have unaspirated stops /t, k/ as coda consonants. The nasal and vocalic segments following the oral stops are simply part of their realization in coda position. But if we consider the underlying phonemic structure, then the stem syllables in (119) and (120) have the structure CVC or CVCʔ.

10.2. Prefix syllables

Prefix syllables may have the shapes C, V, (C)CV(:), and (C)CVC. CV:C does not occur in prefix syllables; the only prefixes with that shape are incorporated roots (10.3).

10.2.1. Onset of prefix syllables

Prefix syllables usually have one onset consonant, but there are also prefix syllables with complex onsets or with no onset consonant at all.

10.2.1.1. Simple onsets Most prefix syllables have one onset consonant. (121) illustrates all consonants that are attested in the onsets of prefix syllables.

(121) One onset consonant

a.	/t̪͜θʰ/	'he fell into the fire' (N)	tthidaltth'ät	/t̪͜θʰitalt̪͜θ'ʌtʰ/
b.	/t̪͜θ'/	'it flew straight' (N)	tth'ineet'ak	/t̪͜θ'inè:t'akʰ/
c.	/tʰ/	'[boat] sank' (T)	tinįįłaat	/tʰinĩ:ɬa:tʰ/
d.	/t/	'I'm hungry'	dihtsįį	/tih.t͡sʰĩ:/
e.	/t'/	'I threw them down'	t'a'akdeeł	/t'aʔakʰtè:ɬ/
f.	/t͡sʰ/	'let's go'	tsuudeeł	/t͡sʰu:tè:ɬ/
g.	/t͡s/	'we're playing'	dzelxoh	/t͡selxoh/
h.	/t͡s'/	'we are small'	ts'įįtsuul	/t͡s'ĩ:t͡sʰú:l/
i.	/t͡ʃʰ/	'I will dance'	chagndzüh	/t͡ʃʰakt͡səh/
j.	/t͡ʃ/	'I want to sing'	jok-'a'	/t͡ʃokʰʔàʔ/
k.	/t͡ʃ'/	'I'm dancing'	ch'agndzüh	/t͡ʃ'akt͡səh/
l.	/kʰ/	'I climbed'	ki'ihshyah	/kʰìʔìhʃʲah/
m.	/k'/	'split SG it!'	k'idįįttheeł!	/k'itĩ:t̪͜θʰè:ɬ/

n.	/ð̆/	'I'm sick'	dhakts'iik	/ð̆akʰt͡s'iːkʰ/
o.	/ɬ/	'they argued'	łidahdetxą̨ą̨	/ɬitahtetxãː/
p.	/ʃ/	'they told me'	shihinih	/ʃihinih/
q.	/m/	'with her'	mbeh	/mèh/
r.	/n/	'with you SG '	neh	/nèh/
s.	/j/	'with her'	yeh	/jèh/

Some conjunct prefixes (see chap. 24.1 for a discussion of this term) do not contain an onset consonant. When these prefixes occur in word-initial position, an epenthetic [ʔ] is usually inserted (121).

(122) Epenthetic onset consonant

a.	'I'm running'	agntthäł	/akt̪θʰʌɬ/	[ʔaŋ.t̪θʰʌɬ]
b.	'you SG are walking'	į̨į̨haał	/ĩːhaːɬ/	[ʔĩːhaːɬ]
c.	'she's laughing'	edloh	/e.t͡ɬòh/	[ʔe.t͡ɬòh]
d.	'I should chop it'	uhttheeł	/uh.t̪θʰèːɬ/	[ʔuh.t̪θʰèːɬ]

Epenthetic [ʔ] is also inserted when a vowel-final prefix precedes a vowel-initial prefix (123).

(123) Epenthetic onset consonant

a.	'she came back'	nii'inshyah	/nìː.ʔìn.ʃʲah
b.	'I threw them down'	t'a'akdeeł	/t'a.ʔakʰ.tèːɬ/
c.	'he was boating around'	na'atkeeł	/na.ʔat.keːɬ/

10.2.1.2. Syllables without onset consonant A few prefixes consist only of a vowel and do not require insertion of an initial epenthetic consonant (124).

(124) Prefix syllables without onset consonant

a.	'her father'	uta'	/u.tʰàʔ/
b.	'she sees him'	ineh'į̨h	/i.neh.ʔĩh/

10.2.1.3. Complex onsets Onset clusters in prefixes occur when a prefix consisting only of a consonant precedes a consonant-initial prefix (125).

(125) Two onset consonants

a.	'they started off'	hteedeeł	/htʰèː.tèːɬ/
b.	'he is following me'	shnaahaał	/ʃnaː.haːɬ/
c.	'you PL will see it'	tnah'į̨į̨ł	/tʰnah.ʔĩ̀ːɬ/

There are also a few prefixes with complex onsets (126). The initial consonant there is always /s/ in contemporary Upper Tanana, but comparison with the data in Kari (1997b) suggests that the initial consonant was originally /ɬ/, a reduced form of the reciprocal object prefix *niɫ-*, *ɫi-*.[1]

(126) Two onset consonants

a. ‘she went away again’ staa’atshyah /stʰaː.ʔat.ʃʲah/
b. ‘she split [the wood]’ sdziidehtʼoh /st͡siː.teh.tʼoh/
c. ‘she went across’ skinįįshyah /skʰi.nì̃ː.ʃʲah/

10.2.2. Rhyme of prefix syllables

10.2.2.1. Nucleus The nucleus of a prefix syllable may be a vowel or, rarely, a syllabic consonant.

10.2.2.1.1. Vocalic nucleus The nucleus of a prefix syllable is usually a short or long oral vowel (127, 128). /ʌ, ɘ, i͡a, i͡o/ and most nasal vowels (with the exception of /ĩ, ĩː, õ, õː/) never occur in prefixes.

(127) Oral vowels in prefix syllables

a. /i/ ‘they played’ hihdelxoh /hih.del.xoh/
b. /iː/ ‘they said to him’ hiiyehnih /hiː.jeh.nih/
c. /e/ ‘she’s laughing’ edloh /e.t͡ɬòh/
d. /eː/ ‘they started off’ hteedeeɫ /htʰèː.tèːɬ/
e. /a/ ‘you PL will see it’ tnah’įįɫ /tʰnah.ʔì̃ːɬ/
f. /aː/ ‘he is following me’ shnaahaaɫ /ʃnaː.haːɬ/
g. /o/ ‘I want to eat them’ ogndeel /ok.teːl/
h. /oː/ ‘she will walk around’ ɫootaahaaɫ /ɬoːtʰaː.haːɬ/
i. /u/ ‘I want to drink it’ ushnaan /uʃ.naːn/
j. /uː/ ‘he should go there’ ni’uushya’ /nì.ʔuː.ʃʲah/

(128) Nasal vowels in prefix syllables

a. /ĩ/ ‘make it!’ įhtsayh /ĩh.t͡sʰaj̊/
b. /ĩː/ ‘you SG are walking’ įįhaaɫ /ĩːhaːɬ/
c. /õ/ ‘you SG should make it’ ǫhtsay /õh.t͡sʰaj/
d. /õː/ ‘you SG should walk there’ ni’ǫǫshya’ /nì.ʔõː.ʃʲaʔ/

10.2.2.1.2. Consonantal nucleus /n/ is the only consonant that may be the nucleus of a prefix syllable. The second-person singular possessor or object prefix *n-* can constitute a syllable by itself when the noun or postposition stem begins with a consonant (129).

(129) Syllabic /n/

a.	'your SG father'	nta'	/n.tʰàʔ/
b.	'your SG mother'	nnąą	/n.nãː/
c.	'in front of you SG '	nttheh	/n.t͜θʰeh/
d.	'away from you SG '	nch'a'	/n.t͡ʃ'aʔ/

In verbs, syllabic /n/ also occurs either as the second-person singular direct object prefix before a consonant (130a), as the distributive prefix (130b), or as the consonantal allomorph of the Ø-perfective (130c).

(130) Syllabic /n/ in verbs

a.	'I see SG you'	nnak-'įh	/n.nakʰ.ʔĩh/
b.	'we're dancing'	nts'eldzüh	/n.t͡s'el.t͡səh/
c.	'it is good'	nsǫǫ	/n.sõː/

10.2.2.2. Coda of prefix syllables Prefix syllables with a vocalic nucleus may have one coda consonant. Usually coda consonants occur only when the prefix vowel is short. Only the following consonants are attested in codas of prefix syllables (131).

(131) Coda consonants in prefix syllables

a.	/tʰ/	'he flew back'	nat̲net-t'ak	/natʰ.net.t'ak/
b.	/t/	'she's working'	et̲nah	/et.nah/
c.	/kʰ/	'I see you'	nnak̲-'įh	/n.nakʰ.ʔĩh/
d.	/k/	'I'm running'	ag̲ntthäł	/ak.t͜θʰʌɬ/
e.	/ɬ/	'we took care of each other'	nił̲k'ats'enelta'	/niɬ.k'à.t͡s'e.nel.tàʔ/
f.	/l/	'she's running'	al̲tthäł	/al.t͜θʰʌɬ/
g.	/s/	'I got well again'	nadhis̲-sǫǫ	/na.ðis.sõː/
h.	/ʃ/	'I am drinking it'	is̲h̲nąą	/iʃ.nãː/
i.	/h/	'I am small'	ih̲tsuul	/ih.t͡sʰúːl/
j.	/n/	'I will take you down'	nan̲takteeł	/nan.tʰakʰ.tʰeːɬ/
k.	/j/	'she punched her up'	łay̲nehgot	/ɬaj.neh.kotʰ/

10.3. Incorporated roots

Incorporated roots conform neither entirely to the criteria for stem syllables nor to those for prefix syllables but have some characteristics of either type.

CV, CVː, CVC, CVːC, and even CVːCʔ are all allowed in incorporated roots, whereas C and V (which are allowed in prefixes) do not occur. The shape CV, however, is characteristic of prefixes but not of stems. The possible syllable types in incorporated roots are illustrated in (132).

(132) Incorporated roots

a.	CV	'head'-	tthi-	/t̪θʰi/-
b.		'hand'-	ła-	/ɬa/-
c.	CV:	'mind'-	nii-	/nì:/-
d.		'knot'-	shyia-	/ʃʲi͡a/-
e.	CVC	'laugh'-	dloh-	/t͡ɬòh/-
f.		'cry'-	tsüh-	/t͡sʰɘh/-
g.	CV:C	'eye'-	naak-	/na:kʰ/-
h.		'trap'-	'eeł-	/ʔe:ɬ/-
i.	CV:Cʔ	'arm'-	gaan'-	/kà:nʔ/-

Most incorporated roots of the shape CV refer to body parts. The noun stems related to the incorporates all contain the inalienable possessive suffix -', which serves as a stem formative. Forms like (132a, b) provide strong evidence to treat incorporates as roots rather than stems (see also chap. 33.3).

CV:, CVC, and CV:C are very common syllable types for incorporates.

(132j) is the only incorporate with the shape CV:Cʔ attested in my corpus; the form is taken from Tyone (1996). The final /ʔ/ is likely the inalienable possessive suffix; *gaan'*- is thus more properly considered a stem than a root. All speakers with whom I have worked use *gą̨ą̨'*- /kà̰:ʔ/-, which suggests that CV:C may be the maximal syllable for an incorporate in contemporary speech.

Regarding the inventory of sounds allowed in incorporated roots, the examples in (132) demonstrate that in this respect incorporates resemble stem syllables. /ʃʲ/ and /t͡ɬ/ in (132d, e) do not occur in the onset of prefix syllables. The diphthong /i͡a/ in (132d) and the vowel /ɘ/ in (132f) also are characteristic of stem syllables.

Incorporates thus generally have the shape of stem syllables, although complex codas are dispreferred and CV syllables are allowed.

10.4. Summary

In this chapter the structure of Upper Tanana syllables is described. There is a distinction between stem syllables and prefix syllables. Stem syllables may have the shapes CV:, CVC, CV(:)C, CV(:)Cʔ; prefix syllables may have the shapes C, V, (C)CV(:), and (C)CVC, but never CV:C. Stem and prefix syllables also differ with respect to the consonants and vowels that may occur therein; generally the inventory of sounds allowed in stem syllables is greater than that allowed in prefix syllables. Incorporated roots share phonotactic characteristics of both syllable types.

Notes

1. One Northway speaker recently commented that /ɬ/-initial clusters were "Tetlin speech," suggesting that the change to /s/ began earlier in Northway than in Tetlin. Nowadays, however, all Tetlin speakers that I know also have /s/-initial clusters.

11 Light and heavy stems

Upper Tanana, like other Dene languages in the region (Leer 1996c, 200), has absorbed vocalic suffixes into the stem syllable, which results in "heavy" stems. Unsuffixed stems are known as "light." There are several synchronic and diachronic suffixes that participate in this process: Leer (1996c, 200) lists the nominalizing suffix on verbs as well as the inalienable and alienable possessive suffixes and two other historic vocalic suffixes on nouns. In Upper Tanana the negative and imperative verbal suffixes also participate in this process. The suffixes differ in their synchronic productivity. Many nouns, such as /tʰuːt/ 'bald eagle/, /tʰʌt/ 'night', or -/nàːkʔ/ 'eye', are the result of historic suffixation processes and in contemporary speech only exist in their suffixed form. Other suffixes, such as the alienable possessive suffix -v̀', the nominalizing suffix -v, or the negative suffix -v́ are still productive; the resulting heavy stems have light counterparts.

11.1. Heavy stems as the result of synchronous suffixation

Many heavy stem syllables are the product of synchronous suffixation processes. Often the effect on noun stems differs in subtle ways from that on verb stems; for this reason noun and verb stems are discussed separately. Note that some vocalic suffixes contain additional information such as (low or high) tone and glottalization. These are represented in the phonemic representations but not discussed further, as they are not integral to the distinction between light and heavy stems.

The suffixes themselves are described elsewhere in this grammar: see chap. 13.2.1.1 for the historical noun suffix -v, chap. 22.2.1 for the alienable possessive suffix -v̀' and the inalienable possessive suffix -', and chap. 37 for the verbal suffixes.

The following discussion is organized by stem-final segment.

11.1.1. No or glottal coda consonant

If a light verb stem ends in a long oral vowel, diphthong, or /ʔ/, no changes take place (133a–d). If a light stem ends in a long nasal vowel, then the corresponding heavy stem will contain a denasalized long vowel followed by /n/ (133e, f). If the stem ends in (historical) /h/, then the final consonant is deleted and the vowel is lengthened (133g, h). The nominalized stems in (133i–k) show that these stems historically end in /j̊/ (see section 11.1.2), even though they have a final /h/ in contemporary speech (erosion of stem-final consonants is touched upon in chap. 8). All heavy stems in (133) are derived via the nominalizing suffix -v.

(133) Vowel lengthening and deletion of final /h/ in verb stems

	English	*Light*		*Heavy*	
a.	'PL stand IPV'	dee	/te:/	dee	/te:/
b.	'be round IPV'	xia	/x͡ia/	xia	/͡ia/
c.	'SG go OPT'	shya'	/ʃʲàʔ/	shya'	/ʃʲàʔ/
d.	'knock PFV'	don'	/tònʔ/	don'	/tònʔ/
e.	'be hungry IPV'	tsį̨į̨	/t͡sʰĩ:/	tsiin	/t͡sʰi:n/
f.	'exercise IPV'	k'į̨ą̨	/k'ĩ͜ã/	k'ian	/k'͡ian/
g.	'be brown IPV'	tth'oh	/t͜θ'oh/	tth'oo	/t͜θ'o:/
h.	'cry IPV (T)'	tsah	/t͡sʰah/	tsaa	/t͡sʰa:/
i.	'SG go PFV'	shyah	/ʃʲah/	shyay	/ʃʲaj/
j.	'classify PL.O IPV'	dlah	/t͡ɬah/	dlay	/t͡ɬaj/
k.	'tie IPV'	tl'uh	/t͡ɬ'uh/	tl'uy	/t͡ɬ'uj/

In noun stems ending in a long vowel or diphthong the addition of a vocalic suffix causes no change (134a–c). (134c, d) illustrate that nasal vowels and diphthongs remain nasal. In /h/-final noun stems, the final consonant is deleted (134d–g); if the nucleus vowel is short, then it is lengthened (134f, g). In /ʔ/-final noun stems, the vowel is lengthened and the final consonant is retained (134h, i). All heavy stems in (134) are formed using the alienable possessive suffix -v̀'.

(134) Vowel lengthening and deletion of final /h/ in noun stems

	English	*Light*		*Heavy*	
a.	'rock' (N)	tthee	/t͜θʰe:/	-tthee'	-/t͜θʰè:ʔ/
b.	'knot' (N)	shyia	/ʃʲì͜à/	-shyia'	-/ʃʲì͜àʔ/
c.	'worm' (N)	gǫǫ	/kõ:/	-gǫǫ'	-/kõ̀:ʔ/
d.	'raft' (N)	xį̨ą̨h	/xĩ̀͜ã̀/	-xį̨ą̨'	-/xĩ̀͜ã̀ʔ/

e.	'leech' (N)	tl'üüh	/t͡ɬ'ɔː/	-tl'üü'	-/t͡ɬ'ɔ̀ːʔ/
f.	'feather' (N)	t'ah	/t'ah/	-t'aa'	-/t'àːʔ/
g.	'grass' (N)	tl'oh	/t͡ɬ'oh/	-tl'oo'	-/t͡ɬ'òːʔ/
h.	'louse' (N)	shya'	/ʃʲàʔ/	-shyaa'	-/ʃʲàːʔ/
i.	'gun' (N)	k'a'	/k'àʔ/	-k'aa'	-/k'àːʔ/

11.1.2. Stems ending in /n̥, j̊, ɬ/

For light stems ending in /n̥, j̊, ɬ/, the corresponding heavy stem ends in voiced /n, j, l/. This is demonstrated in (135) for nouns and the alienable possessive suffix -v̀'. All forms in (135) are taken from the nontonal Tetlin dialect.

(135) Voicing of /n̥/, /j̊/, /ɬ/ in heavy noun stems

	English	*Light*		*Heavy*	
a.	'lake' (T)	manh	/man̥/	-mann'	/manʔ/
b.	'stick' (T)	dichinh	/tit͡ʃʰin̥/	-dichinn'	/tit͡ʃʰinʔ/
c.	'snowshoe' (T)	aayh	/ʔaːj̊/	-aayy'	/ʔaːjʔ/
d.	'canoe' (T)	ts'ayh	/t͡sʰaj̊/	-ts'ayy'	/t͡sʰajʔ/
e.	'rope' (T)	tl'uuł	/t͡ɬ'uːɬ/	-tl'uul'	/t͡ɬ'uːlʔ/
f.	'sled' (T)	xał	/xaɬ/	-xal'	/xalʔ/

Note that the two voiced sonorants /n/ and /j/ in (135a–d) are represented in the orthography with double consonant symbols preceding glottal stop so as to distinguish them from forms ending in a sonorant plus glottal stop that do not contain a vocalic suffix. This contrast is illustrated in (136).

(136) Noun stems ending in /jʔ/, /nʔ/

	English	*Light*		*Heavy*	
a.	'fly'	dąy'	/tã̀jʔ/	-dąyy'	/tã̀jʔ/
b.	'land'	nan'	/nànʔ/	-nann'	/nànʔ/

Minoura (1994, 171) suggests that /n/ and /j/ in this environment are lengthened to /n·/ and /j·/, respectively, but this cannot be confirmed phonetically. In this instance the orthography reflects a morphological distinction that does not have a phonetic realization.

(137) contrasts light and heavy verb stems ending in /n̥, j̊, ɬ/; the suffix is the nominalizing suffix -v.

(137) Voicing of /n̥, j̊, ɬ/ in heavy verb stems

	English	*Light*		*Heavy*	
a.	'smell IPV'	tsänh	/t͡sʰʌn̥/	tsän	/t͡sʰʌn/

b.	'freeze IPV'	tänh	/tʰʌn̥/	tän	/tʰʌn/
c.	'be black IPV'	sąyh	/sãj̊/	sąy	/sãj/
d.	'speak IPV'	heeyh	/he:j̊/	heey	/he:j/
e.	'PL move IPV'	deeł	/tè:ɬ/	deel	/tè:l/
f.	'holler IPV'	säł	/sʌɬ/	säl	/sʌl/

Note that heavy verb stems with sonorant codas are not spelled with double consonant symbols.

11.1.3. Stems ending in /tʰ, kʰ/

For light stems ending in /tʰ, kʰ/, the corresponding heavy stems end in /t, k/. In this environment their fully voiced allophones [d, g] are used. All examples in (138) are from the Northway dialect.[1]

(138) Voicing of /tʰ, kʰ/ in noun stems

	English	*Light*		*Heavy*		
a.	'cane' (N)	tät	/tʰʌ̀tʰ/	-tädn'	/tʌ̀tʔ/	[tʌ̀dnʔ]
b.	'coat' (N)	eek	/e:kʰ/	-eegn'	/ʃʔè:kʔ/	[ʃʔè:gŋʔ], [ʃʔè:ŋʔ]

(139) illustrates the same variation for verb stems using the nominalizing suffix -v. Again all examples are from the Northway dialect.

(139) Vowel lengthening and deletion of final /h/

	English	*Light*		*Heavy*		
a.	'punch IPV' (N)	got	/kòtʰ/	godn	/kòt/	[kòdn]
b.	'SG go IPV CUST' (N)	haak	/ha:kʰ/	haagn	/ha:k/	[ha:gŋ], [ha:ŋ]

11.2. Inherently heavy stems

Heavy stems may also be the product of historical affixation. In that case corresponding light stems may no longer exist.

Inherently heavy noun stems contain one of several historical suffixes. Most obligatorily possessed nouns contain the inalienable possessive suffix -'; the unsuffixed root occurs only as an incorporate, if it occurs at all. While Holton (2000, 143) observes that the cognate suffix in Tanacross does not create heavy syllables, -' often has that effect in Upper Tanana, as discussed in chap. 22. A few examples in the Northway dialect are given in (140).

(140) Inherently heavy noun stems I

a.	'tongue'	-tthuul'	-/t̪θʰù:lʔ/
b.	'arm'	-gaan'	-/kà:nʔ/
c.	'heart'	-dzeey'	/t͡sè:jʔ/

d. ‘hearing’ -dziidn /t͡sì:t/
e. ‘eye’ -naagn’ /nà:kʔ/

The historical suffixes *-ə or *-i: (Leer 1996c, 200) also result in inherently heavy stems (141). None of these stems have a light counterpart. Only Northway forms are given in (141).

(141) Inherently heavy noun stems II

a.	‘bald eagle’	tudn	/tʰut/
b.	‘ant’	naadodn	/na:tòt/
c.	‘fish’	łuugn	/ɬu:k/
d.	‘moose’	diniign	/tini:k/
e.	‘white-winged scoter’	näl	/nʌ̀l/
f.	‘dwarf spruce’	tthaay	/t̪θʰa:j/
g.	‘women’	ts’exeey	/t͡s’èxe:j/
h.	‘child’	ts’iinlin	/t͡s’i:ni:n/

Inherently heavy verb stems are lexicalized negative stems. All of them have the high tone characteristic of the negative suffix (see chap. 26).

(142) Inherently heavy verb stems

a.	‘not know IPV’	niign	/ní:k/
b.	‘be sad, grieving IPV’	dąy	/tã́j/
c.	‘be small IPV’	tsuul	/t͡sʰú:l/
d.	‘be few IPV’	tsiin	/t͡sʰí:n/

The verb stems in (142a, b) have light (affirmative) counterparts (*nayh* ‘feel, know’ and *dįį* ‘learn’, respectively); the ones in (142c, d) do not.

11.3. Summary

Upper Tanana shows a systematic opposition between light (unsuffixed) and heavy (suffixed) stems. Light stems end in long vowels, glottal consonants /h/ and /ʔ/, aspirated oral stop /tʰ, kʰ/, or voiceless /n̥, ɬ, j̊/. Heavy stems also may end in long vowels or /ʔ/, unaspirated oral stops /t, k/, or voiced /n, l, j/.

Most heavy stems are the product of synchronic suffixation processes with a vocalic suffix; all of these have light counterparts. Only a few heavy stems are the result of historic suffixation with a vocalic suffix. For many of these no light counterpart exists in the contemporary language.

Notes

1. See chap. 5.1.2.1 for more examples and chap. 3.2.3 for the dialectology.

12 The practical orthography

There are several practical orthographies in use for Upper Tanana. After a brief comparison between the different spelling systems as they relate to the phoneme inventory presented in chap. 5–7, I briefly comment on some of the conventions I follow in this grammar, namely the representation of /a/ versus /ʌ/ across dialects, tone, lenis fricatives, and vowel-initial words.

12.1. Comparison of orthographies

An orthographic system was originally developed by Reverend Milanowski (1961) for the Tetlin dialect and modified subsequently by Leer (1974) for the Northway dialect. In the mid-1990s further modifications were done by the Alaska Native Language Center (ANLC) as outlined by Kari in Tyone (1996, xi-xvi); these modifications were adopted and implemented in Milanowski (2011). The Yukon Native Language Centre (2009) (YNLC) employs a slightly modified system based on that developed by the ANLC. The different orthographies are contrasted in the following sections.

12.1.1. Spelling of consonants

In the orthographic representation of consonants, the following conventions typical of Alaskan Dene languages are followed: voiceless symbols are used to represent aspirated and ejective stops and affricates; voiced symbols are used for unaspirated stops and affricates. The barred-l <ł> is used for the lateral fricative. Voiceless sonorants are written with the sonorant symbol followed by <h>, and the representation of interdental sounds is inspired by the representation of English /θ/. The glottal stop is represented by an apostrophe rather than by <ʔ>, as is done in some Canadian Dene languages. Table 12.1 contrasts the three orthographies.[1]

IPA	Milanowski	ANLC	YNLC
/ʔ/	’	’	’
/m/	m, b	m, mb	m, b, mb
/n/	n, nd	n	n, nd
/n̥/	n̲	nh	nh
/t/	d	d	d
/tʰ/	t	t	t
/t’/	t’	t’	t’
/ð/	dh	dh	dh
/θ/	th	th	th
/t͜θ/	d̲h	ddh	ddh
/t͜θʰ/	t̲h	tth	tth
/t͜θ’/	t̲h’	tth’	tth’
/l/	l	l	l
/ɬ/	ł	ł	ł
/t͡ɬ/	dl	dl	dl
/t͡ɬʰ/	tł	tl	tl
/t͡ɬ’/	tł’	tl’	tl’
/s/	s	s	s
/t͡s/	dz	dz	dz
/t͡sʰ/	ts	ts	ts
/t͡s’/	ts’	ts’	ts’
/ʃʲ/	shy	shy	s̲h̲
/ʃ/	sh	sh	sh
/t͡ʃ/	j	j	j
/t͡ʃʰ/	ch	ch	ch
/t͡ʃ’/	ch’	ch’	ch’
/j/	iy	y	y
/j̊/	ih	yh	yh
/x/	x	x	x
/k/	g	g	g
/kʰ/	k	k	k
/k/	k’	k’	k’
/h/	h	h	h

Table 12.1. Comparison of orthographies (consonants)

The differences between the three writing systems compared in table 12.1 are relatively minor. The various representations of the nasal consonants /m/ and /n/ are caused by different pronunciations, as discussed in chap. 5.3.2.1.

Milanowski's orthography was developed in the time of the typewriter, when underlining was an easy way to distinguish similar sounds. With the arrival of computers, underlined characters became less convenient, hence the change of <dh, th, th'> to <ddh, tth, tth'> and <n> to <nh>.

The change from <ih> and <iy> in the Milanowski system to <yh> and <y> in the subsequent systems had to do with the recognition that these sounds are consonants, not the second part of a diphthong (this is discussed in some detail in Leer [1982]). Another difference is the use of <l> rather than <ł> in the aspirated and ejective lateral ejectives; this appears to be general ANLC practice, as it is a feature of the writing system of all Alaskan Dene languages.

Additional differences in writing systems not shown in table 12.1 include the use of underlined symbols for lenis fricatives (see chap. 9) in the system used by the YNLC, and the use of <wu> for /u/ in word-initial position when not preceded by a glottal stop in the orthographies of both language centers. These points are discussed in 12.2.3 and 12.2.4 in greater detail.

12.1.2. Spelling of vowels

The different orthographies as pertaining to vowels are compared in table 12.2.

IPA	Milanowski	ANLC	YNLC
/a/	a	a	a
/ʌ/	–	ä	ä
/e/	e	e	e
/i/	i	i	i
/o/	o	o	o
/u/	u	u	u
/ɘ/	u	ü	ü
/ɪ͡a/	ia	ia	ia, ea
/ɪ͡u/	io	iu, io	io
/aː/ etc.	aa	aa	aa
/ã/ etc.	ą	ą	ą
/à/ etc.	–	a	à
[á] etc.	a	a	a̋

Table 12.2. Comparison of orthographies (vowels)

Again the differences between the orthographies are minor. All systems represent short vowels by single vowel symbols, long vowels by double vowel symbols, and nasality by an ogonek. The ANLC changed the spelling of the /ɔ/ from an <u̲> to <ü> and added <ä> for /ʌ/ in the dialects where it occurs. The YNLC orthography is the only one that represents low tone; their materials also indicate the existence of a rising tone represented with <ǎ> and some other, not clearly specified, tonal distinction represented with <ā>. High tone is represented as <ắ>, etc., in YNLC materials and as <á> in many materials by Milanowski, but not in materials created by the ANLC.

12.2. The orthography used in this grammar

Throughout this grammar I use the writing system developed by Kari and the ANLC. In the following sections I briefly comment on a few features of this writing system that require more explanation.

12.2.1. <ä> and <a>

As discussed in chap. 6 and 8, the vowels /ʌ/ and /a/ have merged into /a/ in the Tetlin dialect but remain separate phonemes in the Northway, Scottie Creek, and Beaver Creek dialects. In spelling this sound, I recognize the dialect difference and spell it for Tetlin and <ä> for the other dialects (143). /ɑ/ is written in both dialects.

(143) Spelling of /ʌ/ and /a/

		N, S, B	T
a.	'blood'	däł	dał
b.	'firewood'	tsät	tsat
c.	'towards P'	P+nts'ą̈'	P+nts'ą'
d.	'boat'	ts'ayh	ts'ayh
e.	'my father'	shta'	shta'

12.2.2. Tone

Even though the Northway, Scottie Creek, and Beaver Creek dialects are low-marking (see chap. 7), I follow the tradition (implicit in Kari [1997a, 1997b] and explicit in Tyone [1996]) of not indicating tone in orthographic transcriptions due to the low functional load of tone, as discussed in chap. 7.2. This leads to minor ambiguities; Leer (1974) suggested the two verbs in (144) as a minimal pair.[2]

(144) Tone minimal pair

		Leer (1974)	IPA
a.	‘get up!’	ní’įįhaaih	/niʔĩːhaːj̊/
b.	‘go to point (and stop)!’	ni’į́įhaaih	/nìʔĩːhaːj̊/

In the orthography used here both these words are represented with the same spelling—*ni’įįhaayh*. Of course, this spelling obscures the tonal contrast and the associated meaning difference, which could be taken as an argument in favor of writing tone. I find instead that the tiny amount of clarity gained by writing these contrasts is insignificant when compared to the effort of teaching individuals to write tone correctly (see also Bird [1999] on the challenges of writing tone in Dschang, a Bantu language of Cameroon).

When discussing the spelling system to be used in the Northway story collection by Sam, Demit-Barnes, and Northway (forthcoming), I consulted with the contributors to this grammar about the question of representing tone. Two of them professed not to care; two others were opposed to writing tone, saying that it “looked harder.” Balancing the advantages of writing tone against the difficulties and the speakers’ wishes, I decided to follow ANLC convention in not writing it.

12.2.3. Lenis fricatives

Lenis fricatives are morphologically conditioned allophones of voiceless fricatives (see chap. 9). They are written with underlined voiceless symbols in the YNLC orthography; in the other writing systems they are written with voiceless symbols. An exception is the lenis fricative /ʃ̬/, which seems to be a separate phoneme from (fortis) /ʃ/. Some examples are given in (145). The data in the column labeled “YNLC” comes from Sam (2000), a set of language lessons originally developed by Mrs. Avis Sam together with ANLC linguist James Kari, later retranscribed by the Yukon Native Language Centre; the spellings in the column “ANLC” are taken from Kari (1997b).

(145) Representation of final sonorants in heavy syllables

		YNLC	ANLC
a.	‘it is nice’	hǫǫs̱ǫǫ	hǫǫsǫǫ
b.	‘it (e.g., weather) is, exists’	hǫǫł̱įį	hǫǫłįį
c.	‘snow’	s̱ẖüh	shyüh
d.	‘you want P’	P iynįįṯẖanh	P iynįįthänh
e.	‘she is playing’	delx̱oh	delxoh

I follow the practice of not distinguishing lenis from fortis fricatives orthographically, since their presence is largely predictable.

12.2.4. Word-initial glottal stop, <w> and <y>

One of the few issues where I deviate from the ANLC orthography is word-initial <w> and <y>. They are used to distinguish between vowel-initial and glottal-initial words. There is a general requirement that syllables have an onset consonant (see also chap. 10), yet word-initial glottal stop is never written (146). When a word begins with a vocalic prefix (146d–f), an epenthetic glottal stop is inserted.

(146) Syllable-initial glottal stop

a.	'coat'	eek	/ʔeːkʰ/	[ʔeːkʰ]
b.	'dipnet'	üh	/ʔɘ̀h/	[ʔɘ̀h]
c.	'the outside area'	ogn	/ʔók/	[ʔók]
d.	'she is running'	altthäł	/alt̪͡θʰʌɬ/	[ʔalt̪͡θʰʌɬ]
e.	'I'm working'	ishnah	/iʃnah/	[ʔiʃnah]
f.	'I want to eat'	ogndeel	/okteːl/	[ʔoɡɪeːl]

Thus, generally, the absence of a word-initial consonant should be interpreted as the presence of an unwritten glottal stop. There are a few prefixes, however, that are truly vowel-initial and never cause glottal stop insertion (147).

(147) Vowel-initial prefixes

a.	'she saw him'	ineh'į̨h	/inehʔĩh/	[inehʔĩh]
b.	'3SG away from 3SG'	its'änh	/it͡sʰʌn̥/	[it͡sʰʌn̥]
c.	'his mother'	unąą	/unãː/	[unãː]
d.	'for her'	uxah	/uxah/	[uxah]

To distinguish cases like (147) from those in (146), ANLC and YNLC suggest writing an initial glide, so that the forms in (147) are spelled *yineh'į̨h, yits'änh, wunąą*, and *wuxah*, respectively. I have found that speakers strongly resist this spelling, especially insofar as it pertains to <w>: since there is no labial or labiovelar glide in Upper Tanana, speakers find it counterintuitive in this context.

The other way of marking the contrast, namely using an apostrophe to mark word-initial glottal stop similar to current practice in Ahtna, is also not acceptable to the speakers with whom I work. As this is another issue with low potential for ambiguity, I follow their practice.

12.2.5. Capitalization

In Upper Tanana, as in other Alaskan Dene languages, the first letter of a sentence as well as the initial letters of all personal names and place-names are capitalized (148).

(148) Capitalization in Upper Tanana: UTOLVDN07Nov2803:001-002

a. *Ts'įįtsuul dą' Nahk'ade dą' ch'ale ts'eneeshyaan,*
1PL:be.small:IPV when fish.trap at FOC 1PL:grow.up:PFV:NOM
shaadeh iin shoondaa iin shchil iin
1SG:older.sister PL 1SG:older.brother PL 1SG:younger.brother PL
shdia' iin eɫ shnąą shta' eɫ.
1SG:younger.sister PL and 1SG:mother 1SG:father and
'When we were little, we grew up in Last Tetlin, with my older sisters, my older brothers, my younger brothers, my younger sisters and my parents.'

b. *Aadaat du' Tommy Paul dits'iikeey iin*
NTRL:downriver:PNCT CT Tommy Paul REFL:children PL
di'aat eɫ hihdeltth'ih ay iin du'.
REFL:wife with 3PL:PL.stay:IPV 3 PL CT
'Down there lived Tommy Paul and his wife and children.'

12.2.6. Phonological variation and standardization

In chap. 3, 5, and 6, I describe the considerable phonological variation in Upper Tanana, which could make standardization desirable.

In all my work on this language I made the decision to honor variation at the expense of standardization. The late Mrs. Cora H. David pronounced the word for 'fish' variably as [ɬuːg], [ɬuːgə], or [ɬuːgŋ]—I spell this as *ɬuug*, *ɬuuge*, or *ɬuugn*. Her husband Mr. Roy H. David Sr. strongly denasalizes nasal consonants—I spell the word for 'man' *dindeh* in transcriptions of his recordings, but *dineh* in hers. Several speakers weaken final /j̊/ to [h]—thus I may spell 'be saved' as *shyiyh* in one instance and as *shyih* in the next. I also represent dialect differences as accurately as possible, writing 'my older brother' as *shoondaa* in a text from Tetlin, but as *shǫǫnüü* in a text from Northway.

While standardization has some benefits—not least the ability to look up words in a dictionary—it can lead to a mismatch between the orthographic representation of a word and its actual pronunciation in a given instance, which makes deciphering a text harder for language learners. But most importantly standardization would require that I make a decision of which phonological variant is the "standard," implying that all other variants are nonstandard and offending both speakers and learners in the process. I do not feel that I have the necessary understanding of Upper Tanana varieties to make this type of decision, but even if I did, I do not think it is my place to do so.

12.3. Summary

In this chapter the different writing systems of Upper Tanana are described. There are three systems: the one developed by Reverend Paul Milanowski in the 1960s, the one developed by the ANLC in the 1990s, and a modification of the ANLC system by the YNLC. In this grammar I use the ANLC system with one minor modification. I also briefly explain my preference for the documentation of variation over standardization.

Notes

1. In tables 12.1 and 12.2 I refer to the orthographies by the name or the institution that developed them. "Milanowski" refers to the system used in Milanowski and John (1979); "ANLC" refers to the system used in Tyone (1996); and YNLC refers to that used by in Yukon Native Language Centre (2009).
2. In this initial report on a literacy workshop, Leer (1974) writes high tone rather than low tone; he of course changed his analysis in subsequent documents.

Part III

Lexical categories

13 Nouns

Upper Tanana nouns can be defined structurally, distributionally, and semantically. Structurally they are words that can be inflected for possession. Distributionally they can head noun phrases that serve as arguments of a clause or postposition. Semantically they refer to concepts that are relatively stable over time such as humans, animals, places, objects, or abstract entities.

Nouns consist minimally of a root. As observed by Edward Sapir (1923, 141) in comparative Dene work, the formal distinction between "verb stems" and "noun stems" is often tenuous; the same root may be used to form noun or verb stems. Some examples are presented in (149); this is not an inclusive list. All noun stems in this list are free, while all verb stems are bound.

(149) Noun and verb stems from same root

	Noun stem		*Verb stem*	
a.	chą̨ą̨	'rain'	chą̨ą̨	'rain'
b.	ch'oh	'quills'	ch'oh	'have hurt feelings'
c.	dzee, dzeek	'pitch, spruce gum'	dzeek	'caulk, smear with pitch'
d.	giat	'aufeis'	giat	'freeze and overflow'
e.	kon'	'fire'	kon'	'get warm'
f.	kuyh	'vomit'	kuyh	'vomit'
g.	łoh	'fish hook'	łoh	'fish with fish hook'
h.	mbah	'warrior'	mbaa	'fight'
i.	t'iah	'charcoal'	t'ia	'roast'
j.	tsayh	'ochre'	tsayh	'paint with ochre'

Noun stems may also be derived by (overt) suffixes and prefixes (13.2). There are some disyllabic noun stems that are synchronically unanalyzable (13.3). Nouns may also be formed by compounding, i.e., by concatenation of more than one stem (13.4). Many nouns are derived from verbs (13.5). A few nouns have been borrowed from Russian, French, English, and indigenous languages of Alaska (13.6). The inflectional properties of nouns are discussed in chap. 22. The structure of noun phrases and their functions within the clause are described in volume 2.

13.1. Stem nouns

Upper Tanana has a large number of monosyllabic noun stems consisting merely of a root and no further affixes. (Rice [1989, 161], discussing Slave, analyzes this as a suffixation with -Ø). These are often called "stem nouns" in the literature. A small sample of stem nouns is presented in (150); this list is not inclusive. Nouns of this type usually denote ancient concepts including words for animals and plants, landscape features, traditional technology, weather, celestial bodies, and so forth.

(150) Stem nouns

a. saa 'sun'
b. dziin 'day'
c. mänh 'lake'
d. nän' 'earth'
e. ddhäł 'mountain'
f. tthee 'rock'
g. tuu 'water'
h. shoh 'black bear'
i. tsa' 'beaver'
j. tl'oh 'grass'
k. jiyh 'mittens'
l. 'aayh 'snowshoe'
m. thüh 'belt'
n. xį̨ąh 'raft'

13.2. Affixed stems

Both suffixation and prefixation play a role in noun formation. Some affixes have a clear semantic contribution; others are bleached of meaning.

13.2.1. Suffixed stems

There are three noun stem formative suffixes: the nominalizing suffix -v, the instrumental suffix *-ł*, and the inalienable suffix -'. None of these suffixes are productive.

13.2.1.1. Suffix -v Some nouns have an obligatory suffix -v, which creates a heavy stem syllable (see chap. 11). Cognates of this suffix are mentioned in

Leer (1996c) for Gwich'in and Rice (1989) for Slave. Both authors treat it as a historical nominalizing suffix that is no longer productive in modern languages. A sample of nouns containing this suffix is given in (151). In almost all cases no unsuffixed forms are attested in the language. The exceptions are (151g, h): *shyinh* is the verb stem 'make magic IPV'; *ts'iik* is the verb stem 'be sick IPV'.

(151) Noun stems derived with -v

a.	ddhuugn	'favorite child'
b.	dlegn (N), dlag (T)	'tree squirrel'
c.	jign	'berry'
d.	łuugn	'fish'
e.	tudn (N), tudi (T)	'bald eagle'
f.	shyin	'medicine, medicine song'
g.	ts'iign	'sickness, pain'

13.2.1.2. Suffix *-ł* Many nouns denoting tools or instruments contain a historical *-ł* suffix with an instrumental meaning (this suffix was originally described by Li [1956] for Dëne Sųłiné; see also Rice [1989, 163] for Slave or Kari [1990, 262] for Ahtna). In contemporary Upper Tanana this suffix is not productive. (152) contains a fairly inclusive list of nouns derived with *-ł*. For the nouns in (152a–e) a related unsuffixed stem exists in the language. The nouns in (152f–k) possibly also contain this suffix, but since no related unsuffixed stems are attested, this cannot be stated with certainty.

(152) Noun stems derived with *-ł*

a.	teeł	'mat'	tee	'handle AO s. sleep'
b.	tl'uuł	'rope'	tl'uu	'tie'
c.	tsiił	'bridge, weir'	tsįį	'make SG.O'
d.	nihtsįįł	'subterranean house'	tsįį	'make SG.O'
e.	xeeł	'pack'	xee	'pack'
f.	'eeł	'trap'	eeł	'trap'
g.	gąął	'snare'		
h.	mįįł	'moose snare'		
i.	säł	'gaff hook'		
j.	tthäł	'awl'		
k.	theeł	'box'		

13.2.1.3. Suffix -' Many obligatorily possessed nouns referring to body parts contain the inalienable possessive suffix -'. Holton (2000, 143) observes that in closely related Tanacross, the inalienable possessive suffix does not voice stem-final consonants; in Upper Tanana it sometimes does and sometimes does not (see chap. 22.2.1.2). It always modifies the stem tone.

(153) contains a small selection of stems containing the inalienable possessive suffix. The unsuffixed root is also given if it is attested elsewhere in the language (e.g., as incorporated root, part of a compound, or part of a prefixed stem). Tone is indicated in (153) to show the effects of the suffix. All stems and roots in (153) are bound. The suffixed stems are restricted to the possessive construction (see chap. 22); the unsuffixed roots occur either as incorporates or as part of complex noun stems.

(153) Noun stems derived with -’

	Suffixed		*Unsuffixed*	
a.	-nààgn’	‘eye’	naak-	‘eye’
b.	-tthì’	‘head’	tthi(i)-	‘head’
c.	-xà’	‘hair’	xa-	‘hair’
d.	-dà’	‘beak’	da-	‘mouth’
e.	-kè’	‘foot’	ke-, ki-	‘foot’
f.	-dzììt	‘inner ear’	dzii-	‘hearing’
g.	-dzììdn’	‘moose gut, bible’	dziit	‘?’, ch’indziit ‘bumblebee’
h.	-xə̀l’	‘leg’		

13.2.2. Prefixed stems

There is a large number of nouns consisting of a prefix and a stem. The most common prefixes in noun formation are listed in the following sections.

13.2.2.1. Prefix *ch’*- The indefinite possessor prefix *ch’*- is commonly used as a derivational prefix. It contributes no meaning. The list in (154) is not inclusive. The nouns in (154a, b) consist of the indefinite possessor prefix *ch’*- and the root. (154c, d) additionally contain the nominalizing suffix -v discussed in 13.2.1.1, and (154e–g) contain the inalienable possessive suffix -’ discussed in 13.2.1.3. (154h, i) may contain the instrumental suffix *-ł* described in 13.2.1.2.

(154) Noun stems derived with *ch’*-

	Noun stem		*Related stem*	
a.	ch’i’än	‘shelter, cave’	’än (*n.*)	‘den’
b.	ch’idzik	‘wild chives’		
c.	ch’igugn	‘fork’		
d.	ch’itth’ąy	‘mosquito’		

e.	ch'i'el'	'placenta, afterbirth'	P+eł (*pp.*)	'with P'
f.	ch'inayy'	'mushroom'		
g.	ch'ixia'	'egg'	xia (*v.*)	'round'
h.	ch'itįįł	'can, container, coffin'		
i.	ch'inch'aał	'snowshoe footstrap'		

13.2.2.2. Prefix *įį-*, *ii-* Several obligatorily possessed noun stems contain a prefix *įį-* or *ii-*. The list in (155) is fairly complete. Some of these stems additionally contain the inalienable possessive suffix -'.

(155) Nouns derived with *įį-*, *ii-*

a.	-iinįį'	'thinking'	nįį- 'mind' (*inc.*)
b.	-įįnįį'	'face'	
c.	-įįtsįį	'nose'	tsįhxüü' 'snot' (lit.: 'nose pus')
d.	-įįchil'	'ridge nose'	
e.	-ingǫǫł	'nostrils'	tsįhgǫǫł 'nostrils'
f.	-įįła', -iła'	'hand'	ła- 'hand' (*inc.*)
g.	-iixąą', -inxąą'	'hump'	-tthiixąą' 'brain'

13.2.2.3. Prefix *hu-* The areal possessor prefix *hu-* is also used as a derivational prefix. It is not very common in Upper Tanana; the list given in (156) seems to be inclusive.

(156) Nouns derived with *hu-*

a.	hunik	'news'	nek (N), nak (T) 'speak'
b.	hutsäł	'moisture'	tsäł 'be moist'
c.	huhttheen	'pubescent person'	thįį 'observe puberty rites IPV'

13.2.2.4. Prefix *ǫǫ-*, *oo-* Some nouns are derived using the prefix *ǫǫ-* or *oo-*. The list in (157) seems to be complete. The meaning of *ǫǫ-* or *oo-* cannot be determined based on these few examples, but it is noticeable that all of these are abstract concepts, which suggests that the areal prefix may be involved, as well as possibly the formative *įį-* described in 13.2.2.2. All of these nouns are obligatorily possessed and contain the inalienable possessive suffix -'.

(157) Nouns derived with *ǫǫ-*, *oo-*

a.	-ǫǫk'ją'	'reflection, soul'		
b.	-ǫǫsį'	'name'	si'	'call o's name, read'
c.	-ǫǫshyign'	'picture'	shyiign	'shadow'
d.	-oonįį'	'mind'	nii-	'mind' (*inc.*)
e.	-ooniign'	'news'	nek (N), nak (T)	'speak'

13.2.2.5. Adverbial prefixes Several adverbial prefixes typically associated with the formation of directional adverbs (see chap. 17) or motion verbs (see chap. 25.2.1 and 35) are also used in noun derivation.[1] (158–160) are fairly inclusive for the three adverbial prefixes involved in noun formation. (158) illustrates noun stems derived via the adverbial prefix *dah-* 'up' (in verbs, it usually has the form *da-*). (159) contains noun stems derived by *teh-* 'underwater' (in verbs, this prefix usually has the form *ti-*). (160) contains the only noun derived by the adverbial prefix *tth'i-* 'straight', which has the same form when occurring in verbs. There may be other adverbial prefixes involved in noun derivation.

(158) Nouns derived with *dah-* 'up'

a.	dahmįįł	'baby swing'	mįįł	'snare'
b.	dahdzäł	'drying rack'	dzäł	'?'
c.	dahshyit	'roof, tarpaulin'	shyiit	'down there'
d.	dahshyüü'	'branch snow'	shyüh	'snow'
e.	dahtsaa	'cache'	tsaa	'bury, cache'

(159) Nouns derived with *teh-* underwater'

a.	tehmįįł	'drag net'	mįįł	'snare'
b.	tehtl'ąy	'water spear'		
c.	tehtsaa'	'predaceous diving beetle'	'tsa'	'beaver'
d.	tehts'ogn	'spruce in water'	ts'ǫǫ	'spruce'
e.	tehts'ǫǫdn	'mink'		

(160) Nouns derived with *tth'i-* 'straight'

a. tth'itu' 'river' tuu 'water'

13.2.2.6. Prefix *n-* The prefix *n-* is a common noun formative. According to Kari (1990, 285), it is related to the *n-* qualifier, which denotes small, round entities—clearly an apt description for many of the entities denoted by the nouns in (161). This list is fairly inclusive. (161a–g) consist of just the *n-* prefix and a stem; (161h–l) also contain the indefinite prefix *ch'-* discussed in 13.2.2.1.

(161) Nouns derived with *n-*

a.	nkaał (U)	'salmonberry'		
b.	ntl'ät	'lowbush cranberry'		
c.	nchǫǫ	'rosehip'		
d.	nłuut	'unripe berries, hail'	łuut	'ice'
e.	ntsį̨ą	'otter'	nahtsį̨ą	'wolverine'

f.	ndzäl'	'canvasback'		
g.	ndziił	'flicker'		
h.	ch'indziit	'bumblebee'	-dziit	'moose gut, bible'
i.	ch'įįk'onn'	'dentalium'		
j.	ch'inxät	'fine snow shoe webbing'		
k.	ch'inxoh	'soapberries'		
l.	ch'intthe'	'seed'	tthee	'rock' ?

13.2.2.7. Prefix *di-* Another common derivational prefix, or set of prefixes, is *di-*. (162) contains nouns derived using a *di-* prefix that seems to be related to the *d-* qualifier, which marks gender of nouns to do with wood or skin (see chap. 30.4). This list is fairly inclusive.

(162) Nouns derived with *di-* (I)

a.	dichinh	'stick'		
b.	ditl'uun	'calico, canvas'	-tl'uu	'tie'
c.	-diła'	'branch tips'	-ła'	'hand'

(163) contains nouns derived via a different prefix of the same form (semantically, it is unlikely that this *di-* is related to the *d-* qualifier).[2] This prefix is very productive.

(163) Nouns derived with *di-* (II)

a.	dibee	'sheep'
b.	dineh	'man, person'
c.	diniign	'moose'
d.	dishyüü	'cow moose'
e.	dits'än	'duck'
f.	dinayh	'bearberry'

13.2.2.8. Prefix *nah-*, *naa-* A number of nouns contain the prefix *nah-* or *naa-*.[3] A sample of noun stems formed with this prefix is given in (164); this list is not inclusive.

(164) Nouns derived with *nah-*, *naa-*

a.	nahtsį̨ą̨	'wolverine'	ntsį̨ą̨	'otter'
b.	nahdaa	'great grey owl'		
c.	naht'ia	'blackberry'		
d.	naagädn	'fox'		
e.	naadodn	'ant'		
f.	naatl'ädn	'bead'	tl'ät	'dark, dark blue'

g. naaxąy 'frog' xąy 'croak'
h. naambah 'war' mbah 'warrior, go to war'

13.2.2.9. Prefix *ni-*, *nii-*, *nih-* Nouns may also be derived using the derivational prefix *ni-*, *nii-* or *nih-*. The list in (165) is inclusive; it is possible that several different prefixes are combined here.

(165) Nouns derived with *ni-*, *nii- nih-*
 a. nichoon 'bull moose'
 b. niiduuy 'lynx'
 c. nihbaay 'weasel'
 d. nihchǫǫ (N) 'rosehip'
 e. nimbaał (shyah) 'shelter made with blankets'
 f. niitsįįł, nihtsįįł 'subterraneous house'

13.3. Other disyllabic stems

A small number of disyllabic stems do not contain any of the formatives described so far. A relatively complete inventory is given in (166). The nouns in (166a–d) are all indicators of social status, the nouns in (166e–k) are kinship terms (*łįįts'ee* 'female dog, bitch' in [166m] is included here because of its structural similarity to the preceding two nouns), and the nouns in (166m–p) describe human beings. The remaining nouns (166q–x) are names of animals, most of them birds. While this list contains the more common disyllabic stems, it is not inclusive.

(166) Disyllabic noun stems
 a. haskeh 'chief'
 b. ts'uttheet 'ancestors'
 c. huyaa'aat, kuy'aat 'rich person'
 d. xaashyaa 'widow'
 e. -ǫǫnüü, -ǫǫndaa (T) 'older brother'
 f. -aadeh 'older sister'
 g. -ee'eh 'maternal uncle'
 h. -aak'ay 'maternal aunt'
 i. -uudee 'cross cousin'
 j. -ełegn' 'partner, paternal relative'
 k. -beets'e' 'mother-in-law'
 l. -yaats'e' 'woman's daughter'
 m. łįįts'ee 'female dog, bitch'
 n. ts'exeh 'woman'

o.	ts'ist'e' (N, T)	'old lady'
p.	ts'enät (S)	'old lady'
q.	ts'iiniin	'child'
r.	ch'uudzüüdn	'horned owl'
s.	tthi'dzüüdn	'hawk owl'
t.	thuhshyiidn	'boreal owl'
u.	ts'uugaay	'bird'
v.	ts'igąąk	'chickadee'
w.	mbohk'ąąy	'sea gull'
x.	udzih	'caribou'

These stems are to some degree historically analyzable. The forms in (166h–q), for example, all contain a morpheme *ts'e(e)(')*, which Leer (1996a) reconstructs as *tš̌'ʳe 'female', and the nouns in (166r, t) share a stem reconstructed as *džʳa·džʳ 'matted, tangled'. In contemporary Upper Tanana, however, these morphemes are neither productive nor transparent to speakers; thus I treat them as unanalyzable disyllabic stems.

13.4. Compound nouns

Compound nouns consist of two or more lexical stems. Compounds may consist of two nouns, or of a noun followed by a verb stem, a modifier, or a postposition.

Spelling of compounds in Upper Tanana is irregular. Most compounds are spelled as separate words, while others are spelled as one word. Given the low native-language literacy, it does not seem to be a priority at the moment to attempt to standardize compound spelling. In the following sections, the spelling in Kari (1997b) is followed.

13.4.1. Noun + noun compounds

Compounds consisting of two or more nouns are very common. Two types can be distinguished: compounds where the two nouns are in a possessor relationship, (which is indicated by a possessive suffix on N_2), and compounds where the two nouns are not in a possessor relationship. (167) illustrates both types. In all words N_2 is *jign* 'berry'. In (167a–c) it occurs in the nonpossessed form but in (167d) the word for 'berry' occurs in its possessed form *jign'*. It is not clear what causes this difference (see in particular the contrast between [167c] and [167d], which are semantically quite similar).

(167) a. *nän jign*
earth berry
'bog cranberry'

b. *xay jign*
winter berry
'silverberry'

c. *łįį jign*
dog berry
'soapberry'

d. *shoh jign'*
bear berry:POSS
'northern black currant'

The two types are described in the following sections.

13.4.1.1. Noun + noun:POSS (168) demonstrates noun-noun compounds where the two nouns are in a possessor relationship: N_1 possesses N_2. The formal marker of this construction is the possessive suffix on N_2. In all of these compounds N_2 serves as the head of the compound. This type of compounding is extremely productive.

(168) a. *tsąą' dąyy'*
excrement fly:POSS
'dung fly'

b. *dąy xia'*
fly egg:POSS
'fly eggs'

c. *tuh - t'aann'*
water - leaf:POSS
'water plant, moose food'

d. *thay tu'*
bottom.snow water:POSS
'snow water'

e. *ts'oo nayy'*
spruce mushroom:POSS
'spruce mushroom'

f. *tsät gų̨ų̨'*
wood worm:POSS
'wood worm'

g. *dits'än k'aa'*
duck gun:POSS
'shotgun'

h. *łoh shyi'*
hook meat:POSS
'fish bait'

i. *k'a' tthee'*
gun rock:POSS
'bullet'

j. *ts'iiniin shyiign'*
child shadow:POSS
'doll'

k. *łuut dzägn'*
ice ear:POSS
'moraine'

l. *stsǫǫ mį̨įl'*
1:SG:grandmother snare:POSS
'spiderweb'

m. *saa-mį̨įl'*
sun-snare:POSS
'rainbow'

Semantically, the compounds in (168) are diverse. (168a–h) are compositional; N_1 expresses a property, or possessor, of N_2 (note that the compounds in [168g, h] are lexicalized differently in English). In the compounds in (168i–k), N_1 also expresses a property or possessor of N_2, but semantic shift of N_2 has taken place; the 'bullet' in (168i) is so named because of the physical resemblance between bullets and rocks; the word *dzägn'* in (168k) refers to the shape of a moraine rather than to an actual ear, and so forth. In (168l, m) the meaning of the compounds is not predictable from its parts, and considerable semantic shift has taken place. (168l), for example, is an allusion to the Butterfly story, where one of the main characters is called *Tsǫǫ Kelahdzeey* 'my grandmother Spider'.

This type of compound cannot be possessed using the possessive morphology described in chap. 22. It is likely that this is an inflectional restriction, since the head of the compound already is morphologically (if not semantically) possessed.

13.4.1.2. Noun + noun There is also a (smaller) number of noun-noun compounds where the two nouns are not in a possessor relationship (169). In these compounds the nouns are simply juxtaposed, and N_2 does not bear the possessive suffix.

(169) a. *dlaat shyah*
moss house
'moss house'

b. *kon' k'eet*
fire cavity
'(abandoned) campsite'

c. *tuu-tįįł*
water-container
'cup'

d. *t'uu thüh*
breast pouch
'bra'

e. *ddhäł ts'igąągn*
mountain chickadee
'boreal chickadee'

f. *tl'ų̈ų̈h tįįł*
leech container
'land snail'

It is not entirely clear whether (169a) is unpossessed, since the possessed form of N_2 *shyah* 'house' is identical to its unpossessed form. All other nouns in (169) do have corresponding possessed forms that exhibit the typical word-final glottal stop and (in the tonal dialects) low tone (see chap. 22).

Semantically all but (169f) are quite transparent, with N_1 expressing a property, or purpose, of N_2. These compounds also clearly are right-headed (again, with the exception of [169f]).

This type of compound can be possessed using the possessive morphology described in chap. 22 (170).

(170) *shtuutįįl'*
sh-tuutįįł-v'
1SG.PSR-cup-POSS
'my cup' UTOLAF14Nov2001:003

13.4.2. Noun + verb

Noun + verb compounds consist of a noun stem followed by a verb stem, which often but not always, bears the nominalizing suffix. This type of compounding is extremely common; there are hundreds of nouns with this structure. A small selection is presented in (171).

(171) a. *k'ąy' ch'idn*
willow strong:NOM
'twisted willow, diamond willow'

b. *naagät sąy*
fox black:NOM
'silver fox'

c. *tuu-thäł*
water-hot
'broth, soup'

d. *tth'itu' biat*
river shiny
'large gull'

e. *che-l-nia*
tail-?-long(:NOM?)
'long-tailed mouse'

f. *taa-ch'il*
water-rip:NOM
'kingfisher'

The compounds in (171a–c) are semantically transparent but left-headed with the verb stem modifying the nominal head. (171d–f) are exocentric and instead evoke typical images: gulls on a river reflect the light, the vole described in (171e) has indeed a very long tail, and (171f) describes the motion made by the kingfisher when diving for fish.

Note that the verb stem is sometimes nominalized (171a, b, f) and sometimes not (171c, d) (in the case of [171e], it is impossible to tell whether the verb stem is nominalized).

The origin of these compounds is phrasal; bare or nominalized verb stems are frequently part of complex noun phrases (see volume 2 for more discussion).

13.4.3. Noun + modifier compounds

Noun compounds may also consist of a noun plus a modifier (see chap. 18.2 for more information on modifiers). As pointed out by Lovick and Rice (2015), these compounds are of phrasal origin and could alternatively be viewed as nouns with a derivational evaluative affix that is derived from the modifier. Some examples are given in (172) and (173). Note that within each set of words, the meanings become progressively more lexicalized.

(172) a. *naadodn choh*
ant big
'carpenter ant'

b. *jǫǫ choh*
camprobber big
'goshawk'

c. *Dziin Choh*
day big
'Christmas'

(173) a. *ts'iiniin gaay*
child small
'baby'

b. *łįį-gaay*
dog-small
'puppy'

c. *dzänh gaay*
muskrat small
'whirligig' (insect)

Noun + modifier compounds can be morphologically possessed. The possessive morphology then attaches to the stem of the head noun, not to the modifier.

(174) *shch'įįtįįl' choh*
sh-ch'įįtįįł-v' *choh*
1:SG.PSR-can-POSS big
'my coffee can' UTOLVDN10Jul2724:071

13.4.4. Noun + postposition compounds

Nouns may also be formed by compounding a noun with a postposition (175).

(175) a. *chin-shyiit*
stick-inside
'pole cache, high cache'

b. *taa-maagn*
water-edge
'lake shore'

c. *xał-ts'ą̈'*
darkness-toward
'evening'

d. *dziin shyiit*
day inside
'Sunday'

e. *tsäł shyii*
brush inside
'woods man'

This type of compound is relatively rare; (175) contains more than half of the examples found in Kari (1997b). They are semantically transparent yet morphologically exocentric.

These noun + postposition compounds have nominal distribution, e.g., the compound *chinshyiit* 'pole cache' can function as the direct object (176a) or postpositional object (176b).

(176) a. *Dii hiitaa'aal chinshyiit datnehdok.* (T)
what 3PL>3SG:eat:IPV:NOM pole.cache 3SG:stuff.into.INC:PFV
'He stuffed the pole cache [with] food.'
UTOLAF13May2403:078

b. … *chinshyiit shyiit <łahtthegn nts'ą̈'> dahiinįįdlah.* (N)
cache in all 3PL>3PL:put.PL.O.up:PFV
'… they brought it all up into the cache.'
UTOLVDN13May2003:046

13.4.5. Compounding as a recursive process

Compounding is a highly productive and recursive process. Some examples for recursion are given in (177).

(177) a. *jign tu' thäł*
berry water:POSS pants
'jeans' (lit.: 'berry juice pants')

b. *ch'idzaa thüh kee*
INDF:upright.pole skin footwear
'caribou legging mukluks' (lit. 'legbone skin footwear')

While complex compounds like those in (177) are possible, they are relatively rare in natural speech.

13.5. Deverbal nouns

Deverbal nouns consist of fully inflected verb forms plus the nominalizing suffix -v (see chap. 37). They are formally indistinguishable from relative clauses, but unlike relative clauses, they serve as arguments of a clause. (178a) illustrates a relative clause '[the ones] that had been dried' modifying *ch'ithüh* 'skins'. In (178b–d), nominalized forms function as arguments of the main clause: the one in (178b) is a subject in canonical position, the one in (178c) is a subject in postposed position, and the one in (178d) functions as direct object.

(178) a. *Ch'ithüh nelgąy ditthi' k'et*
INDF:skin 3PL:be.dry:PFV:NOM REFL:head on
daheedlak nts'ą'… (T)
3PL:have.PL.O.up:IPV:CUST and
'They kept dried skins over their heads…'
UTOLAF09Jun2402:008

b. *Hugn nan' k'it t'oo nishyeey hugn t'eey*
there earth on even 3PL:grow:IPV:NOM there even
na'etk'an' nts'ą'. (T)
3PL:burn:IT:PFV and
'Even things growing on the land were burning.'
UTOLAF09Jun2402:004

c. *Ndee nts'ą' hihteenah needach'įįxaan*
where to 3PL:move:INC:PFV INDF>1PL:kill.PL.O.off:PFV:NOM
iin du'... (T)
PL CT
'Where did they go, the ones who killed us off...'
UTOLAF13May2403:102

d. ... *jee'aan diitth'ak.* (T)
3SG:sing:IPV:NOM 3SG:hear:IPV
'... he heard singing.' UTOLAF08Apr2804:002

Based on the argument structure of the underlying verb, several different types of nominalization can be distinguished: subject nominalization (13.5.1), direct object nominalization (13.5.2), and postpositional object nominalization (13.5.3). Deverbal nouns also may be part of compounds (13.5.4).

Nominalization of verbs is a very common, productive noun formation process that is used extensively in creating words denoting objects of acculturation. Some of them are nonce-formations, others have become lexicalized.

13.5.1. Subject nominalization

Deverbal nouns formed by subject nominalization usually have the meaning 'the one that *verbs*'. They can be formed from intransitive (179) or transitive (180) verbs.

(179) a. *dǫǫ ehts'ay* (T)
upriver:ABL 3SG:be.windy:IPV:NOM
'north wind' (lit. 'the one that is windy from upriver')
UTOLAF09Jun2404:004

b. *tuu dzina'įįłąy* (N)
water 3SG:flow.down.over.edge:PFV:NOM
'waterfall' (lit. 'water flowing down over the edge')
UTOLAF12Jul1201:049

c. *nanetshyeey* *iin* (T)
3PL:grow:IT:IPV:NOM PL
'the new generation' (lit. 'the ones growing now')
UTOLAF07Nov2602:008

d. *neldzeegn* (T)
3SG:be.bright:IPV:NOM
'lamp' (lit. 'the bright thing') UTOLAF15May0608:060

(180) a. *dide'* *na'eldeel*
REFL:horns 3SG:eat.PL:IPV:NOM
'long-horned beetle' (lit. 'the one that eats its own horns') Kari (1997b)

b. *k'ahtsäl* *aałeel*
spoon 3SG:handle.PL.O:IPV:PROG:NOM
'2-3 year old bull moose' (lit. 'the one who carries around spoons')
Kari (1997b)

c. *ch'įįttheel*
3SG>INDF:chop:PFV:NOM
'woodpecker' (lit. 'the one who chops something') Kari (1997b)

When subject nominalizations contain a free noun phrase (179b; 180a, b), the noun phrase is interpreted as coreferential with the absolutive argument.

13.5.2. Direct object nominalization

Direct object nominalizations can be formed only from transitive verbs. They are fairly rare (Holton [2000, 139] states that they do not exist at all in Tanacross) and usually have the meaning 'the one that S *verbs*'.

(181) a. *xay* *tah* *nadzelshyaagn* (T)
winter when 1PL:carry.around.PL.O:IPV:CUST:NOM
'winter parkas' (lit. 'what we wear in winter')
UTOLVDN07Nov2803:031

b. *dii* *tah'aal* (T)
whatever 2PL:eat:FUT:NOM
'your PL food' (lit. 'what you PL will eat')
UTOLAF07Nov2602:023

A special case of direct object nominalization are deverbal nouns derived from verbs that have been passivized (182) (see chap. 27.3.2.1.1 for more information).

(182) a. *ch'utkeed* *dą'* (T)
INDF:buy:PASS:IPV:NOM at
'store' (lit. 'where things are bought') UTOLAF12Jul0701:009

b. *dettl'oon* (T)
3SG:weave:IPV:NOM
'canvas' (lit. 'the thing that has been woven')
UTOLAF09Jun2902:005

13.5.3. Postpositional object nominalization

Deverbal nouns formed from postpositional object nominalization are very common, particularly in naming objects of acculturation. They usually can be translated as 'the thing with which S *verbs*'.

(183) a. *uk'e* *dats'edaag* (dialect unknown)
3SG:on IMPSL:SG.sit.on:IPV:CUST:NOM
'chair' (lit. 'the thing one sits on') Kari (1997b)

b. *meh* *dzelxoo* (T)
3SG:with IMPSL:play:IPV:NOM
'toys' (lit. 'things one plays with') Cora David (2011, 38)

c. *meh* *nats'elmoo* (N)
3SG:with IMPSL:roll.around:IPV:NOM
'truck' (lit. 'the thing one rolls around with')
UTOLAF09Aug12:005

d. *hiishyiit* *dal'iad* (T)
3PL>3SG:in step:PFV:NOM
'their footwear' (lit. 'the thing they step into')
UTOLVDN07Nov2804:008

Postpositional object nominalizations have usually *ts'*- as a subject prefix (183a–c). In those cases *ts'*- has its (original) function of an impersonal subject prefix rather than the much more common function of marking first-person plural subject (see chap. 31.1.3.1.4 for discussion of the impersonal subject prefix). Evidence for this comes from (183a), where the singular stem for sitting is used.

13.5.4. Deverbal nouns in compounds

Given that both compounding and nominalization are very productive processes, it is not surprising that they work together to create new words. The deverbal noun always acts as N_1 of noun-noun compounds.

(184) a. *hooniideey* *shyah* (dialect unknown)
3PL:pray:IPV:NOM house
'church' (lit. 'praying house') Kari (1997b)

b. *ch'utkeed* *dą'* (N)
INDF:buy:PASS:IPV:NOM at
'store' (lit. 'where things are bought')
UTOLVDN07Nov2804:016

c. *naxanelshyee* *saa* (U)
3SG:hair.grow:IT:IPV:NOM month
'August-September' (lit. 'hair growing back month') Kari (1997b)

13.6. Loanwords

There is a small number of loanwords in Upper Tanana. Many of these have been recorded by Kari in the 1980s and 1990s but seem to be no longer in use. All loanwords refer to objects of acculturation, i.e., items that white people brought with them when colonizing Alaska and the Canadian Northwest.

In spite of its brief colonial history Upper Tanana contains loanwords from three European languages. Loanwords from Russian probably came into the language via Ahtna, since the Russian fur traders never visited the Upper Tanana area. About half of the Russian loanwords recorded by Kari (1997b) are still in use; these are bolded in (185). The Russian word is included where it is identifiable; ? signals that the Russian word is uncertain.

(185) Loanwords from Russian

a.	'tobacco'	**lasgih**	laskoviy	'tender, pleasing'
b.	'butter'	**baslah**	maslo	'butter'
c.	'tea'	**tseey**	chay	'tea'
d.	'teapot'	**tseeyniik**	chaynik	teapot
e.	'devil'	**yaambäl**	d'yavol	'devil'
f.	'playing cards'	galdas	karta	'cards'
g.	'coffee'	gahtthay	kofe	'coffee'
h.	'cross'	jeliis	krest	'cross'

i. 'credit' keel ?
j. 'frying pan' keemän ?

French loanwords probably reached the Upper Tanana in a similarly indirect fashion as Russian words—although Francophone fur traders from Canada made it as far west as to enter traditional Gwich'in, Slave, and Tłįchǫ territory, they did not visit the Upper Tanana area themselves. Most loanwords from French include the French definite article *le* or *la*, which surfaces either as /l/ (more common in Tetlin) or /n/ (more common in Northway). The bolded French loanwords in (186) are used commonly.

(186) Loanwords from French

a.	'tea'	**ndil, ldil**	le thé
b.	'key'	**ndlen, ldlin**	la clé
c.	'money'	**nsüü, lsüü**	l'argent
d.	'sugar, pop'	**tsǫǫgąy'**	(le) sucre
e.	'salt'	lseel	le sel

Direct contact with English began in the late nineteenth century. None of the words in (187) are used any longer. When discussing objects of acculturation, Upper Tanana speakers are more likely to do one-word code-switches into English, which differ from loanwords in that they are not phonologically integrated into Upper Tanana; speakers will say *clock* rather than *dlak*.

(187) Loanwords from English

a.	**kut**	'coat'
b.	eemen	'amen'
c.	dlak	'clock'
d.	sdoo	'stove'
e.	sdoogin	'stocking'
f.	silek	'silk'
g.	sool	'salt'
h.	xoos	'horse'

The only exception to this is *kut* in (187a), which is not only integrated phonologically (the English diphthong /͡ɔʊ/ is changed to the short monophthong [ʊ], a common realization of Upper Tanana /u/) but also may occur with possessive morphology (188):

(188) … *shkud' t'eey idhagndaa.* (T)

sh-kud' *t'eey* *i-dhag-ndaa*
1SG.PSR-coat:POSS ADVZR PP-DH.PFV:1SG.S:L-forget:PFV
'… I forgot my coat.' UTCBAF13Nov1510:018

Even though all neighboring groups of the Upper Tanana are Dene, there are a few loanwords from non-Dene indigenous languages of Alaska. It is likely that they came into the language via contact with the Ahtna; certainly all of these words (as well as their origin) can be found in Kari (1990). Only the first of these occurs in my data; the others are cited following Kari (1997b).

(189) Loan words from Alaskan Native languages

a.	'fermented fish'	**dzinah**	cin'aq (Alutiiq)	'fermented fish' (Kari 1990, 173)
b.	'abalone button'	yuxaa	guha (Tlingit)	'abalone' (Kari 1990, 188)
c.	'window'	yalo	gaaleq (Alutiiq)	'window' (Kari 1990, 435)

13.7. Summary

In this chapter noun formation is described. Stem nouns consist of merely a root without any affixes; these nouns are always monosyllabic. There are also nouns consisting of a stem and a stem formative; some of these are suffixes, some are prefixes. Suffixed nouns are monosyllabic, while prefixed ones are disyllabic. There are also disyllabic nouns with less clear structure; these are treated as unanalyzable here. Both compounding and nominalization are highly productive processes. There are several types of compounds in Upper Tanana. Noun + noun compounds are right-headed, while noun + verb compounds are left-headed or exocentric and of phrasal origin. Noun + postposition compounds are exocentric. Deverbal nouns are common. Based on the argument structure of the verb theme, subject nominalizations, direct object nominalizations, and postpositional object nominalizations can be distinguished. Upper Tanana also has a small number of loanwords from Russian, French, English, and other indigenous languages of Alaska; most of these loanwords are no longer used.

Notes

1. Kari (1990) treats cognate nouns as compounds; since the morphemes are, however, clearly affixes, I prefer to treat them as derived nouns.
2. Kari (1990, 147) classifies cognate nouns as compounds, but since no meaning of this element can be identified, I treat it as a derivational prefix.
3. Kari (1990, 292) states that the Ahtna morpheme *na-* occurs in compounds but does not give a meaning for this morpheme and admits that it may derive from "distinct roots or affixes." Since no meaning can be identified for this morpheme in Upper Tanana, I treat it as a derivational prefix.

14 Verbs

Upper Tanana verbs can be defined in several ways. Structurally, they are words that can be inflected for conjugation and mode. Distributionally, they head predicative or attributive verb phrases. Semantically, verbs describe events or states.

14.1. Structure

Almost all verb forms in Upper Tanana are morphologically complex. The verb structure can be represented with the template in table 14.1. Morphemes required in all verb forms are bolded; a verb form thus minimally consists of five morphemes (six if the verb is transitive).

12	11	10	9	8	7	#	**6**	5	**4**	**3**	**2**	**1**	**0**	-1
Postpositional object	Postposition	Adverbial-derivational	Iterative	Incorporate	Distributive	– Disjunct boundary –	**Pronominal**	Qualifier	**Conjugation**	**Mode**	**Subject**	**Voice/valence**	**Stem**	Suffix

Table 14.1. The Upper Tanana verb, represented as a template

The basic lexical unit of the verb is the verb theme, which consists of often discontinuous morphemes including minimally the voice/valence marker and a verb stem, and optionally additional prefixes. Verb themes are obligatorily inflected for subject (marked either in position 2 [190a, d] or in position 6 [190b, c]), mode (position 3), and conjugation (position 4). Transitive verbs (190c) are additionally inflected for direct object (position 6), and verb themes containing an incorporated postposition (190d) for postpositional object (position 12). There are no nonfinite verb forms.[1]

(190) a. *uhtsüü* (N)
uh-tsüü
OPT:1SG.S:Ø-cry:OPT
'I want to cry, feel like crying' UT Notebook #3, 69

b. *hįįtsia'* (N)
hįį-tsia'
3PL.S:AA.PFV:Ø-cry:PFV
'they cried' UT Notebook #3, 70

c. *shigot* (N)
sh-i-got
1SG.O-3SG.S:I.PFV:Ø punch:PFV
's/he punched me' UT Notebook #3, 87

d. *hu'ich'ak'aał* (N)
hu-i-ch'ak-'aał
3PL.P-PP-INDF.O-:Ø.IPV:1SG.S:H-feed:IPV
'I am feeding them (something)' UT Notebook #3, 71

More information on verb morphology can be found in chap. 26–36.

14.2. Semantics

Upper Tanana verbs express events or states. The semantic distinction between events and states is reflected by the morphological distinction between active and neuter verbs.

14.2.1. Active verbs

Active verbs describe dynamic situations. Morphologically they are characterized by imperfective morphology in the imperfective mode—i.e., all imperfective forms of an active verb contain the imperfective prefix Ø-, regardless of conjugation marker (191).

(191) a. *ts'etnah* (N)
ts'et-nah
1PL.S:Ø.IPV:D-work:IPV
'we are working' UTOLAF14May0801:010

b. *danįįhaayh* (T)
da-nįį-haayh
inside-N.IPV:2SG.S:Ø-SG.go:IPV
'come in!' UTOLAF08Apr2805:068

c. *altthał* (T)
al-tthał
3SG.S:AA.IPV:L-SG.run:IPV:PROG
'ѕ/he is running' UTCBAF13Nov0501:153

14.2.2. Neuter verbs

Neuter verbs describe states and properties. They are characterized by perfective morphology in the imperfective mode, i.e., all semantically imperfective neuter verb forms contain the perfective prefix *į-* (which has the allomorph *n-*). This is most clearly visible in forms with a Ø- conjugation marker (192a, b) or a *n-* conjugation marker (192c). (192d) illustrates a neuter verb form requiring a *dh-* conjugation marker, which obscures the presence of the perfective prefix.

(192) a. *nsǫǫ* (N)
n-sǫǫ
3SG.S:Ø.PFV:Ø-be.good:IPV
'it is good' UTOLAF09Aug1201:013

b. *ts'įįtsuul* (T)
ts'įį-tsuul
1PL.S:Ø.PFV:Ø-be.small:IPV
'we are small' UTOLAF09Jun2901:001

c. *nįįłąyh* (N)
nįį-łąyh
3SG.S:N.PFV:Ø-flow:IPV
'it is flowing' UTCBVDN13Nov0804:045

d. *dhihdah* (T)
dhih-dah
DH.PFV:1SG.S:Ø-SG.sit:IPV
'I'm sitting' UTOLAF09Jun2902:009

Neuter verb themes may be intransitive or transitive.

The distinction between active and neuter verb themes, as well as a more fine-grained classification system of verb themes, is discussed in more detail in chap. 25.

14.3. Functions

Verbs head verb phrases, which have two primary functions: as predicates and as attributes of nouns.

14.3.1. Verb phrases as predicates

Verb phrases usually function as predicates. Since all verb forms are inflected for subject (and many for direct or postpositional object), a single verb form may be a complete clause as shown in (193a), although clauses may of course be more complex than that (193b–d).

(193) a. *Hu'idatdeemaak,* *I know.* (N)
3sg>3pl:fight.verbally:inc:pfv I know
'She bawled them out, I know.' UTOLVDN07Aug2205:119

b. *Ay ch'a ch'udzüüt, ch'udzüüt gaay haniit'ak ay eh.* (N)
and foc boreal.owl boreal.owl small 3sg:sg.fly.out:pfv and
'And then a small boreal owl flew out.'
UTOLVDN07Aug2205:009

c. … *shįłaa eh ch'ixia' kah nadagnnay.* (N)
1sg:hand with indf:eggs for 1sg:feel.around:pfv:nom
'… I felt with my hands around for eggs.'
UTOLVDN07Aug2205:012

d. *Tl'oh tah ts'änh jah ch'ixia' ts'uudiidlay,*
grass in from here indf:eggs 1pl:find.pl.o:pfv:nom
dits'än xia'. (N)
duck eggs
'In the grass we found eggs, ducks' eggs.'
UTOLVDN07Aug2205:005

14.3.2. Verb phrases as attributes

Verb phrases also are used as attributes in noun phrases. They are always nominalized in this construction. Not surprisingly, neuter verbs expressing property concepts are particularly common in this function (194a, b), but active verbs (then usually translated as relative clauses) also are used in this fashion (194c).

(194) a. *Ay t'eey ch'a dineh hǫǫshyaan huk'eh*
and even FOC man 3SG:be.smart:IPV:NOM 3PL:following
natedaak... (T)
3SG:SG.go.around:IPV:CUST
'And that smart man followed them around...'
UTOLVDN07Oct2604:020

b. *That ch'iik'on k'it tthee deldliad eh t'eey*
that necklace on rock 3SG:be.bright:IPV:NOM with ADVZR
uk'it eedlah. (T)
3SG:on 3SG:classify.PL.O:IPV
'On that necklace was a bright stone.'
UTOLVDN13May2909:164

c. *"Naadeh dhelxiin du' niithaad t'eey*
2SG:older.sister 3SG:kill.SG.O:PASS:PFV:NOM CT long.time ADVZR
natnįl'įįł," yehnih. (T)
2SG:see:IT:FUT 3SG>3SG:say:IPV
'"It'll be a long time [before] you see your older sister again who was killed," she said to her.' UTOLVDN14Nov2301:537

14.4. Summary

In this chapter some properties of verbs are briefly discussed. Structurally, verbs are characterized by great morphological complexity. They are the only lexical category that can be inflected for conjugation and mode. Semantically, verbs express events or states. This semantic distinction corresponds to the morphological distinction between active and neuter verbs. Verbs function as heads of verb phrases. Verb phrases are usually used predicatively but can also be used attributively.

More information on the structure of verbs can be found in chap. 26–36. Their syntactic functions as well as their semantics are described in volume 2.

Notes

1. A few verb stems occur without inflection; they are interpreted as third-person imperfective forms. See chap. 24.6.2.

15 Free postpositions

In this chapter free postpositions are described. They can be distinguished from bound (thematic) postpositions, which are part of the verb theme and affect the verb theme's valency; see chap. 36. Free postpositions, on the other hand, are not part of the verb theme and do not affect its valency. The properties of free postpositions are described in 15.1. The bulk of this chapter contains an inventory of free postpositions (15.2). Many free postpositions may also serve as conjunctions and subordinators; these functions are mentioned briefly in the present chapter but are described in more detail in volume 2.

The free postposition plus its object together form a postpositional phrase. The postpositional object may be expressed through inflection, a free noun phrase, adverbial, or a clause. Postpositional inflection is described in chap. 23; the other types of postpositional objects are described in volume 2.

15.1. Properties

Free postpositions have the following characteristics that differentiate them from bound postpositions: (1) they may combine relatively freely with verb themes; (2) they can be separated from the verb theme; (3) in almost all cases the presence of a free postposition has no impact on the morphology of the verb through changes of conjugation marker or voice/valence prefix.

15.1.1. Compatibility with verb themes

Because free postpositions are not part of the verb theme, they are compatible with a great variety of verb themes. This is most pronounced in highly polysemous postpositions such as P+*xah, aa* 'for P, about P' and P+*eh, eł* 'with P' (see examples in 15.2.3.1 and 15.2.3.2, respectively), but is true for many spatial postpositions as well. P+*k'it* 'on P' combines frequently with motion (195a) and positional themes (195b) but can also be used with the descriptive theme in (195c) or the conversive-reversative theme in (195d).

(195) a. … *neek'it tatnaaxüü…* (T)
1PL:on 3SG:LRO.move.indepently:FUT
'… it is going to fall on us…' UTOLAF09Jun2202:040

b. … *ik'it shyi' eł neetsay shyi' diniign eł udzih*
3SG>3SG:on meat and bear meat moose and caribou
shyi' gah tah ik'it danetdog. (T)
meat rabbit too 3SG>3SG:on stuff.inside:PASS:IPV:NOM
'… and onto it were stuffed meat, bear meat and moose and caribou meat and rabbit too.' UTOLAF09Jun2202:032

c. *Dǫǫndaa k'it ts'ihǫhdąy.* (T)
REFL:older.brother on 3SG:miss:IPV
'She misses her older brother.' UTOLVDN07Oct2602:035

d. *Ahdogn ts'oo k'it tah daach'ettl'uh…* (T)
NTRL:up.vertically:AR spruce on among 3SG:set.snare:IT:PFV
'He set snares up there in the spruce trees…'
UTOLAF09Jun2202:026

Even postpositions with an extremely narrow semantic range such as P+*kįį'* 'subsisting on P, depending on P' are compatible with a variety of different verb themes. (196a) illustrates the most common use of this postposition with a positional theme; almost as common is its use with the conversive theme n+Ø+shyąą 'grow up' in (196b). (196c) shows, however, that P+*kįį'* 'subsisting on P, depending on P' can also occur with a descriptive theme.

(196) a. *Nahugn ch'itdul ntsaan' kįį' tihdaał…* (N)
there trash 2SG:poop:POSS subsisting.on 1SG:SG.live:FUT
'I'm going to live on trash and your poop…'
UTOLVDN10Jul2714:017

b. *Hiikįį' neeshyaan eh.* (T)
3PL>3SG:subsisting.on grow.up:PFV:NOM and
'They grew up on it.' UTOLVDN13May2801:117

c. *Łąą' t'eey T'oodįht'ay kįį' hdįįt'eh.* (N)
truly ADVZR God depending.on 3PL:be.thus:IPV
'They truly depend on God.' UTOLAF10Jul0901:007

15.1.2. Separability of free postpositions

Free postpositions may be separated from the verb theme. (197) illustrates lexical material intervening between the postpositional phrase and the verb.

(197) a. *Igaan' t'aat naann' t'eey dehk'aa ha'…* (T)
3SG>3SG:arm under across:ALL ADVZR shoot:PFV EMPH
'He shot it right under the arm…' UTOLAF09Jun2201:014

b. *Ay tl'aan ut'aat łät ts'ehoh'įįgn.* (N)
and.then 3SG:under smoke 1PL:do:IPV:CUST:NOM
'And then we put smoke under it.' UTOLVDN07Aug2001:008

Postpositional phrases formed with free postpositions are often moved to the postverbal position (198).

(198) a. *Hǫǫ't'eey įltthał uch'a', …* (T)
still 2SG:SG.run:IPV:PROG 3SG:from
'Keep running from him, …' UTCBAF13Nov0501:173

b. *Shin shyįį' t'eey neetsay nts'ą' na'ihthat, k'a' gaay*
1SG only even bear toward 1SG:SG.stand:IPV gun small
eł. (T)
with
'I was standing up to the bear by myself, with a small gun.'
UTOLAF09Jun2201:007

15.1.3. Free postpositions and conjugation markers

Most free postpositions do not impact the conjugation markers. The basic verb motion theme Ø+deeł 'PL move' requires (n, n) conjugation prefixes in its primary derivation (199a). Adding the free postpositional phrase *huxah* 'for them' in (199b) does not affect this, while adding the bound postpositional phrase *hut'a-* 'meeting them, catching up to them' (199c) requires a change to an *aa*-conjugation marker.

(199) a. … *camp ts'inįįdeeł.* (T)
camp ts'-nįį-deeł
camp 1PL.S-N.PFV:Ø-PL.move:PFV
'… we came to the camp.' UTOLVDN13May2004:106

b. *Mbah dindeey iin huxah nįįdeeł.* (T)
mbah dindeey iin hu-xah nįį-deeł
war men PL 3PL.P-for 3PL.S:N.PFV:Ø-PL.move:PFV
'Warriors came for them.' UTOLAF13May2403:010

c. *T'axoh hut'aheedeel eh.* (T)
t'axoh hu-t'a-hee-deel eh
finally 3PL.P-catch.up-3PL.S:DH.PFV:Ø-PL.move:PFV:NOM and
'In the end they caught up with them.'
UTOLVDN13May2909:047

There is one exception: the free postposition P+*tüh* 'over P' triggers a change of conjugation prefix; see 15.2.1.14.

15.2. Inventory

The following list of postpositions is roughly organized by semantic field. Four groups can be distinguished: postpositions of location (15.2.1), postpositions of time (15.2.2), postpositions introducing additional participants (15.2.3), and postpositions that occur in the comparative construction (15.2.4).

15.2.1. Postpositions of place

Postpositions of place describe the location, destination, or point of origin of an entity. Some postpositions of place also have temporal or participant-introducing meanings; these meanings are described in the appropriate sections.

15.2.1.1. P+*dą'* 'at P' P+*dą'* 'at P' expresses that an entity is located at a point in space (200). It is an extremely common postposition.

(200) a. *Niithoo t'eey Sh'aat Niign dą' dzaltth'i'.* (T)
long.time ADVZR 1SG:wife creek at 1PL:PL.stay:PFV
'We stayed at Wife Creek for a long time.'
UTOLVDN08Mar1311:007

b. *Nushyign', tth'itu' nįįłąy ddhäł dą'*
MED:AR:down:ALL river 3SG:flow:IPV:NOM mountain at
nt'ay, nushyign' tah eedah. (N)
3SG:be:IPV:NOM MED:AR:down:ALL among 3SG:SG.sit:IPV
'Down there where the river is flowing, down the mountain, in the area down there it was sitting.' UTOLAF09Aug1201:036

P+*dą'* is also used with spatial adverbs. In (201a), it follows the allative directional *adegn'* 'an unspecified distance toward vertically up' to form the complex adverb 'at an unspecified distance vertically up', while in (201b) it follows the lexicalized punctual directional *ishyiit* 'down there, there' to form a complex adverb with the meaning 'there, at that point'.

(201) a. *Adegn' dą' dineh na'ethat.* (T)
NTRL:up.vertically:ALL at man 3SG:SG.stand:IPV
'Up there the man kept standing.' UTOLVDN14May0703:102

b. *"Ishyiit dą' delttħ'ih!" hu'ehnih.* (T)
there at 3PL:PL.stay:IPV 3SG>3PL:say:IPV
'"They are still here!" he told them.' UTOLAF09Jun2202:063

P+*dą'* is also used following numerals to create the meaning 'X times' (202).

(202) *Taagn dą' hiikah tinįįdeet...* (T)
three times 3PL>3SG:looking.for PL.go:PFV
'Three times they went out looking for him...'
UTOLAF09Jun2202:010

In its spatial use, P+*dą' P* 'at P' does not take clauses as object; the subordinator *dänh* 'at the place where' is used instead. Temporal uses of P+*dą'* are discussed in 15.2.2.1.

P+*dą'* 'at P' does not change the verb's conjugation marker.

15.2.1.2. P+*dänh, danh* 'at P' P+*dänh, danh* 'at P' has the same meaning as P+*dą'* 'at P'. It does not affect the verb theme's conjugation marker and can be separated from the verb (203).

(203) a. *Ashyuugn keey dänh hihdelxoh.* (T)
NTRL:down:AR village at 3PL:play:IPV
'They were playing down there by the village site.'
UTCBAF14Jul1805:008

b. *Tl'aan Stephen Northway shyah ha'ah'aat dänh*
and.then Stephen Northway house ADJ:NTRL:out:PNCT at
ishyiit jah. (N)
there here
'And Stephen Northway's house is next door there.'
UTCBVDN13Nov0804:016

c. *Ay* *t'oot'eey* *unąą* *taagn* *danh* *manh* *maagn*
and but 3SG:mother three times lake around
shiijiinildzüh... (T)
3SG:dance.without.cease:IPV
'But his mother danced around the lake three times without stopping...' UTOLAF10Jul0801:021

15.2.1.3. P+*tah* 'among P, in the area of P' P+*tah* 'among P, in the area of P' indicates location in an area or among several entities (204). It contrasts with P+*dą'* in 15.2.1.1, which indicates punctual location.

The object of P+*tah* is almost always a full noun phrase; (204b) is one of only a handful of examples where P+*tah* takes a pronominal object. This postposition does not influence the choice of conjugation prefix.

(204) a. *Nahdǫǫ* *ddhäł* *tah* *nįįshyah.* (N)
MED:up.vertically:ABL mountain among 3SG:SG.go:PFV
'He came down from among the mountains.'
UTOLVDN10Jul2703:002

b. ... *jign* *utah* *xee* *yaa* *nii'inkąą.* (T)
berry 3SG:among grease 3SG>3SG:for carry.OOC:IT:PFV
'... he brought back a bowl with berries mixed with grease for him.'
UTOLVDN08Mar1302:018

P+*tah* can also have an allative interpretation 'in the direction of P, into P':

(205) a. *Dikeey* *tah* *nahindeeł.* (T)
REFL:village into 3PL:PL.go:IT:PFV
'They came back to their village.' UTCBAF13Nov0501:026

b. *Ch'aldzeeg* *shyiit* *nts'ą'* *tah* *teeshyah.* (T)
moon in to among 3SG:SG.go:INC:PFV
'He went into the moon.' UTOLAF09Jun2202:070

(205b) demonstrates also that P+*tah* 'among P, in the area of P' can combine with other postpositional phrases. This example is particularly interesting, since three postpositions are stacked here: P+*shyiit* 'inside P', P+*nts'ą̈'* 'toward P', and P+*tah* 'among P, in the area of P'. P+*tah* frequently combines with other postpositions, although its semantic contribution is not always clear.

The object of P+*tah* can also be an adverb (206). Comparison to similar sentences not containing *tah* in (207) demonstrates that the semantic contribution of *tah* following adverbs is not clear.

(206) a. *"Jah tah didhaltth'ih," hu'ehnih.* (T)
here among 2PL:PL.stay:IPV 3PL>3PL:say:IPV
'"You PL can stay here," they said to them.'
UTOLAF07Nov2602:016

b. … *hanuhshyign' tah dzina'altth'ät.* (N)
ADJ:MED:AR:down:ALL among 3SG:fall.down.over.edge:PFV
'… [the bear] tumbled down over the edge.'
UTOLAF09Aug1201:033

(207) a. *Shǫǫnüü Carl jah eedah de',*
1SG:older.brother Carl here 3SG:SG.stay:IPV if
neek'anehta'. (N)
3SG>1PL:take.care:IPV
'When my older brother Carl was staying here, he took care of us.'
UTCBAF13Nov1203:015

b. *Noshyign', noshyign' dzinatagntth'äł…* (N)
MED:AR:down:ALL MED:AR:down:ALL 1SG:fall.down.over.edge:FUT
'I'm going to fall down, down over the edge…'
UTOLAF12Jul1201:021

P+*tah* is also used as a temporal postposition, as described in 15.2.2.3.

15.2.1.4. P+*ts'änh* 'from P' P+*ts'änh* 'from P' indicates the source of movement (208). P+*ts'änh* may take a postpositional phrase as its object (208c). P+*ts'änh* 'from P' does not change the verb theme's conjugation marker.

(208) a. *Ts'iit Tthee Niign nts'änh Ch'uhtl'ąyh niign nts'ą̈' ch'ale'*
porcupine rock creek from reflects creek to FOC
ts'idegn. (N)
1PL:PL.go:IPV:CUST:NOM
'From Porcupine Rock Creek we would go to Reflects Snow Creek.'
UTOLAF08Feb1908:003

b. *Dzihyu iin du' udzih ts'anh hadįįdeeł.* (T)
Dzihyu PL CT caribou from 3PL:PL.go:PFV
'The Dzihyu [clan] comes from the caribou.'
UTOLAF11Aug0201:014

c. *Ts'oo t'aa, ts'oo t'aa ts'anh tay' nts'ą' ts'iiniin gaay tay'*
spruce under spruce under from again and baby again
t'eey etsaa hihdįįtth'ak. (T)
ADVZR 3SG:cry:IPV:NOM 3PL:hear:IPV
'Under a spruce, from under a spruce they heard again a small child crying.' UTOLVDN13May2801:039

15.2.1.5. P+*ch'a'* 'from P' P+*ch'a'* 'from P' describes motion away from a reference point (209).

(209) a. *Ts'oo k'it ich'a' ki̯'eltthät.* (N)
spruce on 3SG>3SG:from SG:run.up:PFV
'It quickly climbed the spruce away from him.'
UTOLVDN10Jul2701:006

b. *Ay dindah shiinaltthał ich'a'.* (T)
and meanwhile 3SG:SG.run.hard:IPV:PROG 3SG>3SG:from
'And meanwhile she keeps running hard away from him.'
UTOLVDN14Nov2301:313

While semantically similar to P+*ts'änh* 'from P' (15.2.1.4), P+*ch'a'* 'from P' has connotations of danger and avoidance that P+*ts'änh* 'from P' lacks. It can be used to tell someone to run away from a dangerous dog (210a), which P+*ts'änh* 'from P' cannot (210b). Conversely, P+*ts'änh* 'from P' can be used to indicate the source of movement (211a), while one speaker commented that (211b) "sounds like you just got away from her" (Roy Sam, personal communication).

(210) a. *uch'a' stanįltthiit!* (N)
3SG:from 2SG:SG.run.away:IPV
'run SG away from [the dog]!' UT Notebook #5, 74

b. * *uts'änh stanįltthiit* (N)
Intended: 'run SG away from [the dog]!' UT Notebook #5, 74

(211) a. *Sherry shyah ts'änh ihhaał* (N)
Sherry house from 1SG:SG.go:IPV:PROG
'I'm coming from Sherry's house' UT Notebook #5, 74

b. * *Sherry shyah ch'a' ihhaał* (N)
Intended: 'I'm coming from Sherry's house' UT Notebook #5, 74

This postposition introduces an avertive clause (212); see volume 2 for more information.

(212) *Łahtthegn nts'ą̈' hiiyįhmbiah tatxol ch'a'. (N)*
all 3PL>3PL:boil:PFV 3PL:break:FUT AVERT
'They boiled all [the eggs] lest they break.'
UTOLVDN07Aug2205:060

(209) illustrates that,unlike the adverbial-derivational prefix *ch'a-* 'away, from' discussed in 35.2.1.1, P+*ch'a'* 'from P' does not trigger (n, n) conjugation prefixes; instead the verb theme retains the same conjugation prefixes it would take if P+*ch'a'* 'from P' was absent. (209b) also illustrates that P+*ch'a'* 'from P' can be separated from the verb. This differs from what Kari (1990, 121–22) describes for the bound postposition *c'a* 'from' in Ahtna.

15.2.1.6. P+*nts'ą̈'* 'toward P' P+*nts'ą̈'* 'toward P' is the opposite of both P+*ch'a'* 'away from P' and P+*ts'änh* 'from P'. The initial consonant /n/ is present only when the object is a free noun phrase (213a). In motion verbs P+*nts'ą̈'* 'toward P' describes motion in the direction of P and does not entail that P is actually reached. It tends to co-occur with the progressive (213a) or the inceptive perfective (213b). It may also be used figuratively to introduce the addressee of verbs of speaking (213c).

(213) a. *Shoh shoh nts'ą̈' agntthäl eh.* (N)
bear bear toward 1SG:SG.run:IPV:PROG:NOM and
'I was running toward the bear.' UTOLAF09Aug1201:026

b. *Atthan' huts'ą' nateltthat.* (T)
NTRL:waterwards:ALL 3PL:to 3SG:SG.run:IT:INC:PFV
'He started running back toward the water to them.'
UTCBVDN13Nov1502:037

c. *Ay xah huts'ą̈' hǫǫheey.* (N)
3SG about 3PL:to 3SG:talk:IPV:NOM
'He talked to them about that.' UTOLVDN11Aug0802:034

Like P+*ts'änh* 'from P', P+*nts'ą̈'* 'toward P' frequently combines with other postpositions (214).

(214) a. *It'oh shyiit nts'ą̈' idehnąyh.* (N)
3SG>3SG:nest inside toward 3SG>3SG:throw.CO:PFV
'She threw it into the nest.' UTOLVDN11Aug0802:049

b. … *mänh choh k'it ts'ą' teeshyah…* (N)
lake big on toward 3SG:SG.go:INC:PFV
'… he went onto a big lake…' UTOLAF12Jul1203:103

It does not change the conjugation marker of the verb.

15.2.1.7. P+*ttheh* 'in front of P' The postposition P+*ttheh* 'in front of P' is related to several other stems with similar meaning: the postposition P+*naattheh* 'long before P (temporally)' (15.2.2.5), the imperative-only lexeme *tthee!* 'wait!', and the noun *ts'uttheet* 'ancestors'. P+*ttheh* 'in front of P' is one of several postpositions describing the spatial arrangements of entities along a line (see also 15.2.1.8). Combined with P+*tah* 'among P, in the area of P' as in (215c), it has the meaning 'in the general area ahead of P'.

(215) a. *Carl, nttheh uhhaal!* (N)
Carl 2SG:in.front 1SG:SG.go:OPT:PROG
'Carl, I want to go ahead of you SG!'
UTOLVDN13May2004:028

b. *Huttheh xatjettąą…* (T)
3PL:in.front 3SG:SG.hunt:PFV
'He was hunting ahead of them…' UTOLVDN14May0703:074

c. *Shttheh tah nahatkeeł.* (N)
1SG:in.front among 3PL:go.around.by.boat:IPV:PROG
'They were boating around ahead of me.'
UTOLVDN07Aug2205:104

P+*ttheh* also has a temporal meaning 'before P' described in 15.2.2.4.

15.2.1.8. P+*k'eh* 'behind P, following P' P+*k'eh* 'behind P, following P' is related to the bound noun *-k'eh* 'tracks'. Like P+*ttheh* 'in front of P', P+*k'eh* 'behind P, following P' describes the arrangement of objects along a trajectory (216); when objects are located behind the back of something, the postposition P+*nänht'agn, naht'aagn* 'behind P's back' (described in 15.2.1.23) is used instead.

(216) a. … *shk'eh nagąą'htelshyah.* (N)
1SG:following 3PL:PL.run:PFV
'… they ran after me.' UTOLAF09Aug1202:033

b.

Ik'eh	*ch'inil'įį,*	*hąą?* (N)
3sg>3sg:following	sneak:pfv	right

'She sneaked after him, right?' UTOLVDN10Jul2713:024

c.

…	*ay*	*chih*	*dik'eh*	*t'eey*	*na'įhxal*	*eh.* (B)
	3	too	refl:behind	even	3sg:throw.lro:pfv:nom	and

'… those, too, she threw behind herself [while she keeps running].' UTOLAF10Jul0202:133

P+*k'eh* 'behind p, following p', does not impact the conjugation prefix (216b). (216c) demonstrates that P+*k'eh* can be separated from the verb.

P+*k'eh* has several other meanings; see 15.2.3.3 and 15.2.4.1.

15.2.1.9. P+*k'e'* 'not reaching p' P+*k'e'* 'not reaching p, short of p' occurs only rarely (217).

(217)

Ay	*t'oot'eey*	*hiiyunihdak*	*hiik'e'*	*tah*
and	however	3pl>3sg:shoot.at:pfv	3pl>3sg:short.of	among

hiik'e'	*tah.* (T)
3pl>3sg:short.of	among

'But anyway they shot at him, [but the arrows fell] short of him, short of him.' UTOLVDN13May2909:075

A more common usage of P+*k'e'* 'not reaching p, short of p' is described in section 15.2.4.2.

15.2.1.10. P+*k'üü* 'next to p' The postposition P+*k'üü* 'next to p' expresses adjacency. It can express movement toward next to the reference point (218a) or location next to the reference point (218b). When combined with the postposition P+*tah* 'in the area of p, among p', the complex postpositional phrase acquires the reading 'in the area next to p' (218c).

(218) a.

…	*adogn*	*ts'at*	*eł*	*dats'ehłeek*	*tl'aan*
	ntrl:up:ar	blanket	and	1pl:put.up.pl.o:ipv:cust	and

ch'ik'on'	*uk'üü*	*dats'ehłeek…* (T)
dentalium	3sg:beside	1pl:put.up.pl.o:ipv:cust

'When we have a potlatch, we collect blankets and we put dentalium beside it…' UTOLAF11Aug0207:001

b.

Nah'ogn	*huk'üü*	*kon'*	*deek'an'*	*hǫǫ't'eey,*	*elo::k!* (N)
med:outside:ar	3pl:beside	fire	3sg:burn:ipv	still	hot

'Next to them the fire was still burning, it was hot!' UTOLVDN14Apr2601:016

c. ... *tąy k'üü tah natedaak.* (T)
trail beside among 3SG:SG.go.around:IPV
'... he was walking around beside the trail.'
UTOLVDN07Oct2604:015

P+*k'üü* 'next to P' does not influence the conjugation marker (218b).

15.2.1.11. P+*t'aat, t'aa* 'underneath P' P+*t'aat, t'aa* 'underneath P' does not change the conjugation marker (219). Both forms are attested in both dialects.

(219) a. *Shke' t'aat unah'įh!* (N)
1SG:foot underneath 2PL:look:IPV
'Look PL under my feet!' UTOLVDN10Jul2703:009

b. *Ts'oo t'aa hihdeltth'ih...* (T)
spruce under 3PL:PL.sit:IPV
'They were sitting under a spruce...'
UTOLVDN14Nov2301:114

15.2.1.12. P+*k'it* 'on top of P' P+*k'it* 'on top of P' can describe the location of objects in relation to the reference point (220a), their movement over the surface of the reference point (220b), or movement toward the surface of the reference point (220c).

(220) a. *Hugn nan' k'it huniishyeey hugn t'eey na'etk'an'*
there earth on AR:grow:PFV:NOM there even 3PL:burn:IT:PFV
nts'ą'. (T)
and
'Even things growing on the land burned.'
UTOLAF09Jun2402:004

b. *Hunaann' tsiił k'it daheedeeł nts'ą' ...* (T)
AR:across:ALL bridge on 3PL:PL.go.on:PFV and
'They went across on the bridge...' UTOLVDN07Oct2602:013

c. *Ik'it iłüh.* (N)
3SG>3SG:on urinate:PFV
'He peed on him.' UTOLVDN10Jul2701:013

Usually it is possible to determine from context whether movement across a surface (220b) or onto a surface (220c) is intended. When, however, both interpretations could be possible—for example, when combined with a motion verb—then the postposition P+*nts'ą̈'* 'toward P' can be added to unambiguously create a directional reading. (221a) illustrates movement across a surface, and the (221b) movement onto the surface.

(221) a. *Anaa:::n' manh k'it aahaał.* (T)
NTRL:across:ALL lake on 3SG:SG.go:IPV
'He is walking way across on the [frozen] lake.'
UTOLVDN13May2805:026

b. ... *hanugn mänh choh k'it ts'ą' teeshyah...* (N)
NTRL:upland:AR lake big on to 3SG:SG.go:INC:PFV
'... and he went onto a big lake in the upland area...'
UTOLAF12Jul1203:103

When the object referent is a mountain, P+*k'it* is usually translated with 'in the mountains' (222). The notion of 'on top of the mountain' is expressed using the postposition P+*tthiit'aagn* (see 15.2.1.24).

(222) *Dihthaadn ddhäł, ddhäł k'it ch'a huushyah hǫǫłįį.* (N)
nearby.place mountain mountain in FOC 3PL:house AR:be:IPV
'At Nearby Place (Mansfield) in the mountains they had a house.'
UTOLAF09Aug1202:002

P+*k'it* 'on P' does not influence the choice of conjugation prefix.

15.2.1.13. P+*shyiit* 'inside P, into P' The postposition P+*shyiit* 'inside P, into P' is ambiguous between directional (223a) and positional (223b) meaning. It also combines with other postpositions (223c).

(223) a. *Ushyiit ihshyah tl'aan shyiign' dhihdah.* (T)
3SG:inside 1SG:SG.go:PFV and down:ALL 1SG:SG.sit:IPV
'I went inside [the canoe] and sat down.'
UTOLAF09Jun2902:009

b. *Ch'udzüüt xia' ushyiit deedlah.* (N)
owl egg 3SG:inside 3PL:classify.PL.O:IPV
'Owl eggs were lying inside it.' UTOLVDN07Aug2205:014

c. *It'oh shyiit nts'ą̈' idehnąyh.* (N)
3SG>3SG:nest inside toward 3SG>3SG:throw.CO:PFV
'She threw it into its nest.' UTOLVDN11Aug0802:049

P+*shyiit* 'inside P' does not affect the verb's conjugation marker.

15.2.1.14. P+*tüh* 'over, across' P+*tüh* 'over, across P' is used to describe movement (224).

(224) a. ... *k'at'eey dineh eegn' tüh tah'üh...* (N)
NEG man coat:POSS over 2PL:step:FUT:NEG
'... you PL may not step over men's coats...'
UTOLAF14May0807:035

b. ... *atthiit Tak'at tüh*
NTRL:waterwards:PNCT Clearwater across
huhįįdlah. (T)
3PL>3PL:handle.PL.O:PFV
'... at that point toward the water they took them across the Clearwater.' UTCBAF14Jul1805:020

c. *Nahdǫǫ ddhäł tüh nįįshyah.* (N)
MED:up:ABL mountain across 3SG:SG.go:PFV
'He came from up there across the mountains.'
UTOLVDN10Jul2703:002

In related languages postpositions cognate to P+*tüh* 'over P' trigger (Ø, aa) conjugation prefixes (e.g., Ahtna P+*tes* in Kari [1990, 334] and Koyukon P+*teł* in Jetté and Jones [2000, 509]). In Upper Tanana, P+*tüh* 'over P' triggers this change only in the Tetlin dialect (224b; this verb form has an *aa*- perfective); in the Northway dialect, the verb theme retains its *n*- conjugation prefix in the perfective (224c).

15.2.1.15. P+*taagn, tag* 'meandering through P' P+*taagn, tag* 'meandering through P' does not impact the choice of conjugation marker and can be separated from the verb (225a).

(225) a. *Chinh tag taht'eey yahedak*
flat meandering also 3PL:PL.keep.going:IPV:CUST
hǫǫ't'eey. (T)
still
'They kept walking through the flats.'
UTOLVDN13May2909:019

b. *Hutaagn aahaał nts'ą̈' huts'ą̈' hǫǫheey.* (N)
AR:meandering 3SG:SG.go:IPV:PROG and 3PL:to 3SG:talk:IPV:NOM
'He is going all over [the world] and talks to them.'
UTOLVDN11Aug0802:022

15.2.1.16. P+*aanah* 'around (in a circular motion)' P+*aanah* 'around (in a circle)' can be used to indicate the position of objects extending in a circle, such as the string of dentalium tied around the boy's head in (226a), or for circular motion, e.g., such as when paddling around the edge of a slough in (226b). In (226c) it describes the state of being surrounded by fire. P+*aanah* 'around (in a circle)' does not impact the choice of conjugation marker.

(226) a. *Utthi' aanah ch'ik'on' eł naneltl'ǫǫ.* (T)
3SG:head around dentalium with 3SG:tie.around:PASS:PFV
'Dentalium was strung around his head.'
UTOLAF10Jul0801:015

b. *Ayshįį' neets'ayy' tats'įįdlah tl'aan ay*
finally 1PL:canoe:POSS 1PL:put.PL.O.into.water:PFV and 3SG
aanah natsetkeek. (N)
around 1PL:go.around.by.boat:IPV:CUST
'Finally we put out boats into the water and started to paddle around it.' UTOLVDN07Aug2205:044

c. ... *hu'aanah łahtthegn łät t'eey hudiik'ąą.* (N)
3SG:around all smoke even AR:burn:IPV
'... around them everything was burning and smoky.'
UTOLVDN14Apr2601:005

15.2.1.17. P+*maagn* 'around P, at the edge of P' The postposition P+*maagn* 'around P' is related to the noun stem *-maagn'* -'edge'. It describes movement along (227a) or location at (227b) the edge of an entity. P+*maagn* does not influence the choice of conjugation prefix.

(227) a. ... *yimaagn sts'akiteltthak...* (T)
3SG>3SG:around.shore SG.run.in.circle:INC:PFV
'... he ran all the way around [the lake]...'
UTOLAF08Apr2805:053

b. ... *kon' maagn dzeltth'iik...* (N)
fire around 1PL:PL.sit:IPV:CUST
'... we were sitting around the fire...'
UTOLVDN13May2003:043

15.2.1.18. P+*aaxah* 'in the vicinity of P' The postposition P+*aaxah* expresses spatial proximity but not necessarily adjacency, although the two can of course be hard to separate (228b). P+*aaxah* does not change the conjugation prefix.

(228) a. *Ts'iikeey iin k'a hii'aaxah łootaahaal,*
children PL NEG 3PL>3SG:in.vicinity SG.walk.around:FUT:NEG
įįjih, henih. (T)
forbidden 3PL:say:IPV
'Children may not walk close to it, that's forbidden, they say.'
UTOLAF11Aug0207:011

b. *Dzinal'iin aaxah dhihdah...* (N)
window in.vicinity 1SG:SG.sit:IPV
'I was sitting next to the window...' UTOLVDN14Apr2602:040

15.2.1.19. P+*ch'ąą* 'opposite P, a little ways from P' P+*ch'ąą* 'opposite P, a little ways from P' is frequently used when describing clan relations. Upper Tanana society is divided into two moieties, each of which consists of several clans. The relation between the moieties is often described as being seated opposite one another (see Guédon [1974] for a detailed description of the Upper Tanana clan system). One of the clans even takes its name from this relation; the clan name *Ch'ąą iin* 'Seagull people' is analyzed as coming from the postposition P+*ch'ąą* (229a). (229b) is the only example of P+*ch'ąą* outside the context of the clan system; it was given as the opposite of the phrase *kon' nia* 'close to the fire, in the middle of the fire' during the transcription of a text.

(229) a. *Ch'ąą iin du' Naltsiin iin, "Neech'ąą didhaltth'ih,"*
opposite PL CT Naltsiin PL 1PL:opposite 2PL:PL.stay:IPV
henay xah t'eey hǫǫ hu'ǫǫsi'. (T)
3PL:say:IPV:NOM because ADVZR thus 3PL:name
'As for the Seagull tribe, the Naltsiin [the first clan] said "Stay on the opposite side from us," that's why this is their name.'
UTOLAF11Aug0201:006

b. *kon' ch'ąą* (T)
fire opposite
'a little ways away from the fire' UTOLVDN13May2806:006

Based on the few available examples, P+*ch'ąą* 'opposite P' does not impact the conjugation marker.

15.2.1.20. P+*ahch'aa* 'far from P' P+*ahch'aa* 'far from P' is the opposite of P+*aaxah*. It may be related to P+*ch'ąą* 'a little ways from P, opposite P'. It is attested only once in the corpus; the verb form is in the future, so it is impossible to tell whether the postposition impacts the conjugation markers (230).

(230) … *ts'exeey iin ahch'aa łoohtaahaał.* (T)
women PL far.from 3PL:SG.go.around:FUT
'… they have to walk around far away from women.'
UTOLVDN11Jul2901:023

15.2.1.21. P+*daachiit* 'blocking P's way' The complex postposition P+*daachiit* 'blocking P's way' appears cognate to Ahtna P+*dacaex* 'blocking P's way', which according to Kari consists of the adverbial prefix *da-* 'into orifice' and the postposition P+*caex* 'catching up with P' (Kari 1990, 111). The simple postposition P+*caex* does not seem to have a cognate in Upper Tanana, and only one example for P+*daachiit* 'blocking P's way' can be found in my corpus (231). Judging from this example, P+*daachiit* 'blocking P's way' does not impact the conjugation marker.

(231) *That ts'exeh du' dii xa ch'a idaachiit eeday?* (N)
that women CT why FOC 3SG>3SG:blocking SG.sit:IPV:NOM
'Why is that woman sitting in his way?' UTOLAF14May0807:017

15.2.1.22. P+*naał* 'in front of P's eyes' P+*naał* 'in front of P's eyes' is likely related to the (noun) stem *-naagn'* 'eye' and also appears to contain the instrumental suffix *-ł*. Both examples in (232) are by the same speaker from Tetlin, but the postposition was recognized by speakers of the Northway dialect also.

(232) a. *Xał t'eey ehxįį shnaał t'eey.* (T)
sled even 3SG:make.SG.O:PFV 1SG:in.front ADVZR
'He made a sled in front of my eyes.'
UTCBVDN13Nov1501:078

b. *Tl'aan ndia' gaay sǫ' sta'uushya'*
and 2SG:younger.sister little PROH 3SG:SG.walk.away:OPT
nuhnaał t'eey. (T)
2PL:in.front ADVZR
'And don't let your younger sister wander off in front of your eyes.'
UTOLVDN14Nov2301:052

P+*naał* does not change the conjugation prefix and can clearly be separated from the verb theme.

15.2.1.23. P+*nänht'aagn, naht'aag, nuht'aag* 'behind P's back' When describing the location of objects behind the back of a reference entity, P+*nänht'agn, naht'aag, nuht'aag* is used. This is a complex postposition consisting of the noun stem *t'aagn* 'broad surface of'[1] and another morpheme *nänh*, *nah*, or *nuh*. The first of these is likely related to the noun stem *nän'* 'back'; the other two may be related to the stem *nuugn* 'in the upland area' (see also Kari [1990, 296]). The difference between the different forms is unclear and may be idiolectal. The two forms from the Northway dialect (233a, b) are from different speakers. The two forms from the Tetlin dialect (233c, d) were produced by the same speaker; note that there is a slight meaning difference. There are insufficient examples of this postposition in the data to fully understand the variation involved.

(233a–c) all illustrate literal uses of this postposition; (233d) shows that it may also be used figuratively with the meaning 'without p's knowledge'. (233b, c) further illustrate that this postposition may combine with other postpositions.

(233) a. *Shnänht'agn t'eey hiiyeedlah.* (N)
1sg:behind.back even 3pl>3pl:have.pl.o:ipv
'They kept [the guns] behind me.' UTOLVDN07Aug2205:093

b. *K'ąy' k'ąy' gaay unuht'aagn ts'änh hadee'ah.* (N)
willow willow small 3sg:behind.back from 3sg:lo.extend.out:ipv
'Willow, small willows were sticking out from behind his back.' UTOLAF12Jul1203:105

c. … *shnąą naht'aag tah na'ihthat.* (T)
1sg:mother behind.back among 1sg:sg.stand:ipv
'… I stood behind my mother.' UTOLAF09Jun2201:015

d. … *huk'eh hunaat'agn teltthat.* (T)
3pl:following 3pl:without.knowledge 3sg:sg.run:inc:pfv
'… he ran after them without their knowledge.' UTOLAF09Jun2202:053

This postposition does not influence the choice of conjugation prefix.

15.2.1.24. P+*tthiit'aag* 'on top of p' The object referent of P+*tthiit'aag* 'on top of p' is related to the possessed noun *tthiit'aagn* 'top of head', which is a compound consisting of the noun stems *-tthi'* 'head' and *t'aagn* 'broad surface'. P+*tthiit'aagn* 'on top of P' occurs only rarely and P usually refers to a mountain. Both examples in (234) are taken from the same narrative about an evil spirit residing on *Ts'iit Tl'oo Ddhal'* 'Porcupine Grass Mountain'. P+*tthiit'aag* 'on top of P' does not change the conjugation marker of the verb.

(234) a. *Ddhał* *tthiit'aag* *nts'ą'* *ch'uudehshyaa* *k'eh* *niik,*
mountain on.top at 3SG:whistle:IPV like say:IPV:CUST
"Oooooooo," *ndiik.* (T)
ooooo say:IPV:CUST
'Up there on top of the mountain he would make a whistling sound, "Ooooooo," he would make.' UTOLAF09Jun2404:003

b. *Hutthiit'aagn* *natihdaag...* (T)
AR:on.top 1SG:SG.go.around:IPV:NOM
'I went right on top of it...' UTOLAF09Jun2404:019

15.2.1.25. P+*tthiłt'aagn* 'behind P's head' P+*tthiłt'aagn* 'behind P's head' is another complex position consisting of the morpheme *t'aagn* 'broad surface' (also found in P+*nänht'aagn* 'behind P's back'), the noun stem *tthi'* 'head', and what looks like the instrumental suffix *-ł*. It only occurs once in the data; the context is a text about puberty restrictions. (235) states that girls who have entered puberty may not walk around the back of houses, because men traditionally slept with their heads toward the back of the house, away from the entrance. The example is unusual in that there is no postpositional object. (235) is the only example of this postposition; since the verb is in the future, it is impossible to determine whether the postposition changes the conjugation prefix.

(235) *Hugn* *tthiłt'aagn* *t'eey* *k'a* *łoohtaahaal.* (T)
also behind.head ADVZR not 3SG:SG.go.around:FUT:NEG
'Also she may not walk around behind people's head.'
UTOLVDN11Jul2901:020

15.2.1.26. P+*daategn, daatagn* 'between P' P+*daategn* (N), *daatagn* (T) 'between P' is used in contexts where a number of objects are lined up in a row. It is a clearly a complex postposition; Kari (1997b) glosses *tik* (*tek*, using the spelling system employed in this grammar) as 'between' but does not give an analysis for the first portion *daa*. P+*daategn, daatagn* 'between P' does not impact the conjugation marker (236).

(236) a. *Ay tl'aan hudaategn ha'ashyuugn store*
and then AR:between ADJC:NTRL:down:AR store
hiihuhtsįį. (N)
3PL>AR:make.SG.O:PFV
'And then between [the houses of Frank Sam and Elijah Demit] they built a store.' UTCBVDN13Nov0804:008

b. … *yudih'ąą ts'oo daatagn…* (T)
3SG>3SG:find.SG.O:PFV spruce between
'… she found him between spruce trees…'
UTOLAF09Jun2202:013

c. *Shchil iin needaategn.* (N)
1SG:younger.brother PL 1PL:between
'My younger brothers [were] between us.'
UTOLVDN13May2004:016

This postposition may be used only when an object is located between two similar entities: two houses (236a), two spruce trees in (236b), or two people in (236c). It cannot be used when an entity is located between two entities of different types. (237) is the response to the cue 'I'm standing between the house and the lake'; other attempts to elicit P+*daategn, daatagn* 'between P' between different entities had similar results.

(237) *mänh k'üüdn na'ihthät* (N)
lake beside 1SG:SG.:stand:IPV
'I'm standing beside the lake' UT Notebook #5, 31

15.2.1.27. P+*nia* 'in the middle of P' P+*nia* 'in the middle of P' appears to be only used when P is fire. It does not appear to have an impact on the conjugation prefix (238).

(238) a. *Kon' nia tthinįįtthayh.* (T)
fire middle.of 3SG:put.LRO.into.fire:PFV
'He stuck [the iron pole] into the middle of the fire.'
UTOLAF15May0501:057

b. *Ts'ą̈' wunia' huuxeel'*
and 3SG:middle.of.fire 3PL:pack:POSS
naxeełhiyaldäl ay huuts'ą̈'
3PL>3SG:handle.PL.pack:IPV:NOM and 3PL:for
tthidiłeeh. (S)
3SG:put.PL.O:into.fire:IPV
'And then he threw their packs and everything they were carrying into the fire.' Tyone (1996, 73)

15.2.1.28. P+*tth'itohnia, tthitohnia* 'in the middle of P (water)' *Tth'itohnia, tthitohnia* 'in the middle of water' can be used as a noun, but more frequently, it is used as a postposition P+*tthitohnia* 'in the middle of P' where P refers to a body of water. It is possibly a frozen form of *tth'itu'* 'river + *niu* 'in the middle of P'. In the Northway dialect, the initial sound is an ejective affricate (239a), while it is an aspirated affricate in the Tetlin dialect (239b).

(239) a. ... *dahdeltth'ih mänh tth'itohnia.* (N)
3PL:PL.sit.on:IPV lake middle.of
'... they sat [on a raft] in the middle of the lake.'
UTOLVDN14Apr2601:003

b. ... *ts'ayh tthitohnia eł ninihshyay eł t'eey...* (T)
boat middle.of and 1SG:SG.arrive:PFV:NOM and ADVZR
'... as I get to the middle of the boat...'
UTOLAF09Jun2902:027

In (239b), the object of the postposition P+*tthitohnia* is *ts'ayh* 'boat, canoe'. In this example the narrator and her family put a canoe across a creek in order to cross the creek on top of the canoe. This example suggests that for this speaker at least, P+*tthitohnia* has changed its meaning to something like 'halfway along P'. (Because of her son's actions, the narrator falls into the water and almost drowns, so it is clear that at this time she is about halfway across the boat—and thus across the water.)

P+*tth'itohnia, tthitohnia* 'in the middle of P (water)' does not change the conjugation prefix.

15.2.1.29. P+*eekeh* 'halfway up P, on the side of P' P+*eekeh* 'halfway up P, on the side of P' can be used only with mountains (240), not with other entities such as trees. There are no instances of this postposition with a pronominal object. P+*eekeh* 'halfway up P, on the side of P' does not affect the conjugation marker.

(240) a. *Hanadegn' Nahk'ade hanadeg' ddhał*
ADJC:MED:up:ALL fish.trap ADJC:MED:up:ALL mountain
eekeh łat hihneh'įh... (T)
halfway.up smoke 3PL:see:IPV
'Up there toward Fish Trap (Last Tetlin), up there halfway up the mountain, they saw smoke...' UTOLAF07Nov2602:010

b. *Ay tl'aan ditthe' eh di'aat eh yaadegn*
and then REFL:man's.daughter and REFL:wife and DSTL:up:ALL
tayh eekeh shoh nahatxąą tl'aan. (S)
hill halfway.up bear 3PL:PL.become:PFV and
'And then, he and his daughter and his wife became bears again on the side of the hill.' ANLC4122a:079

15.2.1.30. P+*uudih* 'all the way P' The temporal postposition P+*uudih* 'all __ long' in 15.2.2.7 also can take a directional object. It then has the meaning 'all the way P' (241).

(241) a. ... *ts'ihtąy natneh'įįk naan'::: uudih t'eey.* (T)
arrow 3SG:hide:IPV:CUST across:ALL all.the.way ADVZR
'... he was hiding arrows all the way across [the flat].'
UTOLAF13May2403:114

b. *Deg' uudih.* (T)
up:ALL all.the.way
'All the way up [the mountain].' UTOLVDN14Nov2301:067

15.2.2. Temporal postpositions

Many temporal postpositions are related to spatial postpositions.

15.2.2.1. P+*dą'* 'when P (PST)' P+*dą'* 'at P (PST)' (described in 15.2.1.1) is used very frequently with a temporal reading 'when P', where P is a point in time in the past. (242) shows some of the relatively rare examples where the object of *dą'* is a noun.

(242) a. *K'ahdu' ch'itįįł dą' t'axoh nahditįįk*
now potlatch when:PST finally 3PL:carry.LRO:IPV:CUST

tah... (N)
when...

'Recently at potlatch when they carry [the coffin]...'
UTOLAF12Jul1203:044

b. *K'ahmän' dą' tsät įįttheeł?* (N)
morning when:PST wood 2SG:chop:PFV

'Did you chop wood this morning?' UTOLAF14Nov2001:017

More commonly the object of *dą'* is a postpositional phrase (243).

(243) a. *Hudįįk'aan ttheh dą' hutąy' hǫǫłįį.* (N)
AR:burn:PFV:NOM before when:PST 3PL:trail:POSS AR:be:IPV

'At the time before it burned, they had a trail there.'
UTOLVDN14Apr2601:013

b. *Neenaattheh dą' Yamaagn Teeshyaay keey dą'*
1PL:long.before when:PST Yamaagn Teeshyaay village at

nįįshyah. (T)
3SG:SG.go:PFV

'Long before us Yamaagn Teeshyaay arrived at a village.'
UTOLAF08Apr2804:001

Temporal P+*dą'* is also often used with object clauses where it has the meaning 'when (PST)' (244); see volume 2 for more information.

(244) *Ts'at t'aat hatthi'etthay dą' dineh*
blanket under 3SG:extend.head.out.as.LRO:IPV:NOM when:PST man

nįh'įį. (T)
3SG:see:PFV

'When she stuck her head out from under the blanket, she saw the man.' UTOLVDN14Nov2301:221

15.2.2.2. P+*de'* 'when P (FUT)' P+*de'* 'when P (FUT)' does not have a spatial reading. It is used to refer to a point of time in the future. Its object is usually a time of day (245).

(245) a. *K'ahmann' de' nik'oodahłeey...* (T)
morning when:FUT 2PL>AR:check.out:IPV:IMP
'Check it out tomorrow morning...'
UTOLVDN13May2801:020

b. *K'ahdąą'de' utahshyüüt tädn de' t'eey le'.* (N)
tomorrow AR:snow:FUT night when:FUT ADVZR POT
'It's going to snow tomorrow, maybe tonight.'
UTOLAF15Dec0603:015

As *k'ahdąą'de'* 'tomorrow' in (245b) demonstrates, P+*de'* 'when P (FUT)' is also involved in adverb formation (see chap. 16.2.2.2). Most commonly though it is used as a subordinating conjunction with the meaning 'if, when (FUT)' (246); see volume 2 for more information.

(246) *Nshyaats'e' uts'iiniin hǫǫłįį de' ay ch'a hǫǫ utdįįnįįl.* (N)
2SG:woman's.daughter 3SG:child AR:be:IPV if 3SG FOC thus 2SG>3SG:say:FUT
'If your daughter has a baby you have to tell her this.'
UTOLAF12Jul1203:056

15.2.2.3. P+*tah* 'when P' P+*tah* 'among P' also has a temporal reading 'in the temporal area of P' (247). It thus contrasts with P+*dą'* 'at the point in time of P in the past' and P+*de'* 'at the point in time of P in the future'.

(247) a. *Nooɫuut tah elk'ah, ushyi' nsǫǫ!* (N)
falltime when 3SG:be.fat:IPV 3SG:meat 3SG:be.good:IPV
'In the falltime, they are fat, their meat is tasty!'
UTOLAF09Aug12:013

b. *Dziin tah eetįį...* (B)
day when 3SG:SG:sleep:IPV
'He sleeps during the day...' UTOLVDN10Jul2722:011

P+*tah* 'when P' in combination with a noun indicating time of day is ambiguous between 'every P' and 'all P long' (248).

(248) a. *Dziin tah ogn natidaak...* (N)
day when outside:AR 3SG:SG.walk.around:IPV:CUST
'Every day she walks around outside...'
UTOLAF14Nov2203:020

b. *Dziin tah huukol shǫǫnüü eh.* (N)
day when 3SG:be.gone 1SG:older.brother with
'All day they were gone, with my older brother.'
UTCBAF13Nov1203:013

Temporal *tah* is also used as a subordinator 'when' (249); see also volume 2.

(249) *Tädn hǫǫłiin eh tah nats'indeeł.* (N)
night AR:be:IPV:NOM and when 1PL:PL.go:IT:PFV
'When it was night, we went back.' UTOLAF15Dec0606:003

15.2.2.4. P+*ttheh* 'before P' P+*ttheh* 'in front of P, ahead of P' described in 15.2.1.7 can also be used as a temporal postposition with the meaning 'before P' (250). This use of P+*ttheh* is not very common.

(250) a. *Ch'ita' ay ch'ale di'aat ttheh ditthe'e*
INDF:father and FOC REFL:wife before REFL:man's.daughter
t'eey uuniik... (T)
even 3SG:grab:PFV
'The father grabbed his daughter before his wife [could grab her]...'
UTCBAF13Nov0501:366

b. *Nts'aa' neettheh hįįdį' k'eh t'eey hidį'.* (N)
how 1PL:before 3PL:do:PFV like even 3PL:do:IPV
'They did it like they used to do it before us.'
UTOLVDN13May2003:051

Temporal P+*ttheh* is also used as a subordinator (251); see volume 2.

(251) *"Elih hutaałeel ttheh natsutdeeł," henih.* (N)
cold AR:be:FUT:NOM before 1PL:PL.go:IT:INC:OPT 3PL:say:IPV
'"Let's go back before it gets cold," they said.'
UTCBAF15May0403:041

15.2.2.5. P+*naattheh* 'long before P' The postposition P+*naattheh dą'* 'long before P' is derived from P+*ttheh* 'before P'. It is a complex postposition consisting of *naa-* '?', *ttheh* 'before', and the postposition P+*dą'* 'at a point P'. P+*naattheh dą'* 'long before P' only has temporal meaning, never spatial. It is used only in the formulaic expression *neenaattheh dą'* 'long before us, a long time ago', used to introduce myths or long-ago histories (Lovick 2012) as in (252a) or to refer to the time when the old customs and traditions were still strong (252b).

(252) a. *Neenaattheh dą' ts'exeey gaay łaakeey iin hihdelxoo::*
1PL:long.before at girls two PL 3PL:play:IPV
hah'ogn. (T)
NTRL:outside:AR
'Long before us, two girls were playing outside.'
UTOLAF08Apr2805:001

b. *Neenaattheh dą' ts'anh k'at'eey hǫǫ' hidąy.* (N)
1PL:long.before at from NEG thus 3PL.do:IPV:NEG
'They didn't do that before our time.'
UTOLVDN09Jun2302:033

P+*naattheh dą'* 'long before P' does not affect the choice of conjugation marker.

15.2.2.6. P+*k'ehtl'üdn* 'after P's death' It is likely that the postposition P+*k'ehtl'üdn* 'after P's death' consists of P+*k'eh* 'following P' plus *tl'üdn* '?'. (253) contains most of the available examples.

(253) a. … *shk'ehtl'üdn noo' de' t'eey ishyiit sǫ' ni'ųųshya'…* (T)
1SG:after.death long if even there PROH 2SG:SG.go.there:OPT
'… don't go there even long after I'm gone…'
UTOLVDN08Mar1311:004

b. *Shk'ehtl'üüd dineh hasaa'uushya'.* (T)
1SG:after.death man 3SG:SG.be.important.person:OPT
'He is going to be a big (rich, important) man after my death.'
UTCBAF13Nov0401:117

Since both verb forms in (253) are in the optative mode, it is impossible to tell whether P+*k'ehtl'üdn* 'after P's death' influences the conjugation marker. Both examples illustrate, however, that this postposition can be separated from the verb.

15.2.2.7. P+*uudih* 'all P long' The object of P+*uudih* 'all P long' is usually a noun denoting time (254).

(254) a. *Chinhshyiit hiiyidlaak xay xay uudih*
pole.cache 3PL>3PL:keep.PL:IPV:CUST winter winter all.long
yuu'aal xah. (N)
3SG>3SG.eat:OPT PURP
'They keep them in a pole cache so they can eat it all winter long.'
UTOLVDN07Nov2901:078

b. *Dzii::n uudih t'eey huhdzelxuu…* (T)
day all.long ADVZR 1PL:play:IPV:CUST
'All day long we would play…' UTOLAF09Jun2901:012

15.2.3. Participant postpositions

This group of postpositions introduces additional (nonlocation) participants. Participant postpositions usually do not take the areal object prefix.

15.2.3.1. P+*xah, aa* 'for P, about P' P+*xah, aa* 'for P, about P' is one of the most common postpositions. When used with motion verbs, it may express arrival at P that somehow benefits P (255).

(255) a. *Ay dineh nuhxah danįįshyay angel hǫǫłįį*
and man 2PL:for 3SG:SG.come.in:PFV:NOM angel AR:be:IPV
t'eey du'. (N)
ADVZR CT
'And the man who came in for you might be an angel.'
UTCBAF13Nov1203:033

b. *Ay xah neexah nįįshyah.* (T)
3SG because 1PL:for 3SG:SG.come:PFV
'That's why he came to us.' UTCBVDN14Jul1801:067

In all other types of active themes, P+*xah, aa* 'for P, about P' may express that the event takes place to the benefit or detriment of P. The translation of (256a) was suggested by the speaker, who said that it was more good-natured than the English translation 'I laughed at her' suggested by me.

(256) a. *Shdia', shdia' teejuh t'eey mbaa*
1SG:younger.sister 1SG:younger.sister poor ADVZR 3SG:for
ihdloh. (N)
1SG:laugh:IPV
'My younger sister, my poor younger sister, I just laughed for her.'
UTOLVDN14Apr2602:127

b. … *tsat huxah k'idįįttheeł.* (T)
wood 3PL:for 2SG:split:IPV
'… split SG wood for them!' UTCBAF13Nov0501:016

c. *Shaa* *ts'a'hutshyaak.* (N)
1SG:for AR:happen.badly:PFV
'I don't like what happened.' (lit.: 'it happened badly for me')
UTOLVDN14Apr2601:037

P+*xah, aa* 'for P, about P' is also used with neuter themes. In those instances it expresses that the state somehow affects P, or holds with respect to P (257).

(257) a. *Nche'* *naa* *ndüüh* *de'…* (N)
2SG:tail 2SG:for 3SG:be.heavy:IPV if
'If your (SG) tail is too heavy for you (SG)…'
UTCBAF14Jun0301:003

b. *Shaa* *elkąyh.* (T)
1SG:for 3SG:be.tasty:IPV
'This is tasty for me.' UTOLVDN08Mar1302:021

With the verb theme na#ho+L+nek, nak 'tell story', P+*xah, aa* always has the meaning 'about P'.

(258) *Stsǫǫ* *Kelahdzeey* *xah* *nahoholndag* (T)
1SG:grandmother spider about 3PL:tell.story:IPV:NOM
'The story they tell about Grandmother Spider' Cora David (2011, 118)

P+*xah, aa* also has the meaning 'because of P'.

(259) *Naxat* *neechil* *iin* *ch'a* *huxah* *t'eey*
those 1PL:younger.brother PL FOC 3PL:because.of ADVZR
ts'ihunnay, *hinih.* (T)
1PL:be.alive:IPV:NOM 3PL:say:IPV
'We are alive because of our younger brothers, they said.'
UTCBAF15May0403:052

P+*xah, aa* 'for P, about P' has no impact on the conjugation prefix and can be separated from the verb (259).

The allomorphy of P+*xah, aa* 'for P, about P' is phonologically conditioned: *aa* after the prefixes *sh-* '1SG.P'-, *n-* '2SG.P'-, *y-* '3SG.S>3SG.P'-, *d-* REFL.P'- (257, 260); *xah* elsewhere (258, 259).

(260) a. *Dii xah* *daa* *k'a* *eh* *ch'ihmbia?* (B)
why REFL:for NEG ? 3SG>INDF:cook:IPV:NEG
'Why may she not cook for herself?' UTOLVDN10Jul2601:043

b.

…	*yaa*	*chijeltįį…*	(N)
	3SG>3SG:for	pretend.to.sleep:IPV	

'… she pretended to sleep for (= to fool) him…'

UTOLVDN10Jul2713:024

When the object is third-person singular (with a non-third-person subject), both *mbaa* and *uxah* are attested (261). *Mbaa* is quite a bit more common.

(261) a.

Ay	*mbaa*	*tsin'įį*	*dzįįłįį.*	(T)
and	3SG:for	grateful	1PL:be:IPV	

'And we were grateful for him.' UTCBVDN14Jul1801:047

b.

Hugn	*diniign*	*nathü'ehtįį*	*uxah*	*na'inshyah.*	(N)
there	moose	3SG:skin.AO:PFV	3SG:for	3SG:SG.go:IT:PFV	

'She skinned the moose and then she came back for him.'

UTOLVDN13May2907:049

P+*xah, aa* 'for P' also is used as a subordinator introducing purpose (262a) and causal clauses (262b).

(262) a.

Dineey	*ts'uuxaan*	*xah*	*all*	*niigąą'hįlshyah.*	(T)
people	1PL:kill.PL.O:OPT	PURP	all	3PL:PL.arrive.running:PFV	

'They all came running in order to kill people.'

UTOLAF13May2403:024

b.

…	*naann'*	*nts'ą'*	*tseeneey*	*xah*
	across:ALL	to	1PL:move.nomadically:INC:IPV	because

skįiholshyeek.	(T)
3SG:move.PL.O.across:IT:IPV:CUST	

'… he was moving things across because we are moving to the other side.' UTOLAF10Jul0801:011

The formation of causal and purpose clauses is described in volume 2.

15.2.3.2. P+*eh, eł* 'with P' P+*eh* (N), *eł* (T) 'with P' is another very productive postposition. Its semantic range is similar to that of English *with*. With inanimate referents of P, it introduces instruments (263a, b). If P has human reference, P+*eh, eł* receives a comitative interpretation (263c, d). P+*eh, eł* may also introduce a cause (263e).

(263) a. *K'įį eł, k'įį eł seeyh eh t'eey xał tat'eey*
birch with birch with knife with ADVZR sled also
ehxąą. (T)
3SG:make.PL.O:PFV
'With birch, with birch and with a knife he also made sleds.'
UTOLVDN13May2801:101

b. *Sts'ayy', ok k'it t'eey meh*
1SG:canoe:POSS whirlpool on even 3SG:with
tadhihtįį. (N)
1SG:handle.LRO.on.water:PFV
'My canoe, I went onto a whirlpool with it.'
UTOLVDN07Aug2205:095

c. *Niithoo t'eey hu'eh įįda'.* (N)
long.time ADVZR 3PL:with 3SG:SG.sit:PFV
'She stayed with them for a long time.'
UTOLAF15May0501:189

d. *Shta' eh jah shyah ts'ehtsįį.* (N)
1SG:father with here house 1PL:make.SG.O:PFV
'I built this house with my father; my father and I built this house.'
UTOLAF13May2801:045

e. … *łat eł hu'įįtsįį dał t'eey hǫǫłįį.* (T)
smoke because 3PL:nose blood even AR:be:IPV
'… their noses were bleeding because of the smoke.'
UTOLAF09Jun2402:008

The examples also show that P+*eh, eł* can be separated from the verb and does not affect the conjugation prefix.

P+*eh, eł* 'with P' contains an underlying initial glottal stop that is deleted after *sh-* '1SG.P'-, *n-* '2SG.P'-, *y-* '3SG.S>3SG.P'-, *mh-* '3SG.P'-.[2]

P+*eh, eł* 'with P' has been extended in function as a nominal conjunction (264). More information on noun coordination can be found in volume 2.

(264) *Roy eł shin eł shyįį' t'eey hu'eł natsetdak.* (T)
Roy and 1SG and only even 3PL:with 1PL:PL.walk.around:IPV
'Just Roy and I were walking around with them.'
UTOLAF09Jun2902:004

P+*eh, eł* is also used as a subordinator (265); see also volume 2.

(265) *Hǫǫ' neeshyąąn eh hii'etnayh.* (N)
thus 3SG:grow.up:PFV:NOM because 3SG:know:IPV
'He knew things because he had grown up that way.'
UTOLAF12Jul1203:120

When *eh, eł* is combined with the third-person singular free pronoun *ay*, the resulting *ay eh, ay eł* is usually translated as 'and so, and then', as shown in (266). This function of *eh, eł* also is discussed in volume 2.

(266) Excerpt: UTOLAF13May2403:007-008 (T)

a. *"Didhaltth'ih!" hu'ehnih.*
2PL:PL.stay:IPV 3SG>3PL:say:IPV
'"Stay at home!" she said to them.'

b. *Ay eł hihdeltth'ih, k'at'eey tiheehaay.*
and.so 3PL:PL.stay:IPV NEG 3PL:SG.go.outside:IPV:NEG
'And so they stayed at home, they didn't go out.'

15.2.3.3. P+*k'eh* 'like P' The postposition P+*k'eh* 'following P, after P' additionally has the meaning 'like P, in the same way as P' (267).

(267) a. *Shta', shnąą k'eh t'eey dįįt'e' chih.* (N)
1SG:father 1SG:mother like ADVZR 3SG:be.thus:IPV also
'My father, he was like a mother to me.'
UTCBAF13Nov1203:024

b. *Nuhts'ay' chih dineh yuuton', naann' tsiił k'eh uk'it skįtseedeel xah.* (T)
both.sides too man 3SG>3SG:hold:IPV across:ALL bridge like 3SG:on 1PL:PL.go.across:INC:PFV:NOM PURP
'The man held on to both sides [of the canoe] so that we went across [the creek] on it like on a bridge.' UTOLAF09Jun2902:026

P+*k'eh* also has the meaning 'in the language of P' (268). The most common term for the Upper Tanana language is *neek'eh* 'like us'.

(268) … *ay eh ch'ah hǫǫsǫǫ shk'eh hunihheey.* (N)
and.then FOC well 1SG:in.language.of 1SG:speak:IPV:NOM
'… and that's why I speak my language so well.'
UTOLVDN10Jul2724:026

15.2.3.4. P+*kah* 'in quest of P, to get P' P+*kah* 'in quest of P, to get P' introduces a goal (269).

(269) a. *Hiikah* *teedak* *tah* *ch'ikol.* (T)
3PL>3SG:in.quest.of PL.go:IPV:PFV:CUST when INDF:NEGEX
'When they kept looking for him, [there was] nothing.'
UTOLAF09Jun2202:007

b. *Stsiiniin'* *kah* *ts'ihakdąy.* (N)
1SG:child:POSS for 1SG:miss:IPV
'I miss my child.' UTOLAF13May2801:056

P+*kah* 'in quest of P, for P' does not affect the conjugation marker.

15.2.3.5. P+*de' kah* 'to see if P' P+*kah* 'in quest of P, for P' is also part of the complex postposition P+*de' kah* 'to see if there is P, to check for P'. *De'* is probably related to the subordinator *de'* 'if'. P+*de' kah* implies less confidence in a successful outcome than P+*kah* and is thus often used in contexts of hunting to avoid spoiling the hunter's luck by referencing 'hunting' directly. (This is common in talking about the doman of hunting; the verb form in (270a) literally means 'they were carrying weapons around'.) P+*de' kah* 'to see if there is P, to check for P' is also used in cases where there is genuine doubt whether P will be there, as illustrated in (270b), where the nest may or may not contain eggs.

(270) a. *Ishyiit* *ts'änh* *naxach'ihdelshyeek* *shyi'*
there from 3PL>INDF:carry.around.PL.O:IPV:CUST meat
de' kah, *diniign.* (N)
looking.for moose
'From there they would go hunting for meat, moose.'
UTOLVDN13May2003:007

b. … *ch'ixia'* *ushyiit* *de' kah* *hunįh'įį…* (N)
egg 3SG:in check.for 2SG:look.around:IPV:IMP
'… look [and] check if there's eggs in it…'
UTOLVDN07Aug2205:011

Like P+*kah*, P+*de' kah* 'to see if there is P, to check for P' does not influence the choice of conjugation prefix.

P+*de' kah* 'to check for P' is also used as a subordinator (271); see also volume 2.

(271) *Ntthi' elok de' kah dąą' dįįdį'.* (N)
2SG:head hot check.for thus 2SG:do:IPV
'Do like this [gesturing: put hand on forehead] to check if your head is hot.'
UTOLAF13May2801:068

15.2.3.6. P+*doo* 'waiting for P' P+*doo* 'waiting for P' often occurs with positional themes with the meaning 'waiting for P' (272a) but is also used for lying in wait (272b).

(272) a. *Jah kon'k'eet nuhdoo uhda' ts'iikeey iin t'eey*
here village.site 2PL:wait.for 1SG:SG.sit:OPT children PL ADVZR
ch'a... (N)
FOC
'I'm going to wait here for you PL with the children...'
UTOLVDN11Aug0805:009

b. *xahjelshyah hudoo* (T)
3PL>INDF:carry.weapons:PFV 3PL:wait.for
'they were ready for them with weapons'
UTCBVDN14Jul1801:134

P+*doo* 'waiting for P' does not affect the conjugation prefix and may be separated from the verb theme.

15.2.3.7. P+*ehdänh, ehdanh* 'without P, lacking P' P+*ehdänh, ehdanh* 'without P' is a fairly rare postposition (273). It appears to be used only with inanimate objects. P+*ehdänh, ehdanh* 'without P' can be separated from the verb and does not appear to influence the conjugation prefix.

(273) a. *sǫ' kee ehdänh ti'ųųshya'!* (N)
PROH shoe without 2SG:SG.go.outside:OPT
'don't SG go out without shoes!' UTOLAF14Nov2407:001

b. *Ch'itay tuu ehdanh uda' neegąyh.* (T)
old.man water without 3SG:mouth 3SG:be.dry:IPV
'The old man's mouth was dry without water.'
UTOLVDN13May2907:060

15.2.3.8. P+*kįį'* 'subsisting on P' P+*kįį'* 'subsisting on P' usually is interpreted literally (274a) but may also be used metaphorically as in (274b), where it is best translated as 'depending on God'. It does not affect the conjugation prefix.

(274) a. *Hugn dlagn eh gah eh kįį' shyįį' hihdeltth'ih.* (T)
and squirrel and rabbit and subsisting.on only 3PL:PL.live:IPV
'They lived only on squirrels and rabbits.'
UTOLAF13May2403:044

b. *Łąą' t'eey T'oodįht'ay kįį' hdįht'eh.* (T)
truly ADVZR God subsisting.on 3PL:be.thus:IPV
'They truly depend on God.' UTOLAF10Jul0901:007

15.2.3.9. P+*k'įįl* 'on account of P, through P's fault' The postposition P+*k'įįl* 'on account of P, through P's fault' has clear connotations of blame (275). It is attested in only one narrative.

(275) *Neexon ch'a neek'įįl neets'iikeey iin k'at'eey*
1PL FOC 1PL:through.fault 1PL:children PL NEG

hii'etnay. (N)
3PL>3SG:know:IPV:NEG

'Us, it is our fault that our children don't know it.'
UTOLAF12Jul1203:022

15.2.3.10. P+*k'eexaagn* 'on account of P, through P's fault' P+*k'eexaagn* 'on account of P, through P's fault' is also attested only in this one narrative (276). Speakers commented that it is interchangeable with P+*k'įįl* 'on account of P, through P's fault'.

(276) *Neek'eexaagn ch'a ts'iikeey iin, ts'iikeey iin k'at'eey hǫǫsǫǫ*
1PL:through.fault FOC children PL children PL NEG well

dąy. (N)
do:IPV:NEG:NOM

'It is through our fault that the kids, the kids aren't doing well.'
UTOLAF12Jul1203:041

15.2.3.11. P+*k'ia'* 'on account of P' P+*k'ia'* 'on account of P' is another very rare postposition (277). It does not affect the verb theme's conjugation marker and clearly can be separated from the verb (277b).

(277) a. *Sheh shk'ia' ch'įįxąą.*
1SG:with 1SG:on.account.of 3SG>INDF:kill.PL.O:PFV
'He killed someone on account of me.' Kari (1997b)

b. *"Tl'aan shaadeh k'ia' chih ihtsah*
and 1SG:older.sister on.account.of too 1SG:cry:IPV
dhelxiin eł," nih. (T)
3SG:kill.SG.O:PASS:PFV:NOM and say:IPV
'"And I still cry on account of my older sister, since she has been killed," she said.' UTCBAF13Nov0501:305

15.2.3.12. P+*k'etl'aa(t)* 'in P's place, following P' P+*k'etl'aa(t)* 'in P's place, following P' occurs only a few times in the corpus. In both instances in (278) an object hits the place that a person just left. It might be related to P+*k'ehtl'üd* 'after P's death' described in 15.2.2.6.

(278) a. ... *dik'eetl'aat nts'ą' idehnąyh.* (T)
REFL:in.place to 3SG>3SG:throw.CO:PFV
'... she threw [the fish knife] behind herself.'
UTOLAF08Apr2805:049

b. *Ich'a' tehshyaał hu ik'eetl'aa.* (T)
3SG>3SG:from jump:INC:PFV ? 3SG>3SG:in.place
'He jumped away from [the arrow and it hit] in his place (where he had been).' UTOLVDN13May2801:184

15.2.3.13. P+*ch'a'* 'for fear of P, tired of P' P+*ch'a'* 'away from P' described in 15.2.1.5 above is attested with the meaning 'for fear of P'. (279a) is elicited; (279b) comes from a text.

(279) a. *ch'indziidn ch'a' dhihsäł* (N)
bee from 1SG:scream:PFV
'I screamed for fear of the bees.' UTOLAF18Jun0805:039

b. *Chih nah'ogn ni'eełts'ełeek ch'ah t'eey t'axoh*
also out 1PL:set.traps:IPV:CUST FOC even finally
tits'atndak uch'a'.
1PL:be.tired:IPV 3SG:from
'We would be setting traps too out there; finally we'd get tired of it.' UTCBVDN13Nov1501:096

15.2.4. Comparative postpositions

The following postpositions are all used in the comparative construction. The compared item functions as subject, the parameter of comparison is expressed by a verb, and the standard of comparison by a postpositional phrase. When the parameter of comparison is expressed by a dimensional verb theme, the comparative derivation is required. See chap. 25.3.3.1.1.1 for more information about the comparative derivation; see volume 2 about the comparative construction.

15.2.4.1. P+*k'eh* 'like P, as __ as P' P+*k'eh* 'like P, as __ as P' is used in the comparative construction when the compared entities possess the parameter of comparison to a similar degree (280).

(280) a. *Ts'iniin gaay łaakay niłk'eh t'eey hįhdüü.* (N)
baby two RECP:like ADVZR 3PL:be.heavy:IPV
'The two babies are equally heavy.' UTOLAF15Dec0601:009

b. *Aneg', Skate Lake k'eh įhchay manh.* (T)
NTRL:upland:ALL Skate Lake like 3SG:be.big:PFV: lake
'It's about as big a lake as Skate Lake up there.'
UTOLVDN09Jun2303:024

15.2.4.2. P+*k'e'* 'less than P' P+*k'e'* 'less than P' is used in comparisons of inferiority, where the compared item possesses the parameter of comparison to a lesser degree than the standard (281).

(281) a. *Dineh gaay dinąą k'e' įhchaa.* (T)
boy REFL:mother less.than 3SG:be.big:IPV
'The boy is almost as tall as his mother.' UT Notebook #2, 1a

b. *Tl'aan udia' chih ntsuul, moondaa*
and 3SG:younger.sister too 3SG:be.small:IPV 3SG:older.brother
chih uk'e' įhtsuul. (T)
too 3SG:less.than 3SG:be.small:IPV
'And the younger sister was small too, she was also smaller than her older brother.' UTCBAF13Nov0501:009

15.2.4.3. P+*ch'ashyiit* 'more than P' P+*ch'ashyiit* 'more than P' is used in comparisons of superiority, where the compared item possesses the parameter of comparison to a greater degree than the standard (282).

(282) a. *Nch'ashyiit agtthał.* (T)
2SG:more.than 1SG:SG.run:IPV:PROG
'I run faster than you.' UTOLAF15May0609:018

b. *Ishyiit nah'ogn giǫ shch'ashyiit t'eey nįhnia.* (N)
there outside fireweed 1SG:more.than ADVZR 3SG:be.tall:IPV
'Out there the fireweed is taller than me.'
UTOLAF09Aug1202:027

15.2.4.4. P+*ch'ahnoo* 'lots more than P' P+*ch'ahnoo* 'lots more than P' is used in comparisons of superiority, where the compared item possesses the parameter of comparison to a considerably greater degree than the standard. In the Tetlin dialect P+*ch'ahnoo* 'lots more than P' with an areal object is also the response to the attempt to elicit absolute comparison (283c).

(283) a. *That one du' shch'anoo' t'eey hi'etnayh.* (N)
that one CT 1SG:lots.more.than ADVZR 3SG:know:IPV
'That one knew a lot more than me.'
UTOLVDN10Jul2724:029

b. *Ahdegn' sǫǫgay du' ahdegn'*
NTRL:up.vertically:ALL pop CT NTRL:up.vertically:ALL
uch'anoo' elkąy. (T)
3SG:lots.more.than 3SG:be.sweet:IPV
'This pop up here is a lot sweeter than the one up here.'
UTOLAF15May0608:066

c. *Huch'ahnoo' nįįndia.* (T)
AR:lots.more.than 3SG:be.long:IPV
'This is the longest [rope].' UTOLAF15May0609:010

15.3. Summary

In this chapter free postpositions are described. Free postpositions are distinguished from bound postpositions by three criteria: they combine freely with a variety of different verb themes and verb theme categories, they can be separated from or follow the verb word, and they do not influence the choice of conjugation prefix of the verb form. They are thus not considered part of the verb theme.

The majority of this chapter is dedicated to an inventory of free postpositions detailing their semantics and usage. Four major semantic categories of postpositions are identified: postpositions with spatial arguments, postpositions with temporal arguments, postpositions introducing participants, and postpositions used in the comparative construction.

Notes

1. In Upper Tanana this noun stem does not occur in isolation but only as part of several compounds and complex postpositions. According to Kari (1997b), this morpheme is also related to the postpositions P+*t'aat* 'underneath P', P+*t'a-* 'catching up with P, against P' and P+*t'a-* 'obstructing P, snagging on P'.
2. No forms of this postposition inflected for *d-* 'REFL.P'- are attested.

16 | Adverbs

Adverbs are defined here as uninflectable expressions modifying all constituents other than noun phrases (16.1). Structurally they are very diverse, ranging from monosyllabic stems to more or less lexicalized phrases (16.2; adverbs of phrasal origin are described here only if they are strongly lexicalized). In spite of their structural diversity, I choose the label "adverb" for these words because this is a typologically common label for this type of element.

Adverbs fall into several broad semantic categories: spatial, temporal, aspectual, manner, and degree adverbs; see 16.3. A subgroup of spatial adverbs, the directional adverbs or directionals, form a cohesive system and are described in greater detail in chap. 17. The syntax of adverbs is described in volume 2.

16.1. Functions

Upper Tanana adverbs modify clauses (284), verb phrases (285), other adverbs (286), or adjectives and modifiers (287).

(284) a. *Uhtsüh* *inihthänh* *k'ahdu'.* (N)
1SG:cry:OPT 1SG:want:IPV now
'Now I feel like crying.' UTCBAF13Nov1203:041

b. *Ts'ehkah* *t'eey* *ay* *ch'aldzeeg* *shyiit* *dineh gaay*
plainly ADVZR 3SG moon in boy
eeday *tnah'įįł.* (T)
3SG:SG.stay:IPV:NOM 2PL:see:FUT
'You can plainly see that boy up there in the moon.'
UTOLAF09Jun2202:073

c. *Jahxan* *ch'aadeh* *dii* *le'* *hadel'ąy.* (T)
suddenly INDF:older.sister something IGN 3SG:spot:PFV
'Suddenly the older sister spotted something.'
UTCBAF13Nov0501:061

(285) a. *Ts'exeh gaay ishyiit nts'ą' teeshyah.* (T)
girl there to 3SG:SG.go:INC:IPFV
'The girl went over there.' UTOLAF07Oct2512:005

b. *Soo', soo' dįįt'eh,* … (N)
careful careful 2SG:be.thus:IPV
'Careful, be (SG) careful, …' UTOLVDN14Apr2601:019

c. *Ay eh k'ahjil sheh nakecheexał.* (N)
and and almost 1SG:with 3PL:turn.over.LRO:INC:PFV
'And [the guns sliding about] almost turned over [the canoe] with me.' UTOLVDN07Aug2205:100

(286) a. *"Huhnaan' tat'eey shaa lah hunįįthaat ha',"*
NTRL:AR:across:ALL even 1SG:for NEG AR:be.far:PFV NEG
nih. (T)
say:IPV
'"Even all the way across is not too far for me," he said.'
UTOLVDN13May2902:030

b. *Hugn niign tat'eey ch'a k'ahdu' hǫǫ't'eey ts'idąy.* (N)
there that.way also FOC now still 1PL:do:IPV:NOM
'We do it this way still today.' UTCBAF13Nov1203:035

(287) a. *That stsay Aambeet ła' t'eey tsin'įį.* (T)
that 1SG:grandfather Albert truly grateful
'My grandfather Aambeet was truly grateful.'
UTCBVDN13Nov1502:050

b. *Teejuh nts'ą' t'eey eltsiin ts'iniin gaay.* (T)
cute ADVZR 3SG:seem:IPV:NOM baby
'He looked really cute, that baby.' UTOLVDN13May2801:062

Most adverbs precede the element they modify, although some follow it.

16.2. Adverb formation

16.2.1. Stem adverbs

Many adverbs consist of a lexical stem. The list in (288) is not inclusive.

(288) Stem adverbs
a. haagn 'last, previous'

b. chih 'too, also'
c. jah 'here'
d. dąą' 'thus'
e. hǫǫ' 'thus'
f. łą' 'truly'
g. tay' 'again'
h. t'ah 'also'
i. xaa', xa' 'slowly'
j. xan' 'quickly'

These adverbs have syllable structures typical of stems: CV:(C) and CVC (see chap. 10).

16.2.2. Complex adverbs

Complex adverbs fall into three groups. They can consist of a stem and additional morphological material (16.2.2.1), or they can be of phrasal origin, either from a postpositional phrase (16.2.2.2) or from a verb phrase (16.2.2.3).

16.2.2.1. Adverb stem plus other material There are a number of adverbs consisting of a stem and additional morphological material. Some of these seem to be prefixed stems (289); others consist of two stems (290).

(289) Adverbs consisting of a prefixed stem

a.	tat'eey	'also'	ta- '?' + t'eey 'even, INTS'
b.	dishyįį'	'alone, by oneself'	di- 'REFL' + shyįį' 'only'
c.	dihishyįį'	'alone, by themselves'	dihi- 'REFL:PL' + shyįį' 'only'
d.	ch'idänh	'elsewhere'	ch'i- 'different' + dänh 'at'
e.	ch'its'ąą'	'differently, wrong, evil'	ch'i- 'different' + nts'ąą 'how'?

(290) Adverbs consisting of two stems

a.	jahdu'	'right here'	jah 'here' + du' 'CT'
b.	k'ahdu'	'right now'	k'ah 'now?' + du' 'CT'
c.	ttheede'	'later on'	tthee 'wait' + de' 'when:FUT'
d.	hǫǫ't'eey	'still'	hǫǫ' 'thus' + t'eey 'even'?
e.	ha'gaay	'slowly, carefully, a little'	xa' 'slowly' + gaay 'small'
f.	ha'tsuul	'a little bit'	xa' 'slowly' + tsuul 'small'
g.	ha'k'aa	'slowly'	xa' 'slowly' + k'aa '?'
h.	hanteey'	'quickly'	xan 'quickly' + teey' '?'
i.	jahxan	'suddenly'	jah 'here' + xan 'quickly'

j.	saan xa'	'barely'	saan 'barely' + xa' 'slowly'
k.	saan tah	'barely, hardly'	saan 'barely' + tah 'among'?

In (290e–h) the initial consonant /x/ of *xa'* 'slowly' and *xan* 'quickly' is weakened to /h/.

The adverbs in (291) are clearly complex, yet their components are not identifiable.

(291) Complex, opaque adverbs

a.	t'axoh	'finally'
b.	ts'ehkah	'clearly, plainly'
c.	dahniit	'always, forever, all the time'
d.	dinah	'all the while'

16.2.2.2. Adverbs from postpositional phrases Many adverbs are lexicalized postpositional phrases. Some adverbs originate in postpositions prefixed with the indefinite object prefix *ch'-* (292); this list is not inclusive.

(292) Postpositions with indefinite object

a.	ch'ittheh	'first'
b.	ch'ik'eh	'last'
c.	ch'itah	'there, in the group'

Several temporal adverbs are formed in a very regular fashion using the postpositions P+*dą'* 'at P (PST)' and P+ *de'* 'at P (FUT)'. Additionally, the contrastive topic marker *du'* is used sometimes to convey the meaning 'at a point in the present'. The adverbs formed with *du'* 'CT' are ambiguous; e.g., *k'ahmänn' du'* can mean 'this morning right now' or 'in the morning, every morning'. The inventory in (293) is not inclusive.

(293) Complex temporal adverbs

a.	k'ahdąą' dą'	'yesterday'	k'ah 'now'
b.	k'ahdąą' de'	'tomorrow'	
c.	k'ahmänn' dą'	'this morning past'	k'ahmänn' 'morning'
d.	k'ahmänn' de'	'tomorrow morning'	
e.	k'ahmänn' du'	'this morning right now'	
f.	dziin dą'	'earlier today'	dziin 'day'
g.	dziin de'	'later today'	
h.	dziin du'	'today'	

16.2.2.3. Adverbs from verb phrases A few verb forms have been lexicalized as adverbs (294).

(294) Deverbal adverbs

a.	hǫǫchaa	'very, very much'
b.	hǫǫsǫǫ, hǫǫsu'	'well'
c.	hǫǫdlaan	'many times'
d.	niithaad	'a long time ago'
e.	niithoo'	'many times, a long time'

The morphological structure of the adverbs in (294a–c) is given in (295a), and that of the adverbs (294d, e) is given in (295b). It is unclear why *hǫǫdlaan* 'many times' and *niithaad* 'a long time ago' contain the nominalizing suffix while the others do not.

(295) a. *hǫǫchaa*
hǫǫ-chaa
AR:Ø.PFV:Ø-be.big:IPV
'very, very much'

b. *niithaad*
nii-thaad
3SG:N.PFV:Ø-be.far:IPV:NOM
'a long time ago'

These adverbs may be used together with the adverbializers *t'eey* and *nts'ą̨' t'eey* described in 16.2.3.

16.2.3. Adverbializers

There are several adverbializers. *T'eey* may be used as an adverb of intensity (see 16.3.5), but oftentimes, it seems to be largely bleached of meaning and simply transforms the preceding phrase into an adverbial. In (296a) the preceding phrase is a verb phrase, in (296b) a noun phrase, and in (296c) a postpositional phrase.

(296) a. *Hugn* *nts'ą̨'* *tsaadįįl* *t'eey,* *hǫǫ'* *nee'ehnih.* (N)
whatever how 1PL:do:FUT ADVZR thus 3SG>1PL:say:IPV
'Whatever we're going to do, thus he told us.'
UTCBAF13Nov1203:003

b. *Ay hunu' t'eey titaahaal nt'eh.* (N)
and AR:hole ADVZR 3SG:SG.go.out:FUT ASRT
'He will certainly go out through that hole.'
UTCBAF15May0401:021

c. *Hǫǫsǫǫ t'eey nich'ak-'aał...* (T)
well ADVZR 1SG>2SG>INDF:feed:IPV:CUST
'I always feed you well...' UTOLVDN13May2901:018

Nts'ą̈' t'eey 'ADVZR' seems largely to be restricted to verb phrases (297a); this function is then often extended to that of a subordinator (297b). (297c) is a very rare instance where *nts'ą̈' t'eey* 'ADVZR' follows a nonverbal element *taagn* 'three'.[1]

(297) a. ... *hǫǫsu' nts'ą' t'eey niihu'ahłeek*
nicely ADVZR 2PL>3PL:receive.PL.O:IPV:CUST
hu'ich'ah'aał. (N)
2PL>3PL>INDF:feed:IPV:CUST
'... you PL [must] receive and feed them nicely.'
UTOLAF10Jul0901:038

b. *Dii ch'ihdeh'ąą ts'ą̈' t'eey k'a hi'agnnayh.* (N)
what 3PL>INDF:sing:IPV ADVZR NEG 1SG:remember:IPV:NEG
'I don't remember what they were singing.'
UTCBVDN14Jul2105:043

c. *Taag nts'ą' t'eey łahtthagn nts'ą' t'eey ishnah.* (T)
three ADVZR all ADVZR 1SG:work:IPV
'I have done all my three chores.' (= I have worked all three times.)
UTOLAF12Jul0601:017

The adverbializer *niign* 'the way that, the direction that' always follows a verb phrase (298). For that reason it might be more appropriately considered to be a subordinator; see volume 2 for discussion and examples.

(298) a. *"Nduu tneet'ak niign įįhaał!"* (N)
where:AR 3SG:SG.fly:INC:PFV the.way 2SG:SG.go:IPV:PROG
'Go SG in the direction where it is flying!'
UTOLAF08Feb1906:009

b. *Nts'aa' ndihnih niign tįįdiił!* (T)
how 1SG>2SG:say:IPV the.way 2SG.do:FUT
'You (SG) will act in the way that I tell you!'
UTOLVDN08Mar1307:014

c. *Sheł naholndak niign ch'a dihnay.* (T)
1SG:to 3SG:tell.story:IPV the.way FOC 1SG:say:IPV:NOM
'I say it the way she told me the story.' UTOLAF09Jun2402:002

The subordinating functions of the three adverbializers discussed here are described in volume 2.

16.3. Semantic categorization

There are five major categories of adverbs: adverbs of space, adverbs of time, aspectual adverbs, adverbs of manner, and adverbs of degree. In the following sections the most common adverbs in each category are briefly described. The discussion is limited to stem adverbs and complex adverbs; adverbs created by one of the adverbializers are not discussed here.

16.3.1. Spatial adverbs

The inventory of spatial adverbs in Upper Tanana is quite large due to the existence of a systematic subgroup, the directional adverbs, which are described in chap. 17. Most of the following adverbs do not belong to the directional system; exceptions are (299e, f), both of which are semantically bleached directional forms. *Ishyiit* 'there' is the punctual form of the directional *shyign'* 'downhill'; *ahshyuugn* 'on the ground' is the areal form of the same directional.

(299) Spatial adverbs

a. jah 'here'
b. jah du' 'right here'
c. jah dugn 'hereabouts'
d. ch'idänh 'elsewhere, in a different place'
e. ishyiit 'there'
f. ahshyuugn 'on the ground'

Spatial adverbs usually occur in preverbal position (300).

(300) a. *Shǫǫnüü* *Carl* *jah* *eedah* *de',*
1SG:older.brother Carl here 3SG:SG.stay:IPV if
neek'anehta'. (N)
3SG>1PL:take.care:IPV
'When my older brother Carl was there, he would take care of us.'
UTCBAF13Nov1203:016

b. *Ts'exeh gaay* *ishyiit* *nts'ą'* *teeshyah.* (T)
girl there to 3SG:SG.go:PFV
'The girl went over there.' UTOLAF07Oct2512:005

16.3.2. Temporal adverbs

Many adverbs situating an event in time derive from postpositional phrases (see 16.2.2.2); these are not discussed here. The adverbs listed in (301) are not transparent. Note that this inventory is not inclusive; only the more common adverbs are listed here.

(301) Temporal adverbs

a.	haagn	'last, previous'
b.	niithaad	'a long time ago'
c.	niithoo'	'many times, a long time'
d.	ts'ehłoo	'once'
e.	jahxan	'suddenly'

There are also several spatial adverbs that are ambiguous between a spatial and a temporal reading (302).

(302) Spatial-temporal adverbs

a.	ishyiit dą'	'here'	'now'
b.	noo'	'a long ways ahead'	'a long time from now'
c.	jah	'here'	'now'
d.	jahdu'	'right here'	'right now'

Temporal adverbs setting the time of the event usually occur in clause-initial position, which is consistent with their scope over the entire situation (303).

(303) a. *Jahxan* *t'eey* *didia'* *tay'* *t'eey*
suddenly ADVZR REFL:younger.sister again ADVZR
yiteembaak. (T)
3SG>3SG:fight:INC:PFV
'Suddenly she again began to fight her younger sister.'
UTCBVDN13Nov1101:035

b. *K'ahdu' ts'iikeey iin hǫǫ't'eey hits'ihetniign.* (N)
now children PL still 3PL:not.know:IPV
'Right now, the children still don't understand.'
UTOLAF12Jul1203:040

When they occur in pre-predicate position, they have scope only over the predicate (304).

(304) *Łuugn he'aal, k'ahdu' łuugn*
fish 3PL:eat:IPV:CUST:NOM now fish
hahehłeegn he'aal, k'ahdu'
3PL:take.out.PL.O:IPV:CUST:NOM 3PL:eat:IPV:CUST:NOM now
diniign hehxaan, hugn įįjih. (T)
moose 3PL:kill.PL.O:IPV:CUST:NOM also forbidden
'Eating fish, eating freshly caught fish or freshly killed moose is also forbidden.' UTOLVDN11Jul2901:012

16.3.3. Aspectual adverbs

There are a number of aspectual adverbs; the list in (305) is not inclusive.

(305) Aspectual adverbs
a. t'axoh 'finally, almost, already'
b. dahniit 'forever, always'
c. dinah 'meanwhile, in the meantime'
d. hǫǫ't'eey 'still'
e. tth'ih 'still'
f. tay' 'again'
g. k'ahjil almost'

Aspectual adverbs scope over the verb phrase, which is reflected in their usual placement right before the verb phrase (306).

(306) a. *U'aat t'axoh ts'ehłagn neehaał mbookol.* (T)
3SG:wife already one 3SG:spend.night:PFV 3SG:NEGEX
'His wife had already been gone for one day.'
UTOLVDN13May2907-058

b. *Eh hǫǫ't'eey ihsäł.* (N)
and still 1SG:holler:IPV
'And I was still hollering.' UTOLAF09Aug1202:034

c. ... *tay'* *mbeh* *nadzaltth'i'.* (N)
again 3SG:with 1PL:PL.stay:PFV
'... we stayed another night with him.'
UTOLVDN10Jul2724:048

Only *dinah* 'meanwhile' tends to follow the verb (307).

(307) *Hutthan'* *yaahetdak* *dinah.* (T)
AR:waterwards:ALL 3PL:PL.keep.walking:IPV:CUST meanwhile
'In the meantime, they kept on walking downhill.'
UTCBVDN13Nov1101:039

16.3.4. Manner adverbs

The following adverbs describe the manner in which an event takes place. The list in (308) is not inclusive.

(308) Manner adverbs

a.	hǫǫsu', hǫǫsǫǫ, su'	'well, nicely'
b.	saan xa'/tah/t'eey	'barely'
c.	tsehkah	'plainly, in plain sight'
d.	xan, hanteey'	'quickly'
e.	xa', ha'gaay	'slowly, carefully'
f.	soo', suu'	'carefully'
g.	shyąą' t'eey	'for nothing, for no reason'
h.	ch'its'ąą'	'different, wrong, evil'
i.	naadlįh, naadlii	'instead, by mistake'
j.	dąą'	'thus' (when demonstrating)
k.	hǫǫ'	'thus' (when speaking/doing)

Dąą' 'thus, like that' is often used in demonstrations, while *hǫǫ'* co-occurs with verbs of speaking and thinking and the verb theme d+Ø+dį' 'do' (309).

(309) a. *Dąą'* *ts'eh'įįk* *tl'aan* *eegąy* *de'* *dąą'*
thus 1PL:do:IPV:CUST and 3SG:become.dry:PFV when:FUT thus
tat-'įįł. (N)
3SG:look.like:FUT
'We do like this, and when it has dried, it'll look like that.'
UTOLVDN07Aug2001:004

b. *"Sǫ' hǫǫ' dahdį' t'axoh," hu'ehnih.* (N)
PROH thus 2PL:do:IPV finally 3SG>3PL:say:IPV
'"Don't PL do that again!" he said to them.'
UTOLAF09Aug1202:041

c. *Shnąą hǫǫ' shehnih.* (T)
1SG:mother thus 3SG>1SG:say:IPV
'My mom told me that.' UTOLAF12Jul0601:026

Most manner adverbs precede the predicate or the verb (310), although they may also follow it (311).

(310) a. *I mean udzih ch'its'ąą' iholnayh ha le'.* (T)
I mean caribou different 3SG:taste:IPV maybe
'I mean, maybe caribou tastes different.'
UTOLVDN13May2401:040

b. ... *"Ayaa! Shyąą t'eey ch'a dįįnay!"*
mean for.nothing ADVZR FOC 2SG:say:PFV:NOM
shehnih. (N)
3SG>1SG:say:IPV
'... "Mean! You said that for nothing!" she said to me.'
UTOLVDN14Apr2602:126

c. *Ts'ist'e' ha' gaay ni'eeshyah.* (T)
old.lady slowly 3SG:S.get.up:PFV
'The old lady got up slowly.' UTOLVDN14Nov2301:430

d. *Nts'aa' nih saan t'eey dihtth'ek.* (N)
how say:IPV barely ADVZR 1SG:hear:IPV
'I can barely hear what he's saying.' UTOLAF13May2801:060

e. *Noodlee k'eh naadlįh hihunayh.* (N)
white.person like instead 3PL:live:IPV
'They instead live like white people.' UTOLAF12Jul1203:075

(311) a. *Iich'eh'aał hǫǫsǫǫ t'eey.* (T)
3SG>3SG>INDF:feed:IPV well ADVZR
'She fed him nicely.' UTOLVDN13May2901:013

b. *Na'ithat ts'ehkah t'eey.* (T)
3SG:S.stand:IPV plainly ADVZR
'It was standing in plain sight.' UTOLVDN13May2907:023

16.3.5. Degree adverbs

There are several degree adverbs; the list in (312) is likely inclusive.

(312) Degree adverbs
a. (nts'ą̈') t'eey 'very'
b. hǫǫchaa (t'eey) 'very'
c. łą' t'eey 'really'

The two adverbializers *t'eey* and *nts'ą̈' t'eey* mentioned in 16.2.3 both also function as intensifiers following the adverb they modify (313).

(313) a. *Niithoo' t'eey ts'ist'e' eedah.* (T)
long.time ADVZR old.lady 3SG:S.stay:IPV
'She stayed [with] the old lady for a very long time.'
UTCBAF13Nov0501:280

b. … *shyi' hǫǫsu' nts'ą' t'eey huxah nahįlshyah.* (N)
meat nicely very 3PL:for 3PL:bring.back.PL.O:PFV
'… they brought the meat back to them very nicely.'
UTCBAF15May0403:016

Hǫǫchaa (t'eey) 'very, a lot' and *łą' (t'eey)* 'really truly' usually precede the verb phrases they modify (314) but may also follow it (315).

(314) a. *Hǫǫchaa t'eey tthahdelxoh.* (T)
very ADVZR 3PL:make.noise:IPV
'They were making lots of noise.' UTOLAF13May2403:004

b. *Hudson łą' t'eey nįįsǫǫ nts'ą̈' t'eey eltsįį.*
Hudson really ADVZR 3SG:be.pretty:IPV ADVZR 3SG:appear:IPV
(N)

'Hudson looks very pretty.' UTOLAF15Dec0601:023

(315) *That ch'aadeh du' eetįį hǫǫchaa t'eey.* (N)
that INDF:older.sister CT 3SG.sleep:IPV very ADVZR
'That older sister was sleeping very hard.'
UTOLAF15May0501:060

16.4. Summary

The adverbs of Upper Tanana do not form a structurally homogeneous group. I choose the label "adverb" because of their functional similarities. Their functions are described in section 16.1; some common strategies of adverb formation are described in section 16.2. Section 16.3 contains an inventory of adverbs. A special set of spatial adverbs, the directionals, is described in chap. 17.

Notes

1. The quantifier *łahtthagn* 'all' is of verbal origin and frequently is followed by *nts'ą̈' t'eey.*

17 Directionals

The directionals constitute an important subgroup of spatial adverbs in Alaskan Dene, forming a cohesive system both semantically and formally. They consist of directional roots referencing a riverine orientation system. There are three sets of paired roots (upriver versus downriver, upland versus waterwards, up above versus down below) and three unpaired ones (across, outside, ahead). These roots are obligatorily suffixed with one of four suffixes expressing allative, ablative, punctual, and areal direction or location. While this process is historically transparent (Leer 1989), the resulting stems are not synchronously transparent to Upper Tanana speakers. Directional stems are optionally prefixed with one or several prefixes indicating distance.

The directional system allows speakers to give very detailed and intricate descriptions of spatial layouts. Directionals are pervasive in discourse and serve a number of functions; some of these are described in Brucks (2015) and Brucks and Lovick (2018). Their complex structure means that they are difficult to translate into English (316).

(316) *Ay hanoshyiit kon'k'eet, ts'iikeey iin tsüh eh shya'eh'ąą.* (N)

ay	*ha-na-hu-shyiit*	*kon'k'eet*	*ts'iikeey*	*iin*
and	ADJC-MED-AR-down.vertically:PNCT	village.site	children	PL

tsüh	*eh*	*shya-eh-'ąą*
cry:IPV	and	noise-3PL.S:DH.PFV:H-classify.CO:IPV

'And down there in the village the children were crying and wailing.'
UTOLVDN11Aug0805:014

It is impossible to give an exact yet even slightly elegant translation of *hanoshyiit* into English: literally it means something like 'next to them at a point in the area a medium distance away vertically down'. The translation 'down there' in (316) is woefully inadequate. Throughout this chapter I attempt to render the directionals as accurately as possible. This has the unfortunate but necessary consequence of very cumbersome translations in several

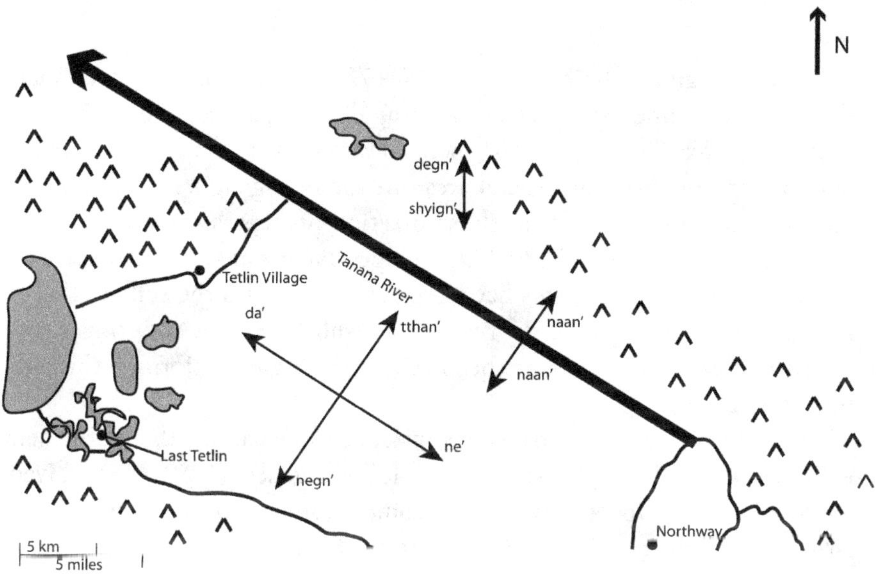

Map 4. Schematic map of the Alaskan part of the Upper Tanana area

places. In the remainder of this grammar I translate directionals less accurately and hope that the glosses convey their intricate meaning sufficiently.

Formation and semantics of directional stems are described in 17.1, prefixes in 17.2. In those sections, morpheme glosses are provided. Directional stems also often bear a high tone; this is described in 17.3.

17.1. Directional stems

The directional system in Alaskan Dene languages is in the terms of Levinson (2003) an absolute landmark-based system, where the GROUND is the major river (Kari 1985, 2010; Berez 2011; Brucks 2015). In the case of Upper Tanana this is the Tanana, which has its origin in the Northway area at the confluence of the Nabesna and Chisana rivers and then flows Northeast. A schematic map is given in map 4.

Underlying the directional system are the four directions *ne'* 'upriver' versus *da'* 'downriver' and *negn'* 'up from shore, upland' versus *tthän'* 'down toward shore, downland, waterward'. There is also the directional *naan'* 'across the river', which is its own opposite. These five directionals are based directly on the flow of the Tanana. The directional stems *degn'* 'up above, uphill' versus *shyign'* 'down below, downhill' are not based on the Tanana but instead reference basic vertical orientation. *Noo'* 'ahead' and *'än* 'off to the side, away' also do not reference the river.

17.1.1. Forms

As observed originally by Kari (1985, 471–72), Alaskan Dene directionals consist of three elements: a prefix expressing distance, a directional root, and one of four suffixes indicating movement toward or away from a place or location in a specific place or general area. In some languages such as Ahtna, unsuffixed roots may occur, and the suffixation process is somewhat transparent to speakers (Kari 1985, 2010). In Upper Tanana unsuffixed directional roots are not attested, and roots have fused so tightly with the suffixes that it is impossible now to separate the two. As a result I treat the resulting stems as indivisible units and consider the allative stem (which is formed through suffixation of *-ə) as basic.

The inventory of directional stems in Upper Tanana, together with their Pre-Proto-Dene (PPD) reconstructions[1] following Leer (1989, 616) is given in table 17.1. All Upper Tanana data comes from my own fieldwork; the ablative stem of the root 'ahead' is not attested in the data.

English	PPD	Upper Tanana			
		Allative	Ablative	Punctual	Areal
'up above'	**dəɢ	degn'	dǫǫ/doo	daat	dogn
'down below'	**yəɢ, yəx	shyign'	shyǫǫ	shyiit	shyuugn
'upriver'	**niʔ	ne'	nǫǫ/noo	niit	nugn
'downriver'	**daʔ	da'	dǫǫ/doo	daat	dugn
'upland'	**nəɢ	negn'	nǫǫ/noo	niit	nogn/nuugn
'downland'	**cənʔ	tthän'	tthǫǫ	tthiit	tthuugn
'ahead'	**nəsd	noo'	?	noot	noogn
'across'	**ŋa·nʔ	naan'	nǫǫ	naat	nuugn
'away'	**ʔɑnʔ	'än'	'ǫǫ	'aat	'ogn/'oogn

Table 17.1. Directional stems in Pre-Proto-Dene and Upper Tanana

Table 17.1 demonstrates that there are quite a few homophones in this set: *nuugn* may mean 'across:AR' or 'upland:AR', *niit* can mean 'upriver:PNCT' or 'upland:PNCT', *dǫǫ* can be either 'up:ABL' or 'downriver:ABL', and so forth. As a result some of these forms are used only rarely (e.g., *nǫǫ* 'upriver:ABL' does not occur in the corpus at all and could be elicited from only one speaker) and are instead replaced with periphrastic expressions. In other cases it appears that speakers do not even notice the resulting ambiguity, presumably because of their detailed knowledge of the surrounding area.

17.1.1.1. *ne'* 'upriver' *Ne'* describes movement or location with respect to a reference point upriver.

The allative form *ne'* 'upriver:ALL' occurs quite frequently. In (317a) the stem is lengthened to indicate that they went a long way. Emphatic lengthening is described in volume 2.

(317) a. *Ay tl'aan ahne:::' tseekįį.* (N)

ay tl'aan ah-ne' tsee-kįį

and.then NTRL-upriver:ALL 1PL.S:INC:DH.PFV:Ø-go.by.boat:PFV

'And then we paddled a long way upriver.'

UTOLVDN07Aug2205:042

b. *Ne' sheh natuudaagn!* (N)

ne' sh-eh na-tuu-daagn

upriver:ALL 1SG.P-with IT-3SG.S:INC:OPT-D:SG.go:OPT

'She should come back upriver with me!'

UTOLVDN10Jul2724:018

The ablative form of *ne'* does not occur in the corpus. When asked about this form directly, one speaker produced (318).

(318) *Nǫǫ ts'ayh eh natihdaał.* (N)

nǫǫ ts'ayh eh na-tih-daał

upriver:ABL boat with IT-INC:AA.IPV:1SG.S:Ø-SG.go:FUT

'I'm going to come back from upriver by boat.' UT Notebook #2.5, 32

Another speaker did not accept this form and instead suggested the periphrastic expression in (319).

(319) *Ande' ts'anh nanishshyah.* (T)

a-nde' ts'anh na-nish-shyah

NTRL-upriver:ALL from IT-N.PFV:1SG.S:D-SG.go:PFV

'I came back from upriver.' UT Notebook #2.5, 26

While this might be a dialect difference, the absence of *nǫǫ* 'upriver:ABL' in the corpus suggests that it is avoided because of its homophony with *nǫǫ* 'upland:ABL' and *nǫǫ* 'across:ABL'.

The punctual form *niit* 'upriver:PNCT' is homophonous with *niit* 'upland:PNCT'. It is not used very frequently, but a few clear cases can be identified. (320a) was uttered in Tetlin; from that perspective, Northway is upriver. Similarly the Scottie Creek area in (320b) is clearly upriver from Northway.

(320) a. *Aniit danh keey danh Naambia.* (T)

a-niit *danh* *keey* *danh* *Naambia*
NTRL-upriver:PNCT at village at Northway

'At a place upriver is the village Northway.'
UTCBAF14Jul1804:001

b. *Ts'oo godn gaay ha'ahniit Scottie Creek nihthänh.* (N)

ts'oo *godn* *gaay* *ha-ah-niit* *Scottie* *Creek*
spruce knee small ADJC-NTRL-upriver:PNCT Scottie Creek

nih-thänh
QUAL:Ø.PFV:1SG.S:Ø-think:IPV

'Little Spruce Knee [is] at a place upriver adjacent to Scottie Creek, I think.' UTOLVDN10Jul2724:009

The areal form *nugn* 'upriver:AR' is illustrated in (321).

(321) a. … *stsay stsǫǫ du' hahnugn tah ishyiit hugn ch'a shǫǫnüü hihnehshyąą.* (N)

s-tsay *s-tsǫǫ* *du'* *hah-nugn*
1SG.PSR-grandfather 1SG.PSR:grandmother CT NTRL-upriver:AR

tah *ishyiit* *hugn* *ch'a* *sh-ǫǫnüü*
among there there FOC 1SG.PSR-older.brother

hih-neh-shyąą
3PL.S-QUAL:DH.PFV:H:raise:PFV

'… and there in the upriver area my grandparents raised my older brother.' UTOLAF12Jul1203:118

b. … *"Anugn mänh tah natsetkeek ch'ixia' de' kah," hinih.* (N)

a-nugn *mänh* *tah*
NTRL-upriver:AR lake among

na-tset-keek *ch'-xia'*
PRMB-1PL.S:INC:Ø.IPV:D-go.by.boat:IPV:CUST INDF.PSR-eggs

de' kah *hi-nih*
check.for 3PL.S:Ø.IPV:Ø-say:IPV

'… "Let's paddle around the lakes in the upriver area to look for eggs," they said.' UTOLVDN07Aug2205:032

17.1.1.2. *da'* 'downriver' The allative form is illustrated in (322).

(322) a. *Hada' Delta, Delta naheltąyh.* (N)

ha-da' *Delta* *Delta*
NTRL-downriver:ALL Delta Delta

na-hel-tąyh
IT-3PL.S:AA.PFV:L-make.trips:IPV:CUST

'They would make trips downriver to Delta.'

UTCBVDN13Nov0805:006

b. *Tth'itu' niign da' tayahteeł.* (N)

tth'itu' niign *da'*
river downriver:ALL

ta-yah-teeł
water-3SG.S>3SG.O:AA.PFV:H-handle.AO:IPV:PROG

'The river was carrying her downstream.'

UTOLAF12Jul1201:039

The form *dǫǫ* 'downriver:ABL' is homophonous with *dǫǫ* 'up:ABL'. In (323a) it is used to describe travel along the Tanana River, while in (323b) it describes the arrangement of houses in the old Northway village.

(323) a. *Ay tl'aan Teedląy ts'änh jah duhdǫǫ Northway nahetdek.* (N)

ay tl'aan *Teedląy* *ts'änh* *jah* *d-uh-dǫǫ* *Northway*
and.then Tetlin from here PROX-AR-downriver:ABL Northway

na-het-dek
IT-3PL.S:Ø.IPV:D-PL.go:IPV:CUST

'And then from Tetlin, from the area a little ways downriver they would return to Northway.' UTCBVDN13Nov0805:014

b. *Ha'ahdǫǫ neeshyah nts'ą̈' dǫǫ, ha'ashyign' shee'eh Stephen eeday…* (N)

ha-ah-dǫǫ *nee-shyah* *nts'ą̈'* *dǫǫ,*
ADJC-NTRL-downriver:ABL 1PL.PSR-house toward downriver:ABL

ha-a-shyign' *sh-ee'eh* *Stephen*
ADJC-NTRL-down:ALL 1SG.PSR-maternal.uncle Stephen

ee-day
3SG.S:DH.PFV:Ø-SG.sit:IPV:NOM

'The next one from downriver toward our house, down from where my uncle Stephen was staying, …' UTCBVDN13Nov0804:015

(324) illustrates the stem *daat* 'downriver:PNCT'.

(324) a. *Ay tl'aan adaat mänh aanah ushyah hǫǫłįį dänh…* (N)

ay tl'aan *a-daat* *mänh* *aanah* *u-shyah*
and.then NTRL-downriver:PNCT lake next.to 3SG.PSR-house

hǫǫ-łįį *dänh*
AR.S:Ø.PFV:Ø-be:IPV at

'And then at the place downriver, next to the lake where her house was, …' UTOLVDN14Apr2602:092

b. *Stsǫǫ du' hashyign' tanel'ah hadaat…* (N)

s-tsǫǫ *du'* *ha-shyign'*
1SG.PSR-grandmother CT NTRL-down:ALL

ta-nel-'ah *ha-daat*
to.side-3SG.S:N.PFV:L-extend:IPV NTRL-downriver:PNCT

'And downriver there on the ground my grandmother was sitting…' UTOLVDN10Jul2724:050

There is only one clear example of *dugn* 'downriver:AR' (325). This stem is homophonous with (or possibly related to) the vague spatial adverb *dugn* 'there' (see chap. 16).

(325) *Ishyiit ts'änh tah hadugn Herman Kessler dii ay telshyeegn <noodlee iin hiiyeldeel> ishyiit nts'ą̈' tah iyuukeet…* (N)

Ishyiit *ts'änh* *tah* *ha-dugn* *Herman* *Kessler*
there from among NTRL-downriver:AR Hermann Kessler

dii ay telshyeegn *<noodlee iin hiiyeldeel>* *ishyiit* *nts'ą̈'* *tah*
groceries white.man's.food there from among

i-uu-keet
3SG>3SG-CON:Ø.IPV:Ø-buy:IPV

'And from there in the downriver area Herman Kessler would buy groceries, white man's food…' UTCBVDN13Nov0805:007

17.1.1.3. *negn'* 'upland, up the shore' The allative stem *negn'* 'upland:ALL' is illustrated in (326).

(326) a. *Ldil kah negn' na'įįdaał.* (N)

ldil *kah* *negn'* *na-įį-daał*
tea for upland:ALL IT-2SG.S:AA.IPV-D:SG.go:IPV:PROG

'Go back upland for tea.' UTOLAF09Aug1202:024

b. … *neg' Nahk'ade nts'ą' neekeey nts'ą' natsetnaa.* (T)

neg' *Nahk'ade* *nts'ą'* *nee-keey* *nts'ą'*
upland:ALL fishtrap to 1PL.PSR-camp to

na-tset-naa
IT-1PL.S:INC:DH.PFV:D-move.nomadically:PFV

'… we moved back upland to our camp at Fish Trap (Last Tetlin).'
UTOLAF09Jun2902:001

The ablative stem has the form *nǫǫ* 'upland:ABL' (327).

(327) a. *Stsǫǫ: "Hahnǫǫ ntsay na'atkeeɬ," nee'ehnih.* (N)

s-tsǫǫ *ah-nǫǫ* *n-tsay*
1SG.PSR-grandmother NTRL-upland:ABL 2SG.PSR-grandfather

na-at-keeɬ *nee-eh-nih*
IT-3SG.S:AA.IPV:D-go.by.boat:IPV:PROG 1PL.O-3SG.S:Ø.IPV:H-say:IPV

'My grandmother said to us, "Your grandfather is coming back from upland."' UTOLAF12Jul1203:106

b. … *nǫǫ ts'ant'ąy t'eey shnaahaal…* (T)

nǫǫ *ts'ant'ąy* *t'eey*
upland:ABL devil even

sh-naa-haal
1SG.O-3SG.S:AA.IPV:Ø-SG.go:IPV:PROG:NOM

'… from upland the devil is following me…'
UTOLVDN14Nov2301:403

The punctual stem *niit* 'upland:PNCT' is not used very frequently (320). Brucks (2015, 50) lists this stem as *noot* based on elicitation but does not provide an example illustrating this form. The rarity of *niit* 'upland:PNCT' is possibly due to the fact that it is homophonous with *niit* 'upriver:PNCT'.

(328) a. *Aniit uts'iiniin' ts'exeh Ida Wilson mǫǫsi' ishyiit chih store hǫǫɬe'.* (N)

a-niit *u-ts'iiniin'* *ts'exeh* *Ida* *Wilson*
NTRL-upland:PNCT 3SG.PSR-child:POSS woman Ida Wilson

m-ǫǫsi' *ishyiit* *chih* *store* *hǫǫ-ɬe'*
3SG.PSR-name there also store AR.S:AA.PFV:Ø-be:PFV

'At a place upland his daughter, Ida Wilson she is called, had a store there.' UTCBVDN13Nov0804:056

b. … *niit tah shnąą naht'aag tana'ihthat.* (T)

niit *tah* *sh-nąą* *naht'aag*
upland:PNCT at 1SG.PSR:mother behind

ta-na-ih-that
upland-CONT-I.PFV:1SG.S:Ø-SG.stand:IPV

'… and I stood upland behind my mother.'
UTOLAF09Jun2201:015

Occasionally speakers will use *negn' tah* 'upland:ALL at' rather than *niit* 'upland:PNCT', presumably to avoid confusion with *niit* 'upriver:PNCT' (329).

(329) *Anegn' tah łįį choh eedah, that delgay…* (N)

a-negn' *tah* *łįį* *choh* *ee-dah* *that*
NTRL-upland:ALL at dog big 3SG.S:DH.PFV:Ø-SG.sit:IPV that

del-gay
3SG.S:QUAL:Ø.PFV:L-be.white:IPV

'The big dog, the white one, is sitting at a place up there…'
UTOLVDN13May2004:053

The areal stem *nogn* 'upland:AR' is illustrated in (330). Milanowski and John (1966) transcribes this stem as *núúgn*; this may be a variant form. (The high tone is a characteristic of many directionals; see 17.3 below.)

(330) a. *Handog łuugn xah dzaltthi' dą' xah Nahk'ade dą' nats'iholndak.* (T)

ha-ndog *łuugn* *xah* *dzal-tthi'*
NTRL-upland:AR fish for 1PL.S:QUAL:AA.PFV:L-PL.stay:PFV

dą' *xah* *Nahk'ade* *dą'* *na-ts'i-hol-ndak*
when for fishtrap at IT-1PL.S-QUAL:Ø.IPV:L-tell.story:IPV

'Let's tell the story of how we were staying in the upland area at Fish Trap (Last Tetlin) for fish.' UTOLVDN10Jul0701:009

b. *Ay hu'eh eeday jah dugn hihnįįnąą tl'aan hanogn łuugn keey.* (N)

ay *hu-eh* *ee-day* *jah dugn*
and 3PL.P-with 3SG.S:DH.PFV:Ø-SG.sit:IPV:NOM there

hih-nįį-nąą *tl'aan* *ha-nogn*
3PL.S-N.PFV:Ø-move.nomadically:PFV and NTRL-upland:AR

łuugn *keey*
fish camp

'And while he stayed with them, they moved here, [they had a] fish camp in the upland area.' UTOLAF12Jul1203:101

17.1.1.4. *tthän'* 'downland, toward water' (331) demonstrates the allative stem of this directional.

(331) a. *Hahtthän' eeł idlaak…* (N)

hah-tthän' *eeł* *i-dlaak*

ADJC-waterward:ALL traps 3PL.S:Ø.IPV:Ø-classify.PL.O:IPV:CUST

'Next to toward the water they used to have traps…'

UTCBVDN13Nov0804:021

b. *Atthan' huts'ą' nateltthat…* (T)

a-tthan' *hu-ts'ą'* *na-tel-tthat*

NTRL-waterward:ALL 3PL.P-to IT-3SG.S:INC:DH.PFV:L-SG.run:PFV

'He ran waterward to them…' UTCBVDN13Nov1502:037

The ablative stem has the form *tthǫǫ* (332).

(332) a. *Ahtthǫǫ haats'atdeeł…* (N)

ah-tthǫǫ *ha-na-ts'at-deeł*

NTRL-waterward:ABL out-IT-1PL.S:AA.PFV:D-PL.go.out:PFV

'From waterward we came back out…'

UTOLVDN13May2004:107

b. *Shee'eh, ahtthǫǫ ts'anh ch'aadał.* (T)

sh-ee'eh *ah-tthǫǫ* *ts'anh*

1SG.PSR-maternal.uncle NTRL-waterward:ABL from

ch'aa-dał

INDF.S:AA.IPV:Ø-PL.go:IPV:PROG

'My uncle, people are coming from waterward.'

UTCBVDN13Nov1502:031

The punctual form *tthiit* 'waterward:PNCT' is illustrated in (333).

(333) a. *Atthiit ch'itay shaadeh dhehxįį…* (T)

a-tthiit *ch'itay* *sh-aadeh*

NTRL-waterward:PNCT old.man 1SG.PSR-older.sister

dheh-xįį

3SG.S:QUAL:DH.PFV:H-kill.SG.O:PFV

'Down there by the water an old man killed my older sister…'

UTCBAF13Nov0501:140

b. *Ha'atthiit shoh dat-sąy its'ą̈' na'ithät...* (N)

ha-a-tthiit *shoh*
ADJC-NTRL-waterward:PNCT bear

dat-sąy *its'ą̈'*
3SG.S:QUAL:AA.PFV:D-be.black:IPV:NOM 3SG.S>3SG.P:TO

na-i-thät
CONT-I.PFV:Ø-SG.stand:IPV

'And right there down by the water there was a black bear standing facing them...' UTOLAF09Aug12:017

The areal form *tthuugn* 'waterward:AR' is illustrated in (334).

(334) a. *Ha'atthuugn doo le' eeday.* (N)

ha-a-tthuugn *doo* *le'* *ee-day*
ADJC-NTRL-waterward:AR who IGN 3SG.S:DH.PFV:Ø-SG.sit:IPV:NOM

'Down there by the water someone was sitting.'
UTOLAF15May0501:028

b. *Ay chih ch'ale ahtthuugn, ahtthuugn ts'anh Toochinh ts'anh nahatdał nts'ą'...* (T)

ay *chih* *ch'ale* *ah-tthuugn,* *ah-tthuugn* *ts'anh*
and also FOC NTRL-waterward:AR NTRL-waterward:AR from

Toochinh *ts'anh* *na-hat-dał* *nts'ą'*
Midway.Lake from IT-3PL.S:AA.IPV:D-PL.go:IPV:PROG and

'And also as they are coming from the water, from Midway Lake...'
UTOLAF09Jun2404:002

17.1.1.5. *degn'* 'up above, uphill' In (335) the allative form of *degn'* is illustrated.

(335) a. *Shnąą eh shta' eh Ladue Hill degn' neehtiłeek xay tah.* (N)

sh-nąą *eh* *sh-ta'* *eh* *Ladue* *Hill* *degn'*
1SG.PSR:mother and 1SG.PSR:father and Ladue Hill up:ALL

nee-hti-łeek *xay* *tah*
1PL.O-3PL.S:INC:Ø.IPV:Ø-handle.PL.O:IPV:CUST winter when

'My parents would take us uphill into the Ladue Hills in winter.'
UTOLVDN07Nov2901:001

b. *Ay tl'aan deg' huneh'į̨h.* (T)
ay tl'aan deg' hu-neh-'į̨h
and.then up:ALL 3SG.S>AR.O-QUAL:Ø.IPV:H-look:IPV
'And then he looked straight up.' UTOLVDN13May2801:205

The ablative form expresses movement away from a location straight up, such as from a high cache in (336a), or in the hills (336b).

(336) a. ... *nahdǫǫ nahal'uuk* ... (T)
nah-dǫǫ na-hal-'uuk
MED-up:ABL down-3PL.S:AA.PFV:L-fall.in.pieces:PFV
'... and it all fell down in pieces...' UTOLAF09Jun2202:040

b. *Nahdǫǫ ddhäł tüh nį̨shyah.* (N)
nah-dǫǫ ddhäł tüh nį̨-shyah
MED-up:ABL mountain across 3SG.S:N.PFV:Ø-SG.go:PFV
'Down the hill he came over the mountains.'
UTOLVDN10Jul2703:002

As *dǫǫ* 'up:ABL' is homophonous with *dǫǫ* 'downriver:ABL', speakers sometimes use a periphrastic construction *deg' ts'änh* 'up:ALL from' to disambiguate, as shown in (337).

(337) *Ahdeg' ts'anh dzina'į̨shyah tl'aan.* (T)
ah-deg' ts'anh dzi-na-į̨-shyah tl'aan
NTRL-up:ALL from over.edge-down-3SG.S:AA.PFV:Ø-SG.go:PFV and
'She came down over the edge from up there.'
UTOLVDN14Nov2301:541

There are no clear examples of *daat* 'up:PNCT', which is homophonous with *daat* 'upriver:PNCT'.

The stem *dogn* 'up:AR' is quite common. (338a) describes an event taking place overhead, (338b) one in the uphill area.

(338) a. *Deeł hadogn sts'akenaat'ah*... (T)
deeł ha-dogn sts'ake-naa-t'ah
crane NTRL-up:AR circling-3SG.S:AA.IPV:Ø-SG.fly:IPV:PROG
'A crane was circling overhead...' UTOLAF07Oct2512:020

b. … *hanadogn ddhäł k'it, jign kah nanita'.* (N)

ha-na-dogn *ddhäł* *k'it* *jign* *kah*
ADJC-MED-up:AR mountain on berries for

na-ni-ta'
IT-3SG.S:Ø.IPV:Ø-look.for:IPV

'... right up there in the mountains he looked for berries.'
UTOLVDN11Aug0805:003

17.1.1.6. *shyign'* 'down below, downhill' The allative form *shyign'* 'down:ALL' is illustrated in (339).

(339) a. *Shyign' t'eey aahaał.* (T)

shyign' *t'eey* *aa-haał*
down:ALL even 3SG.S:AA.IPV:Ø-SG.go:IPV

'She was going down.' UTCBAF13Nov0501:341

b. … *hanuhshyign' tüh dzina'altth'ät.* (N)

ha-na-huh-shyign' *tüh*
ADJC-MED-AR-down:ALL over

dzina-al-tth'ät
down.over.edge-3SG.S:AA.PFV:L-CO.fall:PFV

'... it tumbled down the slope a little ways away down over the edge.'
UTOLAF09Aug12:028

(340) contains most of the examples of *shyǫǫ* 'down:ABL' in the corpus. (340a) describes movement vertically up from out of the water, while (340b) describes movement onto the bank from the frozen surface of a lake.

(340) a. *Tatlogn unįį' k'it ditthi' k'it hashyǫǫ tuu shyiit haanal'ah, oh!* (N)

tatlogn *u-nįį'* *k'it* *di-tthi'* *k'it* *ha-shyǫǫ*
algae 3SG.PSR-face on REFL.PSR-head on NTRL-down:ABL

tuu *shyiit* *ha-na-nal-'ah* *oh*
water in out-IT-3SG.S:AA.PFV:L:extend:PFV oh

'Algae were on her face and on her head when she stuck it back out of the water, oh!' UTOLVDN14Apr2602:105

b. *Nashyǫǫ datl'a'įįshyah de'…* (T)

na-shyǫǫ *datl'a-įį-shyah* *de'*
NTRL-down:ABL ashore-3SG.S:AA.PFV:Ø-SG.go:PFV if

'When he gets onto the shore...' UTOLVDN13May2801:169

Examples where *shyiit* really has the meaning 'down:PNCT' as in (341) are quite rare. More frequently, it has the meaning 'there' (see 17.1.2.6 and chap. 16 for examples).

(341) a. *Nashyiit tah unąą eh uta' eh u'ǫǫnüü eh.* (N)

na-shyiit *tah* *u-nąą* *eh* *u-ta'* *eh*
MED-down:PNCT among 3SG.PSR-mother and 3SG.PSR-father and

u-ǫǫnüü *eh*
3SG.PSR-older.brother and

'Down there [there were] her mother and her father and her older brother.' UTOLAF15May0501:202

b. *Ay eh t'eey hashyiit łigaay iin xah nagnjit.* (N)

ay eh *t'eey* *ha-shyiit* *łigaay* *iin* *xah*
and ADVZR ADJC-down:PNCT puppy PL for

nagn-jit
1SG.S:QUAL:Ø.PFV:Ø-be.scared:IPV

'I'm scared for the puppies down there closeby [the bear].' UTOLVDN13May2004:077

The areal stem *shyuugn* 'down:AR' can be used to refer to a location vertically down ([342a] is uttered while looking down from the sky onto the earth) or to a location at the bottom of a hill ([342b] describes what the parents find in the village upon their return from the hills).

(342) a. … *shyuugn tah tahshyüü nts'ą'* … (T)

shyuugn *tah* *tah-shyüü* *nts'ą'*
down:AR among 3SG.S:INC:AA.IPV:Ø-snow:FUT and

'… it will snow down there…' UTOLAF08Apr2805:099

b. *Hahshyuugn ts'iikeey iin du' hunaagn' łahtthegn nts'ą' kol.* (N)

hah-shyuugn *ts'iikeey* *iin* *du'* *hu-naagn'* *łahtthegn* *nts'ą'*
NTRL-down:AR children PL CT 3PL.PSR-eyes all

kol
NEGEX

'In the downhill area, the children's eyes were all gone.' UTOLVDN11Aug0805:019

17.1.1.7. *naan'* 'across' The allative form is illustrated in (343).

(343) a. *Gary, "Jan shyiit t'eey naan' skįts'uudeeł," shehnih.* (T)

Gary jan shyiit t'eey naan' skį-ts'uu-deeł,
Gary DEM here ADVZR across:ALL across-1PL.S:OPT:Ø-PL.go:OPT
sh-eh-nih
1SG.O-3SG.S:Ø.IPV:H-say:IPV
'Gary said to me, "This is how we're going across."'
UTOLAF09Jun2902:006

b. *And naan' shaak'ay iin shyah ts'ą̈' tidhihshyah...* (N)

and naan' sh-aak'ay iin shyah ts'ą̈'
and across:ALL 1SG.PSR-maternal.aunt PL house to
t-dhih-shyah
INC-DH.PFV:1SG.S:Ø-SG.go:PFV
'And I went across to my aunties' house...'
UTOLAF09Aug1202:010

The ablative stem *nǫǫ* 'across:ABL' is homophonous with *nǫǫ* 'upriver:ABL' and *nǫǫ* 'upland:ABL'. In both cases in (344), it is certain that *nǫǫ* is 'across:ABL' rather than one of the two homophones, as illustrated by the translations.

(344) a. *John Hajdukovich nǫǫ ninįįnaa.* (N)

John Hajdukovich nǫǫ ni-nįį-naa
John Hajdukovich across:ABL TERM-3SG.S:N.PFV:Ø-move:PFV
'John Haijdukovich moved from across [the Nabesna].'
UTCBVDN13Nov0804:050

b. *Ahnǫǫ nche' skįnįįshyiił!* (N)

ah-nǫǫ n-che' skį-nįį-shyiił
NTRL-across:ABL 2SG.PSR-tail across-N.IPV:2SG.S:Ø-extend.LRO:IPV
'From across stretch your tail across [the river]!'
UTOLAF15May0501:101

The punctual form *naat* is illustrated in (345). In (345a) the speaker of the quoted speech asks to be taken back to the shore from the other side of the lake. In (345b) the speaker of the quoted speech tries to get the other hunters to follow him across the flat.

(345) a. *Naat niishnįlteeyh...* (N)

naat *ni-na-sh-nįl-teeyh*
across:PNCT TERM-IT-1SG.O-N.PFV:2SG.S:Lhandle.AO:IPV
'Take SG me back to the place across...'
UTCBAF14May2001:005

b. *Ishyiit nts'ą' "Anaat! Shints'ą' ahdał!"* (T)

shyiit *nts'ą'* *a-naat* *sh-nts'ą'*
there at NTRL-across:PNCT 1SG.P-to
ah-dał
AA.IPV:2PL.S:Ø-PL.go:IPV:PROG
'And there, "Over there at the point across! Come PL to me!"'
UTOLAF09Jun2202:062

The areal form *nuugn* 'across:AR' is illustrated in (346). In (346b) it refers to the opposite side of a tent.

(346) a. *Ahnuugn nǫǫgaay natedaak.* (T)

ah-nuugn *nǫǫgaay* *na-te-daak*
NTRL-across:AR fox PRMB-3SG.S:INC:Ø.IPV:Ø-SG.walk:IPV:CUST
'On the other side a fox was walking about.'
UTCBAF13Nov0501:155

b. *Hahnuugn t'eey tth'idhalt'ay.* (T)

hah-nuugn *t'eey* *tth'i-dhal-t'ay*
NTRL-across:AR ADVZR straight-DH.PFV:2PL.S:L-be:IPV:IMP
'Stretch PL out on the other side!' UTCBAF13Nov0501:076

17.1.1.8. *noo'* 'ahead' The allative form *noo'* 'ahead:ALL' is the most frequent form of this directional. It is illustrated in (347).

(347) a. *Noo shttheh na'ǫǫ ts'änh jah dii le' sheh ha'atdädn.* (N)

noo *sh-ttheh* *na-'ǫǫ* *ts'änh* *jah* *dii*
ahead:ALL 1SG.P-in.front MED-outside:ABL from here something
le' *sh-eh* *ha-at-dädn*
IGN 1SG.P-with out-3SG.S:AA.PFV:D-animal.run:PFV:NOM
'Ahead in front of me out there some animal came running by me.'
UTOLAF09Aug1202:029

b. *Hanoo' nts'ą̈' ts'almbeet iin ditth'ek huhnoo' tateeshyah.* (N)

ha-noo' *nts'ą̈'* *ts'almbeet* *iin*
NTRL-ahead:ALL to loon PL

di-tth'ek *huh-noo'*
3SG.S:QUAL:QUAL:Ø.PFV:Ø-hear:IPV AR-ahead:ALL

ta-tee-shyah
waterward-3SG.S:INC:DH.PFV:Ø-SG.go:PFV

'In the direction ahead he heard loons and he went in the area ahead [to them].' UTCBVDN13Nov1401:023

The ablative form of this directional is not attested in the data. The punctual form *noot* 'ahead:PNCT' occurs only once (348).

(348) … *ay t'axoh noot niits'indeeł.* (N)

ay *t'axoh* *noot* *ni-na-ts'in-deeł*
and finally ahead:PNCT TERM-IT-1PL.S:N.PFV:D-PL.go:PFV

'… and we went to a place ahead there.'
UTOLVDN14Apr2602:091

The areal form *noogn* 'ahead:AR' does not occur in naturalistic speech.

17.1.1.9. *'än* 'out' The allative stem *'än'* 'outside:ALL' is illustrated in (349).

(349) a. … *hah'än hunak-'įh.* (N)

hah-'än *hu-nak-'įh*
NTRL-outside:ALL AR-QUAL:Ø.IPV:1SG.S:H-look:IPV

'I was sitting next to the window and looked outside.'
UTOLVDN14Apr2602:040

b. *Nah'an' ti'uhshya'!* (T)

nah-'an' *ti-uh-shya*
MED-outside:ALL out-OPT:1SG.S:Ø-SG.go:OPT

'I want to go outside!' UTOLAF08Apr2805:038

The ablative stem *'ǫǫ* 'outside:ABL' is illustrated in (350).

(350) a. *Nah'ǫǫ dathinįįtthayh tl'aan…* (N)

nah-'ǫǫ *da-thi-nįį-tthayh*
MED-outside:ABL in-head-3SG.S:N.PFV:Ø-move.CO.quickly:PFV

tl'aan
and

'He peeked in from outside and…' UTOLAF15May0501:155

b. *Ay t'eey shee'eh ha'o̜o̜ danįįshyah dahdzäł.* (N)

ay *t'eey* *sh-ee'eh* *ha-'o̜o̜*
and even 1SG.PSR-maternal.uncle NTRL-outside:ABL

da-nįį-shyah *dahdzäł*
in-3SG.S:N.PFV:Ø-SG.go:PFV fish.rack

'And my maternal uncle came into the fish rack from outside.'
UTOLVDN10Jul2724:051

The punctual stem *'aat* 'outside:PNCT' occurs relatively rarely (351).

(351) a. *Ha'aat tsät įįttheeł ch'a!* (N)

ha-'aat *tsät* *įį-ttheeł* *ch'a*
NTRL-outside:PNCT wood Ø.IPV:2SG.S:Ø-chop:IPV FOC

'Chop wood at a place outside!' UTOLAF13May2804:047

b. *Nah'aat nan' k'it shaa k'iinųųttheeł,* … (T)

nah-'aat *nan'* *k'it* *sh-aa* *k'ii-nųų-ttheeł*
MED-outside:PNCT earth on 1SG.P-for hole-OPT:2SG.S:Ø-chop:IPV

'Chop a hole in the ground for me at a place a little ways away…'
UTOLVDN13May2909:134

The most common form of this directional is *ogn* 'outside:AR' (352).

(352) a. … *hah'ogn dzelxoh.* (N)

hah'ogn *dzelxoh*
NTRL-outside:AR 1PL.S:QUAL:Ø.IPV:L-play:IPV

'… we played in the area outside.' UTOLAF08Feb1906:005

b. … *nah'ogn k'ąy' ts'oo t'eey na'etk'an'.* (T)

nah-'ogn *k'ąy'* *ts'oo* *t'eey* *na-et-k'an'*
MED-outside:AR willow spruce even IT-3PL.S:DH.PFV:D-burn:IPV

'… out there, willows and even spruce were burning.'
UTOLAF09Jun2402:003

17.1.2. Semantics

The semantics of the directionals are explored by looking both at the oppositions in which they participate and at their context.

17.1.2.1. *ne'* 'upriver, backward' This directional has the primary meaning of 'upriver' applied to the major river. From Northway this includes the Scottie Creek and Beaver Creek area as well as the eastern part of the Wrangell

Mountains; from Tetlin this also includes the Northway area. This was illustrated clearly in (328) above. *Ne'* is also used for motion in the upriver direction even after the Tanana River drainage has been left. (353) describes how two girls from Tetlin are taken to the coast by warriors.

(353) Excerpt: UTOLVDN07Oct2602:020-022 (T)

a. *Hugn k'ąy' t'eey tah nde' tatneetsak ne' haadał niig.*

hugn	*k'ąy'*	*t'eey*	*tah*	*nde'*
also	willow	even	among	upriver:ALL

ta-tnee-tsak	*ne'*
to.side-3PL.S:INC:QUAL:DH.PFV:Ø-twist:PFV	upriver:ALL

haa-dał	*niig*
3PL.S:AA.IPV:Ø-PL.go:IPV:PROG	the.way

'They also twisted willow [branches] in the upriver direction as they were going upriver.'

b. *Nduu haadał nts'ą' t'eey hiihitnąy, hunaagn' hunaagn' k'eh ch'ehuhdehchüü eł.*

nduu	*haadał*	*nts'ą' t'eey*
where	3PL.S:AA.IPV:Ø-PL.go:IPV:PROG	ADVZR

hi-hit-nąy,	*hu-naagn'*	*hu-naagn'*
?-3PL.S:NEG.PFV:D-know:IPV:NEG	3PL.PSR-eyes	3PL.PSR-eyes

k'eh	*ch'-hu-hdeh-chüü*	*eł*
around	INDF.O-?-3PL.S:QUAL:DH.PFV:H-tie:PFV:NOM	because

'They didn't know where they were going because they had blindfolded them.'

c. *Ne::' nahatdał, ndiit mbah manh choh <hiiyinih> manh choh ay maagn nihnįįdeeł eł.*

ne'	*na-hat-dał,*	*ndiit*
upriver:ALL	IT-3PL.S:AA.IPV:D-PL.go:IPV:PROG	upriver:PNCT

mbah	*manh choh*	*hiiy-i-nih*	*manh choh*	*ay*
warrior	ocean	3PL.S>3SG:P-Ø.IPV:Ø-say:IPV	ocean	and

maagn	*ni-hnįį-deeł*	*eł*
shore	TERM-3PL.S:N.PFV:Ø-PL.go:PFV	and

'They kept going upriver until at a place upriver, warriors, to what they call ocean, ocean, they arrived at the shore.'

When it has this meaning, *ne'* 'upriver' is paired with *da'* 'downriver'. This opposition is also exploited when speakers want to express a back-and-forth motion (354).

(354) *Utthi' da' ne', shoh ch'a.*

u-tthi' *da'* *ne',* *shoh* *ch'a*
3SG.PSR-head downriver:ALL upriver:ALL bear FOC

'Its head [went] this way and that, the bear's.'

UTOLAF09Aug1201:037

Ne' also is used to express 'backward, the way one came'. In those contexts it is paired with *noo'* 'ahead, into the open, forward'. (355) illustrates this contrast. In the text the speaker discusses the proper way of putting fish onto the fish rack to ensure that the fish keep coming.

(355) Excerpt: UTOLVDN11Jul2903:005-006 (T)

a. *Utthi' ts'ąy' ne' nts'ą' dadhahdlah de' k'at'eey łuugn utaałeel.*

u-tthi' *ts'ąy'* *ne'* *nts'ą'*
3SG.PSR-head side backward:ALL to

da-dhah-dlah *de'* *k'at'eey* *łuugn*
up-DH.PFV:2PL.S:H-have.PL.O:IPV if NEG fish

hu-taa-łeel
AR.S-INC:AA.IPV:Ø-classify.PL.O:FUT:NEG

'If you have [the fish] up [on the drying rack] with the sides of their heads backward, there won't be any fish.'

b. *Utthi' ts'ąy noo nts'ą' dadhahdlah de' shyįį' łuugn utaałeeł heniik.*

u-tthi' *ts'ąy* *noo* *nts'ą'*
3SG.PSR-head side forward to

da-dhah-dlah *de'* *shyįį'* *łuugn*
up-DH.PFV:2PL.S:H-classify.PL.O:IPV if only fish

hu-taa-łeeł *he-niik*
AR.S-INC:AA.IPV:Ø-classify.PL.O:FUT:NEG 3PL:Ø.IPV:Ø-say:IPV:CUST

'Only if you have [the fish] up [on the drying rack] with the sides of their heads forward will there be fish, they used to say.'

Ne' also describes backward (back-first) movement. (356a) describes how the narrator's sister fell backward into the water; (356b) was a response to my walking backward.

(356) a. *Ishyiit ta'įįtaal eh boom hane' shyign' tah [laughs].* (N)

ishyiit *ta-įį-taal* *eh* *boom*
there water-3SG.S:AA.PFV:Ø-burst:PFV:NOM and boom

ha-ne' *shyign'* *tah*
NTRL-backward:ALL down:ALL among

'Boom, there she fell backward down into the water.'

UTOLVDN14Apr2602:103

b. *Ne' nts'ą' na'ihdaał.* (T)

ne' *nts'ą'* *na-ih-daał*
backward:ALL ADVZR PRMB-1SG.S:AA.IPV-D:SG.walk:IPV

'I'm walking around backwards.' UT Notebook #2.5, 23

17.1.2.2. *da'* 'downriver' The semantics of *da'* are simple. It is only used to refer to the downriver direction, i.e., where Tok, Tanacross, Delta, and Fairbanks are located. *Da'* 'downriver:ALL' is only paired with *ne'* 'upriver:ALL'. Examples are given in section 17.1.1.2.

17.1.2.3. *negn'* 'upland, up the shore, back (in a boat, house)' *Negn'* has a variety of meanings. Its basic meaning is 'upland', i.e., away from the major river. From both Tetlin and Northway this is usually the area toward the Wrangell Mountains.[2] Examples for this interpretation are given in 17.1.1.3; *negn'* 'upland' contrasts in these cases with *tthän'* 'waterward'.

Nogn 'upland:AR' is also used to refer to the back area of a house (357), since houses were traditionally built with the entrance facing the river (Leer 1989, 577). In this sense it is again in opposition to *tthän'* 'waterward' according to Leer, but no examples for this opposition can be found in the data.

(357) *Ts'exeh gaay hahnogn huts'adn' shyiit įįda'.* (T)

ts'exeh gaay *hah-nogn* *hu-ts'adn'* *shyiit*
girl NTRL-upland:AR 3PL.PSR-bag inside

įį-da'
3SG.S:AA.PFV:Ø-SG.sit:PFV

'That girl in the back [of the house] remained in their bag.'

UTOLAF08Apr2805:084

Negn' can also be used to express movement toward the shore when one is located on the water (358a). With this meaning *negn'* is in semantic opposition with *noo'* 'ahead:ALL' (358b). This opposition is also reconstructed for

Proto-Dene (Leer 1989, 613).

(358) a. *Hahnegn' nishnįhteeyh mänh maagn.* (N)

hah-negn'	*ni-sh-nįh-teeyh*
NTRL-toward.shore:ALL	TERM-1SG.O-N.IPV:2SG.S:ø-handle.AO:IPV

mänh	*maagn*
lake	shore

'Put me back up there on the lake edge.'

UTCBVDN13Nov1401:049

b. *Noo' ch'ats'inįįkįin eł...* (T)

noo'	*ch'a-ts'-nįį-kįin*	*eł*
into.open:ALL	out-1PL.S:N.PFV:ø-go.by.boat:PFV:NOM	and

'We go out into open water and...' UTOLAF09Jun2902:011

This opposition is then extended to boats. Thus *negn'* is used to refer to the position at the stern of the boat (359a), while *noo'* 'ahead, into the open' refers to the prow (359b). (The original transcription of [359a] from Milanowski and John [1966] is retained in the text line but not in the morpheme breakdown; see chap. 12 for a discussion of the various orthographic conventions.)

(359) a. *JESUS duu' hahnúúgn ts'ath shiit t̲hu'aał et̲hinel'ąą dan̲ ehtįį.* (T)

JESUS	*du'*	*hah-nuugn*	*ts'ayh*	*shyiit*	*tthu'aał*
Jesus	CT	NTRL-stern:AR	boat	in	pillow

i-tthi-nel-'ąą	*danh*
PP-head-3SG.S:QUAL:DH.PFV:L-classify.CO:PFV	at

eh-tįį
3SG.S:DH.PFV:H-SG.sleep:IPV

'Jesus was in the back of the boat, sleeping with his head on the pillow.' Milanowski and John (1966, 28; Mark 4:38)

b. *Noo' dii du' tach'et'oh dą' eedah.* (T)

noo'	*dii*	*du'*	*ta-ch'e-t'oh*	*dą'*
front:ALL	?	CT	water-3SG.S>INDF.O:ø.IPV:ø-paddle:IPV	at

ee-dah
3SG.S:DH.PFV:ø-SG.sit:IPV

'He sat in the prow where he could paddle.'

UTOLAF09Jun2902:010

17.1.2.4. *tthän'* 'downland, toward water' The directional *tthän'* indicates that the direction of movement or the location is downland, or toward the main drainage. It is in opposition to *negn'* 'upland'. Examples for the use of *tthän'* are given in section 17.1.1.4. It has no other meanings.

17.1.2.5. *degn'* 'up above, uphill' The directional *degn'* indicates that the direction of movement or the location of an entity is up a steep incline, e.g., up a hill or up a tree. Examples for the use of *degn'* with these meanings are given in 17.1.1.5. *Degn'* 'uphill' is in semantic opposition with *shyign'* 'downhill', as illustrated in (360).

(360) *Tay' t'eey shyign' degn' tay' t'eey shyign' tl'aan degn' tay' t'eey yaa'atmįįh.* (N)

tay' *t'eey* *shyign'* *degn'* *tay'* *t'eey* *shyign'* *tl'aan*
again ADVZR down:ALL up:ALL again ADVZR down:ALL and

degn' *tay'* *t'eey* *ya-na-at-mįįh*
up:ALL again ADVZR up.out-IT-3SG.S:AA.PFV:D-swim:PFV

'Again down and up and again down and then he swam back up again.'
UTCBVDN13Nov1401:046

17.1.2.6. *shyign'* 'down below, downhill, on the ground' *Shyign'* 'down below, downhill' is the opposite of *degn'*. It is also vague, indicating movement to or from a location either down a slope or down vertically. Examples for these meanings are given in 17.1.1.6.

The punctual stem *shyiit* 'down:PNCT' is probably the most frequently used directional of all. Most of the time it is part of the adverb *ishyiit* 'there' (361).

(361) *Eł Yamaagn Teeshyaay ishyiit na'ethat.* (T)

eł *Yamaagn* *Teeshyaay* *ishyiit* *na-e-that*
and Yamaagn Teeshyaay there CONT-3SG.S:I.PFV:Ø-SG.stand:IPV

'And Yamaagn Teeshyaay stood there.' UTOLAF08Apr2804:009

The areal stem *shyuugn* 'down:AR' also has the meaning 'on the ground' (362).

(362) *Ay eł ashyuugn eedah.* (T)

ay eł *a-shyuugn* *ee-dah*
and NTRL-down:AR 3SG.S:DH.PFV:Ø-SG.sit:IPV

'And he was sitting on the ground.' UTOLAF08Apr2804:015

17.1.2.7. *naan'* 'across' *Naan'* indicates movement toward or a location on the other side of a body of water. It is consequently its own opposite. This is illustrated in (363). Both examples are taken from a story where a girl, pursued by an old man, comes to a river. On the other side of the river is a fox (363a). In the story units between (363a) and (363b), she crosses the river on the fox's tail. When she has reached the other side, she tells the fox about her pursuer who has not yet crossed the river. In (363), the same directional stem *naat* 'across:PNCT' is used to refer to the side of the river that is opposite to that where the girl (the main character of this story) is located.

(363) UTOLAF10Jul0202:089, 104

a. *Nagäd du' hanaat t'eey ich'a' edloh.*

nagäd	*du'*	*ha-naat*	*t'eey*	*i-ch'a'*
fox	CT	NTRL-across:PNCT	even	3SG.A>3SG.P-from

e-dloh
Ø.IPV:Ø-laugh:IPV

'On the other side the fox was laughing at her.'

b. *Ay tl'aan naxat naagät, "Naat ch'itay shk'eh aahaał!"*

ay tl'aan	*naxat*	*naagät*	*naat*	*ch'itay*	*sh-k'eh*
and.then	that	fox	across:PNCT	old.man	1SG.P-following

aa haał
3SG.S:AA.IPV:Ø-SG.go:IPV:PROG

'And then to that Fox: "On the other side an old man is following me!"'

While the core meaning of *naan'* 'across' has to do with crossing rivers or lakes, is also used when traversing an open space such as a flat (364a) or a room (364b).

(364) a. *Naan' chinh k'it skįnihshyah.* (N)

naan'	*chinh*	*k'it*	*skį-nih-shyah*
across:ALL	flat	on	across-1SG.S:N.PFV:Ø-SG.go:PFV

'I walked across the flat.' UTOLAF15Dec0605:011

b. *Ahnaan' tah dadhįįdah.* (N)

ah-naan'	*tah*	*da-dhįį-dah*
NTRL-across:ALL	among	up-2SG.S:DH.PFV:Ø-SG.sit:IPV

'Sit SG across the room.' UTOLAF14Nov2402:006

17.1.2.8. *noo'* 'ahead, into the open, by the hearth, a long way away, a long time in the future' The semantics of this directional are hard to capture, as has already been observed by Kari (2010) and Berez (2011) for Ahtna. Its most common translation in Upper Tanana is 'ahead, forward', which usually refers to movement or location in space. Examples for this meaning are given in 17.1.1.8. When *noo'* is used in this sense, it is paired with *ne'* 'upstream, backward', as illustrated in 17.1.2.1.

Noo' also is used with the meaning 'out into the open'. Prototypically, this is the open expanse of a river or lake. In this sense *noo'* is in semantic opposition to *negn'* 'upland, toward shore (from water)'. It may also be used on land however, e.g., when coming out onto a flat or out of the brush (365).

(365) *Hahnoo' chinh k'it tthidzįįdeeł.* (N)
hah-noo' *chinh* *k'it* *tthi-dzįį-deeł*
NTRL-into.open:ALL flat on out-1PL.S:QUAL:AA.PFV:Ø-PL.go:PFV
'We came out on the flats.' UTOLVDN13May2004:014

When applied to the inside of a dwelling, *noo'* has the meaning 'by the hearth, by the fire' (this polysemy between 'out into open space' and 'toward the fire' is common in languages of the Pacific Rim, as pointed out by Fortescue [2011]). When used in this sense, *noo'* 'by the fire' is again not paired with another directional (366).

(366) a. *Tädn tah, tädn tah hanoo' tth'än' nahe'aal.* (N)
tädn *tah,* *tädn* *tah* *ha-noo'* *tth'än'*
night when night when NTRL-by.fire:ALL bone
na-he-'aal
IT-3PL.S:Ø.IPV:Ø-eat:IPV:NOM
'At night, at night they eat bones by the fire.'
UTOLVDN10Jul2713:017

b. *K'ahdu' t'eey tseeyniik noo' kon' nia tthidįhdeeł.* (N)
k'ahdu' *t'eey* *tseeyniik* *noo'* *kon'* *nia*
now ADVZR teapot by.fire:ALL fire middle.of
tthi-dįh-deeł
by.fire-3SG.S:QUAL:AA.PFV:H-put.PL.O.quickly:PFV
'Straight away he put the teapot onto the fire.'
UTOLVDN10Jul2724:039

Noo' also is used to indicate that movement covers a great distance (367).

(367) a. *Manh hahnoo' t'eey ni'įltthat.* (T)
manh *hah-noo'* *t'eey* *ni-įl-tthat*
lake NTRL:long.way:ALL ADVZR TERM-3SG.S:N.PFV:L-SG.run:PFV
'She ran a long way to a lake.' UTOLAF08Apr2805:046

b. … *hanoo' natsetneek.* (N)

ha-noo' *na-tset-neek*
NTRL-long.way:ALL IT-1PL.S:INC:Ø.IPV:D-move.nomadically:IPV
'… we moved a long way back [to the village].'
UTOLVDN13May2003:023

This meaning 'a long way' probably underlies the temporal use of *noo'* 'a long time in the future' (368).

(368) a. … *shk'ehtl'üdn noo' de' t'eey ishyiit sǫ' ni'ųųshya'…* (T)

sh-k'ehtl'üdn *noo'* *de'* *t'eey* *ishyiit* *sǫ'*
1SG.P-after.death long.time when:FUT ADVZR there PROH
ni-ųų-shya'
TERM-OPT:2SG.S:Ø-SG.go:OPT
'… don't go there even long after I'm gone…'
UTOLVDN08Mar1311:004

b. *"Jah ts'anh noo' huhnay noo' t'eey k'a hǫǫ natdindiil," iiyehnih.* (T)

jah *ts'anh* *noo'* *huh-nay*
here from long.time:ALL AR.O-Ø.IPV:1SG.S:Ø:say:IPV:NOM
noo' *t'eey* *k'a* *hǫǫ* *na-tdin-diil*
ahead even NEG thus IT-INC:QUAL:AA.IPV:2SG.S:D-do:FUT:NEG
iiy-eh-nih
3SG.S>3SG.P-Ø.IPV:H-say:IPV
'"From here on and now on you will not do this again," he said to him.'
UTOLAF09Jun2404:014

In this sense—a long way away spatially or temporally—*noo'* is not paired with any other directional.

17.1.2.9. *'än'* 'out, away, off to the side' This directional is unique in that it is not paired with any of the other directionals (Leer 1989). While Leer (1989) glosses this directional as 'outside, off to the side', in Upper Tanana the meaning 'outside (a dwelling)' is considerably more common. Examples for this sense are given in 17.1.1.9.

Another common meaning is 'away'. This describes an unspecified location a little removed from the reference point, or movement to or from that location (369).

(369) a. *Tl'aan Stephen Northway shyah ha'ah'aat dänh ishyiit jah.* (N)

tl'aan *Stephen* *Northway* *shyah* *ha-ah-'aat* *dänh*
and Stephen Northway house ADJC-NTRL-away:PNCT at

ishyiit *jah*
there here

'And Stephen Northway's house is next door there.'

UTCBVDN13Nov0804:016

b. *Nah'aat nan' k'it shaa k'iinųųttheeł, …* (T)

nah-'aat *nan'* *k'it* *sh-aa*
MED-outside:PNCT earth on 1SG.P-for

k'ii-nųų-ttheeł
hole-QUAL:OPT:2SG.S:ø-chop:IPV

'Chop a hole in the ground for me at a place a little ways away..'

UTOLVDN13May2909:134

With this sense also, *'än'* is not in opposition to any directional.

17.2. Prefixes

Directional adverbs contain optional prefixes. In most related languages the directional prefixes specify the distance from the reference point (usually speaker location). Upper Tanana is somewhat unusual among these languages in that directionals allow several prefixes at the same time. These prefixes occur in a strict order; Brucks (2015, 57) represents this as a prefix template given in table 17.2. The inventory of prefixes in table 17.2 is inclusive.

Prefix 1	Prefix 2	Prefix 3	Stem
ha- 'ADJC'-	*da-* 'PROX' *na-* 'MED'- *ya-* 'DSTL'- *ha-/a-* 'NTRL'	*u-/o-* 'AR'- *tth'ii-* 'straight'	stem

Table 17.2. Directional prefixes in Upper Tanana, from Brucks (2015, 57)

Any of these prefixes may be followed by an epenthetic /h/ when it directly precedes the directional stem.

17.2.1. Prefix order

The prefix *ha-* 'ADJC'- precedes all other prefixes in directional adverbs. (370a) shows it with the neutral distance prefix *(h)a-* and (370b) with the medium distance prefix *na-*. There are no examples of *ha-* 'ADJC' co-occurring with either the distal prefix *ya-* or the proximal prefix *da-*.

(370) a. *Ha'atthuugn doo le' eeday.* (N)

ha-a-tthuugn *doo* *le'*
ADJC-NTRL-waterward:AR someone IGN

ee-day
3SG.S:DH.PFV:Ø-SG.sit:IPV:NOM

'Down there by the water someone was sitting.'
UTOLAF15May0501:028

b. *Hanadegn' Nahk'ade hanadeg' ddhał eekeh łat hihneh'įh…* (T)

ha-na-degn' *Nahk'ade* *ha-na-deg'* *ddhał*
ADJC-MED-up:ALL fishtrap ADJC-MED-up:ALL mountain

eekeh *łat* *hih-neh-'įh*
halfway.up smoke 3PL.S-QUAL:Ø.IPV:H-see:IPV

'At a medium distance uphill next to Nahk'ade (Last Tetlin), halfway up the mountain, they saw smoke…' UTOLAF07Nov2602:010

The four distance prefixes are largely mutually exclusive, although there are a few instances where the distal prefix *ya-* precedes the medial prefix *na-* (371). There are not enough instances to fully understand the semantics of this combination.

(371) a. *Teedląy keey yanadegn' nadegn' tąy hǫǫłįį shiin tąy.* (T)

Teedląy *keey* *ya-na-degn'* *na-degn'* *tąy*
Tetlin village DSTL-MED-up:ALL MED-up:ALL trail

hǫǫ-łįį *shiin* *tąy*
AR.S:Ø.PFV:Ø-be:IPV summer trail

'A long way up there at Tetlin village, up there there is a trail, a summer trail.' UTOLVDN07Oct2602:005

b. *"Yahna'ne' ch'ixia' kah natsitdek," neehinih.* (N)

yah-na-ne' *ch'-xia'* *kah*
DSTL-MED-upriver:ALL INDF.PSR-egg for

na-tsit-dek *nee-hi-nih*
PRMB-1PL.S:Ø.IPV:D-PL.go:IPV 1PL.O-3PL.S:Ø.IPV:Ø-say:IPV

'"Let's go look for eggs way over in the upriver direction," they said to us.' UTOLVDN07Aug2205:002

The areal prefix follows the distance prefixes, with which it also coalesces (372). (372a) illustrates the co-occurrence of the adjacency prefix *ha-*, the medial distance prefix *na-*, and the areal prefix *hu-*.

(372) a. *Baadeh: "Dutthan' du' tsaadal!"* (T)

b-aadeh *da-hu-tthan'* *du'*
2SG.PSR-older.sister PROX-AR-waterward:ALL CT

tsaa-dal
1PL.S:INC:AA.IPV:Ø-PL.go:FUT:IMP

'The older sister: "Let us go down there!"'
UTOLVDN14Nov2301:158

b. … *hanuhshyign' tüh dzina'altth'ät.* (N)

ha-na-uhshyign' *tüh*
ADJC-MED-AR-down:ALL among

dzi-na-al-tth'ät
over.edge-down-3SG.S:AA.IPV:L-CO.move.quickly:PFV

'… it tumbled down the area a little ways away down over the edge.'
UTOLAF09Aug12:028

(373) shows that *tth'ii-* 'straight out' follows the neutral distance prefix; I thus place *tth'ii-* 'straight out' in the same prefix slot as *hu-* 'AR'- (see Brucks [2015, 57] for a differing analysis).

(373) … *ha' guuy nts'ą' hooniign t'eey ditth'iik atth'iidegn' ddhał tthiit'aagn nts'ą'.* (T)

ha' guuy *nts'ą'* *hooniign* *t'eey* *di-tth'iik*
little ADVZR noise ADVZR 3SG.S:QUAL:QUAL:Ø.PFV:Ø-hear:IPV

a-tth'i-degn' *ddhał* *tthit'aagn* *nts'ą'*
NTRL-straight-up:ALL mountain on.mountaintop at

'… he hears every little noise they make straight up there on top of the mountain.' UTOLAF09Jun2404:002

In a fashion the rigid order of prefixes in a directional adverb is reminiscent of the more complex template often used to represent verb structure in this language family.

17.2.2. Semantics of directional prefixes

I discuss these prefixes in the order of increasing distance from the stem.

17.2.2.1. *hu-* 'AR'- The semantics of the areal prefix as opposed to the areal suffix in directionals is hard to capture in English. The difference looks quite subtle in translation even though it is not at all subtle in Upper Tanana, since the areal prefix and the areal suffix are used to describe fundamentally different spatial layouts as illustrated in (374).

(374) a. *Mbookol hanogn tah stach'inįl'įį, ch'iliitthoo'.* (N)

mb-ookol	*ha-nogn*	*tah*
3SG.O-NEGEX	NTRL-upland:AR	among

sta-ch'-nįl-'įį,	*ch'iliitthoo'*
away-INDF-3SG.S:N.PFV:L-hide:PFV	grizzly

'He was gone, he was hiding in the upland area, that grizzly.'
UTOLVDN13May2004:030

b. ... *hunegn' uk'eh t'eey natsetdeeɬ.* (N)

hu-negn'	*u-k'eh*	*t'eey*
AR-upland:ALL	3SG.P-following	ADVZR

na-tset-deeɬ
PRMB-1PL.S:INC:DH.PFV:D-PL.go:PFV

'... we followed him into the area of the upland direction.'
UTOLVDN13May2004:099

The two examples in (374) are taken from a story where a girl (the storyteller) and her brothers are sent to pack meat back to the village. Upon their arrival at the drying rack, they find that a grizzly has taken all the meat and is now hiding in the brush somewhere upland of the children (374a). As the drying rack is located on a flat (an open space), there is an area between the rack and the brush where the bear clearly is *not*: he is hiding in an area upland of the children that is separated by the flat from the place where the children are standing. The areal suffix thus defines a bounded area not contiguous with the reference point or area.

After the children wound the bear by shooting him in the belly, he runs off in the upland direction where he eventually dies. The children follow him (374b) to make sure that he does not double back to attack them. In order to do so, the children need to traverse the whole area upland between their point of origin and the moving bear. Thus the areal prefix defines an area that is contiguous with the reference area. The contrast between the forms in (374) is illustrated in figure 17.1.

17.2.2.2. *tth'i-* 'straight out' There are only two instances of *tth'i-* 'straight out' in the corpus ([373] above and [375]) below; both of them are in the Te-tlin dialect. The Ahtna cognate *ts'i-* 'straight out' is quite common (Kari

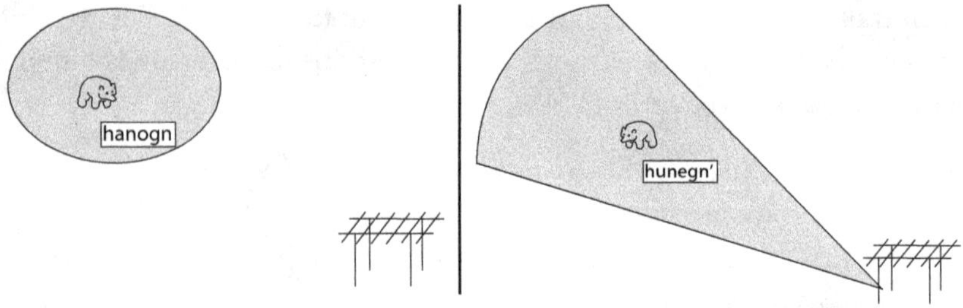

Figure 17.1. The meaning difference between the areal suffix (in the form *hanogn* 'an area upland'; left panel) and the areal prefix (in the form *hunegn'* 'the upland area'; right panel)

2010); possibly its use in Tetlin is due to the influence of Ahtna.

(375) ... *tth'iinoo' nts'ą' hukah nineh'įįk naa::n' udih.* (T)

tth'ii-noo'	*nts'ą'*	*hu-kah*
straight-ahead:ALL	to	3PL.P-for

ni-neh-'įįk	*naan'*	*udih*
TERM-3SG.S:QUAL:Ø.IPV:H-do:IPV:CUST	across:ALL	all

'... straight ahead he kept doing this for them all the way across.'
UTOLVDN13May2801:159

17.2.2.3. Distance distinction: *da-, na-, ya-, a-* Upper Tanana directionals exhibit a four-way distance distinction: *da-* indicates a proximate distance, *na-* indicates an intermediate one, and *ya-* a very great distance. The prefix *a-* indicates a neutral, unknown, or irrelevant distance.

Da- 'PROX'- is used for distances up to maybe five meters (fifteen feet). (376a) is uttered by Raven, who is bragging about his flying skills. He wants to fly particularly low so he can show off better. (376b) describes how the speaker was sitting in a truck and looking out from there for black bear at the sides of the road; she is thus only marginally higher up than the bear she is looking for. (376c) is uttered by a story character who is standing at a crossroads indicating which trail to take.

(376) a. *Dahdogn naa natnusht'ay ay shnųh'įh.* (N)

dah-dogn n-aa na-tnush-t'ay
PROX-up:AR 2SG.P-for PRMB-INC:OPT:1SG.S:D-SG.fly.around:OPT
ay sh-nųh-'įh
and 1SG.O-QUAL:OPT:2SG.S:H-see:OPT

'I want to fly around a little ways overhead for you and I want you to see me.' UTOLVDN10Jul2710:014

b. *Dahdǫǫ shoh dat-sąy kah hach'edagn'įį.* (N)

dah-dǫǫ shoh dat-sąy kah
PROX-up:ABL bear 3SG.S:QUAL:AA.PFV:D-be.black:IPV:NOM for
ha-ch'e-dagn-'įį
out-INDF-QUAL:Ø.IPV:1SG.S:L-look:IPV

'From a little ways uphill I was looking around for black bear.' UTOLAF09Aug1201:011

c. *Sǫ', sǫ' tąy nteel sǫ' dahtthan' tahdeel!* (T)

sǫ', sǫ' tąy n-teel sǫ'
PROH PROH trail 3SG.S:Ø.PFV:Ø-be.wide:IPV:NOM PROH
dah-tthan' tah-deel
PROX-waterward:ALL INC:Ø.IPV:2PL:Ø-PL.go:IPV:IMP

'Don't, don't go a little ways toward the water on the wide trail!' UTOLVDN14Nov2301:130

On the horizontal plane *na-* is used for distances that can be covered by a brief walk there and back (in the same day). In (377a) the people go from Tetlin toward the hill where the Che' T'iin (Tailed People) live; as the crow flies, this is maybe a kilometer and a half (a little over a mile). (377b) describes Raven's arrival in a village. He tricks the villagers to go to the place he came from so he can eat their children's eyes in their absence. They can only hear their children's wailing upon their return to the village. This is from an old-time story where no place-names are used (Lovick 2012), thus distances are harder to evaluate, but it seems likely that *na-* indicates a distance of at least half a mile (eight hundred meters) or more. When applied to the vertical plane, the distance described by *na(h)-* is shorter; *na-* is often used to describe the location of food on drying racks or high caches or, as in (377c), that of a person in a tree.

(377) a. *Dineey iin hǫǫ ehnąy eɬ natthan' Naataybneetkayh nts'ą' hiteedeeɬ.* (T)

dineey iin hǫǫ eh-nąy eɬ na-tthan'
men PL thus 3SG.S:Ø.IPV:H-say:IPV:NOM and MED-waterward:ALL

Naatayhneetkayh nts'ą' h-tee-deeɬ
dried.up.hill to 3PL.S-INC:DH.PFV:Ø-PL.go:PFV

'He told the people that, and they went a medium distance toward the water to Naatayhneetkayh.' UTOLVDN07Oct2604:030

b. *Nahdǫǫ ddhäɬ tüh nįįshyah.* (N)

nah-dǫǫ ddhäɬ tüh nįįs-hyah
MED-up:ABL mountain across 3SG.S:N.PFV:Ø-SG.go:PFV

'Down the hill he came over the mountains.'
UTOLVDN10Jul2703:002

c. *Ts'ehɬegn k'it detxol nashyign' tah.* (N)

ts'ehɬegn k'it det-xol na-shyign'
one on 3SG.S:QUAL:DH.PFV:D-break:PFV:NOM MED-down:ALL

tah
among

'One [of the branches] broke and a medium distance down [he fell].'
UTOLVDN07Aug2205:074

The distal prefix *ya(h)-* 'DSTL'- describes great distances such as a walk that takes all day (378a). It is also used to describe smaller distances that are somehow unusually large, e.g., the distance covered by the speaker after jumping a long way out of the truck to shoot a bear (378b) or a young man picking spruce bows very high up in the tree (378c).

(378) a. *Yanoo:: huniithaadn eh natsetdek, dziin udih nee'eh hǫǫɬe'.* (N)

ya-noo hu-nii-thaadn eh
DSTL-ahead:ALL AR.S-N.PFV:Ø-be.far:IPV:NOM and

na-tset-dek, dziin udih nee-'eh
IT-1PL.S:INC:Ø.IPV:D-PL.go:IPV:CUST day all 1PL.O-with

hǫǫ-ɬe'
AR.S:Ø.PFV:Ø-be:PFV

'We went back a long way, it took us all day.'
UTOLVDN07Aug2205:020

b. … *ya'än' tah tinagntthät k'a' eh.* (N)

ya-'än' *tah* *ti-nagn-tthät* *k'a'* *eh*
DSTL-out:ALL among out-N.PFV:1SG.S:L-run.out:PFV gun with

'… I ran out with the gun.' UTOLAF09Aug1201:024

c. *Ch'itth'ąy yadog ts'oo k'it ts'anh inehts'ayh…* (T)

ch'itth'ąy *ya-dog* *ts'oo* *k'it* *ts'anh*
dry.branch DSTL-up:AR spruce on from

i-neh-ts'ayh
3SG.S>3SG.O-QUAL:Ø.IPV:H-pick:IPV

'He was picking dry spruce boughs way up there from the spruce…' UTOLVDN14May0703:089

The most common distance prefix is *(h)a-* 'NTRL'-, which indicates a neutral or unspecified distance. In all three examples in (379) the speaker knows the distance involved from personal experience, but as it is not important for the development of the narrative, *(h)a-* 'NTRL'- is used rather than one of the more specific distance prefixes.

(379) a. *Ay tl'aan adaat mänh aanah ushyah hǫǫłįį dänh…* (N)

ay tl'aan *a-daat* *mänh* *aanah* *u-shyah*
and.then NTRL-downriver:PNCT lake next.to 3SG.PSR-house

hǫǫ-łįį *dänh*
AR.S:Ø.PFV:Ø-be:IPV at

'And then at the place downriver, next to the lake where her house was, …' UTOLVDN14Apr2602:092

b. … *ahnogn nts'ą' ch'itay iin eł ts'ist'e' iin eł hetsaa:: hesal hihdiitth'ak.* (T)

ah-nogn *nts'ą'* *ch'itay* *iin* *eł* *ts'ist'e'* *iin*
NTRL-upland:AR at old.man PL and old.woman PL

eł *he-tsaa::* *he-sal*
and 3PL.S:Ø.IPV:Ø-cry:IPV:NOM 3PL:Ø.IPV:Ø-holler:IPV:NOM

hih-dii-tth'ak
3PL.S-QUAL:QUAL:Ø.IPV:Ø-hear:IPV

'… in the upland area they heard old men and women cry and holler.' UTOLAF10Jul0801:006

c. *Hanaat dahdzäł da'ee'ąą, ts'ineh'įh łahtthegn nts'ą̈' shyi' t'eey kol.* (N)

ha-naat *dahdzäł* *da-ee-'ąą,*
NTRL-across:PNCT rack up-3SG.S:DH.PFV:Ø-classify.CO:IPV

ts'-neh-'įh *łahtthegn* *nts'ą̈'* *shyi'* *t'eey* *kol*
1PL.S-QUAL:Ø.IPV:H-see:IPV all meat even NEGEX

'Across [the flat] where the meat rack is, we saw that all the meat was gone.' UTOLVDN13May200:025

It is not clear what determines the use of *(h)a-* 'NTRL' as opposed to no distance prefix at all. The same spatial situation is described in the two utterances in (380); both were uttered in Tetlin and reference events at Last Tetlin. Yet (380a) contains the neutral distance prefix while (380b) does not.

(380) a. *Handog łuugn xah dzaltthi' dą' xah Nahk'ade dą' nats'iholndak.* (T)

ha-ndog *łuugn* *xah* *dzal-tthi'*
NTRL-upland:AR fish for 1PL.S:QUAL:AA.PFV:L-PL.stay:PFV

dą' *xah* *Nahk'ade* *dą'* *na-ts'i-hol-ndak*
when for fishtrap at IT-1PL.S-QUAL:Ø.IPV:L-tell.story:IPV

'Let's tell the story of how we were staying in the upland area at Fish Trap (Last Tetlin) for fish.' UTOLVDN10Jul0701:009

b. ... *negn' Nahk'ade dą', dineey iin, stsay iin, stsǫǫ iin stsǫǫ iin nahugn hihdeltth'ii eł t'eey.* (T)

negn' *Nahk'ade* *dą',* *dineey* *iin,* *s-tsay* *iin,*
upland:ALL fish.trap at men PL 1SG.PSR-grandfather PL

s-tsǫǫ *iin* *s-tsǫǫ* *iin* *nahugn*
1SG.PSR-grandmother PL 1SG.PSR-grandmother PL there

h-del-tth'ii *eł* *t'eey*
3PL.S-QUAL:DH.PFV:L-PL.stay:IPV:NOM and even

'... upland at Fish Trap (Last Tetlin) people: my grandparents, my grandmothers were staying out there.' UTOLAF10Jul0801:001

17.2.2.4. *ha-* 'ADJC'- *Ha-* 'ADJC'- refers to a location adjacent to the reference point (381). In the absence of other distance prefixes, *ha-* 'ADJC'- is also easily confused with the neutral distance prefix *(h)a-*.

(381) a. … *hanuhshyign' tüh dzina'altth'ät.* (N)

ha-na-uh-shyign' *tüh*
ADJC-MED-AR-down:ALL over

dzina-al-tth'ät
down.over.edge-3SG.S:AA.IPV:L-CO.fall:PFV

'… it tumbled down the area a little ways away down over the edge.' UTOLAF09Aug12:028

b. *Ha'ahdǫǫ neeshyah nts'ą̈' dǫǫ, ha'ashyign' shee'eh Stephen eeday…* (N)

ha-ah-dǫǫ *nee-shyah* *nts'ą̈'* *dǫǫ,*
ADJC-NTRL-downriver:ABL 1PL.PSR-house toward downriver:ABL

ha-a-shyign' *sh-ee'eh* *Stephen*
ADJC-NTRL-down:ALL 1SG.PSR-maternal.uncle Stephen

ee-day
3SG.S:DH.PFV:Ø-SG.sit:IPV:NOM

'The next one from downriver toward our house, down from where my uncle Stephen was staying, …' UTCBVDN13Nov0804:015

Ha- 'ADJC'- is much more common in the Northway dialect; there are only a handful of examples of this prefix in the Tetlin dialect.

17.3. High tone on directional stems

Directional stems frequently bear a high tone (see chap. 7.3). While it remains uncertain whether this tone is phonemic, it is marked by acute accents already in Milanowski and John (1966), which reflects its salience. (382) contains the original transcription in the first line followed by a transliteration into the orthography used in this grammar.

(382) … *ut̲huul' chih t̲h'iindóó nii'inxal.* (T)

utthuul' *chih* *tth'indoo* *nii'inxal*
3SG:tongue also straight:ahead:ALL 3SG:club.moves.to.point:IT:PFV

'… his tongue also moved straight out again.' Milanowski & John (1966, 51), Mark 7:35

As discussed in chap. 7, high tone is realized consistently in the Northway and Tetlin dialects. Figure 17.2 illustrates the realization of the high tone of the directional stem *degn'* 'up:ALL' in (383) in the Tetlin dialect. figure 17.3, a pitch track of (384), illustrates it for the Northway dialect.

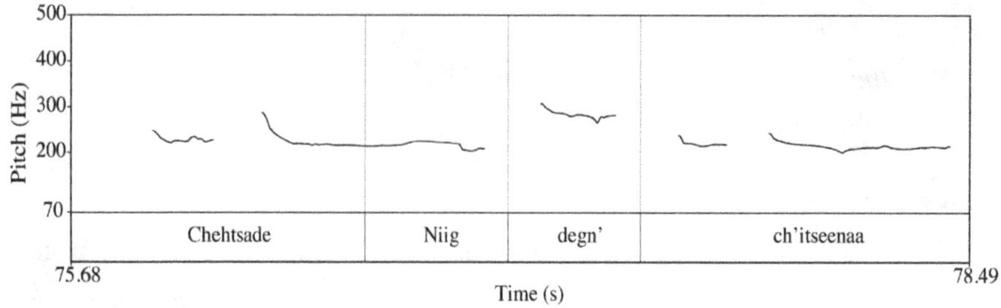

Figure 17.2. High tone on *degn'* 'up:ALL', speaker: Mrs. David (T)

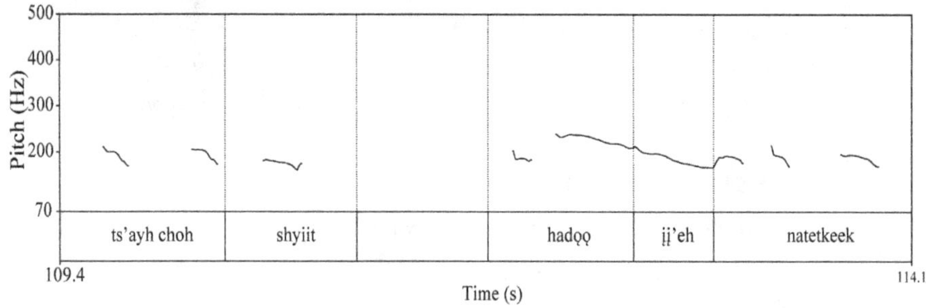

Figure 17.3. High tone on *hadǫǫ* 'NTRL:downriver:ABL', speaker: Mrs. Demit-Barnes)

(383) *Ay* *tl'aan* *eɬ* *Chehtsade* *Niig* *degn'*
and then and mouse creek up:ALL
ch'itseenaa. (T)
1PL:move.nomadically:INC:PFV
'And then we moved up to Mice Creek.'
UTOLVDN08Mar1311:009

(384) … *ts'ayh* *choh* *shyiit* *hadǫǫ* *įį'eh*
boat big in NTRL:downriver:ABL etc.
natetkeek. (N)
3PL:go.by.boat:IT:INC:IPV:CUST
'… and then they would return from downriver in the barge.'
UTCBVDN13Nov0805:007

In the Scottie Creek dialect, directional stems also bear a high tone, as illustrated in figure 17.4, a pitch track of the second part of (385). Both directional stems in this example bear a high tone.

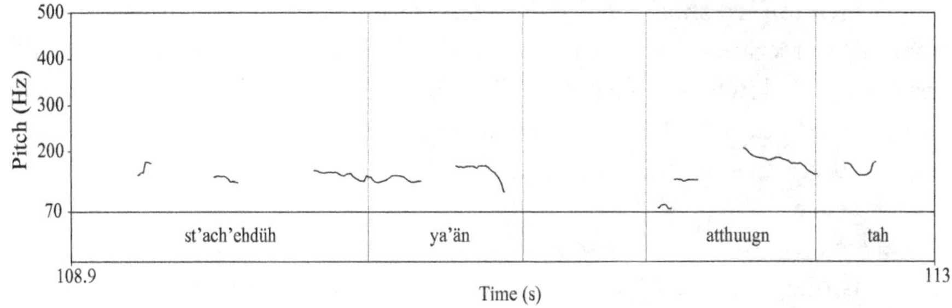

Figure 17.4. High tone on *ya'än* 'DSTL:out:ALL' and *atthuugn* 'NTRL:waterward:AR', speaker: Mrs. Tyone (S)

(385) *Uche',* *uche'* *chį̨'* *st'ach'ehdüh* *ya'än*
3SG:tail 3SG:tail tip 3SG:jump.up:PFV DSTL:out:ALL
atthuugn *tah.* (S)
NTRL:waterward:AR at
'The tip of his tail jumped up, a long ways out, down there by the water.' ANLC4122a:019

It remains an open question whether the high tone on directional stems is phonemic. It is present on most directional stems in the speech of all speakers (excepting strongly lexicalized forms such as *ishyiit* 'there' or *ashyuugn* 'on the ground'), and its realization is quite consistent, as discussed in chap. 7.5, but it still could be an intonational pattern. So far there are no clear diagnostics allowing me to answer this question.

The origin of high tone on directional stems also remains unclear; unlike the high tone on the negative suffix, which is reported for Upper Koyukon (Siri Tuttle, personal communication), Lower Tanana (Tuttle 1998, 111)[3] and Tanacross (Holton 2000, 81-83), the high tone on directional stems appears to be an Upper Tanana innovation.

17.4. Summary

In this chapter the directional adverbs of Upper Tanana are described. They are a subgroup of spatial adverbs; I discuss them separately because they form a cohesive system.

The directional system of Upper Tanana is based on a riverine orientation system, where the Tanana, the major river of the area, serves as reference point. Based on the northeasterly flow of the river, the following distinctions are made: *ne'* 'upriver' versus *da'* 'downriver', *negn'* 'up from shore' versus *tthän'* 'down toward shore', and *naan'* 'across', which is its own opposite. The remaining directionals do not reference the Tanana: *degn'* 'up above, uphill' versus *shyign'* 'down below, downhill', *'än* 'off to the side, away', and *noo'* 'ahead'. In addition to these basic meanings, many directionals have multiple senses and are in semantic opposition with different directionals depending on each sense.

Directional adverbs consist of a root indicating one of these nine directions plus one of four suffixes expressing movement toward or away from or location at a specific place or in a general area. The roots are tightly fused with the suffixes forming allative, ablative, punctual, or areal stems.

Directional adverbs also optionally contain one or more prefixes that can be arranged in a template similar to the verbal template. There are six prefixes in three 'slots'. The first slot contains a prefix expressing adjacency. The second slot contains one of four prefixes indicating distance, and the third slot contains an areal prefix or a prefix with the meaning 'straight out'.

Directional stems are characterized by high tone, which is present in the speech of all Upper Tanana speakers for whom data is available and is realized very consistently. The phonemic status of this tone is uncertain, and it appears that it is an Upper Tanana innovation.

The combination of roots, suffixes, and stems allows speakers to give very precise information about the relative location of entities or the direction of movement, which is difficult to capture adequately in English. A description of the use of directionals is beyond the scope of this grammar; see Brucks (2015) on Upper Tanana and Kari (2011) for Ahtna.

Notes

1. Pre-Proto-Dene reconstructions are marked by two asterisks, e.g., **dəɢ 'up above', while Proto-Dene reconstructions are marked with only one asterisk.
2. The area north of the Tanana River, the Ladue country, is usually referred to as *degn'* 'uphill' rather than *negn'* 'upland'.
3. Tuttle treats this negative morpheme as an enclitic in Lower Tanana.

18 Adjectives and modifiers

Upper Tanana has a small number of uninflected words describing property concepts.[1] Based on their syntactic distribution, they fall into two groups: *adjectives* (also called "predicative adjectives" by Kari [1990, 1997b] or Hargus [2007]), which may occur as predicates, and *modifiers* (termed "evaluative morphemes" in Lovick and Rice [2015]), which modify a noun. Some of them also can occur by themselves as interjections. Many of them are related to other stems, but not all of them are.

The distinction between adjectives and modifiers is not absolute. The word *choh* 'big', for example, is used as adjective in (386a) and as modifier in (386d). In (386b, c) the status of *choh* is less clear.

(386) a. … *hutthi' choh hudzag choh tat'eey.* (T)
3PL:head big 3PL:ear big also
'… their heads [are] big and their ears [are] big, too.'
UTCBAF14Jul1805:005

b. *Ts'ehłegn dineh choh nłįį.* (N)
one man big 3SG:be:IPV
i. 'One man [of the two] is tall.'
ii. 'One of them is a tall man.' UTOLAF12Jul1202:007

c. … *dineh choh eltsįį.* (T)
man big 3SG:become:PFV
i. '… the person became big.'
ii. '… he became a big man.' UTOLAF09Jun2202:016

d. *Haniig choh ts'exeh ni'iltthat.* (T)
river big woman 3SG:arrive.running:PFV
'And the girl arrived running at a big river.'
UTOLAF09Aug1101:001

It would be possible to classify *choh* in (386b, c) as an adjective, resulting in the complex predicates *choh nłįį* 'he is big' and *choh eltsįį* 'he became big', as in the (i) translations. This is the approach taken by Hargus (2007, 318), who calls words with a comparable function in Witsuwit'en "predicate adjectives." Alternatively one could say that *choh* in (386b and c) is part of the noun phrase *dineh choh* 'a big man', as done in the (ii) translations. Speaker judgments show that both options are acceptable, although in any given example, one interpretation is preferred—(i) in the case of (386b), but (ii) in the case of (386c).

Choh 'big' is the only word in Upper Tanana that occurs in all of the constructions demonstrated in (386). Most other nonverbal property concept words can be relatively clearly determined to be an adjective or a modifier, but words in either category allow constructions similar to (386b, c).

Adjectives are described in 18.1, modifiers in 18.2.

18.1. Adjectives

Adjectives are property concept words that function as predicates or as interjections. The class of adjectives in Upper Tanana is very small with only nine members: *abah* 'ouch', *elih* 'cold', *elok* 'hot', *idzii'* 'scary', *įįjih* 'forbidden', *choh* 'big', *teejuh* 'poor thing', *t'ayaadn* or *ayaa* 'filthy', and *tsin'įį* or *tsinah'įį* 'grateful'.

18.1.1. Functions

Adjectives can function as predicates (387).

(387) a. *Hah'ogn* *shaa* *elok.* (N)
NTRL:outside:AR 1SG:for hot
'It's hot outside for me.' UTCBAF13May2401:037

b. *Ayaa* *t'eey* *ch'a* *dineh* *aldeel!* (S)
yuck ADVZR FOC human 2PL:eat:IPV:NOM
'It is disgusting the way you PL eat people!' ANLC4122a:068

Adjectives frequently combine with a form of the verb theme Ø+łįį 'be', Ø+t'eh 'be', or L+tsįį 'seem, become' to become a complex predicate (388).

(388) a. *Ayaa* *nt'eh!* (B)
yucky 3SG:be:IPV
'This is yucky!' UTOLAF10Jul0202:065

b. … *elih* *hǫǫłįį* *tat'eey* *di'eel'* *nts'ą̈'*
cold AR:be:IPV but REFL:trap:POSS to
natetshyah. (T)
3SG:SG.go:IT:INC:PFV
'… it was cold but he walked back to his trap.'
UTOLAF13May2801:012

c. *Teejuh* *nts'ą'* *t'eey* *eltsiin* *ts'iniin* *gaay.* (T)
cute ADVZR 3SG:look:IPV:NOM child small
'He looked really cute, that baby.' UTOLVDN13May2801:062

Some adjectives also can occur in isolation as interjections. The punctuation in (389) reflects the phonetic isolation of the adjectives.[2]

(389) a. *Abah!* (N)
'Ouch!' (Uttered when speaker pricked her finger while sewing.)

b. *Ayaa!* *Dii xa* *dįh'ąy?* (T)
yuck why 2SG:do:IPV:NOM
'Yuck! Why are you doing this?' UTOLVDN08Mar1302:010

Most adjectives cannot be used to modify noun phrases; the exceptions are *choh* 'big' and *teejuh* 'poor, pitiful', which also can function as modifiers.

18.1.2. Inventory

Most adjectives are disyllabic with the stress on the second syllable. They tend not to be related to other stems in the language.

18.1.2.1. *abah* 'ouch' *Abah* 'ouch, painful' is not related to any other stem in the language. It is the only word in Upper Tanana containing a bilabial stop that is consistently denasalized in the speech of all speakers. It can be used as an interjection (390a) or a predicate (390b).

(390) a. *T'axoh* *itthii'ts'al'* *eh* *yeh* *tikįi'et-łuuk.*
enough 3SG:hair with 3SG>3SG:with drag.off.trail:IT:IPV:CUST
Abah! *Itthii'ts'al'!* (T)
ouch 3SG:hair
'Finally she dragged her off the trail by her hair. Ouch! Her hair!'
UTCBVDN13Nov1101:030

b. *Ushyiit* *abah* *nts'ą'* *na'etkuyh.* (T)
3SG:inside ouch and 3SG:vomit:IPV
'Her insides hurt and she vomited.' UTOLVDN10Jul0701:037

18.1.2.2. *elih* 'cold' *Elih* 'cold' is related to the verb stem *dlih* 'be cold IPV' (391a). The adjective can be used as a predicate or as an interjection. No reference is provided for (391b) because it is taken from observation; this word is used quite frequently in complaints about the winter weather (often accompanied by exaggerated shivering).

(391) a. *Elih, natidhihdlih.* (N)
cold 1SG:be.cold:IPV
'[It is] cold, I am cold.' UTOLAF13May2801:062

b. *Eli:::h!* (N, T)
'[It's] cold!'

18.1.2.3. *elok* 'hot' *Elok* 'hot' can be used by itself as an interjection or as predicate. This word is not related to any other stem in the language; the regular themes for 'hot' are n+L+ch'ok 'be hot (weather)', n+L+kon' 'be hot (fire)', n+Ø+thäł 'be hot (food)', and n+L+tthia 'be red-hot (metal)'. *Elok* can be used to describe temperature of all sorts of things: (392a) describes elevated body temperature, (392b) describes the heat of the fire, and (387a) above describes the weather. Generally *elok* indicates that the temperature is considered excessive or unpleasant.

(392) a. *Ntthi' elok de' kah dąą' dįįdį'.* (N)
2SG:head hot to.check thus 2SG:do:IPV
'Do like this to check if your forehead is hot.'
UTOLAF13May2801:068

b. … *ishyiit chih "Elok, elok, elok!," niign.* (S)
there too hot hot hot say:IPV:CUST:NOM
'… there they would say "Hot, hot, hot!"' ANLC4122a:046

18.1.2.4. *idzii'* 'scary' *Idzii'* 'scary' may be related to the interjection *edzee'* 'goodness, surprise' (see chap. 21.2.2). It usually occurs as a predicate (393).

(393) a. *Tuu idzii'!* (T)
water scary
'The water [is] scary!' UTOLVDN13May2907:089

b. *Ch'aldzeek tida'įį'aan idzii' dadhahdąy!* (N)
moon 3SG:be.eclipse:PFV:NOM scary 2PL:behave:IPV:IMP
'The lunar eclipse is scary, behave yourselves!'
UTCBVDN14Jul2105-062

18.1.2.5. *įįjih* 'taboo, forbidden' The importance of *įįjih* 'taboo, forbidden' is discussed in chap. 4.1. The adjective *įįjih* is not transparently related to any other Upper Tanana stem. It occurs rarely as an interjection (394a) but is almost always used as a predicate (394b).

(394) a. *Sǫ', įįjih, nił'ihdetniik.* (T)
PROH forbidden 3PL>RECP:tell:IPV:CUST
'Don't, [it is] forbidden, they tell each other.'
UTCBAF14Jul1804:058

b. *Nahugn hiiye'aal hut'eey įįjih.* (T)
whatever 3PL>3SG:eat:IPV:NOM whatever taboo
'Whatever they eat [is] taboo as well.'
UTOLVDN11Jul2901:003

18.1.2.6. *choh* 'big' *Choh* 'big' is related to the verb stem *chaa* 'be big IPV'. It is only used as a predicate, not as an interjection (395).

(395) a. *Nshyaa' choh.* (T)
2SG:lice:POSS big
'Your lice [are] big.' UTOLAF07Feb1302:078

b. *Kon' choh, elok!* (T)
fire big hot
'The fire [was] big and hot!' UTOLAF09Jun2402:005

There is no adjective for the opposite concept 'small'; instead a form of the verb Ø+tsuul 'small' is used.

18.1.2.7. *teejuh* 'poor, pitiful, cute, respectful' *Teejuh* 'poor, pitiful, cute, respectful' is usually used as an interjection (396a), but it occasionally also functions as an adjective (396b). When used as an adjective, its meaning varies widely between 'poor', 'pitiful', 'cute', or, together with the postposition P+*xah, aa* 'respectful of P, feeling respect for P' (396c).

(396) a. *Gee, teejuh!* (T)
gee poor.thing
'Gee, that poor thing!' UTCBAF13Nov0501:089

b. *Teejuh nts'ą' t'eey eltsiin ts'iniin gaay.* (T)
cute ADVZR 3SG:seem:PFV:NOM baby
'He looked cute, that baby.' UTOLVDN13May2801:062

c. *Huxah teejuh shyįį' t'eey teejuh.* (T)
3PL:for respect only even respect
'They feel deep respect for them.' UTOLVDN13May2905:039

It appears that *teejuh* is a fossilized third-person inceptive perfective verb form. One speaker produced the form in (397); otherwise, the stem *juh* is not attested.

(397) *ti'ahjuh!* (N)
t-ah-juh
INC-Ø.IPV?:2PL.S:Ø-be.poor?:IPV?
'you poor people!' UT Notebook #5, 49

18.1.2.8. *t'ayaadn, ayaa* 'filthy, disgusting' *T'ayaadn* 'filthy, disgusting, dirty' is not related to any other stem. It can be used by itself as an interjection similar to English 'Yuck!' (see [389b] above), but it can also be used as a predicate as shown in (398). *T'ayaadn* seems to be stronger than *ayaa*.

(398) a. *Gǫǫh t'ayaadn.* (T)
worm disgusting
'Worms are disgusting.' UTOLVDN08Mar1302:014

b. *Nan k'it du' ayaa.* (T)
earth on CT dirty
'The land is polluted.' UT Notebook #2, 14

18.1.2.9. *tsin'įį, tsinaa'įį* 'thank you (very much), (very) grateful' *Tsin'įį* 'thank you, grateful' is most often used by itself (399a), as is its more intensive counterpart *tsinaa'įį* 'thank you very much' (399b). *Tsin'įį* 'grateful' also may be used as a verbal complement (399c) or, very rarely, as a nonverbal predicate (399d). *Tsinaa'įį* is not attested in these constructions, but this may be an accidental gap.

(399) a. *Tsin'įį, shdhįhshyiiy.* (T)
thank.you 2SG>1SG:save:PFV:NOM
'Thank you, you SG saved me.' UTOLVDN13May2909:129

b. *"Hǫǫsu' t'eey ay nach'ih'aal; tsinaa'įį," nih.* (T)
well ADVZR and 1SG:eat:IPV:NOM thank.you say:IPV
'"I am eating very well, thank you very much," he said.'
UTOLVDN08Mar1302:022

c. *"... shtlą̨ą̨ iin hutl'atiht̵eeł tsin'į̨į̨ hihnuutłe'*
1SG:partner PL 1SG>3PL:handle.SG.O:IPV thankful 3PL:be:OPT
xah," nih. (T)
PURP say:IPV
'"... I will give things to my partners so they will be grateful," he said.' UTCBAF13Nov0401:052

d. *Mǫǫndaa tat'eey tsin'į̨į̨ xah t'eey.* (T)
3SG:older.brother just grateful ? even
'Her older brother [was] just so grateful.'
UTCBAF13Nov0501:373

18.2. Modifiers

Modifiers are uninflectable property concept words that modify a noun phrase. There are seven modifiers: *choh* 'big', *gaay* 'young, small', *guuy* 'small, tiny', *su'* or *suu'* 'pretty, good', *shyuh* 'full, complete', *teejuh* 'poor', and *tleegn* 'rotten, mushy, dirty'.

18.2.1. Functions

Modifiers in Upper Tanana function as attributes to a noun phrase. A few modifiers may occur by themselves as interjections, but most do not. Modifiers follow the head noun (400).

(400) *Tuu itl'a'į̨į̨ką̨ą̨, gǫǫ gaay ishyiit delttth'ih.* (N)
water 3SG>3SG:give.OOC:PFV bugs small inside 3PL:PL.stay:IPV
'She gave him water, there were lots of little bugs in it.'
UTCBVDN13Nov1401:055

18.2.2. Inventory

All modifiers apart from *teejuh* 'poor' are monosyllablic. Most modifiers are related to other stems in the language.

18.2.2.1. *choh* 'big' The modifier *choh* 'big' is formally identical to the adjective with the same meaning and related to the verb stem *chaa* 'big'. It is often pronounced with extra-high pitch and a lengthened vowel (401a). It can be applied to all types of physical entities.

(401) a. *Tthee cho::h!* (T)
rock big
'A huge rock!' UTCBAF13Nov0501:308

b. *Haniig choh ts'exeh ni'iltthat.* (T)
river big woman 3SG:arrive.running:PFV
'The girl ran to a big river.' UTOLAF09Aug1101:001

c. *Anegn' tah łįį choh eedah...* (N)
NTRL:upland:ALL at dog big 3SG:SG.sit:IPV
'Up there is the big dog...' UTOLVDN13May2004:053

18.2.2.2. *gaay* 'young, small' *Gaay* 'young, small' is related to the verb theme D+gaay 'be born' and to the obligatorily possessed noun stem *-gaay* 'young one, offspring'. Its most common use is in collocation with animate referents where it then has the meaning 'young' rather than 'small'. In (402a) it occurs two times with this meaning 'young' (a 'young woman' is a girl, and a 'young crane' is a baby crane). More rarely, it has the meaning 'small with respect to physical size' in collocation with animate referents (400, 402b). The expression *dineh gaay* usually means 'boy', but in (402b) the meaning 'a man of small physical size' is intended.

(402) a. *Ts'exeh gaay du', "Deeł gaay ch'ale hiiyeh'ąy!"* (T)
woman small CT crane small FOC 3PL>3SG:act:IPV:NOM
'The girl [said]: "They're messing with a baby crane!"'
UTOLAF07Oct2512:010

b. *Dineh gaay nłįį, ntsuul.* (T)
man small 3SG:be:IPV 3SG:be.small:IPV
'He was a small man, he was tiny.' UTOLVDN13May2902:012

With animate referents, *gaay* denotes small physical size (403).

(403) a. *Hanteey' t'eey ts'ayh gaay shyiit huts'ą' hihteedeeł*
quickly ADVZR canoe small in 3PL:to 3PL:PL.go:INC:PFV
eł. (T)
and
'Quickly, in a small boat, they went to them.'
UTOLAF10Jul0801:007

b. *Shin shyįį' t'eey <neetsay> nts'ą' na'ihthat, k'a'*
1SG only even 1PL:grandfather to 1SG:SG.stand:IPV gun
gaay eł.
small with
'I stood up to the bear by myself, with a small gun.'
UTOLAF09Jun2201:007

18.2.2.3. *guuy* 'small, tiny' *Guuy* 'small, tiny' does not seem to be related to any other stem in the language. This stem is usually pronounced with extra-high pitch and is very frequently lengthened (404).

(404) a. *Eł ch'ithüh guu::y eł, guu::y eł hiitl'a'įįdlah.* (T)
and INDF:skin tiny and tiny and 3PL>3SG:handle.PL.O:PFV
'And they gave him a tiny, tiny moose skin among other things.'
UTOLAF08Apr2804:017

b. *Ts'iiniin guuy etsaa.* (T)
child tiny 3SG:cry:IPV
'The tiny baby was crying.' UTOLAF09Jun2202:014

c. *Łuugn xah dahdzał guuy chih ts'ehtsiik...* (T)
fish for rack tiny also 1PL:make.SG.O:IPV:CUST
'We would make a tiny drying rack for the fish...'
UTOLAF09Jun2901:011

There is a small semantic difference between *gaay* and *guuy*. *Guuy* cannot be used to mean 'young' but always refers to physical size. This is demonstrated in (405). *Łįįgaay* can be interpreted as a compound meaning 'puppy' or as a modified noun meaning 'small dog'.

(405) a. *łįįgaay* (N)
łįį - gaay
dog - small
'puppy, small dog' UT Notebook #4, 14

b. *łįį guuy* (N)
łįį guuy
dog tiny
'small dog' (e.g., a Chihuahua) UT Notebook #4, 14

c. *łįįgaay guuy* (N)
łįį-gaay guuy
dog-small tiny
'tiny puppies' (e.g., Chihuahua puppies) UT Notebook #4, 14

When used with inanimate referents, the difference between *gaay* and *guuy* is one of degree. The canoe in (406a) is small, but apparently big enough for several people, whereas the canoe in (406b) is so tiny that the narrator ends up sitting up to her waist in water when trying to cross a creek in it.

(406) a. *Hanteey' t'eey ts'ayh gaay shyiit huts'ą' hihteedeeł*
quickly ADVZR canoe small in 3PL:to 3PL:PL.go:INC:PFV
eł. (T)
and
'Quickly, in a small boat they went to them.'
UTOLAF10Jul0801:007

b. ... *ts'ayh guuy shyį̨' shyiign eetąą...* (T)
canoe tiny only there 3SG:classify.LRO:IPV
'... only a tiny canoe was lying there...'
UTOLAF09Jun2902:005

Generally *guuy* 'small, tiny' is used when the degree of smallness is somehow unusual or excessive.

18.2.2.4. *su', suu'* 'pretty, good' *Su', suu'* 'pretty, good' is related to the verb stem *su'* 'good, beautiful PFV'. When applied to humans, this modifier is ambiguous between the two readings 'good' and 'pretty'. The name *Ts'exeh Su'* 'beautiful woman' in (407a) references the great physical beauty of Mrs. Avis Sam, but *su'* is also used to refer to internal qualities (407b).

(407) a. *Ishyiit ch'ale' k'at'eey Avis shǫǫsi' Ts'exeh Su' shǫǫsi'.* (N)
then FOC NEG Avis 1SG:name woman beautiful 1SG:name
'At that time, my name was not Avis, it was Beautiful Woman.'
UTOLVDN14Apr2602:145

b. *Ts'į̨keey suu' hį̨łį̨.* (T)
children good 3PL:be:IPV
'They were good children.' UTOLVDN14Nov2301:042

c. ... *ts'at su' t'eey k'it t'eey tth'idhalt'ay!* (T)
blanket nice even on even 2PL:stretch.out:PFV:IMP
'... stretch yourselves out on the nice blankets!'
UTCBAF13Nov0501:076

18.2.2.5. *shyuh* 'full, complete' The modifier *shyuh* 'full complete' is attested only in one expression: the self-designation of the Upper Tanana people (408). Its gloss is uncertain; Kari (1997b) comments that it is 'said to mean full, complete'.

(408) *dineh shyuh*
person complete
'Upper Tanana person, Native person' Kari (1997b)

18.2.2.6. *teejuh* 'poor, pitiful' *Teejuh* 'poor, pitiful' is an unusual modifier in several respects. First, it can function both as an adjective (see 18.1.2.7) or as a modifier (409). Second, it can both precede (409a) and follow (409b) the noun without an apparent change in meaning—all other modifiers always follow the noun.[3] Third, it is the only disyllabic modifier.

'Poor' in the glosses should be interpreted as in 'poor thing', not as in the lack of material goods.

(409) a. *Ay teejuh ch'itay ay t'oot'eey yetnąą.* (T)
and poor old.man and though 3SG>3SG:drink:IPV
'And the poor old man would still drink it.'
UTOLVDN13May2907:010

b. *Shdia', shdia' teejuh t'eey mbaa*
1SG:younger.sister 1SG:younger.sister poor even 3SG:for
ihdloh. (N)
1SG:laugh:IPV
'My younger sister, my poor younger sister, I just laughed at her.'
UTOLVDN14Apr2602:127

18.2.2.7. *tleegn* 'dirty, rotten' *Tleegn* 'dirty, rotten' is related to the verb stem *tleek* 'mushy, rotten, deteriorated'.[4]

The modifier *tleegn* is as close to an expletive as a respectable elder would come (at least in my presence). In (410a) the speaker is reprimanding her niece for kicking up a fuss over a marmot. (410b) is part of the response to a video where a young man throws his coat on the floor, an action considered *įįjih*.[5] The speaker pretended to be very upset with the young man. While the original translations of *n'eegn' tleegn* and *dineh tleegn* were 'your funny coat' and 'funny man', the meaning of these expressions is much closer to that given in the glosses.

(410) a. *Ay k'ąąy tleegn!* (N)
and marmot dirty
'Just a dirty marmot!' UTOLAF09Aug1202:036

b. *Nts'ąą' dįįdį' ch'a hashyugn nts'ą̈' t'eey n'eegn'*
how 2SG:do:IPV FOC NTRL:down:AR ADVZR 2SG:coat:POSS
tleegn natįįłeegn? (N)
dirty 2SG:handle.PL.O:PRMB:CUST:NOM
'What are you doing, throwing your dirty coat on the ground around here?' UTOLAF14May0807:041

c. *Dineh tleegn uhłe' nįįthän?* (N)
man dirty 1SG:be:OPT 2SG:want:IPV
'Do you want to be a bum?' UTOLAFMay0807:043

18.3. Summary

In this chapter adjectives and modifiers are described. Both categories contain uninflected words expressing property concepts, but they have different functions: adjectives are used as nonverbal predicates or as interjections, while modifiers are used as attributes of nouns. There are nine adjectives and seven modifiers in Upper Tanana; two lexical items belong in both categories.

Notes

1. Most property concepts in this language are expressed by neuter verbs; see chap. 25.
2. No reference is given for (389a) since this example is drawn from observation.
3. (409a, b) are from different dialects; both word orders are attested in both dialects.
4. In related languages this stem has the meaning 'shabby, scruffy' (Kari personal communication).
5. The goal of showing these videos was to elicit negative directives; see Lovick and Tuttle (2019).

19 Pronouns

Upper Tanana has personal pronouns, demonstrative pronouns, and interrogative pronouns (other interrogative proforms are described in this chapter as well). The interrogative proforms also function as indefinite and negative proforms. Personal pronouns are described in 19.1 and demonstrative pronouns in 19.2. Interrogative, indefinite, and negative proforms are described in 19.3.

19.1. Personal pronouns

The inventory of personal pronouns is quite small, and their functions are rather limited.

19.1.1. Inventory

Table 19.1 contains the inventory of personal pronouns in the Tetlin, Northway, and Scottie Creek dialects; the only dialect difference is in the first-person singular personal pronoun. All dialects use several forms for third-person (singular and plural) personal pronouns depending on the construction (see 19.1.2).

	Tetlin	Northway	Scottie Creek
1SG	shin	shiy	shiy
2SG	nan	nän	nän
3SG	ay, di-	ay, di-	ay, di-
1PL	neexon	neexon	neexon
2PL	nuhxon	nuhxon	nuhxon
3PL	ay iin, dihi-	ay iin, dihi-	ay iin, dihi-

Table 19.1. Personal pronouns

19.1.2. Functions

Since arguments are obligatorily marked on the verb or postposition, the use of personal pronouns is restricted to a few marked constructions. In the collection of narratives by Mary Tyone (1996), the personal pronoun *shiy* '1SG' occurs twenty-two times; in that by Cora C. David (2011), *shin* '1SG' only thirteen times. Personal pronouns are limited to very few contexts: identification of individuals, emphasis and contrast, and a construction that translates to 'by Xself'.

19.1.2.1. Identification of individuals Personal pronouns are used occasionally to identify individuals who are present in the speech situation. All natural-language examples of this are first- and second-person pronouns. In (411) and (412) the discourse context is included.

(411) Excerpt: UTOLAF08Apr2805:058-061 (T)

a. *"Doo ch'a tnay?" Kelahdzeey yehnih.*
who FOC make.noise:IPV:NOM spider 3SG>3SG:say:IPV
'"Who is making that noise?" the Spider said to her.'

b. *"Shin! Shin!*
1SG 1SG
'"Me! Me!'

c. *Tsǫǫ, shin diht'eh," nih.*
grandmother 1SG 1SG:be:IPV say:IPV
'Grandmother, it's me!" she said.'

(412) Excerpt: UTOLAF09Aug1202:012-023 (N)

a. *"Tseey! Ii! Tseey ookol!" nih.*
tea oh.no tea 3SG:NEGEX say:IPV
'"Tea! Oh no! There's no tea!" they said.'

b. *"Nän! Negn' shyah nts'ą̈' na'įįdaał tl'aan tseey*
2SG upland:ALL house to 2SG:SG.go:IT:IPV:PROG and tea
kah įįha'," shihinih.
for 2SG:fetch:IPV 3PL>1SG:say:IPV
'"You! Go back upland to the house and get tea," they said to me.'

In the identification context the personal pronoun can occur either in isolation (411b, 412b) or can be accompanied by a form of the verb theme d+Ø+t'eh 'be a certain way' (411c).

This use of personal pronouns is not very frequent in my corpus.

19.1.2.2. Emphasis and contrast Quite a bit more common is the emphatic and contrastive use of personal pronouns. These two functions are hard to separate and thus are discussed together here.

The emphatic function is often signaled by the focus particle *ch'a(le)*, which is present in (413a, b). Although the focus particle usually is present in the emphatic context, (413c) demonstrates that it is not required.

(413) a. *Shiy ch'a Carl kol tah ay shchil iin*
1SG FOC Carl NEGEX when and 1SG:younger.brother PL
k'anakta', shǫǫnüü Carl kol tah. (N)
1SG:take.care:IPV 1SG:older.brother Carl NEGEX when
'Me, when Carl was not there, I took care of my younger brothers when my older brother Carl was not there.'
UTCBAF13Nov1203:015

b. *Łąy eh hatshyąą, ay iin ch'ale hu'ch*
truly and 3PL:be.old:PFV 3SG PL FOC 3PL:with
ihdaagn. (N)
1SG:SG.stay:PFV:CUST:NOM
'They were really old and they are the ones I used to stay with.'
UTOLVDN14Apr2602:159

c. *Jah shnąą iin shta' iin neexon*
here 1SG:mother PL 1SG:father PL 1PL
ha'ashyign' t'eey Frank Sam neexah
ADJC:NTRL:downhill:ALL ADVZR Frank Sam 1PL:next.to
eedah. (N)
3SG:SG.stay:IPV
'Right here my mother and father, all of us; and down there Frank Sam was living next door to us.' UTCBVDN13Nov0804:020

The contrastive function may be the most common one; it is often signaled by the contrastive topic marker *du'*. In (414a) the speaker contrasts her own generation with that of her grandchildren; in (414b) the speaker's mother wonders why her daughter is so quiet as opposed to her sons, who are telling big stories. In (414c) a storyteller is trying to encourage her friends to take over. (414c) also illustrates that the contrastive topic marker *du'* is not required.

(414) a. *Neexon du' dą̨ą̨' ch'a ts'eneeshyaan, k'at'eey huk'eh*
1PL CT thus FOC 1PL:grow.up:PFV:NOM NEG 3PL:like
ts'iniishyeel. (T)
1PL:grow.up:NEG:PFV
'Us, this is how we grew up, we did not grow up like them.'
UTOLAF09Jun2901:009

b. *"Nän du'? Dii xah k'a honįįheey?" shehnih.* (N)
2SG CT why NEG 2SG:speak:IPV:NEG 3SG>1SG:say:IPV
'"How about you? Why are you not talking?" she said to me.'
UTOLVDN07Aug2205:111-112

c. *Shtheeg t'ay' kol, hanteey' nuhxon dahdį'.* (N)
1SG:voice strength:POSS NEGEX quickly 2PL 2PL:do:IPV
'My voice is going; come on, you guys take over.'
UTOLVDN10Jul2713:053

In the emphatic and contrastive use, the third-person pronoun *ay* (*iin*) is used (413b). This is probably the most common function of personal pronouns.

19.1.2.3. Pronoun + *shyįį'* 'by oneself' Personal pronouns are also often used in the construction pronoun + *shyįį'* 'by oneself'. By itself *shyįį'* is usually translated as 'only'. In the first and second persons the personal pronouns are used (415a, b). In the third person, bound forms reminiscent of the reflexive possessor prefixes are used (415c, d; see also chap. 22.2.2).

(415) a. *Shin shyįį' t'eey <neetsay> nts'ą' na'ihthat...* (T)
1SG only even 1PL:grandfather to 1SG:SG.stand:IPV
'I stood up to the bear all by myself...' UTOLAF09Jun2201:007

b. *"... diaa nuhxon shyįį' didhaltth'ii?" hu'ehnih.* (T)
why 2PL only 2PL:PL.stay:IPV:NOM 3SG>3PL:say:IPV
'"... why do you PL live all by yourselves?" he said to them.'
UTOLVDN13May2801:106

c. *... ch'itay dishyįį' eeday xah hinįįdeel.* (T)
old.man 3SG:only 3SG:SG.stay:IPV:NOM to 3PL:PL.go:PFV:NOM
'... they came to an old man living all by himself.'
UTOLAF08Apr2805:015

d. *Dihishyįį'* *nahetdaak* *tah* *k'at'eey*
3PL:only 3PL:SG.sit:IT:IPV:CUST when NEG
tthihihaagn. *(N)*
3PL:SG.go.out:IPV:CUST:NEG
'When they stay by themselves they may not go outside.'
UTOLVDN10Jul2602:076

19.2. Demonstrative pronouns

There is only one demonstrative pronoun in each dialect. In the Northway, Scottie Creek, and Beaver Creek dialects the demonstrative pronoun has the form *jin* (416); in the Tetlin dialect the demonstrative pronoun has the form *jan* (417). (It is not clear which form would be used in the Nabesna dialect.) It may be used for inanimate, animate nonhuman, and human referents alike. There is no distance distinction.

(416) a. *Jin* *ch'a* *shtthe'.* (N)
DEM FOC 1SG:man's.daughter
'This one [is] my daughter.' (when identifying one of several women in a photograph) UTOLAF14Nov2001:001

b. *Jin* *ch'a* *ts'eldeel!* (S)
DEM FOC 1PL:eat:IPV:CUST:NOM
'This is what we eat!' ANLC4122b

c. *Jin* *dǫh'a'* *de'!* (B)
DEM 2SG:sing:OPT if
'You SG should sing this [song]!' UTOLAF10Jul0202:196

(417) *Jan* *ch'ale'* *etsaa.* (T)
DEM FOC 3SG:cry:IPV:NOM
'That's the one who cried.' UTOLAF13May2403:063

Jin, *jan* 'DEM' occur very frequently with the focus particle *ch'a(le')*, which triggers nominalization of the verb; see volume 2.

19.3. Interrogative proforms

Upper Tanana has two interrogative pronouns and a number of interrogative pro-adverbs.

19.3.1. Inventory

The inventory is given in table 19.2. Note that the proform for 'who' can be pluralized using the plural enclitic *iin*.

English	Upper Tanana
'who (PL)'	doo (iin)
'what'	dii
'why' (= 'what for')	dii xah
'how, what'	nts'ąą', nts'ą̈', nts'aa', nts'üü
'when:FUT'	ndehde'
'when:PST'	ndehdą'
'where:PNCT'	ndee
'where:AR'	nduugn

Table 19.2. Interrogative proforms

19.3.2. Functions

Interrogative proforms can be used in two contexts. Most frequently they are used as question words in content questions. They also may be used as indefinite and negative proforms.

19.3.2.1. Interrogative proforms in questions The interrogative pronouns are used to inquire about nominal referents (418).

(418) a. *Doo nįh'įį?* (N)
who 2SG:see:PFV
'Whom did you SG see?' UTOLAF14Apr3001:003

b. *"Doo iin ch'a daht'ay?"* *yehnih.* (T)
who PL FOC 2PL:be:IPV:NOM 3SG>3PL:say:IPV
'"Who are you PL?" he said to them.' UTCBAF13Nov0501:069

c. *Dii ch'a dįh'ąy?* (N)
what FOC 2SG:act:IPV:NOM
'What are you SG messing with?' UTOLAF09Aug12:031

Interrogative pro-adverbs inquire after adverbial constituents, such as cause, location, direction, or time. Most of these pro-adverbs are complex. *Dii xah*, often pronounced more like *diaa*, consists of *dii* 'what' and the postposition P+*aa, xah* 'for P'.

(419) *Dii xah neeshyah dhįįtal?* (T)
why 1PL:house 2SG:kick:PFV
'Why did you SG kick our house?' UTOLAF08Apr2804:011

Nts'ąą', nts'ą̈', nts'aa', nts'üü' 'what, how' inquires either about abstract referents, such as thoughts, words, or events, or about the manner in which an event or action takes place (420). The variation is partly dialectal, partly idiolectal.

(420) a. *Nts'ą', nts'ą' tsedąy ch'ale'?* (T)
what what 1PL:do:PFV:NOM FOC
'What, what shall we do?' UTCBAF13Nov0501:047

b. *Nday! Nts'aa' hutshyaak?* (T)
whoah what AR:happen:PFV
'Whoah! What happened?' UTOLVDN07Oct2602:033

c. "… *t'oot'eey nts'aa' iinįįthan,"* *yehnih.* (T)
but what 2SG:think:IPV:NOM 3SG>3SG:say:IPV
'"… but what do you think?" she said to him.'
UTOLAF09Aug1101:006

d. *Nts'aa' haa'atshyah?* (N)
how 3SG:SG.go.out:IT:PFV
'How did he get back out?' UTOLAF08Feb1902:016

Ndehde' 'when FUT' is used when inquiring about future events; it consists of the adverbial stem *ndeh*, tentatively translated with 'when' (it cannot occur in isolation) and the postposition P+*de'* 'when P (FUT)' (421a). *Ndehdą'* 'when PST' is used when inquiring about past events and consists of the same adverbial stem plus the postposition P+*dą'* 'when P (PST)' (421b).

(421) a. *Ndehde' sh'aat niitaadaał?* (T)
when:FUT 1SG:wife 3SG:SG.arrive:IT:FUT
'When is my wife going to come back?'
UTOLVDN13May2907:047

b. *Ndehdą' naninshyah?* (N)
when:PST 2SG:SG.go:IT:PFV
'When did you SG come back?' UTOLAF14Apr2501:032

There are a number of interrogative adverbs inquiring about the location or direction of an event. Location at a place is usually inquired about using plain *ndee* 'where' (422a). Movement from a place is inquired after using *ndee ts'änh* 'where from' (422b). Movement to a place may be inquired after using *ndee nts'ą̈'* 'where to (precisely)' (422c) or *nduugn* 'in which general direction, whereabouts' (422d). *Nduugn* likely is a derivation of *ndee* using the same areal suffix used in directionals (see also chap. 17).

(422) a. *Ndee ntsinul'į'?* (T)
where 1PL:hide:OPT
'Where should we hide?' UTOLAF12Jul1101:009

b. *Dii xah ndee ts'anh ch'ale łįį needehtthay?* (T)
why where from FOC dog 3PL>1PL:bark.at:IPV:NOM
'Why, from where are the dogs barking at us?'
UTOLVDN14Nov2301:186

c. *Ndee nts'ą' tidhahdeeł?* (T)
where to 2PL:PL.go:INC:PFV
'Where (precisely) are you PL going?'
UTCBVDN13Nov1101:006

d. *Nduugn teeshyah?* (N)
whereabouts 3SG:SG.go:INC:PFV
'Whereabouts did he go?' UTOLAFMay0807:064

The formation of content questions is described in volume 2.

19.3.2.2. Indefinite and negative proforms The interrogative proforms are also used as indefinite and negative pronouns. The inventory and meanings of indefinite and negative proforms are given in table 19.3. They can be used in a number of different constructions that are distinguished to some degree by particles. Not all indefinite proforms can participate in all constructions. The following discussion is organized by proform, indicating which range of meanings and functions is attested in the data.

19.3.2.2.1. *doo* 'someone, whoever, nobody' *Doo* may be used as an indefinite pronoun 'someone, whoever' (423). It is often, but not always, followed by *le'* 'IGN', which seems to reinforce the uncertainty regarding the identity of the person being talked about. *Doo* may only be used with human referents. Again, it can be pluralized using *iin* (423c).

English	Upper Tanana
'someone, whoever, no one (PL)'	doo (*iin*)
'something, whatever, nothing'	dii
'however, no way'	nts'ąą', nts'ą̈', nts'aa'
'somewhere, wherever'	nduugn
'at some place, nowhere'	ndee
'somewhere'	nday

Table 19.3. Indefinite and negative proforms

(423) a. *Hah'ǫǫ doo le', hahdǫǫ doo le'!* (N)
NTRL:outside:ABL someone IGN NTRL:uphill:ABL someone IGN
'From out there someone [might be coming], from up there someone [might be coming]!' UTOLVDN14Apr2602:123

b. *Doo ts'inuhshyee yuunąy ay*
whoever IMPSL:raise:OPT 3SG>3SG:want:IPV:NOM 3SG
itnahshyeeyh! (T)
3SG>3SG:raise:FUT
'Whoever wants to raise him, will raise him!'
UTOLAF13May2403:067

c. … *doo iin tah nahtetneek tah.* (N)
someone PL among 3PL:move.around:IPV:CUST when
'… whenever somebody moved [to a different place].'
UTOLAF10Jul0901:023

In negative sentences, *doo* followed by the particle *t'eey* has the meaning 'nobody, (not) anyone' (424). In this construction, *t'eey* appears to be required, although its semantic contribution is unclear.[1]

(424) a. *Doo t'eey hǫǫ' shehniign!* (T)
nobody thus 3SG>1SG:say:IPV:CUST:NEG
'Nobody ever says that to me!' UTCBAF13Nov0501:253

b. *Sǫ' doo t'eey staa'utshya' nuhch'a'!* (N)
PROH anyone 2SG:SG.go.away:IT:OPT:NEG 2PL:from
'Don't let anyone go away from you PL!'
UTOLAF10Jul0901:039

(424a) is a rare instance of a negative declarative without the negative particle *k'a(t'eey)*.

19.3.2.2.2. *dii* 'something, whatever, everything, nothing' When followed by *le'* 'IGN', *dii* is usually translated as 'something'. This use of *dii* is quite rare; more commonly, unidentified (nonhuman) object referents are expressed by the bound indefinite pronoun *ch'-* (see chap. 31 for more information).

(425) a. *Jahxan ch'aadeh dii le' hadel'ąy.* (T)
suddenly INDF:older.sister something IGN 3SG:spot:IPV:NOM
'Suddenly the older sister spotted something.'
UTCBAF13Nov0501:061

b. *Noo' shtthe' na'ǫǫ ts'änh jah dii le'*
ahead 1SG:before MED:outside:ABL from here something IGN
sheh ha'atdädn. (N)
1SG:with 3SG:animal.run.out:PFV:NOM
'Ahead, in front of me, something came running by me.'
UTOLAF09Aug1202:029

Frequently *dii* without any particle heads a relative clause; it is then usually translated as 'whatever (relative clause)' (426).

(426) a. *Jah dii hiiye'aal łahtthegn ntsą̈'*
here whatever 3PL>3SG:eat:IPV:CUST:NOM all
tthiteedeeł. (N)
3PL:PL.move.out:INC:PFV
'And whatever they eat had all run off.'
UTOLVDN14Apr2601:027

b. *Ahugn dii hiiyuukeedn Delta*
and whatever 3PL>3SG:buy:IPV:CUST:NOM Delta
Junction ts'änh naheyelshyeel ishyiit chih
Junction from 3PL>3PL:carry.PL.O:IT:IPV:NOM there too
hahiiłeek. (N)
3PL>3PL:take.out.PL.O:IPV:CUST
'And whatever they had bought in Delta Junction they brought it back here and took it out.' UTCBVDN13Nov0805:013

Dii is often used to mean 'anything, everything'; it is then frequently followed by *t'eey* with uncertain meaning (427).

(427) a. *Dii t'eey t'eey shyi' t'eey <hiidlą̨> hǫǫ't'eey ishyiit*
everything ? meat ADVZR all still there
eedlah. (N)
3PL:classify.PL.O:PFV
'Everything, all the meat was still there.'
UTOLVDN10Jul2725:022

b. *Dii eł t'eey dzelxoh.* (T)
anything with ? 1PL:play:IPV
'We played with anything.' UTOLAF09Jun2901:014

In negative clauses *dii* has the meaning 'nothing'; it is obligatorily followed by *t'eey* '?'. The negative particle *k'a(t'eey)* may precede or follow *dii t'eey*, with no apparent change in meaning (428).

(428) a. *K'at'eey dii t'eey ts'i'aal.* (T)
NEG anything 1PL:eat:PFV:NEG
'We didn't eat anything.' UTOLAF09Jun2402:027

b. *Dii t'eey k'a dihtth'egn.* (N)
anything NEG 1SG:hear:PFV:NEG
'I couldn't hear anything.' UTOLVDN14Apr2602:043

19.3.2.2.3. *nts'ą̨'* 'however, no way' The indefinite proform *nts'ą̨* (and variant forms) has the meaning 'however, whatever'. It often co-occurs with the complementizer *niign* (429).

(429) a. *Nts'aa hidį̨k niign t'eey, "Nuh'eh ts'utnüü," *
whatever 3PL:do:IPV:CUST CMP even 2PL:with 1PL:work:OPT
heniik. (N)
3PL:say:IPV:CUST
'Whatever they are working on, "Can we work with you guys," they would say. UTCBVDN13Nov0804:043

b. *Nts'ą̨' utsǫǫ yehnih tah ch'its'ą̨*
whatever 3SG:grandmother 3SG>3SG:say:IPV when differently
shyį̨' t'eey dį'. (T)
only even do:IPV
'Whatever his grandmother told him, he did differently.'
UTOLAF09Jun2202:018

There are very few examples of *nts'ąą'* (or variant forms) in a negative clause, where it predictably has the meaning 'no way, nothing' (430).

(430) a. *Nts'ąą k'at'eey tsaadįįl niign t'eey ch'a hįįdįį.* (N)
how NEG 1PL:do:FUT:NEG CMP even FOC 3PL:do:PFV
'There is no way we can do what they used to do.'
UTCBVDN13Nov0805:036

b. … *k'at'eey nts'ąą t'eey yehnąy, ts'ist'e'.* (T)
NEG how ADVZR 3SG>3SG:say:IPV:NEG old.lady
'… she didn't say anything to him, the old lady.'
UTOLVDN14Nov2301:418

19.3.2.2.4. *nduugn* 'somewhere, wherever' The indefinite proform *nduugn* is translated with 'somewhere, wherever' (431).

(431) a. … *nduugn hihteeneek.* (N)
somewhere 3PL:move:INC:PFV:CUST
'… they moved somewhere.' UTOLAF08Feb1908:004

b. *Nduugn hihteedak niig t'eey, ts'įįkeey iin xah*
wherever 3PL:PL.go:INC:PFV:CUST CMP ADVZR children PL for
huch'enehtanh, nduugn hihteedak t'eey. (T)
3PL>INDF:teach:IPV:CUST wherever 3PL:PL.go:PFV:CUST ADVZR
'Wherever they went, she was teaching the children wherever they went.' UTCBAF13Nov0501:021

There are no examples of *nduugn* 'somewhere, wherever' in negative clauses. It is unclear whether this is an accidental gap in the corpus.

19.3.2.2.5. *ndee* 'somewhere, any place' As an indefinite proform, *ndee* has the meaning 'some place, any place'. Upper Tanana distinguishes allative *ndee ts'ą̈'* (432a) and locative *ndee dänh* (432b).

(432) a. "… *ndee ts'ą' tokteey," nih.* (T)
some.place to 1SG:handle.AO:INC:OPT say:IPV
'"… I would like to take him somewhere," he said.'
UTOLVDN13May2902:035

b. *Ndee danh łįį shyįį' hehxąą.* (T)
where at dog only 3PL:kill:PL.O:IPV
'In any place they only kill dogs.' UTCBAF14May2503:009

There are no examples of *ndee* 'some place, any place' in negative clauses.

19.3.2.2.6. *nday* 'somewhere' When a specific yet unknown location is discussed, *nday* may be used with the meaning 'somewhere'. There appears to be only one example of this in the data (433). Uses of *nday* with the meaning 'anywhere', 'everywhere', or 'wherever' are not attested, nor are negative contexts with the meaning 'nowhere'.

(433) *Hah'ogn* *nday* *chinel'įį.* (N)
NTRL:OUT:AR somewhere 3SG:hide:PFV
'He hid somewhere out there.' UTOLVDN11Aug0802:047

19.3.2.2.7. No indefinite adverb 'whenever, never' There is no indefinite adverb 'whenever' in Upper Tanana; instead an adverbial clause with *tah* 'when' and a verb in the customary superaspect is used (434).

(434) a. *Nats'inel'įįk* *nts'ą̈'* *t'eey* *mbaa*
1PL>3SG:look.at:IPV:CUST CMP even 3SG:for
ts'edloo. (N)
1PL:laugh:IPV:CUST:NOM
'Whenever we looked at him, we laughed at him.'
UTOLVDN07Aug2205:079

b. … *doo* *iin* *tah* *nahtetneek* *tah.* (N)
someone PL among 3PL:move.around:IPV:CUST when
'… whenever somebody moved [to a different place].'
UTOLAF10Jul0901:023

Similarly the concept of 'never' is expressed by a negated verb form in the customary (435):

(435) a. *Shta'* *k'at'eey* *neets'ą̈'* *ts'anii'elt'eegn.* (N)
1SG:father NEG 1PL:at 3SG:get.mad:IPV:CUST:NEG
'My father never got mad at us.' UTCBAF13Nov1203:010

b. *k'at'eey* *ts'uneh'iign* *diht'eh.* (T)
NEG 1PL>AR:see:IPV:NEG 1SG:ASRT
'We had never seen [a road] before.' UTCBVDN14Jul1801:149

19.4. Summary

In this chapter three types of pronouns (and proforms) are discussed: personal pronouns, demonstrative pronouns, and interrogative pronouns and proforms.

Personal pronouns are used only rarely. They may be used for the identification of individuals, for emphasis and contrast, and in the construction pronoun + *shyįį'* 'by oneself'.

There is only one demonstrative pronoun. It may be used to refer to inanimate, animate nonhuman, or human referents. There is no distance distinction.

Interrogative pronouns and proforms are used in content question formation. They may also be used as indefinite pronouns or proforms and as negative pronouns and proforms. Not all proforms are attested in each construction.

Notes

1. Speakers tend to translate *t'eey* as 'even', which points to its use as a degree adverb; see chap. 16.3.5. It also functions as an adverbializer; see chap. 16.2.3.

20 Numerals

Upper Tanana employs a decimal number system. The inventory of cardinal numerals is described in 20.1; other number words are described in 20.2. The use of numerals is discussed in 20.3. Although numerals up to 100 are available in the language, numerals greater than 4 are hardly ever used, and the numbers 2, 3, and 4 have special significance.

20.1. Cardinal numerals

20.1.1. Dialectal variation

There is considerable dialectal variation in numerals, and the rarity of numerals means that information is incomplete for several dialects. Table 20.1 contains the numerals 1 through 10 for the Tetlin and Northway dialects.

	Tetlin	Northway
1	ts'ehłag	ts'ehłegn
2	łaakeey	łaakay
3	taag	taagn
4	dan	dän
5	ahts'ąy	ahts'ąy
6	łk'etaag łaakeey taag	łk'itaagn
7	ahts'ąy uk'it łaakeey	łk'edänchii
8	łk'edan	łk'edän
9	ts'ehłag deetaan ts'ehłag kol ts'ehłag mbaa kol	ts'ehłegn deetaan ts'ehłegn kol ts'ehłegn mbaa kol
10	ts'ehłag deetaan	ts'ehłegn deetaan

Table 20.1. Numerals 1–10

20.1.2. Morphological structure of numerals

The numerals 1–4 are numeral stems that, even though they may have been morphologically complex at some point in the past, are unanalyzable at this point. The numeral 5 is related to the noun stem *ts'ąy* 'side', referencing the gesture of holding up one hand. The differences between the remaining numerals reflect different mathematical operations performed to arrive at numbers greater than 5. Analyses of the structures involved are illustrated in (436) to (440); the commentary is distilled from conversations with speakers about the meanings of these forms.

The numeral 6 can be formed either by 'putting threes on top of each other' (436a) or by using two sets of three (436b).

(436) a. *łk'itaagn* (N)
nił-k'it-taagn
REC.P-on-three
'three on top of each other = six'

b. *łaakeey taag* (T)
two three
'two threes = six'

The same technique 'putting fours on top of each other' is employed in the formation of the numeral 8 in both dialects (437).

(437) *łk'edan* (T)
nił-k'it-dan
RECP.P-on-four
'four on top of each other = eight'

There are two different forms for the numeral 7. In the Tetlin dialect it is formed through the operation 5 + 2, using again the postposition P+*k'it* 'on P' (438a). The Northway form is somewhat more puzzling, consisting of the numeral 8 plus an element *chii* with uncertain meaning (438b). It may be an allomorph of the noun stem *chįį* 'tip' (this allomorph is attested, for example, in the place-name *Tthee Chii* 'rock point'), but the semantic shift from 'tip' or 'point' to 'subtract one' is not clearly motivated. *Łk'edänchii* 'seven' is the only numeral containing this morpheme.

(438) a. *ahts'ąy uk'it łaakeey* (T)
ahts'ąy u-k'it łaakeey
five 3SG.P-on two
'two on top of five = seven'

b. *łk'edänchii* (N)
nił-k'it-dän-chii
RECP.P-on-four-tip?
'four on top of each other tip? = seven'

The numeral 10 consists of the word for 1 plus the verb form *deetaan* (439). Kari (1997b) translates *deetaan* as 'multiple of ten'; it is a form of the verb theme d+Ø+tąą 'classify LRO', which could be a reference to a counting stick similar to that described by Osgood (1959, 57) for the Ingalik. (Note that in his description of the Upper Tanana, however, McKennan [1959, 113] describes the use of counting strings rather than counting sticks.)

(439) *ts'ehłegn deetaan* (N)
ts'ehłegn dee-taan
one 3SG.S:QUAL:DH.PFV:Ø-classify.LRO:IPV:NOM
'one sticklike object is lying there = ten'

The numeral 9 is formed in two different ways in both dialects. One way is to use the full expression for 10 and indicate that one unit is absent or missing (440a). This results in a fairly cumbersome numeral, so the other option of expressing 9 is to simply indicate the absence of one unit (440b). Several speakers volunteered both forms as response to my question about this numeral, so it is unclear which of these could be considered the preferred form, especially given the fact that the corpus of narratives does not contain a single example of a numeral higher than 4 (see 20.3).

(440) a. *ts'ehłegn deetaan ts'ehłegn kol* (N)
ts'ehłegn dee-taan ts'ehłegn kol
one 3SG.S:QUAL:DH.PFV:Ø-classify.LRO:IPV:NOM one NEGEX
'one sticklike object is lying there with one missing = nine'

b. *ts'ehłegn mbaa kol* (N)
ts'ehłegn mb-aa kol
one 3SG.P-for NEGEX
'one is absent for it = nine'

20.1.3. Numerals greater than 10

The elicitation of numerals greater than 10 is challenging, as most of them are never used. Mrs. Rosa Brewer (Northway) provided the numerals given in table 20.2.

	Northway	Analysis
10	ts'ehłegn deetaan	one ten
20	łaakay deetaan	two ten
30	taagn deetaan	three ten
40	dän deetaan	four ten
50	ahts'ąy deetaan	five ten
100	ts'ehłegn deetaan deetan	one ten ten

Table 20.2. Numerals 10–100, UTOLAF14Nov2401

The numerals 60, 70, 80, and 90 are missing from this list, which may be due to the fact that the first element of these numerals would be complex. McKennan (1959, 113) states that these forms exist and even indicates that it is possible to express multiples of 100 using a similar technique. Unfortunately he did not record any of these forms.

20.1.4. No animacy-based distinction

In many Northern Dene languages (see, e.g., Morice [1932, 1, 153] for Dakelh, Rice [1989, 380–82] for Southern Slavey, Kari [1990, 634] for Ahtna, Kwaraceius [2000, 812] for Koyukon, Cook [2004, 110] for Dëne Sųłiné, Kari [2007, 322–24] for Dena'ina, Cook [2013, 124–26] for Tsilhqút'ín), the form of the numeral is determined by the animacy (or rather: humanness) of the referent, such that different number words are used to refer to three human beings and to three things. Such a distinction is not attested in Upper Tanana.

20.1.5. Fractions

Fractions are not commonly used. Kari (1997b) records the postposition P+*xąą'* 'half of P' (441). No dialect information is available for (441a).

(441) a. *kon' xąą'*
fire half
'type of fly' (lit. 'half-burnt wood') Kari (1997b)

b. *Ts'ehłign shyüh xąą' k'eh t'eey yaa'ogn ts'äł shyii*
one snow half during even DSTL:outside:AR bush in
hidaak tl'aan tah. (S)
3PL:SG.stay:IPV:CUST and among
'They would stay out in the bushes for half a year and then.'
Tyone (1996, 21)

No similar forms are recorded for the Tetlin and Northway dialect.

20.2. Other number words

There are not many other number words in Upper Tanana.

20.2.1. Ordinal numbers

Upper Tanana does not have a separate set of ordinal numbers. Cardinal numbers can be used in this context (442).

(442) a. *Ts'ehłegn du' shee'eh Stephen <ay eh> that shyah*
one CT 1SG:maternal.uncle Stephen and that house
guuy łaakay ay Joe Mark and Jessie Demit Ervin. (N)
tiny two 3SG Joe Mark and Jessie Demit Ervin
'The first one is my mother's brother Stephen['s house] and the little house, the second one, is Joe Mark's and Jessie Demit Ervin's.'
UTCBVDN13Nov0804:031

b. *Taag t'eey hutąy' tl'aan eh dziihal'ah*
three even 3PL:trail:POSS and and 3PL:have.trail.over.edge:IT:PFV
danh hunaan' Tak'at naan'... (T)
at AR:across:ALL cold.water across:ALL
'They had a third trail going back down again across the Cold Water (Clearwater)... '
UTOLVDN13May2803:064

This use of numerals is not very frequent.

20.2.2. X times

There is one number adverb: *ts'ehłoo'* 'once' (Kari 1997b). There is no example of this adverb in my data.

For the other numerals the concepts of 'X times' (443a) and 'for the Xth time' (443b) are often expressed by using the postposition P+*k'eh* in the Northway dialect, P+*dą'* in the Tetlin dialect:

(443) a. *Taagn k'eh t'eey neh tiitishdüh…* (N)
three times even 2SG:with 1SG:dive:IT:FUT
'I will dive with you three times…' UTCBVDN13Nov1401:033

b. *"Tay' hǫǫ' ts'uudįį, taagn k'eh hutaałeeł," nih.* (N)
again thus 1PL:do:OPT three times AR:be:FUT say:IPV
'"Let's do this again, it will be the third time," he said.'
UTCBVDN13Nov1401:040

c. *Taagn dą' hiikah tinįįdeeł…* (T)
three at 3PL>3SG:for PL.go.out:PFV
'Three times they went out looking for him…'
UTOLAF09Jun2202:010

20.2.3. No incorporation of numerals

In some Canadian Dene languages (e.g., Morice [1932, 1, 157] for Dakelh or Cook [2004, 239–40] for Dëne Sųłiné), numerals can be incorporated into a form of the verb theme 'to be thus'. In North Albertan Dane-z̲aa this results in frozen, person-marked numerals (Lovick 2010). Neither productive nor fossilized incorporation of numerals is attested in Upper Tanana.

20.3. Use of numerals

The rarity of numerals was already remarked upon by McKennan (1959, 113), who stated that "the nature of the Upper Tanana culture *does not require the use of large numbers* [emphasis added], but the native system would make their use possible. The simple mathematics required for dealing with the traders seems to give the Indians no trouble."

This has not changed since McKennan's time. (McKennan's fieldwork took place in the late 1920s.) My narrative corpus contains many instances of the numerals 1–4, but not a single example of a numeral greater than that. English numerals are used instead (444), but even that happens only occasionally.

(444) a. *Shta'* *nee'eh* *naholnek* *ay* *tl'aan* *shta'*
1SG:father 1PL:to 3SG:tell.story:IPV and then 1SG:father

eighty I don't remember eighty-some years old *shta'*
... 1SG:father

mbookol. (N)
3SG:gone

'My father told us the story, and then my father, [he was] eighty, I don't remember, eighty-some years old, my father passed away.'
UTOLVDN14Apr2601:050

b. *Tl'aan* *tagoh* *du'* *seven, seven foot tall, that's the tallest man,*
and swan CT ...

tagoh. (T)
swan

'And Swan was seven foot tall, the tallest man.'
UTOLVDN13May2902:016

c. *Neekeey,* *neeshyah* *gaay* *nts'ą'* *nineteen fifty six I think I have to*
1PL:village 1PL:house small to

say that in English because nobody knows how to say that in our language,
...

but nineteen fifty six we were *noo'* *nats'atdał...* (T)
... ahead:ALL 1PL:PL.go:IT:IPV:PROG

'Our village, to our house, in 1956, I have to say that in English because nobody knows how to say that in our language, but in 1956 we were walking back...' UTOLAF09Jun2201:001

It should be noted that the three speakers represented in (444) are (or were) extremely strong speakers, so this code-switching is not indicative of limited linguistic competence. The speaker in (444a) does not even appear to notice her switch, since she is preoccupied with trying to remember the age of her father when he passed away. The other two speakers are aware of this issue; Mr. Roy H. David, Sr. in (444b) pauses for eight seconds before he utters the English numeral, and then laughs apologetically. His late wife Mrs. Cora H. David explicitly states that there is no way of expressing large numbers such as 1956. English numerals smaller than 10 are usually back-translated into Upper Tanana during the transcription process; e.g., (444b) was amended by the speaker to (445).

(445) *Tl'aan tagoh du' łats'ąy eh nohts'ąy łaakay nts'ą' ke'*
and swan CT hand.side with other.side two and foot
ninehshyąą, dindeh nchaa, tagoh.
3SG:grow:PFV man 3SG:be.big:IPV swan
'And Swan had grown to seven feet tall, he was a big man, Swan.'
UTOLVDN13May2902:016

It thus seems that enumeration simply was not particularly important in the traditional culture, which leads to an only marginally elaborated semantic domain and also to a lack of instances in natural speech. When this skill became important with the arrival of white traders, speakers simply adopted the English vocabulary rather than extending the Upper Tanana one. This technique had the added benefit of not requiring translation, which made communication with traders that much easier.

Numerals are used only when the exact number of an entity is for some reason very important. The use of numerals is always semantically marked and implies some sort of contrast. In (446a) one of the *gǫǫ* escapes but all others are killed. In (446b) the narrator stresses the lack of ammunition.

(446) a. *Ay du' ts'ehłag gǫǫ etshyiiyh.* (T)
and CT one gǫǫ 3SG:save:PASS:PFV
'Thus, one of the *gǫǫ* was saved.' UTOLVDN13May2909:090

b. *Ts'ehłegn, ts'ehłegn k'a' eh jah eedah…* (N)
one one shot with here 3SG:SG.sit:PFV
'He had only a single shot…' UTOLVDN13May2004:063

The other numerals that occur in texts—mostly 2, 3, and 4—are used only when the exact number is for some reason relevant for the development of the narrative.

20.3.1. Numbers of special significance

In many cultures there are important or even sacred numbers, such as the number 3 in Christianity. Scollon and Scollon (1979, 1981) advance the claim that Dëne Sųłiné (called Chipewyan in their work), and by extension all Dene groups organize their narratives in four parts, rather than the three parts common in the European tradition. I am not sure that this claim can be confirmed or disconfirmed for Upper Tanana,[1] but it certainly appears that 4 as as well as 2 and 3 have special significance in Upper Tanana culture. Events in traditional stories typically take place four times, and they very frequently happen to two people. Spiritual events often happen in sets of three.

20.3.1.1. Four times In traditional stories events are often repeated four times. In (447) a grandmother and her two granddaughters hear a crying baby somewhere outside the village. Only the fourth attempt to find him is successful.

(447) Excerpt: UTOLAF09Jun2202:010-013 (T)

a. *Taagn dą' hiikah tinįįdeeł t'oot'eey k'at'eey*
three times 3PL>3SG:for PL.go.out:PFV but NEG
hiiyudih'aay.
3PL>3SG:find.SG:PFV:NEG

'Three times [the granddaughters] went out looking for him but couldn't find him.'

b. *Dan dą' etsaa eł hutsǫǫ, "Shin tah ukah*
four times 3SG:cry:IPV and 3PL:grandmother 1SG also 3SG:for
honuk-'įį'.
1SG:look:OPT

'For the fourth time be cried and their grandmother [said], "I myself am going to look for him.

c. *Sǫ' shk'eh tahdeeł." hu'ehnih.*
PROH 1SG:following 2PL:PL.go:OPT:NEG 3SG>3PL:say:IPV
'Don't follow me," she said to them.'

d. *Ikah an tinįįshyah nts'ą' ikah*
3SG>3SG:for out:ALL SG.go.out:PFV and 3SG>3SG:for
natetdaag eł yudih'ąą ts'oo
SG.go.around:IPV:NOM and 3SG>3SG:find.SG.O:PFV spruce
daatagn ǫǫ tah ha'įįt'ay.
between out:ABL among 3SG.AO:sticks.out:IPV:NOM

'She went out for him and she was walking about looking for him and she found him lying between two spruce trees.'

(448) describes an unsuccessful attempt to find two girls:

(448) Excerpt: UTOLVDN14Nov2301:089-092 (T)

a. *Tthiigąą'įlshyah hukohnįh'ąy t'eey hu'ookol.*
3PL:PL.run.out:PFV 3PL>3SG:look.for:IPV but 3PL:NEGEX

'They ran straight out again looking for them, but they were gone.'

b. *Ddhał tüh all hįįdeeł.*
mountain across all 3PL:PL.go:PFV
'They went all across the mountains.'

c. *Ałts'ą' tsąy ddhał łaakay ddhał.*
left side mountain two mountain
'Left side mountain, two mountains.'

d. *Taag ddhał ay tüh t'eey all hįįdeel dan*
three mountain and over even all 3PL:PL.go:PFV:NOM four
t'eey. (T)
even
'They went over three mountains, even four.'

In (449) a Loon cures an old man's blindness by diving with him. They dive three times, but the old man is still blind. After another three dives, the man's vision is partially restored. Then, the Loon dives with the old man *four* times, which finally cures the old man (449e, f).

(449) Excerpt: UTCBVDN13Nov1401:033-048 (N)

a. *"Taagn k'eh t'eey neh tiitishdüh," ch'itay ehnih.*
three times even 2SG:with 1SG:dive:FUT old.man 3SG:say:IPV
'"I will dive with you three times," [the Loon] said to the old man.'

b. [9 lines omitted]

c. *"Taagn k'eh t'eey hǫǫ' ts'uudįį."*
three times ADVZR thus 1PL:do:OPT
' "We should do this a third time," [the Loon said].'

d. *Noo' tay' natetmįįh.*
ahead:ALL again 3PL:swim:INC:IT:PFV
'They swam back into the open water.'

e. *Shyiign' tah tuu shyiit tl'aan degn' yaahatmįįh*
down:ALL among water in and up:ALL 3PL:swim.up:IT:PFV
tl'aan tay' shyiign' tah tl'aan degn' tah
and again down:ALL among and up:ALL among
yaahatmįįh.
3PL:swim.up:IT:PFV
'Down into the water and then they swam back up and out and again down and they swam back up and out.'

f. *Tay' t'eey shyign' degn' tay' t'eey shyign' tl'aan*
again ADVZR down:ALL up:ALL again ADVZR down:ALL and
degn' tay' t'eey yaahatmįįh.
up:ALL again ADVZR 3PL:swim.up:IT:PFV
'Again they swam down and back up and out, and down and back up and out.'

g. *"Nday?" yehnih.*
what 3SG>3S"'G:say:IPV
'"Well?" [the Loon] said to [the man].'

h. *"Hunak-'įh hǫǫsu' t'eey hunak'įh," Ts'almbeet ehnih.*
1SG:see:IPV well ADVZR 1SG:see:IPV loon 3SG:say:IPV
'"I can see, I can see really well," he said to the Loon.'

There are other ways in which the significance of the number 4 manifests itself in traditional stories: the two girls in the story about Grandmother Spider encounter four helpful characters (Chickadee, the Stump, Fox, and Grandmother Spider), and Nedzeegn commits four transgressions against cultural norms (both stories can be found in Cora H. David [2017]).

20.3.1.2. Two people While events tend to happen in sets of four, they tend to happen *to* sets of two. Many stories begin with a grandmother and her two granddaughters. In the most recent collection of stories by Cora H. C. David (2017) this particular constellation is present in three stories: *Ts'ist'e' dichaay iin eł nahembaa iin k'ii hitdeeł* 'A grandmother and her granddaughters met with warriors', *Dlagn xa nahogndak* 'I talk about squirrels', and in *Nedzeegn xa nahogndak* 'I talk about Nedzeegn'. *Stsǫǫ Kelahdzeey Xa Nahoholndak*, 'The story they tell about Grandmother Spider' features two girls following a butterfly. And while an individual figures out how to defeat the Tailed People, he does that after they steal and eat two hunters (*Che' T'iin iin Nahogndak* 'I talk about the Tailed People'). The same tendency can be observed in narratives by other storytellers.

20.3.1.3. Three units of time Sets of three—or multiples of three—are used in spiritual contexts. (450a) describes the length of time a young girl would be sequestered at the onset of puberty. (450b) is taken from a text about a funeral potlatch, where the main feasting and gift giving take place on the third day. (450c) describes the actions of a mother whose son drowned in Butterfly Lake.

(450) a. *Taagn hǫǫłįį nts'ą' niithoo t'eey taagn*
three AR:be:IPV and long.time ADVZR three
hǫǫłįį nts'ą' t'eey k'at'eey hah'ogn t'eey
AR:be:IPV ADVZR NJEG NTRL:outside:AR ADVZR
łoohtaahaal nts'ą' shyah shyiit shyįį' hihdaltth'iił. (T)
3PL:SG.go.around:FUT:NEG and house in only 3PL:PL.stay:FUT
'For three days, for thirty days they may not walk around outside, they have to stay inside the house.' UTOLVDN11Jul2901:019

b. *Taagn hǫǫłįį de' shyi' eł hugn dii eł*
three AR:be:IPV when:FUT meat and etc. what and
hehmbiadn eł. (T)
3PL:cook:IPV:NOM and
'On the third day they cook meat and other stuff.'
UTOLAF11Aug0207:006

c. *Ay t'oot'eey unąą taagn danh manh maagn*
and but 3SG:mother three times lake around
shiijiinildzüh nts'ą' etsah. (T)
3SG:dance.ceaselessly:PFV and 3SG:cry:IPV
'But his mother danced around the lake three times and cried.'
UTOLAF10Jul0801:021

But while the examples in (450) all describe situations with strong traditional spirituality, this use of the number three could also be due to Christian influence. The Christian influence in the Upper Tanana valley is very strong, so it is possible that elements of Christianity have become incorporated into older traditions. The narrator of (450a) says that puberty sequestration lasts for thirty days, yet another speaker suggested that it might be three times thirty days, and Tyone (1996, 21) states that her own sequestration lasted about half a year. Similarly the feasting and dancing associated with a traditional potlatch lasts three days nowadays, but Simeone (1995, 142) suggests that formerly, singing and dancing would last "for days on end."

20.4. Summary

In this chapter the numeral system of Upper Tanana is described. Upper Tanana has a decimal number system. While numerals up to 100 can be formed, their elicitation proves difficult, and there are very few examples of numerals in natural speech. Apart from the cardinal numbers, there is no other set of number words such as ordinal numbers. Expressions meaning 'X times' or 'for the Xth time' are formed using postpositional phrases.

Generally numerals are rarely used. Almost all naturally occurring examples of numerals are the words for 1–4. This is not a recent development but was already observed by McKennan (1959) almost a century ago. English numerals are borrowed in most instances where a numeral greater than 4 is required, although the numeral may be back-translated into Upper Tanana during transcription and translation.

Because of their rarity, numerals are quite marked when they do occur. The numeral 'one' expresses unexpected singularity. Narrated events tend to occur in sets of four, characters in narratives in sets of two. There is also a trend for spiritual events to take place three times, although I suspect that this may be a more recent Christian influence.

The domain of numerals in Upper Tanana is generally not very well elaborated, which makes these cultural uses of numerals all the more interesting.

Notes

1. I do not find the organization of narratives into "parts" to be a straightforward task.

21 Other minor word categories

There are several additional minor word categories in Upper Tanana: non-verbal predicates, interjections, one-word responses, quantifiers, conjunctions, and so forth. In the present chapter an inventory of the most common members of each category is presented. By including these lexical categories in the same chapter, I do not wish to imply that they share similarities beyond uninflectability.

21.1. Non-verbal predicates

Upper Tanana has a very small class of non-verbal predicates. Their inventory is given in (451). With the exception of (451c), they are all monosyllabic expressions functioning as imperative-only lexemes (Aikhenvald 2010, 317).

(451) Non-verbal predicates

a. (O) *nde'* 'give me o'
b. (O) *nda'* 'take o, here is o'
c. *aan* 'come in'
d. *an* 'away, out'
e. *duk* 'get ready, go'
f. *(t)thee* 'wait'
g. O+*kol* 'o NEGEX, there is no o'

21.1.1. O *nde'* 'give me o'

O *nde'* 'give me o' is used in requests. As shown in (452b), it replaces an active classificatory verb form inflected for second-person imperfective: the cup in (452a) would require the stem *kaayh* 'handle OOC IPV', the antlers in (452b) would require the stem *shyeeyh* 'handle PL.O IPV', and the scissors in (452c) would require *teeyh* 'handle LRO IPV'.[1]

(452) a. *Shtuutįįl'* *nde'!* (N)
1SG:cup:POSS give.me
'Give me my cup!' UT Notebook #1, 29

b. *Ude'* *nde',* *ǫǫ* *shaa* *nii'alshyeeyh!* (T)
3SG:antlers give.me outside:ABL 1SG:for 2PL:bring.PL.O:IT:IPV
'Give me his antlers, bring them back for me from outside!'
UTOLVDN14May0703:148

c. *Nde'!* [pointing at scissors] (N)
give.me
'Give me those!' Interaction on June 19, 2007

While *nde'* 'give me' usually co-occurs with a noun phrase (452a, b), it can also be used in isolation (452c). It is then accompanied by pointing to the desired object.

21.1.2. O *na'* 'take o, here is o'

O *na'* 'take o, here is o' is used in requests to take something (453a, b) or in presentational sentences (453c). It can be used in plural (453a) and singular (453b) requests. It usually occurs with an overt object noun phrase (453a, c), but it may also occur in isolation (453b).

(453) a. *Nuhch'il'* *na'!* (T)
2PL:clothes:POSS take.it
'Pick up your PL clothes!' UTOLAF07Feb1302:092

b. *Ay* *stsǫǫ* *du'* *dii* *ts'änh* *hach'įįgąąt* *tl'aan*
and 1SG:grandmother CT what from 3SG:tear.off:PFV and
"Nda', įhnay," *shehnih.* (N)
take.it 2SG:taste:IPV 3SG>1SG:say:IPV
'And my grandmother tore some off and, "Here, taste it," she said to me.' UTOLVDN10Jul2724:061

c. *Atthiit* *Naataybneetkayh* *dą'* *ch'a* *ishyiit* *ch'a*
NTRL:downriver:PNCT dried-up.hill at FOC there FOC
hukeey *na'.* (T)
3PL:village take.it
'Down there by the river, at Dried-up Hill, is their village.'
UTOLVDN07Oct2604:023

Na' also replaces a verb form; the speaker who produced (453a) suggested (454) as an alternate way of phrasing it.

(454) *Nuhch'il* *nanahtsayh!* (T)
2PL:clothes:POSS 2PL:pick.up:IT:IPV
'Pick up your PL clothes!' UTOLAF07Feb1302:093

21.1.3. *aan* 'come in, come here'

The imperative-only lexeme *aan* 'come in' replaces a motion verb. It takes no arguments but may occur with a vocative noun phrase. It (455a) it functions as predicate of the consequence clause in a conditional construction; in (455b) it participates in asyndetic clause coordination.

(455) a. *Nnaag' kol de', aan!* (T)
2SG:eye NEGEX if come.in
'If you are blind, come here!' UTOLVDN13May2907:088

b. *Ts'exeh Su', aan, nee'eh nach'įį'aał!* (T)
woman beautiful come.in 1PL:with 2SG>INDF:eat:IPV
'Ts'exeh Su', come in [and] eat with us!'
UTOLVDN14Apr2602:146

21.1.4. *duk* 'get ready, go'

Duk 'get ready, go' takes no arguments. Its semantic range is illustrated in the textual example (456), where a woman guides her blind husband shooting a moose.

(456) Excerpt: UTOLVDN13May2907:030–034 (T)

a. *"Duk" dikąy' yehnih, unaagn' kol t'oot'eey.*
get.ready REFL:husband 3SG:say:IPV 3SG:eyes NEGEX although
'"Get ready!" she said to her husband, even though he was blind.'

b. *"Duk!"*
get.ready
'"Get ready!"'[the wife said]

c. *"Duk shdǫǫni' de' shyįį'," di'aat ehnih.*
go 2SG>1SG:say:OPT if only REFL:wife 3SG:say:IPV
'"Just tell me when," he said to his wife.'

d. [one line omitted]

e. *"Duk!" ehnih, he let go.*
go 3SG:say:IPV
'"Shoot!" she said, and he let go.'

21.1.5. *(t)thee' (de')* 'wait'

Tthee' (de') 'wait' is attested both with initial *th* (457a) and initial *tth* (457b). The contribution of *de'* in (457b) is unclear; it is possibly related to the particle *de'* in requests in the optative mode described in Lovick (2016, 269) (an instance of this construction also occurs in the second clause *udǫǫni' de'* 'make sure you tell him' in [457a]).

(457) a. *Ch'itay dąą tl'uuł itinayh de', "Ina', ina', hǫǫ't'eey*
old.man thus rope 3SG>3SG:shake:IPV if no no still
thee'," udǫǫni' de', ... (N)
wait 2SG>3SG:say:OPT ? 3SG>3SG:say:IPV
'When that old man shakes the rope, make sure you tell him, "No, no, wait," ...' UTOLAF15May0501:087

b. *Tthee' de'! Nuhshyah eł tuu niihąą de', k'at'eey*
wait ? 2PL:house with water 3SG:be.flooded:PFV if NEG
nuhshyah suu hutaałeel.
2PL:house nice AR:classify.PL.O:FUT:NEG
'Just wait! When your PL house gets flooded, you PL won't have a nice house any longer!' UTOLAF07Nov2602:022

21.1.6. O+*kol* 'O NEGEX, there is no O'

I include O+*kol* 'O NEGEX, there is no O' among the non-verbal predicates since it does not fit very well into any other lexical category. According to (Kari 1990, 244), the Ahtna stem *kol* 'absent, none' is a "reanalyzed root from *ko* area, *lae* be, plus *(h)e* negative" (emphasis in the original). O+*kol* is used in existential negation. In Upper Tanana it is best analyzed as a negative verb stem as it contains the high tone associated with negative stems ([kʰól]). O+kol 'O NEGEX, there is no O' is a defective verb theme; it can be inflected for object (458b), for inceptive perfective (458b), for future (458c), or not at all (458a). When inflected, it usually contains the *u*-qualifier.

(458) a. *Diniign udzih iin t'eey kol.* (T)
moose caribou PL even NEGEX
'There were no moose, no caribou.' UTOLAF09Jun2402:014

b. *T'axo:::h t'axoh shuuteekol.* (N)
finally finally 1SG:NEGEX:INC:PFV
'Finally, finally I was near death.' (lit.: 'I was about to be gone.')
UTOLVDN14Apr2602:012

c. *Hut'ay' utaakol…* (T)
3PL:strength NEGEX:FUT
'They will not be strong…' (lit.: 'their strength will be absent')
UTOLVDN11Jul2902:007

More information on the use of O+*kol* 'O NEGEX, there is no O' in existential negation is given in volume 2.

21.2. Interjections

Interjections or exclamations are words that usually form a syntactic unit by themselves. In addition to the interjections given in (459), several adjectives can also function as interjections (see chap. 18.1.2).

(459) Interjections
a. iih 'oh no! yuck!'
b. edzee' 'oh my! goodness!'
c. adzu' 'oops! oh!'
d. ohįį 'if only!'
e. ayt'oo 'OK, all right'
f. ayshyįį' 'that's enough'
g. hǫǫshyįį' 'that's all'

21.2.1. *iih* 'oh no! yuck'

Iih 'oh no! yuck!' is only attested in the Northway dialect. It is used when one makes an unpleasant discovery such as the absence of tea in the camp (460a) or the presence of a flying insect in the house (460b).

(460) a. *"Tseey! Ii! Tseey ookol!" nih.* (N)
tea oh.no tea NEGEX say:IPV
'"Tea! Oh no! There's no tea!" she said.'
UTOLAF09Aug1202:022

b. *Iih! iih! Where did it go!* (N)
yuck yuck
'Yuck! Yuck! Where did it go!' UTOLAF18Jun0101:029

21.2.2. *edzee'* 'oh my! goodness!'

Edzee' 'oh my! goodness!' can be used to express both positive or negative surprise. (461a) describes a speaker's joyful amazement at seeing a message; (461b) expresses dismay at another person's behavior.

(461) a. *Edzee'! Shaa le' nt'ay!* (N)
surprise 1SG:for IGN 3SG:be:IPV:NOM
'Surprise! It must be for me!' UTOLVDN14Apr2602:052

b. *Edzee'! Nts'ą̈' dįįdį' xah ch'a dįįdąy!*
goodness how 2SG:do:PFV for FOC 2SG:do:IPV:NOM
'Goodness! Why did you do what you did!'
UTOLAF14May0807:009

21.2.3. *adzu'* 'oops! oh!'

Adzu' 'oops! oh!' also expresses surprise, but additionally conveys affection toward the addressee. According to one speaker, it is what one would say if a toddler just learning to walk would fall down (UT Notebook #5, 89). In the only textual example of this interjection (462), an abducted girl is both surprised and happy that her brothers have come to save her. One speaker commented that the meaning of *adzu'* in this example was similar to *teejuh* 'poor thing'.

(462) Excerpt: UTOLVDN13May2909:053–055 (T)

a. ... *ch'idia' dǫǫndaa hadel'įh.*
INDF:younger.sister REFL:older.brother 3SG:spot:PFV
'... the younger sister spotted her older brother.'

b. *Adzu'!*
oh.my
'Oh my!'

c. *Shǫǫndaa!*
1SG:older.brother
'My older brother!'

21.2.4. *ohįį* 'if only'

Ohįį 'if only' is attested only in the Northway dialect. It is used when wishing for the impossible; the speaker in (463a) wishes for a boat, while the one in (463b) wishes her brother were still alive.

(463) a. *Ohįį! Neets'ayy' hǫǫłįį de'!* (N)
if.only 1PL:boat:POSS AR:be:IPV if
'Oh, if only we had a boat!' UTOLAF15Dec0701:019

b. *Ohįį shoonüü ts'ihogndayh dą',...* (N)
oh 1SG:older.brother 1SG:miss:IPV at
'Oh, I miss my older brother...' UTOLVDN10Jul2724:030

21.2.5. *ayt'oo* 'okay, all right'

Ayt'oo 'okay, all right' is used when asking permission (464), when granting it (465), or when offering encouragement (466).

(464) *Ayt'oo ishyiit da'uhda'?* (N)
all.right there 1SG:SG.sit.on:OPT
'Is it okay if I sit on [the chair] there?' UTOLAF14Nov2402:009

(465) Excerpt: UTOLVDN07Aug2205:033–034 (N)

a. *"Nuh'eh tuhshya'," hudihnay.*
2PL:with 1SG:SG.go:INC:OPT 1SG>3PL:say:IPV:NOM
'"I want to go with you guys," I said to them.'

b. *Ay shnąą, "Ayt'oo," nih, "nuh'eh natuudaagn,"*
and 1SG:mother all.right say:IPV 3PL:with 2SG:SG.go.around:OPT
hu'ehnih. (N)
3SG>3PL:say:IPV
'And my mother, "All right," she said, "she can go with you guys," she said to them.'

(466) *"Ti'uhduu," nih, "ayt'oo," nih.* (T)
1SG:crawl.out:OPT say:IPV all.right say:IPV
"I'm going to crawl out," he said, "it's okay," he said.'
UTOLVDN13May2907:066

21.2.6. *hǫǫ'shyįį', ayshyįį'* 'that's all'

Hǫǫ'shyįį' and *ayshyįį'* 'that's all' are often used to end narratives. (467) and (468) contain the last two utterances of two narratives. The use of either interjection is not indicative of a dialect difference, nor have I been able to determine a meaning difference.

(467) Excerpt: UTOLAF08Apr2805:112–113 (T)

a. *Ishyiit etsah.*
there 3SG:cry:IPV
'She cried right there.'

b. *Hǫǫ'shyįį' t'eey.*
that's.all even
'That's all.'

(468) Excerpt: UTOLVDN07Aug2205:120–121 (N)

a. *Hu'idatdeemaak, I know.*
3SG>3PL:fight.verbally:PFV
'She bawled them out, I know.'

b. *T'axoh ayshyįį'.*
finally that's.all
'That's all.'

21.3. One-word responses

There are several lexical items that are used as one-word responses to questions or requests. *Ayt'oo* 'okay, it's alright' in 21.2.5 falls into this group, as do the items below.

21.3.1. *ąą* 'yes'

Ąą 'yes' is used to answer polar questions. While (469b) contains a full clause, answering just with *ąą* 'yes' is possible as well.

(469) Excerpt: UTOLAF09Aug1201:042–043, (N)

a. *"Shoh aldeeł dii xah ch'a dįh'ąy?" shehnih.* (N)
bear 2PL:eat:IPV why FOC 2SG:do:IPV:NOM 3SG>1SG:say:IPV
'"Are you SG doing this because you PL eat bear?" he said to me.'

b. *"Ąą, shiy ch'ale agndeel," udihnih.*
yes 1SG FOC 1SG:eat.PL.O:IPV:NOM 1SG>3SG:say:IPV
'"Yes, as for me, I eat them," I said to him.'

21.3.2. *duka'* 'all right, okay'

Duka' 'all right, okay' is used to signal acquiescence to a request (470).

(470) UTOLAF09Aug1202:015–016 (N)

a. *"Nee'eh įįhaał!" shihinih.*
1PL:with 2SG:SG.go:IPV 3PL>1SG:say:IPV
'"Come with us!" they said to me.'

b. *"Duka'!" hudihnih.*
okay 1SG>3PL:say:IPV
'"O'"kay!" I said to them.'

21.3.3. *ina', ena'* 'no'

Ina', ena' 'no' also is used to answer polar questions (471), but it can also be used to refuse requests (472) or instead of uttering a negative request (473).

(471) Excerpt: UTOLVDN14Apr2602:076–077 (N)

a. *"Nts'ą̈' hidį' nts'ą̈' hii'innay," shehnih.*
what 3PL:do:IPV what 2SG:know:IPV:NOM 3SG>1SG:say:IPV
'"Do you know what they did?" she said to me.'

b. *"Ina'."*
no
'"No." ' [I said to her.]

(472) Excerpt: UTOLAF15May0501:077–078, (N)

a. *"Nahshyign' t'eey nashyuugn t'eey*
MED:down:ALL ADVZR MED:down:AR ADVZR
tinįįhaay!"
2SG:SG.go.to.toilet:IPV:IMP
'"Right here, go to the toilet right here on the floor!" [the old man said to the girl.]'

b. *"Ina'! Ina'! Stsay uunihshyąą!"*
no no 1SG:grandfather 1SG:be.shy:IPV
'"No! No! Grandfather, I'm shy!" [the girl said to the old man.]'

(473) Excerpt: UTCBAF13Nov0501:111–112 (T)

a. *K'ahmann' uteełeey, shaadeh tsi'okthiidn!*
morning AR:be:INC:PFV 1SG:older.sister 1SG:wake.up:OPT
'It is morning, I want to wake up my older sister!' [the younger sister said.]

b. *"Ena', hǫǫ't'eey uute',"* *yehnih.*
no still 3SG:sleep:OPT 3SG>3S:say:IPV
'"No, let her sleep some more," he said to her.'

21.3.4. *sǫ'* 'don't'

The prohibitive particle *sǫ'* also may be used in isolation (474):

(474) Excerpt: UTOLAF10Jul0202:022–023 (N)

a. *"Jin tąy ts'uudäł!"*
this trail 1PL:PL.go:OPT
'"Let's go on this trail!" [the older sister said.]'

b. *"Sǫ'!" that ch'idia' ehnih,* ...
PROH that INDF:younger.sister 3SG:say:IPV
'"Let's not!" that younger sister said...'

21.3.5. *le'e, le'* 'I don't know'

Le'e 'I don't know' is used as a response to questions (475).

(475) Excerpt: UTCBAF13Nov0501:048–049 (T)

a. *Natehxeeł t'oot'eey ch'a' ts'idąy?*
3SG:get.dark:IT:INC:PFV although FOC 1PL:do:IPV:NOM
'Even though it's getting dark, what are we doing? [said the older sister.]'

b. *"Le'e," that ts'exeh gaay du' nih.*
don't.know that girl CT say:IPV
'"I don't know," said that girl [the younger sister].'

21.4. Miscellaneous function words

The words in this section can be loosely organized into several different categories. Their syntactic and discourse functions are described in volume 2.

21.4.1. Quantifiers

Most nonnumeral quantifiers in Upper Tanana are nominalized verb forms, but as they are strongly lexicalized, I provide a list in (476).

(476) Quantifiers

a.	ndlaan	'a lot, many'
b.	ntsiin	'a few, few'
c.	łahtthegn nts'ą̈'	'all'

21.4.2. Coordinating conjunctions

There are only a few coordinating conjunctions in Upper Tanana (477).

(477) Conjunctions

a.	eh, eł	'and'	noun phrases, clauses
b.	nts'ą̈'	'and'	noun phrases, clauses
c.	įį'eh (tah)	'and'	noun phrases
d.	(ay) tl'aan	'and then'	clauses
e.	t'oot'eey	'but'	clauses

There are also a number of subordinators, most of them formally identical to postpositions.

21.4.3. Discourse markers

There are also several discourse markers regulating information flow. The most common ones are listed in (478).

(478) Discourse markers

a.	ch'a(le)	'focus'
b.	du'	'contrastive topic'
c.	shyįį'	'only'
d.	t'eey	'even'

21.4.4. Modal particles

The most common modal particles are given in (479).

(479) Modal particles

a.	nt'eh	'for sure, ASRT'
b.	le'(e)	'maybe, IGN, POT, MIR'
c.	de'	'make sure'
d.	lah	'Q'
e.	hąą	'right?'

21.4.5. Polarity particles

There are two polarity particles. *K'a(t'eey)* 'NEG' is used to negate declaratives; *sǫ'* 'PROH' negates commands (480).

(480) a. *K'at'eey ts'iniljidn nts'ą'.* (T)
NEG 1PL:be.scared:IPV:NEG and
'We were not scared.' UTOLVDN10Jul0701:071

b. *Sǫ' shinoljidn!* (N)
PROH 2SG>1SG:be.scared.of:OPT
'Don't be scared of me!' UTOLVDN11Aug0802:030

Negation is discussed in volume 2.

21.4.6. Plural enclitic *iin*

The plural enclitic *iin* is illustrated in (481); its use is discussed in greater detail in volume 2.

(481) *Atshyąą iin t'eey k'a naholndii.* (T)
old.person PL even NEG 3PL:tell.story:IPV:CUST:NEG
'Even the old people don't tell stories.' UTOLAF09Jun2402:040

21.5. Summary

In this chapter a brief overview of several minor word categories is given. All of them cannot be inflected; most of them function at the clause or discourse level. More information on all these items can be found in volume 2.

Notes

1. Scissors in Upper Tanana are classified as a singular long rigid object, not as a plural object.

Part IV

Morphology

22 | Possessor inflection

This chapter describes possession, the only inflectional category of nouns. As discussed in chap. 13, Upper Tanana distinguishes between obligatorily and optionally possessed noun stems (22.1).

Possession is marked by possessive suffixes (22.2.1) as well as by possessor prefixes (22.2.2). Effects of possessive morphology on stems are described in 22.2.3, and some restrictions on possessive morphology are discussed in 22.2.4. The phenomenon of "double possession" described for related languages does not exist in Upper Tanana (22.2.5).

While possessive morphology is the most common way to express possession, there are two other constructions available (22.3).

The syntax of possession is briefly discussed in 22.4.

22.1. Different types of possession

Like related languages, Upper Tanana exhibits a distinction between obligatorily and optionally possessed nouns. Semantically this distinction corresponds to some degree to that between inalienable and alienable possession described in 22.2.1.

22.1.1. Obligatorily possessed nouns

Obligatorily possessed nouns are morphologically bound. They cannot occur without an overt possessor that may be expressed by a noun phrase (482a) or by a possessive prefix (482b).

(482) a. *Dzänh che' xah naholnek.* (N)

dzänh *che'* *xah* *na-hol-nek*
muskrat tail about IT-3PL.S:QUAL:Ø.IPV:L-tell.story:IPV

'They tell a story about Muskrat's tail.'

UTOLVDN10Jul2720:002

b. … *uche' maa ndüüh!* (N)

u-che' *m-aa* *n-düüh*
3SG.PSR-tail 3SG.P-for 3SG.S:Ø.PFV:ø-be.heavy:IPV
'… his tail was too heavy for him!' UTOLVDN10Jul2720:033

Semantically obligatorily possessed nouns fall into four broad categories: kinship terms (483a–g), body parts (483h–l), other concepts that are part of living beings (483n–r), and landscape features (483q, t). All forms in (483) are given in the first-person singular form *sh*____ 'my ____', with the exception of the nouns in (483s, t). All four categories include many more nouns than the ones given in this example.

(483) Obligatorily possessed nouns

a.	'my mother'	shnąą
b.	'my grandmother'	stsǫǫ
c.	'my daughter (woman speaking)'	shyaats'e'
d.	'my younger brother'	shchil
e.	'my mother's sister, father's brother's wife'	shaak'ay
f.	'my husband'	shkąy'
g.	'my friend, (hunting) partner'	shtląą
h.	'my head'	shtthi'
i.	'my voice'	shtheegn'
j.	'my heart'	sdzeey'
k.	'my belly, stomach'	stsaal'
l.	'my ankle'	shkeechin'
m.	'my mind'	shoonįį'
n.	'my shadow, soul'	shǫǫk'įą'
o.	'my breath'	shshyia
p.	'my language'	shaaneegn(')
q.	'nest'	-t'oh
r.	'branch (of a tree)'	-thuuchin'
s.	'ascending ridge line on mountains'	-aak'iign
t.	'above timberline'	-naadok

22.1.2. Optionally possessed nouns

Most other nouns are optionally possessed. This includes items from all semantic categories with the exception of those listed in the previous section. A sample of optionally possessed nouns is given in (484); this list is, of course, not inclusive. Importantly, bodily fluids are not obligatorily possessed (484a–c).

(484) Optionally possessed nouns

	English	*Unpossessed*	*Possessed*
a.	'blood'	däł	shdäl'
b.	'saliva'	seek	sseegn'
c.	'urine'	łüh	shłüü'
d.	'coat'	eek	sh'eegn'
e.	'moccasin'	kentsį̨ą̨	shkentsį̨ą̨'
f.	'knife'	seeyh	sseey'
g.	'gun'	k'a'	shk'aa'
h.	'boat'	ts'ayh	sts'ayy'
i.	'sled'	xał	shxal'
j.	'pack'	xeeł	shxeel'
k.	'louse'	shya'	shshyaa'
l.	'dog'	łį̨į̨	shliign'
m.	'house'	shyah	shshyah

There are also some nouns that cannot be possessed; those are discussed in 22.2.4.1.

22.2. Possessive morphology

Morphological possession is marked in two places in the noun. Most nouns take one of two possessive suffixes (see 22.2.1). In the absence of an overt possessor noun phrase, nouns also take a possessive prefix (see 22.2.2).

Morphological possession affects the form of the stem as described in 22.2.3. Semantic and morphological restrictions on possessive morphology are discussed in 22.2.4.

22.2.1. Possessive suffixes

There are two possessive suffixes. The inalienable possessive suffix -' attaches to many obligatorily possessed noun stems such as kinship terms or nouns referring to body parts. The alienable possessive suffix -v̀' attaches to most other nouns.

Apart from Tanacross and Upper Tanana, the distinction between two possessive suffixes is attested only in Slave (Rice 1989, 212–15). In Athna (Kari 1990, 66) and Koyukon (Jetté and Jones 2000, 10), there is only one possessive suffix of the shape *-e'*, which has the shape *-'* after a vowel. Dena'ina has an alienable possessive suffix *-'a* but no inalienable one (Boraas 2012, 13–15). In the Canadian languages for which data is available, there is only one possessive suffix (see Hargus [2007, 242–45] for Witsuwit'en and Saxon and Wilhelm [2016, 38] for Dëne Sųłiné and Tłįchǫ).

22.2.1.1. Alienable possessive suffix The alienable possessive suffix has the form -v̀'. The -v in the representation of this suffix refers to a vocalic element that has the effect of creating a heavy syllable (see chap. 11); the tone mark indicates that this suffix causes the stem tone to be low. All unpossessed syllables in (485) are light; all possessed syllables are heavy. All possessed syllables are low-toned, regardless of whether the unpossessed stem is unmarked (485a–g) or low-marked (485h–n). All examples are from the (tonal) Northway dialect; tonal information is included to illustrate the contrasts.

(485) Effects of the alienable possessive suffix

	English	*Unpossessed*	*Possessed*
a.	'firewood'	tsät	-tsä̀dn'
b.	'coat'	eek	-'èègn'
c.	'stick'	dichinh	-dichìnn'
d.	'mitten'	jiyh	-jìyy'
e.	'rope'	tl'uuł	-tl'ùùl'
f.	'knife'	seeyh	-sèèyy'
g.	'lake'	mänh	-mä̀nn'
h.	'belt'	thǜh	-thǜǜ'
i.	'hat'	tthììshyòò	-tthììshyòò'
j.	'cane'	tä̀t	-tä̀dn'
k.	'gun'	k'ä̀'	-k'ä̀ä̀'
l.	'trap'	èèł	-'èèl'
m.	'fish hook'	sä̀ł	-sä̀l'
n.	'dipnet'	ǜh	-'ǜǜ'

Syllables that are already heavy due to the presence of historical suffixes remain heavy when the alienable possessive suffix is added. (486) contains forms from the Northway dialect that include tonal information.

(486) Possession in stems containing heavy syllables

	English	*Unpossessed*	*Possessed*
a.	'child'	ts'iinììn	-ts'iinììn'
b.	'children'	ts'ìkeey	-ts'ìkèèy'
c.	'fire'	kòn'	-kòn'

22.2.1.2. Inalienable possessive suffix The inalienable possessive suffix -' consists only of a glottal stop and no vocalic element. According to Holton (2000, 143), in Tanacross this suffix affects the stem tone but does not cause voicing of the stem final consonant. In Upper Tanana this suffix also affects the stem tone, but in contrast to Tanacross, it frequently does cause voicing of the stem final consonant, thus creating a heavy stem syllable (487a–f). In (487h–k) the inalienable possessive suffix only lowers the stem tone but does not cause voicing of the stem final consonant; the glottal stop is not detectable in these stems. Some words are variably pronounced with voiced or voiceless stem-final consonant (487g). (487l, m) illustrate the inalienable possessive suffix in vowel final stems, where it does not cause lengthening. All examples in (487) are from the Northway dialect, and tone information is indicated.

(487) The inalienable possessive suffix -’

	English	*Possessed*
a.	‘face’	-įįnį̀į̀’
b.	‘tongue’	-tthùùl’
c.	‘arm’	-gààn’
d.	‘heart’	-dzèèy’
e.	‘eye’	-nààgn’
f.	‘ear’	-dzàgn’
g.	‘liver’	-thȁt
h.	‘knee’	-gòt
i.	‘torso’	-sàk
j.	‘skin’	-thȕh
k.	‘hearing’	-dzììt, -dzììdn
l.	‘father’	-tà’
m.	‘younger sister’	-dìà’

The data in (487) suggests that in Upper Tanana, the distinction between the two possessive suffixes is in the process of disappearing.

The inalienable possessive suffix is part of many obligatorily possessed nouns. This group includes kinship terms as well as body parts and nouns referring to concepts such as ‘mind,’ ‘soul,’ ‘shadow,’ or ‘language’. There are also some obligatorily possessed nouns that do not contain the inalienable possessive suffix as evidenced by the lack of final glottal stop and low tone (488).

(488) Obligatorily possessed nouns without inalienable possessive suffix

a.	‘nose’	-įįtsįį
b.	‘mother’	-nąą
c.	‘grandmother’	-tsǫǫ
d.	‘fat’	-k’ah
e.	‘neck’	-k’oh
f.	‘older sister’	-aadeh

22.2.2. Possessor prefixes

The possessor prefixes are almost identical to the direct and postpositional object prefixes; see table 23.1 for a comparison. Different groups of possessor prefixes can be distinguished.

22.2.2.1. First- and second-person possessor prefixes

22.2.2.1.1. First-person singular *sh-* The first-person singular possessor prefix has the form *sh-* (489a, b). Before the onset consonants /s, t͡s, t͡sʰ, t͡s'/ it assimilates to [s] (489c, d). Following *sh-* '1sg.psr', stem-initial fricatives become almost always lenis (489b, d) (see chap. 9).

(489) a. *shaadeh* [ʃa:teh] (T)
sh-aadeh
1sg.psr-older.sister
'my older sister' UTCBAF13Nov0501:305

b. *shxeel'* [ʃχ̬e:lʔ] (T)
sh-xeeł-v'
1sg.psr-pack-poss
'my pack' UTOLAF07Feb1302:134

c. *stsǫǫ* [st͡sʰõ:] (T)
s-tsǫǫ
1sg.psr-grandmother
'my grandmother' UTCBAF13Nov0501:331

d. *ssal'* [ss̬alʔ] (T)
s-sał-v'
1sg.psr-hook-poss
'my fish hook' UTOLAF07Feb1302:024

22.2.2.1.2. Second-person singular *n-* The second-person singular possessor prefix has the form *n-*. In stems beginning with a consonant (490b, d), *n-* forms a syllable of its own. *N-* sometimes causes lenition of the stem-initial consonant.

(490) a. *naadeh* [na:.teh] (T)
n-aadeh
2sg.psr-older.sister
'your sg older sister' UTCBAF13Nov0501:367

b. *nxeel'* [n.χ̬e:lʔ] (T)
n-xeeɬ-v'
2SG.PSR-pack-POSS
'your SG pack' UTOLAF07Feb1302:136

c. *nɬiign'* [nɬi:kʔ] (T)
n-ɬiign'
2SG.PSR-dog:POSS
'your SG dog' UTOLAF07Feb1302:017

d. *ntsǫǫ* [n.t͡sʰõ:] (T)
n-tsǫǫ
2SG.PSR-grandmother
'your SG grandmother' UTOLAF08Apr2805:109

22.2.2.1.3. First-person plural *nee-* The first-person plural possessor prefix always has the form *nee-*. When the noun is vowel-initial (491a), an epenthetic glottal stop is inserted. The first-person plural possessor prefix does not usually cause stem-initial fricative lenition (491b), but see (491c) for an exception.

(491) a. *nee'ǫǫndaa* [ne:ʔõ:nᵈa:] (T)
nee-ǫǫndaa
1PL.PSR-older.brother
'our older brother' UTCBVDN13Nov1101:028

b. *neexeel'* [ne:χe:lʔ] (T)
nee-xeeɬ-v'
1PL.PSR-pack-POSS
'our pack' UTOLAF07Feb1302:146

c. *neeseeyy'* [ne:s̬e:jʔ] (T)
nee-seeyh-v'
1PL.PSR-knife-POSS
'our knife' UTOLAF07Feb1302:055

d. *neenąą* [ne:nã:] (T)
nee-nąą
1PL.PSR-mother
'our mother' UTOLVDN11Jul2901:044

22.2.2.1.4. Second-person plural *nuh-* The second-person plural possessor prefix always has the form *nuh-*. In nouns without an onset consonant (492a), the /h/ of the prefix coda does not move into the onset of the following syllable; instead a glottal stop is inserted in stem-initial position. *Nuh-* sometimes causes lenition of stem-initial fricatives (492b, d).

(492) a. *nuh'ǫǫndaa* [nuhʔõːnᵈaː] (T)
nuh-ǫǫndaa
2PL.PSR-older.brother
'your PL older brother' UTOLAF13May2403:069

b. *nuhxeel'* [nuhχ̬eːlʔ] (T)
nuh-xeeł-v'
2PL.PSR-pack-POSS
'your PL pack' UTOLAF07Feb1302:145

c. *nuhłiign'* [nuhɬiːkʔ] (T)
nuh-łiign'
2PL.PSR-dog:POSS
'your PL dog' UTOLAF07Feb1302:020

d. *nuhnąą* [nuhnãː] (T)
nuh-nąą
2PL.PSR-mother
'your PL mother' UTCBAF13Nov0501:081

22.2.2.2. Third-person possessor prefixes

22.2.2.2.1. Third-person singular *u-/mb-* The third-person singular possessor prefix *u-/mb-* usually occurs when the possessor is human or animate. It appears as *mb-* in vowel-initial stems (493a) and as *u-* elsewhere. No epenthetic glottal stop is inserted before *u-*; see chap. 10.2.1.2. *U-/mb-* '3SG.PSR' sometimes causes lenition of stem-initial fricatives (493b).

(493) a. *mbǫǫndaa* [mbõːnᵈaː] (T)
mb-ǫǫndaa
3SG.PSR-older.brother
'his/her older brother' UTOLVDN14Nov2301:549

b. *uxeel'* [uχ̬e:lʔ] (T)
u-xeeɬ-v'
3SG.PSR-pack-POSS
'his/her pack' UTOLAF07Feb1302:142

c. *useeyy'* [use:jʔ] (T)
u-seeyh-v'
3SG.PSR-knife-POSS
'his/her knife' UTOLAF07Feb1302:054

d. *unąą* [unã:] (T)
u-nąą
3SG.PSR-mother
'his/her mother' UTCBAF13Nov0501:029

22.2.2.2.2. Third-person plural *hu*- The third-person plural possessor prefix *hu*- is the plural counterpart to *u-/mb-*. It is typically used when the possessor is human or animate. When it is used with vowel-initial stems, a glottal stop is inserted (494a). *Hu*- '3SG.PSR'- rarely causes lenition of stem-initial fricatives (494b).

(494) a. *hu'ǫǫndaa* [huʔõ:nᵈa:] (T)
hu-ǫǫndaa
3PL.PSR-older.brother
'their older brother' UTOLVDN07Oct2602:040

b. *huxeel'* [huχ̬e:lʔ] (T)
hu-xeeɬ-v'
3PL.PSR-pack-POSS
'their pack' UTOLAF07Feb1302:144

c. *huɬiign'* [huɬi:kʔ] (T)
hu-ɬiign'
3PL.PSR-dog:POSS
'their dog' UTOLAF07Feb1302:021

d. *hunąą* [hunã:] (T)
hu-nąą
3PL.PSR-mother
'their mother' UTCBAF14Jul1805:011

22.2.2.2.3. Disjunct third-person (singular) *i-/y-* The possessor prefix *i-/y-* is relatively rare. Its use is restricted both syntactically and semantically. It may be used only when the subject of the clause is also third person and always has disjunct reference, i.e., the possessor may not be coreferential with the subject. I thus treat it as a portmaneau morpheme similar to the related postpositional object and direct object prefixes (see chap. 23 and 31 for more information). Semantically, *i-/y-* occurs usually with nonhuman referents (but see [496] for an exception). *I-/y-* does not usually cause stem initial fricative lenition.

(495) a. *Igaan' t'aat naann' t'eey dehk'aa ha...* (T)

i-gaan' *t'aat* *naan'* *t'eey*
3SG.S>3SG.PSR-arm under across:ALL even

deh-k'aa *ha*
3SG.S:QUAL:DH.PFV:H-shoot:PFV:NOM EMPH

'He shot [the bear] right under its arm...'

UTOLAF09Jun2201:014

b. *iche' k'it daa'edaak tah* (N)

i-che' *k'it* *da-na-e-daak* *tah*
3SG.S>3SG.PSR-tail on up-IT-Ø.IPV-D:SG.go:IPV when

'when he$_i$ went onto his$_j$ tail' UTOLAF10Jul0202:110

The allomorph *i-* is used before a consonant (495), the allomorph *y-* before a vowel (496).

(496) ... *ch'itay du' yaadeh ehxį̨į̨...* (B)

ch'itay *du'* *y-aadeh* *eh-xį̨į̨*
old.man CT 3SG.S>3SG.PSR-older.sister DH.PFV:H-kill.SG.O:PFV

'he killed her older sister' UTOLAF10Jul0202:046

22.2.2.2.4. Disjunct third-person plural *hii-* *Hii-* is the plural counterpart of *i-/y-*. It also is restricted to clauses with a third-person (human) subject. The possessor is usually nonhuman; as a result possessor number is not overtly expressed. In (497a) the possessor is plural; in (497b) it is singular. (497a) demonstrates that *hii-* '3PL.S>3SG.PSR'- does not usually cause lenition of stem-initial fricatives.

(497) a. *Ay tl'aan hiithüh* [hi:θə̀h] eł jiyh ch'i'ehxaan… (T)

ay *tl'aan* *hii-thüh* *eł* *jiyh*
and then 3PL.S>3PL.PSR-skin with mittens
ch'i-eh-xaan
INDF.O-Ø.IPV:H-make.PL.O:IPV:CUST:NOM
'And then they make mittens out of their skins…'
UTOLVDN07Nov280:-012

b. *Łįį iin du' hiishyi' ineljit.* (B)

łįį *iin* *du'* *hii-shyi'* *i-nel-jit*
dog PL CT 3PL.S>3PL.PSR-food PP-QUAL:Ø.PFV:L-be.scared:IPV
'The dogs are scared of his [the wolf's] food.'
UTOLVDN10Jul2714:020

22.2.2.3. Coreferential possessor and subject

22.2.2.3.1. Reflexive *d-* The possessor prefix *d-* 'REFL.PSR'- is used when the possessor is coreferential with the clausal subject. There is no number distinction; the same prefix is used when the subject (and possessor) is singular (498b–c) or plural (498d). (This is different from the reflexive direct object prefix, which distinguishes singular and plural; see chap. 31.2.3. Other Alaskan Dene languages distinguish reflexive possessor number; see, e.g., Kari [1979, 35] for Ahtna or Boraas [2012, 14] for Dena'ina.) The possessor prefix serves as the onset consonant for vowel-initial nouns (498b). In consonant-initial nouns an epenthetic /i/ is inserted between the possessor prefix and the noun stem (498c, d). (498a) shows that *d-* 'REFL.PSR'- does not usually cause lenition of stem-initial fricatives.

(498) a. *dixeel'* [tixe:lʔ] natdehnąyh (N)

d-xeel' *na-tdeh-nąyh*
REFL.PSR-pack-POSS down-3SG.S:INC:QUAL:DH.PFV:H-throw:CO:PFV
'he's thrown off his pack' UTOLAF08Feb1906:008

b. *dǫǫndaa k'it ts'ihǫhdąy* (T)

d-ǫǫndaa *k'it* *ts'i-hǫh-dąy*
REFL.PSR-older.brother on PEJ-3SG.S:AR:Ø.PFV:H-miss:IPV
'she misses her older brother' UTOLVDN07Oct2602:035

c. *Ditsǫǫ xah niiyiltįį...* (T)

d-tsǫǫ	*xah*
REFL.PSR-grandmother	for

ni-na-y-il-tįį
TERM-IT-3SG.S>3SG.O-N.PFV:L-handle.AO:PFV

'He brought [the dead puppy] back to his grandmother...'
UTOLAF09Jun2202:022

d. *Dik'aa' sts'ayy' shyiit hiiyįįdlah...* (N)

d-k'a-v'	*s-ts'ayh-v'*	*shyiit*
REFL.PSR-gun-POSS	1SG.PSR-boat-POSS	in

hiiy-įį-dlah
3PL.S>3PL.O-AA.PFV:Ø-handle.PL.O:PFV

'They put their guns into my canoe... '
UTOLVDN07Aug2205:114

The reflexive possessor prefix does not seem to affect the voice/valence marker like the reciprocal possessor prefix in 22.2.2.3.2 does (498a, b, d). In (498c) the verb has an L- voice/valence marker rather than its thematic H- voice/valence marker, but this is likely be caused by the iterative prefix (see chap. 27).

22.2.2.3.2. Reciprocal *nił-* The reciprocal possessor prefix is used when the plural subject referents act on each other's possessee. (499) contains all examples of this prefix in the corpus.

(499) a. *Niłchah ch'ihett'üü tl'aan niłhugaay hahełeeg.* (S)

nił-chah	*ch'-het-t'üü*	*tl'aan*
RECP.PSR-abdomen	INDF.O-3PL.S:Ø.IPV:D-cut:IPV:CUST	and

nił-ugaay	*ha-he-łeeg*
RECP.PSR-baby	out-3PL.S:Ø.IPV:Ø-handle.PL.O:IPV:CUST:NOM

'They cut each other's abdomen open and take each other's babies out.'
ANLC4122a:254

b. *nił'ehłaadn hinłįį* (N)

nił-ehłaadn	*hin-łįį*
RECP.PSR-paternal.relatives	3PL.S:Ø.PFV:D-be:IPV

'they are each other's paternal relatives' UTOLAF12Jul1203:008

Note that the reciprocal possessor prefix changes the voice/valence marker of intransitive verbs from ø- to D- in (499b) and the first verb form in (499a), but not in the second verb form in (499a).

22.2.2.4. Other possessor prefixes

22.2.2.4.1. Areal *hu-* The areal possessor prefix does not occur very frequently. (500) contains one of the few examples.

(500) *Huts'änh ay ch'ale' Naambia eh K'ehtthiign Niign hu'ǫǫsį'.* (N)
hu-ts'änh ay ch'ale' Naambia eh K'ehtthiign Niign hu-ǫǫsį'
AR.P-from and FOC Naambia and K'ehtthiign Niign AR.PSR-name
'From that its name is Naambia (Northway) and K'ehtthiign (fish camp) river.' UTCBAF14May2501-010

22.2.2.4.2. Indefinite *ch'-* The indefinite possessive prefix is used when the identity of the possessor is unknown or when it is considered irrelevant. It occurs particularly frequently on inalienably possessed nouns. In (501a) the identity of the possessor of the leg bone (i.e., the animal that the leg used to belong to) is not known, but since 'leg' is obligatorily possessed, the indefinite possessive prefix is required. (501b, c) are both taken from a story about two sisters. The identity of the possessor is known in both instances but is not considered important—important is only which of the sisters does what.

(501) a. *Ch'ixol' tth'än nohshyign' ee'aan…* (N)
ch'-xol' tth'än noh-shyign'
INDF.PSR-leg bone MED:AR-down:ALL
ee-'aan
3SG.S:DH.PFV:Ø-classify.CO:IPV:NOM
'There was a leg bone lying down there…'
UTOLVDN10Jul2713:035

b. *Ch'aadeh du' du' łą' t'eey ti'atnagn eh …* (T)
ch'-aadeh du' du' łą' t'eey
INDF.PSR-older.sister CT CT truly ADVZR
ti-at-nagn eh
tired-3SG.S:AA.PFV:D-be.tired:IPV:NOM and
'The older sister was really tired…' UTCBAF13Nov0501:083

c. *That ch'idia' du' hǫǫshyąą.* (T)
that ch'-dia' du' hǫǫ-shyąą
that INDF.PSR-younger.sister CT 3SG.S:AR:Ø.PFV:Ø-be.smart:IPV
'The younger sister though was smart.'
UTCBAF13Nov0501:084

(501b) also demonstrates that this prefix moves into the onset of vowel-initial nouns. When the noun stem begins with a consonant, the epenthetic vowel /i/ is inserted (501c, a).

22.2.3. Effects on the stem

Possessive morphology has the following effects on the noun stem: the creation of heavy stem syllables by addition of the (alienable) possessive suffix, lowering the stem tone, and lenition of stem-initial fricatives. The first two effects are described in sections 22.2.1.1 and 22.2.1.2 above. Lenition of stem-initial fricatives is briefly described in 22.2.3.1. Irregular possessed stems are described in sec. 22.2.3.2.

22.2.3.1. Stem-initial fricative lenition In many Dene languages stem-initial fricatives become voiced in the possessive construction (see, e.g., Rice [1989, 215] for Slave or Cook [2004, 117] for Dëne Sųłiné). In Tanacross (Holton 2001) and Upper Tanana (Minoura 1994) this is usually treated as a fortis/lenis distinction (see also chap. 9). Examples are given in (502); lenis consonants are marked by [̬] underneath the consonant symbol. Data in (502) is given in orthographic as well as phonetic transcription. (502i) shows that in the case of /ʃʲ/ the lenis consonant is used both in the unpossessed and in the possessed form.

(502) Stem-initial fricative lenition

	English	*Unpossessed*		*Possessed*	
a.	'belt'	thüh	[θɔh]	-thüü'	-[θ̬ɔ̀:ʔ]
b.	'pack'	theeł	[θe:ɬ]	-theel'	-[θ̬è:lʔ]
c.	'fish hook'	łoh	[ɬòh]	-łoo'	-[ɬ̬ò:ʔ]
d.	'urine'	łüh	[ɬɘh]	-łüü'	-[ɬ̬ɘ̀:ʔ]
e.	'gaff hook'	säł	[sʌ̀ɬ]	-säl'	-[s̬ʌ̀lʔ]
f.	'knife'	seeyh	[se:j̊]	-seey'	-[s̬e:jʔ]
g.	'pack'	xeeł	[xe:ɬ]	-xeel'	-[x̬è:lʔ]
h.	'raft'	xįąh	[xĩ͜ãh]	-xįą'	-[x̬ȉ͜ȁʔ]
i.	'louse'	shyà'	[ʃʲàʔ]	-shyàà'	-[ʃʲà:ʔ]

As described in chap. 9, this process applies regularly only in forms containing the first-person singular possessor prefix *sh*-.

22.2.3.2. Irregular possessed stems A handful of optionally possessed nouns have an irregular possessed stem.

A few nouns do not use the alienable possessive suffix in possessive constructions. In these words the possessed form is identical to the unpossessed form; not only is there no final glottal stop, but the stem tone is not affected. I do not know whether the list in (503) is inclusive.

(503) No possessive suffix

	English	*Unpossessed*	*Possessed*
a.	'house'	shyah	-shyah
b.	'village'	keey	-keey
c.	'trail'	tąy	-tąy

The following nouns have unpredictable possessed stems (504). This list is inclusive.

(504) Irregular possessed stem

	English	*Unpossessed*	*Possessed*
a.	'dog'	łįį	-łiign'
b.	'pants'	thäł	-ahtle', -ehtle'

Apart from those exceptions, possession is a very regular process.

22.2.4. Restrictions on possessive morphology

There are both semantic and morphological restrictions on possessive morphology.

22.2.4.1. Semantic restrictions The inalienable possessive suffix is restricted to entities that do not naturally occur without a possessor such as body parts and kinship terms. It cannot be used with other entities.

While inalienable possession of humans as relatives is obligatory, alienable possession of humans is generally not appropriate.

The alienable possessive suffix can be applied to most other entities. Claiming ownership of a wild animal, however, is *įįjih*, and the only domesticated animal is traditionally the dog. Thus, while it is acceptable to say *shliign'* 'my dog', speakers routinely refuse to produce forms corresponding to 'my rabbit' (with either the interpretation of 'my pet rabbit' or 'the rabbit that I snared'), 'my duck', and even more so 'my caribou' or 'my moose'. Speakers marginally accept *shluugn'* 'my fish' with the interpretation 'the fish that I caught', but they are quick to point out that this is not a good thing to say, since it implies a refusal to share the fish.

There is also a certain reluctance to claim ownership of plants and plant materials. 'My spruce' and 'my grass' were not acceptable (although one speaker once told a visitor in my presence to not leave his marijuana in her cabin, using the form *ntl'oo'* 'your SG grass', a calque from English). Plant materials intended for specific uses may however be possessed:

(505) a. *neexayy'* (T)
nee-xayh-v'
1PL.PSR-spruce.root-POSS
'our spruce roots' (for making baskets)
UTOLAF07Feb1302:131

b. *hutsädn'* (N)
hu-tsät-v'
3PL.PSR-firewood-POSS
'their firewood' UTCBVDN13Nov0805:034

Other concepts that cannot be possessed by individuals are landscape features; thus 'my lake' and 'my mountain' are unacceptable. In place-names, however, such stems frequently occur in their possessed form, as illustrated in (506).

(506) a. *Tehshyüü Männ'*
tehshyüü *mänh-v'*
humpback.whitefish lake-POSS
'Humpback Whitefish lake (Wellesley Lakes)' Tyone (1996, 7)

b. *Tehshyüü Ddhäl'*
tehshyüü *ddhäł-v'*
humpback.whitefish mountain-POSS
'Humpback Whitefish mountain (Wellesley Mountain)' Tyone (1996, 7)

See Kari (1997a) for numerous additional examples of morphologically possessed landscape features.

22.2.4.2. Morphological restrictions The possessive morphology described above can be used with stem nouns, prefixed or suffixed nouns, most types of compound nouns, and loanwords. Numerous examples of possessed stem nouns are given above. Possession of suffixed nouns is illustrated in (507); both nouns contain the (nonproductive) instrumental suffix *-ł* described in chap. 13.2.1.2.

(507) a. *di'eel'* (N)
d-eeł-v'
REFL:trap-POSS
'his/her own trap' UTOLVDN13May2804:037

b. *ssal'* (T)
s-sał-v'
1SG.PSR-fish.hook-POSS
'my fish hook' UTOLAF07Feb1302:024

Possession of prefixed nouns also is possible, although it does not seem to be very productive. (508a) illustrates possession of a noun stem prefixed with *ch'-* 'INDF.PSR',[1] (508b, c) noun stems containing adverbial prefixes.

(508) a. *shch'įįtįįl' choh* (N)
sh-ch'įįtįįł-v' *choh*
1SG.PSR-coffee.can-POSS big
'my big coffee can' UTOLVDN10Jul2724:071

b. *neetehmbiil'* (T)
nee-tehmbiił-v'
1PL.PSR-gillnet-POSS
'our gillnet' UTOLVDN10Jul0701:058

c. *shdahdzäl'* (N)
sh-dahdzäł-v'
1SG.PSR-smokehouse-POSS
'my smokehouse' UTOLVDN14Apr2602:148

I am not sure how semantically acceptable these forms are outside their context. (508a) is from a story where Mrs. Darlene Northway describes her own ignorance as a child. In the original narrative she used the phrase in English ("My coffee can!")[2] to describe how she grabbed a coffee can away from her grandmother after first refusing to try the contents. Both the original refusal of the food and the open display of greed are not considered appropriate behavior even for a child. The audience thought this story hilarious, since by the time she told it, Mrs. Northway was a respected elder who certainly would not behave in this fashion.

Similar concerns hold for (508b) and (508c). Such forms are attested only in the negative existential construction.

While some types of compounds may be morphologically possessed, others may not. Morphological possession tends to be possible for noun + noun compounds (509).

(509) a. *nke' tl'uul'* (N)

n-ke' tl'uuł-v'
2SG.PSR-shoe rope-POSS
'your SG shoelace' UT Notebook #4, 30

b. *shtuutįįl'* (N)

sh-tuutįįł-v'
1SG.PSR-cup-POSS
'my cup' UTOLAF14Nov2001:003

(508a) illustrates a possessed noun + modifier compound; another example is given in (510). (510a) is particularly interesting because the modifier *gaay* 'small' is suffixed with the alienable possessive suffix, while the modifier *choh* 'big' in (508a) and (510b) is not suffixed.

(510) a. *shlįįgaay'* (N)

sh-lįįgaay-v'
1SG.PSR-puppy-POSS
'my puppy' UT Notebook #6, 5

b. *n'eegn choh* (N)

n-eek-v' choh
2SG.PSR-coat bit
'your SG parka' UTOLAF18Jun0101:038

Possessive morphology may apply to loanwords (511).

(511) a. *stseeyniign'* (N)

s-tseeyniik-v'
1SG.PSR-teapot-POSS
'my teapot' UT Notebook #2, 56

b. *nelsüü'* (N)

n-elsüü-v'
2SG.PSR-money-POSS
'your SG money' UTOLAF12Jul1203:016

Deverbal nouns cannot be possessed in this fashion; see 22.3.2 for more information.

22.2.5. Double possession (not attested)

Some Dene languages allow what is called "double possession," where an inalienably possessed entity is possessed in an alienable fashion.

(512) illustrates this phenomenon in Witsuwit'en, (513) in Dena'ina.

(512) a. *c'əluh*
c'ə-luh
INDF.PSR-bladder
'bladder, fish skin bag'

b. *nts'ɛtah nc'əluh?*
nts'ɛtah n-c'ə-luh
where 2SG.PSR-INDF.PSR-skin.bag
'where's your skin bag?' Hargus (2007, 236)

(513) a. *k'ts'en*
k'-ts'en
INDF.PSR-meat
'meat'

b. *shts'en*
sh-ts'en
1SG.PSR-flesh
'my flesh, flesh from my body'

c. *shk'ts'en*
sh-k'-ts'en
1SG.PSR-INDF.PSR-meat
'my meat (from something else)' Lovick (2005, 60)

Lovick (2005, 60) points out that in Dena'ina this is only possible if the inalienable possessor is indefinite. Although Rice (1989, 227–28) in her discussion of double possession in Slave does not explicitly state that the inalienable possessor has to be indefinite, her examples certainly suggest so. Thompson (1996, 66), discussing this construction in Koyukon, argues that the indefinite possessor prefix serves to alienate the entity from the inherent possessor.

Forms comparable to (512b) and (513c) are not possible in Upper Tanana. There are no instances of two possessor prefixes in the corpus, and elicitation of such forms consistently failed. Double possession appears not to exist in this language.

22.3. Other possessive constructions

When the morphological possessive construction is for some reason blocked, there are several other strategies to indicate ownership.

22.3.1. __ P+*ts'änh* '__ belonging to P, P's __'

The most common strategy to indicate ownership is to use an inflected form of the postposition P+*ts'änh* 'from P, belonging to P'. This construction is uncommon in natural discourse, quite possibly because claiming ownership can be problematic. (514a) is the only clear naturalistic example; all others come from elicitations. In (514a) the possessee cannot participate in the morphological possessive construction for semantic reasons (eggs are inalienably possessed by the bird that laid them). (514b) is a noun + noun compound, and (514c) is a lexicalized deverbal noun.

(514) a. *Ay tl'aan dii ch'ixia' ts'uudiidlay neexunh neets'änh taałeeł.* (N)

ay	*tl'aan*	*dii*	*ch'-xia'*
and	then	whatever	INDF.PSR-egg

ts'uu-dii-dlay	*neexunh*	*nee-ts'änh*
1PL.S:CON-QUAL:I.PFV:Ø-find.PL.O:PFV:NOM	1PL	1PL.P-from

taa-łeeł
3PL.S:INC:AA.IPFV:Ø-classify.PL.O:FUT

'And all the eggs we found were ours to keep.'
UTOLVDN07Aug2205:023

b. *xałtįį sts'anh* (T)

xałtįį	*s-ts'anh*
sled.handle	1SG.P-from

'my sled handle' UTOLAF07Feb1302:122

c. *uk'it dats'idaagn sts'änh* (N)

u-k'it	*da-ts'i-daagn*	*s-ts'änh*
3SG.P-on	up-IMPSL:Ø.PFV:Ø-SG.sit:IPV:CUST:NOM	1SG.P-from

'my chair' UT Notebook #2, 58

This construction may also be used in words where the morphological possessive would be possible (515). In those instances there appears to be a slight meaning difference between the periphrastic construction and the morphological one. While the morphological construction simply indicates possession, the periphrastic one has emphatic meaning.

(515) a. *ay theeł sts'änh nt'eh* (N)

ay theeł s-ts'änh n-t'eh
3SG box 1SG.S-from 3SG.S:Ø.PFV:Ø-be:IPV
'this is *my* box' (compare *shtheel'* 'my box') UT Notebook #4, 6

b. *ay xį̨ąh sts'änh nt'eh* (N)

ay xį̨ąh s-ts'änh n-t'eh
3SG raft 1SG.S-from 3SG.S:Ø.PFV:Ø-be:IPV
'this is *my* raft' (compare *shxį̨ą'* 'my raft') UT Notebook #4, 5

22.3.2. Possession of deverbal nouns

While (514c) demonstrates that deverbal nouns can be possessed using N P+*ts'änh* 'N of P, P's N', a more common strategy is to inflect deverbal nouns for one of their arguments. As described in chap. 13.5, deverbal nouns describing objects are usually inflected for impersonal/first-person plural subject or third-person plural subject. The subject inflection can be changed to indicate the actual possessor (516).

(516) *"Ndugn tahdak tah hahdogn nuhts'adn dii dii tah'aal eł dii shyii tahtiadn eł nuhch'il eł da'ahdlaak shyiit," nee'ehnih.* (T)

ndugn tah-dak tah hah-dogn
somewhere INC:Ø.IPV:2PL.S:Ø-PL.go:IPV:CUST when NTRL-up:AR

nuh-ts'adn' dii dii tah-'aal eł
2PL.PSR-blanket what what INC:AA.IPV:2PL.S:Ø-eat:FUT:NOM and

dii shyii tah-tiadn eł
what in INC:AA.IPV:2PL.S:Ø-PL.sleep:FUT:NOM and

nuh-ch'il eł da-ah-dlaak shyiit
2PL.PSR-clothes and up-Ø.IPV:2PL.S:Ø-handle.PL.O:IPV:CUST in

nee-eh-nih
1PL.O-3SG.S:Ø.IPV:H-say:IPV

'"When you go somewhere, keep your blankets, what you're going to eat, what you're going to sleep in, and your clothes in a high place," she said to us.' UTOLAF07Nov2602:023

Nuhts'adn' 'your PL blankets' and *nuhch'il* 'your PL clothes' both are formed using possessive morphology and are translated accordingly. *Dii tah'aal*, translated by the speaker as 'your PL food' consists of an indefinite pronoun plus a relative clause 'whatever you PL will eat', as does *dii shyii tahtiadn* 'whatever you PL will sleep in'.

(517) contrasts a nonpossessed use of the deverbal noun for 'chair' with a possessed one.

(517) a. *Ahugn uk'it daatsidaagn k'it dadhḭḭdah.* (N)

ahugn u-k'it da-dzi-daagn k'it
there 3SG.P-on up-IMPSL.S:QUAL:Ø.IPV:D-SG.sit:IPV:CUST:NOM on
da-dhḭḭ-dah
up-DH.PFV:2SG.S:Ø-SG.sit:IPV
'Sit SG over there on a chair.' UTOLAF14Nov2408:004

b. *Ts'exeh dadidaak tah dii xah ik'it da'ḭḭdaay ut'aat hadḭhthay?* (N)

ts'exeh da-di-daak tah
woman up-3SG.S:QUAL:Ø.IPV:Ø-SG.sit:IPV:CUST when
dii xah i-k'it da-ḭḭ-daay u-t'aat
why 3SG.S>3SG.P-on up-AA.PFV:Ø-SG.sit:PFV:NOM 3SG.P-under
ha-dḭh-thay
out-QUAL:AA.PFV:2SG.S:H-move.LRO.quickly:PFV:NOM
'When that woman was sitting, why did you pull out her chair (lit.: 'what she had been sitting on') from under her?'
UTOLAF14May0807:010

The word for 'chair' is a deverbal noun that could be translated literally as 'the thing someone customarily sits on'. A morpheme breakdown is given in (517a). In (517b) the woman has temporary ownership of the chair by trying to sit down in it. This is reflected in the speaker's use of a third-person singular form, rather than the (more common) impersonal form. Note also that the deverbal noun in (517a) is in the imperfective customary, while the one in (517b) is in the perfective.

The examples in (518) come from elicitation and demonstrate the systematicity of this process.

(518) a. *ih'aal*(T)

ih-'aal
1SG.S:Ø.IPV:Ø-eat:IPV:NOM
'[what] I eat, my food' UTOLAF07Feb1302:062

b. *ḭḭ'aal*

ḭḭ-'aal
2SG.S:Ø.IPV:Ø-eat:IPV:NOM
'[where] is your SG food?' UTOLAF07Feb1302:064

c. *ye'aal*
y-e-'aal
3SG.S>3SG.O-Ø.IPV:Ø-eat:IPV:NOM
'[this is] his/her food' UTOLAF07Feb1302:063

In contrast to using the morphological possessive construction, changing the subject inflection seems to indicate more transient ownership: while I might have brought the food along, I will share it, and while I may currently be using this chair, I do not claim ownership over it in perpetuity.

22.4. Syntactic comments

In this section, the syntax of possession is briefly explored. More information on this topic can be found in volume 2.

22.4.1. Noun phrases and possessor prefixes

In the alienable possessive construction, possessor prefixes are mutually exclusive with possessor noun phrases (519). The noun stem contains the alienable possessive suffix regardless of whether the possessor is expressed pronominally or by a full noun phrase.

(519) a. *Uts'ayy' titeeɬaak k'eh eltsį̨į̨.* (N)
u-ts'ayh-v' *ti-tee-ɬaak* *k'eh*
3SG.PSR-canoe-POSS underwater-3SG.S:INC:DH.PFV:Ø-sink:PFV like
el-tsį̨į̨
3SG.S:DH.PFV:L-appear:IPV
'His boat looked as if it was about to sink.'
UTOLAF12Jul1203:108

b. *Stsay stsay du' ts'ayy' ishyiit ts'änh k'ąy' hadį̨į̨'ah...*
s-tsay *s-tsay* *du'* *ts'ayh-v'* *ishyiit*
1SG.PSR-grandfather 1SG.PSR-grandfather CT boat-POSS there
ts'änh *k'ąy'* *ha-dį̨į̨-'ah*
from willow out-3SG.S:QUAL:AA.PFV-LO.extend:IPV
'My grandfather, from my grandfather's boat willow is sticking out...' UTOLAF12Jul1203:110

In the inalienable possessive construction, possession may be marked by just the possessor prefix (520a). When the possessor is expressed by a free noun phrase, however, the possessor prefix may be used (520b) but is not required (520c, d). Note that this is not affected by whether the body part is still attached to its possessor (520c) or has been severed (520d).

(520) a. *Unąą iin uta' atshyąą!* (N)

u-nąą iin u-ta' at-shyąą
3sg.psr-mother pl 3sg.psr-father 3pl.s:aa.pfv:d-grow.old:pfv
'Her mother and father had gotten old!'
UTOLAF10Jul0202:184

b. *Shta' ugaan' łahtthegn nts'ą̈' eet'eh.* (N)

sh-ta' u-gaan' łahtthegn nts'ą̈'
1sg.psr-father 3sg.psr-arm all
ee-t'eh
3sg.s:dh.pfv:ø-get.burned:pfv
'My father's arm got burned all over.'
UTOLVDN14Apr2601:024

c. *Jǫǫ tthi' kon' shyiit nįįshyil eł.* (T)

jǫǫ tthi' kon' shyiit nįį-shyil
camprobber head fire into 3sg.s:n.pfv:ø-push.lro:pfv:nom
eł
and
'He pushed Camprobber's head into the fire.'
UTOLVDN08Mar1304:003

d. *Dindeey tthi' eh hihdelxoh…* (T)

dindeey tthi' eh hih-del-xoh
people head with 3pl.s-qual:ø.ipv:ø-play:ipv
'They were playing with people's [severed] heads…'
UTCBAF14Jul1805:009

22.4.2. Recursion

Possession is a recursive process. The possessor of the head noun *shyah* 'house' in (521a) is in its turn possessed by the speaker. (521b) has three nested possessors and is further complicated by the presence of the conjoined noun phrase *uta' eh unąą* 'her father and mother'.

(521) a. *shta' shyah* (N)

sh-ta' shyah
1sg.psr-father house
'my father's house' UTCBVDN13Nov0804:035

b. *shnąą uta' eh unąą hushyah* (N)

sh-nąą 1SG.PSR-mother *u-ta'* 3SG.PSR-father *eh* and *u-nąą* 3SG.PSR-mother

hu-shyah 3PL.PSR-house

'my mother's father and mother's house'

UTOLAF09Aug1202:009

Constructions such (521) are very common, since Upper Tanana speakers prefer to refer to their relatives with a kinship term rather than with a personal name (Scollon and Scollon 1981).

22.5. Summary

In this chapter possession is described. Upper Tanana distinguishes obligatorily possessed nouns from optionally possessed ones. This corresponds to some degree with the morphological distinction between nouns that take the inalienable possessive suffix -' and nouns that take the alienable possessive suffix -v̀'. Both suffixes are absorbed into the stem; they differ in that the alienable possessive suffix creates a heavy syllable, whereas the inalienable one does not. The possessor is usually indicated by a possessor prefix.

Possessive morphology occasionally causes lenition of stem initial fricatives. There are also some stems that do not require any possessive suffix, and some where the possessed stem cannot be derived from the unpossessed one via regular rule.

Not all nouns can take possessive morphology. There are some semantic restrictions—most living things other than relatives cannot be possessed—and morphological restrictions. Unlike several related languages Upper Tanana also does not allow "double possession," i.e., the co-occurrence of two possessor prefixes in the same word.

Possession of nouns that cannot take possessive morphology can be indicated in two ways: by using a periphrastic construction N P+*ts'änh* 'P's N' or (in the case of deverbal nouns) by changing the subject inflection.

Possessive prefixes alternate with free possessor noun phrases when the possessee is alienably possessed. When the possessee is inalienably possessed, possessive prefixes may co-occur with free noun phrases.

Possession is a recursive process, and it is common to have two or even three nested possessors.

Notes

1. This seems to be the only example of this type in the data.
2. The noun phrase was only later translated back into Upper Tanana; I unfortunately do not recall whether this was done by Mrs. Northway herself or by another speaker.

23 Inflection of postpositions

In this chapter postpositional inflection is described. Inflection is the same for free (chap. 15) and bound (chap. 36) postpositions. The pronominal prefixes used in postpositional inflection are formally almost identical to the direct object prefixes and the possessor prefixes. The three sets of prefixes are compared in table 23.1.[1]

	Possessor	Postp. object	Direct object
1SG	sh-	sh-	sh-
2SG	n-	n-	n-
1PL	nee-	nee-	nee-
2PL	nuh-	nuh-	nuh-
3SG	u-/mb-	u-/mb-	–
3PL	hu-	hu-	hu-
3SG.S>3SG	i-/y-	i-/y-	i-/y-
3PL.S>3SG	hii-	hii-	hii-
REFL	d-	d-	id-
RECP	nił-	nił-/łi-	nił-/łi-
AR	hu-	hu-	hu-
INDF	ch'-	ch'-	ch'-

Table 23.1. Possessor, postpositional object, and direct object prefixes

Postpositional object prefixes referring to speech act participants are described in 23.1, those referring to third-person referents in 23.2, and those used when subject and postpositional object are coreferential in 23.3. The areal and indefinite postpositional object prefixes are described in 23.4.

23.1. First- and second-person postpositional objects

Postpositional object prefixes referring to first- and second-person referents are mutually exclusive with free noun phrases.

23.1.1. First-person singular *sh-*

The first-person singular postpositional object prefix has the form *sh-* (522). Before postpositions beginning with /s, t͡s, t͡sʰ, t͡s'/ it assimilates to /s/ (522b).

(522) a. *Sheh na'įįdaał!* (T)

sh-eh *na-įį-daał*
1sg.p-with it-aa.ipv:2sg.s-d:sg.go:ipv:prog
'Come back with me!' UTCBAF13Nov0501:336

b. *Ay łįį sts'ą̈' tetdät...* (N)

ay łįį s-ts'ą̈' tet-dät
and dog 1sg.p-to 3sg.s:inc:dh.pfv:d-animal.runs:pfv
'And the dog started running to me...'
UTOLVDN14Apr2602:088

23.1.2. Second-person singular *n-*

The second-person singular postpositional object prefix always has the form *n-* (523). Before consonant-initial postpositions, /n/ forms a syllable of its own (523b).

(523) a. *naa nsǫǫ* (N)

n-aa *n-sǫǫ*
2sg.p-for 3sg.s:ø.pfv:ø-be.good:ipv
'it is good for you s' UTOLAF15May0703:002

b. *K'at'eey nkah* (/n.kʰah./) *hutnak-'įįl...* (T)

k'at'eey n-kah hu-tnak-'įįl
neg 2sg.s-for ar-inc:qual:aa.ipv:1sg.s:h-look:fut:neg
'I'm not going to look around at you sg...'
UTOLAF08Apr2805:063

23.1.3. First-person plural *nee-*

The first-person plural postpositional object prefix always has the form *nee-* (524).

(524) a. *Nee'eł dįlxoh nah'ogn!* (T)

nee-'eł dįl-xoh nah-'ogn
1pl.p-with qual:ø.ipv:2sg.s:l-play:ipv med:outside:ar
'Play with us outside!' UTOLAF12Jul0601:024

b. *That shaak'ay neexah ets'üh.* (N)

that sh-aak'ay nee-xah e-ts'üh
that 1SG.PSR-auntie 1PL.P-for 3SG.S:Ø.IPV:Ø-cry:IPV
'My auntie was crying for us.' UTOLVDN13May2004:112

23.1.4. Second-person plural *nuh-*

The second-person plural postpositional object prefix always has the form *nuh-* (525).

(525) a. *Nuhxah tuuthał oktsay!* (T)

nuh-xah tuuthał ok-tsay
2PL.P-for soup OPT:1SG.S:H-make.SG.O:OPT
'I'm going to make soup for you PL!' UTOLAF08Apr2805:020

b. *Jah tädn t'eey nuh'eh natahshyüü.* (N)

jah tädn t'eey nuh'eh natahshyüü
this night even 2PL.P-with IT-3SG.S:INC:AA.IPV:Ø-SNOW:FUT
'Tonight it is going to snow for you PL'
UTOLVDN14Apr2601:038

23.2. Third-person postpositional objects

In the absence of coreferential free noun phrases, third-person postpositional objects are always marked overtly. This distinguishes them from direct object prefixes, which are unmarked under certain circumstances (see chap. 31.2.2).

23.2.1. Third-person singular *u-/mb-*

The third-person singular prefix *u-/mb-* is used when the subject is first- or second-person. In this constellation *u-/mb-* may have an animate (526a) or an inanimate (526b) referent. (In [526b], plural number of the inanimate referent is indicated by the classificatory verb stem; number is not usually marked pronominally for inanimate referents.) The allomorph *mb-* is used before a vowel (526a), *u-* before a consonant (526b).

(526) a. ... *tay' mbeh nadzaltth'i'.* (N)

tay' mbeh nadzaltth'i'
again 3SG.S-with IT-1PL.S:AA.PFV:L-PL.stay:PFV
'... we stayed another night with him.'
UTOLVDN10Jul2724:048

b. *Ay du' dąą' uk'it dats'idlaak.* (N)
ay du' dąą' u-k'it da-ts'i-dlaak
and ct thus 3sg.p-on up-1pl.s:ø.ipv:ø-keep.pl.o:pfv:cust
'And we would have [the leaves] on it like this.'
UTOLVDN07Aug2004:032

U-/mb- is also used when the subject is third person (527).

(527) a. *Uch'a' t'eey staa'inshyah.* (N)
u-ch'a' t'eey sta-na-in-shyah
3sg.s-from even away-it-3sg.s:n.pfv:d-sg.go:pfv
'She went away from him again.' UTCBVDN13Nov1401:017

b. *Ch'iik'on k'it tthee deldliad eh t'eey uk'it eedlah.* (T)
ch'iik'on k'it tthee del-dliad eh
dentalium on rock 3sg.s:qual:ø.pfv:l be.shiny:ipv:nom and
t'eey u-k'it ee-dlah
even 3sg.p-on 3sg.s:dh.pfv:ø-classify.pl.o:ipv
'On the dentalium necklace, gold nuggets too were on it.'
UTOLVDN13May2909:164

The prefix *u-/mb-* also is used in the rare instances where the subject is areal or indefinite (528).

(528) a. *Ts'ełegn du' uk'it ch'ik'eh hǫǫłįį.* (N)
ts'ełegn du' u-k'it ch'-k'eh hǫǫ-łįį
one ct 3sg.p-on indf.psr-tracks ar.s:ø.pfv:ø-be:ipv
'One [trail] had tracks on it.' UTOLAF10Jul0202:018

b. *Ch'aadeh ushyiit ch'įįshyah ch'idanh tah.* (T)
ch'-aadeh u-shyiit ch'įį-shyah
indf.psr-older.sister 3sg.p-into indf:s:aa.pfv:ø-sg.go:pfv
ch'idanh tah
different
'Something different (like an evil spirit) got into the older sister.'
UTOLVDN14Nov2301:139

23.2.2. Third-person plural *hu-*

The prefix *hu-* is the plural counterpart of *u-/mb-*. It is required with first- and second-person subjects (529a), as well as with areal subjects (529b), and is used commonly with third-person subjects (529c). *Hu-* may only be used with animate, typically human, referents; inanimate third-person plural referents are encoded with *u-/mb-* (526b).

(529) a. … *ishyiit hu'eh dzelttth'ih.* (N)
ishyiit hu-'eh dzel-tth'ih
there 3PL.P-with 1PL.S:QUAL:Ø.PFV:L-PL.stay:IPV
'… we stayed there with them.' UTOLAF09Aug1202:009

b. *huxah hǫǫsǫǫ* (T)
hu-xah hǫǫ-sǫǫ
3PL.P-for AR.S:Ø.PFV:Ø-be.good:IPV
'they liked it' UTOLAF09Jun2901:007

c. … *huch'a' teeshyah.* (S)
hu-ch'a' tee-shyah
3PL-from 3SG.S:INC:DH.PFV:Ø-SG.go:PFV
'… he went away from them.' ANLC4122a-070

23.2.3. Disjunct third-person (singular) *i-/y-*

The prefix *i-/y-* is used when both subject and postpositional object are third-person singular (or unmarked for number, as are most nonhuman referents). Like the direct object prefix of the same shape (chap. 31.2.2.3), it is treated here as a portmanteau morpheme with disjunct reference, expressing both subject and (postpositional) object. As a consequence the subject is indicated in the gloss only on the postposition, not on the verb itself (530).

(530) a. *Itüh įį'ia.* (T)
i-tüh įį-'ia
3SG.S>3SG.P-over AA.PFV:Ø-step:PFV
'He stepped over it.' UTOLVDN13May2803:011

b. *yaa chijeltįį* (N)
y-aa chi-jel-tįį
3SG.S>3SG.P-for pretend-INDF:QUAL:Ø.IPV:L-SG.sleep:IPV
'she faked sleep for him' UTOLVDN10Jul2713:025

I-/y- only occurs when there is no adjacent noun phrase that is coreferential with the postpositional object. When *i-/y-* does occur immediately following a free noun phrase, then this noun phrase is interpreted either as subject or as direct object, never as postpositional object.

(531) a. *Ts'iiniin gaay yaa danįįshyah.* (T)

ts'iiniin gaay yaa da-nįį-shyah
child small 3SG.S>3SG.P-for in-N.PFV:Ø-SG.go:PFV

'The small child went inside to him.' (*He went inside to the small child.) UTOLVDN13May2801:199

b. *Tsüü yaa na'elshyeek shyįį'...* (N)

tsüü y-aa na-el-shyeek shyįį'
roots 3SG.S>3SG.P-for IT-Ø.IPV:L-handle.PL.O:IPV:CUST only

'He brought back only roots for her...' (*He brought them back for edible roots...) UTOLVDN10Jul2713:008

The allomorph *i-* occurs before a consonant (532a); *y-* occurs before a vowel (532b).

(532) a. *Alkał łahtthegn ixeel' hǫǫsǫǫ ik'it na'ehtsįį tl'aan.* (N)

Alkał łahtthegn i-xeel' hǫǫ-sǫǫ i-k'it
Alkał all 3SG.S>3SG.PSR-pack:POSS nicely 3SG.S>3SG.P-on

na-eh-tsįį tl'aan
IT-DH.PV:Ø-fix:PFV and

'He [made] Alkał's pack nicely and fixed it on him.' UTOLVDN10Jul2724:107

b. *Noo tah yeh natnett'ak.* (N)

noo tah y-eh
ahead:ALL among 3SG.S>3SG.P-with

na-tnet-t'ak
IT-INC:QUAL:N.PFV:D-SG.fly:PFV

'He started to fly back south with her.' UTOLAF08Feb1902:007

23.2.4. Disjunct hird-person plural *hii-*

The prefix *hii-* is used when the subject is third-person plural and the postpositional object is third-person singular (or unmarked for number). Like *i-/y-*, *hii-* is a portmanteau morpheme; when a postposition is prefixed with *hii-*, the plural subject marker *h-* usually does not occur again within the verb ([533], see also Cook [1996]).

(533) a. *Ay tl'aan hii'eł chaldzüh.* (T)

ay *tl'aan* *hii-'eł* *chal-dzüh*
and and 3PL.S>3SG.P-with INDF:INC:AA.IPV:L-dance:FUT
'And then they will dance with [their potlatch gifts].'
UTOLAF11Aug0207:018

b. *Natelsüü iin hiixah edloh.* (T)

na-tel-süü *iin* *hii-xah*
IT-3PL.S:INC:DH.PFV:L-hunt:PFV:NOM PL 3PL.S>3SG.P-for
e-dloh
ø.IPV:ø-laugh:IPV
'The hunters laughed at him.' UTOLAF09Jun2202:049

Only occasionally is the (plural) subject prefix present both as part of the portmanteau and in the verb (534).

(534) … *ay t'oot'eey hiik'eh haadał.* (T)

ay *t'oot'eey* *hiik'eh* *haadał*
and but 3PL.S>3PL.P-following 3PL.S:AA.IPV:ø-PL.go:IPV:PROG
'… but they kept following them.' UTOLVDN13May2909:009

23.3. Coreferential postpositional object and subject

The reflexive postpositional object prefix *d-* and the reciprocal prefix *nił-/łi-* both express coreferentiality between subject and postpositional object.

23.3.1. Reflexive *d-*

The reflexive postpositional object has the form *d-*, regardless of the person or number of the subject. Both verb themes in (535) contain bound postpositions.

(535) a. *t'axo:::h dich'agn'aal t'eey hidishniih* (N)

t'axoh *d-i-ch'-agn-'aal* *t'eey*
finally REFL.P-PP-INDF.O-ø.IPV:1SG.S:L-feed:IPV:NEG CMP
h-i-d-ish-niih
?-PP-QUAL-AA.PFV:1SG.S:D-fail:PFV
'finally I couldn't feed myself' UTOLVDN14Apr2602:036

b. *k'at'eey hǫǫsǫǫ dik'ahnelta'* (N)

k'at'eey *hǫǫsǫǫ*
NEG well

d-k'a-hnel-ta'
REFL.P-care-3PL.S:QUAL:Ø.IPV:L-take.care:IPV:NEG:NOM

'they do not take good care of themselves'

UTOLVDN10Jul2602:049

The reflexive postpositional object triggers a change in voice/valence marker from H- to L- (535) and from Ø- to D-; see chap. 27.3.2.1.2.

23.3.2. Reciprocal *niɬ/ɬi-*

The reciprocal postpositional object usually has the form *niɬ-*. This is the only form used by Northway speakers (536a, b) and is common in the Tetlin (536c) and Beaver Creek dialects as well.

(536) a. *Nuun eh tsa' eh niɬts'ą' hahatdeel.* (B)

nuun *eh* *tsa'* *eh* *niɬ-ts'ą'*
porcupine and beaver and RECP.P-to

ha-hat-deel
out-3PL.S:AA.PFV:D-PL.go:PFV

'Porcupine and beaver came out to each other.'

UTOLVDN10Jul2721:008

b. *Ay t'oot'eey hǫǫsu' niɬk'ats'enelta'.* (N)

ay *t'oot'eey* *hǫǫsu'* *niɬ-k'a-ts'e-nel-ta'*
and but well RECP.P-care-1PL.S:QUAL:Ø.IPV:L-take.care:IPV

'We used to take good care of each other though.'

UTCBAF13Nov1203:014

c. … *hǫǫ' niɬ'eh hdetk'įą* (T)

hǫǫ' *niɬ-'eh* *hdet-k'įą*
thus RECP.P-with 3PL.S:QUAL:Ø.IPV:D-exercise:IPV

'… in this way they exercise together.' UTCBAF14Jul1805:032

The reciprocal postpositional object prefix also has the allomorph *ɬi-* in the Beaver Creek and Tetlin dialects (537). It is unclear what conditions this variation.

(537) a. *ɫi'eh hdetnih (B)*
ɫi-'eh hdet-nih
RECP.P-to 3PL.S:QUAL:Ø.IPV:D-say:IPV
'they said to each other' UTOLAF10Jul0202:171

b. *ɫits'ą' hihut-heey* (T)
ɫi-ts'ą' h-hut-heey
RECP.P-to 3PL.S-AR:Ø.IPV:D-speak:IPV:NOM
'they talked to each other' UTOLVDN13May2901:043

Like the reflexive prefix, the reciprocal postpositional object prefix triggers a voice/valence prefix change from H- to L- (536b) and from Ø- to D- (536a, 537). See chap. 27.3.2.1.4.

23.4. Other postpositional object prefixes

The areal prefix *hu-* and the indefinite prefix *ch'-* also occasionally serve as postpositional object prefixes.

23.4.1. Areal *hu-*

The areal postpositional object prefix has the form *hu-* (538). It has no allomorphs.

(538) a. *Hutthiit'aagn natihdaag…* (T)
hu-tthiit'aagn na-tih-daag
AR.P-on.top PRMB-INC:Ø.IPFV:1SG.S-D:SG.go:IPV:CUST:NOM
'I would go on top of [the hill]…' UTOLAF09Jun2404:019

b. *Ay tl'aan jah humaagn hats'eht'üh.* (N)
ay tl'aan jah hu-maagn ha-ts'eh-t'üh
and.then here AR-around out-1PL.S:Ø.IPFV:H-cut:IPV
'And then we cut it out around the edge [of the basket].'
UTOLVDN07Aug2001:006

The areal postpositional object prefix can refer to landscape features such as a mountain (538a) or to general areas (538b). Temporal uses of areal *hu-* as a postpositional object are not attested.

23.4.2. Indefinite *ch'-*

The indefinite prefix *ch'-* also may be used as a postpositional object (539). It has no allomorphs.

(539) a. *Shiy shyįį' ch'itah ts'ehxeh ihłįį.* (N)

shiy shyįį' ch'-tah ts'ehxeh ih-łįį

1SG only INDF.P-among girl ø.PFV:1SG.S:ø-be:IPV

'I was the only girl among there [in the family].'

UTOLAF10Jul0901:027

b. *Ch'ittheh k'a hushyaay iin hihteedeeł.* (T)

ch'-ttheh k'a hu-shyaay iin

INDF.P-ahead NEG 3PL.S:AR:NEG.PFV:ø-be.smart:IPV:NEG:NOM PL

hih-tee-deeł

3PL.S-INC:DH.PFV:ø-PL.go:PFV

'The ones who weren't very smart went first.'

UTOLVDN13May2803:028

The referent of *ch'-* in (539a) is known to both speaker and hearer—the speaker talks about her own family here—but it is not important at this point of the narrative. Important is only that the speaker was the only female in her family after her mother's passing. The referent of *ch'-* in (539b) is an unspecific group of people whose identity is not important to the development of the narrative. *Ch'-* as a postpositional object prefix can thus be used when the identity of the postpositional object referent is either unspecific (539b) or not important at the moment (539a).

Postpositions inflected with *ch'-* have a high tendency to become lexicalized as adverbs; see chap. 16.

23.5. Summary

In this chapter postpositional object inflection is described. Postpositional object prefixes are almost identical to the direct object prefixes and to the possessor prefixes. They are affected by very few morphophonemic processes. Postpositional object prefixes cannot co-occur with coreferential noun phrases.

Notes

1. The formal similarity between these sets does not reflect similar behavior. Both functional and morphophonemic differences can be identified as discussed throughout chap. 22, 31, and the present chapter.

24 | Verbal morphology: An overview

Upper Tanana verbs, like those of related languages, are complex in several respects. They are morphologically complex and often represented using a verbal template like the one given in table 24.1. They are morphophonologically complex, since many prefixes fuse tightly. They are also semantically complex because much of the propositional content of any utterance is contained in the verb. As argued by Rice and Saxon (1994) and Rice and Saxon (2005), Dene verbs also have internal syntax. This chapter focuses on the morphological and semantic structure of the verb; verb morphophonemics is described in the chapters describing each position class. Verb-internal syntax is discussed in volume 2.

12	11	10	9	8	7	#	6	5	4	3	2	1	0	-1
Postpositional object	Postposition	Adverbial-derivational	Iterative	Incorporate	Distributive	– Disjunct boundary –	**Pronominal**	<u>Qualifier</u>	**Conjugation**	**Mode**	**Subject**	**Voice/valence**	**Stem**	Suffix

Table 24.1. The Upper Tanana verb, represented as a template

Upper Tanana is overwhelmingly prefixing. Prefixes fall into two domains divided by the disjunct boundary # (24.1). The stem consists historically of a root and aspectual suffixes (Leer 1979), but in Upper Tanana root and aspectual suffixes have fused so tightly that the resulting stems are no longer transparent. The aspectual variation of verb stems is described in chap. 26.

Verbs have enormous derivational potential as described in 24.4. Inflectional properties of verbs are described in 24.5, and discontinuous morphology in 24.3.

24.1. Conjunct and disjunct prefixes

Verbal prefixes fall into two domains: the disjunct domain to the left of # in table 24.1 above and the conjunct domain to the right of #.

This distinction as well as the terms "disjunct" and "conjunct" go back to Li (1946), who observed a phonological boundary within the verb in Dëne Sųłiné (then known as Chipewyan). The concept of the disjunct boundary (# in the template above) was expanded by Kari (1975), drawing on examples from Navajo and Dena'ina (then spelled Tanaina). Kari demonstrated that in both languages, disjunct and conjunct prefixes trigger different allomorphs of several conjunct prefixes. The same observation holds for Upper Tanana; see chap. 28, 29, 30, and 31.

There are additional phonological differences between conjunct and disjunct prefixes. Conjunct prefixes may have the shapes C, V, CV, or V:. They are subject to extensive morphophonemic changes; position classes 4, 3, 2, and 1 in particular tend to coalesce into one monosyllabic portmanteau morpheme (with the form CV, CVC, or CCVC), but many changes also affect morphemes from position 5 and 6. Disjunct prefixes, on the other hand, are minimally of the form CV, but CV, CVC and CV:C are also attested. Most disjunct prefixes are not subject to morphophonemic changes. Finally, there are semantic differences between conjunct and disjunct prefixes. The meaning of many conjunct prefixes is impossible to determine or very vague, while most disjunct prefixes have very clear and well-defined meanings.

24.2. The verb theme

The verb theme is the basic lexical unit of the Upper Tanana verb. It is a discontinuous unit, consisting minimally of a voice/valence-prefix and a verb stem (540). Verb themes are listed with their imperfective stem.

(540) Minimal verb theme
  a. Ø+tsüh 'cry'
  b. D+nah 'work'
  c. Ø+dah 'SG sit'
  d. L+tthiit 'SG run'

Other verb themes contain additional prefixes (541).

(541) More complex themes
  a. n+L+jit 'be scared'

b. O+H+t'iah 'fry O'
c. O+n+H+'i̜h 'see O'
d. O+u+Ø+niik 'grab O, marry O'
e. na#L+xi̜i̜ 'thaw'
f. na#ho+L+nek 'tell story'
g. na#O+G+Ø+ch'ot 'wash O'
h. na#Ø+thät 'SG stand'
i. ni+'eeł#Ø+łeeyh 'set multiple traps'
j. P+i#O+H+'aał 'feed O to P'

The *n*- prefix in (541a, c), the *u*- prefix in (541d), the *ho*- prefix in (541f), and the G (for "gender") in (541g) are qualifiers (position 5). The O in (541b, c, d, g, j) indicates that these verb stems require a direct object. The *na*- prefix in (541e–g) is the iterative prefix (position 9), while *na*- in (541h) is the continuative prefix of position 10. (541i) also contains an adverbial-derivational prefix of position 10 as well as an incorporate of position 9. (541j) is a ditransitive verb theme where the P argument of position 12 is introduced by an incorporated postposition of position 11. The hash sign in themes here and elsewhere refers to the disjunct boundary discussed in 24.1.

Each verb theme is specified for a verb theme category (Kari 1979), an aspectual category with recognizable semantic content. Verb theme categories are described in chap. 25.

24.3. Morpheme order and discontinuous morphology

The template given in table 24.1 consists of fourteen numbered position classes that reflect the very rigid morpheme order of Upper Tanana. Changes of morpheme order are not generally possible.

Discontinuous morphology is extremely common in the Upper Tanana verb. Many of the verb themes listed in (541) are discontinuous. This is demonstrated in table 24.2 by mapping the morphemes making up a sample of verb themes onto the template. Table 24.2 shows that lexical morphemes cluster in three areas of the verb: at the right edge (stem and voice/valence marker), at the left edge of the conjunct zone, and throughout the disjunct zone. This intercalation of thematic, derivational, and inflectional elements in the Dene verb word has long been a problem for morphological theory; see, e.g., Kari (1979), McDonough (1990, 1999), Rice (2000), or Holden (2013) for different approaches to this problem.

12	11	10	9	8	7	#	6	5	4	3	2	1	0	
Postpositional object	Postposition	Adverbial-derivational	Iterative	Incorporate	Distributive	– Disjunct boundary –	Pronominal	Qualifier	Conjugation	Mode	Subject	Voice/valence	Stem	
												D	nah	‘work’
								n				L	jit	‘be scared’
							O					H	t’iah	‘fry o’
							O	n				H	’įh	‘see o’
							O	uu				Ø	niik	‘grab o’
			na									L	xįį	‘thaw’
		na						ho				L	nek	‘tell story’
		na					O	G				Ø	ch’ot	‘wash o’
		sta	na									D	shyah	‘sg go away again’
		ni		’eeł								Ø	łeeyh	‘set multiple traps’
P	i						O					H	’aał	‘feed o to p’

Table 24.2. Some verb themes mapped onto the template

24.4. Derivation

Upper Tanana (and Dene) verbs in general have great derivational potential. Different types of derivation can be distinguished following Kari (1979, 59–62). Most broadly, aspectual, non-aspectual, and superaspectual derivational processes can be distinguished.

24.4.1. Aspectual derivation

Aspectual derivation is achieved using aspectual derivational prefix strings, i.e., sets of discontinuous morphemes affecting not only a verb theme's meaning but also its theme category and thus stem variation. Kari (1979, 28) observes that aspectual prefix strings are mutually exclusive. Aspectual prefix strings are specified for conjugation pattern, (stem) aspect, and verb theme category. This is illustrated in (542). The basic theme is Ø+haayh 'SG go'. This theme belongs to the motion theme category; its basic aspect is the momentaneous. It requires *n*- conjugation prefixes in the imperfective and perfective mode; this is abbreviated as (n, n) throughout.

(542) Derivations of Ø+haayh 'SG go'

	Theme	*Meaning*	*Theme cat.*	*Aspect*	*Cnj.*
a.	Ø+haayh	'SG go'	motion	MOM	(n, n)
b.	ke#Ø+haayh	'SG go up, climb'	motion	MOM	(Ø, aa)
c.	ski#Ø+haayh	'SG go across'	motion	MOM	(n, n)
d.	ni#Ø+haayh	'SG go to point, arrive'	motion	MOM	(n, n)
e.	na+ke#Ø+haah	'SG go around in circle'	motion	REV	(Ø, dh)
f.	łoo#Ø+haał	'SG walk around'	motion	PRMB	(aa, n)

24.4.2. Non-aspectual derivation

Non-aspectual derivations have no effect on a verb theme's aspect, conjugation pattern, or verb theme category. There are many types of non-aspectual derivation such as the formation of subthemes using incorporates (543) or gender prefixes (544), valency-related operations such as causativization (545) and passivization (546), the inceptive perfective (547), the iterative (548), or the addition of certain bound postpositions in position 11 (549).[1]

(543) Incorporation

	Theme	*Meaning*	*Theme cat.*	*Aspect*	*Cnj.*
a.	d+L+xoh	'play noisily'	operative-repetitive$_2$	REP$_2$	(Ø, aa)
b.	thah#d+L+xoh	'PL speak'	operative-repetitive$_2$	REP$_2$	(Ø, aa)
c.	tthe#d+L+xoh	'bark'	operative-repetitive$_2$	REP$_2$	(Ø, aa)

(544) Gender

	Theme	Meaning	Theme cat.	Aspect	Cnj.
a.	Ø+'ąą	'classify CO'	classificatory	NEUT	(Ø, aa)
b.	n+Ø+'ąą	'classify CO' (*n*-GEN)	classificatory	NEUT	(Ø, aa)
c.	d+Ø+'ąą	'classify CO' (*d*-GEN)	classificatory	NEUT	(Ø, aa)
d.	hu+Ø+'ąą	'classify CO' (*hu*-GEN)	classificatory	NEUT	(Ø, aa)

(545) Causativization

	Theme	Meaning	Theme cat.	Aspect	Cnj.
a.	Ø+gąyh	'become dry'	conversive-conclusive	CONCL	(Ø, dh)
b.	O+H+gąyh	'dry O'	conversive-conclusive	CONCL	(Ø, dh)

(546) Passivization

	Theme	Meaning	Theme cat.	Aspect	Cnj.
a.	O+Ø+xąą	'kill PL.O'	operative-durative	DUR	(Ø, aa)
b.	O+D+xąą	'PL.O is killed'	operative-durative	DUR	(Ø, aa)

(547) Inceptive Perfective

	Theme	Meaning	Theme cat.	Aspect	Cnj.
a.	O+Ø+xąą	'kill PL.O'	operative-durative	DUR	(Ø, aa)
b.	O+t+Ø+xąą	'start to kill PL.O'	operative-durative	DUR	(–, dh)

(548) Iterative derivation

	Theme	Meaning	Theme cat.	Aspect	Cnj.
a.	Ø+keeyh	'go by boat'	motion	MOM	(n, n)
b.	na#D+keeyh	'go back by boat'	motion	MOM	(n, n)

(549) Non-aspectual derivation with postposition

	Theme	Meaning	Theme cat.	Aspect	Cnj.
a.	O+Ø+'aał	'eat O'	operative-durative	DUR	(Ø, aa)
b.	P+i#O+H+'aał	'feed O to P'	operative-durative	DUR	(Ø, aa)
c.	n+L+jit	'be scared'	descriptive	NEUT	(Ø, aa)
d.	P+i#n+L+jit	'be scared of P'	descriptive	NEUT	(Ø, aa)

All non-aspectual derivations are highly productive, although not all of them can apply to all verb theme categories. See chap. 25.

24.4.3. Superaspectual derivations

Superaspectual derivations are similar to aspectual derivations in that they require particular conjugation and stem variation patterns, but they differ from them in not being mutually exclusive with aspectual derivational strings (Kari 1979; Axelrod 1993). Upper Tanana has five superaspects of varying productivity. The customary (550) and the progressive (551) are very productive; the distributive (552), the distributive-customary (553), and the errative (554)[2] much less so.

(550) Superaspectual derivation: customary

	Theme	*Meaning*	*Theme cat.*	*Aspect*	*Cnj.*
a.	O+n+H+'įh	'see O'	operative-durative	DUR	(Ø, aa)
b.	O+n+H+'įįk	'see O CUST'	operative-durative	DUR	(Ø, aa)
c.	sta#Ø+haayh	'SG go away'	motion	MOM	(n, n)
d.	sta#Ø+haak	'SG go away CUST'	motion	MOM	(Ø, aa)

(551) Superaspectual derivation: progressive

	Theme	*Meaning*	*Theme cat.*	*Aspect*	*Cnj.*
a.	Ø+keeyh	'go by boat'	motion	MOM	(n, n)
b.	Ø+keeł	'be boating around'	motion	MOM	(aa, –)
c.	sta#Ø+haayh	'SG go away'	motion	MOM	(n, n)
d.	sta#Ø+haał	'SG be going away'	motion	MOM	(aa, –)

(552) Superaspectual derivation: distributive

	Theme	*Meaning*	*Theme cat.*	*Aspect*	*Cnj.*
a.	na#t+n+D+t'ah	'SG fly around'	motion	PRMB	(aa, dh)
b.	na+n#t+n+D+t'ah	'SG flutter around'	motion	PRMB	(Ø, dh)
c.	ta#O+Ø+łe'	'distribute O'	motion	MOM	(Ø, aa)
d.	ta+na#Ø+łeek	'distribute O'	motion	MOM	(Ø, aa)

(553) Superaspectual derivation: distributive-customary

	Theme	*Meaning*	*Theme cat.*	*Aspect*	*Cnj.*
a.	da#O+n+H+tl'uu	'tie a snare closed'	motion	MOM	(Ø, dh)
b.	da(+na)#O+H+tl'uuk	'tie snares CUST'	motion	MOM	(Ø, aa)
c.	ta#O+Ø+łe'	'distribute O'	motion	MOM	(Ø, aa)
d.	ta(+na)#L+shyeek	'distribute O CUST'	motion	MOM	(Ø, aa)

(554) Superaspectual derivation: errative

	Theme	*Meaning*	*Theme cat.*	*Aspect*	*Cnj.*
a.	O+Ø+ttheeł	'chop O'	successive	DUR	(Ø, aa)
b.	O+t+n+Ø+ttheeł	'chop O erroneously'	successive	MOM	(Ø, aa)
c.	sta#Ø+deeł	'PL go away'	motion	MOM	(n, n)
d.	sta#t+n+Ø+deeł	'PL get lost'	motion	MOM	(Ø, dh)

24.5. Inflection

Each verb form must be inflected for subject (either in position 2 or 6) as well as for conjugation and mode (positions 3 and 4). Transitive verbs must also be inflected for direct object (in position 6) and verbs containing a postposition (position 11) for postpositional object (position 12). Crucially there are no nonfinite verb forms.

All forms in (555) illustrate subject, conjugation, and mode inflection; (555b, c, e) illustrate direct object inflection, and (555d, e) illustrate postpositional object inflection.

(555) a. *tihteeł* (N)
tih-teeł
INC:AA.IPV:1SG.S:Ø-SG.sleep:FUT
'I will sleep' UTOLAF10Jul0202:041

b. *jiyh dhįhtsįį* (N)
jiyh dhįh-tsįį
mitten DH.PFV:2SG.S:H-make.SG.O:PFV
'you SG made a mitten' UTOLAF14Apr2501:051

c. *hunįh'įį* (N)
hu-nįh-'įį
3PL.O-3SG.S:QUAL:AA.PFV:H-see:PFV
'she saw them' UTOLAF10Jul0202:185

d. *Sǫ' shinoljidn!* (T)
sǫ' sh-i-nol-jidn
PROH 1SG.P-PP-QUAL:OPT:2SG.S:L-be.scared:OPT
'don't SG be scared of me' UTOLVDN11Aug0802:030

e. *hu'ich'ah'aał* (N)
hu-i-ch'ah-'aał
3PL.P-PP-INDF.O:Ø.IPV:2PL.S:Ø-feed:IPV
'feed PL them (something)' UTOLAF10Jul0901:038

24.6. Verbs without (overt) prefixes

The minimal verb in Upper Tanana consists of four prefixes (conjugation, mode, subject, voice/valence) and one stem. In some instances all four prefixes are phonologically empty; in this case, a peg prefix is added (24.6.1). Some verb stems are used without a peg prefix (24.6.2).

24.6.1. The peg prefix

All obligatory prefixes of a verb form can be phonologically empty: many verbs take a Ø- voice/valence prefix; the imperfective morpheme has the shape Ø- as does the Ø- conjugation prefix; and third-person subject is most commonly also unmarked. Like most related languages, however, Upper Tanana has a requirement that each verb form be at least disyllabic.[3] In verbs with no overt prefixes, this requirement is filled through insertion of a "peg" element /ʔe/- or /ʔi/, represented orthographically as *e-* or *i-*. The peg prefix thus is the overt realization of a portmanteau morpheme consisting of the unmarked third-person singular subject, the Ø- conjugation marker, the Ø-imperfective prefix, and the Ø- voice/valence prefix, glossed as '3SG.S:Ø.IPV:Ø'- (556).

(556) *etsüh* or *itsüh* (N)
e-tsüh
3SG.S:Ø.IPV:Ø-cry:IPV
'[the dog] cried' UTOLVDN14Apr2602:089

This peg prefix is also inserted when the only overt prefix is a voice/valence prefix, which has no syllabic allomorph (557). In these cases the peg prefix always has the form /ʔe/-, never /ʔi/.

(557) a. *łuugn eldeel* (T)
łuugn el-deel
fish 3SG.S:Ø.IPV:L-eat:IPV
'he eats fish' UTOLVDN07Oct2602:049

b. *etnah* (N)
et-nah
3SG.S:Ø.IPV:D-work:IPV
'she is working' UTOLAFMay0807:032

c. *shyi' ehmbiah* (N)
shyi' eh-mbiah
meat 3SG.S:Ø.IPV:H-cook:IPV
'he cooked meat' UTOLVDN10Jul2724:040

24.6.2. Bare stem verbs

There are a few high-frequency verbs that do not contain a peg prefix (558).

(558) a. *"Nday!" nih.* (T)
what say:ipv
'"What!' he said.' UTCBAF13Nov0501:161

b. *Hǫǫ't'eey dį'.* (T)
still do:IPV
'She kept doing that.' UTOLVDN13May2907:013

These and comparable forms are always interpreted as having a third-person subject; the stems indicate that they are imperfective. They are thus finite verb forms even though they violate the disyllabicity constraint.

24.7. Summary

The structure of the Upper Tanana verb can be represented using a templatic model. Two prefix domains can be identified, separated by the disjunct boundary.

The verb theme is the primary lexical unit of the Upper Tanana verb. It consists minimally of a stem and a voice/valence prefix, but many verb themes contain additional "thematic" morphemes. More complex themes may be derived from primary verb themes using aspectual, non-aspectual, or superaspectual derivation.

Verbs are obligatorily inflected for subject, mode, and conjugation. Transitive verbs have to be inflected for direct object, verbs including an incorporated postposition for postpositional object.

Notes

1. Adding other bound postpositions may result in aspectual derivation; see chap. 36.
2. The errative is limited to momentaneous themes. In (554a), the primary theme belongs to the successive verb theme category and requires the durative aspect; for the errative derivation to occur, a momentaneous derivation needs to have occurred first, such as O+Ø+ttheeł (MOM) 'chop O to point'.
3. Exceptions to this are Dena'ina and Ahtna, which do not require peg syllables. The form for 's/he is crying' in those languages is the bare imperfective stem—*chegh* in Dena'ina, *tsagh* in Ahtna.

25 Verb theme categories

The term "verb theme categories" was introduced by Kari (1979) for the description of verb classes in Ahtna and other Dene languages. Verb themes belonging to the same verb theme category share a common structure; e.g., many members of the motion verb theme category such as 'SG run', 'SG go', 'go by boat' are intransitive and have a Ø- voice/valence prefix, while members of the successive verb theme category, such as 'chop O', 'shake O', 'hit O with club', are transitive and have a Ø- or H- voice/valence prefix. Verb theme categories are associated with particular stem aspects that determine its verb stem variation pattern (see chap. 26). The verb theme category of a theme determines its derivational potential (i.e., the types of aspectual derivations it allows) and can predict its conjugation pattern: basic motion themes are in the momentaneous aspect and require an *n-* imperfective and an *n-* perfective, basic operative-durative themes are in the durative aspect and require a Ø- imperfective and an *aa-* perfective, and so on. (The terminology and observations here are based on Kari.)

In his groundbreaking work on Ahtna, Kari (1979, 67) identifies ten major verb theme categories; four of these are active theme categories, six are neuter. The same theme categories can be identified in Upper Tanana, although the languages differ to some degree with respect to which verb themes belong to which theme category.

Kari (1979) focuses largely on morphological criteria (verb stem variation, conjugation patterns, and derivational potential) for the identification of verb theme categories and does not make a strong case for a semantic analysis of these categories, even though he claims that they have a semantic basis (Kari 1979, 66). More detailed semantic analyses of aspectual categories touching on verb theme categories can be found in Axelrod (1993) for Koyukon, Smith (1991) for Navajo, and Wilhelm (2007) for Dëne Sųłiné. The latter author points out (72–73) that the four active verb theme categories identified by Kari are reminiscent of the situation types in the Vendler model, but also notes that this could only be confirmed after rigorous semantic analysis, which has not yet been done. She suggests instead that verb theme categories may be similar to "the noun classes of the Bantu languages: while they have a (perhaps historical) semantic basis, each class also contains a large number of semantically arbitrary members" Wilhelm (2007, 73). Judging from the data presented below, the same is true for Upper Tanana: assignment of verb themes to verb theme categories is to some degree semantically motivated, but many verb themes are not core representatives of the category to which they belong.

25.1. Active versus neuter verb theme categories

The semantic difference between active and static situation types is reflected morphologically as the distinction between active and neuter verb themes. Active themes always have the imperfective prefix Ø- in the imperfective mode, while neuter verbs contain the perfective prefix *į-* in the imperfective mode (559). Neuter imperfective forms are thus morphologically perfective.

(559) a. *etsüh*
e-tsüh
3SG.S:Ø.IPV:Ø-cry:IPV
'he's crying' Kari (1997b)

b. *įįtsia'*
įį-tsia'
3SG.S:AA.PFV:Ø-cry:PFV
'he cried' Kari (1997b)

c. *nsǫǫ*
n-sǫǫ
3SG.S:Ø.PFV:Ø-be.good:IPV
'he is good' Kari (1997b)

d. *įįsu'*
įį-su'
3SG.S:AA.PFV:Ø-be.good:PFV
'he used to be good (but no longer is)' Kari (1997b)

(559a) and (559c) demonstrate the difference between active and neuter verbs in the imperfective mode. While the active verb has a Ø- imperfective and thus contains the peg prefix *e-* in the pre-stem syllable, the neuter verb has the consonantal allomorph *n-* of the perfective prefix *į-*. In the *aa-* perfective forms in (559b) and (559d), the vocalic allomorph of the perfective prefix *į-* is clearly visible, while the conjugation marker is deleted. (The morphophonemics of the conjugation/mode prefixes are described in chap. 29.)

Another indication that neuter imperfective verbs are formally perfective comes from their stem shape. The same classificatory roots are used in a subset of motion verbs (an active theme category) and in classificatory verbs (a neuter verb theme category). (560) contrasts imperfective and perfective forms of the active theme O+Ø+'aayh 'handle compact round object' and the neuter theme Ø+'ąą 'compact round object is in position'. The imperfective neuter stem *'ąą* in (560c) is formally identical to the perfective active stem in (560b). In fact, (560c) is a formally perfective form with an imperfective meaning. This is semantically plausible: if a pack is in a position, as in (560c), then this is the result of an earlier, completed event of putting the object into this position, such as (560b).

(560) a. *xeeł nįį'aayh*
xeeł nįį-'aayh
pack N.IPV:2SG.S:Ø-handle.CO:IPV
'bring SG the pack' Kari (1997b)

b. *xeeł nįį'ąą*
xeeł nįį-'ąą
pack N.PFV:2SG.S:Ø-handle.CO:PFV
'you SG brought the pack' Kari (1997b)

c. *xeeł ee'ąą*
xeeł ee-'ąą
pack 3SG.S:DH.PFV:Ø-classify.CO:IPV
'the pack is there' Kari (1997b)

d. *įį'a'*
įį-'a'
3SG.S:AA.PFV:Ø-classify.CO:PFV
'it used to be there (but no longer is)' Kari (1997b)

With the exception of the presence of the *į-* perfective prefix in semantically imperfective forms, neuter verbs are inflected exactly like active verbs.

Semantically, most neuter themes encode static situations, and most active themes encode active ones. (561) contains a small selection of active themes,

(562) one of neuter themes. All active themes express active situation types, but note that some of the neuter themes do not encode static situations (562d). Most neuter themes are intransitive, but see also (562e).

(561) Active themes

a.	Ø+haayh	'SG go'
b.	O+Ø+ttheeł	'chop O'
c.	D+nah	'work'
d.	d+L+tsiat	'creak'
e.	O+G+H+tl'uuł	'braid O'

(562) Neuter themes

a.	ske#Ø+'ah	'linear entity extends across'
b.	d+L+tth'ih	'PL sit'
c.	Ø+chaa	'be big'
d.	ch'+d+I I+'ą̨ą̨	'sing, be singing'
e.	O+d+Ø+tth'ek	'listen to O'

In the remainder of this chapter, each verb theme category is described briefly with respect to its primary aspectual prefix strings and conjugation patterns, semantics, and derivational potential.

25.2. Active verb theme categories

Active verb theme categories describe active situations. There are four major active verb theme categories: motion, successive, operative, and conversive.

25.2.1. Motion themes

Motion themes describe motion events and can be intransitive or transitive. Kari (1979, 79) points out that this theme category is "the most complex theme category in terms of derivational potential." This is due to a large number of aspectual prefix strings that may apply to motion themes; see chap. 35.2.1. There are also several non-aspectual derivational processes (gender marking, incorporation, inceptive, or causativization) affecting motion themes as well as superaspectual derivations.

The primary aspectual prefix string of motion verbs is the momentaneous aspect, and the conjugation pattern associated with this is (n, n). The momentaneous has punctual, telic meaning. As a result, perfective forms of a motion verb have the meaning 'arrived in the manner specified in the verb theme'—e.g., arrived walking, by boat, or carrying a blanket. Imperfective forms of verb themes in the momentaneous aspect are largely restricted to requests.

There are several lexical pairs of singular versus plural motion themes (563a–d), but not all motion themes are paired like this (563e, f). A subset of transitive motion themes is formed using classificatory stems (563g–j); these are known as classificatory motion themes. Finally, some motion themes contrast regular (563k) with rapid (563l) motion.

(563) Motion themes

a.	Ø+haayh	'SG go'
b.	Ø+deeł	'PL go'
c.	n+Ø+t'ah	'SG fly'
d.	n+Ø+deeł	'PL fly'
e.	ch'+n+L+'įį	'sneak'
f.	Ø+nah	'move nomadically'
g.	O+Ø+'aayh	'handle compact O'
h.	O+Ø+tįįh	'handle long rigid O'
i.	O+H+teeyh	'handle animate O'
j.	O+Ø+deeł	'handle PL.O'
k.	Ø+niik	'move hand'
l.	Ø+ttheet	'move hand quickly'

25.2.1.1. Aspectual derivations of motion themes Primary motion themes such as the ones listed in (563) may conflate NUMBER (singular and plural), FIGURE (e.g., compact versus long versus animate object), and MANNER (e.g., walking versus flying, slow versus rapid motion). Crucially as Kari (1979, 80) points out, PATH is not expressed in primary motion themes; it is added instead by aspectual prefix strings. Each aspectual prefix string consists of derivational material (one or more conjunct or disjunct prefixes), a conjugation pattern, and an aspectual stem suffixation formula. While the primary aspect of motion themes is the momentaneous with (n, n) conjugation prefixes, there are many directional prefix strings requiring different conjugation patterns (564).

(564) Aspectual derivations of motion themes

	Prefix string		*Derived theme*	
a.	ni#(n, n)	'to a point'	nihnįįdeeł	'they arrived'
b.	P+t'a#(Ø, aa)	'catch up with P'	ut'a'įįdeeł	'he caught up with her'
c.	tth'i#(dh, dh)	'straight out'	tth'iteedeeł	'they ran straight out'
d.	łoo#(aa, n)	'here and there'	łoonihshyah	'I went all over'
e.	nake#d(Ø, dh)	'turning around'	nakedeeshyah	'he turned around'
f.	t (Ø, dh)	'starting off'	tidhihshyah	'I started off'

(564a–c) demonstrates derivations in the momentaneous aspect with different conjugation patterns. (564d) illustrates the perambulative (which actually uses two different prefix strings; see chap. 35.2.1.10.1 for more discussion). (564e) shows a derivation in the reversative, and (564f) shows the inceptive derivation. An inclusive inventory of directional prefix strings applying to motion themes is given in chap. 35.2.1; the inceptive derivation is described in chap. 30.6.1.1.

25.2.1.2. Non-aspectual derivations of motion themes In addition to aspectual prefix strings, there are a number of non-aspectual derivations that can apply to motion verbs.

Transitivization (565a, b) or more idiosyncratic derivations (565c) can be indicated by changing the voice/valence prefix from Ø- to H-.

(565) Voice/valence prefix changes in motion themes (I)

	Primary		*Transitivized*	
a.	Ø+deeł	'PL move'	O+H+deeł	'handle PL.O'
b.	Ø+haayh	'SG go'	O+n+Ø+haayh	'SG follows O'
c.	O+n+Ø+'įį	'steal O'	O+n+H+'įį	'hide O'

Transitive motion themes also may be passivized, again using voice/valence prefix changes from Ø- to D- and from H- to L- (566a, b). This change may also result in more idiosyncratic semantics (566c).

(566) Voice/valence prefix changes in motion themes (II)

	Primary		*Passivized*	
a.	O+H+teeyh	'handle animate O'	na#d+L+teeyh	'be born'
b.	O+Ø+łeeyh	'handle PL.O'	ha#uu+d+D+łeeyh	'PL hatch'
c.	O+n+H+'įį	'hide O'	ch'+n+L+'įį	'sneak'

Incorporation often yields highly lexicalized (motion) themes (567).

(567) a. *Ndehde' jah dakįch'ihtalshyaał?* (N)

ndehde' *jah*
when:FUT here

da-kį-ch'-h-tdal-shyaał
up-feet-INDF-3PL.S-INC-QUAL:AA.IPV:L-handle.PL.O.FUT

'When are they going to relax?' (lit. 'kick their feet up')
UTCBVDN13Nov0805:032

b. *yits'ą̈' hatthidalną̈yh* (S)
yi-ts'ą̈' *ha-tthi-dal-ną̈yh*
3SG.S>3SG.P-to out-head-3SG.S:QUAL:AA.PFV:L-CO.move:PFV
'he stared at him' (lit. 'his head moved out toward him') Tyone (1996, 30)

The conjugation pattern and aspect in (567) are determined by the prefix strings; da# 'inside' derives momentaneous themes with (n, n) conjugation prefixes, ha# 'up and out' momentaneous themes with (Ø, aa) conjugation prefixes. The presence of an incorporate has no effect on this.

25.2.1.3. Superaspectual derivations All five superaspectual derivations can apply to motion themes.

The customary superaspect can be applied to all active verb themes. It can combine with all four modes as illustrated in (568), although future and optative customary forms are quite rare. Note also that it can combine with aspectual prefix strings, e.g., sta# (n, n) 'away' in (568a, b) or the perambulative string na#D (aa, dh) in (568c). In that case the conjugation prefix is determined by the superaspect, not by the aspectual prefix string.

(568) a. *.22 eh sta'ihhaak tl'aan...* (N)
.22 eh *sta-ih-haak* *tl'aan*
.22 and away-ø.IPV:1SG.S:ø-SG.go:IPV:CUST and
'I would go out with the .22 and...' UTOLVDN14Apr2602:141

b. *staats'alshyeek* (T)
sta-na-ts'al-shyeek
away-IT-1PL.S:AA.PFV:L-handle.PL.O:PFV:CUST
'we used to put [the pieces of meat] away'
UTOLVDN07Nov2804:006

c. *Hahnaan' mänh k'it natinkeek?* (N)
hah-naan' *mänh* *k'it*
NTRL-across:ALL lake on
na-tin-keek
PRMB-INC:AA.IPV:2SG.S:D-go.by.boat:FUT:CUST
'Are you going to keep paddling around on the lake?'
UTOLAF14Nov2001:016

d. *shiy ch'ittheh natuhdaagn* (N)

shiy ch'ittheh na-tuh-daagn
1SG first PRMB-INC:OPT:1SG.S-D:SG.go:OPT:CUST
'I always want to go in front' UTOLVDN13May2004:100

The progressive superaspect is mostly restricted to motion verb themes in the imperfective. Unlike the punctual momentaneous imperfective (the primary aspect of motion themes), the progressive is durative and atelic. It may co-occur with aspectual prefix strings (569b, c).

(569) a. *naat'ah* (N)

naa-t'ah
3SG.S:QUAL:AA.IPV:Ø-SG.fly:IPV:PROG
'it is flying' comment on UTOLAF08Feb1906:011

b. *taatsąą' dog daanaat'ah* (N)

taatsąą dog da-na-naa-t'ah
raven up:AR up-IT-3SG.S:QUAL:AA.IPV:Ø-SG.fly:IPV:PROG
'the raven was flying around up there' UTOLAF08Feb1906:006

c. *Deeł hadogn sts'akenaat'ah...* (T)

deeł ha-dogn sts'ake-naa-t'ah
crane NTRL-up:AR circling-3SG.S:QUAL:AA.IPV:Ø-SG.fly:IPV:PROG
'The crane was circling overhead...' UTOLAF07Oct2512:020

There are a few optative forms in the progressive (570).[1]

(570) a. *ǫǫhaal* (T)

ǫǫ-haal
OPT:2SG.S:Ø-SG.go:OPT:PROG
'you SG should be walking' UTOLVDN13May2907:086

b. *nttheh uhhaal* (N)

n-ttheh uh-haal
2SG.P-before OPT:2SG.S:Ø-SG.go:OPT:PROG
'I want to walk ahead of you SG' UTOLVDN13May2004:028

The distributive superaspect is characterized by (sometimes) the iterative prefix *na-*,[2] (Ø, dh) conjugation markers, and the distributive stem variation. The distributive seems to be restricted to motion themes (571).

(571) a. *nat'u'ahłe'* (T)
na-t'u-ah-łe'
IT-skin-Ø.IPV:2PL.S:Ø-handle.PL.O:IPV:DSTR
'skin PL them!' UTOLVDN07Nov2803:012

b. *Ay tl'aan hah'ogn ts'ist'e' deltth'ii iin tats'iłe'.* (N)
ay tl'aan *hah-'ogn* *ts'ist'e'*
and.then NTRL-out:AR old.lady
del-tth'ii *iin*
3PL.S:QUAL:DH.PFV:L-PL.stay:IPV:NOM PL
ta-ts'i-łe'
distribute-1PL.S:Ø.IPV:Ø-handle.PL.O:IPV:DSTR
'And then we distributed [the fish] among the old ladies staying there.' UTOLVDN14Apr2602:137

The distributive-customary superaspect also contains the distributive prefix *na-*, but combines with (Ø, aa) conjugation markers and the customary stem variation. In (572b) the distributive prefix triggers a change of voice/valence marker, which is more typical of the iterative prefix. See chap. 34 for more discussion. The distributive-customary superaspect seems to be restricted to motion themes.

(572) a. *daach'ehtl'uuk* (T)
da-na-ch'-eh-tl'uuk
closed-IT-INDF.O-3SG.S:Ø.IPV:H-tie:IPV:DSTR:CUST
'he would set several snares' UTOLVDN13May2801:076

b. *Taahiyįlshyeek.* (N)
ta-na-hii-įl-shyeek
distribute-IT-3PL.S>3PL.O-AA.PFV:L-handle.PL.O:PFV:PFV:DSTR:CUST
'They used to distribute [the meat].' UTCBAF15May0403:006

The errative (described in chap. 30.3.1.1) consists of the prefix string n+D and requires (Ø, dh) conjugation prefixes. Kari (1979, 93) points out that it may not occur in primary themes; instead it is restricted to derived verb themes in the momentaneous (573).

(573) a. *staniłtsenetdeeł* (T)
sta-nił-ts-net-deeł
away-together-1pl.s:inc-qual:dh.pfv:d-pl.go:pfv
'we went astray together, we got lost together'
UTCBAF13Nov0501:073

b. *neeshyah k'ihutnįįttheel* (T)
nee-shyah k'i-hu-tnįį-ttheel
1sg.psr-house split-ar.o-inc:qual:n.pfv-chop:pfv:nom
'you sg, chopping our house apart by mistake'
UTOLVDN13May2805:052

25.2.2. Successive themes

Successive[3] themes describe punctual, repeated events (574). The primary aspect of this verb theme category is the durative, which is characterized by (Ø, aa) conjugation prefixes. All successive themes are transitive. In related languages many successive themes require gender prefixes, but due to the erosion of the gender system in Upper Tanana (see chap. 30), this is not the case here.

(574) Successive themes (durative)
a. O+Ø+ttheeł 'chop o'
b. O+Ø+t'üüt 'cut o'
c. O+Ø+got 'stab o, punch o'
d. O+n+Ø+dät 'spin o, twist o'
e. O+H+xoł 'break o'
f. O+Ø+tał 'shove o with foot'
g. O+G+H+t'oh 'detach, split o'
h. O+H+diih 'shoot repeatedly (at) o'

25.2.2.1. Derivations All successive themes allow a semelfactive derivation, which describes a punctual, not repeated event (575). In the semelfactive derivation, successive themes require in most forms the *i*- conjugation marker; in perfective forms containing an inner subject, they require a *dh*- conjugation marker (see chap. 29).[4]

(575) Successive themes (semelfactive)
a. O+Ø+tthäł 'chop o once'
b. O+Ø+t'üh 'cut o once'
c. O+Ø+got 'stab, punch o once'

d. O+Ø+tał 'shove o with foot once'
e. O+H+dayh 'shoot o'

Successive themes can undergo further derivation using aspectual prefix strings (576).

(576) Aspectual derivations of successive themes

	Primary		*Derived*	
a.	k'i#(Ø, n)	'severing'	tsat k'idįįttheeł	'chop wood!'
b.	k'ii#(n, n)	'hole'	nan' k'iinįįttheeł	'chop a hole into ground!'
c.	tthi#(n, n)	'to pieces'	ch'ichąąg tthinįįttheeł	'she chopped up ribs'
d.	ta#(n, n)	'down'	ts'oo taanįįttheeł	'he chopped down spruce'
e.	ła#t (?, n)	'to chips'	łatnįįttheeł	'he made it into chips'

Kari (1979, 123) points out that many aspectual prefix strings applying to motion themes can be applied to successive themes as well, and, indeed, most of the prefix strings in (576) occur in both verb theme categories.

Successive themes can also take the customary, which is characterized by (Ø, aa) conjugation markers and its own stem variation (577).

(577) a. *Ay ishyiit łuugn iht'üü da'ihdlaak.* (N)

ay *ishyiit* *łuugn* *ih-t'üü*
and there fish Ø.IPV:1SG.S:Ø-cut:IPV:CUST:NOM

da-ih-dlaak
up-Ø.IPV:1SG.S:Ø-classify.PL.O:IPV:CUST

'And there I would cut fish and put it up.'

UTOLVDN14Apr2602:149

b. *Ch'oondah du' tsat huxah k'iidet-tthiił...* (T)

ch'-oondah *du'* *tsat* *hu-xah*
INDF.PSR-older.brother CT 3PL.P-for wood

k'i-na-det-tthiił
severing-IT-3SG.S:QUAL:Ø.IPV:D-chop:IPV:CUST

'The older brother would chop wood for them...'

UTOLVDN14Nov2301:047

25.2.3. Operative themes

Operative themes also require (Ø, aa) conjugation prefixes and describe durative situations. They differ from successive themes in that they do not describe repeated punctual events (such as chopping, hitting, or shooting) but instead describe activities that are sustained over a period of time, such as seeing, having a potlach, or rustling. Operative verb themes may be transitive or intransitive, and some require gender marking although, again, gender marking in Upper Tanana is not very productive. Kari (1979, 124–26) points out that the operative theme category is quite heterogenous; based on their primary aspectual prefix strings he subsumes several different theme categories under the label "operative."

25.2.3.1. Operative-durative themes Operative-durative is the largest operative theme category. These verb themes take the durative as their primary aspectual prefix string. A selection of operative-durative themes is given in (578).[5]

(578) Operative-durative themes

a.	d+Ø+nih	'say'
b.	D+naa 'work'	'work'
c.	O+uu+Ø+sih	'call o's name'
d.	O+n+H+'įį	'see o'
e.	O+Ø+'aał	'eat, chew o'
f.	O+L+deeł	'eat PL o'
g.	O+uu+Ø+keet	'buy o'
h.	ho+Ø+tįįɫ	'be potlatch'
i.	na#ho+L+nek	'tell'
j.	na#O+n+H+ts'ų'	'kiss o'

25.2.3.1.1. Derivations Operative-durative strings have quite limited derivational potential. Valency-affecting derivations are attested for some themes (579).

(579) Voice/valency derivations of operative-durative themes

	Primary		*Derived*	
a.	d+Ø+nih	'say'	O+d+D+nih	'be told'
b.	O+n+H+'įh	'see o'	O+n+L+'įh	'be seen'
c.	O+uu+Ø+sih	'call o's name'	na#d+D+sih	'name oneself'
d.	O+n+H+'įh	'see o'	P+i#O+n+H+'įh	'show o to P'
e.	O+Ø+'aał	'eat, chew o'	P+i#O+H+'aał	'feed o to P'

There is also the derivational string k'e# 'quit', exemplified in (580). This string derives verb themes in the momentaneous aspect; the form in (580) is the only example of this in my corpus.

(580) Other derivations of operative-durative themes

a. O+D+nąą 'drink o' k'e#D+nąą 'quit drinking'

Many operative-durative verb themes allow the customary superaspect (581):

(581) Customary superaspect in operative-durative themes

	Primary		*Derived*	
a.	d+Ø+nih	'say'	O+d+Ø+niik	'customarily say'
b.	O+n+H+'įh	'see o'	O+n+H+'įįk	'customarily see o'
c.	O+H+mbiah	'cook o'	O+H+mbiah	'customarily cook o'
d.	O+Ø+'aał	'eat, chew o'	O+Ø+'iił	'customarily eat o'
e.	O+D+nąą	'drink o'	O+D+niik	'customarily drink o'

25.2.3.2. Operative-onomatopoetic themes The operative-onomotapoetic verb theme category includes, as the name suggests, verb themes describing sounds. These themes share the morphological structure d+L+stem and take (Ø, aa) conjugation prefixes. (582) contains a small selection of operative-onomatopoetic verb themes.

(582) Operative-onomatopoetic themes

a. d+L+theeł 'ring (of a phone, church bell, door bell)'
b. d+L+ts'äł 'crackle (of a fire)'
c. d+L+ch'oh 'hiss, sizzle'
d. d+L+ts'iat 'creak'
e. d+L+tl'iat 'rustle'

25.2.3.2.1. Derivations Kari (1979, 133) reports a semelfactive derivation possible for some operative-onomatopoetic verb themes in Ahtna, but no examples of this can be found in Upper Tanana. No other derivations are attested for this verb theme category.

25.2.3.3. Operative-repetitive$_1$ themes Kari (1979, 135–39) recognizes two operative-repetitive verb theme categories. The differentiation is due to different stem suffixation formulas (see chap. 26.2.1). Like all operative verb themes, the operative-repetitive$_1$ and the operative-repetitive$_2$ take (Ø, aa) conjugation prefixes. Operative-repetitive$_1$ verb themes have invariable stems (583).

(583) Operative-repetitive$_1$ themes

a. d+L+koh 'cough'
b. d+L+xoh 'play (noisily)'
c. P+i#D+nayh 'know p'
d. D+shyiiyh 'breathe'

Kari (1979, 136) presents a longer list of operative-repetitive$_1$ themes in Ahtna, but I have not been able to find cognates for most of them in Upper Tanana. The dearth of operative-repetitive$_1$ themes in Upper Tanana may suggest that this theme category has merged with another one (given the semantics and morphology, the operative-onomatopoetic category discussed in 25.2.3.2 is a likely candidate for such a merger.)

25.2.3.3.1. Derivations At least some operative-repetitive$_1$ themes allow a customary derivation (584). No other derivations are attested.

(584) *Dzii::n uudih t'eey huh dzelxuu…* (T)
dziin uudih t'eey huh dzel-xuu
day all ADVZR ? 1PL.S:QUAL:Ø.IPV:L-play:IPV:CUST
'All day long we would play…' UTOLAF09Jun2901:012

25.2.3.4. Operative-repetitive$_2$ themes Operative-repetitive$_2$ verb themes differ from operative-repetitive$_1$ ones with respect to stem variation: operative-repetitive$_1$ stems are invariable; operative-repetitive$_2$ have suffixed stems in the imperfective, future, and optative modes and unsuffixed perfective stems (see chap. 26.2.1). Semantically they are similar. A few themes from this category are given in (585). The other themes listed in Kari (1979, 137–38) are not attested in Upper Tanana.

(585) Operative-repetitive$_2$ themes
a. O+uu+d+H+keet 'ask o'
b. ch'+L+dzüh 'dance'
c. na#L+shyiit 'rest'

25.2.3.4.1. Derivations There are no derivations attested.

25.2.3.5. Operative-reversative themes This very small group of verb themes is again defined over its stem suffixation formula (see chap. 26.2.1). Like all operative themes, operative-reversative themes take (Ø, aa) conjugation prefixes. As Kari (1979, 140) observes, they describe processes involving a change of state. The list of operative-reversative themes in (586) is inclusive.

(586) Operative-reversative themes
a. O+H+theeh 'tan o'
b. O+d+l+dįįh 'learn o'
c. na#L+xįį 'melt, thaw'
d. na#D+shyee 'heal'

25.2.3.5.1. Derivations No derivations are attested.

25.2.3.6. Operative-persistive themes Operative-persistive themes describe "reversible, back-and-forth action" (Kari 1979, 141). The persistive is a productive aspect of motion verbs in related languages, but does not seem to exist in Upper Tanana. There are two operative-persistive themes in Upper Tanana (587).

(587) Operative-persistive themes
  a. dzi#Ø+teeyh 'SG dances a mourning dance'
  b. dzi#L+shyeeyh 'PL dance a mourning dance'

25.2.3.6.1. Derivations These verb themes allow the customary derivation (588).

(588) *Ay eł dzihelshyiih.* (T)
  ay eł *dzi-hel-shyiih*
  and.then mourn-3PL.S:Ø.IPV:L-PL.mourn.dance:IPV:CUST
  'And then they would do the mourning dance.'
  UTOLAF11Aug0207:004

25.2.4. Conversive themes

Conversive themes are durative and have a natural completion or end point (see, however, Wilhelm [2007] for a different view). Morphologically they are characterized by (Ø, dh) conjugation prefixes. There are transitive and intransitive conversive themes. The conversive theme category is complex with several subcategories distinguished by stem suffixation patterns.

25.2.4.1. Conversive-conclusive themes The largest subcategory of the conversive theme category is the conversive-conclusive group. Their primary aspectual prefix string is the conclusive aspect. The actions and events in (589) all take time but have a natural completion point.

(589) Conversive-conclusive themes
  a. O+H+tsayh 'make SG.O'
  b. O+dh+H+xeh 'kill SG.O'
  c. na#D+tl'uu 'get dressed'
  d. O+H+tl'uuł 'braid O'
  e. O+H+t'iah 'fry O'
  f. Ø+tsanh 'defecate'
  g. n+L+tänh 'freeze'

In his discussion of conversive-conclusive verb themes in Ahtna, Kari (1979, 150) notes that some of them have two perfective forms: one in the conclusive aspect, with an *s*- conjugation marker (the cognate of Upper Tanana *dh*-) and one in the durative aspect, with a *gh*- conjugation prefix (the cognate of Upper Tanana *aa*-). In those verb themes ('defecate, string beads, fart, braid, urinate, vomit, boil, caulk'), the durative perfective form then describes a repeatedly performed action. This is illustrated in (590); note that the Ahtna forms have been rendered in the practical orthography, not in the phonemic orthography used in Kari (1979).

(590) Ahtna conversive themes with two perfective forms

a. *z-lets*
3SG.S:S.PFV:Ø-urinate:PFV
'he urinated' Kari (1979, 148)

b. *ghi-lets*
3SG.S:GH.PFV:Ø-urinate:PFV
'he repeatedly urinated' Kari (1979, 150)

In Upper Tanana, this does not seem to be the case. The verb themes Ø+łüh 'urinate', na#D+kuyh 'vomit', and O+H+mbiat 'boil o' in Upper Tanana allow only the *aa*- perfective as shown in (591) (and might thus better categorized as operative-durative, rather than conversive-conclusive verb themes), while the verb themes H+tsanh 'defecate', O+n+Ø+'iah 'string O', H+jeet 'fart', Ø+tl'iit 'fart', and O+Ø+dzeek 'caulk o' all require the *dh*-perfective.

(591) *į̨łia'*
į̨-łia'
3SG.S:AA.PFV:Ø-urinate:PFV
'he urinated' Kari (1997b)

25.2.4.1.1. Derivations Conversive-conclusive themes may take the customary superaspect (592).

(592) a. *Łuugn xah dahdzał guuy chih ts'ehtsiik...* (T)
łuugn xah dahdzał guuy chih ts'eh-tsiik
fish for rack tiny also 1PL.S:Ø.IPV:H-make.SG.O:IPV:CUST
'We would make a tiny drying rack for the fish...'
UTOLAF09Jun2901:011

b. *Hutsay iin nts'ąą' ch'ihdhehxeek tah…* (N)

hu-tsay	*iin*	*nts'ąą'*
3PL.PSR-grandfather	PL	how

ch'-h-dheh-xeek	*tah*
INDF.O-3PL.S-QUAL:Ø.IPV:H-kill.SG.O:IPV:CUST	when

'When their grandfathers kill [a moose], …'

UTOLAF12Jul1203:081

Other than that, conversive-conclusive themes are not derivationally productive.

25.2.4.2. Conversive-reversative themes Conversive-reversative themes are characterized by a different stem suffixation formula than conversive-conclusive themes (see chap. 26.2.1). Semantically they are similar to conversive-conclusive themes in that they are durative and telic (593).[6]

(593) Conversive-reversative themes

a. n+Ø+shyeeh/shyąą 'grow'

b. Ø+łee 'become'

25.2.4.2.1. Derivations These themes allow the customary superaspect (594).

(594) *Xay nootet-łeek…* (N)

xay	*na-hu-tet-łeek*
winter	IT-AR.S-INC:DH.PFV:D-become:PFV:CUST

'It would become winter again...' UTOLVDN13May2003:023

The theme in (593a) also allows a transitive derivation O+n+H+shyeeh 'raise o' (595).

(595) *Doo ts'inuhshyee yuunąy ay itnahshyeeh!* (T)

doo	*ts'-nuh-shyee*
who	IMPSL.S-QUAL:OPT:H-raise:OPT

y-uu-nąy

3SG.S>3SG.O-CON:Ø.PFV:Ø-want:IPV:NOM

ay	*i-tnah-shyeeh*
3SG	3SG.S>3SG.O-INC:QUAL:AA.IPV:H-raise:FUT

'Whoever wants to raise him, will raise him!'

UTOLAF13May2403:067

25.2.4.3. Conversive-continuative themes In Ahtna conversive-continuative themes are characterized by the presence of the *n*- distributive prefix in addition to continuative stem variation. (596) compares Ahtna and Upper Tanana themes (Ahtna themes are taken from Kari [1979, 154] and have been rendered in the practical orthography) and demonstrates that in some themes in Upper Tanana, the distributive prefix has simply disappeared (596a) whereas it has been replaced by the iterative prefix *na*- (596b, c) in others.

(596) Ahtna and Upper Tanana conversive-continuative themes

	Ahtna	*Upper Tanana*	
a.	n#O+Ł+k'aak	O+H+k'aak	'filet o'
b.	n#O+Ł+'ał	na#O+H+'oł	'butcher o'
c.	n#ko+Ł+'aen	na#ho+H+'įį	'sense a spirit'

25.2.4.3.1. Derivations No derivations of these themes are attested in my corpus.

25.2.4.4. Conversive-repetitive$_2$ themes There is one conversive-repetitive$_2$ verb theme attested in Upper Tanana (597). (There are two in Ahtna, but one of them does not seem to occur in Upper Tanana.) Conversive-repetitive$_2$ themes take the stem variation typical of repetitive$_2$ aspect, but the conversive conjugation pattern.

(597) Conversive-repetitive$_2$

a. O+n+Ø+'įį 'steal o'

25.2.4.4.1. Derivations The customary stem of this verb theme is indistinguishable from the regular stem.

25.3. Neuter verb theme categories

The term "neuter" in Dene linguistics includes a large number of verb themes describing static situations, i.e., stable situations without internal change holding for a period of time (Smith 1991, 37). Descriptions differ in the number of neuter verb theme categories they posit. Kari (1979) distinguishes six neuter verb theme categories in Ahtna based on conjugation patterns, semantic properties, and derivational potential, as does Rice (1989) in her description of Slave, while Axelrod (1993) argues in favor of distinguishing only three neuter theme categories, several of which have multiple subcategories. I follow Kari and Rice here.

25.3.1. Extension themes

Alone among the neuter themes, extension themes require (n, aa) conjugation prefixes in their primary derivation. They describe the linear arrangements of entities in space (598).

(598) Extension themes

- a. Ø+'a' 'long rigid o extends'
- b. L+tąy 'trail extends'
- c. Ø+łąyh 'current flows'
- d. d+H+tąą 'body of water lies'
- e. H+ts'ayh 'be windy'
- f. H+chąą 'rain'
- g. H+shyüh 'snow'
- h. d+L+güh 'be forked'

Primary extension themes are intransitive and impersonal, as suggested by the glosses in (598).

25.3.1.1. Derivations Extension themes vary in their productivity. (598a–c) are extremely productive, (598d) not nearly as much. Many aspectual prefix strings applying to motion themes can apply to extension themes as well (599); see chap. 35.2.1 for more discussion.

(599) Aspectual derivation of extension themes

	Prefix string		*Derived theme*	
a.	ni#(n, aa)	'to a point'	utsįį ninįį'ah	'her scent extends up to here'
b.	ski#(n, aa)	'across'	tl'oh skinįį'ah	'grass extends across [the trail]'
c.	ha#(n, aa)	'up and out'	k'ąy' hadįį'ah	'willow was sticking up and out'
d.	ta#(n, aa)	'upland'	łat ta'įį'ah	'smoke extended upland'

Extension themes frequently take incorporates (600); (600a) contains two extension themes with incorporate.

(600) a. *Hanashyig that ts'ist'e' niigot-'įį'ah ay tl'aan haananhųh'ah.*

ha-na-shyig *that* *ts'ist'e'*
ADJC-MED-down:ALL that old.woman

ni-na-got-įį-'ah *ay* *tl'aan*
TERM-IT-knee-3SG.S:AA.PFV:Ø-LO.extend:PFV and then

ha-na-nan-hųh-'ah
out-IT-back-AR.O:3SG.S:AA.PFV:H-LO.extend:PFV

'Down there that old woman was kneeling and she was humpbacked.' UTCBAF13Nov0501:225

b. *Uts'ą̈' dziitidhak- 'ah.* (N)
u-ts'ą̈' *dzii-t-dhak-'ah*
3SG.P-toward hearing-INC-DH.PFV:1SG.S:H-extend:LO:IPV
'I extend my hearing toward him, I listen to him.'
UTOLAF13May2801:061

25.3.2. Neuter verb themes with (dh, aa) conjugation prefixes

Several neuter verb theme categories take (dh, aa) conjugation prefixes in their primary derivations. These include the classificatory neuter themes, positional neuter themes, and stative themes. Axelrod (1993, 127), who subsumes these three categories under the label "stative", states that "the *l*[7] neuter-primary stative themes are used to imply the achievement of a particular position or condition." For example, classificatory and positional neuter themes describe the state that holds after a motion event has been completed, while a stative theme (such as 'be cold' or 'be bent') also describes the outcome of a process such as a weather change or the act of bending something. Axelrod (1993) contrasts this with neuter themes with (Ø, aa) conjugation prefixes in their primary derivation (see 25.3.3) that describe inherent qualities of an entity, i.e., qualities that are not the result of a prior action.

25.3.2.1. Classificatory themes Classificatory neuter themes are paired with classificatory motion themes (see 25.2.1 above). The classificatory neuter theme category is a small theme category containing only the verb themes in (601); these themes classify their argument by FIGURE, i.e., properties such as shape (compact versus long), rigidity (rigid versus flexible) and enclosedness, as well as ANIMACY and NUMBER. A semantic analysis of this system in Western Apache can be found in Basso (1990); the noun classification of Upper Tanana is described in volume 2 of this grammar. (601) pairs the classificatory neuter themes with the corresponding transitive motion themes. Classificatory themes take (dh, aa) conjugation prefixes in their primary derivation.

(601) Classificatory neuter and motion themes

	Neuter		*Motion*	
a.	Ø+'ąą	'CO is in position'	O+Ø+'aayh	'handle CO'
b.	Ø+tąą	'LRO is in position'	O+Ø+tįįyh	'handle LRO'
c.	Ø+kąą	'OOC is in position'	O+Ø+kaayh	'handle OOC'
d.	Ø+niik	'FO is in position'	O+Ø+niiyh	'handle FO'
e.	Ø+tįį	'AO is in position'	O+Ø+teeyh	'handle AO'
f.	Ø+dlah	'PL.O or RO is in position'	O+Ø+łeeyh	'handle PL.O or RO'

The inventory of classificatory verbs in Upper Tanana is unusually small. Related languages usually have verb themes classifying mushy objects (see, e.g., Tenenbaum [1978, 134] for Dena'ina, Kari [1979, 157] for Ahtna, Rice [1989, 903] for Slave, or Cook [2004, 243] for Dëne Sųłiné); Kari (1979, 157) additionally identifies a verb theme identifying burning objects and Cook (2004, 243) one identifying loose textured objects. Similar verb themes do not seem to exist in Upper Tanana.

25.3.2.1.1. Derivations Like their paired motion themes, classificatory themes have great derivational potential, allowing, for example, a transitive neuter derivation with the meaning 'have O in position, keep O in position' (602; see also chap. 27.3.1.2). Note that (602a, b) are derived with an H- voice/valence prefix, while (602c) is derived with a Ø- voice/valence marker.

(602) a. *Ishyiit tah dahdzäł choh da'eh'ąą stsay.* (N)
ishyiit tah dahdzäł choh da-eh-'ąą
then among rack big up-3SG.S:DH.PFV:H-classify.CO:IPV
s-tsay
1SG.PSR-grandfather
'Back then, my grandpa had a big fish rack.'
UTOLAF12Jul1203:102

b. … *üh ti'ehtąą.* (S)
üh ti-eh-tąą
dipnet underwater-3SG.S:DH.PFV:H-classify.LRO:IPV
'… he was holding a dipnet in the water.' ANLC4122a:145

c. *Sdzeey shyiit dhihdlah, shtthi' chih.* (N)
s-dzeey shyiit dhih-dlah sh-tthi'
1SG.PSR-heart inside DH.PFV:1SG.S:Ø-classify.PL.O:IPV 1SG.PSR-head
chih
too
'I kept [these words] in my heart, in my head too.'
UTOLAF13May2804:015

Classificatory verb themes also allow aspectual derivations, e.g., (602a, b) above.

Classificatory verbs also take the *i-* transitional aspectual prefix string, which is characterized by an *i-* conjugation prefix in the perfective. The meaning of neuter classificatory verbs in the transitional aspect is 'to remain, to be left behind' (603). This derivation seems to be quite rare in Upper Tanana.

(603) *chįį'aay ii'a'*
chįį'aay ii-'a'
axe 3SG.S:I.PFV:Ø-classify.CO:PFV
'the axe was left, remained' Kari (1997b)

25.3.2.2. Positional themes The positional themes differ from the classificatory ones in that they are not paired with a classificatory motion. Like classificatory themes, they indicate that their only argument is in position and require (dh, aa) conjugation prefixes (604).

(604) Positional themes

a.	Ø+dah	'SG sit'
b.	d+L+tth'ih	'PL sit'
c.	Ø+tįį	'SG sleep'
d.	H+tiat	'PL sleep'
e.	ta#n+L+'ah	'sit'

25.3.2.2.1. Derivations Positional themes have more limited derivational potential than classificatory themes. (605b, c) illustrate aspectual prefix strings that also occur in motion themes (where, however, they take different conjugation markers; see chap. 35 for details). (605d, e) are both derived using incorporates. The derived theme in (605e) is a motion theme.

(605) Derivations of positional themes

	Prefix string		*Derived theme*	
a.	da# (dh, aa)	'up high'	da'eedah	'she sat [on chair]'
b.	ta# (dh, aa)	'in water'	tadeltth'ih	'they sat in the water'
c.	dzii# d+D (?, ?)	'listening'	dziidishdah	'I sit listening'
d.	ni+tl'a#d+D (?, ?)	'on buttocks'	nitl'adetdah	'he sat down'

Some positional theme allow also non-aspectual derivations such as transitivization (606).

(606) a. *dadhihdah* (N)
da-dhih-dah
up-DH.PFV:1SG.S:Ø-SG.sit:IPV
'I am sitting [in a chair]' UTOLAF15Dec0701:036

b. *Ts'iiniin gaay naat dadhakdah.* (N)
ts'iiniin gaay *naat* *da-dhak-dah*
baby across:PNCT up-DH.PFV:1SG.S:H-SG.sit:IPV
'I have the baby sitting [in a chair] across [the room].'
UTOLAF15Dec0701:039

While Kari (1979, 163) reports that positional themes in Ahtna can take the transitional derivation, this is not attested in my corpus.

25.3.2.3. Stative The stative verb theme category is negatively defined. Verbs belonging to this verb theme category also take (dh, aa) conjugation prefixes but are neither classificatory nor positional. Semantically they do not describe location or position of entities but temporary qualities (607).

(607) Stative themes
a. n+Ø+k'ät 'be cold'
b. n+L+kon' 'be hot'
c. n+Ø+gon' 'be lukewarm'
d. H+ts'iik 'be sick'
e. n+Ø+xäł 'be crazy'
f. d+Ø+k'an' 'be burning'
g. ch'+d+h+'ąą 'be singing'
h. d+L+'ia 'wear footwear'
i. ch'+t+n+l+'įį 'hide oneself'

25.3.2.3.1. Derivations Another difference between classificatory and positional verb themes, on the one hand, and stative themes, on the other, is the limited derivational potential of the latter Kari (1979, 164). Some stative themes allow a transitional derivation, as shown in (608), but not all of them do (e.g., n+Ø+xäł 'be crazy' or d+Ø+k'an' 'be burning' do not).

(608) a. *huniik'üü'*
hu-nii-k'üü'
AR.S-QUAL:I.PFV:Ø-be.cold:PFV
'it got cold' Kari (1997b)

b. *hunilkǫǫ'*
hu-nil-kǫǫ'
AR.S-QUAL:I.PFV:L-be.warm:PFV
'it became warm, hot' Kari (1997b)

Some stative themes have paired transitive themes with a causative meaning. These can be active (609a) or also neuter (609b).

(609) a. *Isabel shnįhxał.* (T)
Isabel sh-nįh-xał
Isabel 1SG.O-3SG.S:QUAL:AA.PFV:H-drive.crazy:PFV
'Isabel drove me crazy.' UT Notebook #2, 25

b. *Kon' cho::::h hihdehkan'.* (T)
kon' choh h-deh-k'an'
fire big 3PL.S-QUAL:DH.PFV:H-be.burning:IPV
'They had a big fire going.' UTOLVDN13May2909:030

25.3.3. Neuter verbs with (Ø, aa) conjugation markers

There are two neuter verb theme categories with (Ø, aa) conjugation prefixes: dimensional and descriptive verb themes. Both express property concepts. These similarities lead Axelrod (1993) to subsume them into one theme category, "descriptive," which has two subcategories. Kari (1979) instead distinguishes two major theme categories with (Ø, aa) conjugation pattern: dimensional themes, which can take comparative derivational strings, and descriptive themes, which cannot.

25.3.3.1. Dimensional The class of dimensional verb themes can be defined semantically as well as morphologically. Semantically it includes themes expressing inherent property concepts such as size, shape, quality, or color (Kari Kari 1979, 167). Morphologically, dimensional themes differ from other neuter themes in that they alone take the comparative derivational prefix strings (see 25.3.3.1.1.1).

Two groups of dimensional themes can be identified. (610a–e) all seem to contain a *d-* qualifier; (610f–k) do not contain this prefix but sometimes contain a gender prefix instead.[8]

(610) Dimensional themes
a. d#H+tayh 'be strong'
b. (d+)L+mbaa 'be grey'
c. (d+)L+gayh 'be white'
d. d+D+sąy 'be black'
e. d+D+shyįǫt 'be furry'
f. D+xąą 'be moldy'
g. (G)+Ø+sǫǫ 'be good'

h. (G+)Ø+düü 'be heavy'
i. (G+)Ø+tsuul 'be small'
j. (G+)Ø+tsiin 'be few'
k. L+tlät 'be slippery'

Kari (1979, 167–68) observes that in Ahtna as well as Dena'ina, dimensional themes have a *gh-* prefix that he identifies as a conjugation marker (cognate to the conjugation marker *aa-* in Upper Tanana). It is unclear whether the same is true for Upper Tanana because of the morphophonemics of the *aa-* conjugation marker, which disappears before Ø- and H- voice/valence markers in all morphologically perfective forms (see chap. 29.2.2). In these forms only the perfective prefix *į-* is visible with its consonantal allomorph *n-* (611). I treat these forms as Ø-perfective throughout this grammar.

(611) Dimensional themes with Ø- or H- voice/valence prefix: Ø- or *aa-* conjugation prefix

a. nsǫǫ 'it is good'
b. ndüü 'it is heavy'
c. ts'įįtsuul 'we are small'
d. dįhtayh 'he is strong'
e. įhthįą 'it is numb'

Dimensional themes containing a D- voice/valence marker) have an *aa-* conjugation marker in the imperfective (612).

(612) Dimensional themes with *aa-* conjugation prefix

a. dat-sąy 'it is black'
b. atchįǫ 'it (skin) is soft'
c. atxąą' 'it is moldy'

In dimensional themes with an L- voice/valence prefix, neither the conjugation marker nor the perfective prefix are detectable in any form (613). This suggests that these verbs are morphologically Ø- perfective in their imperfective forms, since the *aa-* conjugation prefix is usually visible before an L- voice/valence prefix (see also chap. 29.2.2).

(613) Dimensional themes with L- voice/valence prefix: Ø- or *aa-* conjugation prefix

a. delgayh 'it is white'
b. deldliat 'it is (light) blue/green, bright'
c. elk'ah 'he is fat'
d. hultlät 'it is slippery'

Like all neuter verb themes, dimensional themes require the *aa-* conjugation prefix in the perfective (614). Perfective dimensional themes occur only rarely, which may be due to the fact that some are formally indistinguishable from imperfective forms, e.g., *ts'į̨įtsuul* 'we are/were small' can be analyzed as a perfective or as an imperfective form.

(614) a. *That's why dineh iin neenaattheh dą' hį̨įsu'!* (N)

that's	*why*	*dineh*	*iin*	*nee-naattheh*	*dą'*
that's	why	human	PL	1PL.P-before	at:PST

hį̨į-su'
3PL.S:AA.PFV:Ø-be.good:PFV
'That's why people long before us used to be good!'
UTOLVDN10Jul2602:047

b. *į̨įdüü'*
į̨į-düü'
3SG.S:AA.PFV:Ø-be.heavy:PFV
'it was heavy' Kari (1997b)

25.3.3.1.1. Derivations Dimensional themes can take several derivations.

25.3.3.1.1.1. Comparative derivation The comparative derivation is the primary diagnostic for dimensional themes. There are several comparative prefix strings as listed in (615); "__" in those entries stands for the stem as well as for the translation of the verb theme.

(615) Comparative prefix strings

a. P+ch'ashyiit##H+__ 'be more __ than P'
b. P+ch'anoo'##H+__ 'be a lot more __ than P'
c. P+k'e'##H+__ 'be less __ than P'
d. P+k'eh##H+__ 'be as __ as P'
e. k'a(t'eey) su'##H+__ 'be not very __'
f. nts'ąą'##H+__? 'how __ is S?'
g. da#t+H+__ 'how __ S is!' (admiringly)

Similar comparative derivations are attested in related languages, see, e.g., Morice (1932, 148) for Dakelh, Kari (1979, 171), or Rice (1989, 930) for Slave. An admirative prefix string comparable to (615f) is reported only for Dakelh. More information on comparison can be found in volume 2.

25.3.3.1.1.2. Transitional derivation Dimensional themes also may take the transitional derivational string (with the meaning 'to become __'). Transitional forms require the transitional stem variation formula and are further characterized by the presence of the *i-* conjugation marker in the imperfective; in the perfective, some verb themes take a *i-* conjugation prefix while others take *dh-*. The reason for this variation is not understood at this time; there are even a few verbs that allow both patterns (see, e.g., the forms in [616c] and [617c], which appear to be interchangeable). The transitional derivation also often changes the voice/valence marker to D- (e.g., in [616b] and [617a], both of which require L- in their primary derivation). Again, it is not clear what causes this change.

(616) a. *iisu'*
ii-su'
3SG.S:I.PFV:Ø-be.good:PFV
'she became good' Kari (1997b)

b. *ditdliat*
dit-dliat
3SG.S:QUAL:I.PFV:D-be.blue:PFV
'it turned blue' Kari (1997b)

c. *dilgayh*
dil-gayh
3SG.S:QUAL:I.PFV:L-be.white:PFV
'it turned white' UTOLVDN08Mar1304:005

(617) a. *dett'iił*
det-t'iił
3SG.S:QUAL:DH.PFV:D-be.red:PFV
'it turned red' Kari (1997b)

b. *det-sį̨į'*
det-sį̨į'
3SG.S:QUAL:DH.PFV:D-be.black:PFV
'it turned black' Kari (1997b)

c. *delgayh*
del-gayh
3SG.S:QUAL:DH.PFV:L-be.white:PFV
'it turned white' Kari (1997b)

The transitional derivation appears to be a lot less productive than in other languages. Kari (1997b) contains only a handful of examples beyond those shown in (616) and (617), and only one form (616c) occurs in my corpus.

25.3.3.2. Descriptive The descriptive theme category contains themes with (Ø, aa) conjugation prefixes that do not allow the comparative prefix strings. In his study of Ahtna verb theme categories Kari (1979, 174) considers this theme category to be semantically not very coherent; Axelrod (1993, 132), on the other hand, finds that in Koyukon most descriptive themes are "adjectival," i.e., express a property concept. A selection of descriptive themes is given in (618).

(618) Descriptive themes
a. L+tl'ik 'be swift'
b. na#i+Ø+thät 'stand'
c. d+Ø+tsįį 'be hungry'
d. H+ts'iik 'be sick'
e. L+tsįį 'seem, be like'
f. Ø+łįį 'be'
g. Ø+t'eh 'be a certain way'
h. ts'a+nii#L+t'eh 'be mad'
i. d+L+dąyh 'know a skill'
j. L+choh 'have hurt feelings'
k. n+L+jit 'be scared'
l. hu+Ø+shyąą 'be wise'
m. O+n+Ø+thänh 'think, want o'
n. O+d+i+Ø+tth'ek 'listen to o'

The properties expressed by descriptive verbs can range from physical (618a–e) to psychological states (618e–n).

25.3.3.2.1. Derivations Most descriptive themes have very limited derivational potential. Some allow the transitional derivation described for dimensional verb themes in 25.3.3.1.1.2; only the *dh-* perfective appears to be used (619).

(619) a. *U'aat mbaa huushya'...* (N)

u-'aat *mb-aa* *huu-shya'*
3SG.PSR-wife 3SG.P-for 3SG.S:QUAL:DH.PFV:Ø-become.smart:PFV
'His wife caught on to him...' (lit. 'became smart for him')
UTOLVDN10Jul2713:011

b. *Eh dhakts'iik.* (N)

eh *dhak-ts'iik*
and DH.PFV:1SG.S:H-be.sick:PFV
'And I got sick, was sick.' UTOLVDN14Apr2602:002

In some cases the transitional forms with *dh-* perfective seem to have replaced the primary neuter forms. While *akts'iik* 'I am sick' can be elicited, all naturally occurring forms of this verb are in the transitional aspect, even where a static situation is being described, as in (620a). The same is true for L+tsįį 'seem, be like' (620b).

(620) a. ... *nithoo t'eey u'aat chih ehts'iik.* (T)

nithoo *t'eey* *u-'aat* *chih* *eh-ts'iik*
long.time ADVZR 3SG.PSR-wife too 3SG.S:DH.PFV:H-be.sick:PFV
'... his wife was sick for a long time.'
UTOLVDN14Nov2301:014

b. *Shiy du' nidanh k'eh dhagntsiin?* (N)

shiy *du'* *nihdanh* *k'eh* *dhagn-tsiin*
1SG CT brainless like DH.PFV:1SG.S:L-be.like:PFV:NOM
'Do I look like I have no brain?' UTOLAF15May0703:022

25.4. Summary

In this chapter the verb theme categories were briefly introduced. Each verb theme category is characterized by particular semantic and morphological properties. Semantic properties include typical meaning as well as primary aspect. Morphological properties include conjugation pattern, stem suffixation formula (determined by aspect), and derivational potential.

There are four active verb theme categories: motion, successive, operative, and conversive. While the motion and successive verb theme categories are relatively homogeneous, the operative and conversive verb theme categories can be further split into several minor verb theme categories.

There are six neuter verb theme categories: extension, classificatory, positional, stative, dimensional, and descriptive. Each neuter verb theme category is relatively homogeneous, and no minor theme categories can be identified.

On a comparative note, the Upper Tanana verb theme category system closely resembles that of Ahtna as described by Kari, which supports his claim that the verb theme category system was already present in Proto-Dene (Kari 1979, 7). But while the *systems* are fundamentally similar in the two languages, they differ with respect to many details. Even though the verb theme categories are semantic classes, they have sufficiently fuzzy boundaries to allow categorization of a particular verb theme in one verb theme category in, say, Ahtna, but in a different category in Upper Tanana. Specific morphological developments such as the reanalysis of the distributive prefix in Upper Tanana result in the partial loss of distinctions that require this prefix, and phonological developments obscure stem suffixation patterns, which may lead to the recategorization of individual themes or even to a merger between subtheme categories.

Notes

1. I am grateful to Bill Poser for asking me whether such forms are possible: clearly they are!
2. This is unusual; related languages mark the distributive and the distributive-customary with the distributive prefix *n*-. See chap. 32 for discussion.
3. Axelrod (1993, 66) uses the term "consecutive" rather than "successive."
4. Kari (1979, 118–21), discussing Ahtna, glosses the *i*- prefix as 'transitional' and distinct from the conjugation prefixes.
5. Some of these themes are somewhat different in Upper Tanana than in related languages. The theme in (578c) has a *gh*- qualifier in Ahtna (Kari 1979, 127) and Dena'ina (Tenenbaum 1978, 156). In Upper Tanana, the *gh*- qualifier has been completely lost (Kari 1993). The themes in (578f, g) contain a gender prefix in Ahtna (Kari 1979, 127) and Koyukon (Jetté and Jones 2000, 66, 121) but not in Upper Tanana.
6. Kari (1979, 153) lists six themes in Ahtna, but not all of them are attested in Upper Tanana.
7. *L* is the Koyukon cognate of Upper Tanana *dh*.
8. It is unclear when gender prefixes do occur in these verb themes; hence G is listed in parentheses.

26 Verb stem

In this chapter some properties of the verb stem (position 0 in the Upper Tanana verb template; see table 24.1) are described. Verb stems are bound stems that may only occur in fully inflected forms (see chap. 24 for more information and exceptions).

Phonological properties of verb stems are described in 26.1. 26.2 gives a brief overview over aspectual and superaspectual stem variation. Stem suppletion is addressed in 26.3.

26.1. Phonology

Upper Tanana verb stems consist of an obligatory onset consonant, a long or short vowel nucleus, and a coda consonant. The coda consonant is optional if the stem vowel is long (either a long monophthong or a diphthong); if the stem vowel is short, the coda consonant is obligatory. Upper Tanana contrasts light (unsuffixed) and heavy (suffixed) verb stems; see chap. 11. Verbal suffixes are described in chap. 37.

26.1.1. Verb stems with variable onset consonant

Several high-frequency verb stems in Upper Tanana have variable onset consonants. These stems are reconstructed as vowel-initial, but since Dene stem syllables have to have an onset consonant (see chap. 10), a consonant had to be inserted into this position. Table 26.1 shows a selection of verb stems reconstructed without an onset consonant. In the verb stems in the first three rows, the inserted consonant is /h/.

		IPV	PFV	FUT	OPT
op.	'talk'	heeyh	ha'	heeł	heel
mot.	'spend the night'	haał	haał	hoł	haał
mot.	'stretch'	huu	huu	huu	huu
mot.	'SG go'	haayh	shyah	haał	shya'

Table 26.1. Vowel-initial verbs

Using yet another vowel-initial verb root ('SG go'), Krauss (1969) shows for the Dene language family that the onset consonant of a verb stem formed from this root is not always epenthetic but may also have its origin in another verbal prefix. A partial stem set of the Upper Tanana reflex of this root is given in the fourth row of table 26.1. The imperfective and future stems show the epenthetic consonant /h/, similar to the verb stems in the preceding three rows. Krauss (1969, 62) proposes that the onset consonant *shy* of the perfective stem (reconstructed as *y-) has its origin in an old allomorph triggered by the *s-* perfective (*dh-* perfective in Upper Tanana), whereas the onset consonant of the optative stem seems to derive from a vestigial optative morpheme *y- (Krauss 1969, 70-71).

When the verb form contains a D- voice/valence prefix, this prefix moves into the onset of the stem syllable (Krauss 1969, 61) and /h/ insertion does not take place. In (621), the voice/valence prefix is changed to D- in the presence of the iterative prefix *na-*.[1]

(621) a. *aahaał* (N)
aa-haał
3SG.S:AA.IPV:Ø-SG.go:IPV
'he is going along' UTOLVDN11Aug0802:019

b. *na'aadaał* (N)
na-aa-daał
IT-3SG.S:AA.IPV-D:SG.go:IPV
'she is returning' UTOLVDN11Aug0802:035

The same is true for other verb stems reconstructed without onset consonant (622).

(622) a. *shyiit nahhaał* (T)
shyiit nah-haał
here QUAL:Ø.IPV:2PL.S:Ø-spend.night:IPV
'spend PL the night here...' UTCBAF13Nov0501:076

b. *Tay' nee'eh nanahdaał, …* (N)
tay' nee-eh na-nah-daał
again 1PL.P-with IT-QUAL:Ø.IPV:2PL.S-D.spend.night:IPV
'Spend PL another night with us, …' UTOLVDN10Jul2724:048

Such forms then inflect like verbs with a Ø- voice/valence prefix rather than like verbs with a D- voice/valence marker, as comparison between the singular forms of na#D+haał 'SG return IPV PROG' and na#D+keeł 'return by boat IPV PROG' in table 26.2 shows.

	Ø+haał 'SG go IPV PROG'	na#D+haał 'SG return IPV PROG'	na#D+keeł 'return by boat IPV PROG'
1SG	ihhaał	na'ihdaał	na'ishkeeł
2SG	įįhaał	na'įįdaał	na'inkeeł
3SG	aahaał	na'aadaał	na'atkeeł

Table 26.2. Inflection of verbs with D-voice/valence marker in themes with a stem without an onset consonant

Another common vowel-initial root is 'classify L.O, RO'. The first line in table 26.3 shows the stem set of the motion theme in forms with a Ø- voice/valence prefix. The initial *ł* in forms of the motion theme with a Ø- voice/valence prefix has its origin in the Ł- voice/valence prefix (see Jetté and Jones [2000, 406] for relevant discussion of Koyukon; the Upper Tanana cognate of Ł- is H-). In all formally perfective stems containing a Ø- voice/valence marker (i.e., in the perfective stem of the motion theme as well as in all stems in the classificatory set), the initial consonant has been changed to *dl.* (As Kari [1990, 266–69] shows, this tendency also exists in Ahtna, but *dl-* initial stems are more restricted in that language.)

		IPV	PFV	FUT	OPT
mot. Ø-	'handle PL.O, RO'	łeeyh	dlah	łeeł	łe'
clas.	'PL.O, RO is in position'	dlah	dla'	dlaał	dla'
mot. L-	'handle PL.O, RO'	shyeeyh	shyah	shyeeł	shye'

Table 26.3. Onset variation in 'classify PL.O, RO'

While this stem behaves synchronically in many verb themes like a *ł-* or *dl-* initial stem requiring a Ø- voice/valence prefix, the origin of the stem-initial consonant as a Ł- (H-) voice/valence marker becomes apparent in all forms showing a D-effect. In these forms, the voice/valence prefix changes to L- rather than D-, and the onset consonant of the stem changes from *ł* or *dl* to *shy* ([623]; see also the last row of table 26.3).

(623) a. *dogn dats'eɬeeg* (T)
dogn da-ts'e-ɬeeg
up:AR up-1PL.S:Ø.IPV:Ø-handle.PL.O:IPV:CUST:NOM
'we put them up [on the meat frame]'
UTOLVDN07Nov2803:013

b. *daats'elshyeek*
da-na-ts'el-shyeek
up-IT-1PL.S:Ø.IPV:L-handle.PL.O:IPV:CUST
'we put them up [in the cache]' UTOLVDN07Nov2804:004

(623a) describes the process of hanging fileted muskrat up to dry, while (623b) refers to the process of putting the dried muskrat strips into the cache. The iterative prefix *na-* in (623b) causes a change in voice/valence-prefix (see chap. 27.3.2.2). The change from Ø- to L- is the only indicator that this verb theme underlyingly has an H- voice/valence prefix. Synchronically it is easier to analyze it as an irregular verb theme with a variable onset consonant and unusual voice/valence prefixes.

26.2. Morphology: Verb stem variation

All Dene verb stems are themselves morphologically complex, consisting of a root followed by aspectual suffixes (Kari 1979; Leer 1979). This leads to what has been called verb stem variation—from one underlying (abstract) root, a number of different stems are formed. Leer (1979, 21) argues that stem variation in Dene languages is the result of "originally rather simple and direct rules," which is supported by the Ahtna data presented in Kari (1979, 1990). Due to the erosion of stem-final consonants described in chap. 8, the resulting synchronic variation in Upper Tanana is, however, quite complex.

Aspectual verb stem variation is described in 26.2.1 and superaspectual variation in 26.2.2. All verb stems formed from the same root form a *stem set*. Stem sets have been studied by Leer (1979) for Proto-Dene and Kari (1979) for Ahtna; Kari (1990) lists many stem sets in Ahtna and Jetté and Jones (2000) in Koyukon. The following discussion is based on Kari's work on Ahtna (Kari 1979) and Upper Tanana (Kari 1997b) and informed by Leer's reconstructions.

In his lexicographical work on Upper Tanana, Kari (1997b) compiled many aspectual stems, but even though I continue to add to this file, there remain many gaps in the documentation of verb stem variation in this language. Some aspects are fairly rare, e.g., the persistive, for which I have not been able to find more than two examples. Identifying stem variation patterns in these aspects would require intricate elicitation work on the scale as that done by Kari (1979) for Ahtna, which is beyond the scope of this grammar.[2] Thus much of the data for this section comes from the stem file created by Kari (1997b) or from texts. It is likely that a more thorough analysis of the recorded texts would allow us to fill in some of the gaps in the discussion below, but for now the discussion of verb stem variation in Upper Tanana remains incomplete.

26.2.1. Aspectual variation

According to Leer (1979, 3), Dene verb stems are formed from underlying roots through "regular phonological modification of the vowel nucleus and/or suffixation." The resulting aspectual stems are further modified for mode (imperfective, perfective, future, and optative) and superaspect (customary, progressive, distributive, distributive-customary, errative; see 26.2.2).

Aspect and mode suffixation of verb roots is a historical process. In the contemporary Dene languages the root has to be considered an abstract entity, and the suffixes are not productive. In Upper Tanana verb stem morphology is not transparent to speakers; thus no forms for underlying roots are given in the data tables that follow. Stem suffixation formulae are based on Kari's (1979) Ahtna data, although adjustments have been made to describe the Upper Tanana data. Lowercase letters (e.g., *-yh*, *-ł*) indicate overt suffixes, while uppercase letters describe processes such as vowel lengthening (-L), spirantization of final obstruents (-X), or the perfective suffix (-N). In many aspects, different formulae apply to different root types; this is indicated in the data.

Note that optative forms in general are often characterized by voicing of the stem-final consonant, which is not predicted from comparison with related languages. I suspect that voicing is caused by overgeneralization of the imperative suffix (chap. 37) to all optative forms.

26.2.1.1. Stem variation in the neuter The neuter is the primary stem aspect of all neuter verbs, i.e., of all verb themes in the extension, classificatory, positional, stative, dimensional, and descriptive verb theme categories. A few examples are presented in table 26.4. The left column of table 26.4 indicates the verb theme category. Empty cells indicate that this stem is not attested in the data.

Most neuter stems contain the perfective suffix -N in imperfective stems; the second group of stems in table 26.4 constitutes exceptions. In the other modes open and closed roots take different stem suffixation formulae. All

	Theme		IPV	PFV	FUT	OPT
	open		-N	-ʔ	-ɬ	-ʔ
clas.	Ø+’ąą	‘classify CO’	’ąą	’a’	’aał	’a’
pos.	Ø+tįį	‘SG sleep’	tįį	te’	teeł	te’
dim.	Ø+sǫǫ	‘be good’	sǫǫ	su’	suuł	su’
desc.	L+tsįį	‘seem’	tsįį		tsiił	tsay
	open		Ø-	-ʔ	-ɬ	-ʔ
ext.	ski#n+Ø+’ah	‘LO extend across’	’ah	’a’	’aał	’a’
clas.	Ø+dlah	‘classify PL.O’	dlah	dla’	dlaał	dla’
pos.	da#Ø+dah	‘SG sit on [chair]’	dah	da’	daał	da’
	closed		-N	-N	-N	-N
clas.	Ø+niik	‘classify FO’	niik	niik	niik	niik
pos.	Ø+tiat	‘PL sleep’	tiat	tiat	tiat	tiadn
stat.	hu+n+Ø+k’ät	‘be cold’	k’ät	k’ät	k’ät	k’ät
stat.	ch’+Ø+xot	‘be crooked’	xot	xot	xot	xot
dim.	L+k’ah	‘be fat’	k’ah	k’ah	k’ah	k’ah
desc.	d+Ø+tth’ek	‘hear O’	tth’ek	tth’ek	tth’ek	tth’ek
	irregular					
ext.	H+ts’ayh	‘be windy’	ts’ayh	ts’ayh	ts’ayh	ts’ayh
ext.	Ø+łąy	‘flow’	łąy	łąy	łąy	łąy
dim.	Ø+ndüüh	‘be heavy’	ndüüh	ndüüh	ndüüh	ndüü
			ndüü	ndüü’	ndüü	ndüü’

Table 26.4. Stem variation in the neuter

open roots are suffixed with -ʔ in the perfective and optative, and with *-ɬ* in the future, whereas closed roots take the suffix -N in all forms.

The stems in the final group are somewhat irregular. The first two stems (*ts’ayh* and *łąy*) are historically open and thus expected to take the stem variation pattern -N -ʔ -ɬ -ʔ, but they are invariable in Upper Tanana (all forms have been confirmed with several speakers). As all of them are extension verbs, it is possible that their non-imperfective forms are so rare that the imperfective form has been generalized; certainly elicitation of the non-imperfective modes proved to be challenging. The last verb stem *ndüüh* ‘heavy’ is particularly interesting. It is historically closed as can be seen from comparison with Ahtna *des* ‘be heavy’, but the final consonant has been simplified to /h/ or deleted entirely. The alternative forms suggest that the stem is reanalyzed by some speakers as being an open stem, which takes -ʔ in the perfective and optative modes.

26.2.1.2. Stem variation in the transitional While the transitional is a common aspect in related languages, it has been lost almost entirely in Upper Tanana. Kari (1997b) lists a few transitional stem sets, but re-elicitation from contemporary speakers was not usually successful, even when using forms from Kari as prompts. Thus speakers would refuse *dat-t'iiɬ* 'it became red' and produce instead a periphrastic construction *delt'äɬ eltsį̨į̨* (lit. 'it is red it became'), or replace *iisu'* 'it became good' with *į̨į̨su'* 'it used to be good' or *na'et-sǫǫ* 'it became good again', neither of which exhibits the transitional stem variation.

Table 26.5 contains a complete list of the transitional stems found in Kari (1997b); all of them are derivations of dimensional themes. Because of the limited amount of data, the suffixation formula used in the transitional cannot be identified.

	Theme		IPV	PFV	FUT	OPT
stat.	hu+d+Ø+k'ät	'be cold'		k'üü'	k'üh	
dim.	d+L+t'äɬ	'be red'		t'iiɬ	t'iiɬ	t'iil
dim.	d+D+sąy	'be black'		sį̨į̨'	sį̨į̨'	sį̨į̨'
dim.	d+L+gayh	'be white'	gaayh	gaayh	gagn	gaay
dim.	Ø+sǫǫ	'be good'		su'		

Table 26.5. Stem variation in the transitional

26.2.1.3. Stem variation in the momentaneous The momentaneous is the basic aspect of motion themes but is not restricted to this verb theme category. Different suffixation patterns apply to open and closed roots (table 26.6).

Momentaneous stems of open roots usually end in *-yh* in the imperfective, a nasal vowel in the perfective, the suffix *-ɬ* in the future, and either *-ɬ* or a final glottal stop in the optative. The nasalization in the perfective often is accompanied by ablaut. The optative stems for 'SG swim' and 'tie up' in table 26.6 appear to be irregular but have been confirmed with several speakers.

In closed roots spirantization of the final consonant affected all forms other than the perfective. (Perfective stems with affricate codas subsequently underwent further changes as described in chap. 8.1.2.1.2.) Imperfective momentaneous stems of closed roots are characterized by lengthening. Future stems have the suffix *-ɬ* (often accompanied by vowel reduction), and optative stems are lengthened. The last verb stem in table 26.6 is suppletive.

	Theme		IPV	PFV	FUT	OPT
	open		-yh	-N	-ł	-ł or -ʔ
mot.	Ø+keeyh	‘SG go by boat’	keeyh	kį̨į	keeł	keeł, keel
mot.	d+H+k’aayh	‘build fire’	k’aayh	k’ąą	k’ąął	k’ąąl
mot.	ske#O+H+teeyh	‘carry AO across’	teeyh	tį̨į	teeł	te’
mot.	ske#Ø+mbeeyh	‘SG swim across’	mbeeyh	mį̨į	mbeeł	mbeey
mot.	da#O+H+tl’uyh	‘tie up O’	tl’uyh	tl’ųų	tl’uuł	tl’uy
mot.	Ø+haayh	‘SG go’	haayh	shyah	haał	shya’
	closed		-L	-N	-ł	-L
mot.	L+tthiit	‘SG run’	tthiit	tthät	tthäł	tthiidn
mot.	n+Ø+t’ak	‘SG fly’	t’ak	t’ak	t’ah	t’aa
mot.	sta#D+dia	‘animal runs off’	dia	dät	düh	dia
mot.	Ø+deeł	‘PL go’	deeł	deeł	däł	deel
mot.	Ø+’eeł	‘PL swim’	’eeł	’eeł	’oł	’eeł
mot.	Ø+’üh	‘PL animal moves’	’üh	’üüt	’äh	’üü
mot.	Ø+duu	‘crawl’	duu	duu	duu	duu
suc.	P+k’e#Ø+ttheeł	‘chop P in half’	ttheeł	ttheeł	tthäł	ttheel
	irregular					
mot.	O+H+chuut	‘grab O’	chuut	chuut	chiił	chuudn
mot.	na#O+d+L+nąyh	‘drop O’	thiiyh	nąyh	thäł	–

Table 26.6. Stem variation in the momentaneous

26.2.1.4. Stem variation in the durative The durative is the primary aspect of successive and operative verb themes.

Root shape greatly affects durative stem variation, as shown in table 26.7. Axelrod (1993, 63) states that in Koyukon the durative has “the most varied and complex stem set patterning of all aspects.” The same holds for Upper Tanana.

Kari (1979, 127) reports the durative suffixation formula -L -ʔ -ł - ʔ for open stems in Ahtna, but the data in table 26.7 illustrates that the situation in Upper Tanana is quite different. Imperfective durative stems may be lengthened as they are in Ahtna (e.g., Upper Tanana *nąą* ‘drink’ or *xąą* ‘make PL.O’) but are more frequently short. Perfective stems may or may not be glottal-closed. Future stems may end in *ł* or may be identical to the imperfective stems. Optative stems may be glottal-closed, may be lengthened, or may contain a vocalic suffix. In short, it appears from the data in table 26.7 that each open root takes its own durative suffixation formula. Additionally, there is some variation between speakers (not shown in table 26.7).

Roots of the shape CV:X take the formula -Ø -N -Ø -Ø. Roots formerly closed by glottalized consonants retain low tone in the perfective but not in the other modes. There are also a number of invariable stems.

	Theme		IPV	PFV	FUT	OPT
	open		-Ø	-ʔ	-Ø or -ɬ	ʔ or -V
op.	O+D+nąą	'drink O'	nąą	nąą'	nąą	nąą'
op.	O+H+xąą	'make PL.O'	xąą	xąą	xąą	xaan'
op.	d+Ø+nih	'say'	nih	ni'	niił	ni'
op.	O+n+H+'įh	'see'	'įh	'įį'	'įįł	'įį
op.	D+nah	'work'	nah	na'	nah	naa'
op.	O+uu+Ø+sih	'call O's name'	sih	si'	sih	sii
op.	H+chąą	'rain'	chąą, chąą	chąą, chąą	chįįł, chąą	chąą, chąą
op.	H+shyüü	'snow'	shyüüt, shyüüh	shyüüt, shyüü'	shyüüt, shyüüh	shyüüdn, shyüü
suc.	Ø+ttheh	'bark'	ttheh	–	ttheh	tthay
	CV:X		-Ø	-N	-Ø	-V
op.	O+uu+Ø+keet	'buy O'	keet	keet	keet	keedn
op.	na#O+Ø+'aał	'eat O'	'aał	'aał	'aał	'aal
suc.	O+Ø+ttheeł	'chop O'	ttheeł	ttheeł	ttheeł	ttheel
suc.	O+Ø+t'üüh	'cut O'	t'üüh	t'üü', t'üüt	t'üüh	t'üü
	invariable					
op.	O+n+L+ts'ų'	'kiss'	ts'ų'	ts'ų'	ts'ų'	ts'ų'
op.	na#ho+L+nek	'tell story'	nek	nek	nek	nek
op.	ho+Ø+tįįł	'make potlatch'	tįįł	tįįł	tįįł	tįįł
op.	O+L+deeł	'eat PL.O'	deeł	deeł	deeł	deel
suc.	O+Ø+dät	'twist O'	dät	dät	dät	dädn
suc.	O+Ø+xoł	'break O'	xoł	xoł	xoł	xoł
suc.	ch'+H+xał	'drum'	xał	xał	xał	xał
suc.	P+i+ke#H+kayh	'kick P'	kayh	kayh	kayh	kayh

Table 26.7. Stem variation in the durative

26.2.1.5. Stem variation in the semelfactive The semelfactive is restricted to successive verb themes.

Kari (1979, 119) observes that in Ahtna "semelfactive stem sets always have a reduced vowel and a spirantized final consonant." This also holds for Upper Tanana (table 26.8); the final /t/ in some of the stems below derives from a historic affricate *ts, which has been simplified to /t/ in Upper Tanana.

	Theme		IPV	PFV	FUT	OPT
	CV:X		-X	-X	-X	-X
suc.	O+Ø+tthäł	'chop o once'	tthäł	tthäł	tthäł	tthäł
suc.	O+H+t'üh	'cut o once'	t'üh	t'üh	t'üh	t'üh
suc.	O+Ø+'üh	'step on o once'		'üh, 'üt	'üh	'üh
suc.	O+H+got	'punch, stab o once'	got	got	got	got
suc.	O+Ø+tał	'shove o once with foot'	tał	tał	tał	tał
	CVX		-X	-X	-X	-X
suc.	O+Ø+xoł	'break o once'	xoł	xoł	xoł	xoł
suc.	ch'+H+xał	'club, drum once'	xał	xał	xał	xał
suc.	O+H+dayh	'shoot (at) o once'	dayh	dayh	dayh	dayh
suc.	O+Ø+dät	'twist o once'	dät	dät	dät	dät
suc.	O+Ø+ts'ät	'scratch o once'	ts'ät	ts'ät	ts'ät	ts'ät

Table 26.8. Stem variation in the semelfactive

26.2.1.6. Stem variation in the conclusive The conclusive is the primary aspect of the conversive verb theme category. Closed and open roots take -Ø in all modes other than the perfective, which takes the suffix -N. There are also a number of invariable stems (table 26.9).

26.2.1.7. Stem variation in the perambulative The perambulative aspect is limited to motion verbs. The perambulative suffixation formula is identical to the momentaneous formula with the exception of the imperfective; imperfective stems in the perambulative aspect take a *-ł* suffix (and are thus homophonous with stems in the progressive; see 26.2.2.2). Some examples of motion verb stems in the perambulative are given in table 26.10. The perambulative takes two different prefix strings; see chap. 35.2.1.10.1 for more information.

The perambulative aspect is rather rare in Upper Tanana; much more common is the customary derivation of perambulative verb themes (see 26.2.2.1).

26.2.1.8. Stem variation in the continuative While Kari (1979) finds that in Ahtna, the continuative may occur in motion themes as well as in conversive themes, it appears that in Upper Tanana the continuative is restricted to

	Theme		IPV	PFV	FUT	OPT
	open		-Ø	-N	-Ø	-Ø
conv.	O+H+tsayh	'make sg.o'	tsayh	tsįį	tsayh	tsay
conv.	O+dh+H+xeh	'kill sg.o'	xeh	xįį	xeh	xay
conv.	na#D+tl'uh	'get dressed'	tl'uh	tl'ųų	tl'uh	tl'uy
conv.	Ø+tsanh	'defecate'	tsanh	tsąą	tsanh	tsan(h)
	closed		-Ø	-N	-Ø	-Ø
conv.	O+Ø+chiah	'render, melt o'	chiah	chia'	chiah	chiah
conv.	O+n+Ø+'iah	'string o'	'iah	'iah	'iah	'iah
conv.	O+H+t'eh	'fry o'	t'eh, t'iah	t'iah	t'iah	t'iah
conv.	O+H+mbiah	'boil o'	mbiat, mbiah	mbiat, mbiah	mbiat, mbiah	mbiat, mbiah
conv.	na#D+kuyh	'vomit'	kuyh	kuyh	kuyh	kuyh
	invariable					
conv.	O+Ø+dzeek	'caulk o'	dzeek	dzeek	?	?
conv.	O+H+xot	'boil o'	xot	xot	xot	xot
conv.	D+tänh	'freeze'	tänh	tänh	tänh	tänh
conv.	D+gąy	'dry'	gąy	gąy	gąy	gąy

Table 26.9. Stem variation in the conclusive

	Theme		IPV	PFV	FUT	OPT
	open		-ł	-N	-ł	-ł or -ʔ
mot.	na#D+keeł	'sg go by boat'	keeł	kįį	keeł	keel
mot.	na#L+teeł	'carry ao'	teeł	tįį	teeł	te'
mot.	na#daał	'sg go'	daał	D+shyah	daał	D+shya'
mot.	na#D+mbeeł	'sg swim'	mbeeł	mįį	mbeeł	mbeey
	closed		-ł	-N	-ł	-L
mot.	na#D+tthäł	'sg run'	tthäł	tthät	tthäł	tthiidn
mot.	na#n+D+t'ah	'sg fly'	t'ah	t'ak	t'ah	t'aa
mot.	na#D+deeł	'pl go'	däł	deeł	däł	deel
mot.	Ø+'oł	'pl swim'	'oł	'eeł	'oł	'eeł
mot.	Ø+'äh	'pl animal moves'	'äh	'üüt	'äh	'üü

Table 26.10. Stem variation in the perambulative

conversive themes (table 26.11). (In motion themes it seems to have merged with the perambulative, both with respect to stem variation and prefixes. See chap. 25 for more discussion.)

	Theme		IPV	PFV	FUT	OPT
	closed		-ɬ	-N	-ɬ	-L
conv.	O+H+k'aayh	'filet o'	k'aayh	k'aak	k'aayh	k'aayh
	invariable					
conv.	na#O+H+'oł	'butcher o'	'oł	'oł	'oł	'oł

Table 26.11. Stem variation in the continuative

26.2.1.9. Stem variation in the reversative There are only a handful of reversative forms in the Upper Tanana data. Themes requiring the reversative can be found in the motion, conversive, and operative verb theme categories (table 26.12).

	Theme		IPV	PFV	FUT	OPT
	motion/conversive		-h	-N	-h *or* -ɬ	-h
mot.	na+ke#(d)+Ø+'aah	'turn over CO'	'aah	'ąą	aał	'aa
mot.	s+na+ke#+Ø+haah	'SG go in circle'	haah	shyah	haał	haa
mot.	na+ke#O+d+H+nąyh	'flip o'	nąyh	nąy	nąyh	nąy?
conv.	n+Ø+shyeeh	'grow'	shyeeh	shyąą	shyeeh	shyeey
conv.	ha#O+H+t'üü	'cut out o'	t'üü(h)	t'üüt	t'üü(h)	t'üü
	operative		-h	-ʔ	-h	-h
op.	O+d+L+dįįh	'learn o'	dįįh	dįį'	dįįh	dįį
op.	na#D+shye'	'heal'	shye'	shye'	shye'	shye'

Table 26.12. Stem variation in the reversative

The reversative aspect takes different stem suffixation formulae depending on the verb theme category. For Ahtna, Kari (1990, 102) identifies the stem suffixation formula for motion and conversive verb themes in the reversative as -x -N -x -x. In Upper Tanana this seems to be -h -N -h -h, although some stems take *-ɬ* in the future mode. In obstruent-closed stems (*nąyh* and *t'üüh* in table 26.12) the perfective suffix blocks lenition. Operative reversative stems take -ʔ rather than -N in the perfective and *-h* in the nonperfective modes (Kari 1979, 154), while closed stems remain unchanged.

26.2.1.10. Stem variation in the onomatopoetic The onomatopoetic is the primary aspect of the operative-onomatopoetic verb theme category. It is characterized by invariable stems (table 26.13).

	Theme		IPV	PFV	FUT	OPT
			-N	-N	-N	-N
op.	d+L+ttheł	'ring'	ttheł	ttheł	ttheł	ttheł
op.	d+L+ts'äł	'crackle'	ts'äł	ts'äł	ts'äł	ts'äł
op.	d+L+ts'iat	'creak'	ts'iat	ts'iat	ts'iat	ts'iat
op.	d+L+tl'iat	'rustle'	tl'iat	tl'iat	tl'iat	tl'iat

Table 26.13. Stem variation in the onomatopoetic

26.2.1.11. Stem variation in the repetitive$_1$ The repetitive$_1$ is the primary aspect of the operative-repetitive$_1$ verb theme category. It takes the suffix *-yh* (often weakened to *-h*) in all modes (table 26.14).

	Theme		IPV	PFV	FUT	OPT
			-yh	-yh	-yh	-yh
op.	d+L+koh	'cough'	koh	koh	koh	koh
op.	d+L+xoh	'play'	xoh	xoh	xoh	xoh
op.	P+i#D+nayh	'know'	nayh	nayh	nayh	nayh
op.	D+shyiyh	'breathe'	shyiyh	shyiyh	shyiyh	shyiyh

Table 26.14. Stem variation in the repetitive$_1$

26.2.1.12. Stem variation in the repetitive$_2$ The repetitive$_2$ aspect is taken by operative and conversive themes (table 26.15). It takes a suffix *-yh* in the nonperfective modes but -N in the perfective.

	Theme		IPV	PFV	FUT	OPT
	open		-yh	-N	-yh	-yh
conv.	O+n+Ø+'įį	'steal o'	'įį	'įį	'įįł	'įį
conv.	na#O+n+Ø+kąą	'sew'	kąą	kąą'	kąą	kąą
	closed		-yh	-N	-yh	-yh
op.	O+uu+d+H+kat	'ask o'	kat	kat	kat	kat
op.	ch'+L+dzüh	'dance'	dzüh	dziat, dzia'	dzüh	dzüü
op.	na#L+shyiyh	'rest'	shyiyh	shyiat	shyiyh	shyiyh
op.	da#n+Ø+'at	'untie o'	'at	'at	'at	'at

Table 26.15. Stem suffixation patterns in the repetitive$_2$

The form *dzia'* is in the Northway dialect, *dziat* in the Tetlin dialect. Note that the *-yh* suffix is simplified to *-h* in many forms and disappears completely after long vowels and in closed stems.

26.2.1.13. Stem variation in the persistive The persistive is attested only in two operative themes in Upper Tanana (table 26.16). Like the repetive$_1$, it takes *-yh* in all forms, which is often weakened to *-h*.

	Theme		IPV	PFV	FUT	OPT
			-yh	-yh	-yh	-yh
op.	dzi#D+teeyh	'SG do mourning dance'	teeyh	teeyh	teeyh	teey
op.	dzi#L+shyeeh	'PL do mourning dance'	shyeeh	shyeeh	shyeeh	shyeeh

Table 26.16. Stem variation in the persistive

26.2.1.14. Irregular stems A few verb themes have irregular stem variation that does not fit into any of the aspectual categories identified above. The first two themes in table 26.17 are also listed as irregular in Kari (1979, 143). The third theme is regular in Ahtna but not in Upper Tanana.

	Theme		IPV	PFV	FUT	OPT
op.	hu+Ø+heeyh	'talk'	heeyh	ha'	heeł	heel
op.	Ø+tsüh	'SG cry'	tsüh	tsia'	tsüh	tsüü
conv.	Ø+łüh	'urinate'	łüh	łia'	łüh	łia'

Table 26.17. Irregular verb stem variation

26.2.2. Superaspectual stem variation

Superaspectual derivations, like aspectual derivations, are characterized by their own stem suffixation formulae and their own conjugation patterns. They differ from aspectual stem derivations in that they do not replace the aspectual strings; i.e., superaspectual derivations are compatible with aspectual derivations, whereas aspectual derivations are mutually exclusive.

Upper Tanana has two productive superaspects, the customary and the progressive. The productivity of the distributive and distributive-customary superaspects is unclear; while the few examples of the distributive-customary seem to utilize customary verb stems, there seems to be a distinct distributive stem variation. There are also a few instances of the errative in the corpus (see chap. 24.4.3 and 30.3.1.1 for more discussion), but not enough to understand the stem variation patterns associated with this superaspect.

26.2.2.1. Stem variation in the customary The customary indicates that the action or event takes place regularly or habitually. Stem variation in the customary is simple; all stems take a suffix *-k* (table 26.18). In some consonant-closed stems the customary suffix is visible and the root-final consonant is deleted; in other stems the stem-final consonant is retained and the customary suffix is deleted. Note that in quite a few stems, the customary suffix seems to trigger what Leer (1979, 47) calls an "i-effect," a raising of the stem vowel to /i/.

	Theme		IPV	PFV	FUT	OPT
	open		-k	-k	-k	-k
mot.	Ø+keeyh	'SG go by boat'	keek	keek	keek	keek
mot.	ske#Ø+mbeeyh	'SG swim across'	mbeek	mbeek	mbeek	mbeek
mot.	Ø+haayh	'SG go'	haak	haak	haak	haak
op.	d+Ø+nih	'say'	niik	niik	niik	niik
op.	O+n+H+'įh	'see O'	'įįk	'įįk	'įįk	'įįk
conv.	O+H+tsayh	'make SG.O'	tsįįk	tsįįk	tsįįk	tsįįk
conv.	O+H+gąyh	'dry O'	gįį	gįį	gįį	gįį
ext.	ski#n+Ø+ah	'extend across'	'aak	'aak	'aak	'aak
pos.	Ø+dah	'SG stay'	daak	daak	daak	daak
	closed		-k	-k	-k	-k
mot.	N+Ø+t'ak	'SG fly'	t'ak	t'ak	t'ak	t'ak
mot.	ni#Ø+deeł	'PL arrive'	dek	dek	dek	dek
op.	O+H+mbiat	'cook O'	mbiat	mbiat	mbiat	mbiat
suc.	O+Ø+'aał	'eat O'	'iił	'iił	'iił	'iił
suc.	O+Ø+ttheeł	'chop O'	ttheeł	ttheeł	ttheeł	ttheeł
			tthiił	tthiił	tthiił	tthiił
suc.	O+Ø+t'üüh	'cut O'	t'üü	t'üü	t'üü	t'üü

Table 26.18. Stem variation in the customary superaspect

In addition to stem variation, the customary is marked by (Ø, aa) conjugation markers.

26.2.2.2. Stem variation in the progressive The progressive superaspect expresses that a motion event is ongoing. It is limited to members of the motion verb theme category in the imperfective viewpoint and requires an *aa*-conjugation marker. (There are a few instances of progressive verb forms in the optative mode; see volume 2 for discussion.)

Progressive stems are formed through suffixation of *-ł* (table 26.19). The progressive suffix *-ɬ* is overt in all open stems; in obstruent-closed roots the progressive suffix is sometimes dropped (Leer 1979, 45).

	Theme		IPV
	open		-ɬ
mot.	ske#O+H+teeyh	'carry AO across'	teeɬ
mot.	Ø+keeyh	'SG go by boat'	keeɬ
mot.	ch'+n+L+'įį	'sneak'	'įįɬ
mot.	ske#Ø+mbeeyh	'SG swim across'	mbeeɬ
mot.	Ø+haayh	'SG go'	haaɬ
mot.	H+chąą	'rain moves'	chiiɬ
	closed		-ɬ
mot.	L+tthiit	'run'	tthäɬ
mot.	n+Ø+t'ak	'SG fly'	t'ah
mot.	sta#D+dia	'SG animal runs away'	düh
mot.	Ø+deeɬ	'PL go'	däɬ
mot.	Ø+'eeɬ	'PL swim'	'oɬ
mot.	Ø+'üh	'PL animal moves'	'äh
mot.	Ø+duu	'crawl'	duuɬ

Table 26.19. Stem variation in the progressive

26.2.2.3. Stem variation in the distributive The distributive superaspect expresses that a motion event is repeated or replicated several times. It is signaled by the presence of the iterative prefix *na-* or the distributive prefix *n-* (see chap. 32 and 34), (Ø, dh) conjugation markers, and its own stem variation. The data in table 26.20 is incomplete even for the three verb themes attested with several stems in this derivation, but comparison with table 26.6 shows that distributive stems clearly differ from momentaneous ones.

	Theme		IPV	PFV	FUT	OPT
	open		-ʔ	-N	-ʔ	-ʔ
mot.	da+na#O+H+tl'uyh	'tie up O'	tl'u'	tl'ųų	tl'u'	tl'u'
mot.	ta#O+Ø+ɬe'	'distribute PL.O'	ɬe'	dlah		
	closed					
mot.	na+n#t+D+t'ah	'SG fly around'	t'ah	t'ah		

Table 26.20. Stem variation in the distributive

26.3. Suppletive stems

In addition to the historically vowel-initial stems resulting in stem sets with variable onset consonants (see 26.1.1), there are also truly suppletive stem sets, i.e., stem sets originating in more than one root. A few examples are given in table 26.21.

	Theme		IPV	PFV	FUT	OPT
mot.	d+L+__	'CO moves independently'	thiiyh	nąyh	thayh	thiiy
mot.	Ø+__	'PL swim'	'eeł	'eeł	'oł	'eeł
?	D+__	'happen'		shyaak	nił, niił	

Table 26.21. Suppletive stem sets

26.4. Summary

In this chapter phonological and morphological properties of verb stems are described.

Verb stems have the syllable structure of stem syllables:CV:(C) or CVC. Most Dene verb stems are reconstructed with an onset consonant; in the handful of stems that are not, the onset consonant may be filled either by an epenthetic /h/ or by other, sometimes historical, morphological material.

All verb stems are morphologically complex. They consist of an abstract root plus affixes; the affixes indicate both aspect and mode. While the description of stem variation given here remains incomplete, we can make the following observations. The stem suffixation formulae identified by Kari (1979) for Ahtna by and large explain the Upper Tanana forms as well. The ongoing erosion of stem-final consonants in this language, however, obscures some of these processes, yielding more homophonous stems in Upper Tanana than are present in Ahtna. It is possible that the voiced suffix so common in optative stems as well as the unexpectedly large number of future stems ending in *ł* are recent innovations to preserve mode contrasts.

Notes

1. The iterative prefix is described in chap. 34; its effect on the voice/valence marker is described in chap. 27.3.2.2.
2. This further assumes that this type of elicitation work is still possible with the few remaining speakers, of which I am not convinced.

27 Voice/valence markers

In this chapter the prefixes in position 1 of the Upper Tanana verb template (see table 24.1) are described. In the Dene literature these prefixes are often called "classifiers" (Krauss 1969; Holton 2000), but following Rice (2000) and Hargus (2007), I use the term voice/valence markers, which better reflects their synchronic functions.

Depending on the scholar, two (Krauss 1969), three (Hargus 2007), or four (Rice 1989; Kibrik 1993) voice/valence markers are distinguished. The different numbers reflect different approaches rather than linguistic differences: Rice (1989) and Kibrik (1993) posit a Ø- voice/valence marker, while Krauss (1969) and Hargus (2007) treat this as the absence of a voice/valence marker. The difference between the counts of Krauss (1969) and the other authors lies in their different treatment of the L- voice/valence marker: Rice (1989), Kibrik (1993), and Hargus (2007) take a synchronic approach and treat it as a voice-valence marker on a par with D- and Ł-, while Krauss (1969) argues that it derives historically from D + Ł, and thus he treats it as two morphemes. In this grammar I distinguish four voice/valence markers: Ø-, D-, H-, and L-, where the H- voice/valence marker is cognate to Ł- in related languages. In glosses and discussion all voice/valence markers are represented by capital letters.

The phonology of the voice/valence markers is described in 27.1. Like many other conjunct prefixes, voice/valence markers may be thematic (i.e., lexicalized) or derivational. Thematic voice/valence markers are discussed in 27.2, derivational uses in 27.3.

27.1. Phonology

The phonology of the voice/valence markers is quite complex. They are part of a portmanteau morpheme that also includes the inner subject prefix, the mode and conjugation prefixes, and sometimes qualifiers or outer subject prefixes. This portmanteau is described in chap. 28, 29, 30, and 31. In the present section I focus on the interactions between voice/valence-prefixes and stems.

27.1.1. Voice/valence marker Ø-

The Ø- voice/valence marker is always phonologically empty.

27.1.1.1. Lenition after Ø- For some speakers the Ø- voice/valence prefix triggers lenition of the stem-initial fricative (see chap. 9 for discussion and examples).

27.1.1.2. Ø- in verbs with no onset consonant When verb stems reconstructed without an onset consonant occur in themes requiring a Ø-voice/valence prefix, the consonant /h/ is usually inserted. Examples are given in table 27.1. The different forms in the stems for 'stretch' reflect different dialects; the diphthong is retained in the Beaver Creek and Scottie Creek dialects but has been monophthongized in the Tetlin and Northway dialects (see chap. 6.1.9). In the last partial stem set in table 27.1, the onset consonant in the perfective and optative forms derives from other historical morphemes; see chap. 26.1.1 or Krauss (1969) for details.

		IPV	PFV	FUT	OPT
op.	'talk'	heeyh	ha'	heeł	heel
mot.	'spend the night'	haał	haał	hoł	haał
mot.	'stretch'	huu, hiu	huu, hiu	huu, hiu	huu, hiu
mot.	'SG go'	haayh	shyah	haał	shya'

Table 27.1. Insertion of onset consonant

27.1.2. Voice/valence marker D-

The D- voice/valence marker has the form /t/. Unlike other syllable-final /t/, the D- voice/valence marker is never phonetically voiced (see chap. 5). Because of this lack of voicing, it is written <t>.

27.1.2.1. "D-effect": D- before stem-initial consonants The term "D-effect" in Dene linguistics has two meanings. Several scholars writing about Alaskan Dene languages use this term to describe the change from Ø- to D- and from H- (or Ł- in other languages) to L-; e.g., Axelrod (1993, 16) and Jetté and Jones (2000) for Koyukon, or Holton (2000, 256) for Tanacross. These changes are described in 27.3.2.

Scholars of Canadian and Southern Dene languages, on the other hand, use the term "D-effect" to refer to a morphophonological process between the D- voice/valence prefix and the stem initial consonant. The processes in (624) are taken from a description of Dëne Sųłiné (Cook 2004, 71), but similar facts are described by many authors for many languages; e.g., Faltz (1998, 29–31) for Navajo, Rice (1989, 443–45) for Slave, Hargus (2007, 341) for Witsuwit'en, Gessner (2003, 37–45) for Dakelh (an overview about publications addressing the D-effect can be found in Hargus [2010]).

(624) D-effect in Dëne Sųłiné, Cook (2004, 71)

a. D + dh, l, z, y, gh → ddh, dl, dz, j, g/d respectively
b. D + ʔ → t'
c. D + n → d
d. D + C → C (where C = any other consonant)

In Upper Tanana there are no phonological changes comparable to the ones listed in (624), as shown in the following sections.

27.1.2.1.1. Lenition after D- When a D- voice/valence marker co-occurs in a verb theme with a fricative-initial stem, it usually causes lenition of the stem-initial fricative as described in chap. 9.

27.1.2.1.2. D- plus /ʔ/ The D- voice/valence prefix and a following glottal stop remain separate phones, with /t/ in the coda of the pre-stem syllable and /ʔ/ in the onset of the stem syllable. This is indicated orthographically by a hyphen (625). Evidence for this comes from the shortening of the underlyingly long *aa-* conjugation prefix, as can be seen from the contrast between (625) and (626).

(625) *Ay eh dineh säk na'at-'aał* ([na.ʔat.ʔa:ɬ]) tl'aan. (N)

ay eh *dineh* *säk* *na-at-'aał* *tl'aan*
and.then man torso IT-3SG.S:AA.IPV:D-handle.CO:IPV and
'And then she was bringing back a man's torso.'
UTOLVDN11Aug0802:048

(626) *Laalil hǫǫ't'eey niłk'inaat'ay…* ([niɬ.k'i.na:.t'a:j]) (T)

laalil *hǫǫt'eey* *niłk'i-naa-t'ay*
butterfly still zigzag-3SG.S:QUAL:AA.IPV:Ø-SG.fly:IPV:PROG
'The butterfly was still fluttering around…'
UTCBAF13Nov0501:036

In the stop sequence in (625) the /t/ remains in the pre-stem syllable and causes shortening of the pre-stem vowel. In (626) the long vowel in the prestem syllable demonstrates that the pre-stem syllable has no coda consonant.

27.1.2.2. D- in stems without an onset consonant In verb stems that are reconstructed without an onset consonant, the D- voice/valence prefix moves into the stem onset position (table 27.2).

		IPV	PFV	FUT	OPT
mot.	'spend the night'	daał	daał	doł	daał
mot.	'SG go'	daayh	D+shyah	daał	D+shya'

Table 27.2. D- in vowel-initial verbs

Those verbs are inflected as if they had a Ø- voice-valence marker; see chap. 26.1.1.

27.1.3. Voice/valence marker H-

The voice/valence prefix H- is cognate to Ł- in related languages. It is always voiceless.

27.1.3.1. No lenition after H- Following the H- voice/valence-prefix, fricative lenition almost never takes place (see chap. 9).

27.1.3.2. H- in stems without an onset consonant When H- occurs in a verb theme with a stem reconstructed without an onset consonant, it moves into the onset of the stem syllable. This process clearly predates the sound change of the voice/valence-marker from /ɬ/ to /h/, since the resulting stem begins with a /ɬ/, not /h/. An example for that is the classificatory verb stem for plural/ropelike objects, as shown in (627).[1]

(627) *Nts'ayy' shyiit ts'uułeey!* (N)
n-ts'ayy' *shyiit* *ts'uu-łeey*
2SG.PSR-canoe:POSS in 1PL.S:OPT:ø-handle.PL.O:OPT
'Let's put [the guns] into your canoe!' UTOLVDN07Aug2205:091

These forms inflect as if they contained a Ø- voice/valence prefix (note the lengthening of the optative prefix in (627).

27.1.4. Voice/valence marker L-

The voice/valence marker L- usually has the shape /l/-.

27.1.4.1. Lenition after L- In fricative-initial verbs L- occasionally causes lenition (see chap. 9).

27.1.4.2. L- in verb stems without onset consonant In verb stems reconstructed without an onset consonant, the L- voice/valence marker does not move into the stem onset position; Leer (1996a) suggests that a *y was inserted there, which surfaces in Upper Tanana as *shy* (628).

(628) a. *shk'eh nagąą'htelshyah* (N)
sh-k'eh na-gąą'-htel-shyah
1SG.P-after IT-arm-3PL.S:INC:DH.PFV:L-handle.PL.O:PFV
'they started running after me' UTOLAF09Aug1202:033

b. *tth'ee nahnelshyeek* (N)
tth'ee na-hnel-shyeek
sinew IT-3PL.S:QUAL:Ø.IPV:L-handle.PL.O:IPV:CUST
'they kept bringing back sinew' UTOLAF15May0501:193

27.2. Thematic voice/valence markers

Each verb theme is lexically specified for one voice/valence marker, and while no meaning can be identified for the voice/valence markers, no verb theme is complete without one (629–632).

(629) Verb themes with thematic Ø-

a. Ø+tsüh 'cry'
b. O+Ø+'aał 'eat O'
c. Ø+haayh 'SG walk'
d. Ø+dah 'SG sit, stay'

(630) Verb themes with thematic D-

a. D+nah 'work'
b. D+dät 'animal runs'
c. O+D+nąą 'drink O'
d. D+k'įą 'exercise, train self'

(631) Verb themes with thematic H-

a. ta#H+shyaał 'jump into water'
b. ch'+d+h+'ąą 'sing'
c. O+n+H+'įh 'see O'
d. O+Ø+t'iah 'roast O'

(632) Verb themes with thematic L-

a. d+L+xoh 'play'
b. L+k'ah 'be fat'
c. n+L+jit 'be scared'
d. O+G+L+deeł 'eat PL.O'

Hargus (2007, 342) provides counts of the relative frequency of each voice/valence marker in Witsuwit'en verb themes, finding that 46 percent of thematic voice/valence markers are Ø- (what she calls "no voice/valence prefix"), 20 percent are Ł- (cognate to H- in Upper Tanana), 19 percent are L-, and 14 percent are D-. Similar counts do not exist for Upper Tanana, but based on my impressions, I would assume that the distribution of voice/valence prefixes is quite similar to Hargus's observations. Hargus (2007, 343) also finds that the Ł- voice/valence marker is the only one that is more common in transitive than in intransitive themes. According to her counts, themes containing an L- or D- voice/valence marker are predominantly (in about 90 percent of cases) intransitive, as are themes containing a Ø- voice/valence marker (71 percent intransitive). Again similar numbers are not available for Upper Tanana, but based on the productive functions of the voice/valence prefixes, it is likely that the same tendencies hold for Upper Tanana as well.

27.3. Productive (derivational) uses of the voice/valence prefixes

The productive uses of the voice/valence prefixes were originally summarized by Kibrik (1993, 1996). In the first of these papers Kibrik (1993, 50) demonstrates that the voice/valence markers[2] do not have transitive or intransitive meaning per se; instead, their presence indicates a shift in transitivity. A change from a Ø- voice/valence prefix signals a transitivity increase, while a change from Ø- to D- or from H- to L- signals a transitivity decrease. Hargus (2007, 343) points out, however, that not all shifts in voice/valence marker correspond to a transitivity-changing operation but may have to do with other ways of changing participants' affectedness.

27.3.1. Voice/valence prefix changes to H-

Changes of a voice/valence marker to H- are associated with transitivity-increasing operations or with an increase in intensity. All of them have been reported by Kibrik (1993) for Navajo, and most of them are mentioned in the descriptions of other Dene languages as well.

27.3.1.1. Causativization Causativization in Upper Tanana is an extremely productive operation. Many intransitive verb themes can be causativized by a change from a Ø- voice/valence marker to a H- voice/valence marker (633, 634).

(633) a. *eegąyh* (T)
ee-gąyh
3SG.S:DH.PFV:Ø-be.dry:IPV
'it is dry, withered' UTOLVDN07Nov2803:015

b. *hiiyehgąyh* (T)
hiiy-eh-gąyh
3PL.S>3SG.O-DH.PFV:H-dry:PFV
'they dried it' UTOLVDN07Nov2803:028

(634) a. *neeshyąą* (T)
nee-shyąą
3SG.S:QUAL:DH.PFV:Ø-grow:PFV
'he grew up' UTOLAF13May2403:105

b. *shnehshyaan* (T)
sh-neh-shyaan
1SG.O-3SG.S:QUAL:DH.PFV:H-raise:PFV:NOM
'she, raising me' UTCBVDN13Nov1503:002

Transitive themes also may be causativized using H-. (635) illustrates causativization of a transitive theme containing a Ø- voice/valence marker, (636) that of a transitive theme with a H- voice/valence marker. The indefinite object prefix *ch'*- in (636b) is thematic; hence it is able to co-occur with the direct object noun phrase *stsogn* 'my penis'.

(635) a. *ch'e'aał* (T)
ch'-e-'aał
INDF.O-3SG.S:Ø.IPV:Ø-eat:IPV
'she is eating something' UTOLVDN11Jul2901:006

b. *nee'ich'eh'aał* (N)
sh-i-ch'-eh-'aał
1SG.P-PP-INDF.O-3SG.S:Ø.IPV:H-feed:IPV
'he is feeding us something' UTOLVDN10Jul2724:074

(636) a. *nnak-'į̨h* (B)

n-nak-'į̨h

2sg.o-qual:ø.ipv:1sg.s:h-see:ipv

'I see you sg' UTOLAF10Jul0202:140

b. *Hashyign stsogn nich'itnak-'į̨įl.* (T)

hashyign *s-tsogn*

down.there 1sg.psr-penis

n-i-ch'-tnak-'į̨įl

2sg.p-pp-indf-inc:qual:aa.ipv:1sg.s:h-show:fut:nom

'I am going to show you sg my penis.' UTCBAF13Nov0501:247

Causativization of transitive themes is not a very common process.

27.3.1.2. Possessive transitivization Neuter verb themes from the classificatory, positional, and stative verb theme categories also can be transitivized using a voice/valence marker change. The resulting meaning is one of possession, where the subject of the derived form not only instigated but also retains ownership over the resulting state (637, 638).

(637) a. *Hanaat dahdzäł da'ee'ą̨ą̨…* (N)

ha-naat *dahdzäl* *ee-'ą̨ą̨*

ntrl-across:pnct drying.rack 3sg.s:dh.pfv:ø-classify.co:ipv

'Across there was a drying rack…' UTOLVDN13May2004:025

b. … *dahdzäł choo:: heh'ą̨ą̨.* (N)

dahdzäl *choh* *heh-'ą̨ą̨*

drying.rack big 3pl.s:dh.pfv:h-classify.co:ipv

'… they had a big drying rack.' UTOLVDN14Apr2602:148

(638) a. *kon' deek'än'* (N)

kon' *dee-k'än'*

fire 3sg.s:qual:dh.pfv:ø-burn:ipv

'a fire is burning' UTCBVDN13Nov1401:060

b. *kon' utsǫǫ dehk'an'* (T)

kon' *u-tsǫǫ* *deh-k'ą̨ą̨*

fire 3sg.psr-grandmother 3sg.s:qual:dh.pfv:h-burn:ipv

'his grandmother had a fire going' UTOLAF09Jun2202:037

One particularly surprising example of possessive transitivization involves a change from L- to H- voice/valence marker, which is not documented in any other verb theme.[3]

(639) a. … *ts'ist'e' eł ts'exeh gaay dihishyįį' hihdeltth'ih.* (T)

ts'ist'e' *eł* *ts'exeh gaay* *dihishyįį'*
old.lady with girl 3PL:alone
h-del-tth'ih
3PL.S-QUAL:DH.PFV:L-PL.stay:IPV
'… an old lady and a little girl were staying by themselves.'
UTOLAF07Oct2512:002

b. *Łaakeey ts'exeey gaay shyįį' hudehtth'ih.* (T)

łaakeey *ts'exeey gaay* *shyįį'* *hu-deh-tth'ih*
two girls only 3PL.O-3SG.S:QUAL:DH.PFV:H-PL.stay:IPV
'[The old lady] had two girls staying [with her].'
UTOLAF09Jun2202:005

27.3.1.3. Comparative derivation The H- voice/valence marker also is part of the comparative derivational strings, which are unique to dimensional themes. Dimensional themes are intransitive in their primary derivation; the standard of comparison is introduced by the postposition P+*k'e'* 'less than P' in (640).

(640) a. *Tl'aan udia' chih ntsuul…* (T)

tl'aan *u-dia'* *chih* *n-tsuul*
and 3SG.PSR-younger.sister too 3SG.S:Ø.PFV:Ø-be.small:IPV
'And her younger sister was small…' UTCBAF13Nov0501:009

b. … *moondaa chih uk'e' įhtsuul.* (T)

m-oondaa *chih* *u-k'e'*
3SG.PSR-older.brother too 3SG.P-less.than
įh-tsuul
3SG.S:Ø.PFV:H-be.small:IPV
'… she was smaller than her older brother. '
UTCBAF13Nov0501:009

More information on the comparative derivation can be found in chap. 25; comparison is described in volume 2.

27.3.1.4. Other transitivization Some examples of transitivization involve neither causativization nor comparison. The primary themes in (641) and (642) have the structure Ø+stem and describe vocalizations; the derived themes have the structure O+n+H+stem and describe vocalizations directed at O. The added argument thus has the semantic role GOAL.

(641) a. *łįį ettheh* (T)
łįį e-ttheh
dog 3SG.S:Ø.IPV:Ø-bark:IPV
'dogs were barking' UTOLVDN14Nov2301:183

b. *hunehttheh* (T)
hu-neh-ttheh
3PL.O-3PL.S:QUAL:Ø.IPV:H-bark:IPV
'they were barking at them' UTOLVDN14Nov2301:183

(642) a. *ihsäł* (N)
ih-säł
Ø.IPV:1SG.S:Ø-holler:IPV
'I hollered' UTOLAF09Aug1202:032

b. *Roy naksäł* (N)
Roy nak-säł
Roy QUAL:Ø.IPV:1SG.S:H-holler:IPV
'I hollered at Roy' UTOLAF09Aug12:018

In (643), the added argument also has the role GOAL.

(643) a. *Ay nįį'ia!* (T)
ay nįį-'ia
this QUAL:Ø.IPV:2SG.S:Ø-braid:IPV
'Braid this!' UTOLVDN14Nov2301:511

b. *Ashyign' nts'ą' minįh'iah!* (T)
a-shyign' nts'ą' m-i-nįh-'iah
NTRL-down:ALL to 3SG.P-PP-QUAL:Ø.IPV:2SG.S:H-braid:IPV
'Braid it down to it!' UTOLVDN14Nov2301:513

27.3.1.5. Intensification A change from Ø- voice/valence marker to H- can also indicate intensification (644–46). No transitivity increase is involved, yet the affectedness of the object referent increases. In (646), the postposition changes as well.

(644) a. *eetįį* (T)
ee-tįį
3SG.S:DH.PFV:Ø-SG.sleep:IPV
'she was sleeping' UTCBAF13Nov0501:094

b. *ehtįį* (T)
eh-tįį
3SG.S:DH.PFV:H-SG.die:IPV
'she was dead, she died' UTCBAF13Nov0501:098

(645) a. *ch'enee'įį*
ch'-nee-'įį
INDF.O-3SG.S:QUAL:DH.PFV:Ø-steal:PFV
'he stole something' Kari (1997b)

b. *dits'įįkeey tneh'įį*
d-ts'įįkeey tneh-'įį
REFL.PSR-children 3SG.S:INC:QUAL:DH.PFV:H-hide:PFV
'she hid her children' UTOLAF13May2403:025

(646) a. *hiikah nanetah* (T)
hii-kah na-ne-ta'
3PL.S>3SG.P-for IT-QUAL:Ø.IPV:Ø-look:IPV
'they were looking for him' UTOLAF08Jul2801:019

b. *ik'anehtah* (T)
i-k'a-neh-tah
3SG.S>3SG.P-care-QUAL:Ø.IPV:H-take.care:IPV
'she took care of him' UTOLAF09Jun2202:048

27.3.2. Voice/valence prefix changes to D- or L-

Voice/valence prefix changes to D- or L- (called "D-effect" by Axelrod [1993], Jetté and Jones [2000], and Holton [2000]) can be caused by a number of detransitivizing operations (see 27.3.2.1) as well as by some uses of the iterative prefix (see 27.3.2.2; Holton [2000, 190] calls these "aspectual middle constructions"). Changes to D- and L- are equivalent; verb themes with a Ø- voice/valence prefix change to D- (647), while those with an H- voice/valence prefix change to L- (648; see also Kibrik [1996, 261]). Verb themes with a D- or L- voice/valence marker do not undergo further changes (649, 650).

(647) a. *negn' tah teedeeł* (T)

negn' *tah* *tee-deeł*
upland:ALL among 3PL.S:INC:DH.PFV:Ø-PL.move:PFV
'they went upland' UTOLAF08Apr2805:014

b. *nił'eh tetdeek* (N)

nił-eh *tet-deek*
RECP.P-with 3PL.S:INC:DH.PFV:D-PL.move:PFV
'[the guns] began to slide together [to the side]'
UTOLVDN07Aug2205:099

(648) a. *mikedhakkayh* (N)

m-i-ke-dhak-kayh
3SG.P-PP-foot-DH.PFV:1SG.S:H-strike.LRO:PFV
'I kicked him' UT Notebook #4, 11

b. *nił'ikehelkayh* (N)

nił-i-ke-hel-kayh
RECP.P-PP-foot-3PL.S:DH.PFV:L-strike.LRO:PFV
'they kicked each other' UTOLAF13May2801:067

(649) a. *hetk'į̨ą* (N)

het-k'į̨ą
3PL.S:Ø.IPV:D-exercise:IPV
'they are exercising' UT Notebook #3, 87

b. *nił'eh hetk'į̨ą* (N)

nił-eh *het-k'į̨ą*
RECP.P-with 3PL.S:Ø.IPV:D-exercise:IPV
'they are exercising together' (lit. 'with each other') UT Notebook #3, 87

(650) a. *dlagn eł hihdelxoh* (T)

dlagn *eł* *h-del-xoh*
squirrel with 3PL.S-QUAL:Ø.IPV:L-play:IPV
'they were playing with a squirrel' UTOLVDN13May2801:003

b. *nił'eh hihdelxoh* (T)

nił-eh *h-del-xoh*

RECP.P-with 3PL.S-QUAL:Ø.IPV:L-play:IPV

'they were playing with each other' UTCBAF13Nov0501:010

27.3.2.1. Transitivity decrease Four constructions can be distinguished here: passivization, reflexives, self-benefactives, and reciprocals. There are also a few verb themes that differ in transitivity and display the changes from Ø- to D- or from H- to L- but do not fit into either of these categories.

27.3.2.1.1. Passivization The D- and L- voice/valence prefixes can be used for passivization (651, 652).

(651) a. *yįįtsah* (T)

y-įį-tsah

3SG.S>3SG.O-AA.PFV:Ø-bury:PFV

'he buried her' UTOLVDN13May2901:041

b. *Aneg' et-tsah.* (T)

a-neg' *et-tsah*

NTRL-upland:ALL 3SG.O:Ø.IPV:D-bury:IPV

'He is buried up there.' UTOLVDN09Jun2302:027

(652) a. *shtidhehxįį* (T)

sh-t-dheh-xiin

1SG.O-3SG.S:INC-QUAL:DH.PFV:H-kill.SG.O:PFV

'he is about to kill me' UTOLVDN14Nov2301:339

b. *shtidhelxįį* (T)

sh-t-dhel-xįį

1SG.O-INC-QUAL:DH.PFV:L-kill.SG.O:PFV

'I am about to be killed' UTOLVDN14Nov2301:403

Passives in Dene languages are somewhat different from comparable constructions in Indo-European languages. While the AGENT is suppressed, the PATIENT argument is not promoted to subject status but remains in the direct object position. Third-person objects in passives are unmarked (651b).

Evidence from an irregular verb theme shows that this is a true case of AGENT suppression rather than a Ø-marked subject (653). With a first- and second-person subject the theme is P#d+Ø+nih 'say to P'; with third-person subjects it is P#H+nih 'say to P'. Note that the active form in (653a) is formed using the theme for third-person subjects, while the passive form in (653b) is formed from the other theme, indicating that this is not a case of an unmarked third-person subject.

(653) a. *nee'ehniik* (N)
nee-eh-niik
1PL.P-3SG.S:Ø.IPV:H-say:IPV:CUST
'he used to tell us' UTCBAF13Nov1203:004

b. *Hǫǫ' ch'a needatni'.* (N)
hǫǫ' ch'a nee-dat-ni'
thus FOC 1PL.P-QUAL:AA.PFV:D-say:PFV
'Thus we were told.' UTOLAF10Jul0901:013

Passivization is fairly rare in Upper Tanana, and direct elicitatiton usually results in impersonal constructions (654). An active form ('he shot me') is given in (654a). The speakers were then asked how to say 'I was shot'. (654b) contains the impersonal construction produced by the speakers. (654c) is a passive form constructed by me and judged grammatical by the speakers.

(654) a. *shdehk'aa* (N)
sh-deh-k'aa
1SG.O-3SG.S:QUAL:DH.PFV:H-shoot:PFV
'he shot me' UT Notebook #4, 11

b. *shihdehk'aa* (N)
sh-h-deh-k'aa
1SG.O-3PL.S-QUAL:DH.PFV:H-shoot:PFV
'they/someone shot me, I was shot' UT Notebook #4, 11

c. *shdelk'aa* (N)
sh-del-k'aa
1SG.O-QUAL:DH.PFV:L-shoot:PFV
'I was shot' UT Notebook #4, 11

Passivization of verbs with a postpositional object is exceedingly rare, but (655) shows a clear example.

(655) a. *nee'ahdįįni'* (T)
nee-a-hdįį-ni'
1PL.P-PP-3PL.S:QUAL:AA.PFV:Ø-say:PFV
'they taught us' UTOLVDN11Jul2902:013

b. *Hǫǫ t'eey ch'a nee'adatnį' neexon' du'.* (T)

hǫǫ'	*t'eey*	*ch'a*	*nee-a-dat-ni'*	*neexon*	*du'*
thus	ADVZR	FOC	1PL.P-PP-QUAL:AA.PFV:D-say:PFV	1PL	CT

'That's the way we were taught, us.' UTOLVDN11Jul2902:011

Passives formed from verbs with D- or L- voice/valence markers are indistinguishable from verb forms with an unmarked third-person subject; thus no examples can be provided.

27.3.2.1.2. Reflexive Reflexives in Upper Tanana are formed by the reflexive object prefix in the direct object (656, 657) or postpositional object (658) position in addition to a change in voice/valence marker. The reflexive object prefix has the form *id-* (singular) and *ihd-* (plural) in the direct object and *d-* in the postpositional object position.

(656) a. *dihtth'ek* (N)
dih-tth'ek
QUAL:Ø.PFV:1SG.S:Ø-hear:IPV
'I hear him/her' UTOLAF13May2801:059

b. *na'idishtth'ek* (N)
na-id-dish-tth'ek
IT-SG.REFL.O-QUAL:Ø.PFV:1SG.S:D-hear:IPV
'I hear myself' UTOLVDN10Jul2711:010

(657) a. *udihnih* (N)
u-dih-nih
3SG.P-QUAL:Ø.IPV:1SG.S:Ø-say:IPV
'I told her' UTOLAF12Jul1203:110

b. *idishnih* (N)
id-dish-nih
SG.REFL.O-QUAL:Ø.IPV:1SG.S:D-say:IPV
'I told myself' UTOLVDN14Apr2602:052

(658) a. *hiiyich'eh'aał* (T)
hiiy-i-ch'-eh-'aał
3PL.S>3SG.P-PP-INDF.O-Ø.IPV:H-feed:IPV
'they fed him' UTOLVDN13May2801:068

b. *dich'el'aał* (N)
d-i-ch'-el-'aał
REFL.P-PP-INDF.O-3SG.S:Ø.IPV:L-feed:IPV
'he fed himself' UTOLVDN10Jul2713:011

Occasionally reflexivity is implied but not overtly marked with a reflexive direct or postpositional object prefix. In those cases the voice/valence change still takes place. (659) contrasts a nonreflexive (659a), an overt reflexive (659b) and an implied reflexive form (659c).

(659) a. *ik'anehtah* (T)
i-k'a-neh-tah
3SG.S>3SG.P-care-QUAL:Ø.IPV:H-take.care:IPV
'she took care of him' UTOLAF09Jun2202:048

b. *dik'analta'* (T)
d-k'a-nal-ta'
REFL.P-care-QUAL:OPT:2PL.S:L-take.care:OPT
'take care of yourselves, be careful!' UTCBAF13Nov0501:029

c. *Rowena k'aneltah* (N)
Rowena k'a-nel-tah
Rowena care-3SG.S:QUAL:Ø.IPV:L-take.care:IPV
'Rowena takes care of herself, is careful' UT Notebook #4, 19

27.3.2.1.3. Self-benefactives Closely related to the reflexive construction is the self-benefactive construction, where the agent performs the action expressed by the verb theme for his or her own good. The self-benefactive construction consists of the qualifier prefix *d-* and a voice/valence prefix change (660, 661).

(660) a. *tsät etthee*ł (N)
*tsät e-tthee*ł
wood 3SG.S:Ø.IPV:Ø-chop:IPV
'he chopped wood' UT Notebook #4, 8

b. *tsät (daa) det-ttheeł* (N)
tsät *d-aa* *det-ttheeł*
wood REFL.P-for 3SG.S:QUAL:Ø.IPV:D-chop:IPV
'he chopped wood for himself' UT Notebook #4, 8

(661) a. *jign naktsayh* (N)
jign *nak-tsayh*
berries QUAL:Ø.IPV:1SG.S:H-pick:IPV
'I am picking berries' UT Notebook #4, 9

b. *jign dnagntsayh* (N)
jign *dnagn-tsayh*
berries QUAL:QUAL:Ø.IPV:1SG.S:H-pick:IPV
'I am picking berries for myself' UT Notebook #4, 9

(660b) was first uttered with the postpositional phrase *daa*[4] 'for himself', but the speakers accepted it without this phrase as well. Interestingly, self-benefactives of verbs with a D- or L- voice/valence prefix were consistently rejected by speakers. In response to the prompt 'he's hauling water for himself', the speakers suggested (662b) after some discussion. (662c), suggested by me, was unanimously rejected with and without *daa/dixah*.

(662) a. *Tuu kah eltąyh.* (N)
tuu *kah* *el-tąyh*
water for 3SG.S:Ø.IPV:L-haul:IPV
'He's hauling water.' UT Notebook #4, 8

b. *Tuu kah eltąyh dixah.* (N)
tuu *kah* *el-tąyh* *d-xah*
water for 3SG.S:Ø.IPV:L-haul:IPV REFL.P-for
'He's hauling water for himself.' UT Notebook #4, 8

c. **Tuu kah deltąyh (daa, dixah).*
Intended: 'He's hauling water for himself.' UT Notebook #4, 8

27.3.2.1.4. Reciprocals The reciprocal construction also requires a voice/valence prefix change from Ø- to D- and from H- to L- (663–666). In intransitive themes such as (663, 664), the reciprocal direct object prefix is usually translated as 'together'.

(663) a. *stahnįįdeeł* (T)
sta-hnįį-deeł
away-3PL.S:N.PFV:Ø-PL.go:PFV
'they went away' UTOLVDN07Oct2602:003

b. *staniłtsenetdeeł* (T)
sta-nił-tse-net-deeł
away-RECP.O-1PL.S:INC-QUAL:DH.PFV:D-PL.go:PFV
'we wandered away together' UTCBAF13Nov0501:073

(664) a. *ts'utnah* (N)
ts'ut-nah
1PL.S:OPT:D-work:OPT
'let's work' UT Notebook #3, 76

b. *niłts'utnah* (N)
nił-ts'ut-nah
RECP.O-1PL.S:OPT:D-work:OPT
'let's work together' UTOLVDN13May2905:041

(665) a. *stsay ts'ineh'įh* (N)
s-tsay *ts'-neh-'įh*
1SG.PSR-grandfather 1PL.S-QUAL:Ø.IPV:H-see:IPV
'we saw my grandfather' UTOLAF12Jul1203:107

b. *niłts'enel'įh* (N)
nił-ts'-nel-'įh
RECP.O-1PL.S-QUAL:Ø.IPV:L-see:IPV
'we saw each other' UTOLAF13May2801:053

(666) a. *jign ts'uldeel* (N)
jign *ts'ul-deel*
berries 1PL.S:OPT:L-eat:OPT
'let's eat berries' UT Notebook #5, 31

b. *naniłts'uldeel*
na-nił-ts'ul-deel
IT-RECP.O-1SG.S:OPT:L-eat:OPT
'let's eat each other' UTOLVDN13May2905:045

Examples for reciprocal postpositional objects are given in (647–650) above.

There are a few themes that have a lexicalized reciprocal object prefix translated as 'together' (667). Note that the reciprocal prefix in (667a) triggers a voice/valence marker change while the one in (667b) does not.

(667) a. *łidahdetxą̨ą̨* (T)
łi-da-h-det-xą̨ą̨
together-mouth-3PL.S-QUAL:Ø.IPV:D-kill:PL.O:IPV
'they argue' UTOLVDN14Nov2301:161

b. *Ts'ayh gaay iin naann' łits'inuhtl'uh...* (T)
ts'ay gaay iin naann' łi-ts'-nuh-tl'uh
canoe small PL across:ALL together-1PL.S-QUAL:OPT:H-tie:OPT
'Let's tie the small canoes together...' UTOLAF09Jun2902:016

27.3.2.1.5. Other transitivity reduction A final set of voice/valence marker changes cannot be labeled as clearly; transitivity is being reduced, but there is a significant semantic change as well (668–670).

(668) a. *nidhihdät* (N)
n-dhih-dät
QUAL-DH.PFV:1SG.S:Ø-twist:PFV
'I twisted it (e.g., sinew)' UTOLAF15Dec0608:006

b. *tetdät* (N)
tet-dät
3SG.S:INC:DH.PFV:D-animal.run:PFV
'it [animal] started running' UTOLVDN13May2004:089

(669) a. *łį̨į̨ aktsänh* (N)
łį̨į̨ ak-tsänh
dog Ø.IPV:1SG.S:H-smell:IPV
'I smell the dog' UTOLAF13May2801:064

b. *łį̨į̨ miholtsänh* (N)
łį̨į̨ m-i-hol-tsänh
dog 3SG.P-PP-AR:Ø.IPV:L-be.smelly:IPV
'the dog is smelly' UTOLAF13May2801:065

(670) a. *shdhįhshyiy* (T)
sh-dhįh-shyiy
1SG.O-DH.PFV:2SG.S:H-save:PFV:NOM
'you, having saved me' UTOLVDN13May2909:133

b. *na'elshyiyh* (N)
na-el-shyiyh
IT-3SG.S:DH.PFV:L-rest:IPV
'he's resting' UTOLAF15Dec0608:041

The verb stem in (668) is glossed as 'crooked' in the stem file (Kari 1997b); with a Ø- voice/valence prefix, it can occur in intransitive neuter and transitive active themes meaning 'be crooked' and 'twist o', respectively. The verb theme formed with the D- voice/valence prefix refers to the curved body shape that most four-legged animals have when running. The relationship between the themes in (669) is somewhat unclear. The postpositional object prefix in (669b) is coreferential to the dog, but there is also an areal subject. The relationship between the themes in (670) is similarly unclear.

27.3.2.2. Iterative The iterative derivation na#(D) discussed in chap. 34 triggers a change in voice/valence prefix when applied to intransitive themes, but not always when applied to transitive themes. This is indicated by (D) in the prefix string.

27.3.2.2.1. Iterative in intransitive themes The change of voice/valence marker is obligatory in intransitive themes (671, 672) .

(671) a. *etsah* (T)
e-tsah
3SG.S:Ø.IPV:Ø-cry:IPV
'he cried' UTOLVDN13May2801:046

b. *na'et-tsah* (T)
na-et-tsah
IT-3SG.S:Ø.IPV:D-cry:IPV
'she cried again' UTCBAF13Nov0501:328

(672) a. *Tay' t'eey haadał.* (T)
tay' t'eey haa-dał
again ADVZR 3PL.S:AA.PFV:Ø-PL.go:IPV
'Again they are walking.' UTCBVDN13Nov1101:003

b. *Ushe'e na'atdał...*
u-she'e na-at-dał
3SG.PSR-son IT-3PL.S:AA.IPV:D-PL.go:IPV
'Her sons were walking back...' UTCBAF13Nov0501:283

27.3.2.2.2. Iterative in transitive themes The iterative derivation changes the voice/valence prefix in many transitive themes (673, 674).

(673) a. *nnak-'įh* (B)
n-nak-'įh
2SG.O-QUAL:Ø.IPV:1SG.S:H-see:IPV
'I see you' UTOLAF10Jul0202:140

b. *nannagn'įįł*
na-n-tnagn-'įįł
IT-2SG.O-INC:QUAL:AA.IPV:1SG.S:L-see:FUT
'I'll see you again' UT Notebook #1, 3

(674) a. *nishnįhteeyh* (N)
ni-sh-nįh-teeyh
TERM-1SG.O-N.IPV:2SG.S:L-handle.AO:IPV
'put SG me up there' UTCBVDN13Nov1401:049

b. *niishnalteeyh* (N)
ni-na-sh-nal-teeyh
TERM-IT-1SG.O-N.IPV:2PL.S:L-handle.AO:IPV
'take SG me back across' UTCBAF14May2001:005

In other transitive themes (675) and in themes with a postpositional object (676), the iterative derivation does not trigger a change in voice/valence prefixes.

(675) a. *Tl'aan Mary dineh choh uuniik.* (N)
tl'aan Mary dineh choh uu-niik
and Mary man tall 3SG.S:CON:Ø.IPV:Ø-marry:IPV
'Then Mary marries the tall man.' UTOLAF12Jul1202:021

b. *dik'eh eltsiin na'uuniik* (T)

d-k'eh *el-tsiin*
REFL.P-like 3SG.S:DH.PFV:L-appear:PFV:NOM

na-uu-niik
IT-3SG.S:CON:Ø.IPV:Ø-marry:IPV

'he married again [a woman] who looked like him'
UTOLVDN13May2901:064

(676) a. *ntsą' huhheey* (T)

n-ts'ą' *huh-heey*
2SG.P-to AR:Ø.IPV:1SG.S:Ø-speak:IPV:NOM

'I, talking to you' UTOLAFMay0807:074

b. *k'at'eey nts'ą̈' nootihheel* (N)

k'at'eey *n-ts'ą̈'* *na-hu-tih-heel*
EG 2SG.P-to IT-AR-INC:AA.IPV:1SG.S:Ø-speak:FUT:NEG

'I will not speak to you again' UTOLAF12Jul1202:029

Data similar to that presented in (673–676) is reported in Holton (2000) for Tanacross. Holton (2000, 189) suggests, based on personal communication from Michael E. Krauss, that the presence or absence of the change has to do with the affectedness of the object referent: stronger affectedness results in a changed voice/valence prefix marker, weaker affectedness results in no change. Judging from the data presented above, this does not seem to be the case for Upper Tanana; for example, the affectedness in getting married is stronger than that in being seen, which would suggest that a change of voice/valence prefix would take place in the former theme but not in the latter—the opposite of what we observe in the data.

In related languages the iterative derivation does not affect the voice/valence marker in transitive verb themes, as discussed, for example, by Rice (1989, 464–65) for Slave or by Hargus (2007, 440) for Witsuwit'en.

27.3.2.3. Perambulative The perambulative derivation 'around' has the form na#t+D, łoo#(t); the distribution of the two derivational strings is not clear, as discussed in chap. 35.2.1.10.1. Interestingly, the first of these does trigger a change in voice/valence prefix (677), while the second one does not (678).

(677) a. *hu'eł natsetdak* (T)
hu-eł *na-tset-dak*
3PL.P-with PRMB-1PL.S:INC:Ø.IPV:D-PL.go:IPV:CUST
'we were walking around with them' UTOLAF09Jun2902:004

b. *natsatkeeł* (N)
na-tsat-keeł
PRMB-1PL.S:INC:AA.IPV:D-go.by.boat:FUT
'we will boat around' UTOLVDN07Aug2205:086

(678) a. *łoohtedak* (T)
łoo-h-te-dak
PRMB-3PL.S-INC:Ø.IPV:Ø-PL.go:IPV:CUST
'they used to go around' UTCBAF13Nov0501:020

b. *łoonįįshyah* (N)
łoo-nįį-shyah
PRMB-3SG.S:N.PFV:Ø-SG.go:PFV
'she walked around' UTOLVDN13May2003:012

27.4. Summary

There are four voice/valence prefixes: Ø-, D-, H-, and L-. They occur immediately preceding the stem. The voice/valence prefixes are part of the lexical specification of each verb theme; then they have no inherent meaning.

The voice/valence prefixes are also used derivationally. A change from Ø- to H- is indicative of transitivization or intensification. A change from Ø- to D- or from H- to L- is indicative of detransitivization through a variety of processes. The same change is observed in many instances of the iterative and the perambulative derivations.

Notes

1. In perfective stems, the onset consonant is /tł/, as discussed in chap. 26.
2. Kibrik (1993, 1996) uses the term "transitivity indicators" instead of "classifier" or "voice/valence marker."
3. I want to thank Falene Karey-McKenna, who drew my attention to this particular example and its unusual morphology.
4. Both *daa* and *dixah* are attested.

28 Subject marking

In this chapter the subject prefixes in the "inner subject position" in the Upper Tanana verb are described. Like in all other Dene languages, subjects are marked in two different positions in the verb word (Rice 2000, chap. 10).

Inner subjects (first-person singular and second-person singular and plural) are marked in position 2 of the verb template (see table 24.1), immediately to the left of the voice/valence prefix. *Outer* subjects (third-person singular and plural, first-person plural, and indefinite or areal subjects) are marked in the pronominal zone (position 6 in the template). They are described in chap. 31.

The positional split between inner and outer subject prefixes is attested in all Dene languages (see Jung [1999] for a comparative account). Jung observes that this formal split corresponds to a distinction between speech act participants and non-speech act participants and shows that in many Dene languages, first-and second- person singular and plural are all marked in the inner subject position, while all third-person subjects (with the possible exception of third-person singular, which is unmarked) are marked in the outer subject position. Rice (2000, chap. 10) even suggests that the positional split between subject prefixes reflects a categorical distinction, calling the prefixes found in the inner subject position "person inflection," those in the outer subject position "number inflection."

In Upper Tanana, as in all other Alaskan Dene languages, the original first-person plural subject prefix has been lost. The function of denoting first-person plural subject has been taken over by the (historical) human indefinite prefix (Jung 1999), which occurs in the outer subject position (see chap. 31). There are thus only three inner subject prefixes in Upper Tanana: first-person singular, second-person singular, and second-person plural.

The inner subject prefixes coalesce with the following voice/valence prefixes to the point where it is close to impossible to tease voice/valence prefix and subject prefix apart. It is best to consider them portmanteau morphemes, which coalesce in turn with the conjugation and mode prefixes of positions 4 and 3. The inventory of inner subject–voice/valence prefix combinations in the Ø- imperfective (characterized by the absence of overt marking in positions 4 and 3) is given in table 28.1. Portmanteaus resulting from verbs containing other conjugation and mode prefixes are given in chap. 29.

	Ø-	D-	H-	L-
1SG	ih-	ish-	ak-	ag-
2SG	į̨i-	in-	įh-	įl-/il-
2PL	ah-	at-	ah-	al-

Table 28.1. Inner-subject voice/valence prefix portmanteaus in the Ø-imperfective

The phonology and function of each of the three inner subject prefixes is described in 28.1 and 28.2. Their syntactic behavior is described in 28.3.

28.1. First person

Only the first-person singular subject prefix is marked in the inner subject position.

28.1.1. Phonology

The first-person singular subject prefix underlyingly has the form *ih*-. It has this shape only in verb forms with a Ø- voice/valence prefix; with all other voice/valence markers, the first-person singular subject prefix combines with the voice/valence prefix into a portmanteau morpheme (see table 28.1). In these portmanteau morphemes the contribution of each part is not identifiable (679).

(679) a. *ihtsüh* (N)
ih-tsüh
ø.IPV:1SG.S:ø-cry:IPV
'I'm crying' — UT Notebook #3, 71

b. *tseey ishnąą* (N)
tseey ish-nąą
tea ø.IPV:1SG.S:D-drink:IPV
'I'm drinking tea' — UT Notebook #3, 67

c. *shyi' akt'iah* (N)
shyi' ak-t'iah
meat ø.IPV:1SG.S:H-fry:IPV
'I'm frying meat' UT Notebook #3, 68

d. *agnshyak* (N)
ag-shyak
ø.IPV:1SG.S:L-lie:IPV
'I am lying (telling an untruth)' UT Notebook #4, 59

28.1.1.1. Glottal stop insertion Glottal stop insertion takes place when one of these portmanteaus occurs in word-initial position (680a) or follows a prefix ending in a vowel (680b). When the inner subject prefixes follow a consonant, no glottal stop is inserted (680c). All prefixes in (680) are conjunct prefixes.

(680) a. [ʔ]*ihsäł* (N)
ih-säł
ø.IPV:1SG.S:ø-holler:IPV
'I'm hollering' UTOLAF09Aug1202:034

b. *hu'ihxąą* (T)
hu-ih-xąą
3PL.O-AA.PFV:1SG.S:ø-kill.PL.O:PFV
'I killed them' UTCBAF14Jul1805:053

c. *dihnih* (N)
d-ih-nih
QUAL-ø.IPV:1SG.S:ø-say:IPV
'I say' UTCBVDN13Nov0805:001

When an inner subject prefix is preceded by a disjunct prefix, a glottal stop is inserted regardless of whether the disjunct prefix ends in a consonant (681a) or a vowel (681b).

(681) a. *ni'eeł'ihłeek* (N)
ni-'eeł-ih-łeek
TERM-trap-ø.IPV:1SG.S:ø-handle.PL.O:IPV:CUST
'I customarily set traps' UTOLAF15Dec0708:003

b. *na'ihsäł* (N)
na-ih-säł
CONT-Ø.IPV:1SG.S:Ø-holler:IPV
'I kept hollering' UTOLAF09Aug1202:032

28.1.1.2. Nasalization of *ag-* The portmanteau *ag-* '1sg.s:I'- almost always occurs in a postnasalized variant [agŋ] or [aŋ], particularly in the Northway dialect. This is usually represented in the orthography; the form in (679d) is usually written as *agnshyak* 'I am lying' and pronounced [ʔagŋʃʲak] or [ʔaŋʃʲak], although [ʔagʃʲak] is also attested for speakers of the Tetlin dialect.

28.1.2. Functions

The first-person singular subject prefix has two functions: indexing the speaker and indexing the subject of a matrix verb in certain subordinating constructions.

28.1.2.1. Indexing the speaker This is the most common function of the first-person singular subject prefix, illustrated by (679–681) above.

The first-person subject prefix is also used to index the speaker of quoted speech or thought (682).

(682) a. *"Hǫǫsu' t'eey ay nach'ih'aal; tsinąą'įį," nih.* (T)
hǫǫsu' t'eey ay na-ch'-ih-'aal
well ADVZR that CONT-INDF.O-Ø.IPV:1SG.S:Ø-eat:IPV:NOM
ts'inaa'įį nih
thank.you.much say:IPV
'"I am eating really well, thank you very much," he said.'
UTOLVDN08Mar1302:022

b. *Tl'aan, "Hugn tihdaał," iyniinįįthanh.* (T)
tl'aan hugn tih-daał
and.then here INC:AA.IPV:1SG.S:Ø-SG.stay:FUT
i-nii-nįį-thanh
PP-mind-3SG.S:QUAL:Ø.PFV:Ø-think:IPV
'And then, "I'm going to stay here," he thought.'
UTOLVDN13May2901:042

Quoted speech is described in volume 2.

28.1.2.2. Indexing the subject of the matrix clause In certain subordinate clauses the first-person singular subject prefix is coreferential to the subject of the verb in the matrix clause (683).

(683) a. *Ushnaa' inįįthänh?* (N)

ush-naa' *i-nįį-thänh*
OPT:1SG.S:D-work:OPT PP-QUAL:Ø.PFV:2SG.S:Ø-want:IPV

'Do you SG want to work?' UT Notebook #3, 72

b. *Ts'iikeey iin naagn' ogndeel xah, hanadogn ddhäł k'it, jign kah nanetah.* (N)

ts'iikeey *iin* *naagn'* *ogn-deel*
children PL eyes OPT:1SG.S:L-eat.PL.O:OPT:NOM

xah *ha-na-dogn* *ddhäł* *k'it* *jign* *kah*
PURP ADJ-MED-up:AR mountain on berry for

na-ne-tah
IT-3SG.S:QUAL:Ø.IPV:Ø-look.for:IPV

'He looked for berries up on the mountain so he (lit.: I) could eat the children's eyes.' UTOLVDN11Aug0805:003

The different subordinating constructions involved here are described in volume 2.

28.2. Second person

Both second-person subject prefixes are marked in the inner subject position. The phonology of each prefix is described in 28.2.1 and 28.2.2. The functions of both prefixes are described in 28.2.3.

28.2.1. Phonology of the second-person singular subject prefix

The second-person singular subject prefix is *į-*. While this prefix also interacts with the following voice/valence prefix (684), it is usually possible to identify the contributions of each morpheme in the resulting forms shown in table 28.1 above.

(684) a. *įįtsüh* (N)

įį-tsüh
Ø.IPV:2SG.S:Ø-cry:IPV

'you SG cry' UT Notebook #3, 71

b. *tseey innąą* (N)

tseey in-nąą
tea ø.IPV:2SG.S:D-drink:IPV
'you SG drink tea' UT Notebook #3, 67

c. *kee įhtsayh* (N)

kee įh-tsayh
shoes ø.IPV:2SG.S:H-make.SG.O:IPV
'you SG are making shoes' UT Notebook #3, 68

d. *įlshyak* (N)

įl-shyak
ø.IPV:2SG.S:L-lie:IPV
'you SG are lying (telling an untruth)' UT Notebook #4, 59

28.2.1.1. Glottal stop insertion When the second-person singular subject prefix occurs in word-initial position (685a), or if it is preceded by a conjunct prefix ending in a vowel (685b), glottal stop insertion takes place. When preceded by a consonantal conjunct prefix such as the *n*- qualifier, no glottal stop is inserted (685c).

(685) a. [ʔ]*innah* (N)

in-nah
ø.IPV:2SG.S:D-work:IPV
'you SG work' UT Notebook # 3, 76

b. *u'įįniiy* (N)

uu-įį-niiy
CON-ø.IPV:2SG.S:ø-grab:IPV:IMP
'grab SG [the eggs]... UTOLVDN07Aug2205:017

c. *niljit* (T)

nil-jit
QUAL:ø.IPV:2SG.S:L-be.scared:IPV
'you SG are scared' UTOLVDN14Nov2301:457

Glottal stop insertion does take place after disjunct prefixes regardless of their shape (686).

(686) a. *bexał'įįłeey* (N)
b-xał-įį-łeey
3SG.P-club-Ø.IPV:2SG.S:Ø-handle.PL.O:IPV:IMP
'throw clubs at it' UT Notebook #4, 15

b. *na'įįdaał*
na-įį-daał
IT-AA.IPV:2SG.S-D:SG.go:IPV
'you SG are walking back' UTCBAF13Nov0501:336

28.2.1.2. Denasalization before L- The second-person singular subject prefix has a tendency to become denasalized before L-, particularly in the Tetlin dialect (685c).

28.2.2. Phonology of the second-person plural subject

The second-person plural subject prefix is *ah-*. Again it is possible to identify the contributions of both subject prefix and voice/valence prefix in the portmanteau morphemes in table 28.1. No changes take place when the voice/valence prefix is Ø-. When the second-person plural subject prefix is followed by an overt voice/valence prefix (D-, H-, L-), the final consonant of the subject prefix is deleted to avoid a syllable-final consonant cluster (687).

(687) a. *ahtsüh* (N)
ah-tsüh
Ø.IPV:2PL.S:Ø-cry:IPV
'you PL cry' UT Notebook #3, 71

b. *tseey atnąą* (N)
tseey at-nąą
tea Ø.IPV:2PL.S:D-drink:IPV
'you PL drink tea' UT Notebook #3, 67

c. *kee ahtsayh* (N)
kee ah-tsayh
shoes Ø.IPV:2PL.S:H-make.SG.O:IPV
'you PL are making shoes' UT Notebook #3, 68

d. *alshyak* (N)
al-shyak
ø.IPV:2PL.S:L-lie:IPV
'you PL are lying (telling an untruth)' UT Notebook #4, 59

28.2.2.1. Glottal stop insertion Glottal stop insertion takes place when the second-person plural subject prefix occurs in word-initial position (688a) or following a vocalic conjunct prefix (688b). When the second-person plural subject prefix follows a consonantal conjunct prefix, glottal stop insertion does not take place (688c).

(688) a. [ʔ]*alshyak* (N)
al-shyak
ø.IPV:2PL.S:L-lie:IPV
'you PL are lying (telling an untruth)' UT Notebook #4, 59

b. *nihu'ahɫeek* (N)
ni hu ah-ɫeek
TERM-3PL.O-ø.IPV:2PL.S:ø-handle.PL.O:IPV:CUST
'put PL them somewhere' UTOLAF10Jul0901:038

c. *Dii nah'įį?* (N)
dii nah-'įį
what QUAL:AA.PFV:2PL.S:H-see:PFV
'What did you PL see? UTOLAF14Apr3001:007

Glottal stop insertion always takes place following disjunct prefixes (689).

(689) a. *ni'eeɫ'ahɫeeyh* (N)
ni-'eeɫ-ah-ɫeeyh
TERM-trap-ø.IPV:2PL.S:ø-handle.PL.O:IPV
'set PL traps' UT Notebook #5, 33

b. *nat'u'ahɫe'* (T)
nat'u-ah-ɫe'
skin-OPT:2PL.S:ø-handle.PL.O:OPT
'skin PL [the muskrats]...' UTOLVDN07Nov2803:012

28.2.3. Functions of the second-person subject prefixes

The second-person subject prefixes index the (singular or plural) addressee. They can be used in declarative sentences, questions, and requests.

28.2.3.1. Second-person subject in declarative sentences The use of second-person subject prefixes in declarative sentences (690) is not particularly frequent.

(690) a. *k'at'eey įįsuuy* (T)
k'at'eey įį-suuy
NEG NEG.PFV:2SG.S:ø-be.good:IPV:NEG
'you SG are not a good person' UTOLVDN08Mar1307:005

b. *k'a shdahtthagn* (T)
k'a sh-dah-tthagn
NEG 1SG.O-QUAL:NEG.PFV:2PL.S:ø-listen:IPV:NEG
'you PL did not listen to me' UTOLVDN07Nov2802:020

28.2.3.2. Second-person subjects in questions The use of second-person subject prefixes in questions is quite common (691).

(691) a. *dii xah ch'a dįįdąy?* (N)
dii xah ch'a dįį-dąy
why FOC QUAL:ø.IPV:2SG.S:ø-do:IPV:NOM
'why are you SG doing [this]?' UTCBVDN13Nov1401:025

b. *Shoh aldeeł?* (N)
shoh al-deeł
bear ø.IPV:2PL.S:L-eat:IPV
'Do you PL eat bear?' UTOLAF09Aug12:041

Question formation is described in volume 2.

28.2.3.3. Second person subject prefixes in requests Also common is the use of second-person subject prefixes in requests (692a) and negative requests (692b).

(692) a. *Ldil kah negn' na'įįdaał!* (N)
ldil kah negn' na-įį-daał
tea for upland:ALL IT-AA.IPV:2SG.S-D:SG.go:IPV
'Go back up for tea!' UTOLAF09Aug1202:024

b. *Sǫ' hǫǫ' dahdįį' t'axoh!* (N)

sǫ' *hǫǫ'* *dah-dįį'* *t'axoh*
PROH thus QUAL:OPT:2PL.S:Ø-do:OPT:IMP enough
'Don't you guys do that again!' UTOLAF09Aug1202:041

See Lovick (2016) for more on request formation. Requests are also described in volume 2.

28.3. Syntax of inner subject prefixes

In this section all three inner subject prefixes (first-person singular and second-person singular and plural) are discussed together.

28.3.1. Pronominal prefixes

The inner subject prefixes are pronominal prefixes, i.e., a verb form inflected with an inner subject prefix can function as an independent clause without additional noun phrases or free pronouns (693).

(693) a. *Ihtsüh.* (N)

ih-tsüh
Ø.IPV:1SG.S:Ø-cry:IPV
'I am crying' UT Notebook #3, 71

b. *Įįtsüh?* (N)

įį-tsüh
Ø.IPV:2SG.S:Ø-cry:IPV
'Are you SG crying?' UT Notebook #3, 71

c. *Ahtsüh?* (N)

ah-tsüh
Ø.IPV:2PL.S:Ø-cry:IPV
'Are you PL crying?' UT Notebook #3, 71

28.3.2. Inner subject prefixes with free noun phrases

Verb forms inflected with an inner subject prefix do not usually co-occur with coreferential free noun phrases. (694), for example, is not grammatical with a coreferential interpretation. The sentence is marginally acceptable if the free noun phrase refers to the addressee, with a translation such as "Olga, I am crying" (speaker ≠ Olga).

(694) **Olga ihtsüh.* (N)
Olga ih-tsüh
Olga ø.IPV:1SG.S:ø-cry:IPV
Intended: 'I, Olga, am crying.'

In second-person forms, coreferential noun phrases with a vocative function[1] are permitted. The noun and the verb in (695) are separated from the clause by a pause, which is reflected here by the use of commas.

(695) a. *Chaay, utth'an' dah'ogn t'a'įįłeey!* (T)
chaay u-tth'an' dah-'ogn
grandchild 3SG.PSR-bones PROX-outside:AR
t'a-įį-łeey
under-ø.IPV:2SG.S:ø-handle.PL.O:IPV:IMP
'Grandchild, plant his bones outside!' UTCBAF13Nov0501:262

b. *Ts'iikeey iin, łįį ich'ah'aal!* (N)
ts'iikeey iin łįį i-ch'ah-'aal
children PL dog PP-INDF.O:ø.IPV:2PL.S:H-feed:IPV:IMP
'Children, feed the dogs!' UT Notebook #4, 16

The co-occurrence of free noun phrases with inner subject prefixes is also possible in predicative constructions (696).

(696) a. *Ishyiit dą' k'at'eey ihshyaan nts'ą' ts'iiniin ihłiin eł.* (T)
ishyiit dą' k'at'eey ih-shyaan nts'ą'
then at:PST NEG NEG.PFV:1SG.S:ø-grow.up:PFV:NEG and
ts'iiniin ih-łiin eł
child ø.PFV:1SG.S-be:IPV:NOM and
'At that time I wasn't fully grown up, I was a child.'
UTOLAF09Jun2201:016

b. *Tthi' du' dindayh ǫǫłe' de'!* (T)
tthi' du' dindayh ǫǫ-łe' de'
head CT bearberry OPT:2SG.S:ø-be:OPT if
'His head though, you SG shall be bearberries!'
UTCBAF13Nov0501:268

28.3.3. Inner subject prefixes with coreferential free pronouns

Verb forms inflected with an inner subject prefix co-occur occasionally with free pronouns (697).

(697) a. *Nan, nan ch'ale shkeey dach'įįxaan hąą?* (T)

nan *nan* *ch'ale* *sh-keey*
2SG 2SG FOC 1SG.PSR-village

da-ch'įį-xaan *hąą*
completely-INDF.O:AA.PFV:2SG.S:Ø-kill.PL.O:PFV:NOM right

'You, you SG are the who killed off my whole village, right? '
UTOLVDN13May2801:200

b. *shin udak-'aan* (T)

shin *uu-dak-'aan*
1SG CON-QUAL:I.PFV:1SG.S:H-find.CO:PFV:NOM

'I'm the one who found him' UTOLVDN13May2801:065

c. *Diaa nuhxon shyįį' didhaltth'ih...* (T)

diaa *nuhxon* *shyįį'* *d-dhal-tth'ih*
why 2PL alone QUAL-DH.PFV:2PL.S:L-PL.stay:IPV

'Wy do you PL live all by yourselves...'
UTOLAF13May2403:086

Free pronouns are discussed in more detail in chap. 19.

28.4. Summary

In this chapter the inventory of inner subject prefixes (first-person singular subject, second-person singular and plural subject) is described. The three prefixes form portmanteaus with the voice/valence prefixes; while the portmanteaus involving the two second-person subject prefixes are relatively transparent, the ones involving the first-person singular subject prefix are synchronously unanalyzable.

The first-person singular subject prefix indexes the speaker or, in certain subordination contexts, the subject of the matrix clause. The second-person subject prefixes index the addressee; they are used occasionally in declaratives and more commonly in questions and requests. It was shown that syntactically the subject prefixes function as pronominal affixes. They may co-occur with free person pronouns and noun phrases only in appositive or predicative constructions.

Notes

1. The lack of possessor prefix in the obligatorily possessed kinship term *chaay* 'woman's grandchild' is typical of vocatives; see volume 2.

29 Conjugation and mode prefixes

In this chapter the prefixes from position 3 (mode) and 4 (conjugation) of the verb template (see table 24.1) are described. Because the conjugation and mode prefixes are tightly fused with each other and with the surrounding morphological material, they are treated together, even though they are clearly found in separate positions and have very different functions (Rice and Hargus 1989).

As has been pointed out by numerous scholars, the label "mode" is somewhat problematic, since the categories expressed by morphemes found in this position include not just modality but also viewpoint aspect and polarity. It is used here for lack of a better term. There are four mode prefixes: Ø- 'imperfective', *į*- 'perfective', *u*- 'optative', and *ì*- 'negative perfective; transitional'. They are assigned to the same morpheme slot because they are mutually exclusive; a semantic argument for this cannot be made (see, however, Axelrod [1993, 19–20] for a different view in discussing Koyukon). The imperfective and perfective prefixes express viewpoint aspect. The optative expresses that an action, event, or state is desirable. The *ì*- prefix can function as negative perfective or can be used in certain aspectual derivations. More detail on the functions of these prefixes is given in volume 2.

All verb themes can take the perfective, optative, and negative prefixes; the imperfective prefix is limited to active verb themes; see chap. 25.

There are five conjugation prefixes: Ø-, *aa*-, *n*-, *dh*-, and *ì*-. The *aa*-conjugation marker is the reflex of what is called the *gh*- conjugation prefix in other Dene languages (see, e.g., Tenenbaum [1978] for Dena'ina, Kari [1979] for Ahtna, Jetté and Jones [2000] for Koyukon). The *dh*- conjugation marker is the reflex of what is called the *s*- conjugation prefix in Kari (1990), *inter alia*. The *ì*- and *n*- conjugation prefixes have the same label in other sources.

The conjugation markers occur only in perfective and imperfective verb forms; the optative and the negative mode prefixes preclude the occurrence of a conjugation marker. This distinguishes Upper Tanana from languages such as Kaska (Moore 2002) or Slave (Rice 1989), where optative forms also contain a conjugation prefix.

Table 29.1 shows which conjugation and mode combinations are possible, and what they are called in this grammar. The discussion in the remainder of this chapter is based on these distinctions.

Conjugation	Mode	Short label
Ø-	Ø-	Ø- imperfective
aa-	Ø-	*aa*- imperfective
n-	Ø-	*n*- imperfective
ì-	Ø-	*i*- imperfective
Ø-	į-	Ø- perfective
aa-	į-	*aa*- perfective
n-	į-	*n*- perfective
dh-	į-	*dh*- perfective
ì-	į-	*i*- perfective
—	u-	optative
—	ì-	negative-perfective

Table 29.1. Possible conjugation/mode prefix combinations

As alluded to above, the conjugation and mode prefixes are tightly fused in Upper Tanana. The conjugation-mode complex then in turn fuses with the surrounding material, so its surface form is influenced both by the preceding morphemes (usually the conjunct pronominal prefixes of position 6 and qualifiers of position 5, but sometimes disjunct prefixes as well) and the following morphemes (inner subjects of position 2 and voice/valence markers of position 1). In fact, there is a strong tendency for all conjunct prefixes to be "squished" into one pre-stem syllable of the form (C)CV: or (C)CV(C). This syllable is treated throughout this grammar as a portmanteau morpheme and is glossed accordingly. The rules creating these portmanteau prefixes are described in the following sections as well as in chap. 30 and 31.

29.1. Imperfective Ø-

The imperfective prefix has the form Ø- in all forms. It is limited to active verbs marked by one of the conjugation prefixes Ø-, *aa*-, *n*-, or *ì*-. The *dh*-conjugation marker does not co-occur with the imperfective prefix.

29.1.1. The Ø- imperfective

The Ø- imperfective is characterized by a Ø- conjugation prefix; that is, both positions 3 and 4 are phonologically empty. In the absence of qualifier prefixes the pre-stem syllable then consists of just the subject–voice/valence marker complex. Table 29.2 shows the surface forms. The vowel in forms without an inner subject prefix can be phonetically [ɪ] (more common in the Northway dialect) or [ɛ] (more common in the Tetlin dialect) unless it precedes an L- voice/valence marker; they are represented in the orthography as <i> or <e>, respectively.

	Ø-	D-	H-	L-
1SG	ih-	ish-	ak-	ag-
2SG	įį-	in-	įh-	įl-
3SG	e- *or* i-	et- *or* it-	eh- *or* ih-	el-
1PL	ts'e- *or* ts'i-	ts'et- *or* ts'it-	ts'eh- *or* ts'ih-	ts'el-
2PL	ah-	at-	ah-	al-
3PL	he- *or* hi-	het-	heh- *or* hih-	hel-

Table 29.2. Surface forms in the Ø- imperfective

Examples for these forms can be found in chap. 28 and 31. When the verb form contains qualifier prefixes, these interact with the subject–voice/valence marker complexes in the fashion described in chap. 30.

29.1.2. The *aa-* imperfective

The *aa-* imperfective is characterized by an *aa-* conjugation marker and the Ø- imperfective prefix. It has three functions: (1) combined with the perambulative prefix and stem variant, it forms the perambulative aspect; (2) joined with a progressive stem variant, it forms the progressive superaspect; and (3) together with the future stem variant and the inceptive prefix *t-* (see chap. 30.6), it forms the future mode. The semantics of the perambulative, progressive and future are described in volume 2.

The inventory of subject–voice/valence prefix portmanteaus in the *aa-* imperfective is given in table 29.3.

The morphophonemic changes associated with the *aa-* imperfective are as follows. The *aa-* conjugation prefix is deleted before all inner subject prefixes (698a) but is retained in all forms with an outer subject, regardless of voice/valence prefix (this distinguishes it from the *aa-* perfective discussed in 29.2.2 below). In forms without an inner subject prefix, it takes the form

	Ø-	D-	H-	L-
1SG	ih-	ish-	ak-	ag-
2SG	įį-	in-	įh-	įl-
3SG	aa-	at-	ah-	al-
1PL	ts'aa-	ts'at-	ts'ah-	ts'al-
2PL	ah-	at-	ah-	al-
3PL	haa-	hat-	hah-	hal-

Table 29.3. Surface forms in the *aa-* imperfective

aa- in verb themes with a Ø-voice/valence marker (698b) but is shortened to *a-* in all forms containing an overt voice/valence prefix (698c). Glottal stop insertion takes place when syllables without an initial consonant occur in word-initial position (698a) or following a disjunct prefix (698d).

(698) a. *xeeɬ* [ʔ]*ihxeeɬ* (T)
xeeɬ ih-xeeɬ
pack AA.IPV:1SG.S:Ø-pack:IPV:PROG
'I'm carrying a pack' UT Notebook #4, 29

b. *xeeɬ ts'aaxeeɬ* (T)
xeeɬ ts'aa-xeeɬ
pack 1PL.S:AA.IPV:Ø-pack:IPV:PROG
'we are carrying packs' UT Notebook #4, 9

c. *xeeɬ nats'atxeeɬ* (T)
xeeɬ na-ts'at-xeeɬ
pack IT-1PL.S:AA.IPV:D-pack:IPV:PROG
'we are carrying packs back' UT Notebook #4, 29

d. *xeeɬ na'ishxeeɬ* [naʔiʃkʰeːɬ] (T)
xeeɬ na-ish-xeeɬ
pack IT-AA.IPV:1SG.S:D-pack:IPV:PROG
'I am carrying a pack back' UT Notebook #4, 29

29.1.3. The *n-* imperfective

The *n-* imperfective is characterized by an *n-* conjugation prefix and a Ø-mode marker. The *n-* conjugation marker is characteristic of the momentaneous aspect, which is very restricted in the imperfective (see also volume 2).

All naturally occurring forms of the *n-* imperfective are imperatives[1] (table 29.4).

	Ø-	D-	H-	L-
1SG	–	–	–	–
2SG	nįį-	nin-	nįh-	nįl- *or* nil-
3SG	–	–	–	–
1PL	–	–	–	–
2PL	nah-	nat-	nah-	nal-
3PL	–	–	–	–

Table 29.4. Surface forms in the *n-* imperfective

There are no morphophonemic changes associated with the *n-* imperfective beyond optional denasalization of the second-person singular subject prefix before L- (699).

(699) a. *tiniltthiit!* (T)
ti-nil-tthiit
out-N.IPV:SG.S:L-run:IPV
'run SG outside' UTOLAF08Apr2805:079

b. *ch'inįl'įįyh!* (N)
ch'-nįl-'įįyh
INDF-N.IPV:2SG.S:L-sneak:IPV
'sneak SG!' UTCB15Feb2506:001

29.1.4. The *i-* imperfective

The *i-* imperfective is characterized by an *ì-* conjugation marker and the Ø- imperfective prefix. The low tone of this prefix is indicated in examples throughout the present chapter, but not elsewhere in this grammar.

The *i-* imperfective occurs in the semelfactive and transitional derivations as well as in a few momentaneous prefix strings such as u+d 'finding' or ni# 'lifting'. It is also required by certain verb themes. Verbs that require an *i-* imperfective usually require an *i-* perfective as well. While the productive functions of the *i-* imperfective look diverse, they do contain one common semantic element: they describe punctual events. As a result, the *i-* imperfective is largely limited to imperatives. In my corpus only a handful of *i-* imperfectives occur; all of them have either a Ø- or an H- voice/valence marker and are in the second-person singular (table 29.5). Forms that are likely possible yet not attested are indicated with ?;forms thought to be impossible with –.

	Ø-	D-	H-	L-
1SG	–	–	–	–
2SG	į̀į̀-	?	į̀h-	?
3SG	–	–	–	–
1PL	–	–	–	–
2PL	?	?	?	?
3PL	–	–	–	–

Table 29.5. Surface forms in the *i-* imperfective

(700) contains most of the *i-* imperfective forms found in the corpus. It coalesces with the second-person singular prefix to *į̀*; in verb themes with a Ø- voice/valence marker, the portmanteau is lengthened to *į̀į̀* (700a).

(700) a. *ay nidį̀į̀'aay!* (N)

ay ni-dį̀į̀-'aay

3SG up-QUAL:I.IPV:2SG.S:ø-handle.CO:IPV:IMP

'lift SG that up!' UTOLAF15May0501:200

b. *ch'į̀hdayh!* (N)

ch'-į̀h-dayh

INDF-I.IPV:2SG.S:H-shoot:IPV

'shoot SG!' UTCBVDN13Nov1401:007

29.2. Perfective *į-*

All perfective forms contain underlyingly the *į-* perfective prefix as well as one of the five conjugation prefixes.

29.2.1. The Ø- perfective

The Ø- perfective is characterized by a Ø- conjugation marker and the *į-* perfective prefix. The Ø- perfective is limited to the descriptive and dimensional (neuter) verb theme categories; forms containing the Ø- perfective are semantically *im*perfective. The inventory of Ø- perfective forms is given in Table 29.6. There are no themes with a D- voice/valence prefix that take the Ø- perfective; all of them have an *aa-* perfective in the imperfective mode (see chap. 25.3.3.1). The forms are given in parentheses in table 29.6.

	Ø-	D-	H-	L-
1SG	ih-	(ish-)	ak-	agn-
2SG	į̨į̨-	(in-)	įh-	įl-
3SG	n-	(at-)	įh-	el-
1PL	ts'į̨į̨-	(ts'at-)	ts'įh-	ts'el-
2PL	ah-	(at-)	ah-	al-
3PL	hį̨į̨-	(hat-)	hįh-	hel-

Table 29.6. Surface forms in the Ø- perfective

The following morphophonemic rules apply to the Ø- perfective. The perfective prefix *į-* is deleted before all inner subject prefixes (701a, b). In the first- and third- person plural before the Ø- voice/valence marker, the perfective prefix is lengthened to *į̨į̨-* (701c); this does not happen before an overt voice/valence marker (701d). In the third-person singular before the Ø- voice/valence marker, the perfective prefix surfaces as its consonantal allomorph *n-* (701e). In forms with an inner subject prefix and no qualifiers, a glottal stop is inserted at the beginning of the pre-stem syllable (701a).

(701) a. [ʔ]*ihtsuul* (N)
ih-tsuul
ø.PFV:1SG.S:ø-be.small:IPV
'I am small' UTOLAF13May2804:042

b. *daktayh* (N)
dak-tayh
QUAL:ø.PFV:1SG.S:H-be.strong:IPV
'I am strong' UTOLAF13May2804:042

c. *ts'į̨į̨tsuul* (T)
ts'į̨į̨-tsuul
1PL.S:ø.PFV:ø-be.small:IPV
'we are small' UTOLVDN07Nov2803:001

d. *dįhtayh* (N)
dįh-tayh
3SG.S:QUAL:ø.PFV:H-be.strong:IPV
's/he is strong' UTOLAF17Aug1008:006

e. *ntsuul* (T)
n-tsuul
3sg.s:ø.pfv:ø-be.small:ipv
'she is small' UTCBAF13Nov0501:009

The perfective prefix is deleted in all verb forms containing an L- voice/valence prefix (702).

(702) a. *nagnjit* (T)
nagn-jit
qual:ø.pfv:1sg.s:l-be.scared:ipv
'I'm scared' UTOLAF09Jun2201:011

b. *elk'ah* (T)
el-k'ah
3pl.s:ø.pfv:l-be.fat:ipv
'it [bear] is fat' UTOLAF09Aug1201:013

c. *hihneljit*
h-nel-jit
3pl.s-qual:ø.pfv:l-be.scared:ipv
'they were scared' UTOLVDN13May2801:218

When the perfective prefix follows the areal prefix, the two prefixes coalesce into *hǫ-* (703a), which is lengthened in forms containing a Ø- voice/valence prefix (703b). In forms additionally containing the L- voice/valence marker, the prefixes coalesce into *hul-* (703b).

(703) a. *ts'ihǫhdąy* (N)
ts'i-hǫh-dąy
pej-3sg.s:ar:ø.pfv:h-be.sad:ipv
'she was sad' UTOLAF15May0501:199

b. *hǫǫsǫǫ* (N)
hǫǫ-sǫǫ
ar.s:ø.pfv:ø-be.good:ipv
'[the situation] was good' UTOLAF12Jul1202:020

c. *Ch'its'aa' hultsįį.* (T)
ch'its'aa' hul-tsįį
different AR.S:Ø.PFV:L-look:IPV
'It looked different.' UTOLVDN07Oct2602:008

29.2.2. The *aa-* perfective

The *aa-* perfective is characterized by the conjugation marker *aa-* and the perfective prefix *į-*, but there are no forms where both of these prefixes are detectable in the surface form (table 29.7). The realization of the *aa-* conjugation marker and perfective prefix depends not only on the presence of an inner subject prefix but also on the type of voice/valence prefix.

	Ø-	D-	H-	L-
1SG	ih-	ish-	ak-	ag-
2SG	įį-	in-	įh-	įl-
3SG	įį-	at-	įh-	al-
1PL	ts'įį-	ts'at-	ts'įh-	ts'al-
2PL	ah-	at-	ah-	al-
3PL	hįį-	hat-	hįh-	hal-

Table 29.7. Surface forms in the *aa-* perfective

In all forms containing an inner subject prefix, both the conjugation marker and the perfective prefix are deleted (704a, b). In these forms the only indicator of perfectivity is the stem, e.g., perfective *tsia'* instead of imperfective *tsüh* in (704a) or perfective *na'* instead of imperfective *nah* in (704b).

In forms containing an outer subject prefix, the voice/valence prefix determines whether the conjugation marker or the perfective prefix is deleted. In verb themes containing a voiceless (Ø- or H-) voice/valence prefix, the *aa-* conjugation marker is deleted in all forms, but the perfective prefix is retained (704c, d). If the verb theme has a voiced (D- or L-) voice/valence prefix, the *aa-* conjugation is retained, but the perfective prefix *į-* is deleted (704e, f).

(704) a. [ʔ]*ihtsia'* (N)
ih-tsia'
AA.PFV:1SG.S:Ø-cry:PFV
'I cried' UT Notebook #3, 70

b. *inna'* (N)
in-na'
AA.PFV:2SG.S:D-work:PFV
'you SG worked' UT Notebook #3, 72

c. *įįtsia'* (N)
įį-tsia'
3SG.S:AA.PFV:Ø-cry:PFV
'he cried' UT Notebook #3, 70

d. *ts'enįh'įį'* (N)
ts'-nįh-'įį'
1PL.S-QUAL:AA.PFV:H-see:PFV
'we saw him' UTCBAF14Jun0609:005

e. *atna'* (N)
at-na'
3SG.S:AA.PFV:D-work:PFV
'he worked' UT Notebook #3, 72

f. *ch'ihaldzia'* (N)
ch'-hal-dzia'
INDF-3PL.S:AA.PFV:L-dance:PFV
'they danced' UT Notebook #3, 79

In verb themes with invariable stem sets (see chap. 26), forms with an inner subject prefix are ambiguous with respect to viewpoint aspect. An example for such a theme is d+L+xoh 'to play noisily', where both an imperfective and a perfective interpretation are possible (705).

(705) *dagnxoh* (N)
dagn-xoh
QUAL:Ø.IPV:1SG.S:L-play:IPV
QUAL:AA.PFV:1SG.S:L-play:PFV
'I'm playing' *or* 'I'm done playing' UT Notebook #3, 78

29.2.3. The *n-* perfective

The *n-* perfective is characterized by the *n-* conjugation marker and the perfective prefix *į-*. The morphophonemics of the *n-* perfective are quite complex, as shown in table 29.8.

	Ø-	D-	H-	L-
1SG	nih-	nish-	nak-	nag-
2SG	nįį-	nin-	nįh-	nil-
3SG	nįį-	in-	nįh-	įl-
1PL	ts'inįį-	ts'in-	ts'inįh-	ts'il-
2PL	nah-	nat-	nah-	nal-
3PL	hinįį-	hin-	hinįh-	hil-

Table 29.8. Surface forms in the *n-* perfective

In verb themes with voiceless voice/valence prefixes (Ø- and H-), the *n-* conjugation marker is detectable in all forms (706a–d). The perfective prefix *į-* is deleted before inner subject prefixes (706a, b) but retained before outer ones (706c, d).

(706) a. *nihshyah* (T)
nih-shyah
N.PFV:1SG.S:Ø-SG.go:PFV
'I arrived' UTOLVDN14Nov2301:002

b. *O ninaktįį* (N)
O ni-nak-tįį
O TERM-N.PFV:1SG.S:H-handle.AO:PFV
'I put AO into position' UTOLVDN13May2004:062

c. *nįįshyah* (T)
nįį-shyah
3SG.S:N.PFV:Ø-SG.go:PFV
'he arrived' UTOLAF09Jun2202:054

d. *niynįhtįį* (N)
ni-y-nįh-tįį
TERM-3SG.S>3SG.O-N.PFV:H-handle.AO:PFV
'she brought him' UTCBVDN13Nov1401:005

In verb themes with a voiced voice/valence prefix, the perfective marker *į-* is deleted before inner subjects, but the conjugation prefix *n-* is retained (707a, b). In forms without inner subjects, the *į-* prefix is retained, but the *n-* conjugation marker is deleted instead (707c, d). Note also that the D-voice/valence marker is realized as /n/ in all forms without an inner subject prefix (707c).

(707) a. *nanishshyah* (N)
na-nish-shyah
IT-N.PFV:1SG.S:D-SG.go:PFV
'I arrived back' UTOLAF13May2804:002

b. *tinagntthät* (N)
ti-nagn-tthät
out-N.PFV:1SG.S:L-run:PFV
'I ran out' UTOLAF09Aug12:024

c. *na'inshyah* (T)
na-in-shyah
IT-3SG.S:N.PFV:D-SG.go:PFV
'she arrived back' UTCBAF13Nov0501:359

d. *da'iltthat* (T)
da-il-tthat
in-3SG.S:N.PFV:L-run:PFV
'she ran inside' UTCBAF13Nov0501:220

29.2.4. The *dh-* perfective

The *dh-* perfective is characterized by the presence of the *dh-* conjugation marker and (underlyingly) the *į-* perfective prefix. The latter, however, is not detectable in any form, as shown in table 29.9.

	Ø-	D-	H-	L-
1SG	dhih-	dhish-	dhak-	dhag-
2SG	dhįį-	dhin-	dhįh-	dhįl-
3SG	ee-	et-	eh-	el-
1PL	ts'ee-	ts'et-	ts'eh-	ts'el-
2PL	dhah-	nat-	dhah-	dhal-
3PL	hee-	het-	heh-	hel-

Table 29.9. Surface forms in the *dh-* perfective

The *dh-* conjugation prefix has two allomorphs: *dh-* and *ee-*, where *dh-* occurs in forms with an inner subject prefix (708a, b) and *ee-* in all others (708c, d). The vocalic allomorph is shortened before an overt voice/valence prefix (708d).

(708) a. *dhihdah* (T)
dhih-dah
DH.PFV:1SG.S:Ø-SG.sit:PFV
'I am sitting' UTOLAF09Jun2902:009

b. *didhaltth'ih* (T)
d-dhal-tth'ih
QUAL-DH.PFV:2PL.S:L-PL.stay:PFV
'you PL are staying' UTOLAF13May2403:016

c. *eedah* (T)
ee-dah
3SG.S:DH.PFV:Ø-SG.stay:PFV
'she is staying' UTCBAF13Nov0501:280

d. *hihdeltth'ih* (T)
h-del-tth'ih
3PL.S-QUAL:DH.PFV:L-PL.stay:PFV
'they were staying' UTOLAF09Jun2402:023

29.2.5. The *i-* perfective

The *i-* perfective consists of the *ì-* conjugation marker and the perfective marker *į-*. The *i-* perfective, like its imperfective counterpart, is part of the semelfactive and transitional derivations, occurs in several prefix strings, and is thematic in several verb themes. Table 29.10 contains the recorded forms; elicitation of verbs with an L-voice/valence marker such as the verb theme i+L+gayh 'turn white' has been unsuccessful.

	Ø-	D-	H-	L-
1SG	ìh-	ìsh-	àk-	?-
2SG	į̀į̀-	ìn-	įh-	?-
3SG	ì- *or* e-	èt-	ìh- *or* eh-	ìl-
1PL	ts'ì- *or* ts'e-	ts'ìt-	ts'ìh- *or* ts'eh-	?-
2PL	àh-	àt-	àh-	?-
3PL	hì- *or* or he-	hèt-	hìh- *or* heh-	?-

Table 29.10. Surface forms in the *i-* perfective

The perfective prefix *į-* is never overtly present in the *i-* perfective. In forms with an inner subject prefix, the presence of the *i-* perfective is detectable only by low tone on the pre-stem syllable (709a). In the Northway dialect, the *i-* conjugation marker is visible in forms without an inner subject prefix (709b), while in the Tetlin dialect, it is realized as /e/ (709c, d). In forms with a D- voice/valence marker, the *i-* conjugation marker appears as *è-* in forms without an inner subject (709e) in both dialects.

(709) a. *nà'àhdee* (N)
na-àh-dee
CONT-I.PFV:2PL.S:Ø-PL.stand:IPV
'you PL are standing' UT Notebook #3, 84

b. *na'ìthät* (N)
nà-ì-thät
CONT-3SG.S:I.PFV:Ø-SG.stand:IPV
'she is standing' UT Notebook #3, 84

c. *na'ethat* (T)
na-e-that
CONT-3SG.S:I.PFV:Ø-SG.stand:IPV
'she is standing' UT Notebook #5, 84

d. *nidehtįį* (T)
ni-deh-tįį
up-3SG.S:QUAL:I.PFV:H-handle.AO:PFV
'he lifted him up' UTOLVDN13May2804:046

e. *staniinèt-thiit* (N)
sta-nii-nèt-thiit
away-mind-3SG.S:QUAL:I.PFV:D-be.depressed:IPV
'he is depressed, worried' UT Notebook #4, 47

The *ì*-perfective is somewhat unusual in its morphophonemics as it is not lengthened before the Ø- voice/valence marker, as shown in (709b, c).

29.3. Optative *u-*

The optative is characterized by the mode prefix *u-* and an optative stem. Optative forms never contain a conjugation marker. All verb themes allow optative inflection, although there may be cultural restrictions on its use; a speaker once refused to produce an optative form of the verb theme dzi#L+shyeeyh 'do the mourning dance', saying that it was a lack of respect to think about this theme in this fashion—doing the mourning dance is something that "just happens," and the sense of desire or obligation to perform this activity was, in her mind at least, inappropriate in this context. Apart from a few isolated cases like this, the optative can apply to any verb theme.

The morphophonemics of the optative are quite simple. The prefix *u-* 'optative' coalesces with the inner subject–voice/valence prefix complex as shown in table 29.11.

	Ø-	D-	H-	L-
1SG	uh-	ush-	ok-	og-
2SG	ųų-	un-	ųh-	ųl-
3SG	uu-	ut-	uh-	ul-
1PL	ts'uu-	ts'ut-	ts'uh-	ts'ul-
2PL	ah-	at-	ah-	al-
3PL	huu-	hut-	huh-	hul-

Table 29.11. Surface forms in the optative

In all forms other than the second-person plural subject forms, the optative is characterized by a round vowel /o/ or /u/ (710a–d). In the second-person plural subject forms, the optative prefix is not detectable (710d, e); these forms are recognizable as optatives only because of optative stem variants, e.g., *shyi' na'ah'aał* 'you PL are eating meat IPV' versus *shyi' na'ah'aal* 'you PL should eat meat OPT'. In verb themes where the optative stem is identical to the imperfective stem, it is not possible to identify whether a second-person plural form is in the optative or imperfective (710e).

(710) a. *shyi'* [ʔ]*okt'ia*

shyi' ok-t'ia

meat OPT:1SG.S:H-fry:OPT

'I should fry meat' UT Notebook #4, 25

b. *tseey* [ʔ]*utnaa'* (N)

tseey ut-naa'

tea 3SG.S:OPT:D-drink:OPT

'she should drink tea' UT Notebook #3, 68

c. *ts'uutsüü* (N)

ts'uu-tsüü

1PL.S:OPT:Ø-cry:OPT

'we should cry' UT Notebook #3, 69

d. *shyi' na'ah'aal* (N)
shyi' na-ah-'aal
meat IT-OPT:2PL.S:Ø-eat:OPT
'you PL should eat meat' UT Notebook #3, 71

e. *ch'aldzüh* (N)
ch'-al-dzüh
INDF-OPT:2PL.S:L-dance:OPT
INDF-Ø.IPV:2PL.S:L-dance:IPV
'you PL should dance, are dancing' UT Notebook #3, 79

If the optative prefix is in word-initial position (710a), or if it follows a prefix of the form CV (710d), a glottal stop is inserted. The optative prefix is lengthened when the pre-stem syllable does not contain a coda consonant (710c).

29.4. Negative perfective *ì*-

The mode prefix *ì*- forms the negative perfective, which is characterized by the absence of a conjugation marker, the presence of the *ì*- mode prefix, and a negative perfective stem (711a). Imperfective, future, and optative negatives by contrast contain their regular conjugation and mode prefixes; in the Northway dialect, the pre-stem dialect then bears a low tone (711b–d) (see also Leer [2000, 104]). Throughout this section, low tone (on the negative perfective prefix) and high tone (on the negative stems) are marked, even though this is not usually done in Upper Tanana orthography. In addition to the negative morphology, the negative particle *k'a(t'eey)* is obligatorily used.

(711) a. *k'a ìtsíá* (N)
k'a ì-tsíá
NEG 3SG.S:NEG.PFV:Ø-cry:PFV:NEG
'he hadn't cried' UT Notebook #3, 86

b. *k'a ètsǘǘ* (N)
k'a è-tsǘǘ
NEG 3SG.S:Ø.IPV:Ø-cry:IPV:NEG
'he is not crying' UT Notebook #3, 85

c. *k'a tààtsǘǘ* (N)
k'a tàà-tsǘǘ
NEG 3SG.S:INC:AA.IPV:Ø-cry:FUT:NEG
'he will not cry' UT Notebook #3, 86

d. *k'àt'eey ùùtsǘǘ* (N)
k'àt'eey ùù-tsǘǘ
NEG 3SG.S:OPT:Ø-cry:OPT:NEG
'he should not cry' UT Notebook #6, 17

The portmanteau prefixes in the negative perfective are given in table 29.12.

	Ø-	D-	H-	L-
1SG	ìh-	ìsh-	àk-	àg-
2SG	į̀į̀-	ìn-	į̀h-	į̀l-
3SG	ì-	ìt-	ìh-	ìl-
1PL	ts'ì-	ts'ìt-	ts'ìh-	ts'ìl-
2PL	àh-	àt-	àh-	àl-
3PL	hì-	hìt-	hìh-	hìl-

Table 29.12. Surface forms in the negative perfective

The morphophonemics of the negative perfective prefix are simple. The prefix vowel disappears before all inner subject prefixes; in these forms it is only detectable through the low tone (712a, b). In forms without an inner subject prefix, the negative perfective prefix is retained fully (712c, d). Unlike the (positive) perfective prefix, the negative perfective prefix is not lengthened in forms containing an outer subject prefix and a Ø- voice/valence prefix (712d).

(712) a. *k'at'eey tseey ìshnáán*
k'at'eey tseey ìsh-náán
NEG tea NEG.PFV:1SG.S:D-drink:PFV:NEG
'I didn't drink tea' UT Notebook #3, 85

b. *ts'iiniin k'a ich'àh'áál*
ts'iiniin k'a i-ch'àh-'áál
baby NEG PP-INDF.O:NEG.PFV:2PL.S:H-feed:PFV:NEG
'you PL didn't feed the baby' UT Notebook #3, 86

c. *k'a ts'inìljídn*
k'a ts'-nìl-jídn
NEG 1PL.S-QUAL:NEG.PFV:L-be.afraid:PFV:NEG
'we were not afraid' UT Notebook #3, 85

d. *k'àt'eey hah'áát nà'ìthắdn* (N)

k'àt'eey hah-'áát nà-ì-thắdn

NEG NTRL-out:PNCT CONT-3SG.S:NEG.PFV:Ø-SG.stand:IPV

'he is not standing there' UT Notebook #6, 17

29.5. Summary

In this chapter the conjugation and mode prefixes are described. The conjugation and mode prefixes are tightly fused together and form a portmanteau that also includes some following material (inner subject prefix and voice/valence marker) as well as preceding prefixes (qualifiers and outer subject prefixes). There are four mode prefixes (Ø- 'imperfective', *į-* 'perfective', *u-* 'optative', and *ì-* 'negative perfective') and five conjugation markers (Ø-, *aa-*, *n-*, *dh-* and *ì-*).

Notes

1. I use the term "imperative" to refer to second-person directives in the imperfective mode; see also Lovick (2016).

30 Qualifiers

The qualifiers are prefixes of position 5 of the Upper Tanana template (see table 24.1). They are semantically very diverse, ranging from the gender prefixes, which index certain qualities of the verb's arguments, over derivational prefixes with a variety of meanings, to aspectual prefixes such as the inceptive or the conative, which both have to do with phases of the verb. Furthermore, most qualifiers can be used thematically or productively.

(713) and (714) illustrate the difference between productive and thematic uses of the *n-* qualifier. The verb theme O+G+l+deeł 'to eat o' in (713) requires that each verb form include a gender prefix indexing the kind of object being eaten (this is indicated by the capital G in the theme listing). In (713a), the object *łuugn* 'fish' is of unmarked gender, whereas in (713b), the object *jign* 'berries' is of *n-* gender and thus requires an *n-* qualifier. By contrast, the *n-* qualifier in the verb theme O+n+H+'į̨h 'see o, look at o' shown in (714) is thematic. It occurs in all forms of this verb theme regardless of the shape of the object, and as demonstrated in (714c), it may not be left out.

(713) a. *shoh łuugn eldeeł* (T)
shoh łuugn el-deeł
bear fish 3SG.S-Ø.IPV:L-eat.PL.O:IPV
'the bear is eating fish' UTOLVDN13May1903:023

b. *shoh jign neldeeł* (N)
shoh jign n-el-deeł
bear berries 3SG.S:QUAL-Ø.IPV:L-eat.PL.O:IPV
'the bear is eating berries' UTOLAF14Nov2203:006

(714) a. *łuugn nak-'į̨h* (N)
łuugn n-ak-'į̨h
fish QUAL-Ø.IPV:1SG.S:H-see:IPV
'I see a fish' UT Notebook #5, 84

b. *jign nak-'įh* (N)
jign n-ak-'įh
berries QUAL-Ø.IPV:1SG.S:H-see:IPV
'I see berries' UT Notebook #5, 84

c. **łuugn ak-'įh* (N)
łuugn ø-ak-'įh
Intended: 'I see a fish' UT Notebook #5, 84

30.1. Inventory and order

There are seven overt qualifiers in Upper Tanana: *ì-*, *n-*, *d-*, *dh-*, *uu-*, *t-*, and *hu-*. Note that Upper Tanana does not have the *gh-* qualifier reported by Kari (1993) for several other Alaskan Dene languages.

Presumably because of the diverse functions of qualifiers, it is possible for several of them to co-occur in the same verb. This, along with the fact that even closely related dialects of the same language differ with respect to the ordering of qualifiers, leads scholars to talk about the qualifier *zone* rather than the qualifier *position*. The order of Upper Tanana qualifiers proposed by Kari (1993, 52) is given in table 30.1.

Areal	Inceptive	Conative	*d-*	*n-*	Transitional
hu-	*t-*	*uu-*	*d-*	*n-*	*ì-*

Table 30.1. The qualifier zone in the template following Kari (1993, 52)

Kari (1993) does not indicate the position of the *dh-* qualifier as Upper Tanana retains it only in the verb theme O+dh+H+xeh 'kill SG.O' and in a few fossilized prohibitive forms. As discussed in 30.5, it occurs somewhere to the right of the *t-* qualifier, but since it never co-occurs with the *uu-*, *d-*, or *n-* qualifiers, its position relative to these morphemes cannot be determined.

In the following sections, each qualifier is briefly described. Where possible, evidence regarding its position in the qualifier zone is provided.

30.2. The *i-* qualifier

The status of the *i-* qualifier in Upper Tanana is uncertain. Kari (1993, 52) includes it at the right edge of the qualifier zone. In his work on Ahtna, Kari (1979, 1990) notes that it is involved productively in the formation of transitional and semelfactive themes, and occurs thematically in many other verb themes. In that language the *i-* qualifier occurs in all four modes (Kari

1979, 118). In Upper Tanana the *i-* prefix occurs only in the perfective and imperfective[1] modes; in optative and future forms, it is never present (715).

(715) a. *Łįį ittheh.* (N)
łįį i-ttheh
dog 3SG.S:I.PFV:Ø-bark:PFV
'The dog barked (once).' UTOLAF15Dec0607:013

b. *Jah łįį uutthay dia!* (N)
jah łįį uu-tthay dia
here dog 3SG.S:OPT:Ø-bark:OPT if.only
'If only that dog would bark!' UTOLAF15Dec0607:014

c. *Łįį taattheh.* (N)
łįį taa-ttheh
dog 3SG.S:INC:AA.IPV:Ø-bark:FUT
'The dog is going to bark.' UTOLAF15Dec0607:016

The *i-* qualifier differs from the *i-* conjugation marker in that it is retained in negative perfective forms. Neither the negative-perfective prefix *i-* (716a) nor the *i-* qualifier (716b) by themselves are long in forms with a Ø- voice/valence marker. When they co-occur, however, the resulting vowel is lengthened (716c).

(716) a. *k'a itsia'* (N)
k'a i-tsia'
NEG 3SG.S:NEG.PFV:Ø-cry:PFV:NEG
'he hadn't cried' UT Notebook #3, 86

b. *iditth'ek* (N)
i-di-tth'ek
3SG.S>3SG.O-QUAL:QUAL:Ø.PFV:Ø-hear:IPV
'she heard him' UT Notebook #3, 84

c. *k'a idiitth'agn* (N)
k'a i-dii-tth'agn
NEG 3SG.S>3SG.O-QUAL:QUAL:NEG.PFV:Ø-hear:PFV:NEG
'she didn't hear him' UT Notebook #3, 96

30.3. The *n-* qualifier

The *n-* qualifier is located at the right edge of the qualifier zone.

30.3.1. Functions

The *n-* qualifier has several productive functions: it is part of the errative superaspectual derivation, it can be a gender prefix, a derivational prefix with a variety of meanings, or a thematic prefix completely bleached of meaning.

30.3.1.1. Errative The *n-* qualifier is part of the errative superaspectual string n(+D). The errative is only somewhat productive in Upper Tanana. In the form in (717b), the errative might be lexicalized; no form of this verb theme without the errative string is attested in the data.

(717) a. *stahnetdeeɬ* (N)
sta-hnet-deeɬ
away-3PL.S:QUAL:DH.PFV:D-PL.go:PFV:ERR
'they went astray, they got lost' UTOLAF15May0501:010

b. *nelnak*
tth'änh nel-nak
bone 3SG.S:QUAL:DH.PFV:L-choke:PFV:ERR
'he choked on a bone' Kari (1997b)

c. *hanįįshyah* (T)
ha-nįį-shyah
up.out-3SG.S:QUAL:AA.PFV:Ø-SG.go:PFV:ERR
'[Wolverine] came up and out in a bad way'
UTOLVDN13May2804:005

The errative indicates that an action is performed in such a way as to yield undesirable consequences: getting lost instead of going away or choking instead of swallowing. The form in (717c) contrasts with the regular perfective form *ha'įįshyah* 's/he came up and out'; speakers commented that its use was restricted to abominable creatures like Wolverine ("sounds like he crawled out from somewhere").

30.3.1.2. *n-* as gender prefix As a gender prefix the *n-* qualifier indexes objects that are typically small and round, such as berries. An example for the *n-* qualifier as a gender prefix was given in (713) above.

The gender system of Upper Tanana is vestigial. Some verbs still take a gender prefix, but they do not occur nearly as regularly as they do in a language such as Dena'ina, where they are still being used productively (Tenenbaum 1978; Lovick 2015). More information on the gender system as part of the noun classification system is provided in volume 2.

30.3.1.3. Other derivational uses of *n*- The *n*- qualifier is used productively to refer to the face or facial features. (718) contrasts a verb form of the theme d+D+sąyh 'be black' with the theme n+D+sąyh 'have a black face'. In (719) the *n*- qualifier is added to the transitional theme Ø+gąyh 'become dry'.

(718) a. *dat-sąyh* (N)
d-at-sąyh
QUAL-AA.PFV:D
'it is black, it is dark' UT Notebook #1, 11

b. *nat-sąyh* (N)
n-at-sąyh
QUAL-3SG.S:AA.PFV:D-be.black:IPV
'his/her face is black' UT Notebook #1, 11

(719) a. *Dzanh eegąyh, ndlaa::n t'eey.* (T)
dzanh ee-gąyh ndlaan t'eey
muskrat 3PL.S:DH.PFV:Ø-be.dry:IPV lots ADVZR
'The muskrats dried, lots of them!' UTOLVDN07Nov2803:015

b. *Ch'itay tuu ehdanh uda' neegąyh.* (T)
ch'itay tuu ehdanh u-da'
old.man water without 3SG.PSR-mouth
nee-gąyh
3SG.S:QUAL:DH.PFV:Ø-be.dry:IPV
'The old man's mouth became dry without water.'
UTOLVDN13May2907:060

30.3.1.4. *n*- in themes of seeing and hiding The *n*- qualifier also occurs thematically in many verb themes having to do with seeing and hiding. Its use in the theme O+n+H+'įh 'see o' was already illustrated in (714a); another example is its use in the theme for ch'+t+n+L+'įį 'hide oneself' in (720).

(720) *Hah'ogn nday chinel'įį.* (N)
ha-nogn nday ch-nel-'įį
ADJC-upland:AR somewhere INDF:3SG.S:INC-QUAL:DH.PFV:L-hide:PFV
'He hid somewhere in the upland area.'
UTOLVDN11Aug0802:047

30.3.1.5. Lexicalized *n*- qualifier The *n*- qualifier is also used thematically with unclear semantic contribution (721).

(721) a. *yinaa'ax*
yi-naa-'ax
3SG.S>3SG.O-QUAL:AA.IPV:Ø-lead:IPV
'he led him' Kari (1997b)

b. *natnett'ak* (N)
na-tnet-t'ak
IT-3SG.S:INC:QUAL:DH.PFV:D-SG.fly:PFV
'he started to fly back' UTOLAF08Feb1902:007

30.3.2. Phonology

The *n*- qualifier occurs immediately before the conjugation-mode-subject-voice/valence marker portmanteau morpheme and frequently forms the onset consonant of this syllable (722).

(722) a. *jign naktsayh* (T)
jign nak-tsayh
berry QUAL:Ø.IPV:1SG.S:H-pick:IPV
'I am picking berries' UTCBVDN13Nov1503:026

b. *shneh'įh* (N)
sh-neh-'įh
1SG.O-3SG.S:QUAL:Ø.IPV:H-see:IPV
'he sees me' UTOLVDN10Jul2724:097

c. *ineh'įh* (N)
i-neh-'įh
3SG.S>3SG.O-QUAL:Ø.IPV:H-see:IPV
'he sees her, looks at her' UTOLAF12Jul1201:056

In (722a) there are no other prefixes so that the *n*- qualifier occurs in word-initial position. If it follows a fricative as in (722b) or a vowel as in (722c), no changes take place.

When the *n*- qualifier precedes the consonantal allomorph of the *dh*-conjugation prefix (see 29.2.4), an epenthetic vowel [ɪ] is inserted between them as shown in (723).

(723) *ch'inidhih'įį*
ch'-n-dhih-'įį
INDF.O-QUAL-DH.PFV:1SG.S:Ø-steal:PFV
'I stole something' Kari (1997b)

When the *n-* qualifier precedes the *n-* conjugation prefix, the two /n/ coalesce. The verb theme n+Ø+t'ah 'SG fly' contains a thematic *n-* qualifier, which is clearly visible preceding the vocalic allomorph *ee-* of the *dh-* conjugation prefix (724a), but which coalesces with the *n-* conjugation marker in (724b). The resulting /n/ is not lengthened.

(724) a. *tneet'ak* (N)
tnee-t'ak
3SG.S:INC:QUAL:DH.PFV:Ø-SG.fly:PFV
'it started to fly' UTOLAF08Feb1906:009

b. *stanįįt'ak* (T)
sta-nįį-t'ak
away-3SG.S:QUAL:N.PFV:Ø-SG.fly:PFV
'it flew away' UTOLVDN13May2907:116

30.4. The *d-* qualifier

The *d-* qualifier precedes the *n-* qualifier (725a) as well as the *i-* qualifier (725b).

(725) a. *utthiixa' staxadneetth'ik*
u-tthiixa' *sta-xa-dnee-tth'ik*
3SG.PSR-hair away-hair-3SG.S:QUAL:QUAL:DH.PFV:Ø-be.tangled:IPV
'his hair is tangled' Kari (1997b)

b. *łįį iin hihditth'ek* (N)
łįį *iin* *h-di-tth'ek*
dog PL 3PL.S-QUAL:QUAL:Ø.PFV:Ø-hear:IPV
'they heard dogs' UT Notebook #3, 49

30.4.1. Functions

Like the *n-* qualifier, the *d-* qualifier is part of the gender system but is also used in numerous derivations.

30.4.1.1. *d-* as gender prefix The *d-* gender prefix indexes objects from a number of classes. Jetté and Jones (2000, 124) list the following classes taking *d-* gender in Koyukon: "1) stick, tree, leaf, plant, bark, pitch; 2) cup, basket; 3) feather, hair, fur; 4) enclosed liquids or fluids, lake, puddle, pus, afterbirth; 5) word, song, story, news, name; 6) day, day's journey, units of time; 7) fire, smoke, star." The list in Kari (1990) for Ahtna is almost identical, as is that in Tenenbaum (1978) for Dena'ina. (726a) illustrates the productive use of the *d-* qualifier; (726b) shows, however, that the gender prefix is absent in the verb theme O+G+L+deeł 'eat o', illustrating the fragility of the gender system.

(726) a. *Ch'udzüüt xia' ushyiit deedlah.* (N)

ch'udzüüt *xia'* *u-shyiit*
boreal.owl eggs 3SG.P-inside

dee-dlah
3PL.S:QUAL:DH.PFV:Ø-classify.PL.O:IPV

'Owls' eggs were lying in there.' UTOLVDN07Aug2205:014

b. *Ay du' k'a hiiyildeel.* (N)

ay *du'* *k'a* *hii-il-deel*
3S CT NEG 3PL.S>3PL.O-NEG.PFV:L-eat.PL.O:PFV:NEG

'But they do not eat [the owls' eggs].'
UTOLVDN07Aug2205:015

30.4.1.2. *d-* in self-benefactives The *d-* qualifier also occurs productively in self-benefactives, i.e., in verbs describing events in which the subject participates to their own benefit (727). The self-benefactive derivation changes the voice/valence marker of the verb theme; see also chap. 27.3.2.1.3.

(727) a. *didhagnchuut* (N)

d-dhag-chuut
QUAL-DH.PFV:1SG.S:L-save.food:PFV

'I saved food for myself' UT Notebook #4, 16

b. *Ts'exeh uudagn'ąą...* (N)

ts'exeh *uu-d-agn-'ąą*
woman CON-QUAL-AA.PFV:1SG.S:L-find.SG.O:PFV

'I found myself a girl...' UTOLAF15May0501:183

30.4.1.3. Lexicalized *d-* qualifier The *d-* qualifier has a wide range of meaning in all Dene languages for which information is available (see, e.g.,Tenenbaum [1978, 145–50] for Dena'ina, Kari [1990, 13] for Ahtna, or Jetté and Jones [2000, 124] for Koyukon, to list only sources on Alaskan Dene). In some verbs the *d*-qualifier has become thematized; it occurs, for example, in many themes having to do with fire, e.g., d+H+k'ąą 'build a fire' in (728a), and in many themes having to do with speaking or sound, e.g., d+Ø+nih 'say' or d+L+ts'iat '[door] creak' in (728b, c).

(728) a. *kon' dzihk'ąą* (N)
kon' dzįh-k'ąą
fire 1PL.S:QUAL:AA.PFV:H-build.fire:PFV
'we built a fire' UTOLVDN14Apr2602:118

b. *udihnih* (N)
u-dih-nih
3SG.P-QUAL:Ø.IPV:1SG.S:Ø-say:IPV
'I said to him' UTOLAF09Aug12:043

c. *delts'iat* (N)
del-ts'iat
3SG.S:QUAL:Ø.IPV:L-creak:IPV
'[the door] is creaking' UT Notebook #3, 7

The *d*- qualifier is also present in many neuter verb themes (729).

(729) a. *hu'eh dzeltth'ih* (N)
hu-'eh dzel-tth'ih
3PL.P-with 1PL.S:QUAL:DH.IPV:L-PL.stay:IPV
'we were staying with them' UTOLAF09Aug1202:009

b. *dįįtsįį* (N)
dįį-tsįį
3SG.S:QUAL:Ø.PFV:Ø-be.hungry:IPV
'he is hungry' UTCBAF13Nov1203:031

30.4.2. Phonology

The *d*- qualifier often serves as the onset consonant of the pre-stem syllable, both in word-initial position (730a) but also following another prefix (730b) or preceding the *n*- qualifier as shown in (725) above.

(730) a. *delxoh* (T)
del-xoh
3SG.S:QUAL:Ø.IPV:L-play:IPV
'he/she/it is playing' UTCBAF13Nov0501:040

b. *nahdelxoh* (T)
na-hdel-xoh
IT-3PL.S:QUAL:Ø.IPV:L-play:IPV
'they are playing again' UTOLVDN13May2803:014

When the *d-* qualifier precedes the consonantal allomorph of the *dh-* conjugation prefix, a vowel is inserted (731). The inserted vowel in this case is almost always [ɪ], rarely [ə].

(731) a. *Shyign' didhaltth'ih!* (T)
shyign' d-dhal-tth'ih
down:ALL QUAL-DH.IPV:2PL.S:L-PL.stay:IPV
'Stay PL at home!' UTOLAF13May2403:027

b. *seeyh uts'ą̈' dedhaknąyh* (N)
seeyh u-ts'ą̈' d-dhak-nąyh
knife 3SG.P-to QUAL-DH.PFV:1SG.S:H-move.hand.quickly:PFV
'I tossed the knife to him' UTOLAF13May2801:028

When the *d-* qualifier immediately follows the first-person plural subject prefix *ts'-* or the indefinite subject or object prefix *ch'-*, the qualifier is absorbed into the pronominal prefix resulting in [t͡s] (orthographically <dz>) and [t͡ʃ] (orthographically <j>), respectively. Elsewhere in this grammar, I treat the resulting portmanteau as a unit; only in (732) do I show the components.

(732) a. *dzelxoh* (N)
ts'-d-el-xoh
1PL.S-QUAL-Ø.IPV:L-play:IPV
'we are playing' UTOLAF08Feb1906:005

b. *jeh'ąą* (T)
ch'-d-eh-'ąą
INDF.O-3SG.S:QUAL-DH.PFV:H-sing:IPV
'I am singing' UTOLAF07Oct2512:020

30.5. The *dh-* qualifier

Dh- is the rarest of the qualifiers. No meaning can be assigned to it.

30.5.1. Position and function

The *dh-* qualifier occurs in only one verb theme: O+dh+H+xeh 'kill SG.O' (733).

(733) *ntidhakxeh* (N)
n-t-dhak-xeh
2SG.O-INC-QUAL:AA.IPV:H-kill.SG.O:FUT
'I will kill you SG' UTOLAF15May0501:157

It also occurs in a few fossilized prohibitive forms (734).

(734) a. *dadhįh'ąy!* (B)
da-dhįh-'ąy
?-QUAL:Ø.IPV:2SG.S:H-bother:IPV:NEG
'leave SG her alone! don't SG bother her!'
UTOLAF10Jul0202:052

b. *dadhahnąy!* (N)
da-dhah-nąy
?-QUAL:Ø.IPV:2PL.S:Ø-say:IPV:NEG
'be quiet PL! don't PL talk!' UTOLAF15May0703:012

(733) clearly demonstrates that the *dh-* qualifier follows the inceptive prefix *t-*. Its position regarding the other qualifiers is uncertain since there are no forms recorded where these combinations occur.

30.5.2. Phonology

The *dh-* qualifier is homophonous to the *dh-* conjugation marker described in chap. 29, but they have different morphophonemic properties. The *dh-* conjugation prefix has the allomorph *ee-* in verb forms that do not contain an inner subject prefix (735).

(735) a. *kee maa dhaktsįį* (N)
kee m-aa dhak-tsįį
shoe 3SG.P-for DH.PFV:1SG.S:H-make.SG.O:PFV
'I made shoes for her' UTOLAF13May2801:034

b. *kee yaa ehtsį̨į̨* (N)
kee y-aa eh-tsį̨į̨
shoe 3SG.P-for 3SG.S:DH.PFV:H-make.SG.O:PFV
'she made shoes for him' UTOLAF13May2801:035

The *dh-* qualifier, on the other hand, lacks this vocalic allomorph and appears as *dh-* in third-person subject forms such as (736b).

(736) a. *gah deltthoo dhakxį̨į̨* (T)
gah deltthoo dh-dhak-xį̨į̨
rabbit brown QUAL-DH.PFV:1SG.S:H-kill.SG.O:PFV
'I killed the brown rabbit' UTOLAF13May2404:011

b. *gah dhehxį̨į̨* (N)
gah dheh-xį̨į̨
rabbit 3SG.S:QUAL:DH.PFV:H-kill.SG.O:PFV
'he killed the rabbit' UTCBAF13Nov0801:082

In forms containing an inner subject prefix, where the consonantal allomorph of the *dh-* conjugation marker is used, the two *dh-* prefixes coalesce, as shown in (736a).

30.6. The *t-* qualifier

The *t-* qualifier precedes the *d-* and *n-* qualifiers (737) as well as the *dh-* qualifier (733).

(737) a. *Tadn tah shyį̨į̨' tnah'į̨į̨ł…* (T)
tadn tah shyį̨į̨' tnah-'į̨į̨ł
night during only INC:QUAL:AA.IPV:2PL.S:H-see:FUT
'You PL can see [the stars] only at night…'
UTOLVDN14May0703:188

b. *Dii xah ch'a hǫǫ' dį̨į̨niil?* (N)
dii xah ch'a hǫǫ' tdį̨į̨-niil
why FOC thus INC:QUAL:AA.IPV:2SG.S:Ø-say:FUT:NOM
'Why would you SG say that?' UTOLAF15Dec0705:039

30.6.1. Functions of the *t-* qualifier

The *t-* qualifier 'INC'- occurs productively in three constructions. (1) Motion themes in the momentaneous aspect have an inceptive derivation in all modes. (2) In non-motion themes the inceptive prefix together with the *dh*-perfective and a perfective stem forms the inceptive perfective subaspectual derivation. (3) In all verb theme categories, the inceptive prefix plus the *aa*-imperfective and the future stem forms the future. The inceptive future is also used thematically in some verb themes.

30.6.1.1. Inceptive derivations in motion themes Motion themes in the momentaneous aspect have an inceptive derivation t+(Ø, dh) with the meaning 'start to move'. (738) illustrates that the inceptive derivation can apply to a wide variety of motion themes and in all four modes. In the imperfective mode the inceptive derivation is largely restricted to the second person, which is typical for themes in the momentaneous; see chap. 25 and volume 2 for discussion.

(738) a. *Nduugn tįįhaayh?* (N)
nduugn *tįį-haayh*
whereabouts INC:Ø.IPV:2SG.S:Ø-SG.go:IPV
'Where are you SG off to?' [said as someone is leaving]
UTOLAF14Apr2501:042

b. *tidhagntthät* (N)
t-dhagn-tthät
INC-DH.PFV:1SG.S:L-SG.run:PFV
'I ran off' UTOLAF15Dec0602:002

c. *nitsuudeeł* (T)
ni-tsuu-deeł
TERM-1PL.S:INC:OPT:Ø-PL.go:OPT
'let's go there' UTOLVDN14Nov2301:112

d. *hataambeeł* (T)
ha-taa-mbeeł
up.out-3SG.S:INC:AA.IPV:Ø-swim:FUT
'he will swin out onto the surface' UTOLVDN13May2909:072

30.6.1.2. Inceptive perfective The inceptive perfective is a subaspectual derivation affecting all verb themes other than motion themes. Unlike the inceptive derivation of motion themes discussed in 30.6.1.1, the inceptive perfective is limited to the perfective mode. It requires a *dh*- conjugation marker and a perfective stem (739). Its semantics range from 'begin to' (739a) to 'be about to' (739b) and 'be going to' (739c), where it overlaps with the future (see 30.6.1.3), to 'tried (and failed) to' (739d). More detail on the semantics of the inceptive perfective is given in volume 2.

(739) a. *Ay tl'aan dziiteh'ah.* (T)
ay tl'aan dzii-teh-'ah
and then hearing-3SG.S:INC:DH.PFV:H-extend.LO:PFV
'And then he began to listen.' (lit. 'And then he began to extend his hearing in a linear way.') UTOLVDN13May2907:118

b. *Sdzeh'ogn hihteet'üüt.* (N)
s-dzeh'ogn h-tee-tüüt
1SG.PSR-lung 3PL.S-INC:DH.PFV:Ø-cut:PFV
'They were about to do surgery on my lung.'
UTOLVDN14Apr2602:071

c. *"Nts'ą̈' tidhahdįį?" hudihnih.* (N)
nts'ą̈' t-dhah-dįį hu-dih-nih
what INC-DH.PFV:2PL.S:Ø-do:PFV 3PL.P-QUAL:Ø.IPV:1SG.S:Ø-say:IPV
'"What are you PL doing, about to do?" I asked them.'
UTOLAF09Aug1202:012

d. ... *hiiyuteeniig k'at'eey hiiyuunagn...* (T)
hiiy-uu-tee-niig k'at'eey
3PL.S>3SG.O-CON-INC:DH.PFV:Ø-grab:PFV:NOM NEG
hiiy-uu-nagn
3PL.S>3SG.O-CON:NEG.PFV:Ø-grab:PFV:NEG
'... they tried to grab it [but] they didn't grab it..'
UTOLAF09Jun2202:072

30.6.1.3. Future The *t-* qualifier is also part of the future formation, which applies to all verb themes. It consists of the inceptive prefix, the *aa-* imperfective, and a future stem (740). The future has modal function including future time reference (740a), irrealis (740b), (in)ability (740c), and general prohibition (740d).

(740) a. *tahshyüü* (T)
tah-shyüü
3SG.S:INC:AA.IPV:Ø-snow:FUT
'it is going to snow' UTOLAF07Oct2512:014

b. … *nts'aa' utaaniɫ le'.* (T)
nts'aa' hu-taa-niɫ le'
how AR.S-INC:AA.IPV:Ø-happen:FUT IGN
'… I don't know what would have happened.'
UTOLAF09Jun2202:045

c. *K'at'eey nan' t'eey du' tnah'iil…* (T)
k'at'eey nan' t'eey du' tnah-'iil
NEG land even CT INC:QUAL:AA.IPV:2PL.S:H-see:FUT:NEG
'You cannot even see land, …' UTOLVDN13May2909:050

d. *Ay du' k'at'eey mbaa nitahdäl.* (N)
ay du' k'at'eey mb-aa ni-tah-däl
3SG CT NEG 3SG.P-for TERM-INC:AA.IPV:2PL.S:Ø-PL.go:FUT:NEG
'You PL may not go there for it.' UTOLAF17Aug0801:039

The functions of the future mode are described in volume 2.

30.6.1.4. Lexicalized *t*-qualifier The *t-* qualifier is also thematic in some verb themes (741).

(741) a. *K'a' st'atnelgot.* (N)
k'a' s-t'a-tnel-got
gun RECP.P-snagging-3SG.S:INC:QUAL:DH.PFV:L-punch:PFV
'The gun jammed.' (lit. 'it punched snagging on each other')
UTOLVDN13May2004:083

b. *Ik'eh chinil'įį, hąą.* (N)
i-k'eh ch-nil-įį hąą
3SG.S>3SG.O-behind INDF:INC-N.PFV:L-hide:PFV right
'She was sneaking out behind him, right.'
UTOLVDN10Jul2713:024

30.6.2. Phonology

The inceptive prefix may serve as the onset consonant of the conjugation-mode-(inner subject)-classifier complex (740a, b). It may also form a consonant cluster with the *n-* qualifier (740d).

When the *t-* qualifier occurs between two /n/, it is deleted (742).

(742) a. *nannagn'įįł* [nan.nagŋ.ʔĩ:ɬ.] (N)
na-n-t-n-agn-'įįł
IT-2SG.O-INC-QUAL-AA.IPV:1SG.S:L-see:FUT
'I'll see you again' UT Notebook #1, 3

b. *dannaktl'uuł* [tan.nakʰ.tɬ'u:ɬ] (T)
da-n-t-n-ak-tl'uuł
closed-2SG.O-INC-QUAL-AA.IPV:1SG.S:H-tie.up:FUT
'I am going to tie you up' UTOLVDN14Nov2301:278

The realization of the resulting (double) /n/ varies. In (742a), the nasal consonants are not separated, while in (742b) there a brief period of silence between them, which could be the closure of the oral stop /t/ that is then released nasally.

When the *t-* qualifier precedes the *d-* qualifier, the two qualifiers merge into *d* /t/ (743).

(743) a. … *k'ahdu' du' k'a dak-'aal.* (T)
k'ahdu' du' k'a t-d-ak-'aal
now CT NEG INC-QUAL-AA.IPV:1SG.S:H-sing:FUT:NEG
'… for now I will not sing them.' UTOLAF10Jul0801:027

b. *T'axoh hǫǫ' shyįį' dihnįįł.* (N)
t'axoh hǫǫ' shyįį' tdih-nįįł
enough thus only INC:QUAL:AA.IPV:1SG.S:Ø-say:FUT
'That's all I'm going to say.' UTOLAF15Dec0608:025

When the inceptive precedes *dh-*, an epenthetic [ɪ] or [ə], is inserted. The variability of this vowel is reflected in the orthography as <i> or <e>, respectively (744). The pronunciation with [ə] occurs primarily in Tetlin; [ɪ] is common in both dialects.

(744) a. *natidhihdliyh* (N)
na-t-dhih-dliyh
IT-INC-DH.PFV:1SG.S:Ø-be.cold:PFV
'I'm getting cold' UTCBVDN13Nov1401:027

b. *diłiign tedhehxįį* (T)
d-łiign' t-dheh-xįį
REFL.PSR-dog INC-3SG.S:QUAL:DH.PFV:H-kill.SG.O:PFV
'he killed his own dog' UTOLVDN13May2801:091

When the *t-* qualifier immediately follows the first-person plural prefix *ts'-* or the indefinite subject or object prefix *ch'-*, it merges with these prefixes to [t͡sʰ] (orthographically <ts>) and [t͡ʃʰ] (orthographically <ch>), respectively (745).

(745) a. *tseedeeł* (N)
ts'-tee-deeł
1PL.S-INC:DH.PFV:Ø-PL.go:PFV
'we started off' UTOLVDN10Jul2724:032

b. *nachee'aal* (N)
na-ch'-tee-'aal
IT-INDF.O-3SG.S:INC:DH.PFV:Ø-eat:PFV:NOM
'she, being ready to eat something' UTOLAF15May0501:040

30.7. The *u-* qualifier

The *u-* qualifier is known as the "conative prefix" (e.g., Kari [1990, 68]; Jetté and Jones [2000, 12]) or as the "directive prefix" (e.g., Axelrod [1993, 72]; Holton [2000, 234]). I follow Kari's terminology here.

The *u-* qualifier precedes the *t-* qualifier (746).

(746) a. *hii'aa'an ch'uutnel'iik tah* (T)
hii-'aa'an *ch'-uu-tnel-'iik*
3PL.S>3SG.P-by INDF.O-CON-INC:QUAL:Ø.IPV:L-sneak:IPV:CUST
tah
when
'whenever they try to sneak by it' UTOLAF09Jun2404:002

b. *utdakkał* (N)
uu-tdak-kał
CON-INC:QUAL:AA.IPV:1SG.S:H-ask:FUT
'I will ask [him]' UTOLAF15Dec0707:002

The conative prefix regularly moves left into the pronominal zone. In (747a) it occurs between the direct object and outer subject prefix; in (747b) it precedes the direct object prefix; and in (747c) it precedes the outer subject prefix. This happens particularly frequently in the Tetlin dialect, but also in Northway (747c).

(747) a. *nuudzih'ąą* (T)
n-uu-dzih-'ąą
2SG.O-CON-1PL.S:QUAL:I.PFV:H-find:PFV
'we found you SG' UTOLAF13May2403:093

b. *na'uudet-sih* (T)
na-uu-d-et-sih
IT-CON-REFL.O-3SG.S:Ø.IPV:D-name:IPV
'he identified himself' UTOLVDN14Nov2301:117

c. *Dii uhdih'aan...* (N)
dii u-h-d-ih-'aan
what CON-3PL.S-QUAL-I.PFV:H-find.CO:PFV:NOM
'Everything they found, ...' UTOLVDN07Nov2901:091

(747c) and (748) were produced by the same speaker, yet the morpheme order is different.

(748) *ch'ixia' ts'uudidlay* (N)
ch'ixia' ts'-uu-d-i-dlay
egg 1PL.S-CON-QUAL-I.PFV:Ø-find.PL.O:PFV:NOM
'the eggs we found' UTOLVDN07Aug2205:005

It is unclear to which degree this is an idiolectal or dialectal feature. It certainly does not hamper comprehension, and no speaker has ever commented on or corrected the different orders.

30.7.1. Functions

The *u-* qualifier has several functions. Axelrod (1993, 72) states that the "directive prefix" *oo-* in Koyukon (cognate with the *u-* qualifier) "seems to carry the meaning of movement toward an object, but without that movement accomplishing the goal or making the contact." This statement covers almost all uses of the *u-* qualifier in Upper Tanana, excepting where it is lexicalized as part of the theme.

30.7.1.1. The *u-* qualifier in successive verb themes The *u-* qualifier is part of one, or maybe two, prefix string(s) applying to successive verb themes. Several Alaskan Dene languages distinguish between conative and directive derivations. In Ahtna, according to Kari (1990, 68) the conative derivation consists of just the *u-* qualifier, while the directive derivation consists of the *u-* and *n-* qualifiers. Axelrod (1993, 72, 104), discussing Koyukon, uses the terms in the opposite fashion: the directive derivation consists only of the *oo-* qualifier, whereas the conative derivation consists of the *oo-* and *ne-* qualifiers. (Koyukon *ne-* is cognate to Upper Tanana *n-*.) Holton (2000, 240) does not formally distinguish the conative from the directive in Tanacross but claims that both trigger the *n*-conjugation marker in all modes.

In Upper Tanana the distinction between a conative and a directive derivation is unclear at best. (749) contains three forms of the verb theme O+H+dek/dak 'to shoot O'. This is a successive verb theme, which takes the durative aspect in its primary derivation (see chap. 25). (749a) is the semelfactive derivation of this verb theme. In this sentence the subject successfully shot the rabbit. (749b) illustrates the (n, n) momentaneous theme O+u+(n+)H+dek/dak 'shoot at O'; the *n-* qualifier is in parentheses here because it is impossible to determine whether it is present or not—as discussed in 30.3.2, the *n-* qualifier is not detectable before the *n-* conjugation prefix. (749c) is a form of the derived verb theme O+u+H+diih 'customarily shoot at O', which takes (Ø, aa) conjugation prefixes and the customary-directive stem variation. Stem aspect is indicated in (749).

(749) a. *Shke' dhakdayh* (N)
sh-ke' *dhak-dayh*
1SG.PSR-foot DH.PFV:1SG.S:H-shoot:SEM:PFV
'I shot myself in the foot (once)' UTOLAF13May2801:050

b. *gah uunakdegn* (N)
gah *uu-nnak-degn*
rabbit CON-QUAL:N.PFV:1SG.S:H-shoot:MOM:PFV:NOM
'I shot at the rabbit' UTOLAF13May2801:004

c. *agntthäł nts'ą̈' uu'akdiih* (N)
ag-tthäł *nts'ą̈'*
AA.IPV:1SG.S:L-SG.run:IPV:PROG and
uu-ak-diih
CON-Ø.IPV:1SG.S:H-shoot:MOM:IPV:CUST
'I'm shooting [at the bear] while I'm running'
UTOLAF09Aug12:027

The data in (749) suggests that in successive verb themes, the *u-* qualifier can derive (n, n) momentaneous themes as well as (Ø, aa) directive-customary themes. It is, however, not clear whether these are different derivational strings, as suggested by Kari (1990) or Axelrod (1993) or whether this difference is due to the customary superaspect. There are only a handful of verb forms illustrating this derivation in the data, so no conclusions can be drawn at this time.

30.7.1.2. The *u*- qualifier in motion verbs The *uu*-qualifier is also part of a prefix string (P+aa'an##)u 'moving past (bypassing P)' that applies to members of the motion theme category (750).

(750) a. *K'at'eey hii'aa'an hii'uudagn.* (T)
k'at'eey *hii-aa'an*
NEG 3PL.S>3SG.P-by
hii-uu-dagn
3PL.S>3SG.O-CON:Ø.IPV:Ø-PL.move:IPV:CUST:NEG
'They never pass him.' UTOLAF09Jun2404:006

b. *nah'ogn uu'altthadn* (T)
nah'ogn *u-al-tthadn*
outside 3SG.S:CON-AA.PFV:L-run:PFV:NOM
'he, running past outside' UTCBAF13Nov0501:242

Again, there are only a few examples of this prefix string.

30.7.1.3. Lexicalized *u*- qualifier The *u*- qualifier also is lexicalized in many verb themes. As a lexicalized prefix, the *u*- qualifier has no identifiable meaning (751).

(751) a. *hiiyuuteeniig* (T)
hiiy-uu-tee-niig
3PL.S:3SG.O-CON-INC:DH.PFV:Ø-grab:PFV:NOM
'they, trying to grab him' UTOLAF09Jun2202:072

b. *shyi' uutihkeet* (N)
shyi' *uu-tih-keet*
meat CON-INCEP:AA.IPV:1SG.S:Ø-buy:FUT
'I will buy meat' UTOLAF13May2804:044

c. *shuudehkat* (N)
sh-uu-deh-kat
1SG.O-3SG.S:CON-QUAL:Ø.IPV:H-ask:IPV
'he was asking me questions' UTOLAF09Aug12:046

30.7.2. Phonology

The *u-* qualifier is always short in closed syllables but of variable length in open ones. Since it does not contain an onset consonant, glottal stop insertion is required whenever it occurs in word-initial position or following a prefix ending in a vowel (752).

(752) a. *nah'ogn* [ʔ]*uu'altthadn* (T)
nah'ogn uu-al-tthadn
outside 3SG.S:CON-AA.IPV:L-run:IPV:NOM
'he, running past outside' UTCBAF13Nov0501:242

b. *k'a hu'udagkadn* (N)
k'a hu-uu-dag-kadn
NEG 3PL.O-CON-QUAL:NEG.PFV:1SG.S:L-ask:PFV:NEG
'I didn't ask them' UTOLVDN07Aug2205:019

When a vowel-initial prefix follows the *u-* qualifier, the two prefixes are also separated by a glottal stop (752a).

When the *u-* qualifier precedes the perfective prefix *į-*, e.g., in *aa-* perfective forms with a voiceless voice/valence marker, the two prefixes coalesce into *ǫǫ-* (753a); when it precedes the vocalic allomorph *ee-* of the *dh-* conjugation marker, the prefixes coalesce into *uu-* (753b).

(753) a. *ihǫǫkeet* (N)
i-ǫǫ-keet
3SG.S>3SG.O-CON:AA.PFV:Ø-pay:PFV
'he paid him' UTCBAF14May2001-008

b. *yuuniik* (T)
y-uu-niik
3SG.S>3SG.O-CON:DH.PFV:Ø-grab:PFV
'she grabbed it' UTOLVDN14Nov2301:555

30.8. The *hu*-qualifier

In this section, the qualifier *hu-*, *ho-* 'AR'- is described; the areal pronominal prefix with the same shape is described in chap. 31. This is a somewhat artificial separation, since the very proximity of the *hu-* qualifier to the pronominal zone is an indication that this prefix can have multiple functions, and it is not always clear which of these functions is present in any given instance of this prefix. See 30.8.1 for more discussion.

The areal qualifier is found at the left edge of the qualifier zone. (754a) illustrates that the *hu*-qualifier follows the pronominal prefixes and (754b) shows that it precedes the *t*-qualifier.

(754) a. *hihǫǫshyąą* (T)
h-hǫǫ-shyąą
3PL.S-AR:Ø.PFV:Ø-be.smart:IPV
'they were smart' UTOLVDN13May2803:063

b. *Naa nootagndak.* (T)
n-aa na-hu-tagn-dak
2SG.P-for IT-AR-INC:AA.IPV:1SG.S:L-tell.stories:FUT
'I will tell them about you SG.' UTOLVDN13May2902:048

30.8.1. Pronominal or qualifier?

The position of the areal prefix on the border of the pronominal and qualifier zones reflects its participation in both the qualifier and pronominal systems. This accounts for the different fashions in which this prefix is treated in accounts of the Dene verb. Kari (1990, 41) on Ahtna and Hargus (2007, 389–92) on Witsuwit'en discuss it as a member of the qualifier zone, although both authors recognize and demonstrate that it also has properties of a pronominal prefix. Tenenbaum (1978, 67–68) (on Dena'ina) and Rice (1989, 634–36) (on Slave) discuss it in their sections on pronominal prefixes; again both authors recognize that this morpheme also has properties of a qualifier. Thompson (1993) argues explicitly that in Koyukon, the areal should be considered a prefix that participates both in the qualifier and pronominal systems, and Lovick (2005) makes a similar argument for Dena'ina.

In Upper Tanana the areal also has properties both of a qualifier and of a pronominal prefix. As a qualifier, it is part of verb themes (754), and participates somewhat productively in the gender system (see 30.8.1.1). As a pronominal prefix, it can function as subject or direct object (see chap. 31), postpositional object (chap. 23) or possessor (chap. 22).

30.8.1.1. Areal gender As a qualifier the areal prefix participates in the gender system (755). Note, however, that *hu-* could also be interpreted as an areal subject prefix in these examples.

(755) a. *jign nee'ąą*

jign nee-'ąą
berry 3SG.S:QUAL:DH.PFV:ø-classify.CO:IPV
'a berry is there' Kari (1997b)

b. *keey jah huu'ąą* (N)

keey jah huu-ąą
house here 3SG.S:AR:DH.PFV:ø-classify.CO:IPV
'the village was there' UTOLAF09Aug1202:003

The gender system is described in more detail in volume 2.

30.8.1.2. Lexicalized areal The *hu-* qualifier is also a thematic prefix in many verb themes (754, 756).

(756) a. *hǫǫheeyh* (T)

hǫǫ-heeyh
3SG.S:QUAL:QUAL:Ø.IPV:ø-speak:IPV
'she was speaking' UTOLVDN14Nov2301:337

b. *Yeh naholnek.* (T)

y-eh na-hol-nek
3SG.S>3SG.P-to IT-AR:Ø.IPV:L-tell.story:IPV
'She's telling him a story.' UTOLAF13May2801:024

c. *ts'otnah'įįł* (T)

ts'-ho-tnah-'įįł
1PL.S-AR-INC:QUAL:AA.IPV:H-look:FUT
'we are going to look around' UTOLAF13May2403:036

30.8.2. Phonology

The areal qualifier has variably the form *hu-* or *ho-*. This is apparently a case of genuinely free variation; all speakers seem to use the forms interchangeably. Both forms are illustrated in (754) above.

When the areal prefix follows a disjunct morpheme other than the iterative prefix *na-*, or when it precedes a prefix containing an initial consonant, no changes take place.

The areal qualifier coalesces sometimes with the iterative prefix (757). Note however that this is not always the case (756b). It is not clear what determines whether this process applies.

(757) a. … *nts’iikeey iin nchaay iin eh nootinnegn.* (N)

n-ts’iikeey *iin* *n-chaay* *iin* *eh*
2SG.PSR-children PL 2SG.PSR-grandchildren PL and

na-hu-tin-negn
IT-AR-INC:AA.IPV:2SG.S:D-tell.stories:FUT:NOM

‘… you SG have to tell that to your children and grandchildren.’
UTOLAF12Jul1203:077

b. *Hahnde’ noonel’įh…* (T)

hah-nde’ *na-hu-nel-’įh*
NTRL-backwards:ALL IT-3SG.S:AR-QUAL:Ø.IPV:L-look:IPV

‘He looked back…’ UTCBAF13Nov0501:355

The areal prefix is sometimes, but not always, absorbed into the first-person plural subject prefix *ts’*-. Again it is unclear what determines whether this process takes place; (758a, b) were produced by the same speaker, and both instances of the areal prefix are lexicalized as part of the verb theme.

(758) a. *ts’ihotįįł* (T)

ts’-ho-tįįł
1PL.S-AR:Ø.IPV:Ø-have.potlatch:IPV

‘we are having a potlatch’ UTOLAF08Apr2804:019

b. *ts’otnah’įįł* (T)

ts’-ho-tnah-’įįł
1PL.S-AR-INC:QUAL:AA.IPV:H-see:FUT

‘we are going to look around’ UTOLAF13May2403:036

The areal prefix never is absorbed into the third-person plural subject prefix *h*-, presumably because the presence of the subject prefix would then not be detectable. The form *naholnek* in (759b) is only acceptable as a singular form (with an unmarked subject), not as a plural form.

(759) a. *nahiholnek*
na-h-hol-nek
IT-3PL.S-AR:Ø.IPV:L-tell.story:IPV
'they were telling stories' UTOLVDN07Aug2205:109

b. *naholnek*
na-hol-nek
IT-3SG.S:AR:Ø.IPV:L-tell.story:IPV
'she told a story' UTOLAF13May2801:024

When the areal qualifier precedes a prefix beginning with /a/ (such as the *aa-* conjugation marker or the portmanteau *ak-* '1SG.S:H'-, the vowel of the areal prefix is deleted (760a, b). It coalesces with the vocalic allomorph of the *dh-* conjugation prefix into *hu-* (760c). When it precedes a portmanteau involving the *aa-* perfective or the Ø- perfective, they coalesce into *hǫ-* (760d). The coalesced prefixes in (760c, d) are lengthened due to the lack of overt voice/valence prefix.

(760) a. *Nahalndak.* (T)
na-hal-ndak
IT-3SG.S:AR:AA.PFV:L-tell.story:PFV
'She told the story.' UTCBAF13Nov0501:372

b. *Stsiiniin' kah ts'ihakdąy.* (N)
s-tsiiniin' *kah* *ts'i-hak-dąy*
1SG.PSR-child:POSS for PEJ-AR:Ø.PFV:1SG.S:H-miss:IPV
'I miss my child.' UTOLAF13May2801:056

c. *shyah huu'ąą*
shyah *huu-ąą*
house 3SG.S:AR-DH.PFV:Ø-classify.CO:IPV
'a house is there' Kari (1997b)

d. *hihǫǫshyąą* (T)
h-ho-į-shyąą
3PL.S-AR-Ø.PFV:Ø-be.smart:IPV
'they were smart' UTOLVDN13May2803:063

30.9. Summary

In this chapter the qualifiers of position 5 are described. There are seven qualifiers: *i-*, *n-*, *d-*, *dh-*, *u-*, *t-*, and *hu-*. There is no *gh-* qualifier in Upper Tanana.

The qualifiers have diverse functions. All qualifiers can be thematic morphemes and most of them can also be used productively, referencing properties of referents (gender) or aspectual/temporal properties of the event.

Notes

1. As the *i*-prefix has punctual meaning, it is incompatible with the imperfective viewpoint with the exception of imperatives; see chap. 29.1.4.

31 Pronominal prefixes

Pronominal prefixes are marked in position 6 of the Upper Tanana template (see table 24.1). These prefixes fall into two groups: "outer subject prefixes" (third-person singular and plural subject, first-person plural subject, and areal and indefinite subject) and all direct object prefixes. Since the ordering relationships between these two types of prefixes are complex, I do not assume that they occupy different positions in the template. Instead, position 6, just like position 5, can contain several prefixes at the same time, which is why this part of the verb word is sometimes referred to as the pronominal zone (e.g., Kari [1990, 40] for Ahtna or Jetté and Jones [2000, 758] for Koyukon).

Outer subject prefixes are discussed in 31.1; direct object prefixes and the order of outer subject and direct object prefixes are described in 31.2. For a discussion of the difference between inner and outer subject prefixes, see chap. 28.

31.1. Outer subject prefixes

Five subject prefixes can occur here: Ø- '3SG.S-, 3PL.S-', *ts'*- '1PL.S-, IMPSL-', *h*- '3PL.S-', *ch'*- 'INDF.S'-, and *ho*- 'AR.S'-.

31.1.1. Third-person (singular) subject Ø-

The third-person (singular)[1] subject is phonologically empty. Scholars working on related languages disagree whether it should be considered a Ø-prefix or unmarked. Hargus (2007, 403) does not include Ø- in her list of pronominal prefixes in Witsuwit'en in order to not clutter the analysis of each verb with zero-morphemes (Hargus, personal communication). I assume here that third-person singular subject is marked by a zero-morpheme in position 6 of the template, following Rice (2000, 181). I do this less for theoretical reasons (although some are given in Rice and Saxon [1994] as well as Rice [2000]) but as a reminder that every verb form has to be inflected for subject.

31.1.1.1. Functions The third-person singular subject prefix usually refers to singular non-speech act participants. Upper Tanana does not distinguish masculine, feminine, and neuter gender (the gender distinction mentioned in chap. 30 is a shape classification). Out of context, every third person singular form could be interpreted as having any one of the three English genders (761).

(761) *etsüh* (N)
e-tsüh
3SG.S:Ø.IPV:Ø-cry:IPV
'he, she, it is crying' UT Notebook #3, 71

These forms can also be used to refer to plural referents (762).

(762) a. *Ha'ogn dineey iin natetdagn iin...* (T)
ha-'ogn *dineey* *iin*
NTRL-outside:AR people PL
na-tet-dagn
PRMB-3PL.S:INC:Ø.IPV:D-PL.go:IPV:CUST:NOM
'The people walking around out there...'
UTOLVDN13May2803:041

b. *Ashyign ch'a nnąą deltth'ih, ...* (T)
a-shyign' *ch'a* *n-nąą*
NTRL-down:ALL FOC 2SG.PSR-mother
del-tth'ih
3PL.S:QUAL:DH.IPV:L-PL.stay:IPV
'Down there are your parents...' UTCBAF13Nov0501:316

c. *Hu'ootthee utaałeeł, ntl'at tee'aał de'.* (T)
hu-ootthee *hu-taa-łeeł* *ntl'at*
3PL.PSR-strong.period AR.S-INC:AA.IPV:Ø-be:FUT cranberries
tee-'aał *de'*
3PL.S:INC:DH.PFV:Ø-eat:PFV if
'Their periods will be very strong if they eat cranberries.'
UTOLVDN11Jul2901:015

In (762a, b) plurality is indicated in the verb stem. In (762c), plurality is not indicated in the second clause at all: there is no subject noun phrase in this clause, and the verb stem *'aał* 'eat' is not specified for subject number. The plural interpretation is derived solely from context. The text that (762c) is taken from details puberty restrictions for young girls, and young girls are the implied subject of *tee'aał* 'they eat' (note that the possessor prefix of *hu'ootthee* 'their periods' is overtly plural-marked).

Throughout this grammar the third-person (singular) subject prefix Ø- is glossed as '3SG.S'- or '3PL.S'- depending on consultants' preferred translation of the verb form in context.

31.1.1.2. Syntax A verb inflected for third-person singular subject does not require an external noun phrase coreferential with the subject to form a complete sentence (761), provided that the identity of the subject referent is clear from context. At the same time, external noun phrases that are coreferential with the unmarked third-person subject occur quite frequently (763).

(763) a. *Ts'iiniin guuy etsaa.* (T)

ts'iiniin guuy e-tsaa
child tiny 3SG.S:Ø.IPV:Ø-cry:IPV
'The small baby was crying.' UTOLAF09Jun2202:014

b. *Jah ts'änh shta' tąy hohtsiik...* (N)

jah ts'änh sh-ta' tąy
there from 1SG.PSR-father trail
hoh-tsiik
3SG.S:AR.O:Ø.IPV:H-make.SG.O:IPV:CUST
'From there my father would make a trail...'
UTOLAF08Feb1908:005

Very rarely, the third-person singular subject prefix co-occurs with a coreferential free pronoun (764).

(764) *Xan du' ts'anįįtleegn.* (T)

xan du' ts'a-nįį-tleegn
DEM CT PEJ-3SG.S:QUAL:Ø.PFV:Ø-be.ugly:IPV:NOM
'That [person] is ugly.' UTOLAF07Oct2504:013

More information on subject noun phrases can be found in volume 2.

31.1.1.3. Phonology The third-person (singular) subject is phonologically empty. When there are no other conjunct prefixes present (i.e., in the Ø-imperfective without qualifiers or direct object prefixes), a peg syllable is added to ensure that the verb form is disyllabic. The resulting peg prefix /ʔe/ (orthographically <e>) is glossed as '3SG.S:Ø.IPV:_'- (where _ represents the voice/valence prefix) throughout (765).

(765) a. [ʔe]*tsüh* (N)

e-tsüh

3sg.s:ø.ipv:ø-cry:ipv

'he's crying' UT Notebook #3, 71

b. *tseey* [ʔe]*tnąą* (N)

tseey et-nąą

tea 3sg.s:ø.ipv:d-drink:ipv

'she's drinking tea' UT Notebook #3, 67

c. *shyi'* [ʔe]*ht'iah* (N)

shyi' eh-t'iah

meat 3sg.s:ø.ipv:h-fry:ipv

'he's frying meat' UT Notebook #3, 68

d. [ʔe]*lshyak*

el-shyak

3sg.s:ø.ipv:l-lie:ipv

'she is lying (telling an untruth)' Kari (1997b)

This peg syllable also is inserted after a disjunct prefix of the shape CV, as shown in (766).

(766) *na'elshyih* (N)

na-el-shyih

it-3sg.s:ø.ipv:l-rest:ipv

'he's taking a rest' UTOLAF15Dec0608:041

31.1.2. Third-person plural subject *h*-

The third-person plural subject prefix has the shape *h*- and is largely restricted to human referents.

31.1.2.1. Functions The third-person plural subject prefix has two functions. It can refer to a third-person plural referent, usually human (very rarely to animals such as dogs), or it can function as an indefinite human pronoun, 'someone, people'.

31.1.2.1.1. (Human) plural subject prefix *H*- is used most frequently as a subject prefix for plural human subjects (767a). More rarely it is used to refer to multiple animals, usually dogs (767b). Unlike some related languages (e.g., Faltz [1998] for Navajo, Cook [2004] for Dëne Sųłiné, or de Reuse and Goode [2006] for San Carlos Apache), Upper Tanana does not have a dual/plural distinction. (767a) has a dual subject referent (the speaker's two brothers) and (767b) has a plural subject referent.

(767) a. *Shttheh tah nahatkeeł.* (N)
sh-ttheh tah na-hat-keeł
1SG.P-ahead at PRMB-3PL.S:AA.IPV:D-go.by.boat:IPV
'They were paddling ahead of me.' UTOLVDN07Aug2205:104

b. *łįį iin shihdįįnay eł* (T)
łįį iin sh-h-dįį-nay eł
dog PL 1SG.O-3PL.S-QUAL:AA.PFV:ø-move.quickly:PFV:NOM and
'the dogs threw me down and' UTOLAF09Jun2201:005

In traditional narratives animals other than dogs sometimes are referred to with the third person-plural subject prefix. This usually indicates that they are People with customs of their own, capable of speech and rational thinking. (768) is taken from the Traveler story cycle; Tsa' Ushyąą' has been invited on a moose hunt by the No-see-um People, who hunt great grey owls instead of moose.

(768) *Nahdaa nahįlshyah.* (S)
nahdaa na-hįl-shyah
great.grey.owl IT-3PL.S:AA.PFV:L-handle.PL.O:PFV
'[The No-see-um People] brought the great grey owls home.'
ANLC4122a:243

31.1.2.1.2. Nonspecific human subject prefix The third-person plural subject prefix also is used as a nonspecific human subject prefix. (769a) is not about particular individuals who are on their way back to Tetlin from Midway Lake, but rather about anyone traveling on this trail. The subject in (769b) is again nonspecific; hunting for small game such as squirrels in times of famine was done by everyone.

(769) a. … *Toochinh nts'ą' nahatdał tah …* (T)
Toochinh nts'ą' na-hat-dał tah
sticks.in.water from IT-3PL.S:AA.IPV:D-PL.go:IPV:PROG when
'… when people come back from Sticks In Water (Midway Lake)…'
UTOLAF09Jun2404:002

b. *Hushyi' kol de' hah'ogn nuun de' kah staahtatdek, dineh iin.* (N)

hu-shyi'	*kol*	*de'*	*hah-'ogn*	*nuun*	*de' kah*
3PL.PSR-food	NEGEX	if	NTRL-out:AR	animal	to.check

sta-na-h-tat-dek	*dineh*	*iin*
away-IT-3P-INC:AA.IPV:D-PL.go:IPV:CUST	people	PL

'When they had no food, they would go back out looking for small animals, the men.' UTOLVDN07Nov2901:090

The use of the third-person plural subject prefix as a nonspecific human subject prefix is pervasive. It is in fact the most common strategy for suppression of the actor referent, by far more common (not to mention easier to elicit) than the passive construction described in chap. 27.3.2.1.1.

31.1.2.2. Syntax The third-person plural subject marker may occur with or without coreferential noun phrases, both with a specific (767) or nonspecific (769) interpretation.

The third-person human plural subject prefix also co-occurs with free pronouns as shown in (770). This is a very rare construction.

(770) *Ay iin ch'ale ch'a tąy k'ehįįdeeɬ dänh tąy hǫǫteeɬ.* (N)

ay	*iin*	*ch'ale*	*ch'a*	*tąy*	*k'e-hįį-deeɬ*	*dänh*	*tąy*
3	PL	FOC	FOC	trail	on-3PL.S:AA.PFV:Ø-PL.go:PFV	at	trail

hǫǫ-teeɬ
AR.S:Ø.PFV:Ø-be.wide:IPV

'And the trail they were walking on was a wide trail.'
UTOLAF15May0501:012

31.1.2.3. Phonology

31.1.2.3.1. Schwa insertion In Ø- imperfective verb forms with no additional prefixes, a schwa is inserted following the third-person subject prefix. The schwa is realized as [ɛ] in closed syllables and [ɛ] or [ɪ] in open syllables, which is reflected in the orthography (771).

(771) a. *hitsüh* (N)

hi-tsüh
3PL.S:Ø.IPV:Ø-cry:IPV
'they are crying' UT Notebook #3, 71

b. *tseey hetnąą* (N)
tseey het-nąą
tea 3PL.S:Ø.IPV:D-drink:IPV
'they are drinking tea' UT Notebook #3, 67

c. *shyi' heht'iah* (N)
shyi' heh-t'iah
meat 3PL.S:Ø.IPV:H-cry:IPV
'they are frying meat' UT Notebook #3, 68

d. *helshyak*
hel-shyak
3PL.S:Ø.IPV:L-lie:IPV
'they are lying (telling an untruth)' Kari (1997b)

31.1.2.3.2. Expansion to *hih-* When the third-person plural subject prefix in word-initial position precedes a consonantal qualifier, it is almost always expanded to *hih-* (772).

(772) a. *hihdeltth'ih* (N)
h-del-tth'ih
3PL.S-QUAL:DH.IPV:L-PL.sit:IPV
'they were sitting/staying ' UTCBVDN13Nov0804:017

b. *łat hihneh'įh* (T)
łat h-neh-'įh
smoke 3PL.S-QUAL:Ø.IPV:H-see:IPV
'they saw smoke' UTOLAF07Nov2602:010

c. *hihteedeeł* (T)
h-tee-deeł
3PL.S-INC:DH.PFV:Ø-PL.go:PFV
'they went' UTOLAF07Nov2602:011

31.1.2.3.3. Resyllabification of *h-* When the third-person plural subject prefix follows a prefix of the form CV (where the vowel may be underlying or epenthetic), it may be resyllabified as the coda consonant of that prefix (773). The vowel in the first syllable of (773a) is underlying; that in the first syllable of (773b) is epenthetic.

(773) a. *nahdelttb'ih* (T)
na-h-del-tth'ih
IT-3PL.S-QUAL:DH.PFV:L-PL.sit:IPV
'they are sitting again, keep sitting' UTCBAF13Nov0501:289

b. *shihneh'įh*
sh-hneh-'įh
1SG.O-3PL.S:QUAL:Ø.IPV:H-look:IPV
'they looked at me' UTOLAF09Jun2902:014

31.1.3. First-person plural subject *ts'*-

Dene languages differ in which morpheme is used to express first-person plural subjects. Jung (1999, 81) shows in her table 10 that Apachean and Pacific Coast Dene languages use a reflex of a prefix sequence reconstructed as *əŋəʔdəD by Story (1989, 496). This morpheme (often of the shape VVd- in contemporary languages) occurs in the inner subject position. The Canadian Dene languages are split between using this prefix and a reflex of the Proto-Dene impersonal subject prefix, which occurs in the outer subject position. An overview is given by Jung (1999, chap. 2.3).[2] Alaskan Dene languages, with the possible exception of Han and Gwich'in (Story 1989, 496), do not have a reflex of *əŋəʔdəD. Instead they all use a reflex of the impersonal prefix to express first-person plural subject.

The origin of the first-person plural subject prefix as an impersonal prefix is partly responsible for its semantics.

31.1.3.1. Functions The first-person plural subject prefix *ts'*- is used in the following contexts: (1) indexing a group including the speaker, (2) in certain subordinate clauses, indexing the referent of the main clause, (3) as part of a prohibitive construction to express general prohibitions, and (4) as an impersonal subject.

31.1.3.1.1. Indexing group including the speaker In most instances, *ts'*- expresses first-person plural subject (774).

(774) a. … *hah'ogn dzelxoh.* (N)

hah-'ogn	*dzel-xoh*
NTRL-outside:AR	1PL.S:QUAL:Ø.IPV:L-play:IPV

'… we were playing outside.' UTOLAF08Feb1906:005

b. *Ts'įįłįį dą'…* (T)
ts'įį-łįį *dą'*
1PL.S:Ø.PFV:Ø-be.small:IPV when:PST
'When we were small…' UTOLVDN07Nov2803:001

This prefix is also used in comitative constructions including the speaker and at least one other individual (775).

(775) a. *Shta' eh jah shyah ts'ehtsįį.* (N)
sh-ta' *eh* *jah* *shyah* *ts'eh-tsįį*
1SG.PSR-father with here house 1PL.S:DH.PFV:H-make:SG.O:PFV
'I built this house with my father.' UTOLAF13May2801:045

b. *Shchil eh ha'ogn dzelxoh.* (N)
sh-chil *eh* *ha-'ogn*
1SG.PSR-younger.brother with NTRL-outside:AR
dzel-xoh
1PL.S:QUAL:Ø.IPV:L-play:IPV
'I played outside with my younger brother.'
UTOLAF13May2801:044

31.1.3.1.2. Indexing the subject of the matrix clause In some subordinating constructions, the first-person plural subject prefix is coreferential to (or includes) the third-person subject of the verb in the matrix clause (776). The same situation is described with respect to first-person singular subjects in chap. 28.1.2.2.

(776) a. *ts'utl'u' hinįįthanh* (T)
ts'u-tl'u' *h-nįį-thanh*
1PL.S:OPT:Ø-dress:OPT 3PL.S-QUAL:QUAL:Ø.PFV:Ø-want:IPV
'they want to dress' (lit.: 'they want we should dress')
UTOLVDN09Jun2302:122

b. *Those Che' T'iin iin huts'uuxąą xah tl'oh skihdeh'ah.* (T)
those *Che' T'iin* *iin* *hu-ts'uuxąą* *xah*
those Tailed.People PL 3PL.O-1PL.S:OPT:Ø-kill:OPT for
tl'oh *ski-h-deh-'ah*
grass across-3PL.S-QUAL:DH.PFV:H-extend:IPV
'Those Tailed People$_i$ had put grass across the trail so they$_i$ (lit.: we) could kill them$_j$.' UTOLVDN13May2803:009

These subordinating constructions are described in more detail in volume 2.

31.1.3.1.3. *ts'*- in prohibitive constructions The first-person plural subject prefix *ts'*- may be used as part of a prohibitive construction (777).

(777) a. *sǫ' dzulchuudn (S)*

sǫ' *dzul-chuudn*
PROH 1PL.S:QUAL:OPT:L-save.food:OPT:NEG
'don't save food' ANLC4122a:281

b. *Ena', shnąą iin shta' "Hǫǫ' k'a tsaadįįgn!" neeheniik.* (T)

ena' *sh-nąą* *iin* *sh-ta'* *hǫǫ* *k'a*
no 1SG.PSR-mother PL 1SG.PSR-father thus NEG

tsaa-dįįgn
1PL.S:INC:AA.IPV:Ø-do:FUT:CUST:NEG

nee-he-niik
1PL.O-3PL.S:Ø.IPV:Ø-say:IPV:cust

'No, my parents always told us, "Don't do that!"'
UTOLVDN14Nov2301:276

This construction is used in contexts where an outsider is being introduced to unfamiliar customs or rejects actions judged inappropriate. More information on prohibitive constructions can be found in volume 2 or in Lovick (2016).

31.1.3.1.4. Impersonal uses of *ts'*- The Upper Tanana first-person plural subject prefix is cognate to what has been called the "impersonal" subject prefix (Saxon 1993) or the "fourth person" (Akmajian and Anderson 1970) in related languages. Similarly to what Hargus (2007, 407) describes for Witsuwit'en, the impersonal use in Upper Tanana has all but disappeared. It mainly occurs in nominalizations; (778b) gives the breakdown of the Upper dialect word for 'chair' and (778a) for the Tetlin word for 'parka', both of which illustrate the impersonal use of this prefix.

(778) a. *nadzelshyaagn* (T)

na-dzel-shyaagn
PRMB-IMPSL.S:QUAL:Ø.IPV:L-SG.handle.PL.O:IPV:CUST:NOM
'the things one carries around = parka'
UTOLVDN07Nov2803:031

b. *uk'edats'edaag* (U)
u-k'e-da-ts'e-daag
3SG.P-on-up-IMPSL.S:Ø.IPV:Ø-SG.sit:IPV:CUST:NOM
'the thing one sits on = chair' Kari (1997b)

There are few examples of *ts'-* as an impersonal subject outside of nominalizations (779); usually the third-person plural subject prefix is used instead.

(779) a. *Doo ts'inuhshyee yuunąy…* (T)
doo *ts'-nuh-shyee*
who IMPSL.S-QUAL:OPT:H-raise:OPT
y-uu-nąy
3SG.S>3SG.O-CON:Ø.IPV:Ø-want:IPV:NOM
'Whoever wants to raise him…' UTOLAF13May2403:067

b. *"Jah duugn ts'eedah lah?"* (T)
jah duugn *ts'ee-dah* *lah*
hereabouts IMPSL.S:DH.PFV:Ø-SG.sit:IPV Q
'Is there anyone here?' UTOLVDN14Nov2301:402

Functions of reference tracking similar to that described by Akmajian and Anderson (1970) for Navajo or by Saxon (1993) for Tłı̨chǫ are not attested in Upper Tanana.

31.1.3.2. Syntax As discussed in chap. 28, speech act participant subject pronouns do not usually co-occur with coreferential free noun phrases. This is true for the first-person plural subject prefix *ts'-* as well. It may, however, co-occur with predicative noun phrases (780).

(780) *Ts'iikeey ts'į̨įłį̨į nts'ą'…* (T)
ts'iikeey *ts'į̨į-łį̨į* *nts'ą'*
children 1PL.S:Ø.PFV:Ø-be:IPV and
'We were children…' UTOLVDN07Nov2803:006

In the comitative construction, the first-person plural subject prefix *ts'-* may also co-occur with a singular noun phrase that refers to a member of the group referenced by *ts'-*, as shown in (775a) above.

31.1.3.3. Phonology

31.1.3.3.1. Schwa insertion If a first-person plural subject verb form in the Ø- imperfective contains no direct object prefix or qualifier, a schwa vowel is inserted between the subject prefix and the voice/valence prefix (781). The realization of this schwa can be [ɛ] or [ɪ], which is usually reflected in the orthography.

(781) a. *ts'etsüh* (N)
ts'e-tsüh
1PL.S:Ø.IPV:Ø-cry:IPV
'we are crying' UT Notebook #3, 71

b. *tseey ts'etnąą* (N)
tseey ts'et-nąą
tea 1PL.S:Ø.IPV:D-drink:IPV
'we are drinking tea' UT Notebook #3, 67

c. *shyi' ts'eht'iah* (N)
shyi' ts'eh-t'iah
meat 1PL.S:Ø.IPV:H-roast:IPV
'we are roasting meat' UT Notebook #3, 68

d. *ts'elshyak*
ts'el-shyak
1PL.S:Ø.IPV:L-lie:IPV
'we are lying (telling an untruth)' Kari (1997b)

31.1.3.3.2. Qualifier absorption When the first-person plural subject prefix *ts'*- immediately precedes a qualifier of the shape *d*- or *t*-, it merges with the qualifier to yield the portmanteaus *dz*- (782a) and *ts*- (782b), respectively. When both qualifiers are present (e.g., in future forms of verb themes containing a *d*- qualifier), the resulting portmanteau is *dz*- (782c).

(782) a. *dzįįtsįį* (N)
ts'-d-įį-tsįį
1PL.S-QUAL-Ø.PFV:Ø-be.hungry:IPV
'we are hungry' UTOLAF12Jul1203:037

b. *Ishyiit nitsaadał...* (T)
ishyiit ni-ts'-t-aa-dał
there TERM-1PL.S-INC-AA.IPV:Ø-PL.go:FUT
'We will go there...' UTOLAF13May2403:036

c. *ishyiit dzaltth'iił* (N)
ishyiit ts'-t-d-al-tth'iił
there 1PL.S-INC-QUAL-AA.IPV:L-PL.stay:FUT
'we will stay there' UTOLVDN07Nov2901:019

31.1.3.3.3. Indefinite object absorption When *ts'*- co-occurs with the indefinite object prefix *ch'*-, they coalesce into *nts'*-, where the *n*- is the distributive prefix of position 7 of the verb template (783, 784). Third-person plural subject forms are included in these examples to demonstrate the underlying morpheme order.

(783) a. *ch'ihaldziat* (T)
ch'-hal-dziat
INDF.O-3PL.S:AA.PFV:L-dance:PFV
'they danced' UT Notebook #3, 95

b. *nts'aldziat* (T)
n-ch'-ts'-al-dziat
DSTR-INDF.O-1PL.S-AA.PFV:L-dance:PFV
'we danced' UT Notebook #3, 95

(784) a. *ts'iiniin k'a ich'ihih'aal* (N)
ts'iiniin k'a i-ch'-hih-'aal
child NEG PP-INDF.O-3PL.S:NEG.PFV:H-feed:PFV:NEG
'they didn't feed the baby' UT Notebook #3, 86

b. *ts'iiniin k'a ints'ih'aal* (N)
ts'iiniin k'a i-n-ch'-ts'-ih-'aal
child NEG PP-DSTR-INDF.O-1PL.S-NEG.PFV:H-feed:PFV:NEG
'we didn't feed the baby' UT Notebook #3, 86

When the portmanteau consisting of the first-person plural subject and indefinite object prefixes is followed by a *t*- or *d*- qualifier, they coalesce into *nts*- or *ndz*-, respectively, (785) and (786). Again, first- and third-person plural forms are contrasted.

(785) a. *Ndee ch'ihtnel'įį' le'?* (T)

ndee ch'-h-t-nel-'įį' le'
where INDF.O-3PL.S-INC-QUAL:Ø.IPV:L-hide:IPV MIR
'Where can they be hiding?' UTOLAF12Jul1101:022

b. *Ndee ntsinul'į'?* (T)

ndee n-ch'-ts'-t-nul-'į'
where DSTR-INDF.O-1PL.S-INC-QUAL:OPT:L-hide:OPT
'Where can we hide?' UTOLAF12Jul1101:009

(786) a. *ch'ihdįh'a'* (N)

ch'-h-dįh-'a'
INDF.O-3PL.S-QUAL:AA.PFV:H-sing:PFV
'they sang' UT Notebook #3, 74

b. *ndzįh'a'* (N)

n-ch'-ts'-dįh-'a'
DSTR-INDF.O-1PL.S-QUAL:AA.PFV:H-sing:PFV
'we sang' UT Notebook #3, 74

31.1.4. Indefinite subject *ch'*-

The indefinite subject prefix *ch'*- is by far the rarest of the subject prefixes; there are only a handful of examples.

31.1.4.1. Functions The indefinite subject prefix *ch'*- is used especially in contexts where the subject referent is known but is being intentionally avoided: in (787a) the narrator avoids talking directly about an evil spirit, and the character uttering (787b) similarly does not directly reference the enemies that slaughtered her village.

(787) a. *Ch'aadeh ushyiit ch'įįshyah ch'idanh tah.* (T)

ch'-aadeh u-shyiit ch'įį-shyah
INDF.PSR-older.sister 3SG.P-into INDF.S:AA.PFV:Ø-SG.go:PFV
ch'idanh tah
different
'Something different [an evil spirit] got into the older sister.'
UTOLVDN14Nov2301:139

b. *Needach'įįxąą shyiign danh.* (T)

nee-da-ch'įį-xąą *shyiign* *danh*
1PL.P-all-INDF.S:AA.PFV:Ø-kill.PL.O:PFV down:ALL at

'Something killed all of us down there.'

UTCBAF14Jul1805:035

The indefinite subject prefix is also used when the identity of the subject referent is unknown to the speaker (788):

(788) a. *Choyh! ch'etnih.* (T)

choyh *ch'et-nih*
ONOM INDF.S:Ø.IPV:D-be.noise:IPV

'There was a hissing sound.' UTOLVDN14Nov2301:242

b. *Shee'eh, ahtthǫǫ nts'anh ch'aadał.* (T)

sh-ee'eh *ah-tthǫǫ* *nts'anh*
1SG.PSR-maternal.uncle NTRL-waterward:ABL from

ch'aa-dał
INDF.S:AA.IPV:Ø-PL.go:IPV:PROG

'My uncle, people are coming from waterward.'

UTCBVDN13Nov1502-036

In the speech of Mrs. Mary Tyone from Scottie Creek, the indefinite subject prefix *ch'-* is also used in negative constructions with the meaning 'no one':

(789) a. *Shnąą k'aa wuk'it ch'ihol'ay.* (S)

sh-nąą *k'a* *u-k'it* *ch'-hol-'ay*
1SG.PSR-mother NEG 3SG.P-on INDF.S-AR.O:Ø.IPV:L-do:IPV:NEG

'No one could outdo my mother.' Tyone (1996, 9)

b. *Oooh aydu' k'aa wudziiy ch'ehuuheel duuni'.* (S)

oh *ay* *du'* *k'a* *u-dziit*
oh 3SG CT NEG 3SG.PSR-hearing

ch'-huu-heel *duuni'*
INDF.S-QUAL:OPT:Ø-speak:PFV:NEG ?

'Oh, that one, he has no one to tell him stories.' Tyone (1996, 53)

A similar construction is not attested in the Tetlin and Northway dialects.

31.1.4.2. Syntax The indefinite subject prefix never co-occurs with co-referential noun phrases.

31.1.4.3. Phonology (788a) demonstrates that a schwa is inserted if no prefixes occur between the subject prefix and the voice/valence marker. A schwa is also inserted before a consonant-initial prefix (789).

31.1.5. Areal subject *hu-*

As discussed in chap. 30, the areal prefix has dual status as qualifier and pronominal prefix. In the present chapter only its pronominal functions are described.

31.1.5.1. Functions As a referential marker, the areal prefix indexes spatial or temporal referents, as shown in (790).

(790) a. *tąy hǫǫts'eek* (N)
tąy hǫǫ-ts'eek
trail AR.S:Ø.PFV:Ø-be.narrow:IPV
'the trail was narrow' UTOLAF09Aug1202:028

b. *tadn hǫǫłįį* (T)
tadn hǫǫ-łįį
night AR.S:Ø.PFV:Ø-be:IPV
'it was night' UTCBVDN13Nov1101:005

The areal can also reference abstract subjects, such as the scent in (791):

(791) *Jah tah t'eey uts'įį' hunįį'ah!* (T)
jah tah t'eey u-ts'įį' hu-nįį-'ah
here among even 3SG.PSR-scent AR.S-N.PFV:Ø-LO.extends:IPV
'Her scent is right here!' UTCBAF13Nov0501:244

31.1.5.2. Syntax

31.1.5.2.1. Coreferential noun phrases The areal subject prefix can occur with (792a) or without (792b) a coreferential noun phrase. Examples without a coreferential noun phrase are relatively rare.

(792) a. *Shiin hǫǫłįį eh.* (N)
shiin hǫǫ-łįį eh
summer AR.S:Ø.PFV:Ø-be:IPV and
'It was summer time.' UTOLVDN10Jul2710:022

b. … *nts'aa' neh hǫǫt'eh?*
nts'aa' n-eh hǫǫ-t'eh
how 2SG.P-with AR.S:Ø.PFV:Ø-be:IPV
'… how are things with you?' UTOLVDN07Aug2205:110

It can also occur with a modifier:

(793) *elih hǫǫłįį* (N)
elih hǫǫ-łįį
cold AR.S:Ø.PFV:Ø-be:IPV
'it was cold' UTOLAF13May2801:012

31.1.5.2.2. Dummy subject The areal prefix can also serve as a dummy subject in existential clauses. (794a) is an identificational sentence; (794b) is an existential one. As Thompson (1993, 322) points out for Koyukon, one cannot argue that the word *ts'iiniin* 'child, baby' takes Ø- gender in one sentence but not in the other; hence he concludes that *ho-* is a dummy subject in existential sentences such as (794b).

(794) a. *shnąą ts'iiniin nłįį* (T)
sh-nąą ts'iiniin n-łįį
1SG.PSR-mother child 3SG.S:Ø.PFV:Ø-be:IPV
'my mother was a child' UTOLAF07Nov2602:017

b. *Nshyaats'e' uts'iiniin' hǫǫłįį de'…* (N)
n-shyaats'e' u-ts'iiniin' hǫǫ-łįį
2SG.PSR-womans.daughter 3SG.PSR-child:POSS AR.S:Ø.PFV:Ø-be:IPV
de'
if
'If your daughter has a child…' (lit. 'If your daughter's child exists…')
UTOLAF12Jul1203:056

31.1.5.3. Phonology The areal subject marker coalesces both with preceding and with following material.

31.1.5.3.1. Coalescence with iterative prefix When the iterative prefix *na-* of position 8 immediately precedes the areal subject marker *ho-*, the two prefixes often coalesce into *noo-* (795).

(795) a. *nooditk'ąą* (N)
na-hu-dit-kąą
IT-AR.S-QUAL:I.PFV:D-be.burning:IPV
'[the land] was burning' UTOLVDN14Apr2601:001

b. *nootalxįį* (N)
na-hu-tal-xįį
IT-AR.S-INC:AA.IPV:L-melt:FUT
'[the ground] will thaw' UTOLAF13May2804:040

31.1.5.3.2. Coalescence with conjugation and mode markers The areal subject marker coalesces with following material in the same way that the areal qualifier does; see chap. 30.8 for details.

31.2. Direct object prefixes

The inventory of direct object prefixes is almost identical to the postpositional object and possessor prefixes; see chap. 23 for a comparison. Four types of direct object prefixes can be distinguished: (1) first- and second-person object prefixes, (2) third-person object prefixes, (3) prefixes expressing coreferentiality between subject and direct object, and (4) other object prefixes. The following discussion broadly follows this organization. Third-person object marking is, however, quite complex, as the choice of object prefix depends not only on the type and reference of the subject prefix but also on the presence of an overt object noun phrase. For this reason the intricacies of third-person object marking are not discussed in this chapter; more information can be found in volume 2.

31.2.1. First- and second-person direct object prefixes

The form of first- and second-person direct object prefixes is not influenced by the subject marker.

31.2.1.1. First-person singular direct object *sh-* The first-person singular object prefix has the form *sh-*.

31.2.1.1.1. Functions The first-person singular object prefix indexes the speaker or the subject of the main clause in certain subordinating constructions.

31.2.1.1.1.1. Indexing the speaker The referent of a first-person singular object prefix may be the person producing the utterance (796a) or a person within a narrative producing direct speech (796b).

(796) a. *shihnih'į̨h* (T)
sh-hnį̨h-'į̨h
1sg.o-3pl.s:qual-aa.pv:h-look:pfv
'they looked at me' UTOLAF09Jun2902:014

b. *"Ahnoo shnaahaal ch'a'," nih.* (T)
ah-noo *sh-naa-haal* *ch'a'*
ntrl-ahead:all 1sg.o-3sg.s:qual:aa.ipv:ø-sg.go:ipv:nom avert
nih
say:ipv
'"To prevent him from following me," she said.'
UTCBAF13Nov0501:177

31.2.1.1.1.2. Indexing the subject of the matrix clause Very rarely *sh-* may also be the object within a purpose clause with reference shift, as in (797). More information is given in volume 2.

(797) *Eł hǫǫshyą̨ą̨ t'oo ch'a dą̨y' nts'aa' shdutni' xah le' dą̨y'.*
eł *hǫǫ-shyą̨ą̨* *t'oo* *ch'a* *dą̨y'*
and 3sg.s:ar:ø.pfv:ø-be.smart:ipv but foc do:ipv:nom
nts'aa' *sh-dut-ni'* *xah* *le'* *dą̨y'*
how 1sg.o-qual:opt:d-be.told:opt purp mir do:ipv:nom
'He was smart, but he did it anyway [to see] what he (lit.: I) would be told.' UTOLAF09Jun2202:031

31.2.1.1.2. Syntax This prefix does not co-occur with coreferential noun phrases or pronouns.

31.2.1.1.3. Phonology The first-person singular object prefix undergoes only one phonological process. When it precedes the third-person plural subject prefix *h-* (798a), the epenthetic vowel [ɪ] is inserted between the prefixes. When it immediately precedes the voice/valence marker, the epenthetic vowel has the form [ɛ] (798b).

(798) a. *dashihnį̨htį̨į̨* (N)
da-sh-h-nį̨h-tį̨į̨
inside-1sg.o-3pl.o-n.pfv:h-carry.ao:pfv
'they carried me inside' UTOLVDN14Apr2602:034

b. *shehnih* (N)
sh-eh-nih
1SG.O-3SG.S:Ø.IPV:H-say:IPV
'he said to me' UTOLAF09Aug1201:042

Epenthesis does not take place preceding other consonants; see, e.g., (796b) or (797).

31.2.1.2. Second-person singular direct object *n*- The second-person singular object prefix has the form *n*-.

31.2.1.2.1. Functions The second-person singular object marker references the singular listener in a conversation (799a) or in direct speech within a narrative (799b).

(799) a. *nuudakkat* (T)
n-uu-dak-kat
2SG.O-CON-QUAL:Ø.IPV:1SG.S:H-ask:IPV
'I am asking you SG' UT Notebook #4, 9

b. *nantsidhahxeh* (T)
na-n-ts-dhah-xeh
IT-2SG.O-1PL.S:INC-QUAL:AA.IPV:H-kill.SG.O:FUT
'we will kill you SG also' UTOLVDN13May2909:038

There are no other uses of the second-person singular object prefix.

31.2.1.2.2. Syntax This prefix does not co-occur with coreferential noun phrases or pronouns.

31.2.1.2.3. Phonology The second-person singular object prefix does not trigger epenthesis when it occurs before a consonant; instead it occurs in a syllable of its own (800).

(800) a. *nnak-'į̨h* [n.nakʰ.ʔĩh.] (B)
n-nak-'į̨h
2SG.O-QUAL:Ø.IPV:1SG.S:H-see:IPV
'I see you SG' UTOLAF10Jul0202:139

b. *nts'į̨į̨ni'* [n.ts'ĩː.niʔ.] (N)
n-ts'į̨į̨-ni'
2SG.P-1PL.S:AA.PFV:Ø-say:PFV
'we said to you SG' UTOLVDN07Aug2205:080

When the second-person singular object prefix follows a vowel, it is resyllabified as the coda consonant of the preceding syllable (799b).

There are no other phonological processes affecting the second-person singular object prefix.

31.2.1.3. First-person plural direct object *nee-* The first-person plural object prefix has the form *nee-*.

31.2.1.3.1. Functions The first-person plural object prefix references a group including the speaker. This group may include the individual producing the actual utterance (801a) or a group including an individual producing an utterance within a story, as in (801b), where the speaker talks about what happened to her and her older sister.

(801) a. *shta' neenehshyą̨ą̨* (N)

sh-ta' *nee-neh-shyą̨ą̨*
1SG.PSR-father 1PL.O-3SG.S:QUAL:Ø.IPV:H-raise:IPV
'my father raised us' UTCBAF13Nov1203:029

b. *Ahdeg' ch'itay daneenįįdlay...* (T)

ah-degn' *ch'itay*
NTRL-up:ALL old.man
da-nee-nįį-dlay
inside-1PL.O-3SG.S:N.PFV:Ø-handle.PL.O:PFV:NOM
'Up there an old man took us inside...'
UTOLVDN14Nov2301:301

The first-person plural object prefix may also reference a group that the speaker identifies with but is not actually included in. *Nee-* in (802), taken from a traditional story, clearly does not include the speaker—who is still alive—but references all the people in her village who were killed by another tribe. (The subject prefix *ts'-* has impersonal meaning in this example.)

(802) *All neets'įįxą̨ą̨...* (T)

all *nee-ts'įį-xą̨ą̨*
all 1PL.O-IMPSL.S:AA.PFV:Ø-kill.PL.O:PFV
'Someone killed all of us...' UTOLAF13May2403:091

31.2.1.3.2. Syntax This prefix does not co-occur with coreferential noun phrases or pronouns.

31.2.1.3.3. Phonology A glottal stop is inserted between the first-person plural object prefix and a following vowel (803). No other phonological processes affect this prefix.

(803) *k'at'eey hǫǫ' nee'ehnay* (N)
k'at'eey hǫǫ' nee-eh-nay
NEG thus 1PL.O-3SG.S:Ø.IPV:H-say:IPV:NEG
'he didn't tell us' UTOLAF12Jul1203:121

31.2.1.4. Second-person plural direct object *nuh-* The second-person plural object prefix has the form *nuh-*.

31.2.1.4.1. Functions The second-person plural object prefix references a group of people including the addressee. This may be the addressee of the actual utterance (804a) or the addressee of an utterance within a narrative (804b).

(804) a. *Ay ch'ale nuhxon nuhhogndag.* (T)
ay ch'ale nuhxon nuh-hogn-dag
3SG FOC 2PL 2PL.O-QUAL:OPT:1SG.S:H-tell:OPT:NOM
'This is what I want to tell you PL.' UTCBAF13Nov0501:006

b. *k'a nuhhihtaaxą̨* (T)
k'a nuh-h-taa-xą̨
NEG 2PL.O-3PL.S-INC:AA.IPV:Ø-kill.PL.O:FUT:NEG
'they will not kill you PL' UTOLVDN07Oct2602:012

There are no other functions of this prefix.

31.2.1.4.2. Syntax This prefix does not co-occur with coreferential noun phrases or pronouns.

31.2.1.4.3. Phonology No changes take place when *nuh-* precedes a prefix beginning with a consonant (804). When it precedes a prefix beginning with a vowel, such as the *u-* qualifier, a glottal stop is inserted (805).

(805) *nuh'uudehkat* (T)
nuh-uu-deh-kat
2PL.O-3SG.S:CON-QUAL:Ø.IPV:H-ask:IPV
's/he asked you' UT Notebook #4, 9

Presumably the glottal stop in (804b) is inserted to avoid resyllabification of the coda consonant /h/ as the onset of the following syllable. There are no other phonological processes affecting this prefix.

31.2.2. Third-person direct object prefixes

The choice of third-person object prefix depends on several factors including subject person, subject identity, and syntactic factors such as the presence and position of coreferential noun phrases. In the following sections form and functions of the direct object prefixes are described briefly. The syntax of (postpositional and direct) object prefixes is explored in greater detail in volume 2.

31.2.2.1. Unmarked third-person (singular) object With first- and second-person subjects, third person objects are usually unmarked.

31.2.2.2. Third-person plural direct object *hu-* The third-person plural object prefix *hu-* refers to human plural subjects.

31.2.2.2.1. Functions The direct object prefix *hu-* is used when the subject is first or second person (806).

(806) a. *hutsaaxą̨ą̨* (T)
hu-tsaa-xą̨ą̨
3PL.O-1PL.S:INC:AA.IPV:ø-kill.PL.O:FUT
'we will kill them all' UTCBAF14Jul1001:010

b. *nihu'ahłeek* (N)
ni-hu-ah-łeek
TERM-3PL.O-ø.IPV:2PL.S:ø-handle.PL.O:IPV:CUST
'give PL them a place to sit' (lit. 'put them there')
UTOLAF10Jul0901:038

Hu- is also occasionally used with third-person subjects when the plurality of the object reference is important, e.g., when the direct object has a human referent. This is done even when plurality of the object referent is indicated by the choice of verb stem (807).

(807) *hu'įįxą̨ą̨* (T)
hu-įį-xą̨ą̨
3PL.O-3SG.S:AA.PFV:ø-kill.PL.O:PFV
'he killed them' UTCBAF14Jul1001:002

31.2.2.2.2. Syntax The third-person plural direct object marker usually does not co-occur with free noun phrases.

31.2.2.2.3. Phonology When *hu-* is followed by a vowel-initial prefix, a glottal stop is inserted between the vowels. No changes take place when the third-person plural object prefix precedes a consonant-initial prefix.

(808) a. *"Tsin'įį," hu'ehnih.* (T)
tsin'įį *hu-eh-nih*
thank.you 3PL.O-3SG.S:Ø.IPV:H-say:IPV
'"Thank you," she said to them.' UTCBAF13Nov0501:288

b. *dahdzał k'it dahuts'ehłeeg* (T)
dahdzał k'it da-hu-ts'eh-łeeg
fish.rack on up-3PL.O-1PL.S:Ø.IPV:H-handle.PL.O:IPV:CUST:NOM
'we, putting [fish] up on the fish rack' UTOLAF09Jun2901:011

31.2.2.3. Disjunct hird-person (singular) *i/y-* The portmanteau *i/y-* is used when a (singular) third-person subject acts on a (singular) third-person direct object. Since third-person singular subjects are not marked overtly (see 31.1.1), I treat *i/y-* as a portmanteau morpheme expressing both third-person singular object and third-person singular object.

31.2.2.3.1. Functions The prefix *i/y-* expresses disjunct third-person (singular) reference—i.e., it is used when both subject and object are third-person (singular) but not coreferential (809a, b). The word "singular" is in parentheses here because *i-* may also be used for plural referents if plurality either is not important (e.g., for nonhuman referents such as the birds in [809c]) or is expressed elsewhere, e.g., in a coreferential noun phrase or in the verb stem. See volume 2 for more detail.

(809) a. *John ineh'įh* (N)
John i-neh-'įh
John 3SG.S>3SG.O-QUAL:Ø.IPV:H-see:IPV
'John looked at her' UTOLAF12Jul1201:056

b. *yeldeeł* (N)
y-el-deeł
3SG.S>3SG.O-Ø.IPV:L-eat:IPV
'she ate it' UTOLAF15May0501:041

c. *niiyilshyah* (T)
ni-na-y-il-shyah
TERM-IT-3SG.S>3PL.O-N.PFV:L-handle.PL.O:PFV
'he brought them [birds] back' UTOLAF09Jun2202:028

31.2.2.3.2. Syntax The portmanteau prefix *i-* does not usually co-occur with coreferential direct object noun phrases. See volume 2 for more information.

31.2.2.3.3. Phonology The distribution of *i-* and *y-* is phonologically conditioned: in the absence of any disjunct prefixes, *y-* is used before a vowel, *i-* before a consonant. This is demonstrated in (809a, b) above.

Following a disjunct prefix of the form CV, only the allomorph *y-* is used regardless of whether the following sound is a vowel or a consonant.

(810) a. *Huugn tah gǫǫ tayeldeeɬ.* (T)
huugn tah gǫǫ ta-y-el-deeɬ
and among worms CMPL-3SG.S>3SG.O-Ø.IPV:L-eat:IPV
'And there the worms ate her up.' UTOLVDN13May2907:136

b. *naytet-ɬuuk* (N)
na-y-tet-ɬuuk
PRMB-3SG.S>3SG.O-INC:Ø.IPV:D-drag:IPV:CUST
'he dragged it around' UTOLVDN13May2801:093

There are no cases where *i-* follows a disjunct prefix of the form CVC.

31.2.2.4. Disjunct third-person plural *hii/hiiy-* The prefix *hii/hiiy-* is the plural counterpart of *i/y-*. It is composed of the third-person plural subject prefix *h-* and the third-person singular object prefix *i/y-* (see Cook [1996] for a comparative study of this portmanteau morpheme).

31.2.2.4.1. Function Like its counterpart *i/y-*, *hii/hiiy-* has disjunct third-person reference—i.e., it is used when the third-person subject is not coreferential with the third-person object. While it may only be used with plural subjects, the object referent is unspecified for number. (811a) is an example with a third-person singular object. The object in (811b) is clearly plural as indicated by the verb stem *shyeek* 'classify plural object', yet because the referent is inanimate, the (human) third-person plural prefix *hu-* discussed in 31.2.2.2 is not used.

(811) a. *hiidehtsiih* (T)
hii-deh-tsiih
3PL.S>3SG.O-QUAL:Ø.IPV:H-cuss:IPV
'they cussed at him' UTOLAF09Jun2202:059

b. *niihiiyelshyeek* (T)
ni-na-hiiy-el-shyeek
TERM-IT-3PL.S>3SG.O-Ø.IPV:L-classify.PL.O:IPV:CUST
'they brought [the food] back' UTOLAF07Nov2602:026

31.2.2.4.2. Syntax The portmanteau prefix *hii/hiiy-* does not usually co-occur with free direct object noun phrases. See volume 2 for more information.

31.2.2.4.3. Phonology The vowel of this prefix is always long. The allomorph *hii-* is used before a consonant and *hiiy-* before a vowel (812).

(812) a. *hahiidel'įh*
ha-hiiy-del-'įh
spot-3PL.S>3SG.O-QUAL:Ø.IPV:L-see:IPV
'the children spotted him' UTCBAF14Jul1804:004

b. *hiiyįhmbiah* (T)
hiiy-įh-mbiah
3PL.S>3PL.O-AA.PFV:H-boil:PFV
'they boiled them [eggs]' UTOLVDN07Aug2205:061

There are no further phonological processes affecting this morpheme.

31.2.3. Coreferential subject and direct object

There are three prefixes indicating coreferentiality between subject and direct object: *id-* 'SG.REFL.O'-, *ihd-* 'PL.REFL.O-, and *niłłi-* 'RECP.O'-.

31.2.3.1. Reflexive singular direct object *id-* The singular reflexive direct object prefix has the form *id-*.

31.2.3.1.1. Functions *Id-* is used when the singular subject and object are coreferential. Subject person has no impact on the shape of the object prefix as shown in (813).

(813) a. *Jah tsayh eh idnintsay…* (N)
jah tsayh eh id-nin-tsay
here ochre with SG.REFL.O-QUAL:Ø.IPV:2SG.S:D-paint:IPV:IMP
'Here, paint yourself with this ochre…'
UTOLAF15May0501:105

b. *na'itnet-tsät* (N)
na-id-net-tsät
IT-SG.REFL.O-3SG.S:Ø.IPV:D-scratch:IPV
'he scratched himself' UTCBAF13Nov0906:013

The singular reflexive prefix triggers a change in voice/valence prefix (see chap. 27.3.2.1.2).

31.2.3.1.2. Syntax This prefix may co-occur with a coreferential free noun phrase (814).

(814) *Na'uudet-sih jah dindeh.* (T)
na-uu-id-et-sih jah dindeh
IT-CON-SG.REFL.O-3SG.S:Ø.IPV:D-call.name:IPV that man
'He identified himself, that man.' UTOLVDN14Nov2301:117

(814) is also interesting because the *uu-* qualifier precedes the object prefix. In the speech of this individual, this is somewhat common; see chap. 30 for more discussion.

31.2.3.1.3. Phonology Glottal stop insertion takes place when the singular reflexive object prefix follows a disjunct prefix of the shape CV (813b) or occurs in word-initial position (815).

(815) [ʔ]*idnintsay* (N)
id-nin-tsay
SG.REFL.O-QUAL:Ø.IPV:2SG.S:D-paint:IPV:IMP
'paint yourself' UTOLAF15May0501:105

Following a vocalic conjunct prefix, the initial vowel of *id-* is deleted (814).

31.2.3.2. Plural reflexive direct object *ihd-* There is also the plural reflexive object prefix *ihd-*.

31.2.3.2.1. Function The plural reflexive prefix is used when the plural subject is referentially identical to the plural direct object. This prefix is very rare; only two examples occur in the whole corpus. Both examples are in the third-person plural, but it is likely that the prefix would also be used in first- and second-person plural contexts.

(816) a. *K'a ihdetk'į̨ą eł.* (T)
k'a ihd-et-k'į̨ą eł
NEG PL.REFL.O-3PL.S:Ø.IPV:D-exercise:IPV and
'They do not exercise themselves.' UTOLVDN11Jul2901:035

b. *Na'uhdet-sih.* (T)
na-u-ihd-et-sih
IT-CON-PL.REFL.O-3PL.S:Ø.IPV:D-name:IPV
'They introduced themselves.' UTOLVDN14Nov2301:198

The plural reflexive prefix also triggers a change in voice/valence prefix (see chap. 27.3.2.1.2).

31.2.3.2.2. Syntax As there are only two examples of this prefix, it is impossible to say whether it may co-occur with coreferential noun phrases.

31.2.3.2.3. Phonology Due to the dearth of examples, the description of the phonological behavior of this prefix is incomplete. In (816b), the initial vowel of the prefix is elided following the conative prefix. This form, however, is unusual in that for most speakers, the conative prefix (a qualifier) *follows* the pronominal prefixes, whereas in the speech of the individual who produced (816b), it consistently precedes them.

31.2.3.3. Reciprocal object The reciprocal direct object prefix has the form *nił-* or *łi-*.

31.2.3.3.1. Function The reciprocal direct object prefix has two functions: it can be used as a true object prefix in situations where the plural subject referents act upon each other, or it can be used as a lexicalized prefix expressing that the plural subject referents act together. In both cases, the reciprocal object prefix triggers a D-effect as described in chap. 27.3.2.1.4.

31.2.3.3.1.1. Productive use Most frequently the reciprocal object *nił/łi-* is used when plural referents perform an action upon each other (817).

(817) a. *niłhutniik* (T)
nił-hut-niik
RECP.O-3PL.S:CON:DH.PFV:D-marry:PFV
'they got married' UTOLVDN14May0703:017

b. *niłudzilkan* (N)
nił-u-dzil-kan
RECP.O-CON-1PL.S:QUAL:Ø.PFV:L-be.maternally.related:IPV
'we are maternally related to each other'
UTOLAF12Jul1203:004

31.2.3.3.1.2. Lexicalized use The reciprocal direct object prefix is part of some intransitive verb themes, where it has the meaning 'together' (818).

(818) a. *staniłtsenetdeeł* (T)
sta-nił-ts-net-deeł
away-together-1PL.S:INC-QUAL:DH.PFV:D-PL.move:PFV:ERR
'we went astray together' UTCBAF13Nov0501:073

b. *hǫǫ't'eey niłts'etdiik* (T)
hǫǫ't'eey nił-ts'et-diik
still together-1PL.S:Ø.IPV:D-do:IPV:CUST
'we still do stuff together' UTCBVDN13Nov1501:090

The themes in (818) are intransitive despite the presence of a direct object prefix; they have not been transitivized using the voice/valence marker. The verb theme sta#t+n+Ø+deeł 'PL go astray' in (818a) requires a Ø- voice/valence prefix. In a transitivized construction with the meaning of 'lead PL.O astray', we would expect an H- voice/valence marker, which would then be changed to L- under the influence of the reciprocal prefix. Instead the reciprocal prefix in (818a) has triggered a voice/valence marker change from Ø- to D-; this theme has thus remained intransitive. A similar argument can be made for (818b).

31.2.3.3.2. Syntax When the subject is third-person plural, the reciprocal object prefix may co-occur with a coreferential noun phrase (819); with first- and second-person plural subject, it may not.

(819) *Kahdu' Jǫǫ eh chįhttheeł eh łihdetxąą.* (N)
k'ahdu' jǫǫ eh chįhttheeł eh
now camprobber and woodpecker and
łi-hdet-xąą
RECP.O-3PL.S:QUAL:DH.PFV:D-fight:PFV
'And now Camprobber and Woodpecker fought each other.'
UTOLVDN11Aug0803:017

31.2.3.3.3. Phonology The reciprocal direct object prefix has two allomorphs: *nił-* and *łi-*.

31.2.3.3.3.1. Allomorph *łi-* As (817b, 819) above illustrate, the reciprocal direct object prefix has the allomorph *łi-*. It appears that the conditions for using this allomorph differ slightly between dialects. In the Northway dialect it only occurs in strongly lexicalized contexts. (817b) is in fact the only example of the allomorph *łi-* in direct object position in the Northway dialect. There are no examples of this allomorph in direct object position in Tyone (1996), the only collection of narratives in the Scottie Creek dialect.

In the Tetlin dialect, the use of *łi-* seems to be more widespread, although it is not nearly as common as *nił-* (820). The speaker commented that there was no meaning difference between the two forms.

(820) *niłts'elgot, łits'elgot* (T)
nił-ts'el-got
RECP.O-1PL.S:Ø.IPV:L-punch:IPV
'we punch each other' UT Notebook #5, 84

31.2.4. Other direct object prefixes

There are two other direct object prefixes: the areal direct object prefix *hu-* and the indefinite direct object prefix *ch'-*.

31.2.4.1. Areal object *hu-* The object prefix *hu-* references areal (i.e., spatial, temporal, or abstract) referents.

When used as a direct object prefix, the areal usually precedes the outer subject prefixes *ts'-* '1PL.S' and *h-* '3PL.S' as shown in (821), but it may also follow the outer subject prefixes (822).

(821) a. *hudzaldįį'* (N)
hu-dzal-dįį'
AR.O-1PL.S:QUAL:AA.PFV:L-learn:PFV
'we learned it' UTOLVDN13May2003:057

b. *Ay tl'aan that tąy hohįįxaan.* (T)
ay tl'aan that tąy ho-hįį-xaan
and.then that highway AR.O-3PL.S:AA.PFV:Ø-make.PL.O:PFV:NOM
'And then they built that highway.' UTCBVDN14Jul1801:145

(822) a. *hiishyah hihuhtsį̨į̨* (N)

hii-shyah *h-huh-tsį̨į̨*
3PL.S>3SG.PSR-house 3PL.S-AR.O:DH.PFV:H-make.SG.O:PFV
'they built her house' UTCBVDN13Nov0804:012

b. … *teegn tą̨y hihų̨ų̨xaan* … (N)

teegn *tą̨y* *h-hų̨ų̨-xaan*
underwater trail 3PL.S-AR.O:AA.PFV:Ø-make.PL.O:PFV:NOM
'… the underwater trails they had built…'
UTOLVDN10Jul2720:032

It is not clear what causes this variation in morpheme order.

31.2.4.1.1. Functions The areal direct object prefix indexes spatial (823a) or abstract (823b) referents. There is no example of the areal direct object referring to a temporal referent, but this may be due to its syntactic position—humans generally do not act upon temporal referents.

(823) a. *dą̨ą̨' ch'a shyah hutah'aal* (N)

dą̨ą̨' *ch'a* *shyah* *hu-tah-'aal*
thus FOC house AR.O-INC:AA.IPV:2PL.S:H-classify.CO:FUT:NOM
'this is the way you PL will build a house'
UTOLVDN11Aug0802:024

b. *Ch'its'ą̨ą̨' tah huneh'į̨h.* (T)

ch'its'ą̨ą̨' *tah* *hu-neh-'į̨h*
different among AR.O-3SG.S:QUAL:Ø.IPV:H-see:IPV
'She noticed something was wrong.' (lit.: 'She saw that things were different.') UTCBAF13Nov0501:085

31.2.4.1.2. Syntax

31.2.4.1.2.1. Co-occurrence with noun phrases (822) and (823) illustrate that the areal direct object prefix can co-occur with coreferential noun phrases.

31.2.4.1.2.2. Introducing complement clauses Certain verbs taking complement clauses require an areal direct object prefix (824). A detailed description of complement clauses can be found in volume 2.

(824) … *łuugn iht'üü nts'ą̈' akgąy hǫǫ' ch'a hudagndįį.* (N)

łuugn *ih-t'üü* *nts'ą̈'* *ak-gąy* *hǫǫ'* *ch'a*
fish AA.IPV:1SG.S:Ø-cut:IPV and Ø.IPV:1SG.S:H-dry:IPV thus FOC
hu-dagn-dįį
AR.O-QUAL:AA.PFV:1SG.S:L-learn:PFV
'… I learned how to cut and dry fish.' UTOLVDN14Apr2602:133

31.2.4.1.3. Phonology

31.2.4.1.3.1. *ho-* versus *hu-* The areal direct object has variably the vowel [o] or [u]. This appears to be free variation.

31.2.4.1.3.2. Coalescence with iterative When the areal direct object prefix follows the iterative prefix *na-* of position 8, the two prefixes often coalesce into *noo-* (825).[3]

(825) a. *shyah shyiit noodihthat* (T)

shyah *shyiit* *na-hu-dih-that*
house inside IT-AR.O-QUAL:AA.PFV:1SG.S:Ø-sweep:PFV
'I swept inside the house' UTOLAF12Jul0601:018

b. *Nahtthan' nts'ą' tąy teeł noonel'įįk.* (T)

nah-tthan' *nts'ą'* *tąy* *teeł*
MED-waterward:ALL to trail wide
na-hu-nel-'įįk
IT-3SG.S:AR.O-QUAL:Ø.IPV:L-look:IPV:CUST
'She keeps looking down at the wide trail.'
UTOLVDN14Nov2301:140

31.2.4.1.3.3. Coalescence with conjugation markers The areal direct object prefix also coalesces with the conjugation-mode-subject-voice/valence marker complex in the absence of intervening prefixes as shown in (822) above.

31.2.4.2. Indefinite direct object *ch'-* The indefinite object prefix has the form *ch'-*.

31.2.4.2.1. Functions The indefinite direct object marker *ch'-* is used in two contexts: when the object referent is unknown or unelaborated, and when the verb theme contains a lexicalized indefinite object prefix.

31.2.4.2.1.1. Unknown or unelaborated referent Transitive verbs in Upper Tanana require that their object position be filled, even when the speaker chooses not to elaborate the object referent. (826) demonstrates this using the verb theme O+Ø+'aaɬ 'eat o'. (826a) comes from a story about eating rotten fish (which then made Stella ill); the identity of the food is known to speaker and hearer. In the first verb form the object is not expressed at all because of the first-person subject; in the second form it is expressed by *i/y-*. In (826b) the identity of the thing to be eaten is not mentioned; the speaker will eat *something* but chooses not to elaborate. This is expressed by the indefinite object prefix *ch'-*.

(826) a. *Shin du' k'a ih'aal, Stella ye'aaɬ.* (T)

shin	*du'*	*k'a*	*ih-aal*	*Stella*
1SG	CT	NEG	NEG.PFV:1SG.S:Ø-eat:PFV:NEG	Stella

y-e-'aaɬ
3SG.S>3SG.O-Ø.IPV:Ø-eat:IPV

'I didn't eat it, Stella ate it.' UTOLVDN10Jul0701:034

b. *Dziin hǫǫɬįį nachih'aaɬ.* (N)

dziin	*hǫǫ-ɬįį*	*na-chih-'aaɬ*
day	AR.S:Ø.PFV:Ø-be:IPV	IT-INDF.O:INC:AA.IPV:1SG.S:Ø-eat:FUT

'I will eat at noon.' UTOLAF13May2804:019

This low elaboration of object referents can have several causes. Frequently the object referent is simply considered irrelevant (826b) or its identity is not known (827a). In (827b) the indefinite prefix is used in accordance to *įįjih* to avoid referring directly to the animal to be killed—a moose—which runs the risk of spoiling the hunter's luck.

(827) a. *ahnoo' doo le'e ch'aaɬuu*

ah-noo'	*doo*	*le'e*	*ch'aa-ɬuu*
NTRL-up.ahead:ALL	who	IGN	INDF.O:3SG.S:AA.IPV:Ø-drag:IPV

'up there someone is dragging something'
UTOLVDN13May2801:162

b. *Ay tl'aan ch'idhįhxįį de'…*

ay	*tl'aan*	*ch'-dhįh-xįį*	*de'*
and	then	INDF.O-QUAL:AA.PFV:2SG.S:H-kill.SG.O:PFV	if

'And if you SG kill something…' UTOLAF08Feb1906:010

31.2.4.2.1.2. Lexicalized use Frequently the indefinite direct object prefix is lexicalized (828).

(828) a. *ch'aldziat* (T)
ch'-al-dziat
INDF-3SG.S:AA.PFV:L-dance:PFV
'he danced' UT Notebook #3, 95

b. *daach'ettl'uh* (T)
da-na-ch'-et-tl'uh
closed-IT-INDF.O-3SG.S:DH.PFV:D-tie:IPV
'he set snares' UTOLAF09Jun2202:026

c. *ch'inal'iił* (T)
ch'-nal-'iił
INDF.O-3PL.S:AA.IPV:L-sneak:IPV:PROG
'they are sneaking' UTCBAF14Jul1805:041

31.2.4.2.2. Syntax The indefinite direct object prefix never occurs with coreferential noun phrases.

31.2.4.2.3. Phonology

31.2.4.2.3.1. Epenthesis When the indefinite direct object prefix precedes a consonant, the epenthetic vowel [ɪ] is inserted (828c).

31.2.4.2.3.2. Qualifier absorption When the indefinite direct object prefix precedes a *d-* or *t-* qualifier, it coalesces with these qualifiers to *j-* (829) and *ch-* (830), respectively. In both examples, a first-person singular form is compared with a third-person plural form, since the qualifiers become visible only when the third-person plural subject prefix *h-* occurs between the indefinite object prefix and the qualifier.

(829) a. *jok-'a'* (N)
ch'-d-ok-'a'
INDF.O-QUAL-OPT:1SG.S:H-sing:OPT
'I should sing' UT Notebook #3, 74

b. *ch'ihduh'a'* (N)
ch'-h-duh-'a'
INDF.O-3PL.S-QUAL:OPT:H-sing:OPT
'they should sing' UT Notebook #3, 74

(830) a. *tth'ak k'iichaktsał* (T)
tth'ak k'ii-ch'-t-ak-tsał
plate wash-INDF.O-INC-AA.IPV:1SG.S:H-wash:FUT
'I have to wash the dishes' UTOLAF12Jul0601:006

b. *tth'ak k'iich'ihtahtsał* (N)
tth'ak k'ii-ch'-h-tah-tsał
plate wash-INDF.O-3PL.S-INC:AA.IPV:H-wash:FUT
'they have to wash the dishes' UT Notebook #6, 28

When the indefinite object is followed by both the inceptive prefix *t-* and the *d*-qualifier, the three prefixes coalesce into *j-* (831).

(831) a. *jak-'ał* (N)
ch'-t-d-ak-'ał
INDF.O-INC-QUAL-AA.IPV:1SG.S:H-sing:FUT
'I will sing' UT Notebook #3, 74

b. *ch'ihdah'ał* (N)
ch'-h-t-dah-'ał
INDF.O-3PL.S-INC-QUAL:AA.IPV:H-sing:FUT
'they will sing' UT Notebook #3, 74

31.2.4.2.3.3. Absorption into *ts'*- When the indefinite direct object prefix precedes the first-person plural subject prefix, the two coalesce into *nts'*- (see 31.1.3.3.3 above).

31.3. Summary

In this chapter the pronominal prefixes of position 6 are described. Two types of prefixes are identified: outer subject prefixes and direct object prefixes.

Most of the outer subject prefixes refer to third-person referents: Ø- 'third-person (singular) subject'-, *h-* 'third-person plural subject', *ch'-* 'indefinite subject', and *hu-* 'areal subject'. There is also the prefix *ts'-*, the main function of which is first-person plural subject reference.

All direct object prefixes of Upper Tanana are marked in position 6. They fall into four major groups: (1) first- and second-person direct object prefixes, (2) third-person direct object prefixes, (3) direct object prefixes expressing coreferentiality of subject and direct object, and (4) other direct object prefixes. Some prefixes in the last two groups can occur either as direct object prefixes or as thematic prefixes; both of these uses are discussed.

Notes

1. The word "singular" is included in parentheses because Ø- does not always have singular reference, as discussed in 31.1.1.1.
2. While Jung (1999) does not offer a reconstruction for this prefix, she does suggest a possible etymology relating it to a noun meaning 'woman'—if that was correct, the *ts'*- prefix then would be cognate to the word *ts'exeh* 'woman'.
3. I treat the areal prefix in (825b) as an object prefix of the verb theme O+n+H+'į̨h 'look at o' rather than as a qualifier in the verb theme hu+n+H+'į̨h 'look around' because of the translation provided by the speaker: the girl looks directly *at* the trail, she does not look around in the vicinity of a trail.

32 | Distributive prefix

In this chapter the morpheme of position 7 of the verb template (see table 24.1) is described. This position class contains only one prefix: the distributive prefix *n-*. In related languages this prefix has a variety of functions. Kari (1990, 285) states that in Ahtna, distributive *n-* is used in dimensional themes to mark plural subjects, and that it is part of the momentaneous-distributive and continuative derivations as well as several other prefix strings. Jetté and Jones (2000, 461) observe that in Koyukon the distributive prefix *ne-* is part of several superaspectual and aspectual prefix strings. Hargus (2007, 423–25) finds that in Witsuwit'en, the distributive prefix /n/- functions as a general pluralizer, although it is somewhat limited in its applicability. Looking beyond languages where the distributive prefix has the form *n-*, Rice (1989, chap. 24, unit 12) observes for the distributive prefix *yá-* in Slave that it serves as a pluralizer but is aspectual in that it affects the conjugation marker of the verb. In Dëne Sųłiné, the distributive prefix *dá-* serves to distinguish dual (without *dá-*) from plural forms (with *dá-*) (Cook 2004, 119). While one can argue whether *n-, yá-*, and *dá-* are actually the same prefix, it appears that in most of the languages the distributive quantifies over entities (Rice 2000, 59).

In Upper Tanana the distributive prefix *n-* has lost these functions; it is instead used to signal instances of haplology involving the first-person plural subject marker (32.3). Its derivational and lexicalized functions have shifted to other parts of the verb; some are expressed by the iterative prefix *na-* of position 9, while others are expressed only in the verb stem.

32.1. Position

Identifying a position for a morpheme with such a limited distribution is not unproblematic. (832) shows that it follows the incorporated roots in position 8 and precedes the pronominal prefixes of position 6.

(832) *staxandzelshyeek* (N)
sta-xa-n-dzel-shyeek
away-weapon-DSTR-INDF.O:1PL.S:INC:QUAL:Ø.IPV-handle:PL.O:IPV:CUST
'we customarily go out carrying weapons'
UTOLAF17Aug0801:047

32.2. Phonology

When the distributive prefix occurs in word-initial position (833a) or after a prefix CVː (833b), it forms a syllable by itself. When it follows a morpheme of the form CV, it moves into the coda of that syllable (833c).

(833) a. *Ndzeldįį dänh...* [n.tsel.dĩː.] (N)
n-dzel-dįį *dänh*
DSTR-INDF.O:1PL.S:QUAL:Ø.IPV:L-learn:IPV at
'At the school...' (lit. 'at the place where we learn something')
UTCBVDN13Nov0805:003

b. *huk'iintsehtsiił* [hu.k'iː.n.tsʰeh.tsʰiːɬ.] (N)
hu-k'ii-n-tseh-tsiił
3PL.P-wash-DSTR-INDF.O:1PL.S:INC:DH.PFV:H-wash:PFV:CUST
'we used to wash them' UTOLVDN07Aug2004:0212

c. *nants'uu'aał* [nan.ts'uː.ʔaːɬ.] (N)
na-n-ts'uu-'aał
IT-DSTR-INDF.O:1PL.S:OPT:Ø-eat:OPT
'let's eat' UT Notebook #4, 72

32.3. Function

The distributive morpheme occurs regularly in two morphological contexts.

32.3.1. Indefinite object *ch'*- + first-person plural subject *ts'*-

The distributive prefix is used when the first-person plural subject prefix *ts'*- and the indefinite object prefix *ch'*- co-occur. The two prefixes coalesce into /ts'/- and the *n*- distributive is added to the verb. It does not matter whether the indefinite object prefix is thematic (834a) or inflectional (834b).

(834) a. *nts'eldzüh*
n-ch'-ts'el-dzüh
DSTR-INDF.O-1PL.S:Ø.IPV:L-dance:IPV
'we're dancing' UT Notebook #3, 79

b. *nants'e'aał*
na-n-ch'-ts'e-'aał
IT-DSTR-INDF.O-1PL.S:Ø.IPV:Ø-eat:IPV
'we're eating (something)' UTOLVDN10Jul2724:045

This use of the distributive prefix is consistent with the plurality or multiplicity of events alluded to above and described by Rice (2000) for the language family as a whole, but crucially the distributive morpheme never appears in any other plural forms: not in forms containing a second- or third-person plural subject combined with an indefinite object prefix (835), nor in verb forms containing a first-person plural subject prefix with any other type of object prefix (836).

(835) a. *ch'aldzüh (*nch'aldzüh)* (N)
ch'-al-dzüh
INDF-Ø.IPV:2PL.S:L-dance:IPV
'you PL are dancing' UT Notebook #3, 79

b. *ch'iheldzüh (*nch'iheldzüh)* (N)
ch'-hel-dzüh
INDF-3PL.S:Ø.IPV:L-dance:IPV
'they are dancing' UT Notebook #3, 79

(836) a. *shyi' ts'eht'iah (*nts'eht'iah)* (N)
shyi' ts'eh-t'iah
meat 1PL.S:Ø.IPV:H-fry:IPV
'we are frying meat' UT Notebook #3, 68

b. *dzanh iin huts'ehk'aayh (*nhuts'ehk'aayh)* (T)
dzanh iin hu-ts'eh-k'aayh
muskrat PL 3PL.O-1PL.SØ.IPV:H-filet:IPV
'we fileted the muskrat' UTOLVDN07Nov2803:013

32.3.2. Pejorative *ts'*- and first-person plural subject *ts'*-

The distributive prefix also occurs when the pejorative prefix *ts'*- of position 10 immediately precedes the first-person plural subject prefix. (837) compares a first-person plural form of the negative-descriptive verb theme P+i+ts'#D+niign 'not know P' with a third-person plural form.

(837) a. *Hints'etniign.* (T)
h-i-ts'-n-ts'et-niign
?-PP-PEJ-DSTR-1PL.S:DH.PFV:D-not.know:IPV
'We don't know.' UTOLVDN13May2801:058

b. *hits'ihetniign* (N)
h-i-ts'-het-niign
?-PP-PEJ-3PL.S:DH.PFV:D-not.know:IPV
'they don't know' UTOLAF12Jul1203:028

In the first-person plural subject form in (837a), the haplology of the two prefixes *ts'-* is signaled by the distributive prefix *n-*, just like the coalescence of the first-person plural subject prefix and the indefinite object marker is signaled by *n-*.

To summarize, the distributive prefix in Upper Tanana is morphologically conditioned and appears to be almost entirely bleached of meaning.

32.3.3. Exception

There is one exception to this generalization in my corpus. In the form *nantnett'ah* in (838), the distributive morpheme occurs without the first-person plural subject and indefinite object prefixes.

(838) *Kahjil t'eey hiiyuuniik t'oot'eey huch'a' t'eey nantnett'ah.* (T)

kahjil	*t'eey*	*hiiy-uu-niik*	*t'oot'eey*	*hu-ch'a'*
almost	even	3PL.S>3SG.O-CON:DH.PFV:Ø-grab:PFV	but	3PL.P-from

t'eey	*na-n-tnet-t'ah*
ADVZR	IT-DSTR-3SG.S:INC:QUAL:DH.PFV:D-SG.fly:PFV

'They almost caught one, but it/they fluttered away from them.'
UTCBAF13Nov0501:037

This form suggests that multiple events of single flying—encoded by the verb stem *t'ah* rather than its plural counterpart *deeł*—are going on simultaneously. I have not succeeded in eliciting similar verb forms; I suspect that this may be an archaic verb form in a traditional story that may have been learned by the speaker in a formulaic fashion during his youth.

32.4. Redistribution of distributive functions

The functions of the distributive prefix have been redistributed to other parts of the Upper Tanana verb. In some instances of the distributive superaspectual derivation, the distributive morpheme has been lost, and only the stem variation indicates the superaspect. This has occurred regularly in the verb theme ta#O+Ø+łe' 'distribute PL.O' and sometimes in the verb theme da#ch'+Ø+tl'u' 'set multiple snares'. The conversive-continuative verb theme O+Ø+k'aayh 'filet O' also is predicted to contain the distributive prefix but does not.[1]

In other instances the functions of the *n-* distributive prefix have been shifted to the iterative prefix of position 9; see chap. 34.2.3 for examples. In the remainder of this chapter I comment on the process that appears to have taken place in Upper Tanana compared to other Dene languages.

32.4.1. Iterative and distributive

In the Alaskan languages for which there is information, the distributive prefix is clearly distinct from the iterative prefix, as the comparison in table 32.1 shows.

	Iterative	Distributive	Source
Dena'ina	nu-	n-	Tenenbaum (1978, 172, 160)
Ahtna	na-	n-	Kari (1990, 291, 285)
Koyukon	no-	ne-	Axelrod (1993, 96, 91)

Table 32.1. Iterative and distributive morphemes in Alaskan Dene

The order of these morphemes differs slightly in these three languages and, indeed, across the entire language family (Rice 2000, 41–68). In Dena'ina the iterative precedes the distributive (incorporates occur between them.) In Ahtna the iterative and distributive precede the incorporates, but Kari (1990, 40) points out that the order of iterative and distributive is variable. In Koyukon the iterative precedes the distributive, which in turn precedes the incorporates.

Functionally the distributive and iterative prefixes clearly differ in the more conservative Alaskan Dene languages. In Dena'ina the distributive is part of continuative verb themes and is used to mark plurals (Tenenbaum 1978, 160), while the iterative functions very similarly to what is described in chap. 34.2 for the Upper Tanana cognate. Kari (1990) reports a similar distinction for the Ahtna morphemes, and Axelrod (1993) for Koyukon. Rice (2000, 68) notes for the language family as a whole that the distributive quantifies over entities, while the iterative quantifies over events.

In Upper Tanana this distinction is getting lost. The iterative is used not only in the (non-aspectual) iterative derivation (839a), where it quantifies over events, but also in the superaspectual distributive derivation (839b), where it quantifies over entities. Note that the distinction between the non-aspectual and superaspectual derivation is maintained in the verb stems. In both instances, the morpheme involved is clearly the iterative prefix *na-*, which exhibits iterative absorption (see chap. 34.3.1).

(839) a. *nłįįgn' daanįhtl'uh* (N)
n-łįįgn' *da-na-nįh-tl'uh*
2s.PSR-dog:POSS closed-IT?-N.IPV:2SG.S:H-tie:IPV
'tie up your SG dog again!' UTOLAF15Dec0704:017

b. *Daach'ihtl'u'.* (N)
da-na-ch'ih-tl'u'
closed-DSTR?-INDF.O:Ø.IPV:1SG.S:Ø-tie:IPV:DIST
'I'm setting snares' UTOLAF15Dec0607:007

In some instances the meaning of the *na-* prefix is clearly distributive, but it triggers the D-effect that is typical of the iterative (840); note that this does not happen in (839b). See chap. 27.3.2.2 for a discussion of the D-effect and the iterative.

(840) *Gah gaay xah daats'et tl'ųų.* (T)
gah gaay xah da-na-ts'et-tl'ųų
rabbit small for closed-DSTR?-1PL.S:DH.PFV:D-tie:PFV:DIST
'We set snares for small rabbits.' UTOLVDN10Jul0701:027

In cases where the distributive stem is identical to the momentaneous one (e.g., [840] or [841]), this can lead to ambiguity. (840) could be interpreted to mean 'we again set a snare for a small rabbit', and (841) is ambiguous between an iterative-customary interpretation (841i) and a distributive-customary one (841ii). Indeed, in this latter example the semantic difference is very subtle: an iterative-customary interpretation focuses on the iterativity of the event (putting a large amount of fish into the cache requires repeated motion), while a distributive-customary interpretation highlights the fact that the same event takes place with respect to multiple pieces of fish.

(841) *daahiyelshyeek* (T)
da-na-hii-el-shyeek
i. up-IT-3P>3P-Ø.IPV:L-handle.PL.O:IPV:CUST
ii. up-IT-3P>3P-Ø.IPV:L-handle.PL.O:IPV:DIST:CUST
'they used to put [the fish] into the cache'
UTOLVDN07Nov2803:022

Thus while related languages distinguish clearly between quantification over entities and quantification over events, this distinction seems to be disappearing in Upper Tanana.

32.5. Summary

The distributive prefix in Upper Tanana has lost most of its functionality and occurs only in contexts where the first-person plural subject prefix *ts'*- is preceded either by the indefinite object prefix *ch'*- or by the pejorative prefix *ts'*-. There is one exception to this generalization where the distributive seems to express multiple simultaneous events.

Some of the functions of the distributive morpheme have been taken on by the iterative prefix of position 9.

Notes

1. Other conversive-continuative verb themes have the iterative prefix instead; see chap. 34.2.3.2.

33 Incorporated roots

The prefixes of position 8 of the verb template (see table 24.1) are incorporates, lexical roots that are compounded, or incorporated, into the verb theme. In (842) the root *'eeł* is incorporated into the verb theme ni#Ø+łeeyh 'put PL.O'.

(842) *dzanh xah ni'eełhełeegn* (T)

dzanh *xah* *nı-'eeł-he-łeegn*
muskrat for TERM-trap-3PL.S:Ø.IPV:Ø-handle.PL.O:IPV:CUST:NOM
'they set traps for muskrat' UTOLVDN07Nov2803:004

33.1. Position

The incorporates follow the iterative prefix (843).

(843) a. *shk'eh nagąą'htelshyah* (N)

sh-k'eh *na-gąą'-h-tel-shyah*
1SG.P-after IT-arm-3PL.S-INC:DH.PFV:L-handle.PL.O:PFV
'they ran back after me' UTOLAF09Aug1202:033

b. *dzänh nathu'ahłe'* (N)

dzänh *na-thuu-ah-łe'*
muskrat IT-skin-Ø.IPV:2PL.S:H-handle.SG.O:IPV:DIST
'skin out those muskrat!' UT Notebook #4, 17

The incorporate precedes the distributive prefix; see chap. 32.1.

33.2. Inventory of incorporates

Incorporates can be broadly assigned to one of three categories: (1) roots referring to body parts, (2) roots referring to other types of entities or actions, and (3) roots not related to any other stem. The following inventory is organized according to this categorization. Where available, information about related noun or verb stems is included in the description of each incorporate.

33.2.1. Body parts

Most terms for body parts can be used for human and animal referents equally. In some cases incorporates referring to body parts are used metaphorically. Many incorporated roots in this category are also part of noun stems, which then also contain the inalienable suffix -’. The incorporates referring to body parts are roughly organized from head to toe.

33.2.1.1. *tthi*- ‘head’ The incorporated root *tthi*- ‘head’ also is part of the noun stem *-tthi’* with the same meaning (844).

(844) a. *tthihnatgagn ch’a’* (S)
tthi-hnat-gagn *ch’a’*
head-3PL.S:QUAL:AA.PFV:D-turn.white:IPV:NOM AVERT
‘to prevent them getting grey hair’ (lit. ‘lest their heads turn white’)
Tyone (1996, 18)

b. *datthinįįtthayh* (T)
da-tthi-nįį-tthayh
inside-head-3SG.S:N.PFV:Ø-move.quickly:PFV
‘he peeked inside’ (lit. ‘he quickly moved his head inside’)
UTCBAF13Nov0501:238

33.2.1.2. *xa*- ‘hair’ The incorporate *xa*- ‘hair’ is related to the noun stem *-xa’* ‘hair, fur’. There is only one example of this root (845).

(845) *uk’ehts’üü uxa’ shaa xa’ildeeɬ* (S)
u-k’ehts’üü *u-xa’* *sh-aa* *xa-il-deeɬ*
3SG.PSR-elbow 3SG.PSR-hair 1SG.P-for hair-Ø.IPV:2SG.S:L-eat.PL.O:IPV
‘you SG eat his elbow hair for me’ ANLC4122a:094

33.2.1.3. *nii*- ‘mind’ The incorporate *nii*- ‘mind’ is related to the stems *-iinį’*, *-oonįį’* ‘mind’. In contrast to the noun stems, the nucleus vowel of the incorporated root is not nasal. It occurs in a large number of themes having to do with mental activities (846).

(846) a. *ts’anii’elt’eh* (T)
ts’a-nii-el-t’eh
bad-mind-3SG.S:DH.PFV:L-be:IPV
‘he was angry’ UTOLAF09Jun2202:060

b. *inaniich'akthät* (N)
i-na-nii-ch'ak-thät
PP-IT-mind-INDF.O:Ø.PFV:1SG.S:H-think:IPV
'I thought about it, I prayed about it'
UTOLVDN13May2004:085

33.2.1.4. ***naak-* 'eye'** This incorporate is related to the noun stem *-naagn'* 'eye'. The glottal stop in (847b) is the onset consonant of the following syllable, hence the hyphen.

(847) a. *yenaagnetshyah* (N)
y-naak-net-shyah
3SG.S>3SG.P-eye-QUAL:DH.PFV:D-move.PL.O:PFV
'she stared at him' (lit. 'she moved her eyes at him')
UTOLVDN10Jul2713:028

b. *Ts'exeh naak-'uudį̨shyah.* (T)
ts'exeh naak-uu-dį̨-shyah
woman eye-3SG.S:CON-QUAL:AA.PFV:Ø-move.PL.O:PFV
'The woman was wise.' UTCBAF13Nov0501:007

33.2.1.5. ***dzii-* 'hearing, inner ear'** This incorporated root is related to the noun stem *-dziit* 'hearing, inner ear' (848).

(848) a. *dziihteh'aak* (T)
dzii-h-teh-'aak
hearing-3PL.S-INC:Ø.IPV:H-extend.LO:IPV:CUST
'they listened' (lit. 'they customarily kept their hearing extended as a linear object') UTOLAF10Jul0801:005

b. *ts'iiniin gaay dziidetdah* (T)
ts'iiniin gaay dzii-det-dah
child small hearing-3SG.S:QUAL:DH.PFV:D-SG.sit:IPV
'the child sat listening' UTOLVDN13May2801:130

33.2.1.6. ***da-* 'mouth'** The incorporate *da-* 'mouth' is related to the noun stem *-da'* 'beak'. The noun stem may only be used for the beaks of birds (for humans, the noun stem *-thaat* 'mouth' is used instead), but the incorporate *da-* has no such restrictions. It occasionally references the body part (849a) but is most commonly used in verb themes having to do with verbal actions (849b).

(849) a. *tuu shdanįįgąy* (T)
tuu sh-da-nįį-gąy
water 1SG.P-mouth-3SG.S:N.PFV:ø-be.dry:PFV
'I was dehydrated' (lit. 'the mouth dried me [for lack of] water') UTOLVDN13May2907:128

b. *hu'idatdeemaak* (N)
hu-i-da-tdee-maak
3PL.P-PP-mouth-3SG.S:INC:QUAL:DH.PFV:ø-fight:PFV
'she bawled them out' (lit. 'she began to fight with them using her mouth') UTOLVDN07Aug2205:119

33.2.1.7. *thaa-* 'mouth' This incorporate root is related to the noun stem *-thaat* 'mouth'. There are only two examples of this incorporate; no dialect information is available for (850a).

(850) a. *thaadagnnąyh*
thaa-dagn-nąyh
mouth-QUAL:AA.PFV:1SG.S:L-move.quickly:PFV
'I ate it up' Kari (1997b)

b. *Shaadeh, all tha'agdeeł,...* (T)
sh-aadeh all tha-ag-deeł
1SG.PSR-older.sister all mouth-AA.PFV:1SG.S:L-eat:PL.O:PFV
'My older sister, I ate it all up,...' UTOLVDN14Nov2301:213

33.2.1.8. *thah-* 'voice' This incorporate root may be related to the noun stem *-theek* 'voice, throat'. It occurs only in the following theme (851).

(851) *k'at'eey noodlee k'eh thahdzilxoo* (T)
k'at'eey noodlee k'eh
NEG white.person like
thah-dzil-xoo
voice-1PL.S:QUAL:NEG.PFV:L-make.noise:PFV:NEG
'we did not speak English' (lit. 'we did not make voice noises like white people') UTOLVDN07Nov2802:016

33.2.1.9. *thii(n)-* 'neck' This incorporate is related to the noun stem *-thiin* 'neck'. It is not clear what causes the presence or absence of the stem-final /n/ (852).

(852) a. *ch'inikon thiinalshyah k'eh t'eey eltsįį* (N)

ch'inikon' thiin-al-shyah k'eh t'eey
dentalium neck-3SG.S:AA.PFV:L-classify.PL.O:PFV like ADVZR
el-tsįį
3SG.S:DH.PFV:L-look:IPV
'it looks like he wears dentalium on his neck'
UTCBAF14May2001:011

b. *thiich'ehchüh (T)*

thii-ch'eh-chüh
throat-INDF.O:3SG.S:DH.PFV:H-tie:PFV
'he strangled him' UTOLAF09Jun2202:020

33.2.1.10. *dzii-, dzeeyh-* 'heart' The incorporated root *dzii-, dzeeyh-* is related to the noun *-dzeey* 'heart'. It is not clear whether the different forms of the incorporate reflect different dialects; no dialect information is available for the form in (853a).

(853) a. *nadzeeyhdagnnayh*

na-dzeeyh-dag-nayh
IT-heart-QUAL:AA.PFV:1SG.S:L-move.quickly:PFV
'my heart is beating fast; I am scared' Kari (1997b)

b. *chiidziidetdaak* (T)

chi-na-dzii-det-daak
?-IT-heart-3SG.S:QUAL:Ø.IPV-D:S.move:IPV:CUST
'she was amazed' (lit. 'her heart jumped')
UTOLVDN13May2801:103

33.2.1.11. *thu(u)-* 'skin' The incorporated root *thu(u)-* is probably related to the noun stem *-thüh* 'skin'. It occurs in verb themes to do with skinning animals; these verb themes are always in the distributive superaspect. In the Northway dialect *thuu-* may be used for all types of animals; in the Tetlin dialect it is only used for large animals such as moose. (In themes to do with skinning small animals such as muskrat, the aspectual prefix *nat'uu-* is used instead in Tetlin; see chap. 35. The form in (854a) would be *dzanh nat'uu'ahłe'* in the Tetlin dialect.)

(854) a. *dzänh nathu'ahłe'* (N)

dzänh na-thuu-ah-łe'
muskrat IT-skin-Ø.IPV:2PL.S:H-handle.SG.O:IPV:DIST
'skin PL out those muskrat' UT Notebook #4, 17

b. *diniign nathu'ehtįį* (T)

diniign na-thu-eh-tįį
moose IT-skin-3SG.S:DH.PFV:H-handle.AO:PFV:DIST
'she skinned the moose' UTOLVDN13May2907:046

33.2.1.12. *gaan', gąą'*- 'arm' The incorporate *gaan'*- (S), *gąą'*- (N, T) is related to the noun stem *-gaan'* 'arm'. It is one of the few incorporated roots that contains the inalienable possessive suffix. It only occurs in themes describing several humans running (855).

(855) a. *tthigaan'helshyeek* (S)

tthi-gaan'-hel-shyeek
out-arm-3PL.S:Ø.IPV:L-move.SG.O:IPV:CUST
'they ran out' (lit. 'they moved their arms out') Tyone (1996, 44)

b. *shk'eh nagąą'htelshyah* (N)

sh-k'eh na-gąą'-htel-shyah
1SG.P-after IT-arm-3PL.S:INC:DH.PFV:L-handle.PL.O:PFV
'they ran back after me' UTOLAF09Aug1202:033

33.2.1.13. *ła*- 'hand' The incorporated root *ła*- 'hand' is related to the noun stem *-ła'* 'hand'. In (856b) the incorporate refers to a branch of a tree rather than to a hand.

(856) a. *łahet-'aak hiits'ą'* (T)

ła-het-aak hii-ts'ą'
hand-3PL.S:Ø.IPV:D-extend:LO:IPV:CUST 3PL.S>3SG.O-to
'they waved to her' UTOLVDN13May2801:226

b. *sheełajinelthayh*
sh-i-ła-j-nel-thayh
1sg.p-pp-hand-indf.s:qual-qual:ø.ipv:l-strike:ipv
'a branch struck me' Kari (1997b)

33.2.1.14. *tl'a-* 'buttocks, stern' The incorporate *tl'a-* 'buttocks, stern' is related to the noun stem *-tl'a* 'buttocks'. This morpheme is limited to a few directional aspectual prefix strings having to do with coming ashore (see chap. 35.2.1). This meaning originates with boats coming ashore stern first; semantic shift has since taken place, and the prefix string is now used for movement onto shore involving boats or not. The verb form in (857a) describes a loon swimming out of a lake; the one in (857b) describes landing in a boat. There are no examples of the incorporate outside such prefix strings.

(857) a. *datl'a'eemįį* (T)
datl'a-ee-mįį
onto.shore-3sg.s:dh.pfv:ø-swim:pfv
'he swam up onto the shore' UTOLVDN13May2907:107

b. *Ay tl'aan ketl'aatsikeek.* (N)
uy tl'aan ketl'a-na-tsi-keek
and then ashore-it-1pl.s:inc:ø.ipv:ø-go.by.boat:ipv:cust
'And then we would land...' UTOLVDN07Aug2205:049

33.2.1.15. *nän, nan-* 'back' The incorporated root *nän, nan-* 'back' occurs only in one verb theme (858). It is related to the noun stem *-nänn', -nann'* 'back'.

(858) *haananhųh'ah* (T)
ha-na-nan-hųh-'ah
out-it-back-3sg.s:ar:aa.pfv:h-extend:pfv
'she was hump-backed' (lit. 'she had her back extending up and out')
UTCBAF13Nov0501:225

33.2.1.16. *chi-* 'tail' The incorporated root *chi-* 'tail', related to the noun stem *-che'* 'tail', occurs only once in the data (859).

(859) *shaa skechinįįttheeyh* (S)
sh-aa ske-chi-nįį-ttheeyh
1sg.p-for across-tail-n.ipv:2sg.s:ø-strike.lro:ipv
'put sg your tail across for me' Tyone (1996, 28)

33.2.1.17. *got-* 'knee' The incorporate *got-* 'knee' is related to the noun stem *-got* 'knee'. It is attested in only one verb theme (860).

(860) *niigot-'įį'ah* (T)
ni-na-got-įį-'ah
up-IT-knee-3SG.S:AA.PFV:Ø-extend:PFV
'she was kneeling' UTCBAF13Nov0501:222

33.2.1.18. *ki-, ke-* 'foot' The incorporate *ki̠-, ke-* 'foot' is related to the noun stem *-ke'* 'foot'. It occurs in a variety of verb themes (861).

(861) a. *ut'aki̠tdagnthäł* (N)
u-t'a-ki̠-tdagn-thäł
3SG.P-against-foot-INC:QUAL:AA.IPV:1SG.S:L-move.quickly:FUT
'I will stumble over it' UTOLAF12Jul1201:017

b. *daki̠ch'ihtdalshyaał* (N)
da-ki̠-ch'-h-tdal-shyaał
up-foot-INDF.O-3PL.S-INC:QUAL:AA.IPV:L-bounce:FUT
'they will relax' (lit. 'they will kick their feet up')
UTCBVDN13Nov0805:032

33.2.2. Other stems

The incorporates below are organized alphabetically.

33.2.2.1. *'eeł-* 'trap' The incorporated root *'eeł* also is part of the stem *eeł* 'trap' (862).

(862) a. *dzanh xah ni'eełheteegn* (T)
dzanh xah ni-'eeł-he-teegn
muskrat for TERM-trap-3PL.S:Ø.IPV:Ø-handle.PL.O:IPV:CUST:NOM
'they would set traps for muskrat' UTOLVDN07Nov2803:004

b. *tsuugn eł hugn tah ha'eełhedlak* (T)
tsuugn eł hugn tah
marten and etc. among
ha-'eeł-he-dlak
out-trap-3PL.S:Ø.IPV:Ø-classify.PL.O:IPV:CUST
'they customarily have traps for marten and so on'
UTOLVDN07Nov2804:009

33.2.2.2. *chin-* 'moving as a group' The stem *chin-* (N) is cognate to the Ahtna stem *cehw-* '(moving) as a group' (Kari 1990, 113) and related to the adverb *łechin* (N), *niłchin* (T) 'together, into a group'. The L-voice/valence marker in (863) is caused by the reciprocal postpositional object marker; the primary theme has an H- voice/valence marker. (863) is the only example of this incorporate in my corpus.

(863) *Łahtthegn nts'ą' łechinhįldeeł...* (N)
łahtthegn nts'ą' łechin-hįl-deeł
all as.group-3PL.S:N.PFV:L-PL.move:PFV
'They gathered all of them together...'
UTOLVDN11Aug0805:011

33.2.2.3. *dli-* 'cold' This incorporate is related to the verb stem *dliy* 'be cold' as well as to the adjective *elih* 'it is cold'. The verb form in (864) is a curse uttered by Yamaagn Teeshyah toward Wolverine. It is the only instance of this incorporate in the data.

(864) *dlinoltsįį de'* (T)
dli-nol-tsįį de'
cold-QUAL:OPT:2SG.S:L-become:OPT if
'you shall freeze' UTOLVDN13May2805-030

33.2.2.4. *dlįǫ-* 'snare' This incorporate is related to the verb stem *dliu* 'snare' (865). The shape of the incorporate (with a nasalized vowel) suggests that it might be derived from a noun stem rather than the verb (see also Lovick [2011] or, more briefly, chap. 6.1.9), but such a noun stem is not attested in the contemporary language.

(865) *shyign' nän' k'it ts'ą̈' naadlįǫ'įį'ąą* (S)
shyign' nän' k'it ts'ą̈'
down:ALL ground on to
na-na-dlįǫ-įį-ąą
down-IT-snare-3SG.S:AA.PFV:Ø-classify.CO:PFV
'down below a spider web dangled to the ground' Tyone (1996, 32)

33.2.2.5. *dloh-* 'laugh' The incorporated root *dloh* 'laugh' in (866) is related to the verb stem *dloh* 'laugh'. It is attested only in one verb theme.

(866) *nadlohdelshyah* (N)
na-dloh-tdel-shyah
IT-laugh-3SG.S:INC:QUAL:DH.PFV:L-SG.go:PFV
'he went around laughing' UT Notebook #4, 17

33.2.2.6. *kon'*- 'fire' The incorporated root *kon'*- 'fire' is formally identical to the noun stem *kon'* with the same meaning. It is attested only in the verb theme in (867).

(867) … *jahxan hekon'nįįshyiił.* (T)
jahxan he-kon'-nįį-shyiił
suddenly against-fire-3SG.S:N.PFV:Ø-move.LRO.rapidly:PFV
'… suddenly he set fire to it [using a firebrand].'
UTOLVDN13May2803:081

33.2.2.7. *łįǫ'*-, *łǫǫ*- 'drag' Like *dlįǫ*- 'snare' above, the nasal vowel of the incorporate suggests that it is interpreted as a noun rather than a verb (see Lovick [2011]). The origin of the syllable-final glottal stop in (868a) is not clear; in (868b) it is presumably inserted to avoid hiatus. In the Tetlin dialect this incorporate has the shape *łǫǫ*- (868b). Semantically the form in (868b) is more similar to *dlįǫ*- 'snare' in 33.2.2.4, but the incorporate clearly begins with *ł* rather than *dl*.

(868) a. *ch'aachin' hałįǫ'dalnąyh* (S)
ch'aachin' ha-łįǫ'-dal-nąyh
tree stump out-drag-3SG.S:QUAL:AA.PFV:L-move.quickly:PFV
'he yanked out the tree stump' Tyone (1996, 26)

b. *shyign' tah nałǫǫ'idihnąy…* (T)
shyign' tah
down:ALL among
na-łǫǫ-i-dįh-nąy
down-drag-3SG.S>3SG.O-QUAL:AA.PFV:H-move.quickly:PFV:NOM
'she let her down quickly by the rope…'
UTOLAF08Apr2805:102

33.2.2.8. *kał*- 'patch' This incorporate may be related to the verb stem *kat* 'slap'. It appears to occur only in one verb theme (869).

(869) *yikałjehkąą'* (T)
y-i-kał-jeh-kąą'
3SG.S>3SG.P-PP-patch-INDF.O:DH.PFV:H-sew:PFV
'she patched [her mittens]' UT Notebook #5, 52

33.2.2.9. *neeł-* 'group of people' This incorporate may be related to the noun stem *dineh* 'person, man, human'. There is only one example of this incorporate in the data (870).

(870) *Snag tthän' ts'eeneełhįhdeeł* (S)
Snag tthän' ts'ee-neeł-hįh-deeł
Snag waterward:ALL ?-group-3PL.S:AA.PFV:H-PL.move:PFV
'they moved in a group down below to Snag' Tyone (1996, 9)

33.2.2.10. *sa-, saa* 'sun' This incorporated root is related to the noun stem *saa* 'sun'. It occurs primarily in the themes for the sun's rising and setting (871). The length of the vowel is variable even in the speech of individual speakers.

(871) a. *hasaa'įį'ąą* (T)
ha-saa-įį-ąą
out-sun-3SG.S:AA.PFV:Ø-classify.CO:PFV
'the sun rose' (lit. 'the sun came out as a compact object')
UTCBAF13Nov0501:116

b. *nasa'aa'aal* (T)
na-sa-aa-'aal
down-sun-3SG.S:AA.IPV:Ø-classify.CO:IPV:NOM
'at sundown' (lit. 'the sun going down as a compact object')
UTOLVDN07Oct2604:006

33.2.2.11. *säł-* 'hollering' This incorporate is related to the verb stem *säł* 'holler'. There is only one example of this incorporate in the data (872).

(872) *nasałdelshyah* (T)
na-sał-tdel-shyah
PRMB-holler-3SG.S:INC:QUAL:DH.PFV:L-SG.go:PFV
'he walked around hollering' UT Notebook #4, 28

33.2.2.12. *shya-* 'noise' This incorporated root is probably related to the verb stem *shyak* 'lie'. The Ahtna cognate *ya-* of the incorporate is translated as 'noise, talking, howling' (Kari 1990, 425). In Upper Tanana the incorporate seems to occur only in the theme in (873).

(873) *shyaheh'ąą* (T)
shya-heh-'ąą
noise-3PL.S:Ø.IPV:H-handle.CO:IPV
'they were making noise' (about a group of children playing noisily)
UTOLAF07Oct2512:003

33.2.2.13. *shyah-* 'house' This incorporate is related to the noun stem *shyah* 'house'. It is only attested in Kari's (1997b) stem list (874).

(874) *nishyahhunih'ąą*
ni-shyah-hu-nįh-'ąą
TERM-house-3SG.S>AR.O-N.PFV:H-handle.CO:PFV
'he got married' Kari (1997b)

33.2.2.14. *shyia-* 'knot' This root also is attested only in Kari (1997b), who states that it is related to the noun stem *shyia* 'knot' (875).

(875) *niishyianįį'ąą*
ni-shyia-nįį-'ąą
TERM-knot-3SG.S:N.PFV:Ø-handle.CO:PFV
'he put a knot in it' Kari (1997b)

33.2.2.15. *(ch'u)shyoo-* 'whistle' This incorporate is related to the verb stem *shyoh* 'whistle'. The form in (876a) describes the noise made by flying green-winged teals; the context and dialect of (876b) are unknown. The verb stem *shyoh* is used only to describe the noise made by *Gǫǫ* 'Bush Indians', evil creatures that abduct women and children. For that reason both whistling and using words referring to whistling (other than by birds) are *įįjih*.

(876) a. *hishyoodeh'aak* (T)
hii-shyoo-deh-'aak
3PL.S>3SG.P-whistle-QUAL:Ø.IPV:H-extend.LO:IPV:CUST
'they make that whistling sound' UTOLVDN13May2902:061

b. *nach'uushyoohdelshyah*
na-ch'uushyooh-del-shyah
PRMB-whistle-3SG.S:QUAL:DH.PFV:L-SG.go:PFV
'he went around whistling' Kari (1997b)

33.2.2.16. *ta-* 'water' The incorporated root in (877) is related to the noun stem *tuu* 'water' and the adverbial-derivational prefix *ta-* 'into the water' (see chap. 35.2.1.16).

(877) *Tth'itu' niign da' tayahteeł.* (N)
tth'itu' niign *da'*
river downriver:ALL
ta-y-ah-teeł
water-3SG.S>3SG.O-AA.IPV:H-handle.AO:IPV:PROG
'The river is carrying her downriver.' UTOLAF12Jul1201:039

33.2.2.17. *tät-* 'cane' This incorporated root is related to the noun stem *tät* 'cane'. It is attested only once (878).

(878) *łehnaan' tät eh natätjettiin* (S)
łehnaan' *tät* *eh*
both.sides cane with
na-tät-jet-tiin
PRMB-cane-3SG.S>INDF.O:INC:QUAL:Ø.IPV:D-handle.AO:PFV:NOM
'she, going around by using a cane on both sides' Tyone (1996, 8)

33.2.2.18. *tl'uuł-* 'rope' This incorporate is related to the noun stem *tl'uuł* 'rope'. Only one example occurs in the data (879).

(879) *natl'uułch'ihtidaagn* (S)
na-tl'uuł-ch'-h-ti-daagn
down-rope-INDF.O-3PL.S-INC:Ø.IPV-D:SG.go:IPV:CUST:NOM
'they, moving down using the rope' Tyone (1996, 32)

33.2.2.19. *tsaa-* 'cache' The incorporated root is related to the noun stem *tsaa* 'cache'. Again, there is only one example in the data (880).

(880) *łahtthign' ditsaa hatsaahiłeeyh* (S)
łahtthign' di-tsaa ha-tsaa-hi-łeeyh
all REFL.PSR-cache out-cache-3PL.S:Ø.IPV:Ø-handle.PL.O:IPV
'they opened all their caches' Tyone (1996, 63)

33.2.2.20. *tsüh-, tsaa-* 'cry' The form *tsaa-* 'cry' is from the Tetlin dialect; it is *tsüh-* in all other dialects. *Tsüh-, tsaa-* are both related to the stem 'cry', which has the form *tsah* in Tetlin, *tsüh* in the other dialects (881).

(881) a. *taatsaadeldah* (T)
ta-na-tsaa-del-dah
upland?-IT-cry-3SG.S:QUAL:DH.PFV:L-SG.sit:IPV
'he sat there crying' Titus David (2006, 1)

b. *natsühdelshyah* (N)
na-tsüh-tdel-shyah
PRMB-cry-3SG.S:INC:QUAL:DH.PFV:L-SG.go:PFV
'he went around crying' UT Notebook #4, 17

33.2.2.21. *tsüü-* 'whip' The incorporate *tsüü* is related to the verb stem *tsüh* 'whip' (882). There is no explanation for the long vowel.

(882) *niitsüü'iniixał* (T)
ni-na-tsüü-i-nįį-xał
TERM-IT-whip-3SG.S>3SG.O-N.PFV:Ø-club:PFV
'he whipped him' Titus David (2006, 1)

33.2.2.22. *tsiił-* 'snow' The incorporate *tsiił* 'snow' is related to the noun stem *tsiił* 'snow on the ground'. The noun and verb stem for falling snow in Upper Tanana is *shyüh*. Note that the incorporate refers to falling snow in (883); it has thus undergone semantic shift.

(883) *hu'eh naatsiił'įįshyah* (S)
hu-'eh na-na-tsiił-įį-shyah
3PL.P-with down-IT-snow-3SG.S:AA.PFV:Ø-SG.go:PFV
'it snowed heavily on them' Tyone (1996, 63)

33.2.2.23. *tthee-* 'bark' This root is related to the verb stem *ttheh* 'bark' (of a dog). It is only attested in the verb theme in (884).

(884) *ttheehihdelxoh* (S)
tthee-h-del-xoh
bark-3PL.S-QUAL:Ø.IPV:L-make.noise:IPV
'they were barking' Tyone (1996, 24)

33.2.2.24. *tthii-* 'rock' The incorporated root *tthii-* is related to the noun stem *tthee* 'rock'. It can refer to actual rocks (885a) but also occurs in some themes of throwing (885b).

(885) a. *tthee eh mbitthiididhaknayh* (N)
tthee *eh*
rock with
mb-i-tthii-d-dhak-nayh
3SG.P-PP-rock-QUAL-DH.PFV:1SG.S:H-move.CO.quickly:PFV
'I threw a rock at him' UTOLAF13May2801:005

b. *hit'aatthiihiiyetthak* (T)
hi-t'a-a-tthii-hiiy-e-tthak
3SG.P-against-IT-rock-3PL.S>3SG.O-Ø.IPV:Ø-move.quickly:IPV:CUST
'they tossed [the baby crane] high into the air'
UTOLAF07Oct2512:006

33.2.2.25. *xał-* 'sled' The incorporated root *xał-* is related to the free stem *xał* 'sled' (886). It occurs in verb themes describing travel by sled (886).

(886) a. *tiixałnįįtąą* (T)
ti-xał-nįį-tąą
out-sled-3SG.S:N.PFV:Ø-handle.LRO:PFV
'he came out into the open with a sled'
UTCBVDN14Jul1801:018

b. *jah duugn naxałtihtįįk* (T)
jah duugn *na-xał-tih-tįįk*
hereabouts PRMB-sled-INC:Ø.IPV:1SG.S:Ø-handle.LRO:IPV:CUST
'I drive around with a sled' UTCBVDN14Jul1801:024

33.2.2.26. *xał-* 'club' This root is related to the free stem *xał* 'club', which can be used as a noun stem or a verb stem. It occurs only in this verb theme (887).

(887) *bexałdįįłeey* (N)
be-xał-dįį-łeey
3SG.P-club-QUAL:Ø.IPV:2SG.S:Ø-handle.PL.O:IPV:IMP
'throw sticks at it' UT Notebook #4, 15

33.2.2.27. ***xeeł-*** **'darkness'** This incorporate is related to the noun *xeeł* 'darkness'. It seems to occur only in the theme 'to get dark'. No dialect information is available for the form in (888).

(888) *nee'eh naxeełdeltthayh*
nee-'eh *na-xeeł-del-tthayh*
1PL.P-with IT-darkness-3SG.S:QUAL:DH.PFV:L-move.quickly:PFV
'it got dark on us' Kari (1997b)

33.2.2.28. ***xeeł-*** **'pack'** This incorporated root is related to the stem *xeeł* 'pack' (889).

(889) a. *tsaak'eet mba' gąyh naaxeełheldik* (S)
tsaak'eet *mba'* *gąyh*
fish.cache dry.fish dry
na-na-xeeł-hel-dek
down-IT-pack-3PL.S:Ø.IPV:L-PL.move:IPV:CUST
'they packed the dry fish to the caches' Tyone (1996, 62)

b. *unia' huxeel' naxeełhiyaldäl* (S)
unia' *hu-xeel'*
into.fire 3PL.PSR-pack:POSS
na-xeeł-hiy-al-däl
IT-pack-3PL.S>3SG.O-AA.IPV:L-PL.move:IPV:NOM
'he threw them and their packs into the fire' Tyone (1996, 73)

33.2.3. Incorporates with no corresponding free stem

The following incorporates have no corresponding free forms. They are listed as incorporates because they are either identified as such in related languages (e.g., by Kari [1990] in Ahtna or Jetté and Jones [2000] in Koyukon) or because they occur after the iterative prefix.

33.2.3.1. ***chi-*** **'pretend'** This incorporate only occurs as part of the prefix string chi#ch'+d+L 'pretend'. The indefinite prefix *ch'-* is thematic and occurs in transitive (890b) as well as intransitive (890a) themes.

(890) a. *chijeltįį*
chi-jel-tįį
pretend-INDF:3SG.S:QUAL:Ø.IPV:L-SG.sleep:IPV
'she pretended to sleep, she pretended to be dead'
UTCBAF13Nov0501:092, UTOLVDN13May2805:013

b. *chijel'aał* (N)
chi-jel-'aał
pretend-INDF:3SG.S:QUAL:Ø.IPV:L-eat:IPV
'he's pretending to eat' UT Notebook #4, 23

The form *chijeltįį* in (890a) is ambiguous between 's/he pretended to be sleeping' (derived from the theme Ø+tįį 'SG sleep') and 's/he pretended to be dead' (derived from the theme H+tįį 'SG be dead'). The difference between the two themes is erased in the derived form, where both Ø- and H- voice/valence marker are changed to L-.

33.2.3.2. *ch'edzi-* 'quadruped' According to Kari (1990, 175), the Ahtna cognate *c'edzi-* of this incorporate stem observes that it only occurs in two themes in that language. Upper Tanana *ch'edzi-* seems to be similarly restricted and occurs only in the verb theme in (891).

(891) *stach'edzinįįdlah* (T)
sta-ch'edzi-nįį-dlah
away-quadruped-3SG.S:N.PFV:Ø-classify.PL.O:PFV
'[the caribou] ran away' UTOLAF09Jun2202:057

33.2.3.3. *ła-* 'sagging, deteriotating' The incorporate *ła-* may be related to the verb stem *tleek* 'be rotten, mushy'. It is attested only once in the data (892).

(892) *That nałateetleegn eh...* (N)
that na-ła-tee-tleegn eh
that IT-sagging-3SG.S:INC:DH.PFV:Ø-be.rotten:IPV:NOM because
'Because that [house] was falling apart...'
UTCBVDN13Nov0804:036

33.2.3.4. *mbäł-, mbał-* 'sleep' A free stem cognate to *mbäł-, mbał-* 'sleep' is attested in several other languages, but not in Upper Tanana. The verb themes in (893) are very similar; the different translations may be due to the presence of the prefix *t'a-* 'under'- in (893a).

(893) a. *t'aambałyįhtįį* (T)

t'a-na-mbał-y-įh-tįį

under-IT-sleep-3PL.S>3SG.O-AA.PFV:H-handle.AO:PFV

'she fell asleep instantly' UTOLVDN14Nov2301:226

b. *hambäłntahteegn* (N)

ha-mbäł-n-tah-teegn

out-sleep-2SG.O-3SG.S:INC:AA.IPV:H-handle.AO:FUT:CUST:NOM

'you SG might fall asleep' UTOLAF18Jun0803:018

33.2.3.5. *ta-* 'skin' Kari (1990, 324) lists the Ahtna cognate of this root as *ta-* and notes that it might be related to *taan* 'inner skin membrane' and the Eyak word *tah* 'skin'. Jetté and Jones (2000, 518) lists the Koyukon form *to-* as 'inner skin'; the incorporate *to-* in that language is glossed as 'act with, treat skin, hide'. In Upper Tanana there is no cognate free stem, but the incorporated stem occurs in several themes describing the processing of a skin (894).

(894) a. *Huthüh du' tahiidehthoh…* (T)

hu-thüh du' ta-hii-deh-thoh

3SG.PSR-skin CT skin-3PL.S>3SG.O-QUAL:Ø.IPV:H-scrape:IPV:CUST

'They scrape their skins…' UTOLVDN07Nov2804:007

b. *tatnat-thoh* (N)

ta-tnat-thoh

skin-3SG.O:INC:QUAL:AA.IPV:D-tan:PASS:FUT

'[the skin] will be tanned' UTOLVDN07Aug2001:011

33.2.3.6. *thaa-* 'fighting' The incorporate *thaa-* 'fighting' occurs only in a few verb themes; all forms involving this incorporate were produced by the same speaker (895). It is likely cognate with Ahtna *sghae-* 'fighting' (Kari 1990, 213), which derives from the verb stem *ghae* 'kill SG O'. The verb stem has the form *xeh* in Upper Tanana. The initial consonant of the incorporate has been fronted to /θ/ <*th*> in the Great Northern Series Shift (see chap. 8.1.1.1.2). Since *th*-initial consonant clusters are not possible in Upper Tanana, the velar fricative was deleted, although it leaves a trace in the vowel quality of the incorporate.

(895) a. *Ts'exeey <chih> nithaahįhdeek.* (T)
ts'exeey chih ni-thaa-hįh-deek
women also up-fighting-3PL.S:AA.PFV:H-PL.experience:PFV
'The women also rose up fighting.'
UTOLVDN13May2801:164

b. *yathaa'ehthak* (T)
ya-thaa-eh-thak
CONT-fighting-3SG.S:Ø.IPV:H-SG.experience:IPV
'[the grizzly] was really fighting' UTOLVDN13May2909:113

33.2.3.7. *thi-, shi-* 'in fright' The incorporated stem *thi-, shi-* is probably cognate to the Ahtna prefix *si-* 'in fear' (Kari 1990, 463). The different onset consonants appear to be due to different dialects, although this is not usually a differentiating feature (see chap. 3). The verb theme in (896b) appears to be transitivized.

(896) a. *Ishyiit ch'a neetsay shits'ishnihshyah.* (T)
ishyiit ch'a nee-tsay
then FOC 1PL.PSR-grandfather
shi-ts'-sh-nih-shyah
fright-PEJ-1SG.O-3SG.S:N.PFV:H-SG.go:PFV
'This is how a bear really frightened me.' (lit. 'This is how our grandfather came to me in a frightening and bad way.')
UTOLAF09Jun2201:021

b. *stathindakshyay* (N)
sta-thi-nak-shyay
away-fright-N.PFV:1SG.S:H-SG.go:PFV:NOM
'I'm running away (from him) in a frightened way'
UTOLVDN14Nov2301:302

33.2.3.8. *xa-* 'weapon' Kari (1990, 209) lists Ahtna *xa-* as an incorporate meaning 'to act with a weapon (bow, gun)'. In Upper Tanana it usually occurs in a motion theme containing a classificatory verb stem referring to handling one or multiple long rigid objects such as (traditionally) bows or spears or (nowadays) guns; the resulting themes then have the meaning '(SG or PL) move carrying weapons, go hunting' (897).

(897) a. *naxajushtii* (T)
na-xa-jush-tii
PRMB-weapon-INDF.O:QUAL:OPT:1SG.S:D-handle.LRO:OPT
'I want to go hunting' (lit. 'I want to carry around a long weapon')
UTOLVDN13May2801:112

b. *staaxach'ihdelshyeek* (N)
sta-na-xa-ch'-h-del-shyeek
away-IT-weapon-INDF.O-3PL.S-QUAL:DH.PFV:L-handle.PL.O:PFV
'they went away hunting' (lit. 'they carried weapons away')
UTOLVDN13May2003:033

33.2.3.9. *xeeł*- 'cramped, crippled' The Koyukon cognate of this root *ghaał*- 'bundled, wrapped object, crippled, hobbled' is distinct from the cognate of the incorporate discussed in 33.2.2.28, *haał* 'pack' (Jetté and Jones 2000, 213). Because of the loss of voiced fricatives, this distinction is not maintained in Upper Tanana; there is also no corresponding free stem (898).

(898) a. *huuxol' nixeełdelthąy* (S)
hu-xol'
3PL.PSR-leg
ni-xeeł-del-thąy
TERM-crippled-3PL.S:QUAL:Ø.IPV:L-move.quickly:IPV:NOM
'they, getting leg cramps' Tyone (1996, 18)

b. *nixeełdelnayh* (N)
ni-xeeł-del-nayh
TERM-cramp-3SG.S:QUAL:DH.PFV:L-S.experience:PFV
'he's got a seizure' UT Notebook #1, 16

33.3. Incorporated roots, not stems

In many accounts of related languages, the incorporates are called "stems" rather than "roots", e.g., in Rice (1989) on Slave, Axelrod (1990) on Koyukon, Tuttle (2003) on Lower Tanana, Cook (2004) on Dëne Sųłiné, Cook (2013) on Tsilhqút'ín. I follow Hargus (2007) on Witsuwit'en in calling these items "roots." Evidence for this stance comes from two sources: incorporated body parts and roots that are not specified for category.

Body part terms are inalienably possessed. Unincorporated noun stems referring to body parts usually contain the inalienable possessive suffix -'; e.g.,

-tthi' 'head', *-naagn'* 'eye', *-che'* 'tail', or *-ke'* 'foot'. This suffix can be viewed as a stem formative (see chap. 13.2.1.3). The incorporated forms of these and other body parts lack this suffix: *tthi-*, *naak-*, *chi-*, and *ke-* etc (see 33.2.1 for more examples). The only exception to this is the incorporate *gaan'-/gąą'-* 'arm', which does contain the inalienable possessive suffix. Thus, most body part incorporates are morphologically roots.

The second piece of evidence comes from related stems. Some incorporates are clearly related to verb stems; others are clearly related to noun stems. (899) illustrates an incorporate referring to an action where a related verb stem exists, but no related noun stem.

(899) a. *Łįį ettheh.* (N)

łįį e-ttheh
dog 3SG.S:Ø.IPV:Ø-bark:IPV
'The dog is barking.' UTOLAF15Dec0607:008

b. *ay łįį elk'aagn gąy iin t'eey ttheehihdelxoh* (S)

ay łįį el-k'aagn gąy iin t'eey
and dog 3SG.O:DH.PFV:L-split:PFV dry PL ADVZR
tthee-h-del-xoh
bark-3PL.S-QUAL:Ø.IPV:L-make.noise:IPV
'and those dried split dog carcasses were barking' Tyone (1996, 24)

Similarly (900) contrasts the incorporate referring to an entity with a related noun stem referring to the same entity. In this case there is no related verb stem.

(900) a. … *saa chih t'a'įį'ąh.* (T)

saa chih t'a-įį-'ąh
sun also under-3SG.S:AA.PFV:Ø-classify.CO:PFV
'… the sun also went under.' UTOLVDN07Nov2802:007

b. *hasaa'įį'ąą* (T)

ha-saa-įį-ąą
out-sun-3SG.S:AA.PFV:Ø-classify.CO:PFV
'the sun rose' (lit. 'the sun came out as a compact object')
UTCBAF13Nov0501:116

But as pointed out in chap. 13, some roots underlie both nominal and verbal stems. Some are related to incorporated roots; e.g., *eeł*, which can be used as a noun stem (901a), a verb stem (901b), and an incorporate (901c).

(901) a. *sh'eel'* (T)
sh-'eel'
1sg.psr-trap:poss
'my trap' UTOLVDN13May2804:039

b. *Tl'aan niiduuy chih eh'eeł...* (T)
tl'aan niiduuy chih eh-eeł
and lynx also 3sg.s:ø.ipv:h-trap:ipv
'And he also trapped lynx...' UTCBVDN13Nov1501:038

c. *dzanh xah ni'eełhełeegn* (T)
dzanh xah ni-'eeł-he-łeegn
muskrat for term-trap-3pl.s:ø.ipv:ø-handle.pl.o:ipv:cust:nom
'they would set traps for muskrat' UTOLVDN07Nov2803:004

Rice (1989, 161) suggests treating items such as *'eeł* 'trap' as roots that are not specified for lexical category and that are converted into noun or verb stems by stem formation rules. There is no reason to posit a stem formation rule for an incorporate.

Finally, there are instances where the incorporate is related to a stem of one category but seems to have a meaning more typical to that of a different one. The incorporate *tsüü* 'whip', for example, is related to the verb stem *tsüh* 'whip, spank', and a corresponding noun stem is not attested. (There is a related prefixed noun *ch'itsüü* 'willow steambath switch'.) Yet in (902b), the incorporate seems to have instrumental meaning, since the act of whipping or spanking is already contained in the verb stem.

(902) a. *neehehtsüh* (T)
nee-heh-tsüh
1pl.o-3pl.s:ø.ipv:h-whip:ipv
'they spanked us' UTOLVDN07Nov2802:023

b. *niitsüü'iniixał* (T)
ni-tsüü-i-nįį-xał
term-whip-3sg.s>3sg.o-n.pfv:ø-club:pfv
'he whipped him' Titus David (2006, 1)

Thus, I prefer to treat incorporates as roots that are not specified for lexical category.

33.4. Phonological properties

The syllable types of incorporates are described in chap. 10.3. Unlike in related languages, incorporated stems are rarely truncated, but they trigger glottal stop insertion in many instances.

33.4.1. Truncation of incorporates

Several authors working on Canadian languages report truncation of stems to fit them into the CV pattern commonly associated with Dene prefixes (see Cook [2004, 197] for Dëne Sųłıné and Cook [2013, 245] for Tsilhq'útʼín as well as Hargus [2007, 430] for Witsuwit'en). In Upper Tanana this does not usually happen; in fact, incorporates differ from most other prefixes precisely in that many of them do *not* have CV shape (see chap. 10.3). It is possible that some of the variable root shapes in 33.2 are due to truncation, but there are not enough examples to suggest that this might be a general trend.

33.4.2. Glottal stop insertion

When the syllable following the incorporate begins with a vowel, a glottal stop is usually inserted (903).

(903) a. *ni'eeł'ihłeek* (N)
ni-'eeł-ih-łeek
TERM-trap-Ø.IPV:1SG.S:Ø-handle.PL.O:IPV:CUST
'I'm usually setting traps' UTOLAF15Dec0708:003

b. *diniign nathü'ehtįį* (T)
diniign na-thü-eh-tįį
moose IT-skin-3SG.S:DH.PFV:H-handle.AO:PFV
'he skinned the moose' UTOLVDN13May2907:049

33.5. The syntax of incorporates

The syntactic status of incorporated nouns in Upper Tanana is somewhat unusual for a Dene language. Rice (1989, 660–64) gives evidence that incorporates in Slave function as direct objects and subjects. She provides the following diagnostics for the direct object status of Slave incorporates:

1. Many incorporated nouns are in complementary distribution with pronominal or nominal direct objects.
2. If there is a co-occurrence of an incorporated noun and a free noun or pronominal, then the free noun or pronominal must refer to the oblique object.

Third-person subjects in Dene language are usually unmarked, so no morphological evidence for subjecthood of incorporates can be provided. The examples cited by Rice (1989) do however strongly suggest that subject incorporation exists in Slave, and similar points are made by Axelrod (1990) for Koyukon and Tuttle (2003) for Lower Tanana. In Upper Tanana the evidence for the grammatical status of incorporates as arguments is considerably weaker.

33.5.1. Incorporates as arguments

Alternations between incorporated and free stems as described by Rice (1989, 661) for Slave or Tuttle (2003, 1-2) for Lower Tanana occur occasionally. In (904a), the object *'eeɬ-* 'trap' is incorporated into the verb theme, while it occurs as a free nominal in (904b). The examples were produced by the same speaker within the same story. (904a) was produced spontaneously, while (904b) was added at a later date. According to the speaker, the two utterances are roughly semantically equivalent.

(904) a. … *k'at'eey dzanh xah ni'eeɬts'eɬeegn nts'ą'.* (T)

k'at'eey *dzanh* *xah*
NEG muskrat for

ni-'eeɬ-ts'e-ɬeegn *nts'ą'*
TERM-trap-1PL.S:Ø.IPV:Ø-handle.PL.O:IPV:CUST:NEG and

'… we didn't set traps for muskrat.' UTOLVDN07Nov2803:005

b. *K'a łą' eeɬ niits'et-ɬeeg t'oot'eey…* (T)

k'a łą' eeɬ ni-na-ts'et-ɬeeg
NEG truly trap TERM-IT-1PL.S:Ø.IPV:D-handle.PL.O:IPV:CUST:NEG

t'oot'eey
however

'But we did not really set traps, …' UTOLVDN07Nov2803:008

Sentence pairs like (904) are, however, rare. More commonly the incorporate co-occurs with a free noun phrase or a bound pronominal. In (905b) the direct object is expressed using the independent noun *uxa'* 'its hair', yet the verb also contains the incorporated stems *xa-*. The same thing is illustrated in (905a) using the nominal *tthee'* 'rock' and the incorporated root *tthi-* 'rock'.

(905) a. *uk'ehts'üü uxa' shaa xa'ildeeł* (S)

u-k'ehts'üü *u-xa'* *sh-aa*
3sg.psr-elbow 3sg.psr-hair 1sg.p-for

xa-il-deeł
hair-ø.ipv:2sg.s:l-eat.pl.o:ipv

'you sg eat his elbow hair for me' ANLC4122a:094

b. *tthee choh tthits'utthedihnayh* (S)

tthee choh tthi-ts'u-tthe-dih-nąyh
rock big out-?-rock-3sg.s:qual:??.pfv:h-move.co:pfv

'she shoved out a large rock' Tyone (1996, 49)

The same can be observed for postpositional objects. (906a) contains both the incorporated root *ke-* and an inflected noun stem as part of a postpositional phrase *dike' eh* 'with his own foot'. Similarly *tät* 'cane' in (906b) is incorporated into the verb theme but also occurs as free postpositional object.

(906) a. *naan' dike' eh yeketdelthayh* (S)

naan' *di-ke'* *eh*
across refl.psr-foot with

ye-ke-tdel-thayh
3sg.p-foot-3sg.s:inc:qual:ø.ipv:l-strike:ipv

'he kicked it with his foot' Tyone (1996, 63)

b. *łehnaan' tät eh natätjettiin* (S)

łehnaan' *tät* *eh*
both.sides cane with

na-tät-jet-tiin
prmb-cane-3sg.s>indf.o:inc:qual:ø.ipv:d-handle.ao:pfv:nom

'she, going around by using a cane on both sides' Tyone (1996, 8)

There are even some examples where an incorporate co-occurs with an (indefinite) direct object prefix (907). Both the plural and singular themes involving this incorporate—xa#ch'+d+H+tąą 'carry an indefinite lro in way to do with weapons = sg goes hunting' and xa#ch'+d+H+łeeyh 'carry pl.o in a way to do with weapons = pl go hunting' in their basic derivation—are transitive. It appears that *xa-* 'weapon' cannot fill the direct object position; that is filled instead by the indefinite object marker *ch'-*. This suggests that the incorporate does not have status as a nominal and that the themes are lexicalized.

(907) *staaxach'ihdelshyeek* (N)
sta-na-xa-ch'-h-del-shyeek
away-PRMB-weapon-INDF.O-3PL.S-QUAL:DH.PFV:L-handle.PL.O:PFV:CUST
'they went away hunting' UTOLVDN13May2003:033

d s (905), (906), and (907) suggest that in Upper Tanana incorporated roots cannot always fill a verb theme's argument positions, thus necessitating the presence of overt noun phrases. This is an important difference to languages like Slave (Rice 1989) or Lower Tanana (Tuttle 2003), where there is very strong evidence that incorporates may have argument status (see, however, Cook and Wilhelm [1998] for a different view). It is possible that this is due to their status as roots rather than stems (see 33.3), or maybe this is a sign of the waning productivity of the process of incorporation (see 33.6, 33.7).

33.5.2. Incorporates as adverbials

The loss of argument status of incorporated nouns raises the question of their syntactic function. It is well attested in other languages that incorporates, especially incorporated verb roots, may serve as manner adverbials (see, e.g., Kari [1979, 36–38] or Rice [1989, 664–67], and the examples in 33.2.3 above). I suggest that with a few exceptions such as (904) above, all Upper Tanana incorporates, including those related to noun stems, have adverbial function. In (908a) there are three participants: the AGENT, which is part of the portmanteau *hel-* '3PL.S:ø.IPV:L'-, the THEME *mba' gąyh* 'dry fish', and the GOAL *tsaak'eet* 'fish cache'. There is no argument position in this clause that could be filled by the incorporate *xeeł* 'pack'; instead it describes the manner of motion (moving while packing or moving with a pack). In (908b) there are two arguments, the AGENT (not expressed overtly, since it is third person singular) and the PATIENT, *diniign* 'moose'. The incorporated stem *thu-* 'skin' cannot have the role of PATIENT due to selection restrictions of the verb stem 'handle animate object'—a moose is animate, its skin is not. The moose must have the role of PATIENT in this sentence. A more literal translation could be 'she skin-handled the moose' or 'she handled the moose in a way that has to do with its skin'. (908c) also has two participants, the AGENT (again not expressed) and the PATIENT, *teejuh ch'itay* 'the poor old man'. The incorporated stem *ła-* 'hand' has the role of INSTRUMENT, 'she slapped him with her hand'.

(908) a. *tsaak'eet mba' gąyh naaxeełheldek* (S)

tsaak'eet *mba'* *gąyh*
fish.cache dry.fish dry

na-na-xeeł-hel-dek
down-it-pack-3pl.s:ø.ipv:l-pl.move:ipv:cust

'they would pack the dry fish back down to the caches' Tyone (1996, 62)

b. *diniign nathu'ehtįį* (T)

diniign na-thu-eh-tįį
moose it-skin-3sg.s:dh.pfv:h-handle.ao:pfv

'she skinned the moose' UTOLVDN13May2907:046

c. *Teejuh ch'itay łahiidnįįkat.* (T)

teejuh ch'itay łah-ii-dnįį-kat
poor old.man hand-3sg.s>3sg.o-qual:n.pfv:ø-slap:pfv

'She slapped the poor old man.' UTOLVDN13May2907:043

Incorporated verb roots very frequently function as adverbials of manner (909).

(909) a. *nadlohdelshyah* (N)

na-dloh-del-shyah
it-laugh-3sg.s:qual:dh.pfv:l-sg.go:pfv

'he went away laughing' UT Notebook #4, 17

b. *ttheehihdelxoh* (S)

tthee-h-del-xoh
bark-3pl.s-qual:ø.ipv:l-make.noise:ipv

'they were barking' Tyone (1996, 24)

While incorporation in Upper Tanana shows some evidence of being a syntactic process similar to what has been described by Rice (1989) and Tuttle (2003), most of the data suggests that it is a lexical process to do with the formation of new verb themes, as has been already suggested by Kari (1979) for Ahtna.

33.6. Productivity and lexicalization

Kari (1979, 36) considers incorporates in Ahtna to be a type of non-aspectual derivational string, meaning that the process of incorporation has no effect on conjugation, mode, or stem aspect. This is also true for incorporation in Upper Tanana.

As has been shown in the examples in 33.2, the semantic effects of incorporation can be highly transparent or quite unpredictable. A similar observation has been made by Hargus (2007, 427-429) regarding Witsuwit'en, which led her to postulate a distinction between what she calls thematic and productive incorporation. By productive incorporation she means the productive inclusion of a number of different incorporates into the same theme; Kari (1979) calls this process the formation of "subthemes." (910) demonstrates the productivity of the theme inc#d+l+ye 'move performing incorporated oral action' in Witsuwit'en:[1]

(910) Witsuwit'en (Hargus 2007, 429)

a. *nəkwəs dəlye* (incorporate: *kwəs-* 'cold, sickness')
'she's going around coughing'

b. *nədlət dəlye* (incorporate: *dlət-* 'talk loudly and angrily')
'he's going around yelling angrily'

c. *nəcən dəlye* (incorporate: *cən-* 'song')
'he walks around singing'

In the case of thematic incorporation the incorporate is part of the verb theme, and it is not possible to replace a particular incorporate with a semantically similar one. One of Hargus's examples is reproduced in (911). In these verb themes, *tl'a-* 'buttocks' cannot be replaced by another incorporate referring to a body part.

(911) Witsuwit'en (Hargus 2007, 247)

a. *də-tl'a#l-tl'əs* '(buttocks) bounce' (incorporate: *tl'a-* 'buttocks')
dətl'altl'əs
'he's bouncing up and down'

b. *tl'a#d-l-ts'i* 'PL sit down' (incorporate: *tl'a-* 'buttocks')
netl'azdilts'i
'we sat down'

c. *tl'a#l-t'əɣ* 'fall on buttocks, sit down quickly' (incorporate: *tl'a-* 'buttocks')
netl'alt'əɣ
'he sat down fast'

The theme inc#d+L+ye exemplified in (910) and its cognates seems to be highly productive in Northern Dene; it exists at the very least in Slave (Rice 1989, 667), Ahtna (Kari 1990, 424), Lower Tanana (Tuttle 2003), and Tsilhq'útín (Cook 2013), and all authors apart from Cook comment on its productivity. It exists in Upper Tanana as well, see (909, 876b, 881b) above.

Similarly productive is the theme inc#d+L+xoh 'to make noise in the manner of incorporate' (912).

(912) a. *k'at'eey noodlee k'eh thahdzilxoo* (T); incorporate: *thah-* 'voice'-

k'at'eey *noodlee* *k'eh*
NEG white.man like

thah-dzil-xoo
voice-1PL.S:QUAL:NEG.PFV:L-make.noise:PFV:NEG

'we did not speak English' (lit. 'we did not make voice noises like white people') UTOLVDN07Nov2802:016

b. *ttheehihdelxoh* (S); incorporate: *thah-* 'bark'-

tthee-hih-del-xoh
bark-3PL.S-QUAL:Ø.IPV:L-make.noise:IPV

'they were barking' Tyone (1996, 24)

The prefix string containing the incorporate *chi-* 'pretend' is also highly productive (913).

(913) a. *chijel'aał* (N)

chi-jel-'aał
pretend-INDF:3SG.S:QUAL:Ø.IPV:L-eat:IPV

'he's pretending to eat' UT Notebook #4, 23

b. *chijeltįį* (T)

chi-jel-tįį
pretend-INDF:3SG.S:QUAL:Ø.IPV:L-sleep:IPV

'she pretended to sleep' UTCBAF13Nov0501:092

c. *yichijelnih* (T)

y-i-chi-jel-nih
3SG.S>3SG.P-PP-pretend-INDF:QUAL:Ø.IPV:L-say:IPV

'she lied to him' (lit. 'she pretended to say something affecting him') UTCBAF13Nov0501:243

Another highly productive theme is inc#d+G+L+nąyh[2] 'move incorporated body part quickly'; the resulting subthemes (914) are a lot less transparent than the ones in (912) and (913) and could be considered morphological idioms (Holden 2013, 444–52).

(914) a. *ut'akįtdagnthäł* (N); incorporate: *kį-*, *ke-* 'foot'
u-t'a-kį-tdagn-nąyh
3SG.P-against-foot-INC:QUAL:AA.IPV:1SG.S:L-move.quickly:FUT
'I will stumble over it' UTOLAF12Jul1201:017

b. *datthinįįtthayh* (T); incorporate: *tthi-* 'head'
da-tthi-nįį-tthayh
inside-head-3SG.S:N.PFV:Ø-move.quickly:PFV
'he peeked inside' (lit. 'he quickly moved his head inside')
UTCBAF13Nov0501:238

c. *yits'ą̈' hatthidalnąyh* (S); incorporate: *tthi-* 'head'
yi-ts'ą̈' *ha-tthi-dal-nąyh*
3SG.S>3SG.P-to out-head-QUAL:AA.PFV:L-move.quickly:PFV
'he stared at him' (lit. 'his head moved out toward him') Tyone (1996, 30)

Thematic incorporation as described by Hargus (2007, 427–29) is also common in Upper Tanana (915).

(915) a. *That nałateetleegn eh…* (N)
that na-ła-tee-tleegn *and*
that IT-sagging-3SG.S:INC:DH.PFV:Ø-be.rotten:IPV:NOM because
'Because that [house] was falling apart…'
UTCBVDN13Nov0804:036

b. *shk'eh nagąą'htelshyah* (N)
sh-k'eh *na-gąą'-h-tel-shyah*
1SG.P-after IT-arm-3PL.S:INC:DH.PFV:L-handle.PL.O:PFV
'they ran back after me' UTOLAF09Aug1202:033

c. *chiidziidedaak* (T)
chi-na-dzi-de-daak
?-IT-heart-3SG.S:QUAL:Ø.IPV-D:SG.move:IPV:CUST
'she was amazed' (lit. 'her heart jumped')
UTOLVDN13May2801:103

It is apparent from the data in (914) and (915) in particular that incorporation is not always a semantically transparent process. The data presented in this section and also (more implicitly) in 33.2 above has shown that even in productive themes, incorporates have a strong tendency to become lexicalized.

33.7. Incorporation and language endangerment

In concluding this chapter, I wish to make a few brief remarks on Upper Tanana incorporation in light of the severe endangerment of the language. If one analyzes the incorporation data by speaker, it becomes apparent that older or more conservative speakers utilize incorporation more than younger ones, both in terms of frequency and of variety. A text by Titus David from Tetlin, recorded by Paul Milanowski in 1963 (cited here as Titus David [2006]), which is the most recent draft of the transcription) contains more incorporates on a single page than long texts produced by speakers alive today. Many incorporated roots in this section are attested only in Tyone (1996), the texts for which were recorded in the 1980s and 1990s. Today's speakers do not use nearly as many or as broad a variety of incorporates. It is important to note that these are not speakers whose fluency is at all in doubt; all of them have great verbal skill and linguistic sensitivity. They simply use fewer incorporates and hardly ever produce alternations such as given in (904) above. Incorporation in Upper Tanana thus is an example of how language endangerment may result in loss of linguistic complexity.

33.8. Summary

In this chapter incorporation is discussed. There are three groups of incorporates: incorporates referring to body parts, incorporates related to other stems, and incorporates that are not related to other stems in the language. The bulk of this chapter consists of an inventory of incorporates.

Following this inventory I present evidence why incorporates should be considered roots rather than stems in this language, and I make a few remarks about their phonology. I note that syntactically they behave more like adverbials than like arguments of the verb. I also show that incorporation can be productive or thematic, and more or less semantically transparent. The chapter closes with a brief discussion of incorporation and language endangerment.

Notes

1. The spaces after the incorporate are in the original source.
2. This stem set has suppletive forms; see chap. 26 for more information.

34 Iterative prefix

Position 9 of the Upper Tanana template (see table 24.1) contains only one prefix: *na-* 'IT-'. This prefix has the properties associated with the iterative morpheme in related languages, but it additionally has taken on some of the functions of the distributive morpheme (see chap. 32 for discussion).

34.1. Position

The iterative prefix precedes the incorporates; see chap. 33.1. It follows the adverbial-derivational prefixes with which it coalesces: it changes an adverbial-derivational prefix of the shape CV to the shape CV: (916; see also 34.3.1 below).

(916) a. *Ay eh naa'inshyah.* (N)

ay *eh* *na-na-in-shyah*
and and down-IT-3SG.S:N.PFV:D-SG.go:PFV
'And she came back down.' UTOLAF10Jul0202:192

b. *Ahdogn ts'oo k'it tah daach'ettl'u'...* (T)

ah-dogn *ts'oo* *k'it* *tah*
NTRL-up:AR spruce on among
da-na-ch'et-tl'u'
closed-IT-INDF.O:3SG.S:Ø.IPV:D-tie:IPV:DSTR
'He was setting snares up in the spruce trees...'
UTOLAF09Jun2202:026

34.2. Functions

The iterative prefix is often used productively as part of the non-aspectual prefix string na#(D). The different productive functions associated with this prefix string are described in 34.2.1. It is also part of many verb themes (34.2.2). Lastly, this prefix is part of the distributive prefix string described in 34.2.3.

34.2.1. Iterative prefix string

The iterative prefix string na#(D) consists of the iterative prefix and usually, but not always, a changed voice/valence prefix (see chap. 27.3.2.2). The iterative prefix string is non-aspectual, i.e., it affects neither conjugation markers nor stem aspect. The iterative derivation is highly productive with a number of semantic effects depending on the semantics of the original theme. Rice (2000, 65) summarizes the functions of the iterative derivation as follows: simple repetition of an event, movement to a previous location ("returning"), transfer of an object to a previous location, or repetition of an action involving a different object referent. Hargus (2007, 438–39) adds to this that the iterative derivation is often used to describe cyclical events. All these functions are attested in Upper Tanana; additionally the iterative derivation may indicate the return to a previous state.

34.2.1.1. Iterative indicating simple repetition The iterative derivation can signify simple repetition of the event expressed in the verb theme, regardless of the transitivity of the theme (917).

(917) a. *na'ettsah* (T)
na-et-tsah
IT-3SG.S:Ø.IPV:D-cry:IPV
'she cried again' UTCBAF13Nov0501:328

b. *k'at'eey nts'ą̈' nootihheel* (N)
k'at'eey n-ts'ą̈' na-hu-tih-heel
NEG 2SG.P-to IT-AR-INC:AA.IPV:1SG.S:Ø-speak:FUT:NEG
'I will not speak to you again' UTOLAF12Jul1202:029

c. *Nahunelts'ųų eł t'eey.* (T)
na-hu-nel-ts'ųų eł t'eey
IT-3PL.O-3SG.S:QUAL:Ø.IPV:L-kiss:IPV and even
'She was kissing them again and again.'
UTOLAF08Apr2805:105

34.2.1.2. Iterative in transitive themes: 'another o' In transitive verb themes the iterative frequently implies that the action is repeated with a different object referent. In (918a) the man marries a different woman rather than the same one again. In (918b) the girl repeats the action of bringing in wood, but of course not with the same piece of wood over and over again.

(918) a. *dik'eh eltsiin nahuuniik* (T)

d-k'eh *el-tsiin*
REFL.P-like 3SG.S:DH.PFV:L-appear:PFV:NOM

na-uu-niik
IT-3SG.S:CON:DH.PFV:Ø-marry:PFV

'he married again [a woman] who looked like him'

UTOLVDN13May2901:064

b. *Tsat niidelshyeek, tsat niidelshyeek.* (T)

tsat *ni-na-del-shyeek* *tsat*
wood TERM-IT-3SG.S:QUAL:Ø.IPV:L-handle.IPV:CUST wood

ni-na-del-shyeek
TERM-IT-3SG.S:QUAL:Ø.IPV:L-handle.IPV:CUST

'She brought in wood, she brought in wood.'

UTOLAF07Oct2512:018

34.2.1.3. Iterative plus customary superaspect When the iterative derivation occurs with a verb in the customary in a subordinate clause, the resulting reading is 'every time' (or in [919b], where the verb is complementized by *niign* 'where', 'everywhere').

(919) a. *Nats'inel'įįk nts'ą̈' t'eey mbaa ts'edloh.* (N)

na-ts'-nel-'įįk *nts'ą̈'* *t'eey* *m-aa*
IT-1PL.S-QUAL:Ø.IPV:L-see:IPV:CUST and even 3SG.P-for

ts'e-dloh
1PL.S:Ø.IPV:Ø-laugh:IPV

'Every time we see him, we laugh at him.'

UTOLVDN07Aug2205:079

b. ... *natsetndeek niign t'eey anyway t'eey neeheh'įh.* (T)

na-tset-ndeek *niign* *t'eey*
IT-1PL.S:INC:DH.PFV:D-move.nomadically:IPV:CUST where even

anyway *t'eey* *nee-heh-'įh*
anyway even 1PL.O-3SG.S:Ø.IPV:H-do:IPV

'... everywhere we move, they always do that do us.'

UTOLAF09Jun2902:029

34.2.1.4. Iterative in motion themes: return to origin In motion verbs the iterative derivation often signifies return to one's point of origin (920).

Tenenbaum (1978, 173) points out that Dena'ina speakers are "very literal" in the use of this derivation; whenever the connotation of a returning movement is present, the iterative has to be used. The same is true for Upper Tanana.

(920) a. *Ldil kah negn' na'įįdaał!* (N)

ldil	*kah*	*negn'*	*na-įį-daał*
tea	for	upland:ALL	IT-AA.IPV:2SG.S-D:SG.go:IPV:PROG

'Go back upland for tea!' UTOLAF09Aug1202:024

b. *Shta' chih t'axoh tay' staatetshyah…* (N)

sh-ta'	*chih*	*t'axoh*	*tay'*
1SG.PSR-father	too	finally	again

sta-na-tet-shyah
away-IT-3SG.S:INC:DH.PFV:D-SG.go:PFV

'My father quickly got ready again to go back out…'
UTOLAF08Feb1906:007

In (920a) the speakers have just arrived at their location when they remember that they forgot the tea at their point of origin, so they send the addressee back to fetch it. In (920b) the father has just returned from an unsuccessful hunting trip and is about to leave again. (921) illustrates the same interpretation of transitive verb themes.

(921) a. *Shnąą iin shta' iin ndlaa::n dzanh t'eey nahelshyeek.* (T)

sh-nąą	*iin*	*sh-ta'*	*iin*	*ndlaan*	*dzanh*	*t'eey*
1SG.PSR-mother	PL	1SG.PSR-father	PL	lots	muskrat	even

na-hel-shyeek
IT-3PL.S:Ø.IPV:L-handle.PL.O:IPV:CUST

'My mother and father brought back lots of muskrat.'
UTOLVDN07Nov2803:010

b. *Daayįltįį.* (T)

da-na-y-įl-tįį
in-IT-3SG.S>3SG.O-N.PFV:L-handle.AO:PFV

'She brought him back inside.' UTOLAF13May2403:062

34.2.1.5. Iterative in neuter themes: return to a previous state Applied to neuter themes, the iterative derivation often indicates the return to a previous state (922). The addressee in (922a) is cold after walking home wet, while the husband in (922b) pretended to be human for the benefit of his wife.

(922) a. *k'a natįlxiin* (N)
k'a na-tįl-xiin
NEG IT-INC:AA.IPV:2SG.S:L-be.warm:FUT:NEG
'you SG will not warm [yourself] up again'
UTOLAF12Jul1201:058

b. *Ukąy' chih shoh na'et-łįį...* (N)
u-kąy' chih shoh na-et-łįį
3SG.PSR-husband too bear IT-DH.PFV:D-become:PFV
'Her husband had turned back into a bear...'
UTOLVDN10Jul2713:029

34.2.1.6. Iterative in cyclical events The iterative derivation is very common in cyclical events ([923]; see also Hargus [2007, 438–39] for discussion).

(923) a. *Xay nootet-łeek...* (N)
xay na-hu-tet-łeek
winter IT-AR.S-INC:Ø.IPV:D-be:IPV:CUST
'It became winter...' UTOLVDN13May2003:023

b. *Dziin k'ahmän' nahut-łiin eh...* (N)
dziin k'ahmän' na-hut-łiin eh
day morning IT-AR.S:DH.PFV:D-become:PFV:NOM and
'And when it became morning...' UTOLVDN10Jul2724:046

c. *na'įhxeeł* (T)
na-įh-xeeł
IT-3SG.S:AA.PFV:H-get.dark:PFV
'it got dark' UTCBAF13Nov0501:060

The iterative derivation is, however, not required in verb themes describing cyclical events (924).

(924) *k'ahman' huteełeeg (T)*
k'ahman' hu-tee-łeeg
morning AR.S-INC:DH.PFV:Ø-become:PFV:CUST:NOM
'it became morning' UTCBAF13Nov0501:106

It is not clear what determines the use of the iterative derivation in cyclical events—note that (923b) and (924) both describe the same type of event, once with the iterative derivation, once without.

34.2.1.7. Overlaps in meaning Rice (2000, 64-68) points out that the various functions of the iterative derivation often result in ambiguity. I agree with her, although I would choose the term "vagueness" rather than "ambiguity", since several meanings of the iterative may be present at the same time (925).

(925) a. *Tsat niidelshyeek, tsat niidelshyeek.* (T)

tsat *ni-na-del-shyeek* *tsat*
wood TERM-IT-3SG.S:QUAL:Ø.IPV:L-handle.IPV:CUST wood
ni-na-del-shyeek
TERM-IT-3SG.S:QUAL:Ø.IPV:L-handle.IPV:CUST
'She brought in wood, she brought in wood.'
UTOLAF07Oct2512:018

b. *Shta' chih t'axoh tay' staatetshyah...* (N)

sh-ta' *chih* *t'axoh* *tay'*
1SG.PSR-father too finally again
sta-na-tet-shyah
away-IT-3SG.S:INC:DH.PFV:D-SG.go:PFV
'My father quickly got ready again to go back out...'
UTOLAF08Feb1906:007

(918b), repeated here as (925a), was used as an example for a repeated event involving different object referents, but it is also possible that the iterative derivation here refers to the fact that the girl is bringing the wood back to her point of origin. Both interpretations are equally likely and not mutually exclusive. (920b), repeated here as (925b), was cited as an example illustrating movement back to one's point of origin; thus the father goes back out where he came from. It is, however, also possible that this is an example for repeated motion; he went out once without hunting success, and now he is going out again, hoping for better luck. Again, both interpretations are possible simultaneously.

Thus, while the iterative derivation is very productive, it has a variety of functions that are not mutually exclusive, and several functions may be present at the same time.

34.2.2. Lexicalized iterative prefix

The iterative prefix *na-* is part of many verb themes. In these verb themes it does not affect the voice/valence marker. The list in (926) is not inclusive.

(926) Thematic Iterative

a. na#O+G+Ø+ch'ot 'wash o'

b. na#ho+l+nek 'tell story'
c. na#O+H+łoh 'fish for o with hook'
d. na#D+kuyh 'vomit'
e. na#O+H+shyii 'heal o'
f. na#n+Ø+de' 'get sick from grease'
g. na#t+L+süüh 'hunt'

In some of these examples the semantic contribution of the iterative prefix is obvious. The themes in (926a–d) all involve repeated motions or activities. (926e) suggests the return to a previous state. These are not instances of the iterative derivation, since the voice/valence markers Ø- and H- are not affected. The semantic contribution of the iterative prefix in (926g, 926h) is unclear; these verb stems never occur outside the verb themes listed here.

(926) also demonstrates that the thematic iterative prefix may co-occur with all four voice/valence prefixes.

34.2.3. "Distributive" functions

The iterative prefix has taken on some of the functions of the distributive prefix *n-* of position 7.

34.2.3.1. Distributive derivations As stated in chap. 24.4.3 and 25.2.1.3, some motion themes can take the distributive and the distributive-customary superaspects. Both superaspects are characterized by the presence of the distributive prefix in other languages; in Upper Tanana they usually bear the iterative prefix instead.

The distributive indicates that a motion event is replicated several times, possibly involving different patient referents[1] ([927]; note here the semantic overlap with the functions of the iterative derivation described above). The distributive-customary indicates that this replication is customary (928).

(927) a. *K'ahdąą'dą' gah de' kah anogn daach'idhihtl'ųų.* (N)
k'ahdąą'dą' *gah* *de' kah* *a-nogn*
yesterday rabbit to.check NTRL-upland:AR
da-na-ch'-dhih-tl'ųų
closed-IT-INDF.O-DH.PFV:1SG.S:Ø-tie:PFV:DSTR
'Yesterday I set snares for rabbits in the upland area.'
UTOLAF15Dec0607:006

b. *Diniign kah <nts'ą'> nii'eełhełe'.* (T)
diniign *kah* *nts'ą'*
moose for to
ni-na-'eeł-he-łe'
TERM-IT-trap-3PL.S:Ø.IPV:Ø-handle.PL.O:IPV:DSTR
'They set several traps for moose.' UTOLVDN08Mar1311:002

(928) a. *Ts'oo tah naadlįh ḵi'įįhaak tl'aan daach'etl'uuk.* (T)
ts'oo *tah* *naadlįh* *ḵi-įį-haak* *tl'aan*
spruce among instead up-3SG.S:AA.PFV:Ø-SG.go:PFV:CUST and
da-na-ch'e-tl'uuk
closed-IT-INDF.O:3SG.S:Ø.IPV:Ø-tie:IPV:DSTR:CUST
'Instead he would go up into the spruce trees and set snares there.'
UTOLVDN13May2801:076

b. *Ts'at įį'eh tat'eey ǫǫkeet huugn taa'ǫlshyeek de'!* (T)
ts'at *įį'eh tah* *tat'eey* *ǫǫ-keet* *huugn*
blanket as.well also OPT:2SG.S:Ø-buy:OPT etc.
ta-na-ǫl-shyeek *de'*
distribute-IT-OPT:2SG.S:L-handle.PL.O:OPT:DSTR:CUST if
'Buy blankets as well and make sure you distribute them [at potlatch]!' UTCBAF13Nov0401:071

Both derivations are quite rare and due to the similarities with the iterative derivation hard to identify (see chap. 32.4.1 for more discussion) .

34.2.3.2. Lexicalized "distributive" A few conversive-continuative verb themes contain a lexicalized *na-*. Related languages employ the distributive prefix in these verb themes (see Tenenbaum [1978, 160] for Dena'ina or Kari [1979, 154–55] for Ahtna); see also chap. 26.2.1.8. The list in (929) may not be inclusive.

(929) Lexicalized "distributive"
a. na#O+H+'oł 'butcher o'
b. na#ho+H+'įį 'sense a spirit'

34.3. Phonology

Two processes involving the iterative prefix are discussed here: the absorption of the iterative prefix into preceding adverbial-derivational prefixes and coalescence of the iterative and areal prefixes.

34.3.1. Iterative absorption

When the iterative prefix follows an adverbial-derivational prefix (see chap. 35) of the shape CV, it is absorbed into this prefix and lengthens the vowel to CV:. Orthographically, this is represented by double vowel symbols (930).

(930) a. *tay' ich'a' tii'inshyah* (T)

tay' i-ch'a' ti-na-in-shyah
again 3SG.S>3SG.P-from out-IT-N.PFV:D-SG.go:PFV
'he went out away from him again' UTOLVDN13May2805:025

b. *Anaan' nts'ą̈' staa'almoh.* (N)

a-naan' nts'ą̈' sta-na-al-moh
NTRL-across:ALL to away-IT-3SG.S:AA.IPV:L-roll:IPV
'It is rolling over and over, across and away.'
UTOLAF13May2801:033

This process distinguishes the iterative prefix *na-* from several adverbial-derivational prefixes in position 10 that also have the shape *na-* (see chap. 35 for examples). (927b, 928a) demonstrate that iterative absorption also takes place for the "distributive" use of this prefix.

34.3.2. Coalescence with areal prefix

When the areal prefix immediately follows the iterative, the two prefixes merge into *noo-* in casual or fast speech (931); in careful and slow speech (e.g., when asked to repeat the word during transcription), speakers will often but not always pronounce the two morphemes individually.

(931) a. *Naa nootagndak.* (T)

n-aa na-hu-tagn-ndak
2SG.P-for IT:AR-INC:AA.IPV:1SG.S:L-tell:FUT
'I will tell the story about you SG.' UTOLVDN13May2902:047

b. *Hahnde' noonel'įh...* (T)

hah-nde' na-hu-nel-'įh
NTRL-back:ALL IT-3SG.S:AR-QUAL:Ø.IPV:L-look:IPV
'He looked back...' UTCBAF13Nov0501:355

34.4. Summary

The iterative prefix of position 9 occurs in two contexts: it may be thematic or it may be part of the extremely productive non-aspectual iterative prefix string na#(D). This prefix string may apply to almost all verb themes. It has a variety of functions: it can indicate simple repetition of an event or repetition of an event involving different object referents; it may indicate that an event is recurring and cyclical, or that it always takes place. In motion themes it can indicate that the motion goes back to a point of origin. In neuter themes it indicates a return to an original state. In many verb forms several of these meanings of the iterative derivation are present simultaneously.

The iterative morpheme also has taken on some of the functions associated in other languages with the distributive morpheme.

Notes

1. See also Axelrod (1993, 89-91) for discussion of the distributive superaspect in Koyukon.

35 Adverbial-derivational prefixes

Position 10 of the verb template (see table 24.1) contains the adverbial-derivational prefixes. This is a very large group of prefixes with well-defined meaning. As the label suggests, these meanings are frequently adverbial in nature (one of the largest subgroups has directional meanings), and the prefixes feature prominently in the derivational system by being part of aspectual prefix strings.

(932) demonstrates the position of the adverbial-derivational prefixes to the right of the (bound or free) postposition. In (932a) the adverbial-derivational prefix *ts'-* 'pejorative' follows the bound postposition *i-* 'to'; in (932b) the adverbial-derivational prefix *da-* 'up' follows the free postposition *k'it* 'on'.

(932) a. *mits'ishniign* (N)
m-i-ts'-ish-niign
3SG.P-PP-PEJ-NEG.PFV:1SG.S:D-not.know:IPV
'I don't know him' UTOLVDN07Aug2205:016

b. *dahdzał k'it dahuts'ehłeeg* (T)
dahdzał k'it da-hu-ts'eh-łeeg
rack on up-3PL.O-1PL.S:Ø.IPV:H-handle.PL.O:IPV:CUST:NOM
'we put [the leaves] onto the drying rack'
UTOLAF09Jun2901:011

The adverbial-derivational prefixes precede the iterative prefix *na-* (chap. 34).

The role of adverbial-derivational prefixes in the formation of aspectual prefix strings is described in 35.1. The bulk of this chapter consists of an inventory of adverbial-derivational prefixes and of the aspectual prefix strings of which they are part (35.2).

35.1. Adverbial-derivational prefixes and aspectual prefix strings

The adverbial-derivational prefixes are crucially involved in the formation of aspectual prefix strings, defined by Kari (1979, 28) as "sets of discontinuous morphemes that have defined semantic content and apply productively to a number of verbs." Aspectual prefix strings are specified for stem aspect (the aspect system of Upper Tanana is described in volume 2) and a conjugation pattern (933). (933a) contains the primary derivation of a motion verb theme like Ø+mbeeyh 'swim' and D+düh 'sg animal runs'—the primary derivation of these themes contains no additional prefixes, take the momentaneous stem aspect and require an *n*- conjugation marker in the perfective and imperfective modes. (933b–f) contains a sample of prefix strings that can apply to these motion themes. Additional information on each prefix string is included: the verb theme category of the resulting verb theme, its (stem) aspect, and the conjugation markers it requires.

(933) Aspectual prefix strings

	Prefix string	*Meaning*	*Theme category*	*Aspect*	*Conjugation*
a.	–	'arrive'	motion	MOM	(n, n)
b.	sta#	'away'	motion	MOM	(n, n)
c.	ti#	'into water'	motion	MOM	(n, n)
d.	ha#	'up and out'	motion	MOM	(Ø, aa)
e.	na#t+D	'around'	motion	PRMB	(aa, n)
f.	na+ke#(d)	'around in circle'	motion	REV	(Ø, dh)

(934) and (935) show actual verb forms resulting from aspectual derivation of the primary themes Ø+mbeeyh 'sg swim' and D+düh 'sg animal runs' using the strings in (933).[1]

(934) a. *tanįįmįį* (T)
sta-nįį-mįį
away-3SG.S:N.PFV:Ø-swim:PFV
'he swam away' UTOLVDN13May2909:091

b. *tinįįmįį* (T)
ti-nįį-mįį
into.water-3SG.S:N.PFV:Ø-swim:PFV
'he waded into the water' UTOLVDN13May2907:091

c. *haa'atmįį* (T)
ha-na-at-mįį
out-IT-3SG.S:AA.PFV:D-swim:PFV
'he swam back up to the surface' UTOLVDN14Nov2301:381

d. *na'atmeeł* (N)
na-at-meeł
PRMB-3SG.S:AA.IPV:D-swim:IPV
'it was swimming around' UTCBAF13May2301:0933

e. *nake'aambeeł* (T)
nake-aa-mbeeł
in.circle-3SG.S:DH.PFV:Ø-swim:IPV:PROG
'it is swimming in circles' UT Notebook #5, 84

(935) a. *sta'indät* (N)
sta-in-dät
away-3SG.S:N.PFV:D-SG.animal.runs:PFV
'[the fox] ran away' UTOLAF15May0501:128

b. *ti'indät* (T)
ti-in-dät
into.water-
'[the loon] dove into the water' UTCBVDN13Nov1401:045

c. *diniign hutthe hа'atdät* (N)
diniign hu-ttheh ha-at-dät
moose 3PL.P-in.front out-3SG.S:AA.PFV:D-SG.animal.runs:PFV
'a moose jumped out in front of them'
UTOLAF13May2801:002

d. *na'atdüh* (T)
na-at-düh
PRMB-3SG.S:AA.IPV:D-SG.animal.runs:IPV
'it is running around' UT Notebook #5, 84

e. *nakidetdät*
naki-det-dät
around.and.back-3SG.S:QUAL:DH.PFV:D-SG.animal.runs:PFV
'it turned around and ran off' UTOLVDN13May2004:088

(934) and (935) show that the meanings of the derived themes are compositional, even though there are idiosyncratic effects, e.g., when the prefix string ti# 'into water' is added: combined with the verb theme Ø+mbeeyh 'swim' it yields 'wade into the water' (934b), whereas with the stem D+dät 'SG animal runs' it yields 'dive into the water' (935b).

35.2. Inventory

The adverbial-derivational prefixes below are grouped roughly by semantic category: directional, nondirectional, and adjectival. Within each group the prefixes are ordered alphabetically.

For each prefix the aspectual prefix strings of which it is part are included. Individual prefixes are italicized: *da-* 'into', *ke-* 'up'. Aspectual prefix strings, just like verb themes, are not italicized. Within each prefix string, the location of the disjunct boundary as well as the conjugation prefixes are indicated: da# (n, n) 'into dwelling', na+ke#(d) (Ø, dh) 'around and back, around and over'; when possible, conjugation markers in the imperfective and perfective are exemplified. The discussion of each prefix string also contains all available information on verb theme categories it can apply to as well as the aspect of the derived verb themes.

Aspectual prefix strings vary greatly in productivity. Some of them, such as the prefix strings in (933) are remarkably productive and can apply to (almost) all verb themes from a particular verb theme category; others are restricted to one or two themes. For this reason the productivity of each prefix string is indicated when known.

35.2.1. Directional adverbial-derivational prefixes

This subgroup of adverbial-derivational prefixes describes the PATH of a motion event. The strings formed by these prefixes apply widely to motion verbs or derive motion verbs from other verb theme categories.

35.2.1.1. *ch'a-* 'away, out' This prefix derives from the postposition *P+ch'a'* 'from'. It is part of only one prefix string.

35.2.1.1.1. ch'a#(n, n) 'away, out' The prefix string ch'a# (n, n) 'out' derives motion themes in the momentaneous aspect (936).

(936) a. *ch'aydihtįį* (T)
ch'a-y-dįh-tįį
out-3SG.S>3SG.O-QUAL:N.PFV:H-handle.AO:PFV
'she took him out [of between the trees]'
UTOLAF09Jun2202:015

b. *Noo ch'ats'inįįkįin eł...* (T)
noo *ch'a-ts'inįį-kįin* *eł*
ahead out-1PL.S:N.PFV:ø-go.by.boat:PFV:NOM and
'We start out by boat and...' UTOLAF09Jun2902:011

It is unclear what causes the elision of the *n*- conjugation prefix in (936a).

35.2.1.2. *da*- 'orifice' The prefix *da*- 'orifice' is related to the noun stem -*da* 'beak' and is used in a number of different prefix strings.

35.2.1.2.1. da# (n, n) 'into dwelling' The prefix string da# (n, n) 'into dwelling' derives a number of motion themes in the momentaneous (937).

(937) a. *Nuhk'aa' thüh danahłeeyh!* (T)
nuh-k'aa' *thüh* *da-nah-łeeyh*
2PL.PSR-gun:POSS skin inside-N.IPV:2PL.S:ø-handle.PL.O:IPV
'Bring in your PL gun cases!' UTOLVDN07Oct2602:027

b. *danįįshyah* (N)
da-nįį-shyah
inside-3SG.S:N.PFV:ø-SG.go:PFV
'she came in' UTOLAF12Jul1201:046

35.2.1.2.2. da#n (Ø, dh) 'filling, full' The prefix string da#n (Ø, dh) 'filling, full' derives motion themes in the momentaneous aspect (938b). It does not seem to be very productive.

(938) a. *nsaag' shyiit danįhdok!* (T)
n-saag' *shyiit* *da-nįh-dok*
2SG.PSR-sack:POSS in full-QUAL:ø.IPV:2SG.S:H-stuff:IPV
'stuff it into your SG bag!' UT Notebook #5, 85

b. *Tthee dog daneedog...* (T)
tthee *dog* *da-nee-dog*
rock up:AR full-3SG.S:QUAL:DH.PFV:ø-stuff:PFV:NOM
'She stuffed rocks up there...' UTOLAF13May2403:015

35.2.1.2.3. da#t+n (dh, aa) 'full' The prefix string da#t+n (dh, aa) 'full' derives extension and positional themes in the neuter aspect (939).

(939) *Tsin'įį! Neeshyah <łahtthagn nts'ą'> tuu tuu daatneehaan eł...* (T)

tsinįį *nee-shyah* *łahtthagn nts'ą'* *tuu* *tuu*
thank.you 1PL.PSR-house all water water

da-na-tnee-haan *eł*
full-IT-3PL.S:INC:QUAL:DH.PFV:Ø-be.flood:IPV:NOM because

'Thank you! Because our houses are all full of water...'

UTOLAF07Nov2602:014

35.2.1.2.4. da# (Ø, dh) 'closing off' Da# (Ø, dh) 'closing off' derives motion themes in the momentaneous aspect. It occurs primarily in the verb theme da#ch'+Ø+tl'uh 'set snares', which always occurs in the distributive superaspect (940).

(940) a. *Adogn gah kah dach'įįtl'uh!* (T)

a-dogn *gah* *kah*
NTRL-up:AR rabbit for

da-ch'įį-tl'uh
closing.off INDF.O:Ø.IPV:2SG.S:Ø-tie:IPV:DSTR

'Set snares for rabbits up there!' UTOLAF09Jun2202:025

b. *Ahdogn ts'oo k'it tah daach'ettl'u' nts'ą'...* (T)

ah-dogn *ts'oo* *k'it* *tah*
NTRL-up:AR spruce on among

da-na-ch'et-tl'u' *nts'ą'*
closing.off-IT-INDF.O:3SG.S:DH.PFV:D-tie:PFV:DSTR and

'He set snares up there in the spruce trees and...'

UTOLAF09Jun2202:026

35.2.1.3. *da-* 'up, on' *Da-* 'up, on' is not related semantically to *da-* 'orifice' discussed in 35.2.1.2. It is part of several prefix strings.

35.2.1.3.1. da# (?, dh) 'up, ascending' Da# (?, dh) 'up, ascending' derives many motion themes in the momentaneous aspect (941). No imperfective form of this prefix string is attested.

(941) a. *Łįį daats'ehtl'u'.* (N)

łįį *da-na-ts'eh-tl'u'*
dog up-IT-1PL.S:DH.PFV:H-tie:PFV:DSTR

'We tied [packs] on the dogs.' UTOLVDN13May2003:036

b. *Hunaann' tsiił k'it daheedeeł...* (T)
hu-naan' tsiił k'it da-hee-deeł
AR-across:ALL bridge on up-3PL.S:DH.PFV:Ø-PL.go:PFV
'They went across onto the bridge...'
UTOLVDN07Oct2602:013

35.2.1.3.2. da# (dh, aa) 'up, at an elevation' This prefix string derives many positional (942a) or classificatory (942b) themes in the neuter aspect.

(942) a. *Hǫǫ dits'oo' k'it dahdeltth'ih.* (T)
hǫǫ d-ts'oo' k'it da-hdel-tth'ih
thus REFL.PSR-spruce:POSS on up-3PL.S:QUAL:DH.PFV:L-PL.sit:IPV
'Thus they stayed up on their spruce.'
UTOLVDN13May2804:096

b. *Ch'ithüh nelgąy ditthi' k'e daheedlak...* (T)
ch'-thüh nel-gąy d-tthi'
INDF.PSR-skin 3PL.S:QUAL:DH.PFV:L-be.dry:IPV:NOM REFL.PSR-head
k'e da-hee-dlak
on up-3PL.S:DH.PFV:Ø-classify.PL.O:IPV:CUST
'They kept dried skins over their heads...'
UTOLAF09Jun2402:008

35.2.1.3.3. da+tl'a# (Ø, dh) 'up onto shore' This prefix string consists of the adverbial-derivational prefix *da-* 'up'- and the incorporate *tl'a-* 'buttocks; stern'; the whole prefix string is best translated as 'up onto the shore'. This prefix string is semantically similar to ki+tl'a# (Ø, aa) 'ashore' in 35.2.1.7.6. It derives a variety of motion themes in the momentaneous (943).

(943) a. *Datl'a'ahdeeł hǫǫ't'eey!* (T)
datl'a-ah-deeł hǫǫ't'eey
up.shore-Ø.IPV:2PL.S:Ø-PL.go:IPV still
'Come PL onto land anyway!' UTCBAF14Jul1804:018

b. *datl'a'eemįį* (T)
datl'a-ee-mįį
up.shore-3SG.S:DH.PFV:Ø-swim:PFV
'[the loon] swam up onto the shore'
UTOLVDN13May2907:107

35.2.1.3.4. k'i+da#, k'e+da# (?, dh) 'upon' K'i+da#, k'e+da# (?, dh) 'upon' consists of the adverbial-derivational prefix *k'e-* 'on' (likely a reduced form of the postposition P+*k'it* 'on P'; see 35.2.1.8) and the prefix *da-* 'up'. (944a, b) are the only two forms of this prefix string in the corpus; note, however, that they are semantically quite distinct. Both seem to be motion themes in the momentaneous.

(944) a. *jah ndee k'edahtaadał* (T)

jah *ndee* *k'eda-htaa-dał*
here where upon-3PL.S:INC:AA.IPV:Ø-PL.go:FUT
'somewhere where they can land' UTOLAF07Nov2602:006

b. ... *ch'idia' du' hǫǫsǫǫ tąy tah k'idadeltthät.* (N)

ch'-dia' *du'* *hǫǫ-sǫǫ* *tąy* *tah*
INDF.PSR-younger.sister CT AR.S:Ø.PFV:Ø-be.good:IPV trail on
k'ida-del-tthät
onto.trail-3SG.S:QUAL:DH.PFV:L-run:PFV
'... the younger sister ran onto the good trail.'
UTOLAF10Jul0202:023

35.2.1.4. *dzi-* 'dividing' The prefix *dzi-* is part of several prefix strings. Kari (1990, 175, 641) observes that the Ahtna cognate of this morpheme, *dzi-* 'over P (a barrier)', is a postposition. It is likely that the Upper Tanana morpheme originated as a postposition as well, given that it may occur with the reflex *s-* of the postpositional object prefix *nił-, łi-* (see 35.2.1.4.3). Aside from this, *dzi-* occurs without a postpositional object in Upper Tanana and it thus seems more appropriate to treat it as an adverbial-derivational prefix.

35.2.1.4.1. dzi# (?, ?) 'over edge' The prefix string dzi# (?, ?) 'over edge' derives motion themes in the momentaneous aspect. The only instance of this prefix string (945) is in the progressive superaspect, thus no information about conjugation markers is available.

(945) ... *tl'uuł Tsǫǫ Kelahdzeey dzinaałuu.* (T)

tl'uuł *Tsǫǫ* *Kelahdzeey*
rope grandmother spider
dzi-naa-łuu
over.edge-3SG.S:QUAL:AA.IPV:Ø-pull:IPV:PROG
'... Grandmother Spider was pulling the rope over the edge.'
UTCBAF13Nov0501:343

35.2.1.4.2. dzi+na# (Ø, aa) 'down over edge' The prefix string dzi+na# (Ø, aa) 'down over edge' also contains the adverbial-derivational prefix *na-* 'down' (see 35.2.1.11.2). It derives motion themes in the momentaneous (946).

(946) a. *dzina'įljiyh!* (T)
dzina-įl-jiyh
down.over.edge-ø.IPV:2SG.S:L-slide:IPV
'slide SG down!' UT Notebook #5, 85

b. *Tuu dzina'įįłąy dänh noshyign' tah dzina'altth'ät.* (N)
tuu *dzina-įį-łąy* *dänh*
water down.over.edge-3SG.S:AA.PFV:ø-flow:PFV:NOM at
no-shyign' *tah* *dzina-al-tth'ät*
MED:AR-down:ALL at down.over.edge-3SG.S:AA.PFV:L-fall:PFV
'She fell over the edge of the waterfall.' UTOLAF12Jul1201:040

(946b) also illustrates this prefix string in the extension verb theme dzi+na#Ø+łąy 'flow down over edge, be waterfall'.

35.2.1.4.3. sdzi# (Ø, dh) 'split, apart' The prefix string sdzi# (Ø, dh) 'split, apart' is related to the bound postposition P+*dzi-* 'split from P' (36.2.3). It is listed as *łdzi-* in Kari (1997b), where the *ł-* is the reduced form of the reciprocal object prefix *nił-*, *łi-*. In the speech of all speakers I have worked with, the prefix is pronounced with an initial [s]. Sdzi# (?, dh) 'split, apart' derives successive themes in the momentaneous aspect (947).

(947) a. *hǫǫsǫǫ sdzidįht'oh!* (T)
hǫǫsǫǫ *sdzi-dįh-t'oh*
well split-QUAL:ø.IPV:2SG.S:H-split.kindling:IPV
'split SG [the wood] well!' UT Notebook #5, 85

b. *hiiche' sdzi'eetthäl eh*
hii-che' *sdzi-ee-tthäl* *eh*
3SG.S>3PL.PSR-tail split-DH.PFV:ø-chop:PFV:NOM and
'he split all their tails [lengthwise]' ANLC4122a:032

35.2.1.4.4. sdzi# (Ø, aa) 'split' The prefix string sdzi# (Ø, aa) 'split' derives extension themes in the neuter aspect (948).

(948) *Tąy sdzihǫǫ'ah.* (N)
tąy sdzi-hǫǫ-'ah
trail split-AR.S:Ø.PFV:Ø-extend:IPV
'The trail forked.' UTOLAF15May0501:014

35.2.1.5. *ha-* 'up and out' The adverbial-derivational prefix *ha-* is part of two aspectual prefix strings.

35.2.1.5.1. ha# (Ø, aa) 'up and out, out from below' The prefix string ha# (Ø, aa) 'up and out' derives motion themes in the momentaneous. It describes vertical movement out of an enclosure, such as out of a bag (949a), out from underwater (949b), or out from the brush (949c). For horizontal movement out of an enclosure, see the prefix strings listed in 35.2.1.18.

(949) a. *haa'iltthiit!* (T)
ha-na-ıl-tthiit
out-IT-Ø.IPV:2SG.S:L-run:IPV
'run SG out [of the bag]!' UTOLAF09Jun2404:004

b. *Degn' haahatdeel eh...* (N)
degn' ha na hat-deel eh
up:ALL up-IT-3PL.S:AA.PFV:D-PL.go:PFV:NOM and
'They came back up and out [of the water] and...'
UTCBVDN13Nov1401:038

c. *diniign huttheh ha'atdät* (N)
diniign hu-ttheh ha-at-dät
moose 3PL.P-in.front out-3SG.S:AA.PFV:D-SG.animal.runs:PFV
'a moose jumped out in front of them'
UTOLAF13May2801:002

35.2.1.5.2. ha# (Ø, dh) 'off, into a pattern' The prefix string ha# (Ø, dh) 'off, into a pattern' applies to successive verb themes, but the derived themes are compatible with the imperfective mode (950a), which suggests that they are in the conclusive, rather than in the momentaneous aspect. (Most prefix strings that apply to successive verb themes derive verb themes in the momentaneous.)

(950) a. *kee haa'akt'üü* (N)
kee ha-na-ak-t'üü
slippers out-IT-Ø.IPV:1SG.S:H-cut:IPV
'I'm cutting out slippers' UTOLAF15Dec0704:024

b. *ch'itthįį' ts'ehteel ha'ehtsaat* (S)
ch'-tthįį' *ts'ehteel* *ha-eh-tsaat*
INDF.PSR-meat piece off-3SG.S:DH.PFV:H-slice:PFV
'he sliced off a piece of meat' ANLC4122a:102

35.2.1.6. *ha-* '?' There are a few instances of an adverbial-derivational prefix *ha-* with unclear meaning.

35.2.1.6.1. ha# (?, ?) 'turn around' It is impossible to determine the conjugation markers triggered by ha# 'turn around' based on the two examples found in the data: (951a) is in the negative perfective (which blocks the presence of a conjugation marker) and (951b) in the future, which requires an *aa-* imperfective. The theme in (951b) only occurs in this precise form (uttered identically by two different speakers), which makes it hard to identify the other components; the indefinite object prefix might refer to the speaker's eyes being moved toward the addressee, but this is by no means certain.

(951) a. *k'at'eey hahniidal* (T)
k'at'eey *ha-hnii-dal*
NEG turn-3PL.S:QUAL:NEG.PFV:Ø-PL.move:PFV:NEG
'they did not turn around' UTOLVDN07Oct2602:014

b. *nts'ą' hachakthak!* (T)
n-ts'ą' *ha-chak-thak*
2SG.P-toward turn-INDF.O:INC:AA.IPV:1SG.S:H-move.quickly:FUT
'I'm going to turn and look at you' UTOLAF08Apr2805:075

35.2.1.7. *ki-* 'against, up' The adverbial-derivational prefix *ki-* 'against, up' is part of several prefix strings.

35.2.1.7.1. ki# (Ø, aa) 'up, climbing' Ki# (Ø, aa) 'up, climbing' derives motion themes in the momentaneous (952). It is very productive.

(952) a. *Maa ki'įįhaay!* (N)
m-aa *ki-įį-haay*
3SG.P-for up-Ø.IPV:2SG.S:Ø-SG.go:IPV:IMP
'Climb up [the tree] for [the eggs]!'
UTOLVDN07Aug2205:010

b. *Ay eh mbaa ki'ihshyah...* (N)

ay eh mb-aa ki-ih-shyah

and and 3SG.P-for up-AA.PFV:1SG.S:ø-SG.go:PFV

'And I climbed up [the tree] for it...'

UTOLVDN07Aug2205:011

35.2.1.7.2. ski# (n, n) 'across' This prefix string consists of *ki-* 'against' plus a reduced form *s-* of the reciprocal prefix *nił-*, *łi-*. Minoura (1994) and Kari (1997b) both cite the form of this prefix as *łki-*, *łke-*, but in my own data, only [ski]- and [ske]- are attested. Looking at the form *łke-* in a transcript of a story told by the late Mr. Titus David (T), one Northway speaker commented that this was "Tetlin way," which suggests that this variant was used more recently there than in Northway.

One speaker consistently pronounces this prefix without the initial consonant, as illustrated in (953b). Ske#, ski#- (n, n) 'across' derives motion themes in the momentaneous and describes motion over bodies of water or across open spaces.

(953) a. *Ahnǫǫ nche' skinįįshyiił!* (N)

ah-nǫǫ n-che' ski-nįį-shyiił

NTRL-across:ABL 2SG.PSR-tail across-N.IPV:2SG.S:ø-extend:IPV

'From across extend your tail!' UTOLAF15May0501:099

b. *Naan' chinh k'it skinihshyah.* (N)

naan' chin k'it ski-nih-shyah

across:ALL flat on across-N.PFV:1SG.SØ-SG.go:PFV

'I walked across the flat.' UTOLAF15Dec0605:011

c. *iche' k'it t'eey kenįįshyah* (T)

i-che' k'it t'eey ske-nįį-shyah

3SG.S>3SG.PSR-tail on even across-N.PFV:ø-SG.go:PFV

'she crossed [the river] on his tail' UTCBAF13Nov0501:165

35.2.1.7.3. ski# (n, aa) 'across' In extension themes, ski# (n, aa) usually refers to water stretching out across the landscape, such as in the description of the ocean in (954). Again, one speaker does not pronounce the initial consonant.

(954) *Nithaad tah t'eey hutnah'iil tuu tüh tuu tüh ki̠nįį'ah nih.* (T)

nithaad *tah* *t'eey* *hu-tnah-'įįl* *tuu*
long.way among even AR.O-INC:QUAL:AA.IPV:2PL.S:H-see:FUT water

tüh *tuu* *tüh* *ski̠-nįį-'ah* *nih*
across water across across-3SG.S:N.PFV:Ø-extend:IPV say:IPV

'For a long way, as far as you can see, water extends all over, they say.'
UTOLVDN13May2909:049

35.2.1.7.4. sts'a+ke# (?, dh) 'around in a circle' The prefix string sts'a+ke# (?, dh) 'around in a circle' has somewhat obscure structure. It probably consists of the reduced form [s] of the reciprocal prefix *nił-* as well as of the prefix *ke-* 'against'. The origin of *ts'a-* is however unclear; it may be related to the free postposition P+*ts'ą̈'* 'to P'.

This prefix string is only attested in the Tetlin dialect in the speech of the late Mrs. Cora H. David. It derives reversative motion themes. The only imperfective form of this prefix string in (955a) is in the progressive (which requires the *aa-* imperfective), so it is unclear which conjugation marker the prefix string usually requires in the imperfective.

(955) a. *Deeł hadogn sts'akenaat'ah…* (T)

deeł *ha-dogn*
crane NTRL-up:AR

sts'ake-naa-t'ah
around.circle-3SG.S:QUAL:AA.IPV:Ø-SG.fly:IPV:PROG

'The crane was circling above...' UTOLAF07Oct2512:020

b. *sts'akedeexał* (N)

sts'ake-dee-xał
around.circle-3SG.S:QUAL:DH.PFV:Ø-turn:PFV

'[the canoe] capsized' UTOLAF09Jun2902:027

Semantically this prefix string is similar to sna+ke# (?, ?) 'around in a circle' described in 35.2.1.10.3.

35.2.1.7.5. ki+tl'a# (?, dh) 'to shore' This prefix string consists of *ki̠-* 'against' and the incorporate *tl'a-* 'buttocks, stern'. It derives motion themes in the momentaneous aspect. It seems to convey the meaning 'to the shore' but not necessarily onto dry land. Only perfective forms are attested (956).

(956) *taamaagn ḵitl'aadhishkįį* (N)
taamaagn ḵitl'a-na-dhish-kįį
shore ashore-IT-DH.PFV:1SG.S:D-go.by.boat:PFV
'I canoed back toward the shore' UTOLAF15Dec0705:008

35.2.1.7.6. ki+tl'a# (Ø, aa) 'ashore' With (Ø, aa) conjugation markers, the same prefix string has the meaning 'ashore, onto dry land' (957).

(957) a. *ḵitl'ashahteey* (N)
ḵitl'a-sh-ah-teey
ashore-1SG.O-Ø.IPV:2PL.S:H-handle.AO:IPV:IMP
'take SG me ashore' UTCBAF14May2001:004

b. *ketl'a'įįshyah* (T)
ḵitl'a-įį-shyah
ashore-3SG.S:AA.PFV:Ø-SG.go:PFV
'he got onto land' Commentary on UTOLVDN13May2801:169

35.2.1.7.7. ti+ki# (?, aa) 'off trail' The prefix string ti+ki# (?, aa) 'off the trail' is discussed in 35.2.1.18.2 below.

35.2.1.7.8. *he-* (Ø, n) 'against' The prefix string *he-* (Ø, n) 'against' is attested only in the Tetlin dialect. I include it under the prefix strings formed with *ke*, *ḵi-* 'against, up' because the verb theme he+kon'#Ø+shyiił 'put firebrand against' in (958) is clearly cognate to the Ahtna verb theme ke+kon'#G+Ø+yeł with the same meaning (Kari 1990, 435), even though the onset consonant /h/ for the adverbial-derivational prefix is unexpected.[2]

(958) a. *hekon'dahshyiił!* (T)
he-kon'-dah-shyiił
against-fire-QUAL:Ø.IPV:2PL.S:Ø-move.LRO.rapidly:IPV
'set PL fire to it!' UTOLAF17Aug1009:020

b. *hekon'nįįshyiił.* (T)
he-kon'-nįį-shyiił
against-fire-3SG.S:N.PFV:Ø-move.LRO.rapidly:PFV
'he set fire to it [using a firebrand]' UTOLVDN13May2803:081

35.2.1.8. *k'i-* 'on' The semantics of this prefix are not entirely clear. The grouping here follows Kari (1990, 255), who suggests that more than one root may be represented.

35.2.1.8.1. k'i# (?, n) 'to the trail' The prefix string k'i# (?, n) seems to have the meaning 'to the trail'. It derives a motion theme in the momentaneous. There is only one example of this prefix string in the data (959).

(959) *Tąy hǫǫteeł niign k'iits'indeel eh…* (N)
tąy hǫǫteeł niign k'i-na-ts'in-deel eh
highway to.trail-IT-1PL.S:N.PFV:D-PL.go:PFV:NOM and
'When we got back to the highway…' UTOLVDN10Jul2724:111

35.2.1.8.2. k'e# (Ø, aa) 'along the trail' This prefix string is also attested with (Ø, aa) conjugation markers (960). The resulting verb theme is again in the momentaneous. It is unclear whether there is a semantic difference to k'i# (?, n).

(960) a. *Du'an' tąy tah k'e'įįhaay!* (T)
du-'an' tąy tah k'e-įį-haay
PROX:AR-OUT:ALL trail among on-Ø.IPV:2SG.S:Ø-SG.go:IPV:IMP
'Go SG here onto this trail!' UT Notebook #5, 85

b. *Ay iin ch'ale ch'a tąy k'ehįįdeeł dänh tąy hǫǫteeł.* (N)
ay iin ch'ale ch'a tąy k'e-hįį-deeł dänh tąy
3 PL FOC FOC trail on-3PL.S:AA.PFV:Ø-PL.go:PFV at trail
hǫǫ-teeł
AR.S:Ø.PFV:Ø-be.wide:IPV
'And the trail they were walking on was a wide trail.'
UTOLAF15May0501:011

35.2.1.8.3. ti+k'i# (?, aa) 'onto the trail' Somewhat more common than k'e# (?, n) in 35.2.1.8.1 is the prefix string ti+k'i# (?, aa) 'onto the trail', which additionally contains the prefix *ti-*, an adverbial prefix related to the noun stem *tąy* 'trail' (see 35.2.1.18 for other uses). Ti+k'i# (?, aa) derives motion themes in the momentaneous. The conjugation marker in the imperfective required by this prefix string is unclear, since the Ø-imperfective in (961a) is caused by the customary superaspect.

(961) a. *tik'iiyet-łuuk* (T)
tik'i-na-y-et-łuuk
onto.trail-IT-3SG.S>3SG.O-Ø.IPV:D-drag:IPV:CUST
'she dragged her back onto the trail'
UTOLVDN14Nov2301:168

b. *tąy choh tik'ihįįdeeł* (T)
tąy choh tik'i-hįį-deeł
trail large onto.trail-3PL.S:AA.PFV:Ø-PL.go:PFV
'they went onto the wide trail' UTCBVDN13Nov1101:038

35.2.1.8.4. nił+k'i# (Ø, dh) 'back and forth' The prefix string nił+k'i# (Ø, dh) 'back and forth' derives from the (free) postposition P+*k'eh* 'like P, following P' (see chap. 15.2.1.8) inflected for reciprocal object. It may also be related to the bound postposition P+*k'e-* 'trading with P' described in chap. 36.2.6. There are only a handful of forms derived with this prefix string, but they differ considerably in semantics. (962a) illustrates the variant pronunciation *sk'e-*.

(962) a. *Nan' neet'aat sk'e'eljii.* (T)
nun' nee-t'aat sk'e-el-jii
earth 1PL.P-under back.forth-3SG.S:Ø.IPV:L-slide:IPV
'The earth was sliding back and forth underneath us.'
UTOLVDN07Nov2802:005

b. *Laalil hǫǫ't'eey niłk'inaat'ay…* (T)
laalil hǫǫ't'eey
butterfly still
niłk'i-naa-t'ay
back.forth-3SG.S:QUAL:AA.IPV:Ø-SG.fly:IPV:PROG:NOM
'The butterfly, still fluttering back and forth…'
UTCBAF13Nov0501:036

35.2.1.9. *k'i-* 'by the wayside' This prefix is attested in only one prefix string. It is likely cognate with the Koyukon adverb *kk'eł* 'away, discarding, by the wayside' (Jetté and Jones 2000, 356).

35.2.1.9.1. k'e# (?, dh?) 'by the wayside' There is only one instance of this prefix string (963). Speakers suggested the translation given below as the most accurate but commented that the meaning is more like "have fallen into the wrong teachings." This verb may be a *dh-* perfective or a Ø-imperfective, possibly in the customary superaspect.

(963) *Hunąą in hutsǫǫ iin k'iheltth'ek...* (N)

hu-nąą	*iin*	*hu-tsǫǫ*	*iin*
3PL.PSR-mother	PL	3PL.PSR-grandmother	PL

k'i-hel-tth'ek
wayside-3PL.S:DH.PFV?:L-fall:PFV
'Their mothers and grandmothers have fallen by the wayside...'
UTOLAF12Jul1203:074

35.2.1.10. *na-* 'iterative' The iterative morpheme is part of several aspectual prefix strings described below. The non-aspectual iterative derivation is discussed in chap. 34.

35.2.1.10.1. na#t+D (aa, n), łoo#(t) (aa, n) 'perambulative' The prefix string na#t+D, łoo#(t) is referred to as the perambulative. It requires (aa, n) conjugation markers and has its own aspectual stem variation (see chap. 26.2.1.7). Its semantics is described in volume 2.

Kari (1990, 292) states that in Ahtna, the string na#t+D is used in the imperfective and łoo# in the other modes, but in Upper Tanana, as well as in Tanacross (Holton 2000, 261), the distribution is less straightforward. Both prefix strings occur in the imperfective (964a, 965a), the imperfective customary (964b, 965b), and the future (964c, 965c), without a difference in meaning. In the perfective (965d), however, only the prefix string łoo# is permitted; there is no example of the perambulative string na#t+D in the perfective mode in the whole corpus. This may be due to the fact that na#t+D in the perfective would be homophonous with iterative inceptive perfective forms such as *natetshyah* 'he started to go back'). In the optative, only na#t+D is used (964d).

The inceptive prefix is present in all perambulative forms formed with *na-* apart from the imperfective (964a), which would otherwise be indistinguishable from the future. In perambulative forms formed with *łoo-*, the inceptive prefix is only used in the imperfective customary (965c).

(964) a. *Shttheh tah nahatkeeł.* (N)

sh-ttheh	*tah*	*na-hat-keeł*
1SG.P-in.front	amont	PRMB-3PL.S:AA.IPV:D-go.by.boat:IPV

'They were paddling about in front of me.'
UTOLVDN07Aug2205:104

b. *hu'eł natsetdak* (T)
hu-eł *na-tset-dak*
3PL.P-with PRMB-1PL.S:INC:Ø.IPV:D-PL.go:IPV:CUST
'we would walk around with them' UTOLAF09Jun2902:004

c. *Tthitu' Niign t'eey natsatkeeł!* (N)
Tthitu' Niign *t'eey* *na-tsat-keeł*
Chisana River even PRMB-1PL.S:INC:AA.IPV:D-go.by.boat:FUT
'Let's paddle around on the Chisana River!'
UTOLVDN07Aug2205:086

d. *Adogn natuhdaak...* (N)
a-dogn *na-tuh-daak*
NTRL-up:AR PRMB-INC:OPT:1SG.S-D:SG.go:OPT:CUST
'I want to walk around up there...' UTOLAF13May2804:051

(965) a. *Nan ch'ale łoo'įhtįįl!* (T)
nan *ch'ale* *łoo-įh-tįįl*
2SG FOC PRMB-AA.IPV:2SG.S:H-classify.LRO:IPV:NOM
'You are the one carrying [that knife] around!'
UTOLVDN13May2804:074

b. *Dinąą iin eł łoohtedak duugn.* (T)
d-nąą *iin* *eł* *łoo-hte-dak*
REFL.PSR-mother PL with PRMB-3PL.S:INC:Ø.IPV:Ø-PL.go:IPV:CUST
duugn
everywhere
'They used to go around everywhere with their parents.'
UTCBAF13Nov0501:020

c. *dits'ayy' łootaatįįł* (N)
d-ts'ayy' *łoo-taa-tįįł*
REFL.PSR-boat:POSS PRMB-3SG.S:INC:AA.IPV:Ø-handle.LRO:FUT
'she can carry around her own canoe'
UTOLVDN07Aug2205:037

d. *nee'eh łoonįįshyah* (N)
nee-eh *łoo-nįį-shyah*
1PL.P-with PRMB-3SG.S:N.PFV:Ø-SG.go:PFV
'she walked around with us' UTOLVDN13May2003:012

Note that the two prefix strings also differ in their effect on the voice/valence prefix; while na#t+D always changes the voice/valence prefix to D-, łoo#(t) never does. (The same fact is reported by Holton [2000, 191] for Tanacross.)

35.2.1.10.2. na+ke#(d) (Ø, dh) 'around and back, around and over' The prefix string na+ke#(d) (Ø, dh) 'around and back, around and over' is composed of the adverbial-derivational prefix *na-* 'around', *ke-* 'against, up', and, in some forms, the *d-* qualifier. It is not entirely clear what drives the presence or absence of the qualifier.

Na+ke#(d) (Ø, dh) 'around and back, around and over' derives motion themes in the reversative aspect, which has its own stem variation pattern (see chap. 26.2.1.9). The *na*-prefix in this prefix clearly is adverbial-derivational as can be seen from its position preceding another adverbial-derivational prefix.

The conjugation markers required by this prefix string can be seen in the elicited forms (966a, b); the naturally occurring forms of this prefix string (966c, d) all contain additional morphology obscuring the conjugation markers. They are included here to illustrate the semantic range of this prefix string.

(966) a. *Łiat gąy nakidaknayh.* (N)
łiat gąy naki-dak-nayh
pancake around.over-QUAL:Ø.IPV:1SG.S:H-move.CO.quickly:IPV
'I'm flipping pancakes.' UTOLAF15Dec0705:035

b. *Łiat gąy nakididhaknayh.* (N)
łiat gąy naki-didhak-nayh
pancake around.over-QUAL:DH.PFV:1SG.S:H-move.CO.quickly:PFV
'I flipped a pancake.' UTOLAF15Dec0705:034

c. *nakitdetdät* (N)
naki-tdet-dät
around.back-3SG.S:INC:QUAL:DH.PFV:D-animal.runs:PFV
'he turned around and ran off' UTOLVDN13May2004:088

d. *Ay eh k'ahjil sheh nakecheexał.* (N)
ay eh k'ahjil sh-eh
and and almost 1SG.P-with
nake-chee-xał
around.over-INDF:INC:DH.PFV:Ø-LRO.moves.quickly:PFV
'And [the canoe] almost turned over with me.'
UTOLVDN07Aug2205:100

Kari (1990, 292) observes that in Ahtna the prefix string na+ke#(d) 'around and over' often triggers the same voice/valence prefix changes as the iterative derivation; this does not appear to be the case in Upper Tanana.

35.2.1.10.3. sna+ke# (?, ?) 'around in a circle' This prefix string is similar to na+ke#(d) (Ø, dh) 'around and back' but additionally contains a reduced form *s-* of the reciprocal object prefix *niɬ-*. (967) is in the progressive, which requires an *aa-* imperfective. This makes it impossible to determine its regular conjugation pattern. (967) is the only form containing this prefix string.

(967) *Yaanoo yaamaagn nts'ą̈' snake'aahaaɬ...* (S)

yaa-noo *y-aamaagn* *nts'ą̈'*
DSTL-ahead:ALL 3SG.P-around.shore and

snake-aa-haaɬ
around.circle-3SG.S:AA.IPV:Ø-SG.go:IPV

'He went a long way, all around the lakeshore...' ANLC4122a:071

35.2.1.11. *na-* 'down' The adverbial-derivational prefix *na-* 'down' is not related to the iterative prefix. It is involved in several prefix strings.

35.2.1.11.1. na# (Ø, aa) 'down' The very productive prefix string na# (Ø, aa) 'down' derives motion themes in the momentaneous (968).

(968) a. *naa'įįdaay!* (N)

na-na-įį-daay
down-IT-Ø.IPV:2SG.S-D:SG.go:IPV:IMP

'come SG back down!' UT Notebook #6, 15

b. *ts'ant'ay na'al'uuk* (T)

ts'ant'ay na-al-'uuk
devil down-3SG.S:AA.PFV:L-fall.in.pieces:PFV

'the devil fell down in pieces' UTCBAF13Nov0501:257

35.2.1.11.2. na# (dh, aa) 'down' Na# (dh, aa) 'down' is also attested in an extension theme (969).

(969) ... *tsugaay iin na'eet'ayh.* (T)

tsugaay iin na-ee-t'ayh
bird PL down-3PL.S:DH.PFV:Ø-hang:IPV

'... the birds were hanging there.' UTOLAF09Jun2202:026

35.2.1.12. *ni*- 'terminative' The terminative prefix *ni*- derives motion themes and extension themes.

35.2.1.12.1. ni# (n, n) 'to a point, stopping' Ni# derives motion themes in the momentaneous aspect. It is usually glossed as 'TERM' for *terminative* and is a very productive prefix string (970).

(970) a. *tthee shyign' ninįį'aayh* (N)
tthee shyign' ni-nįį-'aayh
rock down TERM-N.IPV:2SG.S:Ø-handle.CO:IPV
'put SG the rock down' UTCBAF14Jun0902:004

b. *Łigaay thiin tl'uuł ninįįdlah...* (T)
łigaay thiin tl'uul ni-nįį-dlah
puppy neck rope TERM-3SG.S:N.PFV:Ø-handle.rope:PFV
'He put a rope around the puppy's neck...'
UTOLAF09Jun2202:020

35.2.1.12.2. ni# (n, aa) 'to a point, stopping' Ni# (n, aa) 'to a point, stopping' also derives extension themes in the neuter aspect (971).

(971) a. *jah nts'ą̈' utsįį ninįį'ah* (N)
jah nts'ą̈' u-tsįį ni-nįį-'ah
here to 3SG.PSR-scent TERM-3SG.S:N.PFV:Ø-extend:IPV
'her scent extends up to here' UTOLAF15May0501:158

b. *taathüh ni'įh'aay* (N)
taadhüh ni-įh-'aay
tent TERM-3SG.S:AA.PFV:H-extend:PFV:NOM
'a tent someone had there' UTOLAF15May0501:134

35.2.1.12.3. ni# (i, i), ni# (Ø, dh) 'up vertically' The prefix string ni# (i, i), ni# (Ø, dh) 'up vertically' derives motion themes in the momentaneous aspect.

(972b, c) demonstrate that there is some uncertainty regarding the formation of the perfective. (972b), produced by a Tetlin speaker, seems to contain a *dh*- perfective; (972c), by a speaker from Northway, an *i*-perfective. This reanalysis of the *i*-modes appears to be a general tendency in the Tetlin dialect; see chap. 29.2.5. Note that it is impossible to determine whether the form in (972a) has an *i*-imperfective or a Ø-imperfective.

(972) a. *Ni'įįhaay!* (N)
ni-įį-haay
up-?.IPV:2SG.S:Ø-SG.go:IPV:IMP
'Get SG up, stand SG up!' UTOLAF15Dec0705:025

b. *Yambaa Teeshyaay nidehtįį...* (T)
Yambaa Teeshyaay ni-deh-tįį
Yambaa Teeshyaay up-3SG.S:QUAL:DH.PFV:H-handle.AO:PFV
'He lifted up Yambaa Teeshyaay...' UTOLVDN13May2804:046

c. *Niydi'ąą...* (N)
ni-y-di-'ąą
up-3SG.S>3SG.O-QUAL:I.PFV:Ø-handle.CO:PFV
'She lifted [the rock]...' UTOLAF15May0501:201

This prefix is also part of the prefix string ni+k'i#hu+d 'figure out' discussed in 35.2.2.5.3.

35.2.1.13. *taa-* 'down' This prefix is attested in only one prefix string.

35.2.1.13.1. taa# (?, n) 'down' Both instances of this prefix string have to do with taking down trees (973). No imperfective forms are attested.

(973) a. *Ts'oo įį'eh tat'eey taachehxüüt...* (T)
ts'oo įį'eh tah taa-cheh-xüüt
spruce etc. down-INDF.O:3SG.S:INC:DH.PFV:H-pull:PFV
'He pulled down spruce...' UTOLVDN13May2803:089

b. *ts'oo taanįįttheel* (N)
ts'oo taa-nįį-ttheel
spruce down-3SG.S:N.PFV:Ø-chop:PFV:NOM
'he chopped down spruce' UTOLVDN13May2003:031

35.2.1.14. *ta-* 'off to the side' *Ta-* 'off to the side' occurs in several prefix strings.

35.2.1.14.1. ta#t+n (?, dh) 'off to the side' The prefix string ta#t+n (?, dh) 'off to the side' is by itself attested only in a few forms (974). It requires the *dh-* perfective which may however be due to the presence of the *t-* inceptive prefix; no imperfective form including this prefix string is attested.

(974) a. *k'ąy' t'eey tah nde' tatneetsak* (T)

k'ąy' *t'eey* *tah* *nde'*
willow even among upstream:ALL

ta-tnee-tsak
off.to.side-3PL.S:INC:QUAL:DH.PFV:Ø-twist:PFV

'they twisted willow [branches] off to the side in the upstream direction' UTOLVDN07Oct2602:020

b. *tsa' k'įįy taatneldeeł* (N)

tsa' *k'įįy* *ta-na-tnel-deeł*
beaver birch off.to.side-IT-3SG.S:INC:QUAL:DH.PFV:L-eat.PL.O:PFV

'the beaver is chewing on birch' UTOLAF14Nov2203:008

35.2.1.14.2. sta# 'away' (n, n) This prefix string consists of the prefix *ta-* 'off to the side' discussed in 35.2.1.14 plus the reduced form *s-* of the reciprocal prefix *nił-*, *łi-*, which assimilates to [s]. It derives motion themes in the momentaneous aspect and is very productive. One speaker pronounces this prefix consistently as [tʰa], without the initial [s] (975c).

(975) a. *An staanįįdaay!* (T)

an *sta-na-nįį-daay*
out:ALL away-IT-N.IPV:2SG.S-D:SG.go:IPV:IMP

'Out, go SG away again!' UTOLAF08Apr2805:074

b. *Dogn stanįįshyah.* (T)

dogn *sta-nįį-shyah*
up:AR away-3SG.S:N.PFV:Ø-SG.go:PFV

'He went up [into the moon].' UTOLAF09Jun2202:032

c. *Ch'its'anh ta'įlch'ee.* (T)

ch'its'anh *sta-įl-ch'ee*
different.place away-3SG.S:N.PFV:L-go.in.anger:PFV

'He walked away in anger to a different place.' UTOLVDN13May2901:046

Sta# 'away' (n, n) can also be used metaphorically (976). These themes are not fully understood at this time.

(976) a. *staniinishthiit* (N)

sta-nii-nish-thiit

away-mind-N.PFV:1SG.S:D-be.depressed:IPV

'I'm depressed, worried' UT Notebook #4, 47

b. *hu'eh stadoodnįį'ąą* (N)

hu-eh *sta-da-ho-dnįį-'ąą*

3PL.P-to away-mouth-3SG.S:AR-QUAL:N.PFV:ø-handle.CO:PFV

'he exaggerated to them' UTOLVDN10Jul2703:008

35.2.1.15. *ta-* 'among' The adverbial-derivational prefix *ta-* (Ø, aa) 'among' is related to the free postposition P+*tah* 'among P'. It is part of only one prefix string.

35.2.1.15.1. ta# (Ø, aa) 'distribute' This prefix string is attested in only one verb theme ta#O+Ø+łe' 'give out (potlatch) gifts'. The stem variation pattern (chap. 26.2.2.3) suggests that this verb theme only occurs in the distributive superaspect (977).

(977) a. *Jah ahshyuugn ch'il tats'ełe'...* (T)

jah *ah-shyuugn* *ch'il*

here NTRL-down:AR cloths

ta-ts'eh-łe'

distribute-1PL.S:ø.IPV:H-handle.PL.O:IPV:DSTR

'We are distributing potlatch gifts down there...'

UTOLAF08Apr2804:014

b. *All k'ahdąądą' shyiit all dindeey iin tach'įįdlah.* (T)

all *k'ahdąądą'* *shyiit* *all* *dindeey* *iin*

all yesterday then all people PL

ta-ch'įį-dlah

distribute-INDF.O:3SG.S:AA.PFV:ø-handle.PL.O:PFV:DSTR

'Yesterday, he passed out all [the potlatch gifts] to people.'

UTCBVDN13Nov1502:032

35.2.1.16. *ta-* 'into the water' This prefix is historically related to the noun stem *tuu* 'water'. It occurs in several prefix strings.

35.2.1.16.1. ta# (Ø, aa) 'into the water' The prefix string ta# (Ø, aa) 'into the water' derives motion themes in the momentaneous aspect. It can also be used when the movement is directed into a liquid other than water (978c).

(978) a. *tach'et'oh* (T)
ta-ch'e-t'oh
into.water-INDF.O:3SG.S:Ø.IPV:Ø-paddle:IPV
'he is paddling' UTOLAF09Jun2902:010

b. *Ts'ayh slough gaay tats'įįtąą.* (N)
ts'ayh slough gaay ta-ts'įį-tąą
boat slough little into.water-1PL.S:AA.PFV:Ø-classify.LRO:PFV
'We put the boat into a little slough.'
UTOLVDN07Aug2205:040

c. … *xee shyiit tats'ełeeg…* (T)
xee shyiit ta-ts'e-łeeg
grease into into.water-1PL.S:Ø.IPV:Ø-classify.PL.O:IPV:CUST:NOM
'… we put [braided pieces of canvas] into grease…'
UTOLVDN07Nov2802:010

35.2.1.16.2. ta# (?, ?) 'upland' This prefix string is related to ta# 'into the water' discussed in 35.2.1.16 (Kari 1990, 324). It derives motion themes in the momentaneous aspect. From the available data in (979), the conjugation markers required by this prefix string cannot be determined, as both forms are in the inceptive perfective and thus require a *dh-* conjugation marker.

(979) a. *taatetshyah* (N)
ta-na-tet-shyah
upland-IT-3SG.S:INC:DH.PFV:D-SG.go:PFV
'she started back upland' UTOLAF12Jul1201:044

b. *nahne' tanatidhagtthat* (T)
nah-ne' ta-na-tidhag-tthat
MED-upstream:ALL upland-IT-INC:DH.PFV:1SG.S:L-run:PFV
'I ran back upstream' UTOLAF09Jun2201:015

35.2.1.16.3. ta# (Ø, aa) 'upland' Ta# (Ø, aa) also derives extension themes in the neuter aspect (980).

(980) *łat ta'įį'ah* (T)
łat ta-įį-'ah
smoke upland-3SG.S:Ø.IPV:Ø-extend:IPV
'smoke extended upland' UTOLAF07Nov2602:010

35.2.1.17. *ti*- 'submerged in water, underwater' The adverbial-derivational prefix is related to the prefix *ta*- 'into water' discussed in 35.2.1.16. It is part of several prefix strings.

35.2.1.17.1. ti# (Ø, n) 'underwater' Ti# (Ø, n) 'underwater' derives a variety of motion themes in the momentaneous aspect (981).

(981) a. *ti'įįhaayh!* (T)
ti-įį-haayh
underwater-ø.IPV:2SG.S:ø-SG.go:IPV
'go SG into the water!' UT Notebook #5,86

b. *tinįįłaat* (T)
ti-nįį-łaat
underwater-3SG.S:N.PFV:ø-sink:PFV
'[the boat] sank' UTOLAF09Jun2902:011

Ti- 'submerged, underwater' is semantically similar to *ta*- 'into the water' discussed in 35.2.1.16. Possibly *ti*- requires total submersion whereas *ta*- does not, but the exact difference between the morphemes and their associated prefix strings remains unclear, and they occur in the same verb themes with the same meaning (982, 983). It is thus likely that there is some degree of overlap between the two prefixes.

(982) a. *Tuu shyiit tatagnttth'äł.* (N)
tuu shyiit ta-tagn-tth'äł
water in into.water-INC:AA.IPV:1SG.S:L-fall:FUT
'I'm going to fall into the water.' UTOLAF12Jul1201:018

b. *tinagntth'at* (T)
ti-nagn-tth'at
underwater-N.PFV:1SG.S:L-fall:PFV
'I fell into the water' UTOLAF09Jun2902:027

(983) a. *taa'etdüh* (S)
ta-na-et-düh
into.water-IT-3SG.S:ø.IPV:D-dive:IPV
'[the fish] dove underwater again' Tyone (1996, 40)

b. *ti'indät* (N)
ti-in-dät
underwater-3SG.S:N.PFV:D-dive:PFV
'[a bird] dove underwater' UTCBVDN13Nov1401:045

35.2.1.17.2. ti# (dh, aa) 'underwater' Ti# (dh, aa) 'underwater' is used to derive neuter themes that require the *dh-* conjugation prefix in the imperfective (984).

(984) *üh ti'ehtąą* (S)
üh ti-eh-tąą
dipnet underwater-3SG.S:DH.PFV:H-classify.LRO:PFV
'he held the dipnet under water' ANLC4122a:145

35.2.1.18. *ti-* 'out of enclosure, out into the open' The prefix *ti-* 'out of enclosure, out into the open' occurs in a number of prefix strings.

35.2.1.18.1. ti# (n, n) 'out into the open' The prefix string ti# (n, n) derives motion themes in the momentaneous (985). It is very productive.

(985) a. *tinįltthiit!* (T)
ti-nįl-tthiit
out-N.IPV:2SG.S:L-run:IPV
'run SG out!' UTOLAF08Apr2805:079

b. *u'aat tiich'inįl'įį ich'a'* (T)
u-'aat ti-na-ch'-nįl-'įį'
3SG.PSR-wife out-IT-INDF.O-3SG.S:N.PFV:L-sneak:PFV
i-ch'a'
3SG.S>3SG.O-from
'his wife sneaked out away from him again'
UTOLVDN13May2907:053

35.2.1.18.2. ti+ki# (Ø, aa) 'off the trail' Ti+ki# (Ø, aa) 'off the trail' consists of *ti-* 'out into the open' and *ke-* 'against', discussed in 35.2.1.7. It derives motion themes in the momentaneous (986).

(986) a. *tiki'įįhaay!* (T)
tiki-įį-haay
off.trail-ø.IPV:2SG.S:ø-SG.go:IPV:IMP
'turn SG off the trail!' UT Notebook #5, 85

b. *tiki'atdät* (N)
tiki-at-dät
off.trail-3SG.S:AA.PFV:D-animal.run:PFV
'[the bear] turned off the trail' UTOLVDN13May2004:105

35.2.1.19. *t'a-* 'under, out and down' This prefix occurs in several prefix strings. It is possible that several different prefixes are involved.

35.2.1.19.1. t'a# (Ø, aa) 'under, out and down' T'a# (Ø, aa) 'under, out and down' derives motion themes in the momentaneous aspect. (987c) does not describe a regular sunset, but instead an occasion where the sun disappeared during an earthquake.

(987) a. *utth'an' dah'ogn t'a'įįłeey* (T)
u-tth'an' dah-'ogn t'a-įį-łeey
3SG.PSR-bone PROX-out:AR out ø.IPV:2SG.S:ø-handle.PL.O:IPV:IMP
'plant SG his bones outside' UTCBAF13Nov0501:262

b. *t'a'akdeeł* (N)
t'a-ak-deeł
down-AA.PFV:1SG.S:H-handle.PL.O:PFV
'I threw [the eggs] out and down' UTOLVDN07Aug2205:018

c. *saa chih t'a'įį'ah* (T)
saa chih t'a-įį-'ah
sun too under-3SG.S:AA.PFV:ø-classify:CO:PFV
'the sun, too, went under' UTOLVDN07Nov2802:007

35.2.1.19.2. t'a# (Ø, aa) '?' There are some examples of the prefix string t'a# (Ø, aa) with uncertain meaning (988).

(988) a. *t'aatthiihiiyetthak* (T)
t'a-na-tthii-hiiy-e-tthak
?-IT-rock-3SG.S>3SG.O-ø:.IPV:ø-move.quickly:IPV:CUST
'they kept throwing it like a rock in the air'
UTOLAF07Oct2512:007

b. *dikąy' t'a'įhxał* (T)
d-kąy' *t'a-įh-xał*
REFL.PSR-husband ?-3S.AA.PFV:H-turn:PFV
'she turned away from her husband'
UTOLVDN13May2907:044

c. *t'aneltth'ät* (S)
t'a-nil-tth'ät
?-3SG.S:N.PFV:L-fall:PFV
'he fell over backward' Tyone (1996, 40)

It is not even clear whether the *t'a-* prefix in these examples is identical to the one discussed above. Note that (988c) uses the *n-* conjugation prefix in the perfective, which suggests that there is also a semantic difference. There are, however, too few examples to understand the semantics of this prefix string.

35.2.1.19.3. s+t'a# (Ø, aa) 'up?' S+t'a# (Ø, aa) '?' is attested only in the verb theme st'a#ch'+H+düh 'inanimate jumps, jerks up'. It may be related to *t'a-* discussed in 35.2.1.19 or to the postposition P+*t'a-* 'snagging on P' described in chap. 36.2.11. In either case the [s] likely derives from the reciprocal prefix *nił-*, *ł-*. The theme category of the verb theme in (989) is unclear; possibly this is a successive theme.

(989) a. *uche' chįį' st'ach'ehdüh* (S)
u-che' *chįį'* *st'a-ch'eh-düh*
3SG.PSR-tail tip:POSS up?-INDF.O:3SG.S:Ø.IPV:H-twist:IPV
'the tip of his tail jumped up' ANLC4122a-024

b. *uche' chįį' st'aach'įhdät* (S)
u-che' *chįį'* *st'a-na-ch'įh-dät*
3SG.PSR-tail tip:POSS up?-IT-INDF.O:3SG.S:AA.PFV:H-twist:PFV
'the tip of his tail jumped up again' ANLC4122a-027

35.2.1.20. *tth'a-* 'out and away' *Tth'a-* 'out and away' is part of one prefix string.

35.2.1.20.1. tth'a# (Ø, aa) 'out and away' Tth'a# (Ø, aa) derives motion themes in the momentaneous (990).

(990) a. *tth'a'įhdeeł!* (N)
tth'a-įh-deeł
away.out-Ø.IPV:2SG.S:H-handle.PL.O:IPV
'throw SG them away!' UT Notebook #5, 82

b. *tth'a'akdeeł* (N)
tth'a-ak-deeł
away.out-AA.PFV:1SG.S:H-handle.PL.O:PFV
'I threw them away' UT Notebook #5, 82

35.2.1.21. *tthi-* 'into the fire, into the open' *Tthi-* 'into the fire, into the open' is part of several prefix strings. The surprisingly common conflation of terms for 'toward the fire' and 'out into the open (sea)' in languages of the Pacific Rim has been commented on by Fortescue (2011).

35.2.1.21.1. tthi#d (Ø, aa) 'into the fire, into the open' The prefix string tthi#d (Ø, aa) 'into the fire' consists of the adverbial-derivational prefix *tthi-* 'into the fire' and the *d-* qualifier, which often refers to fire (see chap. 30.4.1.2). Note that the *d-* qualifier is present also with the meaning 'into the open' (991c). This prefix string derives motion themes in the momentaneous aspect (991).

(991) a. *hanoo' tthidįįkaayh* (N)
ha-noo'   *tthi-dįį-kaayh*
NTRL-toward.fire:ALL   into.fire-QUAL:Ø.IPV:2SG.S:Ø-handle.OOC:IPV
'put it in a bowl over the fire' UTOLAF10Jul0202:145

b. *kon'nia' tthiidįįtthayh* (T)
kon'nia'
middle.of.fire
tthi-y-dįį-tthayh
into.fire-3SG.S>3SG.O-QUAL:AA.PFV:Ø-move.LRO.quickly:PFV
'he stuck [the steel rod] into the middle of the fire'
UTOLAF08Apr2805:029

c. *Hahnoo' chinh k'it tthidzįįdeeł.* (N)
hah-noo'   *chinh*   *k'it*
NTRL-into.open:ALL   flat   on
tthi-dzįį-deeł
into.open-1PL.S:QUAL:AA.PFV:Ø-PL.go:PFV
'We came out onto a flat.' UTOLVDN13May2004:014

35.2.1.21.2. tthi# (n, n) 'out' Some speakers use the prefix string tthi# (n, n) 'out'. It is unclear what distinguishes this prefix string semantically from ti# (n, n) in 35.2.1.18.1 or from tthi#d (Ø, aa) in 35.2.1.21.1. Tthi# (n, n) 'out' derives motion themes in the momentaneous.

(992) a. *Än tthinįįhaay!* (N)

än *tthi-nįį-haay*
outside:ALL out-N.IPV:2SG.S:ø-SG.go:IPV:IMP
'Go SG outside!' UTOLAF15May0501:079

b. *Hah'än tthinįįshyah.* (N)

hah-'än *tthi-nįį-shyah*
NTRL-outside:ALL out-3SG.S:N.PFV:ø-SG.go:PFV
'She went outside.' UTOLAF15May0501:080

35.2.1.22. *tth'i-* 'straight out' *Tth'i-* 'straight out' is part of two prefix strings. This prefix also occurs in directional adverbs (see chap. 17.2.2.2).

35.2.1.22.1. tth'i# (Ø, dh) 'straight out' Tth'i# (Ø, dh) 'straight out' derives motion themes in the momentaneous (993).

(993) a. *ahnoo tah tth'idįhtthiiyh!* (T)

ah-noo *tah*
NTRL-ahead:ALL among
tth'i-dįh-tthiiyh
straight-ø.IPV:2SG.S:ø-move.LRO.quickly:IPV
'throw SG it way out!' UT Notebook #5, 86

b. *Ay saa eh tth'ineet'ak.* (N)

ay *saa* *eh* *tth'i-nee-t'ak*
and sun with straight-3SG.S:QUAL:DH.PFV:ø-SG.fly:PFV
'And he flew straight out with the sun.'
UTOLVDN10Jul2719:035

35.2.1.22.2. tth'i# (dh, aa) 'straight out' Tth'i# (dh, aa) 'straight out' derives positional themes in the neuter aspect (994).

(994) *tth'idhalt'ay (T)*

tth'i-dhal-t'ay
straight-DH.IPV:2PL.S:L-lie:IPV:IMP
'stretch yourselves out' UTCBAF13Nov0501:076

35.2.1.23. *ts'i-* 'wake' This prefix occurs in only one prefix string.

35.2.1.23.1. ts'i# (n, n) 'wake' This prefix string occurs in transitive and intransitive momentaneous themes to do with waking up, or waking up someone. The resulting themes are motion themes in the momentaneous aspect (995).

(995) a. *ts'inįįthiit!*
ts'i-nįį-thiit
wake-N.IPV:2SG.S:Ø-SG.experience:IPV
'wake SG up!' UT Notebook #5, 86

b. *naadeh ts'itakthał* (T)
n-aadeh *ts'i-tak-thał*
2SG.PSR-older.sister wake-INC:AA.IPV:1SG.S:H-SG.experience:FUT
'I am going to wake up your older sister'
UTCBAF13Nov0501:119

35.2.1.24. *ya* 'continuously' *Ya-* 'continuously' occurs in only one prefix string.

35.2.1.24.1. ya# (Ø, ?) 'continously' The prefix string ya# (Ø, ?) 'continuously' combines with motion themes (996). The aspect of the resulting themes is unclear; the stems look identical to stems in the customary superaspect.

(996) a. *hǫǫt'eey ya'embeek* (T)
hǫǫt'eey *ya-e-mbeek*
still continuously-3SG.S:Ø.IPV:Ø-swim:IPV:CUST
'Still he keeps swimming away from them.'
UTOLVDN13May2909:076

b. *ya'ehshyiik shyah k'it* (N)
ya-eh-shyiik *shyah* *k'it*
continuously-3SG.S:Ø.IPV:H-jump:IPV:CUST house on
'he keeps jumping up and down on the roof of the house'
UTOLVDN10Jul2724:101

35.2.1.25. *ya-* 'into air' (Ø, aa) *Ya-* 'into air' derives from the noun *yaa* 'sky'. It appears to be limited to one prefix string.

35.2.1.25.1. ya+ha# (?, aa) 'out into the air' The prefix string ya+ha# 'out into the air' is composed of the prefixes *ya-* 'into the air' and *ha-* 'up and out', discussed in 35.2.1.5. There is only one example of this prefix string in the data. The verb theme belongs to the motion theme category and is in the momentaneous aspect (997).

(997) *yahaa'atmįį*
yaha-na-at-mįį
out.into.air-IT-3SG.S:AA.PFV:D-swim:PFV
'he swam back up to the surface' UTCBVDN13Nov1401:045

35.2.2. Nondirectional adverbial-derivational prefixes

Some adverbial-derivational prefixes do not indicate PATH but instead describe the manner in which an event or action takes place. The prefixes are listed in alphabetical order.

35.2.2.1. *da-* 'ADMIR, excessively'- The prefix *da-* 'ADMIR, excessively' is part of only one prefix string.

35.2.2.1.1. da#t+H (dh, ?) 'ADMIR, excessively' The prefix string da#t (dh, ?) 'ADMIR, excessively' is one of several comparative prefix strings and thus only applies to dimensional verb themes. It indicates that the quality expressed by the verb theme is present in abundance or to a surprising or excessive degree. Like all comparative prefix strings, it changes the voice/valence marker to H- (both verb themes in [998] have a Ø-voice/valence marker in their primary derivation). When followed by the areal prefix, *da-* coalesces with it to *doo-* (998b).

(998) a. *Datehdzaagn!* (T)
da-teh-dzaagn
ADMIR-3SG.S:INC:DH.PFV:H-be.lightweight:IPV
'He was so light!' UTOLVDN14May0703:100

b. *Dootehsu' shyah choh huhtsįį!* (T)
da-hu-teh-su' *shyah* *choh*
ADMIR-AR.S-INC:DH.PFV:H-be.good:IPV house big
huh-tsįį
3SG.S>AR.O:DH.PFV:H-make.SG.O:PFV
'How well he built his big house!' UTCBVDN14Jul1801:049

35.2.2.2. *dzi-* 'mourn'

35.2.2.2.1. dzi# (Ø, aa) 'mourn' The prefix string dzi# (Ø, aa) 'mourn' is restricted to the verb themes dzi#D+teeyh 'SG do mourning dance' and dzi#L+shyeeyh 'PL do mourning dance' (999). These themes require the persistive aspect, which has its own stem variation pattern (see chap. 26.2.1.13).

(999) a. *dzi'etteeyh* (N)
dzi-et-teeyh
mourn-3SG.S:Ø.IPV:D-classify.AO:IPV
'she was doing a mourning dance' UTOLAF15Dec0705:037

b. *Ishyiit dzi'alshyeey xa'.* (T)
ishyiit dzi-al-shyeey xa'
there mourn-3PL.S:AA.PFV:L-classify.PL.O:PFV EMPH
'That's how they mourned.' UTOLAF10Jul0802:006

35.2.2.3. *ha-* 'spot, look around' This prefix occurs in two closely related verb themes.

35.2.2.3.1. ha#d+L (?, n) 'spot' The prefix string ha#d+L (Ø, aa) 'spot, glimpse' consists of the adverbial-derivational prefix *ha-* '?', the *d-* qualifier, and the L-voice/valence marker. It occurs in only one theme in the momentaneous (1000). No imperfective forms of this prefix string are recorded.

(1000) *didia' hadil'įh* (T)
d-dia' ha-dil-'įh
REFL.PSR-younger.sister spot-3SG.S:QUAL:N.PFV:L-glimpse:PFV
'he spotted his younger sister' UTCBAF13Nov0501:355

35.2.2.3.2. P+kah ## ha#ch'+(uu)+d+L (Ø, aa) 'look around for P' Related to the previous prefix string is P+kah ## ha#ch'+(uu)+d+L (Ø, aa) 'look around for P'. P+*kah* is a free postposition 'in quest of P, to get P' (see chap. 15.2.3.4). It is not clear why the *uu-* qualifier is present in some forms but not in others. The only verb theme derived via this string is operative and in the durative aspect (1001). No imperfective forms of this theme are recorded.

(1001) a. *Dahdǫǫ shoh dat-sąy kah hach'edagn'įį.* (N)

dah-dǫǫ *shoh* *dat-sąy* *kah*
PROX-up:ABL bear 3SG.S:QUAL:AA.PFV:D-be.black:IPV for

ha-ch'-dagn-'įį
spot-INDF.O-QUAL:Ø.IPV:1SG.S:L-look:IPV

'From up there I was looking around for black bear.'
UTOLAF09Aug12:011

b. *hukah hach'udal'įį'* (T)

hu-kah *ha-ch'u-dal-'įį'*
3PL.P-for spot-INDF.O:3SG.S:CON-QUAL:AA.PFV:L-see:PFV

'he looked around for them' UTOLVDN07Oct2604:011

35.2.2.4. *ha-* 'completely' (Ø?, aa) This may be the same prefix as the one discussed in 35.2.1.5.

35.2.2.4.1. ha# (?, aa) 'completely' The prefix string ha# (?, aa) 'completely' can apply to a variety of themes; resulting themes are in the momentaneous aspect (1002). No imperfective forms are attested.

(1002) a. *uche' chįį łahtthagn nts'ą' nts'ą' t'eey hadįįk'an* (T)

u-che' *chįį* *łahtthagn nts'ą'* *t'eey*
3SG.PSR-tail tip all ADVZR

ha-dįį-k'an
completely-3SG.S:QUAL:AA.PFV:Ø-burn:PFV

'the tip of his tail burnt up completely'
UTOLVDN08Mar1304:005

b. *udzih ha'įįxąą* (T)

udzih *ha-įį-xąą*
caribou completely-3SG.S:AA.PFV:Ø-kill:PL.O:PFV

'he killed off all the caribou' UTOLAF09Jun2202:056

35.2.2.5. *k'i-* 'severing' This prefix is variably transcribed as *k'i-*, *k'ii-* or *k'e-*, which reflects variable pronunciation.

35.2.2.5.1. k'i#G (Ø, n) 'severing' The prefix string k'i#G contains a gender prefix. In (1003a), an object of *d-* gender is broken; in (1003b), an object of Ø-gender. This prefix string derives successive themes in the momentaneous (1003).

(1003) a. *tsat huxah k'idįįttheeł* (T)

tsat *hu-xah* *k'i-dįį-ttheeł*
wood 3PL.P-for severing-QUAL:Ø.IPV:2SG.S:Ø-chop:IPV
'split SG wood for them' UTCBAF13Nov0501:016

b. *tehtthįįł tįį' k'enakxol* (S)

tehtthįįł *tįį'* *k'e-nak-xol*
axe handle:POSS severing-N.PFV:1SG.S:H-break:PFV:NOM
'I, having broken the axe handle' Tyone (1996, 42)

In semelfactive derivations, it occurs with the *dh-* conjugation prefix in the perfective mode (1004).

(1004) *tthi' k'iiheet'üü* (T)

tthi' *k'ii-hee-t'üü*
head severing-3PL.S:DH.PFV:Ø-cut:PFV:NOM
'they, having cut off their heads' UTOLVDN07Oct2602:010

35.2.2.5.2. k'i# (?, dh) 'figure out' The prefix string k'i# (?, dh) may be related to the one in 35.2.2.5.1 and likely to the one in 35.2.2.5.3. The theme in (1005) is not fully understood. No imperfective forms of this prefix string are attested.

(1005) *Dikąy' k'ineetąą...* (N)

d-kąy' *k'i-nee-tąą*
REFL.PSR-husband figure.out-3SG.S:QUAL:DH.PFV:Ø-handle.LRO:PFV
'She figured her husband out...' UTOLVDN10Jul2713:019

35.2.2.5.3. ni+k'i#hu+d 'figure out' The prefix *k'i-* is also part of the prefix string ni+k'i#hu+d 'figure out', which additionally contains the terminative prefix *ni-* as well as the *uu-* and *d-* qualifiers. The prefix *k'i-* coalesces with *uu-* to *k'uu-* in the Tetlin dialect (1006a) and to *ch'uu-* in the Northway dialect (1006b). The prefix string derives momentaneous themes requiring an *aa-* conjugation prefix in the perfective. No imperfective forms are recorded.

(1006) a. *nik'oodnįįdlah* (T)

nik'i-uu-dnįį-dlah
figure.out-3SG.S:CON-QUAL:N.PFV:Ø-classify.PL.O:PFV
'he figured it all out' UTOLVDN13May2801:111

b. *tąy nik'oodnįįdlah* (T)

tąy nik'i-uu-dnįį-dlah
trail figure.out-3SG.S:CON-QUAL:QUAL:AA.PFV:Ø-classify.PL.O:PFV
'he really inspected that trail' UTOLVDN13May2803:008

c. *nich'uudnįįdlah* (N)
'he really inspected that trail' commentary

The two Tetlin forms in (1006) were produced by the same speaker; the Northway variant in (1006c) was suggested by a speaker of the Northway dialect during the translation of (1006b).

35.2.2.6. *ła*-'completely' This prefix is related to the bound postposition P+*tl'a*- ' exterminating P' (see chap. 36.2.13).

35.2.2.6.1. ła#t+(n) (? dh), ła# (?, n) 'completely' This prefix string consists of *ła*- 'completely', the inceptive prefix *t*-, and frequently the *n*- qualifier. It applies to different verb theme categories (the primary verb theme in [1007a] is stative, that in [1007b] successive) and requires the *dh*- conjugation prefix in the perfective (1007). No imperfective examples of this prefix string are attested.

(1007) a. *unįį' łahtthegn nts'ą̈' łatneek'ąą* (N)

u-nįį' *łahtthegn nts'ą̈'*
3SG.PSR-face all

ła-tnee-k'ąą
completely-3SG.S:INC:QUAL:DH.PFV:Ø-burn:PFV
'his face was all burned up' UTOLVDN10Jul2719:039

b. *łaytnehgot* (T)

ła-y-tneh-got
completely-3SG.S>3SG.O-INC:QUAL:DH.PFV:H-punch:PFV
'she punched her all up' UTCBVDN13Nov1101:036

When ła#(n) occurs without the inceptive prefix, it takes the *n*- perfective (1008). This suggests that the *dh*- conjugation marker in (1007) may be triggered by the inceptive derivation.

(1008) *ch'ithüh łahnįįt'üüt* (N)

ch'-thüh *ła-hnįį-t'üüt*
INDF.PSR-skin completely-3PL.S:QUAL:N.PFV:Ø-cut:PFV
'they cut the skin to pieces' UTOLAF15Dec0706:003

If *ła-* immediately precedes the areal prefix, they coalesce to *łoo-*. The speaker uttering (1009) actually has a false start with *ła-* and then corrects herself to *łoo-*.

(1009) *łahtthegn nts'ą̈' [ła...] łootdeek'aan* (N)
łahtthegn nts'ą̈' ła-ho-tdee-k'aan
all completely-AR.S-INC:QUAL:DH.PFV:Ø-burn:PFV:NOM
'[the land], having all burned up' UTOLVDN14Apr2601:026

The prefix *ła-* 'completely' is also part of the form *łahtthegn, łahtthagn* 'all'.

35.2.2.6.2. ła# (?, n) 'drown' *Ła-* also occurs in the prefix string ła# (?, n) 'drown', which is attested only in the verb theme ła#Ø+that 'SG drowns' (1010). This theme occurs in the momentaneous aspect and requires the *n*-perfective; imperfective forms are impossible to elicit (the imperative form 'drown!', which would likely be in the imperfective, is semantically problematic). It is unclear whether the *ła-* in this prefix string is related to *ła-* in 35.2.2.6.1.

(1010) *k'ahjil t'eey łanihthat* (T)
k'ahjil t'eey ła-nih-that
almost even drown-N.PFV:1SG.S:Ø-SG.experience:PFV
'I almost drowned' UTOLAF09Jun2902:027

35.2.2.7. *na-* 'continuative' This is another use of the iterative prefix as an adverbial-derivational prefix of position 10. Unlike the iterative prefix of position 9, the continuative prefix has no effect on the voice/valence marker.

35.2.2.7.1. na#(t)+D (aa, dh) 'continuative' Kari (1979, 103) and Axelrod (1990, 136–38) note that the continuative consists (both in Ahtna and Koyukon) of the distributive prefix *n-* together with (Ø, s/l)[3] conjugation prefixes. Upper Tanana has largely lost derivational processes involving the distributive prefix (see chap. 32.4.1); instead the continuative prefix has the form *na-* (see also Holton [2000, 264] for comparison to Tanacross). It is compatible with a large variety of active verb themes.

In motion themes the continuative derivation looks identical to the perambulative derivation, but the semantics are different. In (1011a) brothers are following for several days a trail marked by their sister with swan down, and (1011b) describes how the narrator's brothers are paddling on even though their little sister almost capsized. Crucially all motions follow a trajectory from one point to another and are not meandering 'here or there', as a perambulative interpretation would suggest.

(1011) a. … *ay chih nahatdał.* (T)
ay chih na-hat-dał
and too CONT-3PL.S:AA.IPV:D-PL.go:IPV:PROG
'… and they kept walking.' UTOLVDN13May2909:022

b. … *noo tah nahtetdeeł ay.* (N)
noo tah na-htet-deeł ay
ahead:ALL among CONT-3PL.S:INC:DH.PFV:D-PL.go:PFV and
'… they kept going ahead.' UTOLVDN07Aug2205:103

(1012) illustrates the continuative in operative verb themes and demonstrates that the continuous derivation can co-occur with the iterative one (1012b).

(1012) a. *na'ihsäł*
na-ih-säł
CONT-Ø.IPV:1SG.S:Ø-holler:IPV
'I kept hollering' UTOLAF09Aug1202:032

b. *Nan' naa'etnah.*
nan' na-na-et-nah
eart CONT-IT-3SG.S:Ø.IPV:D-work:IPV
'There was an earthquake.' (lit.: 'the earth kept moving again and again') UTOLVDN07Nov2802:002

35.2.2.7.2. k'i+na# (?, aa) 'taking revenge' The iterative prefix is also part of the prefix string k'i+na# (?, aa) 'taking revenge', which occurs only as part of the verb theme P+i+na#O+d+L+shyaak 'taking revenge on P, get even with P' (1013). Kari (1990, 428) classifies the Ahtna cognate of this verb theme as an "*u*-transitional"; the theme category of the Upper Tanana verb theme is unclear to me. All forms of this verb theme were produced by the same Tetlin speaker. No imperfective forms are attested.

(1013) *k'inahu'įlshyaak*
k'ina-hu-įl-shyaak
revenge-3PL.O-3SG.S:AA.PFV:L-get.even:PFV
'… he got even with them.' UTOLVDN13May2801:197

35.2.2.7.3. nat'u# (Ø, aa) 'skinning' The prefix string nat'uu# 'skinning' (Ø, aa) derives motion themes. It consists of the iterative prefix and an unknown prefix *t'uu-*; Tanacross is the only language I am aware of for which a cognate is reported (Holton 2000, 265). The stem shape suggests that the derived themes are in the distributive superaspect. Nat'u# 'skinning' (Ø, aa) is used only when talking about the skinning of small animals, such as rabbits or muskrat (1014).

(1014) a. *Nat'u'ahłe'!* (T)
nat'u-ah-łe'
skinning-Ø.IPV:2PL.S:H-handle.PL.O:IPV:DSTR
'Skin PL [the muskrats] out!' UTOLVDN07Nov2803:011

b. *dzanh nat'u'akte'* (T)
dzanh nat'u-ak-te'
muskrat skinning-AA.PFV:1SG.S:H-handle.AO:PFV:DSTR
'I skinned the muskrat' UT Notebook #5, 86

Two Northway speakers commented that this prefix string is only used in Tetlin (the forms they prefer are given in [1015a, b]), and also that it cannot be used to refer to skinning a moose, because a moose is not skinned in the same way as a muskrat.

(1015) a. *dzänh nathuu'ahłe'* (N)
dzänh na-thuu-ah-łe'
muskrat CONT-skin-Ø.IPV:2PL.S:H-handle.PL.O:IPV:DSTR
'skin PL the muskrats' UT Notebook #4, 17

b. *diniign nathuu'ahte'* (N)
diniign na-thuu-ah-te'
moose CONT-skin-Ø.IPV:2PL.S:H-handle.AO:IPV:DSTR
'skin PL the SG moose' UT Notebook #4, 17

c. * *diniign nat'u'ahte'*
Intended: 'skin PL the SG moose!' UT Notebook #4, 17

35.2.2.8. *shi-* '?' This prefix is attested in several prefix strings.

35.2.2.8.1. shi#n (?, dh) 'intensely' The prefix string shi#n (?, dh) 'intensely' derives motion verb themes in the momentaneous aspect. No regular imperfective forms containing this prefix string are recorded, but (1016b) illustrates a progressive form.

(1016) a. *Łaakaay shineehaał*... (T)
łaakaay shi-nee-haał
two intensely-3SG.S:QUAL:DH.PFV-spend.night:PFV
'She spent two nights...' UTOLVDN13May2907:059

b. *Hǫǫ' shinaltthał*... (T)
hǫǫ' shi-nal-tthał...
still intensely-3SG.S:QUAL:AA.IPV:L-run:IPV:PROG
'He was still running full blast...' UTCBAF13Nov0501:211

35.2.2.8.2. shi#n+L (?, dh) 'ceaselessly, uncontrollably' The prefix string shi#n+L (?, dh) 'ceaselessly, uncontrollably' derives operative (1017a, b) and neuter (1017c) themes in the momentaneous aspect. Again, no imperfective forms are attested. In (1017b), which contains the prefix string shii#n+L, the conjugation marker appears to be *n*- rather than *dh*-. (The stem is harder to identify. *Dzüh* looks like the imperfective stem in the durative aspect, but it is conceivable that the momentaneous perfective stem would have the same form. Kari [personal communication] suggested that this could be an instance of the errative derivation described in 30.3.1.1.)

(1017) a. *shitneltseh* (T)
shi-tnel-tseh
ceaselessly-3SG.S:INC:QUAL:DH.PFV:L-cry:PFV
'she was crying hard, uncontrollably'
UTOLVDN14Nov2301:529

b. *Ay t'oot'eey unąą taagn danh manh maagn shiijiinildzüh*... (T)
ay t'oot'eey u-nąą taagn danh manh maagn
and but 3SG.PSR-mother three times lake around
shii-ji-nil-dzüh
ceaselessly-INDF.O:3SG.S:QUAL-QUAL:?.PFV:L-dance:PFV
'But his mother danced around the lake three times....'
UTOLAF10Jul0801:021

c. *shinelte'* (T)
shi-nel-te'
ceaselessly-3SG.S:QUAL:DH.PFV:L-SG.sleep:PFV
'she slept deeply, unable to wake up' UTCBAF13Nov0501:083

35.2.2.9. *ti-* 'tired' This prefix is not related to any other adverbial-derivational prefixes with the same shape. It occurs in only one prefix string.

35.2.2.9.1. ti# (aa, aa) 'tired' This prefix string occurs only in the neuter verb theme ti#D+nek (N), ti#D+ndak (T) 'be tired' (1018).

(1018) *ti'atndak (T)*
ti-at-ndak
tired-3sg.s:aa.pfv:d-be.tired:ipv
'she was tired' UTCBAF13Nov0501:078

35.2.2.10. *tthi-* 'into pieces' *Tthi-* 'into pieces' occurs in only one prefix string.

35.2.2.10.1. tthi#(?, n) 'into pieces' Tthi# (n, n) derives successive verb themes. It is attested only in one verb theme (1019), which makes it impossible to identify the aspect. No imperfective forms are recorded.

(1019) *ch'ichąągn ch'ishyuutth'än įį'eh tah tthinįįttheeł (N)*
ch'-chąągn *ch'-shyuuth'än'* *įį'eh tah*
indf.psr-ribs indf.psr-brisket as.well
tthi-nįį-ttheeł
pieces-3sg.s:n.pfv:ø-chop:pfv
'she chopped up the ribs and the brisket' UTOLAF12Jul1203:113

35.2.3. Adjectival adverbial-derivational prefixes

The final few adverbial-derivational prefixes are involved in the formation of thematic non-aspectual prefix strings.

35.2.3.1. ts'#__+v́ 'pejorative' The prefix string ts'#__+v́ derives negative-descriptive themes, i.e., descriptive themes that obligatorily contain the negative suffix and are inflected for negative perfective in the imperfective (1020). They never cooccur with the negative proclitic *k'a(t'eey)* . The *hu-* prefix in (1020b), tentatively glossed as 'lazy' here, occurs only in this one verb theme (see also Kari [1990, 246]). The high stem tone is shown in (1020–1022).

(1020) a. *Ohįį' shǫǫnüü ts'ihogndą́y…* (N)
ohįį' sh-ǫǫnüü *ts'i-hogn-dąy*
des 1sg.psr-older.brother pej-neg.pfv:1sg.s:l-miss:ipv
'Oh, I miss my older brother…' UTOLVDN10Jul2724:030

b. *Diniign du' mbihǫǫłeek tah ts'udetníign...* (T)
diniign du' m-i-hǫǫ-łeek tah
moose CT 3SG.P-PP-AR.S:Ø.PFV:Ø-be.born:IPV:CUST when
ts'-hu-det-niign
PEJ-lazy-3SG.S:QUAL:NEG.PFV:D-be.lazy:IPV
'Moose though, when it gets born it's lazy...'
UTOLVDN11Jul2902:002

This prefix exhibits haplology in Upper Tanana: in the first-person plural subject forms, the two *ts'*- coalesce into *ts'*- (1021); see chap.32.3.2.

(1021) *Hints'etníig.* (T)
h-i-ts'-n-ts'et-niig
?-PP-PEJ-DSTR-1PL.S:DH.PFV:D-not.know:IPV
'We don't know.' UTOLVDN13May2801:058

When the pejorative prefix is followed by a prefix of the shape *hu-* , they coalesce to *ts'uu-* (1022).

(1022) *Shiy du' ts'uunihníign...* (N)
shiy du' ts'uu-nih-niign
1SG CT PEJ:AR-QUAL:NEG:1SG.S:Ø-be.stupid:IPV
'Me though, I'm stupid...' UTOLVDN10Jul2724-080

35.2.3.2. *ts'a-* 'bad' The prefix *ts'a-* is used only in a few themes (1023). It does not appear to impact the verb theme's conjugation markers; all themes in (1023) have the same conjugation marker that they would have in their primary derivation.

(1023) a. *Ts'ahǫǫt'eh nts'ą' shyįį' ts'anii'ilt'eh nts'ą'.* (T)
ts'a-hǫǫ-t'eh nts'ą' shyįį'
bad-AR.S:Ø.PFV:Ø-be:IPV how only
ts'a-nii-il-t'eh nts'ą'
bad-mind-Ø.PFV:2SG.S:Ø-be:IPV CMP
'It is bad how you always get mad.'
UTOLVDN08Mar1307:004

b. *Shaa ts'ahutshyaak.*

sh-aa *ts'a-hut-shyaak*

1SG.P-for bad-AR.S:DH.PFV:D-happen:PFV

'I don't like what happened' (lit.: 'it happened in a bad way for me') UTOLVDN14Apr2601:037

Ts'a- 'bad' is also part of one of the words for 'devil' (1024).

(1024) *ts'ant'ay* (T)

ts'a-n-t'ay

bad-3SG.S:Ø.PFV:Ø-be:IPV:NOM

'the bad one, the devil' UTCBAF13Nov0501:368

35.3. Summary

In this chapter, an inventory of adverbial-derivational prefixes and the prefix strings in which they participate is presented. The derivational system of Upper Tanana is very similar to that of related Dene languages. Most of the prefixes and prefix strings reported in 35.2 not only exist in other languages but work in similar ways, deriving the same aspect and mode combinations. The robustness of this system strengthens Kari's (1979, 6–7) claim that this is an ancient system inherited from Proto-Dene.

Notes

1. The speaker who produced (934a) never pronounces the initial *s-* of the morpheme *sta-* 'away'-. See 35.2.1.14.2.
2. Another prefix where Upper Tanana /h/ corresponds to Ahtna /k^h/ is the areal prefix; see chap. 8.1.1.1.2.
3. Ahtna *s-* and Koyukon *l-* correspond to Upper Tanana *dh-*.

36 | Bound postpositions

Postpositions in Upper Tanana may be bound or free. Free postpositions are described in chap. 15; the present chapter is concerned only with bound postpositions. Diagnostics for the distinction between bound and free postpositions are discussed in 36.1. An inventory of bound postpositions is given in 36.2.

Information on postpositional inflection can be found in chap. 23.

36.1. Bound versus free postpositions

Bound postpositions are, as the label suggests, part of the verb theme whereas free postpositions are not. This difference is reflected orthographically, with the former group written as part of the verb word (1025) and the latter written as a separate word (1026):

(1025) a. *hu'ich'ak-'aał* (N)
hu-i-ch'ak-'aał
3PL.P-PP-INDF.O:Ø.IPV:1SG.S:H-feed:IPV
'I feed them' UT Notebook #3, 71

b. *Rowena k'aneltah* (N)
Rowena k'a-nel-tah
Rowena care-3SG.S:QUAL:Ø.IPV:L-take.care:IPV
'Rowena takes care of herself, is careful' UT Notebook #4, 19

(1026) a. *Shaa elkąyh.* (T)
sh-aa el-kąyh
1SG.P-for 3SG.S:Ø.PFV:L-be.tasty:IPV
'This is tasty for me.' UTOLVDN08Mar1302:021

b. *Deeł ugaay eł hihdelxoo…* (T)

deeł u-gaay eł h-del-xoo
crane 3SG.PSR-baby with 3PL.S-QUAL:Ø.IPV:L-play:IPV:NOM
'They, playing with a baby crane…' UTOLAF07Oct2512:006

(1025a, b) are examples of bound postpositions; the verb themes are P+i#O+H+'aał 'feed O to P' and P+k'a#n+H+tah 'care for P', respectively. In these themes the postpositional phrase is required; *ch'ak-'aał* and *neltah* are not grammatical forms. This contrasts with (1026a, b), where the verb themes are L+kąyh 'be tasty' and d+L+xoh 'play', respectively.

Three diagnostics can be applied to determine whether a given postposition is bound or free: separability (36.1.1), voice/valence prefix changes (36.1.2), and effect on conjugation marker (36.1.3). A fourth diagnostic, semantic bleaching, only works in some instances.

36.1.1. Inseparability

An inflected free postposition in canonical position immediately precedes the verb form (1027a), but it may also be separated by an adverbializer such as *t'eey* (1027b) or may occur in postverbal position (1027c).

(1027) a. … *sǫ' utüh tah'ia…* (T)

sǫ' u-tüh tah-'ia
PROH 3SG.P-over INC:AA.IPV:2PL.S:Ø-step:FUT
'… don't PL step over it…' UTOLVDN11Jul2901:036

b. *Ay tüh t'eey įįshyah.* (T)

ay tüh t'eey įį-shyah
3SG over ADVZR AA.PFV:Ø-SG.go:PFV
'He stepped over it.' UTCBAF14Jul1805:43

c. … *iche' k'it t'eey skinįįshyah tth'iitu' tüh ch'a.* (T)

i-che' k'it t'eey ski-nįį-shyah
3SG.S>3SG.PSR-tail on ADVZR across-3SG.S:N.PFV:Ø-SG.go:PFV

tth'iitu' tüh ch'a
river across FOC
'… she went across the river on his tail.'
UTCBAF13Nov0501:165

Bound postpositional phrases cannot be separated from or follow the verb (1028).

(1028) a. *ik'anehta'* (T)
i-k'a-neh-ta'
3SG.S>3SG.P-care-QUAL:Ø.IPV:H-take.care:IPV
'she took care of him' UTOLAF09Jun2202:046

b. * *ik'a t'eey nehta'*
intended: 'she took care of him' UT Notebook #5, 45

c. * *nehta' ik'a*
intended: 'she took care of him' UT Notebook #5, 45

36.1.2. Voice/valence prefix changes

The postpositions P+*i*- 'affecting P' and P+*k'a*- 'taking care of P' change an underlying Ø-voice/valence prefix to H- (the other three voice/valence markers are usually unaffected; see chap. 27). The postpositional object can thus be considered an argument of the verb theme. (1029a, 1030a) illustrate verb themes without a postposition; (1029b, 1030b) corresponding verb themes derived with a postposition.

(1029) a. *ch'e'aal* (T)
ch'e-'aal
INDF.O:3SG.S:Ø.IPV:Ø-eat:IPV:NOM
'she, eating something' UTOLVDN11Jul2901:006

b. *nee'ich'eh'aał* (N)
nee-i-ch'eh-'aał
1PL.P-PP-INDF.O:3SG.S:Ø.IPV:H-feed:IPV
'he fed us something' UTOLVDN10Jul2724:074

(1030) a. *hiikah naneta'* (T)
hii-kah na-ne-ta'
3PL.S>3SG.P-for CONT-QUAL:Ø.IPV:Ø-look.for:IPV
'they were looking for him' UTOLAF10Jul0801:019

b. *hǫǫsǫǫ hiik'anehta'* (T)
hǫǫsǫǫ hii-k'a-neh-ta'
nicely 3SG.S>3SG.P-care-QUAL:Ø.IPV:H-take.care:IPV
'they took good care of them' UTOLVDN14Nov2301:022

Not all bound postpositions trigger a change in voice/valence marker. P+*tl'a-* 'handing to P' introduces a recipient argument but never changes the voice/valence marker (1031).

(1031) a. *Ts'ayh slough gaay tats'įįtąą.* (N)
ts'ayh slough gaay ta-ts'įį-tąą
boat slough small into.water-1PL.S:AA.PFV:ø-handle.LRO:PFV
'We put the boat into the water in a small slough.'
UTOLVDN07Aug2205:040

b. *Jah k'a' itl'a'įįtąą.* (N)
jah k'a' i-tl'a-įį-tąą
here gun 3SG.S>3SG.P-handing.to-AA.PFV:ø-handle.LRO:PFV
'She gave him the gun here.' UTOLAF13May2801:026

The addition of free postpositions to the verb never changes the voice/valence marker (1032).

(1032) a. *Ts'idloo:::!* (N)
ts'i-dloh
1PL.S:ø.IPV:ø-laugh:IPV
'We laughed so hard!' UTOLVDN14Apr2602:096

b. … *shaa idloh.* (N)
sh-aa i-dloh
1SG.P-for 3SG.S:ø.IPV:ø-laugh:IPV
'… she laughed at me.' UTOLVDN10Jul2724:072

c. … *doondaa nts'ą' edloh.* (T)
d-oondaa nts'ą' e-dloh
REFL.PSR-older.brother to 3SG.S:ø.IPV:ø-laugh:IPV
'… she smiled at her older brother.'
UTOLVDN14Nov2301:561

Thus postpositions are bound when their presence affects the voice/valence marker. When it does not, the postposition may be bound or free.

36.1.3. Change in conjugation prefix

Some postpositions change the conjugation prefix. This process is quite common in other Dene languages. Kari (1979), for example, contains long lists of conjugation-prefix-changing postpositions in Ahtna. In Upper Tanana conjugation-changing prefixes are rarer. All verb forms in (1033) are derived from motion themes, which require (n, n) in their basic derivation, but the postpositions in (1033a-c) trigger a change to (Ø, aa), while the one in (1033d) triggers a change to (Ø, dh). The postpositions in (1033a, b, d) are bound postpositions. P+*tüh* 'over P' in (1033c) is the only free postposition that affects the conjugation prefix—in the Tetlin dialect, at least. (In the Northway dialect this postposition seems not to affect the conjugation marker.)

(1033) a. *Dzänh diche' itl'a'į̨tą̨ą̨.* (N)

dzänh *d-che'* *i-tl'a-į̨-tą̨ą̨*
muskrat REFL.PSR-tail 3SG.S>3SG.P-to-AA.PFV:Ø-handle.LRO:PFV
'Muskrat gave [Beaver] his$_{M}$ tail.' UTCBAF14Jun0301:006

b. ... *di'an shyiit k'iihį̨į̨deeɬ all Che' T'iin.* (T)

d-'an *shyiit* *k'ii-hį̨į̨-deeɬ* *all*
REFL.PSR-den in into.hole-3PL.S:AA.PFV:Ø-PL.go:PFV all
Che' T'iin
Tailed.People
'... all the Tailed People went into their dens.'
UTCBAF14Jul1805:046

c. ... *atthiit Tak'at tüh huhį̨į̨dlah.* (T)

a-tthiit *Tak'at* *tüh*
NTRL-waterwards:PNCT Clearwater across
hu-hį̨į̨-dlah
3PL.O-3PL.S:AA.PFV:Ø-handle.PL.O:PFV
'... at that point towards the water they took them across the Clearwater.' UTCBAF14Jul1805:020

d. *T'axoh hut'aheedeel eh.* (T)

t'axoh *hu-t'a-hee-deel* *eh*
finally 3PL.P-catch.up-3PL.S:DH.PFV:Ø-PL.go:PFV:NOM and
'They had almost caught up them.'
UTOLVDN13May2909:047

36.1.4. Semantic bleaching

An additional diagnostic of bound postpositions is semantic bleaching. No meaning can be assigned to P+*i*-; it merely introduces an additional argument. The same is true for P+*k'a*-. P+*tl'a*-, which introduces a recipient, is related to the noun *-įįtl'aa* 'palm'. As a postposition, it has, however, lost its connotations of physical contact with the palm of the recipient. P+*t'a* 'catching on P' has been extended (or merged with another morpheme) to mean 'against P'.

This diagnostic is not entirely reliable—the meaning of bound postpositions like P+*k'ii* 'into P (hole or depression)' is quite specific.

36.2. Inventory

Using the diagnostics discussed in 36.1, we can identify thirteen bound postpositions. The following discussion is organized alphabetically.

36.2.1. P+*a*- 'teaching P'

The postposition P+*a*- 'teaching P' occurs only in the Tetlin dialect and only in one verb theme: P+a#d+Ø+nih 'teach P'. This verb theme takes the same conjugation marker (*aa*-) in the perfective as does the primary theme P#d+Ø+nih 'say to P' (1034).

(1034) a. *Hugn ch'a nuhts'iikeey atdahniil.* (T)

hugn	*ch'a*	*nuh-ts'iikeey*
etc.	FOC	2PL.PSR-children

a-tdah-niil
teach-INC:QUAL:AA.IPV:2PL.S:ø-teach:FUT:NOM

'Things like that, you PL have to teach them to your PL children.'
UTOLAF07Nov2602:018

b. *Unąą chih yadįįni'...* (T)

u-nąą	*iin*	*chih*
3SG.PSR-mother	PL	also

y-a-dįį-ni'
3SG.S>3SG.P-teach-QUAL:AA.PFV:ø-say:PFV

'His mother also taught him...' UTOLVDN14May0703:012

36.2.2. P+*i*-, Ø- 'acting on P'

P+*i*-, Ø- 'acting on P' is a bound postposition that introduces an oblique object and is cognate to what is called the "null postposition" in related languages (see also Faltz [1998, 399] for Navajo, Kari [1990, 64] for Ahtna). I gloss it as 'PP' throughout this grammar, since even 'acting on' suggests more specific meaning than this postposition actually has. P+*i*-, Ø- 'acting on P' is often thematic (1035).

(1035) a. *Mits'ishniign.* (N)
m-i-ts'-ish-niign
3SG.P-PP-PEJ-NEG.PFV:1SG.S:D-not.know:IPV
'I didn't know him.' UTOLVDN14Apr2602:023

b. *sǫ' midaltsadn* (T)
sǫ' m-i-dal-tsadn
PROH 3SG.P-PP-QUAL:OPT:2PL.S:L-touch:OPT
'don't PL touch it' UTOLVDN11Jul2901:037

c. … *Nisüü hu'ich'ihnįį'ąą.* (T)
Nisüü hu-i-ch'-hnįį-'ąą
Nisüü 3PL.P-PP-INDF.O-3PL.S:N.PFV:ø-handle.CO:PFV
'… they named them Nisüü.' (lit.: 'they handled an unspecified abstract object to them') UTOLAF11Aug0201:010

P+*i*-, Ø- may also be used productively to derive verb themes as shown in (1036).

(1036) P+*i*- in derived verb themes

	Primary theme		*Derived theme*	
a.	n+L+jit	'be scared'	P+i#n+L+jit	'be scared of P'
b.	O+Ø+'aał	'eat O'	P+i#O+H+'aał	'feed O to P'
c.	O+uu+Ø+keet	'buy O'	P+i#uu+Ø+keet	'pay P'
d.	chi#ch'+d+L+nih	'lie'	P+i+chi#ch'+d+L+nih	'lie to P'

Note that a change of voice/valence prefix (from Ø- to H-) only takes place when a third argument is introduced as in (1036b), but not when an oblique object is substituted for a direct one, as in (1036c).

In some verb themes, this postposition is phonologically empty. In both verb forms in (1037), a postpositional object prefix immediately precedes an incorporate.

(1037) a. *mbexałdįįłeey!* (N)
mb-xał-dįį-łeey
3SG.P-club-QUAL:Ø.IPV:2SG.S:Ø-handle.PL.O:IPV:IMP
'throw sticks at it!' UT Notebook #4, 15

b. *tuu shdanįįgąy* (T)
tuu sh-da-nįį-gąy
water 1SG.P-mouth-3SG.S:N.PFV:Ø-be.dry:PFV
'I was dehydrated' (lit. 'the mouth dried me [for lack of] water')
UTOLVDN13May2907:128

It is unclear if there is any difference between the overt postposition P+*i*- and the null postposition P+Ø-.

P+*i*-, Ø- does not affect the conjugation marker or verb theme category, making this a case of non-aspectual derivation.

36.2.3. P+*dzi*- 'splitting P'

The corpus contains one instance of the bound postposition P+*dzi*- 'splitting P' (1038). More commonly the reduced form *dzi*- is used as part of an aspectual prefix string (see chap. 35.2.1.4.4).

(1038) *Taag t'eey hutąy' tl'aan niłdzihal'ah danh...* (T)
taag t'eey hu-tąy' tl'aan
three ADVZR 3SG.PSR-trail:POSS and
nił-dzi-hal-'ah danh
RECP.P-split-AR.S:AA.PFV:L-extend:PFV at
'Where the third trail used to split off...'
UTOLVDN13May2803:064

The postposition seems to require an *aa*- conjugation marker in the imperfective form of an extension theme.

36.2.4. P+*k'a*- 'taking care of P'

P+*k'a* 'taking care of P' is a bound postposition that occurs only in the theme P+k'a#n+H+ta' 'take care of P'. This verb theme has (Ø, aa) conjugation prefixes (1039).

(1039) a. *hǫǫsǫǫ hiik'anehta'* (T)
hǫǫsǫǫ hii-k'a-neh-ta'
nicely 3SG.S>3SG.P-care-QUAL:Ø.IPV:H-take.care:IPV
'they took good care of them' UTOLVDN14Nov2301:022

b. *dik'anįlt'a' nt'eh* (T)
d-k'a-nįl-ta' *nt'eh*
REFL.P-care-3SG.S:QUAL:AA.PFV:L-take.care:PFV ASRT
'she certainly took care of herself' UTOLVDN13May2901:037

36.2.5. P+*k'etaa-* 'according to P, as P told S'

The postposition P+*k'etaa-* 'according to P, as P told S' is attested only in the Tetlin dialect. (1040a) suggests that it requires a *dh-* conjugation marker (the verb theme d+Ø+dį' 'do' usually takes a *aa*-perfective). In all examples the postpositional phrase immediately precedes the verb theme.[1]

(1040) a. *Ts'ist'e' k'etaadeedį' that ts'exeh gaay.* (T)
ts'ist'e' *k'etaa-dee-dį'* *that*
old.lady according.to-3SG.S:QUAL:DH.PFV:Ø-do:PFV that
ts'exeh gaay
girl
'The girl did as the old lady [had told her].'
UTOLVDN14Nov2301:499

b. *Hugn t'eey k'a huk'etaatsul'įį nahthan.* (T)
hugn *t'eey* *k'a* *hu-k'etaa-tsul-'įį*
etc. ADVZR NEG 3PL.P-according.to-1PL.S:OPT:L-act:OPT
nah-than
2PL.S:Ø.PFV:L-want:IPV:NEG
'Even those things you PL don't want to do according to [the ancestors].' UTOLVDN11Jul2903:008

In the Northway dialect, the free postposition P+*k'eh* 'like P' is used instead (1041).

(1041) *Ditsǫǫ* *k'eh* *t'eey* *dį'.* (N)
REFL.PSR:grandmother like ADVZR do:IPV
'She did as her grandmother [had told her].'
UTOLAF15May0501:149

36.2.6. P+*k'i-* 'trading with P'

P+*k'i-* 'trading with P' requires an *aa*-perfective (1042a). No imperfective forms are recorded.

(1042) a. *Nitk'idzalshyah teejuh.* (T)

nit-k'i-dzal-shyah *teejuh*
RECP.P-trade-1PL.S:QUAL:AA.PFV:L-handle.PL.O:PFV respect
'We traded respectfully.' UTCBVDN14Jul1801:060

b. *Dzanh dzanh nuhk'itdihteet...* (T)

dzanh *dzanh*
muskrat muskrat
nuh-k'i-tdih-teet
2PL.P-trade-INC:QUAL:AA.IPV:1SG.S:ø-handle.PL.O:FUT
'I will trade muskrat with you PL...' UTCBVDN14Jul1801:057

36.2.7. P+*k'ii*- 'into P (hole, depression)'

P+*k'ii*- 'into P (hole, depression)' requires (Ø, aa) conjugation markers (1043).

(1043) a. *Hu'an hu'an k'idahteey...* (T)

hu-'an *hu-'an*
3PL.PSR-hole 3PL.PSR-den
k'i-dah-teey
hole-QUAL:ø.IPV:2PL.S:ø-handle.PL.O:IPV:NOM
'Put PL [the grass] into their dens...' UTOLAF17Aug1009:020

b. ... *di'an shyiit k'iihįįdeet all Che' T'iin.* (T)

d-'an *shyiit* *k'ii-hįį-deet* *all*
REFL.PSR-den in hole-3PL.S:AA.PFV:ø-PL.go:PFV all
Che' T'iin
Tailed.People
'... all the Tailed People went into their dens.'
UTCBAF14Jul1805:046

c. *Ay k'it dishyi' k'iihiteek...* (N)

ay *k'it* *d-shyi'*
3SG on REFL.PSR-food
k'ii-hi-teek...
into.hole-3PL.S:ø.IPV:ø-handle.PL.O:IPV:CUST
'On top of that they would put their food into the hole...'
UTOLVDN07Nov2901:084

(1043c) suggests that this postposition might be reanalyzed as an adverbial-derivational prefix, given that it does not seem to have an object (*dishyi'* 'their food' is the direct object of the verb form, not a postpositional object).

36.2.8. P+*k'ii*- 'rubbing P'

This postposition appears to occur in only one verb theme: P+k'ii#ch'+G+H+tsał 'wash P'. The verb theme has (Ø, dh) conjugation prefixes (1044).

(1044) a. *Tth'aak k'iijehtsał.* (T)
tth'aak k'ii-jeh-tsał
plate rubbing-INDF.O:QUAL:Ø.IPV:H-wash:IPV
'she's doing the dishes' UTOLAF12Jul0601:007

b. *tth'aak k'iijidhaktsał* (T)
tth'aak k'ii-ji-dhak-tsał
plate rubbing-INDF.O:QUAL-DH.PFV:1SG.S:H-wash:PFV
'I did the dishes' UTOLAF12Jul0601:018

36.2.9. P+*na*- 'around P'

P+*na*- 'around P' is likely related to the iterative prefix. Unlike the iterative prefix, however, it does not trigger a D-effect. It does not appear to change the voice/valence prefix; both the classificatory theme in (1045a) and the motion theme in (1045b) have their usual perfective prefix. The resyllabification of the third-person plural subject marker *h*- as coda consonant in (1045a) suggests that this postposition is bound.

(1045) a. *Ts'ät t'eey hunahdehniik?* (N)
ts'ät t'eey hu-na-hdeh-niik
blanket ADVZR 3PL.P-around-3PL.S:QUAL:DH.PFV:H-keep.FO:IPV
'Did they keep blankets wrapped around them?'
UTCBAF15May0403:025

b. *Dǫǫ danh field k'it hunajįįniik.* (T)
dǫǫ danh field k'it hu-na-jįį-niik
downriver:ABL at field on 3PL.P-around
'Down there in the field they covered themselves.'
UTCBVDN13Nov1502:040

36.2.10. P+*t'a*- 'catching up with P, against P'

P+*t'a*- 'catching up to P, against P' is, according to Kari (1990, 340), related to P+*t'aat* 'under P', discussed in chap. 15.2.1.11. P+*t'a* 'catching up to P, against

P' allows both areal (1046a) and human (1046b, c) referents of P. This seems to impact the choice of conjugation prefix; (1046a) has an *aa-* conjugation marker in the perfective, (1046b, c) both have *dh-*.

(1046) a. … *łįį iin hut'ashihdįhnay eł…* (T)

łįį *iin*
dog PL

hu-t'a-sh-h-dįh-nay *eł*
AR.P-against-1SG.O-3PL.S-QUAL:AA.PFV:H-throw.AO:PFV:NOM and

'… the dogs threw me against [the ground] and…'
UTOLAF09Jun2201:005

b. … *hiit'a'eedeel eh.* (T)

hii-t'a-ee-deel *eh*
3PL.S>3SG.P-catch.up-DH.PFV:Ø-PL.go:PFV:NOM and

'… they caught up with him.' UTOLVDN14May0703:074

c. *Dii xah ut'akįjidhįl'aan…* (N)

dii xah
why

u-t'a-kį-ji-dhįl-'aan
3SG.P-against-foot INDF.O:QUAL-DH.PFV:2SG.S:L-keep.CO:IPV:NOM

'Why are you relaxing like this…' (lit.: 'Why do you have your foot against it…') UTOLAF14May0807:022

(1046c) illustrates this postposition in a neuter verb theme with a *dh-* conjugation marker in the imperfective. No imperfective forms of this postposition in an active theme are recorded.

36.2.11. P+*t'a-* 'obstructing P, snagging on P'

P+*t'a-* 'snagging on P, being blocked by P' is formally distinguished from P+*t'a-* 'catching up to P, against P' by conjugation prefix; P+*t'a-* 'snagging on P, being blocked by P' requires an *n-* conjugation marker in the perfective (1047). (Again, there are no imperfective forms containing this postposition.)

(1047) a. *It'anįltthat.* (T)

i-t'a-nįl-tthat
3SG.S>3SG.O-obstructing-QUAL:N.PFV:L-run:PFV

'He ran up against it; it blocked his way.'
UTCBAF13Nov0501:216

b. ... *ts'ät t'akidilnąy...* (N)

ts'ät
wood

t'a-ki-dil-nąy
snagging.on-foot-3SG.S:QUAL:N.PFV:L-move.quickly:PFV:NOM

'... she tripped over the piece of wood...'

UTOLAF12Jul1201:035

36.2.12. P+*tl'a-* 'handing to P'

P+*tl'a-* 'handing to P' is a thematic postposition that is part of many ditransitive motion verb themes. The postposition is related to the obligatorily possessed noun stem *-įįtl'aa* 'palm' and introduces the recipient of a transfer event. It triggers (Ø, aa) conjugation prefixes and does not affect the voice/valence marker (1048).

(1048) a. *shtl'anįįłeey* (T)

sh-tl'a-nįį-łeey
1SG.P-to-QUAL:Ø.IPV:2SG.S:Ø-handle.RO:IPV:IMP

'give SG me [the rope]' UTCBAF13Nov0501:142

b. *Jah k'a' itl'a'įįtąą.* (N)

jah k'a' i-tl'a-įį-tąą
here gun 3SG.S>3SG.P-to-AA.PFV:Ø-handle.LRO:PFV

'She gave him the gun here.' UTOLAF13May2801:026

36.2.13. P+*tl'a-, da-* 'exterminating P'

The postposition P+*tl'a-* 'exterminating P' is attested only as part of the verb theme P+tl'a#ch'+Ø+xąą, which requires an *aa-* perfective. (No imperfective forms of this verb theme occur in the data.) In most instances this postposition is pronounced /ta/ (1049b); the speaker however repeated it back as /t͡ɬ'a/ during the transcription.[2]

Particularly interesting is (1049c), which appears to combine the postposition P+*tl'a-* 'exterminating P' with the adverbial-derivational string kitl'a# 'onto shore' described in chap. 35.2.1.7.6. The resulting theme has the meaning 'kill PL.O all the way to dry land'. (This example comes from a narrative where a young man on a frozen lake is killing off a whole village.)

(1049) a. *Neetl'ach'atxąą...* (T)
nee-tl'a-ch'at-xąą
1PL.P-exterminate-INDF:AA.PFV:D-kill.PL.O:PASS:PFV
'all of us were killed off' UTOLAF13May2403:092

b. *Hudach'ihxaan eh...* (T)
hu-tl'a-ch'ih-xaan *eh*
3PL.P-exterminate-INDF:AA.PFV:1SG.S:H-kill.PL.O:PFV:NOM and
'I killed them all off and...' UTOLVDN13May2803:106

c. *All hukitl'ach'įįxąą...* (T)
all hu-kitl'a-ch'įį-xąą
all 3PL.P-ashore-INDF.O:3SG.S:AA.PFV:Ø-kill.PL.O:PFV
'He killed all of them all the way up to the shore...'
UTOLAF13May2403:128

36.3. Comparison to Ahtna

The number of bound postpositions in Upper Tanana—thirteen in total—is quite small compared to a more conservative language such as Ahtna, where Kari (1979, 83–87) identifies twenty-four prefix strings involving bound postpositions that can apply to motion themes. Comparison between the languages suggests that two processes are responsible for this difference. Some postpositions are bound in Ahtna but free in Upper Tanana. A small selection of those is given in table 36.1. All Ahtna data in table 36.1 is from Kari (1979, 83–87); it has been retranscribed to match the current orthographic conventions of this language in, for example, Kari (1990). The single hash sign after the Ahtna morpheme signals that these are bound morphemes, whereas the double hash sign in the Upper Tanana form indicates that these are separate words.

Ahtna		Upper Tanana
P+c'a# (n, n)	'from P'	P+ch'a ##
P+tah# (n, n)	'among P'	P+tah ##
P+tes# (Ø, aa)	'over P'	P+tüh ## (Ø, aa)
P+tsi# (s, s)	'ahead of P'	P+ ttheh ##

Table 36.1. Postpositions in Ahtna and Upper Tanana

Other morphemes that function as bound postpositions in Ahtna are used only as adverbial-derivational prefixes that cannot take objects. An example for that is Ahtna P+*ke*- 'climbing P', which corresponds to the Upper Tanana adverbial-derivational prefix *ḵi*- 'climbing, up', which cannot take objects. Still other Ahtna bound postpositions simply do not occur at all in Upper Tanana. There appears to be a general trend away from bound postpositions in Upper Tanana, where postpositions either become free stems or lose their argument-taking functions and become adverbial-derivational prefixes.

36.4. Summary

In this chapter, bound postpositions are described. Bound postpositions are part of the verb theme: they cannot be separated from the verb word, some of them affect the voice/valence prefix of the verb theme, and some require particular conjugation prefixes. I also noted that semantic bleaching has affected some bound postpositions.

Using these diagnostics, thirteen bound postpositions can identified. Each is briefly described.

Notes

1. It is likely cognate to Koyukon P+*kk'aatʉgh* 'according to, confirming with, agreeable to, following P', which is classified as a free postposition in that language (Jetté and Jones 2000, 507).
2. I choose the representation P+*tl'a*- because there is a cognate postposition P+*tl'a*- in Ahtna with the same meaning; see Kari (1990, 359).

37 Verbal suffixes

In addition to the historic suffixes causing stem variation (chap. 26), there are three productive verbal suffixes in Upper Tanana. All are absorbed into the stem (Leer 1996c, 200), creating a heavy stem syllable (see chap. 11).

37.1. Inventory

There are three suffixes: the nominalizing suffix -v, the imperative suffix -v, and the negative suffix -v́.

37.1.1. The nominalizing suffix -v

37.1.1.1. Phonology The nominalizing suffix -v creates a heavy stem syllable (see chap. 11). It does not affect stem tone.

37.1.1.2. Functions The nominalizing suffix -v can be added to any verb form; it is involved in the formation of deverbal nouns (1050a) and relative clauses (1050b). It is also used in verb forms modifying a noun (1050c).

(1050) a. *meh nats'elmoo* (N)

m-eh *na-ts'el-moo-v*
3SG.P-with PRMB-1PL.S:Ø.IPV:L-roll:IPV-NOM
'the thing we roll around with = truck'
UTOLAF09Aug1201:005

b. *Ishyiit ts'ehłagn dineh hugn łuugn eldeel ay ajettsat…* (T)

ishyiit ts'ehłagn dineh hugn łuugn el-deeł-v ay
there one man and fish 3SG:Ø.IPFV:L-eat:IPV-NOM that
a-jet-tsat
?-3SG.S:INDF.O:QUAL:DH.PFV:D-turn:PFV
'There one man turned himself into [a bird] that eats fish…'
UTOLVDN07Oct2602:046

c. *shoh dat-sąy* (N)

shoh dat-sąy
bear 3SG.S:QUAL:AA.PFV:D-be.black:IPV-NOM
'a black bear' UTOLAF09Aug1201:011

Nominalized verb forms are part of many subordinating constructions (1051).

(1051) a. *Shta' ehnay hi'agnnayh.* (N)
sh-ta' eh-nih-v
1SG.PSR-father 3SG.S:Ø.IPV:H-say:IPV-NOM
hi-agn-nayh
?-Ø.PFV:1SG:L-remember:IPV
'I remember her saying that to my father.'
UTOLAF08Feb1906:011

b. ... *ikah natedaagn eł yudih'ąą...* (T)
i-kah na-te-daak-v eł
3SG.S>3SG.P-for PRMB-INC:Ø.IPV:D-SG.go:IPV:CUST-NOM and
y-u-dih-'ąą
3SG.S>3SG.O-CON-QUAL:I.PFV:H-find.CO:PFV
'... as she was walking around [looking] for him she found him, ...' UTOLAF09Jun2202:013

c. *Ay iin du' naxach'ihdelshyeegn xah hu'ookol.* (N)
ay iin du'
3 PL CT
na-xa-ch'-h-del-sheek-v
PRMB-weapon-INDF.O-3PL.S-QUAL:Ø.IPV:L-carry.PL.O:IPV:CUST-NOM
xah hu-ookol
because 3PL.O-NEGEX
'They were gone because they had gone hunting.'
UTOLAF15May0501:177

Nominalization also has discourse functions; it is triggered by the focus particle *ch'a* (1052a) and may occur in (backgrounded) main clauses (1052b); this tendency was already noted by Leer (1996c, 202).

(1052) a. *Dii ch'a dįh'ąy?* (N)
dii ch'a dįh-'įh-v
what FOC QUAL:Ø.IPV:2SG:H-mess.with:IPV-NOM
'What is it you're messing with?' UTOLAF09Aug1201:031

b. *Naan' na'ihdaal; tąy hǫǫts'eek.* (N)

naan' *na-ih-daał-v* *tąy*
across:ALL IT-AA.IPV:1SG.S-D:SG.go:IPV:PROG-NOM trail
hǫǫ-ts'eek
AR.S:Ø.PFV:Ø-be.narrow:IPV
'I'm going back across; the trail is narrow.'
UTOLAF09Aug1202:028

Deverbal nouns are described in chap. 13; more information on the other constructions is given in volume 2.

37.1.2. The imperative suffix -v

37.1.2.1. Phonology The imperative suffix has the same effects as the nominalizing suffix discussed in 37.1.1.

37.1.2.2. Functions Verb forms in positive directives very frequently contain the imperative suffix -v (1053). In fact, I suspect that the voicing so frequently associated with optative stems is due to an overgeneralization of this suffix (see examples in 26.2).

(1053) a. … *ch'ixia' ushyiit de' kah unįh'įį…* (N)

ch'-xia' *u-shyiit* *de' kah*
INDF.PSR-egg 3SG.P-inside to.check
hu-nįh-'įh-v
AR-QUAL:Ø.IPV:2SG.S:H-look:IPV-IMP
'… check if there are eggs in it…' UTOLVDN07Aug2205:011

b. *Mbaa nche' skidǫǫteey tl'aan…* (T)

mb-aa *n-che'*
3SG.P-for 2SG.PSR-tail
skį-dǫǫ-teeyh-v *tl'aan*
across-QUAL:OPT:2SG.S:Ø-classify.LRO:OPT-IMP and
'Extend your SG tail across for him and…'
UTOLVDN14Nov2301:359

The imperative suffix appears to be optional. The two sentences in (1054) were uttered by the same speaker as part of the same story, and she was adamant that there was no meaning difference between the forms.

(1054) a. *Tsǫǫ: "Danįįhaay," yehnih.* (T)

tsǫǫ *da-nįį-haayh-v*
grandmother inside-N.IPV:2SG.S:Ø-SG.go:IPV-IMP
y-eh-nih
3SG.S>3SG.P-Ø.IPV:H-say:IPV
'The grandmother: "Come in," she said to her.'
UTOLAF08Apr2805:062

b. *"Danįįhaayh," yehnih.* (T)

da-nįį-haayh-v *y-eh-nih*
inside-N.IPV:2SG.S:Ø-SG.go:IPV-IMP 3SG.S>3SG.P-Ø.IPV:H-say:IPV
'"Come in," she said to him.' UTOLAF08Apr2805:068

More information on the imperative suffix can be found in volume 2 and in Lovick (2016).

37.1.3. The negative suffix -v́

37.1.3.1. Phonology The addition of the negative suffix creates a heavy stem syllable (chap. 11). This morpheme carries a tonal specification that changes (unmarked or low) stem tone to high.[1] This high tone is indicated in the examples below but not elsewhere.

37.1.3.2. Functions The negative suffix -v́ occurs in all formally negative verb forms. These fall into two types: negative verb forms occurring in clauses negated by the negative particle *k'a(t'eey)* (1055), and verb forms belonging to inherently negative verb themes (1056).

(1055) a. ... *k'at'eey nagnjídn...* (N)

k'at'eey *nagn-jit-v́*
NEG QUAL:Ø.PFV:1SG.S:L-be.afraid:IPV-NEG
'... I was not afraid...' UTOLVDN13May2004:042

b. *Atshyaan iin t'eey k'a naholndíí.* (T)

atshyaan *iin* *t'eey* *k'a*
old.people PL even NEG
na-hol-ndiik-v́
IT-3PL.S:AR:Ø.IPV:L-tell.story:IPV:CUST-NEG
'Even the old people don't tell stories.'
UTOLAF09Jun2402:040

(1056) a. *Mits'ishníígn.* (N)
m-i-ts'-ish-níígn
3SG.P-PP-PEJ-Ø.PFV:1SG.S:D-not.know:IPV
'I didn't know him.' UTOLVDN14Apr2602:023

b. *Dǫǫndaa k'it ts'ihǫhdą́y,...* (T)
d-ǫǫndaa k'it ts'i-hǫh-dą́y
REFL.PSR-older.brother on PEJ-3SG.S:AR:Ø.PFV:H-miss:IPV
'She misses her older brother...' UTOLVDN07Oct2602:035

In (1056) the negative suffix has become lexicalized as part of the verb theme (this is reflected in the gloss), and the negative particle *k'a(t'eey)* is not used.

37.2. Co-occurrence and ordering of suffixes

Since the three verbal suffixes are all absorbed into the stem syllable, it is not possible to provide a morphological argument for their order. In fact, it is not even possible to tell whether more than one suffix is present in any given verb form.

The nominalizing suffix and the imperative suffix may well be mutually exclusive; given their respective functions, it is hard to imagine a situation where both would be used. Negative directives are not morphologically negative and thus do not use the negative suffix (see volume 2 for details); there is no other context where the negative suffix and the imperative suffix might co-occur.

The presence of the nominalizing suffix in negative verb forms is also not detectable; yet an argument for its presence can be made.

The plural enclitic *iin* requires nominalization of the preceding verb form (1057).

(1057) *Dineey hehxaan iin tthi' k'iiheet'üü...* (T)
dineey heh-xą̨ą-v iin tthi'
men 3PL.S:Ø.IPV:H-kill.:PL.O:IPV-NOM PL head
k'i-na-hee-t'üü
severing-3PL.S:DH.PFV:Ø-cut:PFV
'They cut the heads off the men they were killing...'
UTOLVDN07Oct2602:010

We can thus assume that the nominalizing suffix is also present in negative forms followed by *iin* (1058). *K'a hiidláán* 'not many' is a nominalized negated verb form; *ntsíín* is an inherently negative nominalized verb form. Clearly there is no overt trace of the nominalizing suffix even though its presence is required by the plural enclitic *iin*.

(1058) *Hǫǫ ch'ale hediign k'ahdu' dziin, k'a hiidláán nah'ogn ntsíín iin hǫǫ hediik.* (T)

hǫǫ'	*ch'ale*	*he-diign*	*k'ahdu'*	*dziin*
thus	FOC	3PL.D:Ø.IPV:Ø-do:IPV:CUST-NOM	now	day

k'a	*hii-dląą-v́-v*	*nah-'ogn*
NEG	3PL.S:NEG.PFV:Ø-be.many:IPV-NEG-NOM	MED-out:AR

n-tsíín-v	*iin*	*hǫǫ*	*he-diik*
3PL.S:Ø.PFV:Ø-be.few:IPV-NOM	PL	thus	3PL.S:Ø.IPV:Ø-do:IPV:CUST

'That's what they do today, not very many, but some out there [still] do that.' UTOLVDN07Nov2803:025

Since negation is an inflectional category whereas nominalization is derivational, I assume here that the negative suffix precedes the nominalizing one and gloss examples like (1058) accordingly.

37.3. Summary

There are three productive verbal suffixes: the nominalizing suffix -v, the imperative suffix -v, and the negative suffix -v́. All of them are absorbed into the verb stem and create a heavy stem syllable; the negative suffix additionally changes the stem tone to high.

The nominalizing suffix is involved in the formation of deverbal nouns and relative clauses, which are used in several different constructions. The imperative suffix is involved in the formation of positive directives. The negative suffix is present in morphologically negative verb forms as well as in inherently negative verb themes.

The imperative suffix is not compatible with either of the other two suffixes. The nominalizing suffix and the negative suffix are compatible with each other and likely co-occur, but no trace of the nominalizing suffix can be found in such forms.

Notes

1. As discussed in chap. 7.3, the phonemic status of this high tone is uncertain.

References

Aikhenvald, Alexandra Y. 2010. *Imperatives and Commands.* Oxford: Oxford University Press.

Akmajian, Adrian, and Stephen Anderson. 1970. "On the Use of the Fourth Person in Navajo, or Navajo Made Harder." *International Journal of American Linguistics* 36, no. 1: 1–8.

Arnold, Irene, Rick Thoman, and Gary Holton. 2009. *Tanacross Learners' Dictionary: Dihthâad xt'een iin aanděg dínahtlăa'.* Fairbanks: Alaska Native Language Center.

Arppe, Antti, Christopher Cox, Mans Hulden, Jordan Lachler, Sjur N. Moshagen, Miikka Silfverberg, and Trond Trosterud. 2017. "Computational Modeling of the Verb in Dene Languages: The case of Tsuut'ina." In *Working Papers in Dene Languages 2016,* edited by Alessandro Jaker, 51–69. Alaska Native Language Center Working Papers no. 13. Fairbanks: Alaska Native Language Center.

Attla, Catherine. 1990. *K'etetaalkkaanee (The One Who Paddled among the People and Animals): The Story of an Ancient Traveler.* Fairbanks: Alaska Native Language Center.

Axelrod, Melissa. 1990. "Incorporation in Koyukon Athapaskan." *International Journal of American Linguistics* 56, no. 2: 179–95.

———. 1993. *The Semantics of Time: Aspectual Categorization in Koyukon Athabaskan.* Lincoln: University of Nebraska Press.

Basso, Keith H. 1990. *Western Apache Language and Culture: Essays in Linguistic Anthropology.* Tucson: University of Arizona Press.

Berez, Andrea L. 2011. "Directional Reference, Discourse, and Landscape in Ahtna." PhD diss., University of California Santa Barbara.

Bird, Steven. 1999. "When Marking Tone Reduces Fluency: An Orthographic Experiment in Cameroon." *Language and Speech* 42, no. 1: 83–115.

Bochnak, M. Ryan, and Lisa (eds.) Matthewson. 2015. *Methodologies in Semantic Fieldwork*. Oxford: Oxford University Press.

Boraas, Alan. 2012. "An Introduction to Dena'ina Grammar: The Kenai Dialect." Ms. in possession of author.

Bright, William. 2004. *Native American Placenames of the United States*. Norman: University of Oklahoma Press.

Brucks, Caleb D. 2015. "The Creation of Narrative Space: The Directional System of Upper Tanana." Master's thesis, University of Regina.

Brucks, Caleb D., and Olga Lovick. 2018. "Losing One's Way: Geographical and Moral Lessons in the Butterfly Story in Upper Tanana Athabascan." In *Language and Toponymy in Alaska and Beyond: Papers in Honor of James Kari, Language Documentation & Conservation Special Publication 17,* edited by Gary Holton and Thomas Thornton, 97–120. Honolulu: University of Hawai'i Press.

Brucks, Caleb, and Siri G. Tuttle. 2014. "Negative Prosody in Interior Athabascan Languages." International Symposium on Prosody to commemorate Gösta Bruce, University of Lund, Lund, Sweden. June 2–3, 2014.

Case, Martha F. 1986. *Wild Resource Use in Northway, Alaska*. Anchorage: Alaska Department of Fish & Game, Division of Subsistence.

Cook, Eung-Do. 1996. "Third-person Plural Subject Prefix in Northern Athapaskan." *International Journal of American Linguistics* 62, no. 1: 86–110.

———. 2004. *A Grammar of Dëne Sųłiné (Chipewyan). Algonquian and Iroquoian Linguistics – Special Athabaskan Number, Memoir 17.* Winnipeg: Algonquian / Iroquoian Linguistics, University of Manitoba.

———. 2013. *A Tsilhqút'in Grammar*. Vancouver: University of British Columbia Press.

Cook, Eung-Do, and Andrea Wilhelm. 1998. "Noun Incorporation: New Evidence from Athapaskan." *Studies in Language* 22, no. 1: 49–81.

Crowley, Terry. 2007. *Field Linguistics*. Oxford: Oxford University Press.

David, Cora. 2011. *Teedląy t'iin naholndak niign: Stories by the Tetlin People.* Edited by Olga Lovick. Fairbanks: Alaska Native Language Center.

———. 2017. *Teedląy t'iin naholndak niign: Stories by the Tetlin People.* Expanded edition. Edited by Olga Lovick. Fairbanks: Alaska Native Language Center.

David, Titus. 2006. "Niithaadn dą' ts'anh noonagn. Upper Tanana (Tetlin) Old-time Stories." Transcribed and edited by Paul Milanowski, translated by Titus David. Ms. in possession of author.

de Laguna, Frederica, ed. 1995. *Tales from the Dena: Indian Stories From the Tanana, Koyukuk, and Yukon Rivers.* Seattle: University of Washington Press.

de Reuse, Willem Joseph, and Phillip Goode. 2006. *A Practical Grammar of the San Carlos Apache Language.* LINCOM Studies in Native American Linguistics 51. München: LINCOM.

Demit, Ellen, and David Joe. 2010. *The Adventures of Yabaa Teeshaay: First Man Stories from Healy Lake as Told by Ellen Demit and David Joe.* Edited by Constance Ann Friend, Athabascan translated and transcribed by Irene L. Arnold and Richard Thoman. Fairbanks: Alaska Native Knowledge Network.

Dixon, R. M. W. 2009. *Basic Linguistic Theory, vol. 1: Methodology.* Oxford: Oxford University Press.

Dryer, Matthew S. 2006. "Descriptive Theories, Explanatory Theories, and Basic Linguistic Theory." In *Catching Language: The Standing Challenge of Grammar Writing,* edited by Felix K. Ameka, Alan Dench, and Nicholas Evans, 207–34. Berlin: Mouton de Gruyter.

Ellanna, Linda J., and Andrew Balluta. 1982. *Nuvendaltin quht'ana: The People of Nondalton.* Washington DC: Smithsonian Institution.

Fall, James A. 1990. *Upper Cook Inlet Dena'ina Oral Traditions: An Introduction to the Narrative Art of an Alaskan Athabaskan People.* Technical report. Alaska Humanities Forum.

Faltz, Leonard M. 1998. *The Navajo Verb: A Grammar for Students and Scholars.* Albuquerque: University of New Mexico Press.

Fortescue, Michael. 2011. "Where 'Out to Sea' Equals 'Toward the Fire': The Macrocosm-Microcosm Relationship in Languages of the Pacific Rim." *Anthropological Linguistics* 53, no. 1: 1–14.

Friend, Connie, Gary Holton, and Norm Alexander Easton. 2007. "An American - Canadian Traditional Ecological Knowledge Study of the Upper Tanana River Fisheries." Park Science in Central Alaska: Crossing Boundaries in a Changing Environment, *Alaska Park Science* 6, no. 2: 78–82.

Gessner, Suzanne. 2003. "The Prosodic System of the Dakelh (Carrier) Language." PhD diss., University of British Columbia.

Golla, Victor K. 2007. "North America." In *Encyclopedia of the World's Endangered Languages,* edited by Christopher Moseley. London: Routledge.

Guédon, Marie-Françoise. 1974. *People of Tetlin Why Are You Singing?* Mercury Series, Ethnology Division. Ottawa: National Museum of Man, National Museums of Canada.

———. 1981. "Upper Tanana River Potlatch." In *Handbook of North American Indians, vol. 6: Subarctic,* edited by June Helm. Washington DC: Smithsonian Institution.

———. 2005. *Le rêve et la forêt.* Québec: Les Presses de l'Université Laval.

Halpin, Libby. 1987. *Living Off the Land: Contemporary Subsistence in Tetlin, Alaska.* Anchorage: Alaska Department of Fish & Game.

Hargus, Sharon. 2007. *Witsuwit'en Grammar: Phonetics, Phonology, Morphology.* Vancouver: University of British Columbia Press.

———. 2010. "Athabaskan phonetics and phonology." *Linguistic Compass* 4 (10): 1019–40.

Heinrich, Albert. 1957. "Sib and Social Structure on the Upper Tanana." In *Science in Alaska: Proceedings of the Eighth Alaskan Science Conference,* edited by Albert W. Johnson. Anchorage: Alaska Division, American Association for the Advancement of Science.

Helm, June, and Beryl C. Gillespie. 1981. "Dogrib Oral Tradition as History: War and Peace in the 1820s." *Journal of Anthropological Research* 37, no. 1: 8–27.

Hill, Jane H. 2006. "Writing Culture in Grammar in the Americanist Tradition." In *Catching Language: The Standing Challenge of Grammar Writing,* edited by Felix K. Ameka, Alan Dench, and Nicholas Evans, 609–28. Berlin: Mouton de Gruyter.

Holden, Josh. 2013. *Benasní—I Remember: Dene Sųłiné Oral Histories with Morphological Analysis.* Leiden: Brill.

Holton, Gary. 2000. "The Phonology and Morphology of the Tanacross Athabaskan Language." PhD diss., University of California Santa Barbara.

———. 2001. "Fortis and Lenis Fricatives in Tanacross Athapaskan." *International Journal of American Linguistics* 67, no. 4: 396–414.

Jetté, Jules. 1908. "On Ten'a Folk-Lore." *Journal of the Royal Anthropological Institute* 38: 297–367.

Jetté, Jules, and Eliza Jones. 2000. *Koyukon Athabaskan Dictionary.* Fairbanks: Alaska Native Language Center.

Joe, Donald, Alfred John, and Paul G Milanowski. 2013. *T'oodiht'ay aaneegn' (God's Word), Tetlin aaneegn' (in the Tetlin Language).* Tetlin: Native Village of Tetlin.

Jung, Dagmar. 1999. "The Dynamics of Polysynthetic Morphology: Person and Number Marking in Athabaskan." PhD diss., University of New Mexico.

Kari, James. 1975. "The Disjunct Boundary in the Navajo and Tanaina Verb Prefix Complexes." *International Journal of American Linguistics* 41, no. 4: 330–45.

———. 1979. *Athabaskan Verb Theme Categories: Ahtna.* Alaska Native Language Center Research Papers no. 2. Fairbanks: Alaska Native Language Center.

———. 1985. "A Note on Athapaskan Directionals." *International Journal of American Linguistics* 51, no. 4: 471–73.

———. 1990. *Ahtna Athabaskan Dictionary.* Fairbanks: Alaska Native Language Center.

Kari, James. 1993. "Diversity in Morpheme Order in Several Alaskan Athabascan Languages: Notes on the *gh*-Qualifier." *Proceedings of the Nineteenth Annual Meeting of the Berkeley Linguistics Society: Special Session on Syntactic Issues in Native American Languages* 19, no. 2: 50–56.

———. 1997a. *Upper Tanana Place Names Lists and Maps.* Compiled and Edited by James Kari, Alaska Native Language Center. Final Report for the Project "Upper Tanana Athabaskan Place Names in the Vicinity of Wrangell-St. Elias National Park," Sponsored by Wrangell-St. Elias National Park, during 1995–1997.

———. 1997b. "Upper Tanana Stem List." With additions by Olga Lovick. Unpublished Lexware file in possession of author.

———. 2007. *Dena'ina Topical Dictionary.* Fairbanks: Alaska Native Language Center.

———, ed. 2010. *Ahtna Travel Narratives: A Demonstration of Shared Geographic Knowledge among Alaska Athabascans.* Fairbanks: Alaska Native Language Center.

———. 2011. "A Case Study in Ahtna Geographic Knowledge." In *Landscape in Language: Transdisciplinary Perspectives,* edited by David M. Mark, Andrew G. Turk, Niclas Burenhult, and David Stea, 239–260. Amsterdam: John Benjamins Publishing.

———. 2019. "Lexware, Dene Band Labels, and Recent Alaska Dene Lexicography Work." In *Working Papers in Dene Languages 2018,* edited by Siri G. Tuttle, 69–83. Alaska Native Language Center Working Papers no. 15. Fairbanks: Alaska Native Language Center.

Kari, James, and James A. Fall. 2003. *Shem Pete's Alaska: The Territory of the Upper Cook Inlet Dena'ina.* Fairbanks: University of Alaska Press.

Kari, James, and Ben A. Potter, eds. 2010. *The Dene-Yeniseian Connection.* Anthropological Papers of the University of Alaska, vol. 5 New Series, nos. 1–2. Fairbanks: University of Alaska Fairbanks.

Kibrik, Andrej A. 1993. "Transitivity Increase in Athabaskan Languages." In *Causatives and Transitives,* edited by Bernard Comrie and Maria Polinsky, 47–67. Amsterdam: John Benjamins.

———. 1996. "Transitivity Decrease in Navajo and Athabaskan: Actor-affecting Propositional Derivations." In *Athabaskan Language Studies: Essays in Honor of Robert W. Young,* edited by Eloise Jelinek, Sally Midgette, Keren Rice, and Leslie Saxon, 259–303. Albuquerque: University of New Mexico Press.

Krauss, Michael E. 1962. "Letter from Michael Krauss to Paul Milanowski, June 25, 1962." Unpublished Ms., Alaska Native Language Archive no. CA961K1962n. http://www.uaf.edu/anla/item.xml?id=CA961K1962n.

———. 1964. "Proto-Athapaskan-Eyak and the Problem of Na-Dene: The Phonology." *International Journal of American Linguistics* 30, no. 2: 118–31.

———. 1969. *On the Classification in the Athapaskan, Eyak, and Tlingit Verb.* Indiana University Publications in Anthropology and Linguistics, Memoir 24. Baltimore: Waverly.

———. 1982. *Alaska Native Languages Map.* Fairbanks: Alaska Native Language Center.

———. 2000. "Koyukon Dialectology and Its Relationship to Other Athabaskan Languages." In *Koyukon Athabaskan Dictionary,* edited by Jules Jetté and Eliza Jones, l–lxv. Fairbanks: Alaska Native Language Center.

———. 2005. "Athabaskan Tone." In *Athabaskan Prosody,* edited by Keren Rice and Sharon Hargus, 51–136. Amsterdam: John Benjamins Publishing Company.

Krauss, Michael E., and Victor Golla. 1981. "Northern Athapaskan Languages." In *Handbook of North American Indians, vol. 6: Subarctic,* edited by June Helm, 67–85. Washington DC: Smithsonian Institution.

Krauss, Michael E., Gary Holton, Jim Kerr, and Colin T. West. 2010. *Indigenous Peoples and Languages of Alaska.* Map. Fairbanks: Alaska Native Language Center.

Krauss, Michael E., and Jeff Leer. 1981. *Athabaskan, Eyak, and Tlingit Sonorants.* Alaska Native Language Center Research Papers no. 5. Fairbanks: Alaska Native Language Center.

Kwaraceius, Joe. 2000. "Koyukon Numerals." In *Koyukon Athabaskan Dictionary,* edited by Jules Jetté and Eliza Jones, 811–14. Fairbanks: Alaska Native Language Center.

Lahaussois, Aimée, and Marine Vuillermet, eds. 2019. *Methodological Tools for Linguistic Description and Typology, Language Documentation and Conservation Special Publication no. 16.* University of Hawai'i Press.

Leer, Jeff. 1974. "Report on the Upper Tanana Bilingual Workshop." Unpublished Ms., Alaska Native Language Archive no. UT974L1974a. http://www.uaf.edu/anla/item.xml?id=UT974L1974a.

———. 1977. "Stem Syllable Development in Tanacross and Upper Tanana." Unpublished Ms., Alaska Native Language Archive no. TC974L1977. http://www.uaf.edu/anla/item.xml?id=TC974L1977.

———. 1979. *Proto-Athabaskan Verb Stem Variation Part One: Phonology.* Alaska Native Language Center Research Papers no. 1. Fairbanks: Alaska Native Language Center.

———. 1982. "Issues in Tanacross Orthography." Unpublished Ms., Alaska Native Language Archive no. TC974L1982b. http://www.uaf.edu/anla/item.xml?id=TC974L1982b.

———. 1989. "Directional Systems in Athapaskan and Na-Dene." In *Athapaskan Linguistics: Current Perspectives on a Language Family,* edited by Eung-Do Cook and Keren Rice, 575–622. Berlin: Mouton de Gruyter.

———. 1996a. "Comparative Athabaskan Lexicon." Ms., Alaska Native Language Archive no. CA965L1996a. http://www.uaf.edu/anla/item.xml?id=CA965L1996a.

———. 1996b. "Comparative Athabaskan Lexicon Fileslips." Unpublished Ms., Alaska Native Language Archive no. CA965L1996e. http://www.uaf.edu/anla/item.xml?id=CA965L1996e.

———. 1996c. "The Historical Evolution of the Stem Syllable in Gwich'in (Kutchin/Loucheux) Athabaskan." In *Athabaskan Language Studies: Essays in Honor of Robert W. Young,* edited by Eloise Jelinek, Sally Midgette, Keren Rice, and Leslie Saxon, 193–234. Albuquerque: University of New Mexico Press.

———. 2000. "The Negative/Irrealis Category in Athabaskan-Eyak-Tlingit." In *The Athabaskan languages: Perspectives on a Native American language family,* edited by Theodore B. Fernald and Paul R. Platero, 101–38. Oxford: Oxford University Press.

Levinson, Stephen. 2003. *Space in Language and Cognition: Explorations in Cognitive Diversity.* Cambridge: Cambridge University Press.

Li, Fang-Kuei. 1946. "Chipewyan." In *Linguistic Structures of Native America,* edited by Cornelius Osgood and Harry Hoijer, 398–423. Viking Fund Publications in Anthropology no. 6. New York: Viking Fund.

———. 1956. "A Type of Noun Formation in Athabaskan and Eyak." *International Journal of American Linguistics* 22, no. 1: 45–48.

Lovick, Olga. 2005. "Agentivity and Participant Marking: A Text-Based Study." PhD diss., Universität zu Köln.

———. 2010. "Person-Marked Numerals in North Alberta Beaver (Athabaskan)." *Anthropological Linguistics* 52, no. 3–4: 300–309.

———. 2011. "The Upper Tanana Athabascan Vowel System: Taking a Snapshot of a Language." In *Working Papers in Athabaskan Languages 2010,* edited by Siri G. Tuttle and Olga Lovick, 96–105. Alaska Native Language Center Working Papers no. 9. Fairbanks: Alaska Native Language Center.

———. 2012. "The Identification of Narrative Genres in Upper Tanana Athabascan: A Preliminary Study." *Northwest Journal of Linguistics* 6, no. 3: 1–29.

———. 2015. "Dena'ina." In *The Edinburgh Handbook of Evaluative Morphology,* edited by Nicola Grandi and Lívia Körtvélyessy, 536–41. Edinburgh: Edinburgh University Press.

———. 2016. "*Įįjih* and Request Formation in Upper Tanana Athabascan: Evidence from Narrative Text." *Anthropological Linguistics* 58, no. 3: 248–98.

Lovick, Olga, Christopher Cox, Miikka Silfverberg, Antti Arppe, and Mans Hulden. 2018. "A Computational Architecture for the Morphology of Upper Tanana." In *Proceedings of the Language Resources and Evaluation Conference,* 1874–79. http://www.lrec-conf.org/proceedings/lrec2018/pdf/816.pdf.

Lovick, Olga, and Keren Rice. 2015. "Slavey (Dene) and Other Athabaskan Languages." In *The Edinburgh Handbook of Evaluative Morphology,* edited by Nicola Grandi and Lívia Körtvélyessy, 579–94. Edinburgh: Edinburgh University Press.

Lovick, Olga, and Siri G. Tuttle. 2011. "Conversation in Upper Tanana Athabascan: Syntactic and Prosodic Patterns." In *Language Documentation and Description 10,* edited by Niclas Burenhult, Arthur Holmer, Anastasia Karlsson, Håkan Lundström, and Jan-Olof Svantesson, 132–176. London: SOAS.

———. 2019. "Video Elicitation of Negative Directives in Alaskan Dene Languages: Reflections on Methodology." In *Methodological Tools for Linguistic Description and Typology. Language Documentation & Conservation Special Publication no. 16,* edited by Aimée Lahaussois and Marine Vuillermet, 125–54.

McDonough, Joyce. 1990. "Topics in the Phonology and Morphology of Navajo Verbs." PhD diss., University of Massachusetts at Amherst.

———. 1999. "On a Bipartite Model of the Athabaskan Verb." In *The Athabaskan Languages: Perspectives on a Native American Language Family,* edited by Theodore B. Fernald and Paul R. Platero, 139–66. Oxford Studies in Anthropological Linguistics. Oxford: Oxford University Press.

McDonough, Joyce, and Valerie Wood. 2008. "The Stop Contrasts of the Athabaskan Languages." *Journal of Phonetics* 36: 427–49.

McKennan, Robert A. 1959. *The Upper Tanana Indians.* Yale University Publications in Anthropology. New Haven: Department of Anthropology, Yale University.

———. 1969. "Athapaskan Groups of Central Alaska at the Time of White Contact." *Ethnohistory* 16, no. 4: 335–43.

———. 1981. "Tanana." In *Handbook of North American Indians, vol. 6: Subarctic,* edited by June Helm, 562–76. Washington DC: Smithsonian Institution.

Meek, Barbra A. 2007. "Respecting the Language of Elders: Ideological Shift and Linguistic Discontinuity in a Northern Athapascan Community." *Journal of Linguistic Anthropology* 17, no. 1: 23–43.

———. 2010. *We Are Our Language: An Ethnography of Language Revitalization in a Northern Athabaskan Community.* Tucson: University of Arizona Press.

Milanowski, Paul G. 1961. "Sound System of Upper Tanana Athapaskan (a Preliminary View)." In *Science in Alaska, Proceedings of the 12th Alaskan Science Conference.* College, AK: Alaska Division, American Association for the Advancement of Science.

———. 2011. *Naabia Niign aaneegn': Northway Dictionary. 3rd ed.* Alaska Native Language Archive, UT961M2007b. https://www.uaf.edu/anla/collections/search/resultDetail.xml?id=UT961M2007b.

Milanowski, Paul G., and Shirley David Jimerson. 1975. *Nee'aandeegn': Upper Tanana Dictionary.* Anchorage: Alaska Native Education Board.

Milanowski, Paul G., and Alfred John, eds. 1966. *T'oodįht'aiy aandeegn' suu' Mark utneetł'adn haa': The Gospel According to Mark. Upper Tanana and Today's English Version.* New York: American Bible Society.

———, eds. 1972. *T'oodįht'aiy aandeegn. PAUL ainahtł'aa ch'it͟heh eł łaakeiy dan THESSALONICA keiy' koht'iin ts'ą' tł'aan ch'it͟heh eł Łaakeiy dan TIMOTHY ts'ą' tł'aan TITUS ts'ą' tł'aan PHILEMON ts'ą' neetł'at (God's Word. I and II Thessalonians, I and II Timothy, Titus, and Philemon: Upper Tanana and Today's English Version.)* Fairbanks: Wycliffe Bible Translators Inc.

———. 1979. *Nee'aaneegn': Upper Tanana (Tetlin) Junior Dictionary.* Anchorage: National Bilingual Materials Development Center.

Minoura, Nobukatsu. 1994. "A Comparative Phonology of the Upper Tanana Athabaskan Dialects." In *Languages of the North Pacific Rim,* edited by Osahito Miyaoka, 159–96. Hokkaido University Publications in Linguistics no. 7. Sapporo: Department of Linguistics, Faculty of Letters, Hokkaido University.

———. 1997. "A Note on Possessive Construction in Upper Tanana Athabaskan." In *Studies in Possessive Expressions,* edited by Tooru Hayasi and Peri Bhaskararao, 177–96. Tokyo: Institute for the Study of Language / Cultures of Asia / Africa.

———. 2004. "A Preliminary Typology of *wh*-Questions." *Area and Culture Studies* 68: 37–64.

Moore, Patrick J. 2002. "Point of View in Kaska Historical Narratives." PhD diss., Indiana University.

Morice, Adrien-Gabriel. 1932. *The Carrier Language.* Vol. 1. Mödling bei Wien: Verlag der Internationalen Zeitung "Anthropos."

Nelson, Richard K. 1983. *Make Prayers to the Raven: A Koyukon View of the Boreal Forest.* Chicago: University of Chicago Press.

Osgood, Cornelius. 1936. *The Distribution of the Northern Athapaskan Indians: Study of the Dene in Alaska and Canada.* Yale University Publications in Anthropology no. 7. New Haven: Department of Anthropology, Yale University.

———. 1959. *Ingalik Mental Culture.* Yale University Publications in Anthropology. New Haven: Department of Anthropology, Yale University.

Rice, Keren. 1989. *A Grammar of Slave.* Berlin: Mouton de Gruyter.

———. 2000. *Morpheme Order and Semantic Scope.* Amsterdam: John Benjamins.

———. 2006. "Let the Language Tell Its Story? The Role of Linguistic Theory in Writing Grammars." In *Catching Language: The Standing Challenge of Grammar Writing,* edited by Felix K. Ameka, Alan Dench, and Nicholas Evans, 235–68. Berlin: Mouton de Gruyter.

Rice, Keren, and Sharon Hargus. 1989. "Conjugation and Mode in Athapaskan Languages: Evidence for Two Positions." In *Athapaskan Linguistics: Current Perspectives on a Language Family,* edited by Eung-Do Cook and Keren Rice, 265–315. Berlin: Mouton de Gruyter.

Rice, Keren, and Leslie Saxon. 1994. "The Subject Positions in Athapaskan Languages." In *The Morphology-Syntax Connection,* edited by Heidi Harley and Colin Phillips, 173–95. MIT Working Papers in Linguistics, vol. 22. Cambridge: MIT.

———. 2005. "Comparative Athabaskan Syntax: Arguments and Projections." In *The Oxford Handbook of Comparative Syntax,* edited by Guglielmo Cinque and Richard S. Kayne, 698–774. Oxford: Oxford University Press.

Ruppert, James. 1996. "Mary Tyone: An Appreciation." In *Ttheek'ädn ut'iin yaaniidą' ǫǫnign': Old Time Stories of the Scottie Creek People. Stories told in Upper Tanana Athabaskan by Mary Tyone, Ts'ą' Yahnik,* edited by James Kari, ix–x. Fairbanks: Alaska Native Language Center.

Rushforth, Scott, and James S. Chisholm. 1991. *Cultural Persistence: Continuity in Meaning and Moral Responsibility among the Bearlake Athapaskans.* Tucson: University of Arizona Press.

Sam, Avis. 2000. *Upper Tanana Athabaskan Language Lessons: Northway Ddialect.* Whitehorse: Yukon Native Language Centre.

Sam, Avis, Sherry Demit-Barnes, and Darlene Northway. forthcoming. *Ts'exeey iin Naabia Niign xah nahiholnegn: Women Tell Stories about Northway.* Transcribed and translated by Caleb Brucks and Olga Lovick with the help of the storytellers as well as Roy Sam and Rosa Brewer. Edited by Olga Lovick and Caleb Brucks. Fairbanks: Alaska Native Language Center.

Sapir, Edward. 1923. "A Type of Athapaskan Relative." *International Journal of American Linguistics* 2, no. 3/4: 136–42.

Saxon, Leslie. 1993. "A Personal Use for Athapaskan 'Impersonal' *ts'e-*." *International Journal of American Linguistics* 59, no. 3: 342–54.

Saxon, Leslie, and Andrea Wilhelm. 2016. "The "Possessed Noun Suffix" and Possession in Two Northern Dene (Athabaskan) Languages." *International Journal of American Linguistics* 82, no. 1: 35–70.

Scollon, Ronald, and Suzanne B.K. Scollon. 1979. *Linguistic Convergence: An Ethnography of Speaking at Fort Chipewyan, Alberta.* New York: Academic Press.

———. 1981. *Narrative, Literacy, and Face in Interethnic Communication.* Norwood NJ: Ablex.

Simeone, William E. 1995. *Rifles, Blankets, & Beads: Identity, History, and the Northern Athapaskan Potlatch.* Civilization of the American Indian Series. Norman: University of Oklahoma Press.

Smith, Carlota S. 1991. *The Parameter of Aspect.* Dordrecht: Kluwer Academic.

Story, Gillian L. 1989. "The Athapaskan First Duoplural Subject Prefix." In *Athapaskan Linguistics: Current Perspectives on a Language Family,* edited by Eung-Do Cook and Keren Rice, 487–531. Berlin: Mouton de Gruyter.

Tenenbaum, Joan M. 1978. "Morphology and Semantics of the Dena'ina Verb." PhD diss., Columbia University.

Thompson, Chad. 1990. *K'etetaalkkaanee: The One Who Paddled among the People and Animals.* An analytical companion volume. Fairbanks: Alaska Native Language Center.

———. 1993. "The Areal Prefix *hʉ-* in Koyukon Athapaskan." *International Journal of American Linguistics* 59, no. 3: 315–33.

———. 1996. "On the Grammar of Body Parts in Koyukon Athabaskan." In *The Grammar of Inalienability: A Typological Perspective on Body Part Terms and the Part-Whole Relation,* edited by Hilary Chappell and William MacGregor, 651–77. Berlin, New York: Mouton de Gruyter.

Tuttle, Siri G. 1998. "Metrical and tonal structures in Tanana Athabaskan." PhD diss., University of Washington.

———. 2003. "Impurity, Part 1: Notes on Noun and Verb Incorporation in Northern Athabaskan." Unpublished Ms. in possession of author.

Tuttle, Siri G., Olga Lovick, and Isabel Núñez-Ortiz. 2011. "Vowels of Upper Tanana Athabascan." *Journal of the International Phonetic Association* 41, no. 3: 283–312.

Tyone, Mary. 1996. *Ttheek'ädn ut'iin yaaniidą' ǫǫnign': Old Time Stories of the Scottie Creek People. Stories Told in Upper Tanana Athabaskan by Mary Tyone, Ts'ą' Yahnik.* Edited by James Kari. Fairbanks: Alaska Native Language Center.

UNESCO Ad Hoc Expert Group on Endangered Languages. 2003. *Language Vitality and Endangerment (pdf).* https://ich.unesco.org/doc/src/00120-EN.pdf.

Vajda, Edward J. 2010a. "A Siberian Link with Na-Dene Languages." In *The Dene-Yeniseian connection,* edited by James Kari and Ben A. Potter, 33–99. Anthropological Papers of the University of Alaska, vol. 5 New Series, nos. 1–2. Fairbanks: University of Alaska Fairbanks.

———. 2010b. "Yeniseian, Na-Dene, and Historical Linguistics." In *The Dene-Yeniseian Connection,* edited by James Kari and Ben A. Potter, 100–118. Anthropological Papers of the University of Alaska, vol. 5 New Series, nos. 1–2. Fairbanks: University of Alaska Fairbanks.

Wilhelm, Andrea. 2007. *Telicity and Durativity: A Study of Aspect in Dëne Sųłiné (Chipewyan) and German.* Outstanding Dissertations in Linguistics Series. New York: Routledge.

Yukon Native Language Centre. 2009. *Upper Tanana Literacy Session.* February 5–6, 2009. Whitehorse: Yukon Native Language Centre.

CPSIA information can be obtained
at www.ICGtesting.com
Printed in the USA
LVHW040105101220
673765LV00002B/2

9 781496 222275